ESSAYS ON ARISTOTLE'S

ESSAYS ON ARISTOTLE'S
DE ANIMA

edited by

MARTHA C. NUSSBAUM
and
AMÉLIE OKSENBERG RORTY

CLARENDON PRESS · OXFORD

Oxford University Press, Walton Street, Oxford OX2 6DP
Oxford New York
Athens Auckland Bangkok Bombay
Calcutta Cape Town Dar es Salaam Delhi
Florence Hong Kong Istanbul Karachi
Kuala Lumpur Madras Madrid Melbourne
Mexico City Nairobi Paris Singapore
Taipei Tokyo Toronto
and associated companies in
Berlin Ibadan

Oxford is a trade mark of Oxford University Press

Published in the United States by
Oxford University Press Inc., New York

First published 1992
First issued in paperback 1995

British Library Cataloguing in Publication Data
Data available

Library of Congress Cataloging in Publication Data
Essays on Aristotle's De anima / edited by Martha C. Nussbaum and
Amélie Oksenberg Rorty.
Includes bibliographical references and index.
1. Aristotle. De anima. 2. Psychology. I. Nussbaum, Martha
Craven, 1947- . II. Rorty, Amélie.
B415.E87 1991 128—dc20 91-22833
ISBN 0-19-824461-4
ISBN 0-19-823600-X (Pbk)

Printed in Great Britain
on acid-free paper by
Biddles Ltd, Guildford and King's Lynn

CONTRIBUTORS

JULIA ANNAS is at Columbia University

FRANZ BRENTANO (1838–1917) was at the University of Würzburg

M. F. BURNYEAT is at Robinson College, Cambridge

ALAN CODE is at the University of Michigan

S. MARC COHEN is at the University of Washington

DOROTHEA FREDE is at the University of Hamburg

MICHAEL FREDE is at Keble College, Oxford

CYNTHIA FREELAND is at the University of Houston

CHARLES KAHN is at the University of Pennsylvania

L. A. KOSMAN is at Haverford College

G. E. R. LLOYD is at Darwin College, Cambridge

GARETH B. MATTHEWS is at the University of Massachusetts, Amherst

JULIUS MORAVCSIK is at Stanford University

MARTHA C. NUSSBAUM is at Brown University

HILARY PUTNAM is at Harvard University

HENRY S. RICHARDSON is at Georgetown University

AMÉLIE OKSENBERG RORTY is at Radcliffe College and Mt. Holyoke College

MALCOLM SCHOFIELD is at St John's College, Cambridge

RICHARD SORABJI is at King's College London

JENNIFER WHITING is at the University of Pittsburgh

K. V. WILKES is at St Hilda's College, Oxford

CHARLOTTE WITT is at the University of New Hampshire

ACKNOWLEDGEMENTS

The editors are grateful to the Faculty of Classics, University of Cambridge, for permission to reproduce Malcolm Schofield's 'Aristotle on the Imagination', originally published in G. E. R. Lloyd and G. E. L. Owen (eds.), *Aristotle on Mind and the Senses: Proceedings of the Seventh Symposium Aristotelicum* (Cambridge University Press, 1978); to the Regents of the University of California for permission to reproduce Franz Brentano's '*Nous Poiētikos*: Survey of Earlier Interpretations', originally published in *The Psychology of Aristotle*, translated and edited by Rolf George (University of California Press, 1977); and finally to Rolf George for his translation of Brentano's essay, and for the revisions he made to it for this publication.

CONTENTS

I

INTRODUCTION

A. THE TEXT OF ARISTOTLE'S *DE ANIMA*

MARTHA C. NUSSBAUM

I. The Manuscript Tradition

LIKE most other works of Aristotle, the *De Anima* survives in a relatively large number of manuscripts; but none of these is earlier than the tenth century AD. (Fragments of the earlier tradition can in some cases be recovered from citations in the ancient commentators—see Section II below; but it must be remembered that their work itself survives only in manuscripts of the same age as the Aristotle manuscripts—so there is a good deal of room for error to creep in.) The extant manuscripts have probably not been sufficiently described and analysed; there seems to be room for a new critical edition. But in so far as it is possible to say anything without having done the work oneself (and having done comparable work only on the *De Motu Animalium*, which has a somewhat different manuscript tradition, though related in several important cases), I shall try to give a brief sketch of the situation.

The earliest manuscript in which the work survives is E, Parisinus graecus 1853, a manuscript that has long been regarded as an extremely valuable source for the works of Aristotle that it contains. The presentation of *De Anima* in E has one peculiar feature: the second book of the treatise is not in the same hand as the first and third. There are signs that the original second book (scraps of which remain) was torn out and a new version inserted. Moreover, the new version does not seem to derive from the same manuscript family as the other books: for its readings are said to mark it as belonging to the other major family. One should, however, bear in mind that the only other exemplar of the E family that has been said to have independent authority—L, Vaticanus graecus 253—contains only the third book of the treatise; therefore the basis for Ross's claims about the filiation of the readings in the second book in e (his symbol for the version of book 2 in E) should be further scrutinized.[1] In any case, one can agree with Ross that it was certainly misleading to designate the entire manuscript by the single letter E (as Förster did), failing to alert the reader to the problem posed by the two hands.

[1] See Ross in Aristotle (1961*a*), Introduction.

Some editors have treated E as a paradigm, dismissing all the other manuscripts as less valuable. R. D. Hicks, for example, writes, 'The text of the *De Anima* rests mainly on the authority of a single good manuscript, Cod. Parisiensis 1853, better known by the symbol E...'.[2] This practice of looking for a single authority can only lead to confusion; what one needs to do first of all is to look at all the extant manuscripts that have any claim at all to independence, and to produce an exacting analysis of their relationships—as was done, for example, in exemplary fashion by R. Kassel in his work on Aristotle's *Rhetoric*.[3] This task clearly has not yet been completed for the *De Anima*. In the case of the *Rhetoric*, Kassel showed convincingly enough the unreliability of Ross's work (both collations and analysis) near the end of his career; and his *De Anima* work—though the most complete account of the manuscripts we have—is likely to be marred in similar ways. If we may judge, however, from what Ross (and earlier editors such as Förster) do report, then there are quite a few manuscripts other than E that make independent contributions to the establishments of the text. All these with the exception of L, which is close to E, are said to form a single large family, whose archetype does not survive. This family appears to fall, in turn, into two subfamilies. Ross holds that the EL family is of equal importance with the other family, and that the two subfamilies within the other family are of equal importance with one another. In addition, one relatively late manuscript—P,[4] Vaticanus graecus 1339—seems to contain readings from both families.

Additional insight into the text can be gained by examining the paraphrases, lemmata, and citations in the ancient commentaries, which sometimes can be shown to preserve readings deriving from some independent tradition otherwise lost to us. Caution is required, both because the manuscript traditions of *these* authors are themselves complex and because a commentator may combine readings from more than one manuscript. Much the same is true of the literal Latin translation of William of Moerbeke, used by Thomas Aquinas as the basis for his commentary.

Since the text of the *De Anima* is unusually corrupt—above all, in the third book, which is in as bad a condition as any extant work of Aristotle—any text one uses will be bound to contain a fairly large number not only of difficult judgement-calls but also of conjectural emendations. The most ambitious and invasive surgical enterprise was that of Torstrik, who claimed that Aristotle wrote two different versions of book 3, which had somehow become conflated; he attempted to pull them apart and to reconstruct the originals.[5] Most scholars have not been convinced by Torstrik's arguments; but all endeavour in various ways to clear up the problems in book 3. The philosopher/scholar should be especially attentive to the critical apparatus when working on *De Anima*, and should think with more than usual care about the alternatives that have been proposed, using, if possible, more than one edition.

---

[2] Hicks in Aristotle (1907), p. lxxxiii.   [3] Aristotle (1976), reviewed by Nussbaum (1981).
[4] For an account of this manuscript, see Nussbaum (1975, 1976).   [5] Aristotle (1862).

II. The Tradition of Commentary

The *De Anima* was the focus of intense work in the ancient Aristotelian traditions. Theophrastus evidently discussed the work, and a portion of his discussion (concerning the intellect) is preserved in Themistius. Alexander of Aphrodisias (2nd–3rd c. AD) wrote about the *De Anima* in two works of his own: his *De Anima* (of which book 1 is probably genuine, book 2—called the Mantissa —more dubious), and the *Aporiai kai Luseis*, or *Puzzles and Solutions*.[6] Both works, especially the latter, are of considerable philosophical interest. Alexander writes as an acute Aristotelian not committed to any other school; and he is a very probing interpreter. In addition, his citations and lemmata are a valuable textual source.

Themistius (4th c. AD) wrote a paraphrase of Aristotle's treatise; his practice is not to amplify or comment a great deal, but to give in different words the sense of the original. Occasionally, however, he supplements his paraphrase with material drawn from other Aristotelian sources (for example, the *De Motu Animalium*, used in paraphrasing 3. 10). Because he remains relatively close to the text, his work can sometimes be useful in confronting textual problems.

Simplicius and Philoponus (5th–6th c. AD) wrote the two most extensive commentaries on the work that survive from antiquity.[7] Both are Neoplatonists (the former, however, a pagan, and the latter a Christian). They were not allies, but antagonists on central questions of cosmology and metaphysics. Both are influenced in their interpretations by their other philosophical and religious views. But both are also close readers of the text, and highly intelligent interpreters; their suggestions should always be taken seriously. Once again, citations and lemmata are a valuable source for the text. A contemporary author, Priscianus Lydus, wrote a *Metaphrasis in Theophrastum* that is sometimes also consulted for textual material.[8]

The next commentary known to us is by one Sophonias, probably written in the thirteenth century AD or before (to judge from the date of the oldest manuscript). As Fabricius, quoted by Trendelenburg, says (in Latin), 'Who this Sophonias was, and when he lived, we can't say.'[9] The paraphrase is worth examining in working on the text, though it has less philosophical interest than the other works that have been mentioned.

Also produced in the thirteenth century is one of the very greatest commentaries on the work, by Thomas Aquinas. Aquinas, who could not read Greek, worked, here as elsewhere, from an allegedly literal Latin version produced for him by William of Moerbeke, whose knowledge of Greek, though renowned in his day, is not all it might be, and whose principle of supplying a Latin word for every word of the Greek—even for conjunctions and particles

[6] Alexander (1887).   [7] Simplicius (1882), Philoponus (1897).
[8] See the Introductions of Ross and Hicks, and the edition by Bywater (1886).
[9] Trendelenburg, quoted in Aristotle (1907). For the original Latin remark see J. A. Fabricius (1790–1809), vii. 236. I am grateful to Leofranc Holford-Strevens for the reference.

that have no single-word equivalent in Latin—produces a Latin syntax that is frequently unintelligible. But sometimes, used with caution, William's versions can help us to reconstruct a part of the ancient manuscript tradition.[10] Aquinas' commentary itself is very insightful; so too are the extensive remarks about Aristotelian soul–body issues contained in the *Summa Theologiae* (see the discussion in Putnam and Nussbaum).

From this time on, Aristotle's *de Anima* was continually discussed within the philosophical traditions of Europe. Meanwhile, in the Arab world, the treatise was also available, and was the subject of much discussion, especially in the work of Avicenna and Averroës, who focused above all on the doctrine of the intellect (see Brentano). But the Arabic tradition, in this case, does not contribute vital information about the text itself. Among later work one might mention the edition by J. Pacius (Frankfurt, 1596) and the commentary by J. Zabarella (Venice, 1605).

Modern work on the text was pioneered by I. Bekker's Berlin Academy edition of 1831, which, with all its notorious deficiencies in both collation and judgement, still provided a solid basis for further work. The editions of Torstrik (1862), Biehl (1884), and Förster (1912), and textual criticism by Bonitz and Bywater, took things further.[11] The massive edition, translation, and commentary by R. D. Hicks (1907) is useful as a commentary, but not very helpful on textual matters. The French edition, translation, and commentary by G. Rodier (1900) does little textual work (reprinting Biehl's apparatus with little revision); and the interpretations proposed can be eccentric. But the volume is especially useful for its inclusion of many pertinent citations from the ancient commentators. W. D. Ross edited the work for the Oxford Classical Texts in 1956, and again in 1961, with a relatively brief commentary. (The Bibliography mentions other recent commentaries and translations in various languages.)

III. Unity of the Treatise

The fact that the *De Anima*, like other Aristotelian works, did not receive its present form until around 30 BC, with the edition of Andronicus of Rhodes,[12] means that its original form must remain in doubt. In the case of some of Aristotle's other works, we have some (not terribly clear) information about their state in a catalogue of works that can be traced back to either the Alexandrian librarian Hermippus or the Peripatetic scholarch Ariston of Ceos.[13] But in this catalogue *De Anima* is present only in a piece which, according to the convincing arguments of Paul Moraux, is itself post-Andronican, inserted to fill a gap in the original text. Here it is listed among other works dealing with nature, such as

---

[10] For a close study of William's skills and practices as translator, see Nussbaum (1975).
[11] See also the comments of Ross in Aristotle (1961*a*).   [12] On Andronicus, see Plezia (1946).
[13] On the question of the origin of the ancient catalogues, see Moraux (1951), Düring (1956), Keaney (1963), Nussbaum (1975).

Physics, De Gen. et Corr., De Caelo, and the biological works, but the *Metaphysics* is included in the group also. (At most this may be an indication of the order in Andronicus' edition.) In the catalogue of Ptolemy, which probably derives from Andronicus' edition, *De Anima* is listed in the middle of an exclusively physical, psychological, and biological group. Even if we can glean from this a bit of information about Andronicus' ordering of the works, it means that we have no knowledge of what *De Anima* looked like before his edition, and of whether or not it was a unitary work.[14] Well-embedded cross-references to a *Peri Psuchēs* in other genuine Aristotelian works give evidence that there was such an Aristotelian title, possibly in Aristotle's lifetime (since the cross-references are often of dubious authenticity); but they do not enlighten us much about the precise contents, or the ordering of the parts, especially in the messy terrain of book 3.[15]

On account of this uncertain situation, it has been possible for interpreters to question in rather radical ways the compositional unity of the work—especially once it was recognized that chronological development might be a salient feature of Aristotle's work. For a time, in recent decades, scholars found attractive the hypothesis of F. Nuyens, that Aristotle's writing on soul and body fell into three distinct periods: (i) a period of faithful Platonist dualism (represented, allegedly, by the *Eudemus*, a dialogue); (ii) a middle period of 'instrumental dualism', in which Aristotle still holds that the soul and the body are distinct substances, but views the body as a help rather than a hindrance, a 'tool' for the soul (a view allegedly present in some of the biological works, the *Parva Naturalia*, and the *De Motu*); and finally, (iii) a period of hylomorphism, in which the soul is held to be the form of the body (*De Anima*).[16] Nuyens placed the *De Anima* as a whole in the final period. But Ross, noting the fact that 'tool' language is used of soul–body relations, with a cross-reference to the *De Motu*, in 3. 10 (433[b]18–30), made one alteration to Nuyens's general scheme, which on the whole he accepted: he concluded that the material in book 3 must represent the second, rather than the third, period; in consequence he concluded that book 3 was composed before books 1 and 2. He also believed it to be unfinished, remarking that 'Aristotle left the manuscript of the third book less carefully prepared for publication than that of the earlier books.'[17]

Nuyens's rigid schema has by now been generally rejected. Material from a dialogue cannot be straightforwardly used as evidence of what Aristotle himself thought; and one can show that 'tool' (*organon*) language need not be incompatible with a hylomorphic theory of soul and body. On Aristotle's hylomorphic view, particular materials are not essential parts of what the *psuchē* itself is; they are at

---

[14] The earlier lists show that in many respects the corpus did not have the form Andronicus gave it, but consisted, frequently, of smaller units, such as an 'On Motion in Three Books'—presumably the central books of the *Physics*.

[15] The *De Motu Animalium* does, however, appear to refer back to the contents of *DA* 3. 9–11 under the description *Peri Psuchēs*, just as 3. 10 refers forwards to the *De Motu*.

[16] Nuyens (1948).   [17] Ross in Aristotle (1961a), introduction.

most necessary for performing the functions towards which *psuchē* is organized. Thus it is rather natural for Aristotle to speak of bodily parts as tool-like, even though they are not separate from, but rather constitutive of, the organization that is *psuchē*. Tool language abounds in clearly hylomorphic discussions. Indeed, one need go no further than the final definition of *psuchē* in *De Anima* 2.1, the showcase for Nuyens's 'third period'; for *psuchē* is said to be the *entelecheia* of a *sōma phusikon organikon*, a natural tool-like body, or body equipped with useful tool-like parts. This definition is immediately followed by the comment, 'Wherefore one must not ask whether the soul and the body are one, any more than whether the wax and its shape are one, or in general the matter of each thing and that of which it is the matter' (412^b5-8). In other words, tool language is closely linked to the strongest statement Aristotle makes about the hylomorphic unity of soul and body.

This means that the strongest argument that has recently been advanced for the disunity of the treatise is weak indeed. None the less, it is still perfectly clear that book 3 is internally a mess, and that the current sequence of topics may not represent Aristotle's own finished work and/or arrangement—either because the work remains incompletely finished or because of some subsequent damage.

IV. Relationship to Other Parts of the Corpus

The *De Anima* has complex links with other works, such as the *Metaphysics*, the *Physics*, the *Parva Naturalia*, the *De Motu Animalium*, the various biological treatises, the ethical works, and even—on the emotions—the *Rhetoric*. In some cases, one may feel that two treatments of a single topic are incompatible in ways that do suggest revision over time. (I have argued as much for the two treatments of action in *De Anima* 3. 9–11 and the *De Motu Animalium*.[18]) On the other hand, it frequently seems preferable to view putative differences as differences of emphasis in connection with Aristotle's focus on a particular set of problems.[19] Aristotle himself gives an example of this in 3. 10, where he defers the detailed discussion of the physiology of motion for another treatise (summarizing prospectively arguments of the *De Motu Animalium*), suggesting in a general way that it is in the treatises that we call the *Parva Naturalia* (called by him 'the functions common to body and soul') that he will have more to say about the concrete physiology of the life-processes.

[18] See Nussbaum (1983).   [19] For a good treatment of this question, see Kahn (1966).

B. *DE ANIMA*: ITS AGENDA AND ITS RECENT INTERPRETERS

AMÉLIE OKSENBERG RORTY

I. The Agenda of *De Anima*

THE scope of *De Anima* is much broader than that of either contemporary philosophy of mind or contemporary philosophical psychology. It is a metaphysical inquiry into the ontology of *psuchē* and of *nous*;[1] it is philosophical psychology, a general analysis of the activities of *psuchē*; it is philosophical bio-psychology, an investigation of the teleologically organized functions that are common to living bodies. It has sometimes been classified with metaphysics in a group of works on natural philosophy, and sometimes more narrowly with the physical and biological treatises.

Aristotle begins his philosophical psychology by attempting to analyse and arbitrate the opinions of his predecessors. Typically, his principled courtesy leads him to a set of distinctions that are intended to reformulate their questions and preoccupations. He proposes to resolve their controversies about the definition of *psuchē*, its cognitive and motive powers, and the ontological status of *nous*.

By Aristotle's lights, psychology is not, strictly speaking, an independent science, with its own method and subject-matter. He allocates the inquiry into the nature of the soul to the *phusikos* concerned with the principle of living things (*archē tōn zōion*; 402ᵃ7 ff., 403ᵃ27–8). Every scientific inquiry involves some separation, a logical abstraction of the *logos* from the subject-matter under investigation. Those sorts of 'investigations' that do not separate the *logos* of the thing from the thing itself—carpentry or medical practice, for instance—do not strictly speaking fall within the domain of natural science (403ᵇ10 ff.). Most investigations also involve another kind of separation, distinguishing aspects, attributes or 'parts' of a complex substances. These are sometimes analytically separable from one another and from the immediate material cause of the substance without being capable of existing separately; sometimes they are separable both analytically and in fact. If there are any functions of the soul that are capable of existing independently of the functions of the body in fact as well as in thought, they will fall within the province of the metaphysician (*ho prōtos philosophos*; 403ᵇ15).

According to Aristotle, the natural philosopher (*phusikos*) who studies human psychology must specify both the physical conditions and the central cognitions

© Amélie Oksenberg Rorty, 1992.

[1] Because it carries many post-Cartesian connotations, 'mind' is not a felicitous translation of Aristotle's *nous*.

(*logos*) that characterize psychological activities and affections (403ᵇ7 ff.). The affections of the soul (*pathē tēs psuchēs*), for instance, are enmattered *logoi* (*ta pathē logoi enhuloi eisin*); they involve both cognition and the body (*meta sōmatos*; 403ᵃ25). Explaining affections of the soul (*pathē*) therefore requires the co-operation of two specialists. The *phusikos* gives an analysis of the physical condition of the body (a state and movement); but he must absorb the work of the *dialektikos* who specifies the central cognitions—the *logos* and the end (*hou heneka*)—that are constitutively associated with each affect (403ᵃ26, 403ᵇ9 ff.). In one sense the physical and the cognitive accounts are separable from one another, and in another sense they are not. That they are separable in thought is evident from the fact that they are the subject of two distinct types of inquiry, one of which is broadly speaking physiological and the other cognitive. That they are not separable in being or in fact is evident from Aristotle's claim that explanations of such affections of the soul (*tēs psuchēs pathē*) as anger are incomplete unless they include both accounts (403ᵃ25 ff.). Anger involves the boiling of the blood around the heart *and* the person must think himself unjustly injured, to the extent of having a desire for revenge along with the pleasurable expectation of revenge (403ᵃ31, *Rh.* 1378ᵃ31 ff.). If the boiling of the blood around his heart had simply been caused by a feverish illness, without his having the accompanying thoughts, the person would not be angry.

Aristotle suggests that if we want to understand the connection between the material and the cognitive causes of an affect, we must turn to its final cause, the end designated in its *logos*. Drawing an analogy with the description of the essence of a house, he says: 'the *logos* of a house is a shelter against destruction… One [presumably the *phusikos*] describes this as stones, bricks, timber; another [presumably the *dialektikos*] will say it is a form (*eidos*) in that material with that purpose or end (*heneka tōndi*)' (403ᵇ4 ff.) The end of anger—revenge for an unjust injury—is, so to say, fuelled by the *pathos* associated with the boiling of the blood. The conjunction of these causes is required for the *phusikos*'s explanation of the physical motions that are taken in revenge.[2] Although Aristotle introduces the co-operative conjunction of the material, the formal, and the final causes as explanations of the affections of the soul, it is reasonable to suppose that he might extend this kind of analysis for at least some of its activities, for instance, for nutrition and growth.

It is a difficult and disputed question whether—or how—the co-operation among the causal dimensions of explanation is also required for those activities of the soul, which—like perception, desire, and some kinds of locomotion—we call intentional (433ᵇ19). Roughly speaking, we can distinguish three general positions concerning the materiality of *psuchē*:

---

[2] Because the *Rhetoric*'s account of the affects is given by the *dialektikos*, it does not refer to their material causes. Because it is not primarily concerned with the motivational force of the affects, *De Anima* makes only the briefest reference to the ways they involve pleasure and pain (431ᵃ10–14). Despite the ellipsis of the *De Anima*'s account, and the suppresion of the material causes in the *Rhetoric*, the two stories are in general compatible.

(i) Any and every *psuchē* is *logos enhulos* (403ᵃ5 ff.) and every psychological operation involves a particular material change (*kinēsis tēs hulēs*), such as locomotion, growth, or change of size.

(ii) Any and every *psuchē* is *logos enhulos* realized in some or another type of matter. But while psychological functions (perception, desire, *phantasia*) involve material changes, there is neither token nor type correlation between such activities and specific material changes. Nor do psychological functions set constraints on the kind of matter in which they are realized: formally identical psychological functions can be realized in radically distinctive types of matter.

(iii) Any and every *psuchē* is a *logos enhulos* realized in a physical body (*sōma*) of a certain kind, rather than in matter (*hulē*) as it might be described by a theoretical physicist. For example, the *psuchē* of ruminant mammals is expressed in the kind of body that is specific to that type of animal, one whose nutritive functions are physically organized in flesh of a certain kind. While there are general resemblances or analogies between the psychological functions of distinctive types of animals, the full explanation of those functions essentially refers to the specific physiology of a certain type of animal; for example, animals that eat flying insects must have perceptual systems with a certain kind of physical organization, effectively connected to the parts of their bodies that are engaged in locomotion (433ᵇ12–31). The co-operation of the causal dimensions of *psuchē* begins with the final cause: the preservation and maintenance of a specific form (*eidos*) or type of life, such as its being a ruminant or a human. These two—the final and formal causes—taken together, set constraints on the kind of matter— the kind of physical body—in which this form of life can be effectively, actively realized. And this in turn sets further constraints on the details of the material organization of that kind of animal, so that it effectively promotes the motions required for leading its kind of life. If there are some psychological activities that are not *logos enhulos*—if *nous* and its activities are not only analytically but substantially separable—then not all psychological activity involves organic change. Still, we might speculate that thinking could nevertheless so change the whole person—as having realized his highest potentiality—that he became visibly *kalos kagathos*.[3]

Aristotle characterizes *psuchē* as the first actuality (*entelecheia*) of a natural body capable of sustaining life (*sōma phusikon metechon zōēs*) that is, an organism composed of organs (412ᵃ19–21, 412ᵇ4–6). It expresses the living thing's defining essence (*logos*) (412ᵇ10), its *aitia*, *archē*, and *telos* (415ᵇ9–18). *Psuchē* is—as common speech has it—the life and soul of an organism, engaged in its natural activities. An organism does not have life as one of its attributes, along with its size and shape. Rather, the life and soul of a certain kind of body consists in its being active in a certain way, engaged in those activities that constitute its being the sort of thing it is. Life is not a presupposition of activity; rather, to be alive is to

---

[3] I believe that Aristotle holds a highly refined version of the third position, but it would be inappropriate to argue for this claim here.

be actively (endogenously) engaged in those activities which constitute one's nature. Aristotle does not draw a sharp distinction between those vital activities which, like self-nourishment, just keep an organism alive, and those that express the nature of the thing, that constitute a way of living. The view is severe: an organism that can survive but not engage in its 'higher' activities is only equivocally (*all' ē homōnumōs*) a member of its species (412^{b}15).

It is for this reason that the greater part of *De Anima* is devoted to an analysis of the psychological activities of living things are organized to maintain a specific sort of life. Psychological activities are individuated and identified not only by their contributions to sheer maintenance for survival, but also by their contributions to the organism's realizing the potentialities of its species. The *dunamis* of self-nutrition distinguishes living from non-living things: it is a precondition for all other capacities that constitute an organism's living (413^{a}21 ff.). Similarly, animals are distinguished from other living things by their capacity for sensation. But touch is the only sense that all animals have; it is, moreover, a precondition for all other senses (413^{b}4 ff.). It is for this reason that so much of *De Anima* is devoted to the analysis of these functions, as they not only conduce to the sheer survival of an animal, but to its well-being, its fulfilling its potentialities as a specific kind of animal (435^{b}20). Because humans are distinguished from other animals by their *dianoia*, by their capacities for thought and reasoning (415^{a}8–11, 413^{b}13), there is a question of how, if at all, thinking (and its objects) is integrated with other basic human activities and their proper objects. Unfortunately none of the works in the Aristotelian corpus as we have it presents a full discussion of this issue.

Aristotle's account of *psuchē* as the active organizing principle of living bodies sets the agenda for his analyses of the most general principles of organic functioning and of the activities that differentiate animals from other organisms, as well as humans from other animals. His views generate a set of questions that are addressed in *De Anima* 1 and 2. If each species actualizes its basic vital capacities in a physically distinctive way, are there as many kinds of souls, each with its distinctive activities, as there are species (402^{b}1–3 ff.)? If the soul is the source of motion, is it itself moved (408^{a}29 ff.)? How, if at all, are the sense-organs altered in perception (417^{a}15 ff., 425^{b}27)? What is the relation between the cause and the proper objects of perception (418^{a}7 ff.)? How are perceptions co-ordinated in the common sense? Does it have special objects (426^{b}8 ff.)? Is *phantasia* a distinct faculty with special objects, and if so, what is their relation to the objects of the various sense-organs (427^{b}28 ff.)? How is perception related to opinion (427^{a}17 ff.) and in what sense is the perception of proper objects always true (*aisthēsis tōn idiōn aei alēthēs*; 427^{b}12 ff.)? (Analogously, in what sense are desires correct when they are directed to their proper objects (*alētheia homologōs echousa tēi orexei tēi orthēi*; *EN* 1139^{a}24–32, 1143^{b}5)?) In what sense is the object of desire (*orekton*)—as conceived to be genuinely good—the first cause of motion (433^{a}27–^{b}13)? What role does teleology play in these explanations: to what extent are the ends of various psychological activities—including voluntary motions—

necessary to explain the causal force of the *orekton*, as known or imagined to be good?

Nous has a special status within the psychological organization of human beings. It is characterized as a simple and unaffected kind of substance that cannot perish (408^b18, 429^b22) and as a different kind of soul that can exist separately from the body, in the same way that what is everlasting can exist separately from what is perishable (413^b24, 429^a18 ff.). Pure noetic activity in *theōria* does not involve the actualization or fulfilment of any particular part or aspect of the body. It is, rather, the whole man that is perfected or actualized by his thinking (*EN* 1178^a2–8). The full analysis of the noetic functions of the human *psuchē* brings us to the premises that guide Aristotle's metaphysics of epistemology: that there is nothing of which the mind is incapable of thinking (429^a17); that in a sense, the mind does not exist as an independent entity before it thinks (429^a22); that it is, in its first actualization as active (*kat' energeian*) in thought, identical with its objects (*pragmata*; 429^b6–7, 430^a20) and with the forms (*eidē*) in mental images (*phantasmasi noei*; 431^b3 ff.). A full account of *nous* and *dianoia* requires specifying the proper objects of the various forms of cognition: sense-perception, *phantasia*, desire, *dianoia*, and pure thought-thinking itself. To what extent is *aisthēsis* noetic, or as we would say, cognitive? How is it possible for a specific kind of organism to know eternal and unchanging things, without itself having some eternal separable 'part' or function? What is the relation between the kind of human *dianoeisthai* that depends on *phantasia* and pure unembodied or divine *theōrein*? Is *nous* separable from the body in the same way that two substances are separable, capable of existing independently of one another? Or is it separable in the way that geometrical properties are separable, abstractible from bodies without being capable of existing separately?

Because the discussion of *nous* in *De Anima* is so fragmented and apparently incomplete, we must turn elsewhere for its fullest analysis. Since the range of logical works—the *Organon*—articulate the structure of valid thought, they contribute to a philosophical understanding of forms—the *eidē*—of *nous*. In book 6 of the *Nicomachean Ethics*, Aristotle develops an account of the elements of practical reasoning, distinguishing the operations and objects of various types of thinking (*phronēsis*, *logistikon*, *epistēmē*, *bouleusis*, and *sophia*). Unfortunately he does not give us a full account of their interrelations or their relation to *nous*, taken generally. But it is to the *Metaphysics* that we must turn for the most extended treatment of the intellect. It is there, if anywhere, that we can find an account of what Aristotle might mean by characterizing *nous* as a form of forms (*nous eidos eidōn*; 432^a1 ff.) and by drawing an analogy between *psuchē* and the hand as a tool of (for) tools (*organon estin organōn*).

Another relatively independent line of thought connects *De Anima* with Aristotle's ethical works. Besides being capable of intentional voluntary action, at least some human agents are capable of acting deliberately, their choices (*prohaireseis*) and deliberations (*bouleuseis*) being guided and formed by their general ends. Unlike scientific reason, however, practical thinking issues in

action: it is qualified by circumstances and directed to particulars. An understanding of human agency requires an account of the special status of practical
reasoning, of thought that links desire to perception, *phantasia*, and belief.

De Anima has a fragmentary treatment of the integration of *dianoia, aisthēsis,
phantasia,* and *orexis.* Besides the complex history of our version of the text, there
are philosophic reasons for what seems an incomplete discussion. By Aristotle's
lights, a scientific explanation of natural phenomena focuses on their invariable
and universal features. It requires the co-operation of the four causal dimensions,
loosely integrated by reference to final causes. Philosophic ethics analyses the
teleology and the structure of well-formed action (*praxis*). But since its subject-
matter is contingent and particular, it can at best provide qualified generalizations
about 'what is true for the most part'. The phenomena of voluntary action—
of the *telos* and *logos* of virtuous character—are not susceptible to the kind of
scientific explanation that the *phusikos* can provide for phenomena that are
necessary and invariable. There is no general integration of the causal dimensions
of explanation of action, one that would link the logic of practical reasoning to the
biology in which it is realized. The connection between *De Anima* and the theory
of action developed in Aristotle's ethnical works must, in the nature of the case,
remain schematic because ethics is not, according to Aristotle, a psycho-biological
science.

II. The Directions of Recent Interpretations

Not surprisingly, contemporary approaches to *De Anima* reflect a range of
heterogeneous philosophical preoccupations. The confluence of several lines of
investigations that bring scholars to *De Anima* represents the lines of thought that
originally formed the work. They come from primary concerns about problems in
metaphysics, philosophical psychology, philosophical biology, or action theory.
Contemporary scholars who attempt to locate their own views by explicating
those of Aristotle often also find themselves drawn into the task of placing his
views within the larger frame of classical and Hellenistic philosophy, determining
whether he did justice to his predecessors, charting the Platonic strands in his
analysis of *nous,* and specifying its influence on later philosophers.

Many commentators who approach *De Anima* with an interest in Aristotle's
biological treatises attempt to formulate the details of his psychophysicalism, his
account of the role of *psuchē* in the organization and (types of) motion of living
organisms (see the articles by Code and Moravcsik, Matthews, Lloyd in this volume). Others are interested in specific psychobiological problems: the analysis of
the organization and functioning of the various sense modalities, and their integration in the common sense and *phantasia* (Witt, Sorabji, Freeland, Schofield,
D. Frede, Annas). Still a third group are primarily interested in the conceptual
issues raised by biology: what are the material causes of psychological activities
(Whiting)?

A number of philosophers come to *De Anima* from specific issues in contemporary philosophy of mind. Some are particularly interested in a realist analysis of the intentionality of *aisthēsis*. Others defend Aristotle's account of the relationship between form and matter in perception and desire as an ancestor of contemporary functionalism (Nussbaum and Putnam). They attempt to interpret Aristotle's psychophysicalism in such a way as to avoid the difficulties of interactive dualism and reductive materialism, hoping to use functionalism to clarify the under-specified relation between the formal and the material-efficient causes of thought. A lively controversy about the plausibility of drawing such parallels has emerged: some philosophers argue that this attempt is committed to a picture of matter that can no longer be taken seriously (Burnyeat). Their view is that neither Aristotelian *hulē* nor *sōma* corresponds to post-Newtonian matter; and little in contemporary psychology captures the way that biological teleology functions in Aristotle's psychology. Other philosophers hold that the recent advances in biological psychology argue for replacing neo-Cartesian views of the mind with Aristotle's conception of *nous* (Wilkes).

Some commentators focus on Aristotle's discussions of the status and activities of *nous*: its relation to *psuchē* (M. Frede), the activity of thinking (Kahn), and the relation between the active and passive intellect (Kosman).

Still other commentators come to *De Anima* by way of ethics and action theory. Many are interested in the connections between *phantasia* and desire, and in the contribution that *De Anima* might make to our understanding of choice and the role of *dianoia* in practical reasoning (Richardson).

The variety of directions from which commentators come to *De Anima*—the range of interests that brings philosophers to the work—is ample testimony to its fertility. Philosophers do not turn to *De Anima* solely from scholarly piety: many also hope to find insights that could in principle illuminate current issues in the philosophy of biology and the philosophy of mind. But because the book is deeply embedded within the rest of Aristotle's thought, particularly in his metaphysical and biological studies, detaching *De Anima*'s discussions of (as it may be) perception or desire from the extended treatment of related matters elsewhere in the corpus runs the danger of misinterpretation. The read-and-raid school of interpretation often constructs intriguing 'Aristotelian' positions that Aristotle did not himself develop, and that he would have understood only with great difficulty. When they bring Aristotle's discussions to bear on a wide range of current philosophical issues, the authors of the essays in this volume attempt to avoid fanciful, anachronistic reconstructions of his views. They locate their interpretations firmly within the context of the entirety of the Aristotelian corpus. While expounding and explaining his views to the modern reader, they have also attempted to interpret Aristotle in Aristotelian terms.[4]

---

[4] I am grateful to Rüdiger Bittner, Myles Burnyeat, Aryeh Kosman, and Martha Nussbaum—who disagrees with most of my account—for their generous, detailed comments and discussions.

2

IS AN ARISTOTELIAN PHILOSOPHY OF MIND STILL CREDIBLE?

(A DRAFT)

M. F. BURNYEAT

I publish this version of my paper with reluctance. Originally composed in 1983 for a visit to the University of California at Santa Barbara, it is a promissory note for a longer study still in progress. My intention was to provoke discussion and then sit back to reflect on objections and responses before producing a fully argued, properly documented presentation of my case. With this in view I circulated the Santa Barbara draft to a small number of close colleagues, made a few revisions, and read it again to meetings in Birmingham, Cambridge, Durham, Oxford, Pittsburgh, and St Andrews. It was only when refutations of the paper I have not yet written began to appear in print that I became aware of the extent to which copies of the draft were multiplying. It now seems unreasonable not to let everyone have access to the cause of the controversy.

I am grateful for the lively interest my remarks have aroused, and I will continue to reflect on the many objections (both published and unpublished) that I have received. I remain convinced, however, that whatever the meaning of the phrase 'taking on form without matter', it picks out the most basic level of interaction between a perceiver and the object perceived. Accordingly, if taking on form without matter is not the physiological process that Sorabji describes, then in Aristotle's view *there is no physiological process* which stands to a perceiver's awareness of colour or smell as matter to form. The most basic effect on the perceiver is identical with an awareness of colour or smell, as indeed Aristotle asserts at 425ᵇ26–426ᵃ19. This explains why the Sorabji interpretation of taking on form without matter is essential support for the Putnam–Nussbaum interpretation of Aristotle as a functionalist. Without Sorabji, the functionalist can point to no material process that serves for Aristotle as the realization of perception. Without Sorabji, therefore, the Aristotelian theory of perception is neither functionalist nor a theory that any of us could believe.

But of all this, more in the next version.

WHEN Hilary Putnam had worked out his functionalist solution to the mind–body problem, he discovered that it was only a more precise version of Aristotle's view. When Martha Nussbaum recorded a dialogue between Aristotle and Democritus on explanations in psychology, she discovered that Aristotle had borrowed an important example from Putnam in order to make their shared position clear and precise. K. V. Wilkes in her book *Physicalism* is another functionalist who sees herself as restating in modern terms a theory that was already held by Aristotle.[1] What inspires this happy convergence of modern minds is the following thought: Aristotle explains the relation of soul to body as a special case of the relation of form or function to the matter in which it is realized. He aims thereby to escape the difficulties of (Platonic) dualism without relapsing into the crudities of reductive (Democritean) materialism. But Aristotle's problem is ours too. Just read Descartes for Plato, and for Democritus J. J. C. Smart, and any sane philosopher will start looking for a credible middle path. The Putnam–Nussbaum thesis is that the functionalist map of that middle path was authoritatively drawn long ago by Aristotle.

I propose to argue that the Putnam–Nussbaum thesis is false, and that its falsehood is of more than historical interest. The thesis fails as an interpretation of Aristotle because it fails to notice that Aristotle's conception of the material or physical side of the soul–body relation is one which no modern functionalist could share; no modern functionalist could share it because no modern philosopher, whatever his persuasions, could share it. Modern philosophies of mind have taken shape, very largely, as so many ways of responding to Cartesian dualism, but all the fire has been aimed at the mind side of that dualism. My hope is that a historical inquiry into what Aristotle believes about the physical basis of animal life will bring about a sense that the other half of Cartesian dualism, the matter half, remains intact in all of us. Our conception of the mental may be open for discussion and revision, but our conception of the physical is irreversibly influenced by the demolition of the Aristotelian philosophy through Descartes and others in the seventeenth century. Aristotle's solution to the mind–body problem sounds attractive when it is stated in general outline as the view that the mind or soul is a set of functional capacities of the animal body. It becomes less attractive when we find that it is worked out in terms of, and cannot be understood apart from, various physical assumptions which we can no longer share: assumptions, indeed, of such a kind that we can scarcely even imagine what it would be like to take them seriously. Aristotle's philosophy of mind is no longer credible because Aristotelian physics is no longer credible, and the fact of that physics being incredible has quite a lot to do with there being such a thing as the mind–body problem as we face it today.

The context in which I will examine the Putnam–Nussbaum thesis and try to give substance to the historical perspective I have just sketched is the theory of perception. This will involve us in a struggle to understand one of the most mysterious of Aristotelian doctrines, the doctrine that in perception the sense-organ takes on the sensible form of the object perceived without its matter. I choose this context precisely because it is so difficult to understand. I think it is difficult to understand what Aristotle says about perception because it is difficult for us to believe it. In arguing this, I shall be arguing against a rival interpretation of Aristotle's theory of perception, advanced in an influential paper by Richard Sorabji, which makes it all rather easy to understand, and easy in just the particu-

---

[1] Putnam (1975), Nussbaum (1978), Wilkes (1978).

lar way it needs to be if the theory of perception is to conform to and confirm the Putnam–Nussbaum thesis that modern functionalism is genuinely Aristotelian. Let me explain.

The usual way into the form–matter analysis of the soul–body relation is through a series of analogical extensions from the paradigm case of the statue made of bronze:

(1)	(2)	(3)
bronze	shape	a statue
bricks, etc.	arrangement	a house
wood and iron	capacity for chopping	an axe
transparent jelly	capacity for seeing	an eye
body (with organs)	soul	an animal

Now the trouble with proceeding by analogical extension is that it can be unclear which features of the original case you are to hold on to and which you are to discard as you journey to the case you are really interested in. But there is one feature of the statue case which a functionalist reading of Aristotle must hold on to. It is a feature of all artefacts that the relation of matter and form is contingent. The shape is something added to the bronze both in the sense that the bronze might not have been made into that shape and in the sense that the same shape could be realized in different material. Just so, the functionalist says that his psychological states, construed as functional states, must be realized in *some* material or physical set-up, but it is not essential that the set-up should be the flesh and bones and nervous system of *Homo sapiens* rather than the electronic gadgetry of a computer. The artefact model is maintained, Putnam says explicitly that it is purely contingent that human beings are not artefacts, and Nussbaum gives her scholarly endorsement to this being Aristotle's view.

Apply this to the case of perception. If the artefact model prevails, it is a contingent matter whether perception, construed as a functional state, is realized in a physiological set-up such as modern science describes or in the physiological set-up that Aristotle described. It will not then be essential to Aristotle's account of perception that it involves the particular physiological processes he invokes to explain it. We can discard his story about the sense-organ taking on form without matter, on the grounds that it is antiquated physiology, substitute our own physiology, and still claim in good conscience to have an *Aristotelian* theory of perception. We must be able to do this if Aristotle is a functionalist and functionalism is Aristotelian, because the whole point of functionalism is to free our mental life from dependence on any *particular* material set-up. And this is precisely what the Sorabji interpretation of taking on form without matter enables us to do.

According to Sorabji, taking on form without matter is a strictly physiological process in which the organ of sense quite literally takes on the colour or smell perceived. The eye-jelly goes red, something in our nose goes smelly. This process stands to the perceiver's awareness of colour or smell as matter to form. That is, we have

(1)	(2)	(3)
going red	awareness of red	seeing red

The point Sorabji emphasizes is that the form of a thing or process is not a component of it additional to its matter, nor can it be characterized in a Cartesian or any other modern sense as mental in contrast to physical. So Aristotle is seen to have found a way of saying, 'Yes, perception is a physiological process, but remember—it is also an awareness', without involving himself in the difficulties of dualism. His view rather is that the physiological process of taking on the colour (in the eye-jelly) *constitutes* seeing red, as a piece of bronze constitutes a statue or as a particular series of steps constitutes a journey from Athens to Thebes. In favour of his interpretation, Sorabji cites, in particular, the last sentence of 2. 12: 'What then is smelling apart from being affected? Or is smelling also awareness...?' (translating *aisthanesthai*, not unreasonably, as 'awareness'). In this text we have a separate mention of the physiological process, the being affected by sensible forms, and the awareness; the physiology is characterized in intentional terms as an awareness of smell; and it is clear from the word 'also' introducing the characterization that this awareness is not in any simple way reducible to the physical or causal interaction with the object of perception. QED.

So much for the position I want to argue against, which is related to the general Putnam–Nussbaum thesis as a piece of essential support in the particular area of perception.[2] On the other side, opposed to the Sorabji reading of the theory of taking on form without matter, is a rival interpretation whose leading representatives are John Philoponus, Thomas Aquinas, and Franz Brentano, all of them anxious to deny that the colour is literally taken on by the eye-jelly. Rather, the eye's taking on a colour is just one's becoming aware of some colour. Brentano went so far as to identify Aristotle's form taken on without matter with his own idea of the intentional object of mental states, but the question whether that is going too far lies outside the scope of this paper. Instead I shall start from the problem of what the rival interpretation should say about the last sentence of 2. 12.

On the face of it, it is a grave problem for the rival interpretation that there should even be such a question as what it is to smell something, or in general to perceive something, over and above being affected by sensible forms. The question makes good sense if, as the Sorabji interpretation holds, the being affected is the nose literally and physiologically becoming smelly, or the eye-jelly becoming red, etc. But if, as the rival interpretation holds, the being affected is already a cognitive state, in that it is the becoming aware of a colour, a smell, a sound, or whatever, what sense does it make to ask what more there is to perceiving than the becoming aware of a sensible quality? That is the puzzle of the last sentence of 2. 12.

Before embarking on a reading of 2. 12 which will lead to a resolution of this

[2] Nussbaum does accept it.

puzzle, it may be helpful to mention that in an earlier chapter, 2. 5, Aristotle has taken pains to inform us of his view that, although perceiving is a being affected by something, an alteration undergone in a sense-organ, it is so in a very special sense of being affected or being altered. It is not the sort of alteration or change of quality that a cold thing undergoes when it becomes warm or a green thing when it becomes red. That is, it is not the sort of change that Aristotle in his physical works classifies as an alteration. Indeed, it is none of the types of change that Aristotle classifies and analyses in his physical works (change of quality, quantity, place, and substance). All these are in Aristotle's terms the actualization of a potentiality. What 2. 5 explains is that perception is not in this way the actualization of a potentiality; that is, it is not an ordinary change. It has to be understood in terms of a more complicated scheme which Aristotle illustrates by contrasting three cases: (i) a man who has not yet learnt a subject, for example grammar, but who has the capacity of doing so, (ii) a man who has learnt grammar, (iii) a man who is currently using the grammatical knowledge he has learnt. Ordinary alteration or change of quality, as when a green apple goes red, is comparable to the transition from (i) to (ii): a potentiality becomes actual. The alteration involved in perception is alteration in a special sense because it is comparable to the transition from (ii) to (iii). We are already at birth possessed of the capacity to perceive. Actually perceiving is exercising that capacity, and the sense-organ, Aristotle says, is not so much altered as brought into activity. Its nature is not changed but realized.

I take it that this is in fact initial evidence in favour of the rival interpretation and against the Sorabji interpretation. On the Sorabji reading the organ literally and physiologically undergoes an alteration: the eye-jelly turns red, the nose becomes smelly. This ought to be comparable to the transition from (i) to (ii), even if the newly established quality is short-lived and is soon replaced by another as one's perceptual attention switches to something else. If the change involved in perception is not an ordinary alteration but comparable rather to the transition from (ii) to (iii), it cannot be a matter of literally and physiologically becoming red or smelly.

On the other hand, if this evidence does incline us to the rival interpretation, as I think it should, we should notice that it also implies that the physical material of which Aristotelian sense-organs are made does not need to undergo any ordinary physical change to become aware of a colour or a smell. One might say that the physical material of animal bodies in Aristotle's world is already pregnant with consciousness, needing only to be awakened to red or warmth.

That way of putting it may sound excessively lyrical and mysterious, but from a twentieth-century point of view it is matched by equal mysteriousness on the object side of perception. Consider 424^{b}3 ff. The question 'Does colour or does smell have any effect on things which cannot perceive?' brings out, what is amply attested elsewhere, that for Aristotle the 'causal' agent (if such it may be called) of the unordinary change which constitutes perceiving is the colour or the smell itself. This is a world in which colours, sounds, and smells are as real as the primary qualities, and they are the chief factors in the causal explanation of perception. It is not that Aristotle does not make a distinction between light and colour, between sound and the movement of air; 424^{b}10–11 shows that he does. But what produces the perception of red or of middle C is not light striking the retina or the movement of air striking the ear; it is red and middle C. All of which is further grounds for thinking that the unordinary change produced by this unordinary agency, the taking on of sensible form, is not red in your eye or middle C in your ear, in the sense that the Sorabji reading requires, but simply awareness of red and middle C.

What can be confusing here is that Aristotle states on a number of occasions that the sense-organ has to be potentially such as the object of perception is actually, and that the object of perception makes the organ to be such as it already is. There is an especially clear statement of this point at 423^{b}30–4^{a}2. Let us therefore examine this text to see what kind of assimilation of subject to object is being referred to.

Aristotle is arguing that the organ of touch must be in a mean state with respect to sensible opposites like hot and cold, hard and soft. The problem he is facing does not arise with other sense-modalities. The organ of vision, for example, is colourless (the eye-jelly is transparent), the organ of hearing (air walled up in the ear) is soundless, and in this way we are provided with a neutral medium for the reception of visual and auditory qualities. But objects of touch are the qualities which belong to bodies as bodies (423^{b}27). The organ of touch being itself bodily, inevitably possesses some temperature, some degree of hardness. It cannot be temperatureless as the eye can be colourless. Aristotle, therefore, deals with the problem by arguing that the organ of touch has a temperature and a hardness of a mean or intermediate degree between hot and cold, hard and soft. His argument is an argument from blind spots (424^{a}2–5), followed by a restatement of the principle that the organ must be potentially such as the object is actually. The idea—confirmed elsewhere—is that we judge or notice hot and cold, hard and soft, by the contrast between the temperature or hardness of the object and the temperature or hardness of that with which we touch it (so *Mete.* 4. 4, 382^{a}17). Where there is no contrast, we do not notice these qualities. I once thought that the idea of a blind spot like this was more plausible for temperature than for hard and soft, but I take it that Aristotle is not saying that if you put your hands together, palms facing, neither hand will feel the other, but that they will not feel the other *as* hard or soft. But the point I want to emphasize is this: it is one thing to say that it takes a strong hard hand to appreciate the delicate softness of the hand it is holding, quite another to suggest that the strong hard hand softens as it holds the other, or that a hand which touches the pavement literally becomes itself as hard as concrete. The Sorabji reading will have to insist on distinguishing very sharply, as Aristotle in this passage does not appear to do, between the hand and the internal organ of touch, which on Aristotle's theory is the heart. For Sorabji it will be the heart that hardens, not the hand, which on Aristotle's considered view is the medium, not the organ, of touch. The trouble is that Aristotle then loses his argument from blind spots, for it is no longer the common-sense observation it seemed to be that we do not perceive what has the same degree of hardness and hotness as the organ of perception,[3] and we certainly do not judge hard and soft by reference to the hardness or otherwise of our hearts.

Once again, I think, we are forced to conclude that the organ's becoming like the object is not its literally and physiologically becoming hard or warm but a noticing or becoming aware of hardness or warmth. All these physical-seeming descriptions—the organ's becoming like the object, its being affected, acted on, or altered by sensible qualities, its taking on sensible form without the matter— all these are referring to what Aquinas calls a 'spiritual' change, a becoming aware of some sensible quality in the environment.

We are now ready to embark on 2. 12 and to understand why Aristotle's most official statement of his theory that every sense receives sensible forms without matter is illustrated by the model of the wax block: 424^{a}17–24. It is striking that Aristotle should apply to perception a model which Plato used for judgement in contrast to perception. In Plato's *Theaetetus* the mark on the wax block represents the conceptual content of a judgement such as 'That is Theodorus'; it is the identifying knowledge of who Theodorus is. This knowledge, this mark on the block, is originally produced not simply by perceiving Theodorus but by per- ception plus a deliberate act of memorization. One is not aware of Theodorus as Theodorus unless and until one applies the mark on one's block to the renewed perception of him. Anyone familiar with the discussion of perception in the *Theaetetus* will recognize the polemical thrust of Aristotle's appropriating the wax-block model for perception. Plato had contrasted perception with judge- ment. He had argued that there is no awareness in perception itself, just a causal interaction with sensible qualities in the environment; the awareness of what these qualities are is the work of, and can only be the work of, a thinking soul which can make judgements and understand general concepts. Aristotle's apply- ing the wax-block model directly to perception is a way of insisting, against Plato, that perception is awareness, articulate awareness, from the start.

Once grant Aristotle that the awareness in perception is in this sense primitive and it will turn out that he can explain with marvellous economy a great deal of cognitive life which Plato thought could only be due to a thinking soul, and explain it, moreover, without calling on more advanced resources than the five separate senses which (nearly) every animal possesses. But that project of Aristotle's takes us into the third book of the *De Anima*. For the present under- taking, the importance of Aristotle's polemical realigning of the wax-block model is that it confirms for us the two central claims for which I have been arguing.

The first such claim is that the reception of sensible forms is to be understood in terms of becoming aware of colours, sounds, smells, and other sensible

---

[3] Theophrastus, *De Sensibus* 2 makes it perfectly clear that the blind spot phenomenon was a received *endoxon*, independent of particular theories of perception.

qualities, not as a literal physiological change of quality in the organ. And if we think for a moment about wax blocks, we can see that the model is well suited to this idea. Suppose my ring has a circular seal. When I mark the wax with the ring, is the block circular? No, it is not circular but it has in it, it has registered and now displays, a circle. The predicate 'circle' or 'circular' characterizes not the wax itself but the content displayed therein.

The second claim which the opening of 2. 12 confirms for us, as it seems to me, is that no physiological change is needed for the eye or the organ of touch to become aware of the appropriate perceptual objects. The model says: the effect on the organ *is* the awareness, no more and no less. This second point is the one that is puzzling from a modern point of view, the one that is inimical to the Putnam–Nussbaum assimilation of Aristotle to modern functionalism, for it means that in a certain sense an animal's perceptual capacities do not require explanation. For Aristotle such capacities are part of animal life and in Aristotle's world the emergence of life does not require explanation. For Aristotle it is the existence of life which explains why animals have the physical constitutions they do, not the other way round. The unity of science is achieved from the top down, not from the bottom up, which is the way we have seen it since the seventeenth century. Aristotle simply does not have our task of starting from the existence of matter as physics and chemistry describe it and working up to the explanation of the secondary qualities on the one side and animal percep-tual capacities on the other. The secondary qualities (so called by us) are already out there in his world, fully real; these are the sensible forms. All that is needed for perception to take place is for these qualities or forms to act on the corresponding faculties in us to bring about an awareness of themselves. From the fact that this occurs we can derive certain conclusions about the kind of physical organs we must have (in two senses of 'must'): the eye must be made of something transparent, the organ of touch must have an intermediate tempera-ture and hardness. But these are merely necessary conditions for perception to take place. They are not part of a more elaborate story which would work up in material terms to a set of sufficient conditions for the perception of colours and temperature. In Aristotle's view, there is no such story to be told (*DA* 1. 1). Whereas modern functionalism, if I understand it correctly, is designed precisely to leave room for such a story to be told, while recognizing that we are not yet in a position to tell it.

To put the point in more technical terms, Aristotle would insist strongly that the only values a scientist should admit for the predicate variables in a Ramsey sentence are the psychological predicates which the Ramsey sentence so cleverly allows us to eliminate from the scientific story of animal life. What makes it true that animals perceive and that their perceiving plays the part it does in their lives is simply this: they have a faculty of perceptual awareness.

The claim that no physiological change is needed for the eye to see—it just responds to colours of its own nature—may be thought to require further eluci-dation and further support than I have so far given it. I shall provide the support, but first the elucidation. Putnam goes to a good deal of trouble to distinguish between being able to *deduce* our mental functioning from what we may one day know about our material constitution (plus a lot of assumptions) and having an *explanation* of our mental life in terms of physics and chemistry and the sciences of matter. He argues that such a deduction would not be an explanation of mental life, but he does not try to show that the deduction is impossible or in principle misconceived. Nussbaum agrees on Aristotle's behalf when she speaks of there being no gaps in the efficient causal explanations. But Aristotle, in fact, does not have this problem of distinguishing between a deduction and an explanation here because he is entirely confident, as numerous texts will testify, that deduction 'from the bottom up' is impossible.[4]

But this is still to understate the difference between Aristotle's outlook and ours. A modern philosopher who agrees that deduction 'from the bottom up' is impossible has not thereby joined the Aristotelian camp. I take it that a minimum condition for the unity of modern science is this, that in any two worlds where the physical facts are the same, the mental facts are the same; they are the same because the mental facts are supervenient on the physical facts, even if the supervenience is not predictable. This principle, which was put to me by a functionalist who denies deduction 'from the bottom up', is of course imbued with the Cartesian distinction between mental facts and physical facts. And whatever one's qualms about explanation or deduction, it is very difficult, once one is thinking in these Cartesian terms, to doubt that *determination* is 'from the bottom up': the physical facts provide sufficient conditions for the mental facts. That is what supervenience means. But it seems to me equally difficult to doubt that this is something that Aristotle denies.

Thus when one is angry, the blood boils, but that is merely a necessary, not a sufficient condition for anger; hence one's body, as he puts it, can be aroused and in the state it is in when one is angry without one's actually being angry (403^{a}21–2). The extra element needed is that an occasion for retaliation should be noticed by the agent. But here, when we turn from the emotional to the cognitive side of our mental functioning, Aristotle holds, as it seems to me, a much stronger thesis. Not merely is there no deduction from physiology to perception, not merely are there no physiological sufficient conditions for perception to occur, but the only necessary conditions are states of receptivity to sensible form: transparent eye-jelly, still air walled up in the ear, intermediate temperature and hardness in the organ of touch. When these have been specified, the material side of the story of perception is complete. That, at any rate, is my thesis about what Aristotle's thesis about perception is.

Further support for this interpretation is forthcoming as we move on into the chapter and study the passage about plants beginning at 424^{a}32. About this passage Sorabji comments[5] that it confirms the physiological interpretation of taking

---

[4] e.g. *Ph.* 2, *Metaph.* H2.   [5] Sorabji (1974), n. 28.

on form without matter because it says that plants can only take on colour and warmth by admitting into themselves coloured or warm matter. The point about perceiving will then be that it involves becoming coloured or warm in the same sense as a plant does but without having to admit coloured or warm matter. But I submit that this is plainly false about plants. The sun warms the tree without transmitting any warm matter to it, and the leaves of the tree turn brown without absorbing brown-coloured materials of any kind, and there is no evidence that Aristotle thought otherwise. So plants being affected by the matter as well as the form must mean something different from what Sorabji supposes.

After all, if receiving form with matter is absorbing some matter carrying a certain form, receiving form without matter would be absorbing the form without its being carried by a material vehicle. But form is not the sort of thing that can flit from here to there, with or without a material vehicle, and be absorbed. Receiving the form of something just means becoming like it in form. So, receiving the form of something without its matter means becoming like it in form but not becoming like it in matter. Hence also receiving the form of something with its matter means becoming like it in both form and matter. Aquinas gives an excellent account of this: when a kettle or a plant gets warmed by the fire, its matter comes to be disposed in a certain way, the same way as the fire already is. That is what makes this a case of real change; the matter of the thing is assimilated to— becomes like—the matter of the agent, and that is how it acquires the same form and that is the sense in which it is affected by the agent's matter as well.

It follows that receiving the warmth of a warm thing without its matter means becoming warm without really becoming warm; it means registering, noticing, or perceiving the warmth without actually becoming warm. If we find this a baffling way to describe what it is to perceive warmth, that, I suspect, is because we find it difficult to think of warmth as a reality apart from its material basis—that is, we find it difficult to think of warmth as anything other than a secondary, supervenient, phenomenal quality—and hence we find it difficult to think of becoming warm as anything other than becoming warm in a material way. But that is our difficulty, not Aristotle's. In his world, it is taken for granted that warmth and red can bring about 'effects' which are not effects of the material basis of these qualities.

Which brings us to the last section of the chapter and to the question whether colours and smells can have effects other than that of getting themselves perceived. The section is a typical specimen of Aristotle thinking on his feet and modifying his view as he goes along. He starts out with a reply to the question of 424^b5-6: if smell produces any effect, it produces smelling (*osphrēsis*). All a smell can act on is something that can smell and it can act on that only because or in so far as it is sensitive to smell. In other words, smell is a cause that acts only in a special way on a special matter, energizing a first actuality. Then 9 ff. confirms this: cases where you might think that something more was happening are in fact cases of ordinary causal action of the *compound* body on another body, as when (not the thunderclap but) the air of the thunderclap splits a piece of wood.

At 424^{b}12 he backtracks: the objects of the two contact senses, touch and taste, do affect bodies—after all, what agencies of ordinary alteration would be left if the heat of the fire did not warm things or the hardness of stone break things? Aristotle does not here explain the difference between their causation of real change and their causation of perception. But of course in real change they do not affect things *qua* perceptually sensitive (*hēi aisthētikon*) but (as Philoponus 443 says) *qua* bodies *simpliciter* (*hēi sōmata haplōs*), and on the active side they affect them as themselves enmattered compounds.

Aristotle backtracks further at l. 14, asking if the objects of the distance senses do not affect things after all—that is to say, affect things otherwise than perceptually (so Philoponus) and not as themselves enmattered compounds. The answer is: Yes, they do, at least in the case of indeterminate (*aorista*) things like air. What they do to air is make it smell*able*, hear*able*. They do not of course make it smell anything or hear anything. It is, I submit, in the context of causation by form alone that the question is asked: what is smelling over and above being affected? The question is not what we originally, following Sorabji, took it to be, viz. What is the difference between the effect smell has on an organ and smelling? But rather: What is the difference between the sort of effect that scent has on air and the effect it has on an organ? The answer is that the latter effect is the perceiving of something, the former the becoming perceivable. That is all Aristotle says, and that is all he needs to say, because he is not asking: What more is there to smelling than the being affected that goes on in the perceiver when he perceives? but: What more than a case of being affected does the scent effect in our noses, given that a being affected is what scent produces in the air? Answer: in this case it is a special being affected, due to the special capacity of the thing being acted on, viz. a perceiving.

The only thing that obstructs this solution is the word 'also' at l. 17, which suggests that smelling is a certain affection, viz., one in the organ, and also a perceiving. But the answer here is that the word 'also' should not be in the text.[6] In most of the manuscripts the Greek reads *osmasth*ai ais*thanesthai*. But in one MS tradition the scribe wrote *ai ai ai* three times instead of twice, and a nineteenth-century editor, Torstrik, took the middle *ai* to be the remnant of *kai* 'also'. He was wrong. The process in the organ is the perceiving and nothing else than the perceiving of scent. It is not something more than an underlying physiological process, but something more than the change scent produces in the air which is the medium of smell. But if we in the twentieth century want an explanation of that difference, Aristotle will not provide it. Instead he will refer to the difference between the air and the animal. The animal has the faculty of perception, the air, like the plants discussed earlier, does not. That's all—that's where *for Aristotle* explanation comes to a stop. The ultimate thing is the existence of life and mind. Which is just another way of saying that where living

---

[6] The proof is due to Kosman (1975).

things are concerned, the artefact model breaks down. Life and perceptual awareness are not something contingently added to animal bodies in the way in which
shape is contingently added to the bronze to make a statue. Aristotle states
explicitly in 2. 1 that the only bodies which are potentially alive are those that are
actually alive. A dead animal is an animal in name alone. And this homonymy
principle is no mere linguistic ruling. It is a physical thesis to the effect that the
flesh, bones, organs, etc. of which we are composed are *essentially* alive, *essentially*
capable of awareness.

So the Putnam–Nussbaum reading of Aristotle as a functionalist in the modern sense fails. There are in any case strong independent grounds for rejecting,
where proper substances are concerned, the artefact model and the idea of a
merely contingent relation between matter and form. (Ackrill's problem about
specifying the matter side independently of form arises from trying to carry over
this contingency from the original artefact illustrations. My view is that were
Aristotle so much as to try to answer the question as Ackrill puts it, he would be
abandoning his project of beating the Platonists and the Democriteans at one
blow by stopping the question 'What makes this a living thing?' before it can
arise.) But what the details of the theory of perception teach us is how closely the
failure of the functionalist interpretation of Aristotle is bound up with the fact
that Aristotle has what is for us a deeply alien conception of the physical. If we
want to get away from Cartesian dualism, we cannot do it by travelling
backwards to Aristotle, because although Aristotle has a non-Cartesian conception of the soul, *we* are stuck with a more or less Cartesian conception of the
physical. To be truly Aristotelian, we would have to stop believing that the
emergence of life or mind requires explanation.

We owe it above all to Descartes that that option is no longer open to us.
Hence all we can do with the Aristotelian philosophy of mind and its theory of
perception as the receiving of sensible forms without matter is what the seventeenth century did: junk it.[7] Having junked it, we are stuck with the mind–body
problem as Descartes created it, inevitably and rightly so. The modern
functionalist should be grateful to Descartes for having set him the problem to
which functionalism is supposed to be a more satisfactory solution than Cartesian
dualism. For the moral of this paper's history is that new functionalist minds do
not fit into old Aristotelian bodies.

[7] For a very clear appreciation of the point that the Aristotelian theory of perception blocks the
important questions, see Hobbes, *Leviathan*, ch. 1.

3
CHANGING ARISTOTLE'S MIND

MARTHA C. NUSSBAUM
HILARY PUTNAM

WE take up arms together in response to an attack. It is an attack on our interpretation of Aristotle and, through that, on the credibility and acceptability of Aristotle's views of soul and body. Myles Burnyeat, in his paper, 'Is an Aristotelian Philosophy of Mind Still Credible?', discovered in various things that we had written separately a shared view of Aristotle: namely, a defence of the Aristotelian form–matter view as a happy alternative to materialist reductionism on the one hand, Cartesian dualism on the other—an alternative that has certain similarities with contemporary functionalism.[1] Burnyeat argues 'that the Putnam–Nussbaum thesis is false, and that its falsehood is of more than historical interest'. Aristotle's view of mind, he argues, cannot be defended as we defend it, since, properly interpreted, it is wedded to, it 'cannot be understood apart from', a view of the material side of life that we can no longer take seriously. Indeed, we cannot even know what it would be to take it seriously. Burnyeat develops an alternative interpretation of Aristotle in the context of the theory of perception, defending a reading that he also claims to be that of Philoponus, Aquinas, and Brentano. He then argues that this interpretation does have the consequence that Aristotle is wedded to the unacceptable view of matter. Aristotle's philosophy of mind, therefore, must be 'junked'; and, 'having junked it, we are stuck with the mind–body problem as Descartes created it'.

This co-authored paper represents a stage in an on-going dialectical exchange. Burnyeat's paper responded to our earlier work, and we now respond to him— with a revision and expansion of an argument first produced and circulated in 1984. We allude throughout to the 1984 text of Burnyeat's paper, which has now circulated widely in typescript, and is published in this volume as an unfinished work in progress. Although the debate is bound to continue, we hope that this stage of it states the issues sufficiently clearly that the reader will be able (in the words of that peaceable philosopher Parmenides) to 'judge by reason the very contentious refutation'.

First we shall talk briefly about Aristotle's motivating problems—why these are not the problems from which the classic mind–body debate begins, and what significance this has for the understanding of his attitude to material

---

[1] Burnyeat (this volume, ch. 2). His references are to Putnam (1975) and Nussbaum (1978). He notes that Nussbaum refers to Putnam, and Putnam to Aristotle.

reductionism and material explanation. Then we shall look at the texts, defending against Burnyeat an interpretation that distinguishes Aristotle both from materialist reductionism and from the Burnyeat interpretation, according to which perceiving etc. require no concomitant material change, and awareness is primitive. We shall go on to defend Aristotle's position philosophically, as a tenable position even in the context of a modern theory of matter. Explain the doings of natural beings 'neither apart from matter nor according to the matter' —so Aristotle instructs the philosopher of nature (*Ph.* 194ª13–15). So: with 'cannon to right' of us and 'cannon to left', we shall try to forge a middle path that will not, as Burnyeat thinks it must, end up in the 'valley of death'.

I. Aristotle's Problems: Explanation, Nature, and Change

We have chosen the title, 'Changing Aristotle's Mind'. This paper was first written for a conference entitled 'Aristotle's Philosophy of Mind and Modern Theories of Cognition.'[2] The paper to which we reply is entitled 'Is an Aristotelian Philosophy of Mind Still Credible?' The first change we wish to make in Aristotle's mind is to point out that, properly speaking, he does not have a philosophy of mind. This fact has been pointed out before. Nussbaum has discussed the issue in 'Aristotelian Dualism: A Reply to Howard Robinson'. Putnam discusses it in 'How Old is the Mind?' Others have discussed it elsewhere.[3] But it still bears repeating: for only if we understand Aristotle's starting-points and problems can we accurately assess his solution.

The mind–body problem, the problem with which Burnyeat says we are 'stuck', the problem with which he believes any contemporary functionalist must 'inevitably and rightly' begin, starts from a focus on the special nature of mental activity—therefore from just one part of the activity of some among the living beings. It attempts to characterize that specialness. Whether the answer defended is Cartesian, reductionist, functionalist, or of some still other sort, the starting-point is the same. It is the question, how are we to speak about (conscious) awareness and about those aspects of our functioning that are thought to partake in awareness or consciousness? Aristotelian hylomorphism, by contrast, starts from a general interest in characterizing the relationship, in things of many kinds, between their organization or structure and their material composition. It deals with the beings and doings of all substances, including all living beings (plants, animals, and humans alike), all non-living natural beings, and also all non-natural substances (i.e. artefacts). It asks some very global and general questions about all these things, and two questions in particular.[4]

First, it asks: How do and should we explain or describe the changes we see taking place in the world? In particular, which sorts of entities are the primary

[2] At the University of Rochester, spring 1984.
[3] Nussbaum (1984), Putnam (1988); see also, in this volume, the papers by Matthews and Wilkes.
[4] See Nussbaum (1982), and (1978), Essay 1.

subjects or 'substrates' of change, the things that persist through changes of various sorts, on which our explanations of change are 'hung'? Aristotle holds, plausibly (appealing to ordinary discourse and practices) that any coherent account of change must pick out some entity that is the 'substrate', or underlying persistent thing, of that change, the thing to which the change happens and which persists itself as one and the same thing throughout the change. His first question, then, is: What are those primary substrates?

Second, he asks: How do and should we answer 'What is it?' questions asked about the items in our experience? What accounts give us the best stories about the identities of things, as they persist through time? What is it about individuals that makes them the very things they are? And what is it (therefore) that must remain one and the same, if we are going to continue to regard it as the same individual?

Aristotle shows that these two questions are held closely together in our discourse and practices. For any good account of change will need to single out as its underlying substrates or subjects items that are not just relatively enduring, but also relatively definite or distinct, items that can be identified, characterized as to what they are. On the other hand, if we ask the 'What is it?' question of an item in our experience, one thing we are asking is, what changes can that item endure and still remain what it is? One reason why 'a pale thing' is a bad answer to the 'What is it?' question asked about Putnam, while 'a human being' is a good answer, is that Putnam can get a suntan in Spain without ceasing to be himself; whereas if an orang-utan got off the plane we would suspect that someone had done Putnam in.

Aristotle seems to argue, then, that an answer that fails to deal with one of the questions will fail, ultimately, to do well by the other. Matter might look at first like the most enduring substrate, in that it persists through the birth and death of horses, human beings, trees.[5] But if it is not a 'this'—a definite structured item that can be picked out, identified, and traced through time, it is not in the end going to be a very good linchpin for our explanations of change and activity.[6] Indeed, in natural substances at least, matter clearly falls short even earlier on. For the matter of a tree does not in fact stay the same as long as this tree exists; it changes continually. In general, no list of particular materials will give us a substrate as stable and enduring as the form or organization of the tree, since that organization stays while the materials flow in and out. That is the nature of living things—to be forms embodied in ever-changing matter. By the same token, the organization characteristic of the species has the best claim to be the essential nature, or what-is-it, of the thing, since it is what must remain the same so long as that thing remains in existence. If it is no longer there, the identity of the thing is lost, and the thing is no more. When Putnam returns from Spain, he will have assimilated a great deal of fine Spanish food; and this will have produced matter

[5] See *Metaph.* 983[b]6–18.
[6] See *Metaph.* Z3, and the fine account of the argument in Owen (1986).

that he didn't have before he left. Nussbaum will still regard him as the same person, and treat the new bits of matter as parts of him. But if the being who got off the plane had changed in functional organization, and now had the organization characteristic of the aforementioned orang-utan, not of a human, she would call the police.

These are complex issues. We have only alluded schematically to some of our more detailed treatments of them. But we think that even this brief account shows a profound difference between Aristotle's motivations and those of most writers on the 'mind–body problem'. He does not appear to give awareness or the mental any special place in his defence of form. He has a broad and general interest in identity and explanation, and he defends the claim of form over matter with respect to this whole broad range of cases, in connection with these two questions. These are not outmoded philosophical questions; nor is Aristotle's way of pressing them at all remote from the methods and concerns of modern inquiries into substance and identity. Fine contemporary philosophers such as David Wiggins and Roderick Chisholm[7] share Aristotle's belief that the form–matter question can and should be posed in this very general way, in connection with worries about identity and persistence, before we go on to ask what special features the cases of life and mind might have in store for us. Although one of these thinkers defends the Aristotelian position and the other attacks it, neither believes that our possession today of a theory of matter different from Aristotle's alters in a fundamental way the manner in which these questions should be posed, or makes the Aristotelian reply one that we cannot take seriously.[8]

In replying to Burnyeat, then, we think it important to point out that when Aristotle argues against materialist reductionism he could not possibly be relying on the 'primitive' nature of intentionality, or on the inexplicable character of life and mind—for the simple reason that his defence of form is meant to apply (as are Wiggins's similar defence of form and Chisholm's mereological essentialism) across the board to all substances, whether or not they have 'mind', or even life. Both of us, when characterizing Aristotle's general line of anti-reductionist argument, used an artefact as our example, in order to make this point perfectly clear. And we also, for the sake of argument, expressed the example in terms of a modern theory of matter, in order to show that it is independent of pre-modern views. Let us recall the example briefly. We asked the question, why does a bronze sphere of radius r pass through a wooden hoop of radius just slightly greater than r, while a bronze cube of side $2r$ will not pass through? We argued that—no matter whether one thinks in terms of lumps of Aristotelian stuff or in terms of plotting the trajectories of the atoms characteristic of bronze and wood —the relevant answer to this 'why' question will not in fact be one that brings in facts specific to the materials (the bronze and wood) in question. The relevant answer will appeal to general formal or structural features, features that can be

---

[7] Wiggins (1980a), Chisholm (1976).

[8] An even stronger claim is made by Suppes (1974), who argues that Aristotle's theory of matter is *more* nearly adequate to recent developments in particle physics than the old atomic theory.

given in terms of geometrical laws without mentioning matter—though of course any existing cube or sphere must always be realized in *some* suitable matter. The geometrical explanation remains the same no matter whether we make the cube and sphere of bronze, or wood, or plastic (all of which will, of course, very much change an account on the material level, whether in terms of stuffs or atom-charts). The formal account, therefore, is *simpler* and more *general* than the material account; and while the material account omits the *relevant* features and includes many irrelevant features, the formal account introduces only the relevant features.[9]

In short, Aristotle thinks matter posterior to form because of a general view about the nature of scientific explanation—and *not* because matter cannot do a certain special task, the task of 'explaining mind'. We believe that these general arguments against reduction are still sound, although we are also convinced that the case for non-reduction can be bolstered by further arguments where the functions of life are concerned. So we think that any view of Aristotle that criticizes his anti-reductionism on the grounds that mind must be explained in such and such a way in our scientific age risks failing to come to grips with Aristotle.

We are not clear about how Burnyeat would confront the more general Aristotelian arguments, which are explicitly designed to hold whether one uses an ancient or a modern theory of matter. He says cryptically that he does fault them on 'strong independent grounds'; but he does not develop this thesis. We think it will be important for him, if he wants to 'junk' Aristotle on form and matter, to say how and why he 'junks' this general argument, or why, if he does not 'junk' it, he feels confident that Aristotle's whole 'philosophy of mind' can be 'junked' anyhow. In short: beginning where Aristotle begins helps to see exactly why Aristotle feels that the mind–body problem (or rather, the *psuchē*-body problem, which is his closest analogue to that problem) can be bypassed and should not arise. We shall study Aristotle's anti-reductionism with this in mind.

One further point deserves emphasis before we charge in. Aristotle's general arguments against reductionism pertain to all substances, living and non-living, as we said. At least one of these substances is altogether immaterial and unchanging. Another group consists of artefacts, whose principle of motion lies outside themselves. Living beings are a subgroup of the class of natural substances. These are defined in *Ph.* 2. 1 as 'things that have within themselves a principle of change and of remaining unchanged'. In two passages Aristotle tells us that, of necessity, if something is a changing thing it is also a material thing.[10] In *Metaph.* 1026ᵃ2–3, he writes: 'If, in fact, all natural things are accounted for in the same way as the snub [Aristotle's stock example of the inseparability of a form, and its account, from a suitable material substrate]—for example, nose, eye, face, flesh, bone, in general animal, leaf, root, bark, in general plant—for the definition of

---

[9] See Nussbaum (1978), 69–71; compare Putnam (1975), 295–8.
[10] It is notoriously difficult to know where Aristotle wants us to place the necessity operator in claims like this, and whether he firmly grasps the difference. So we give the weaker form.

none of these is without change, but they always have matter—then it is clear how one must seek and define the what-is-it in natural things.' Lest we be hesitant on account of the conditional (*not*, however, a hesitant conditional, but one with an emphatic indicative antecedent), *Metaph.* Z11 asserts the point unconditionally about animals, in a passage to which we shall return in our next section: 'For the animal is a perceptible thing, and it is not possible to define it without change, therefore not without the bodily parts' being in a certain condition' (1036^{b}27 ff.). The inferential pattern in both passages suggests that Aristotle makes an intimate—indeed a necessary—connection between change and materiality. The commentary ascribed to Alexander of Aphrodisias, in fact, takes things all the way to identity, writing on both passages, 'By change, he means matter' (512. 21 and 445. 5).[11] Before Christianity and Cartesianism separated movement from matter, it was apparently taken for granted that change is something that goes on in materials, and indeed that what matter is is the vehicle of change.

We believe that this is still a reasonable position (although we do not go so far as to *identify* change with matter). In our conception, any being that undergoes change is a material being. We cannot prise these two things apart, even in thought, without incoherence. From this it follows that any account that properly gives the what-is-it of such a being must make mention of the presence of material composition—and, as our Z11 passage suggests, of the presence of a material composition that is in some way *suitable* or *in the right state*. This tells us that on pain of incoherence we cannot describe the natural functions that are the essential natures of animals and plants without making these functions (even if only implicitly) embodied in some matter that is suitable to them: matter that is not simply an inert background, but the very vehicle of functioning itself.

All of this is supposed to be true of all the essential beings and doings of natural substances;[12] *a fortiori* (apparently) of the beings and doings of living creatures; *a fortiori* (one might suppose) of perceiving. But there are problems to be dealt with before we can arrive securely at that conclusion. So we turn from the preliminary skirmishing and prepare for the battle.

II. Perceiving is an Enmattered Form

Our argument in this section will have two parts. First, we shall give an account of how we understand and, in general, defend Aristotle's anti-reductionism. Here we shall try to show that Burnyeat has not accurately characterized our position, and that in one important respect Nussbaum's position has shifted since the 1978

---

[11] The commentary is clearly written in part by Alexander (the earlier books), in part by some later philosopher who is closely imitating Alexander; this section is from the later author, but may still derive from Alexander ultimately.

[12] Thinking, of course, is an anomaly, here as elsewhere: see below.

work that Burnyeat cites. Then we shall argue that the psychological activities of living beings, such as perceiving, desiring, and imagining, are realized or constituted in matter, are in fact the activities *of* some suitable matter; and that the relationship between form and matter is one of constitution or realization, not of either identity or mere correlation.

A. *Anti-Reductionism*

Burnyeat ascribes to us two views—both about Aristotle and about mind in general—that seem hard to put together. First, that the relation between life-functions and matter is purely contingent: 'psychological states...must be realized in *some* material or physical set-up, but it is not essential that the set-up should be the flesh and bones and nervous system of *Homo sapiens*, rather than the electronic gadgetry of a computer.' Secondly, that we can state, in material terms, sufficient conditions for the occurrence of psychological processes, such as perception of colours and properties. These are supervenient on material changes, and even if we cannot state the material sufficient conditions now, we can always work towards such an account. There will eventually be an efficient-causal account with no gaps in it.

This puzzles us: for our argument for saying that the link between form and matter was contingent is one that gives us good reasons *not* to think that sufficient conditions will be forthcoming on the material level. It is that living creatures, like many other substances, are *compositionally plastic*. The same activity can be realized in such a variety of specific materials that there is not likely to be *one* thing that is just what perceiving red *is*, on the material level. In our substance examples, the fact that matter continually changes during a thing's lifetime gave us reason to say that matter fails to be *the nature of the thing*; in these examples of life-activity a different and further sort of variability blocks us from having the generality that would yield adequate material explanations. We shall return to this point later. There are numerous passages in Aristotle that make it, in a general way. ('We must speak of the form and the thing *qua* form as being each thing; but the material side by itself must never be said to be the thing' (*Metaph.* 1035ª7–9, and cf. also *PA* 640ª33 ff., ᵇ23 ff., 641ª7 ff., *DA* I. 1, 403ª3 ff., cf. below, *Ph.* 2. 2.)) We originally illustrated it, as we have said, through the example of a bronze sphere, whose doings were explained not by alluding to its specific materials but by speaking of its geometrical properties.

Now, however, we must concede that in her 1978 book Nussbaum did suggest that, although the material account would not have a high degree of generality across cases, we could still, in particular cases at least, give material sufficient conditions for action, belief, perception, and desire—and that we would need to do so, if we wanted to have a genuine causal explanation of actions. This was supposed to be so on the grounds that the logical connections among perception (or belief), desire, and action invalidated these as genuinely explanatory Humean causes of the action.[13] Nussbaum has, however, recanted and criticized this view in two subsequently published papers—'Aristotelian Dualism' and 'The "Common Explanation" of Animal Motion'[14] the latter known to Burnyeat before he wrote the paper we discuss here. In 'The "Common Explanation"' (later revised and expanded as ch. 9 of *The Fragility of Goodness*) she argues that the *sort* of logical connection the intentional *explanantia* have with one another does not really disqualify them from acting as genuine *causes* of the *explanandum*, the action. Aristotle stresses this independence in several ways,[15] and it is all the independence he needs. Indeed, so far from being incompatible, the logical and causal connections are closely linked. It is because what this *orexis* is is an *orexis* for object O, and because what the creature sees before it is this same O, that the movement towards O can be caused in the way it is, by the *orexis* and the seeing. Suppose a dog goes after some meat. It is highly relevant to the causal explanation of its motion that its *orexis* shall be for meat (or this meat) and that what it sees before it it shall also see *as meat*. If it saw just a round object, or if its *orexis* were simply for exercise, the explanatory causal connections that produce the action would be undermined. The dog might for some other reason not have gone for the meat, while having the same desire and belief: in this sense the desire and belief are independent of the goal-directed motion. But their close conceptual relatedness seems very relevant to their causal explanatory role.

Nussbaum then went on to argue that the physiological account *could not*, for Aristotle, provide a causal explanation of an animal action. First, as we have already mentioned here, the connections we might find between a desire for meat and certain concrete bodily changes will lack the generality requisite for Aristotelian explanation. Secondly, and this is what we want to stress here, the physiological feature, *just because* it lacks both the general and the particular conceptual link with the action, links which the intentional items, perception (belief) and desire, do possess, lacks the sort of *relevance* and *connectedness* that we require of a cause when we say, 'This was the thing that made that happen'. In other words, to use Aristotle's terminology, it could not be a *proper cause* of the action.[16] All this suggests that we shall never be in a position to explain action (or

[13] Nussbaum (1978), Essays 1 and 3.

[14] Nussbaum (1984); also (1983), repr. (1986) as ch. 9, with changes.

[15] (i) He says that desire must be combined in the right way with perception in order for movement to follow. (ii) He insists that the cognitive faculties must come up with a possible route to the goal, or else movement will not follow. (iii) He makes it clear that the desire must be not just one among others, but *the* one, the 'authoritative' or 'decisive' one—however we understand this. (iv) He points out that even when all this is true there may be some impediment, in which case movement will not follow.

[16] See *Ph.* 195ᵇ3–4. The example is the relationship between Polyclitus the sculptor and the statue. Aristotle insists that not just any attribute of Polyclitus caused the statue: it was his skill of sculpting. So it is as sculptor (not as human being, or as father, etc.) that he is the cause of the statue. The point is that it is Polyclitus' skill that has the requisite conceptual connection with the production of the statue—although no doubt at every point he had many other properties, and at every point his body was in some suitable physiological condition. There is, Aristotle says, an intimate connectedness (*oikeiotēs*) to the one factor that is lacked by all the others.

indeed presumably the perceptions and desires that cause it) from the bottom up; it is not simply that we do not have the realizing descriptions in each case. If we did have them, they would not have the right sort of explanatory linkage with the *explanandum* and with the other *explanantia*. So we believe that these intentional features are irreducible, and not explicable in terms of material states and activities. We argue for finding this view in Aristotle, and we believe it to be a compelling and largely correct view.[17]

B. *Material Embodiment*

Burnyeat holds that in Aristotelian perception, becoming aware is a primitive phenomenon that has no associated material change:

no physiological change is needed for the eye or the organ of touch to become aware of the appropriate perceptual objects. The model says: the effect on the organ *is* the awareness, no more and no less...Not merely is there no deduction from physiology to perception, not merely are there no physiological sufficient conditions for perception to occur, but the only necessary conditions are states of receptivity to sensible form: transparent eye-jelly, still air walled up in the ear, intermediate temperature and hardness in the organ of touch. When these have been specified, the material side of the story of perception is complete.

In other words, there is in perception a transition from potential to actual awareness that is not the transition of any materials from one state to another. There is psychological transition without material transition. Becoming aware is neither correlated with nor realized in the transitions of matter. It is this feature that is

---

[17] We hold that while embodiment in some sort of suitable matter is essential to animals and their life-activities, the particular material realization is contingent. But caution is in order here. For Aristotle, the organic parts of animals—the heart, the eye, the hand, etc.—are *functionally defined*: the heart is whatever performs such and such functions in the animal, and a disconnected heart or hand is not, he repeatedly insists, really a heart or hand except in name. This means that we could perfectly well say that the life-activities of animal A are necessarily and not contingently realized in a heart, and eye, and so forth, *without ever leaving the formal (functional) level*. What would then be contingent would be the material realization of that organic function at a lower level. Aristotle is less consistent about the 'homoiomerous parts', viz., flesh, blood, bone, etc. Sometimes he takes the same line about them—spilt blood is not really blood, etc.; and sometimes he gives a physiological formula for them, in terms of proportions of earth, air, fire, and water. So again, on the former line, we could say that an animal must have blood, without ruling out the possibility that some non-organic stuff could play that same role in the animal's life. Aristotle's point is that this stuff would then *be blood*: and what would be contingent would be the relation between a certain lower-level chemical composition and being blood. The latter line—if the formulae are really meant as definitions—would imply that blood must be materially composed in such and such a way; but then, the fact that the animal is filled with *blood* would be contingent. We believe that Aristotle's line is the former line, and that the formulae should probably not be taken as definitions. For able discussion of this whole problem, see Whiting's paper in this volume, with which we are largely in agreement. For relevant passages, see *PA* 640^{b}34 ff., 641^{a}18 ff., *DA* 412^{b}18 ff., *Mete.* I. 12, *GA* 734^{b}24 ff., *GC* 321^{b}28, *Metaph.* 1036^{b}22 ff., 1034^{a}6, 1058^{b}7, *Ph.* 193^{a}36 ff., *Metaph.* 1035^{b}16, 1035^{a}18, *GA* 766^{a}8, *Pol.* 1253^{a}21, 24. The position implies that the Jarvik II *is* the heart of the person who receives it, that a transplanted cornea *is* the cornea of the recipient and a full-fledged part of his or her eye; probably also that grafted or even artificial skin, bone, blood is that person's blood, etc.—just in case it does the function that defines each of these.

thought to have the consequence that Aristotle's view is not to be taken seriously by us moderns. Let us examine the thesis, and then this inference.

We now wish to make two preliminary distinctions and two dialectical concessions. First, it is one thing to hold that perception cannot be explained 'from the bottom up', quite another to hold that it is not accompanied by or realized in any material transition. We hold the first, but deny the second. For something to be a causal explanation of something, as we and Aristotle both suppose, far more is required than that it be true and truly linked with the item in question. As we have already said, we believe that our sort of 'functionalism' (the next section will show that Putnam now dissociates himself from functionalism for reasons that bring him even closer to Aristotle) is not only not committed to explanation 'from the bottom up', but is built on the denial of this possibility.

Second, we find that Burnyeat's argument at this point takes a peculiar turn. For suddenly we find little reference to Putnam and Nussbaum, and copious reference to an article by Richard Sorabji.[18] Burnyeat takes our position to be committed to Sorabji's account of what the physiological change involved in perception is: that in perception the sense-organ actually takes on the quality of the object perceived, becoming red, or hard, or whatever. He calls this Sorabji position 'a piece of essential support' for us in the area of perception. Having argued against this view and in favour of a view according to which the eye's becoming *aware* of red does not require its *going red*, he thinks he has damaged our view (and Sorabji's more general thesis, which we do accept) that the becoming aware is realized in (constituted by) a material transition. But it is one thing to argue against a particular story of what the physiological change is, quite another to establish that there need be no physiological change. (Aquinas, as we shall see in Section IV, argues like Burnyeat against the Sorabji physiological story, yet takes it as so evident as not to require argument that each act of perception is of necessity accompanied by *some* physical change (*immutatio*) in the sense-organs.)

Now the dialectical concessions. We shall grant Burnyeat his criticism of Sorabji's physiological thesis, and so forgo that concrete story as to what the physiological change is. We are not sorry to give that up. Indeed, it would be unwelcome to us if Aristotle *did* insist on a monolithic account of what the physiological realization of perception always *consists in*, since we have ascribed to him the view that there *need not be one thing* that it (physiologically) consists in. What we do want to ascribe to Aristotle on the physiological side will become clear in a moment.

Second concession: we grant as well that it is important that perception is not the type of change that Aristotle (speaking strictly[19]) calls a *kinēsis*; it is, rather, the actualization of a potential. This is why we have been using the rather

---

[18] Sorabji (1974). We refer to the strata of Sorabji's position that predate our original paper, not to the modified account included in this volume.

[19] He does not, however, always make this distinction: sometimes he uses *kinēsis* as a very general word for change, covering both *kinēsis* and *energeia* narrowly construed. This is especially likely to be true in a work like *De Motu*, whose purpose is the general explanation of *kinēseis* of many sorts.

mysterious word 'transition' instead of the word 'change'. (Aquinas is not so cautious.) Still, the point is: it does not follow that this transition is not at every point of necessity accompanied by *some material transition*. (Matter has potentialities too, clearly; and these too can be actualized.) We shall argue that it is; indeed, with Sorabji, we believe that the most precise way of characterizing the relationship is that it is a transition *realized in* the matter. The *psuchē* does nothing alone; its doings are the doings *of* the organic body. Perceiving is an activity in matter.[20]

Burnyeat's position is a slippery one to attack, since he is prepared to grant that perception has necessary material conditions, and that these are conditions of the sense-organs. Many of the passages in which Aristotle asserts that the *psuchē* or its activities are 'not without matter' could indeed be understood in this weaker way. We shall now, however, bring forward several that are not so ambiguous.

Exhibit A: De Motu Animalium, *chs. 7–11*[21]   Burnyeat's analysis of perception rests on the evidence of *De Anima* alone. And of course this is a major text, where perception is concerned. On the other hand, it seems especially unwise to regard it as *the* central text, when discussing this particular problem. For Aristotle himself makes a distinction between two types of writings on psychology, according to which the *De Anima* will, on the whole, discuss psychological matters structurally, without reference to their material accompaniments, and another group of treatises will handle the relationship between psychology and physiology. Thus in *DA* 3. 10, discussing the way in which desire produces bodily movements, he writes, 'But as for the equipment (*organōi*) in virtue of which desire imparts movement, this is already something bodily (*sōmatikon*)—so we shall have to consider it in the "functions common to body and soul" ' (433ᵇ18 ff.).[22] There follows a brief summary of the argument of the *De Motu Animalium*. The rubric *ta koina psuchēs kai sōmatos erga* will be discussed below, when we analyse Exhibit B: for it appears to be a general title for the *Parva Naturalia* taken as a group, with the *De Motu* added. Meanwhile, we wish to suggest only that this passage shows any silence on Aristotle's part, in the *De Anima*, about the physiology of psychological processes to be a deliberate strategy, indicating his commitment to non-reductionism about psychological explanation, but showing nothing at all about the issue that divides our view from Burnyeat's. It is not surprising that he should be silent about what he has deferred to another treatise; and someone who wants to find out his view on the problem needs to look closely at that other treatise.

---

[20] We *do* accept Sorabji's suggestion that the characterization of perception as 'receiving the form' of the perceived object 'without the matter' is primarily intended to bring out a contrast with plants —or, we would rather say, with nutritive and digestive activity in both plants and animals. In nutrition and related forms of being affected by the environment, the environmental material affects the animal by entering into it; in perception the animal gets in touch with the object without assimilating it. (See Nussbaum (1978) commentary on ch. 11, and Essay 2, pp. 117 ff.).

[21] On all this, see further details in Nussbaum (1978).

[22] On this passage and the *De Motu*, see Nussbaum (1978), 9 ff.

Moreover, since Burnyeat seems inclined (see below, Exhibit C) to grant something like our position where *desire* is concerned, it is worth pointing out that the *De Motu* cannot be read as treating desire and perception asymmetrically. The treatment of the physiology of desire is more obscure than the physiology of perceiving, and seems to involve reference to the somewhat mysterious *sumphuton pneuma*; by contrast Aristotle (as also in Exhibit B) treats perceiving as the clearest and simplest case of physiological realization. But both are treated perfectly symmetrically, as interlocking elements in a single causal process.

The general approach of the *De Motu*, where physiology is concerned, can be clearly seen from the passage in ch. 10 that introduces the *pneuma*: 'According to the account that gives the reason for motion, desire is the middle, which imparts movement being moved. But in living bodies there must be some *body* of this kind' (703^a4–6). In other words, it is psychology, unreduced, that gives us the reasons for, or explanations of, the (voluntary) movements of animals. But since we are dealing with embodied living creatures (and not, for example, with the activities of god), we know, too, that we will discover *some* physiological realization for the psychological process in each case.

Let us now look at the situation where perception is concerned—and the complex interaction between perceiving and desiring that results in animal movement. At the opening of ch. 7, Aristotle asks the question: how does it happen that cognition of an object is sometimes followed by movement and sometimes not? He answers: because sometimes the animal has a desire for the object it apprehends, and also a feasible route towards getting it through movement, and sometimes not. He describes the complex ways in which different forms of cognition (including *aisthēsis*, *phantasia*, and *noēsis*) interact with different forms of desiring, in order to produce the resulting action (the famous 'practical syllogism'). In the second half of the chapter, however, he turns to a further question: how *can* such psychological processes actually set a large heavy animal body in motion? The answer seems to be: because these processes are themselves functions of and in the body; and they easily and naturally cause other bodily movements that end up moving the limbs. In a famous simile, Aristotle compares animals to automatic puppets, and also to a certain sort of toy cart. In both cases, even a small change in a central part of the mechanism can bring about large-scale and obvious changes in other parts. And such changes (warmings and chillings in the region of the heart above all) are the physiological concomitants of perception and the other forms of cognition, as well as of desire.

We propose to look very closely now at the central text in which this thought is expressed, first interpreting it in what seems to be the most natural and straightforward way, then trying out Burnyeat's position, to see whether it can possibly be made to fit. We shall quote it in Nussbaum's translation, with one difference: the pivotal word *alloiōsis* ('alteration') will remain untranslated. Numbers have been inserted for ease of reference in the subsequent discussion:

(1) The movement of animals is like that of automatic puppets, which are set moving when a small motion occurs: the cables are released and the pegs strike against one another; and

like that of the little cart (for the child riding in it pushes it straight forward, and yet it moves in a circle because it has wheels of unequal size: for the smaller acts like a centre, as happens in the case of the cylinders). For they have functioning parts that are of the same kind: the sinews and bones. The latter are like the pegs and the iron in our example, the sinews like the cables. When these are released and slackened the creature moves. (2) Now in the puppets and carts no *alloiōsis* takes place, since if the inner wheels were to become smaller and again larger, the movement would still be circular. But in the animal the same part has the capacity to become both larger and smaller and to change its shape, as the parts expand because of heat and contract again because of cold, and alter (*alloioumenōn*) (3) *Alloiōsis* is caused by *phantasiai* and sense-perceptions and ideas. For sense-perceptions are at once a kind of *alloiōsis*, and *phantasia* and thinking have the power of the actual things. For it turns out that the form conceived of the pleasant or fearful is like the actual thing itself. That is why we shudder and are frightened just thinking of something. All these are affections (*pathē*) and *alloiōseis*. (4) And when bodily parts are altered (*alloioumenōn*) some become larger, some smaller. It is not difficult to see that a small change occurring in an origin sets up great and numerous differences at a distance—just as, if the rudder shifts a hair's breadth, the shift in the prow is considerable. Further, when under the influence of heat or cold or some other similar affection, an *alloiōsis* is produced in the region of the heart, even if it is only in an imperceptibly small part of it, it produces a considerable difference in the body, causing blushing and pallor, as well as shuddering, trembling, and their opposites. (701^{b}2–32.)

What this *seems* to say, we claim, is that the animal moves as it does because of the fact that its psychological processes are realized in physiological transitions that set up movements that culminate in fully-fledged local movement.

(1) Puppets and little carts move as wholes, just as the result of a change in a central part; this is the way animals also move. For they are equipped with a functional physiology (*organa* in the sense of suitable equipment): their tendons and bones being rather like the strings and wood in the puppets.

(2) But there is a difference. The puppets and carts move simply by a push – pull mechanism that does not involve a (physiological) qualitative change, an *alloiōsis*. Animal parts, however, do undergo such *alloiōseis*, namely changes of shape and size in the parts resulting from heatings and chillings.

(3) These *alloiōseis* are brought about by perception and imagining and thinking. For perceptions just *are* (*ousai*), are realized in, such *alloiōseis*. And although this seems less clear where *phantasia* and thinking are in question, still, the fact that these two produce results similar to those produced by perception shows that the case *is* similar. Just imagining or thinking of something can chill you.[23] And all these are experiences and *alloiōseis*.

(4) When an *alloiōsis* takes place, some parts become larger, others smaller. And this has consequences at a distance.

Now it appears that *alloiōsis*, in this passage, is Aristotle's word for what we have called the material transition. He tells us, both here and in subsequent chapters, that such *alloiōseis* of necessity accompany perceiving and imagining;

[23] Thinking, it turns out, is realized in the body *via* the concomitant *phantasia*.

and ch. 10 completes the picture where desire is concerned. Furthermore, the material transition is not just a concomitant, it is what perception *is*. Nussbaum has argued that this 'is' must be understood (as elsewhere in Aristotle) to indicate material realization or constitution, not full identity. For Aristotle's commitment to explanatory non-reductionism is plain in the treatise as a whole, and there is no sign that a complete causal account could be given on the material level. None the less, the material transition is linked far more closely with psychological activity than Burnyeat's account permits. Whatever the *ousai* means, it clearly means that the material change is intrinsic to what goes on when perceiving takes place, and necessary for a full explanation of animal motion. There are some unclarities about the physiological story: it is not fully clear, for example, whether the *alloiōsis* is the heating (chilling) or the closely linked change of shape. But in a sense the very vagueness of the story is its strength, where our view is concerned. For we would not want Aristotle to suggest that sufficient conditions for motion could be given by mentioning materials alone. The story here is far more pleasingly reticent than the one Sorabji told. But it does show that psychological transitions are, for Aristotle, material transitions, *and* that this embodied status is necessary for the explanation of perception's causal efficacy.

Subsequent chapters confirm this general picture. Ch. 8 argues, once again, that certain heatings and chillings are the necessary concomitants of certain perceptions; the argument is extended to memory. And now we are given a way of handling Burnyeat's point that perceiving is not a *kinēsis*. For we are told that the bodily parts are crafted in such a way as to have by nature the capability of making these transitions—so the transition in question will be the realization of a natural capability, just the sort of transition from potency to actualization that Burnyeat is after on the psychological side. (He seems to suppose that material changes are all *kinēseis*; but matter has its potentialities too.) Ch. 9 argues that the complexity of animal movement requires something like our central nervous system: a central bodily location for stimulus-reception and the initiation of response. The area of the heart is defended by arguments presupposing the general psychophysical picture we have outlined. Ch. 10 fleshes out the picture where desire is concerned, introducing the *pneuma*. Ch. 11 assures us that desire is not necessary for any and every animal motion: some movements of parts are produced by *phantasia* alone, without *orexis*; and some systemic movements (e.g. digestion, the functions of sleep) go on without either perception or desire.[24]

Where can Burnyeat dig in here? It seems to us that he cannot deny that the *alloiōseis* in the crucial parts of the cited passage are material transitions, without making the passage as a whole so riddled with ambiguity as to be hopeless. Nor can he deny, it seems to us, that this natural reading of the passage is consistent with *De Anima*'s insistence that perceiving is an *energeia*, and also consistent with

---

[24] Throughout the *De Motu* account, Aristotle focuses on physiological transitions in the region of the heart, since it is one of his primary purposes to establish the importance of this central 'receptor'; he says less about transitions in the organs, but the conception of the heart area as receptor of stimuli and initiator of the movements that lead to local motion strongly suggests that there are some.

Aristotle's overall non-reductionism about the explanation of animal motion. Our account, based on the passage, is not reductionistic, and it does not propose to build up intentionality from matter. The best hope for Burnyeat's reading, we believe, would be to claim that the *alloiōseis* in question here are material transitions associated not with *all* perceiving, but only with a special sort, the perceiving of the object of desire or avoidance. In other words, it is not perception itself that is realized in matter, it is perception-cum-desire. It is only in so far as desire enters the picture that the body enters it also.

We have already said that we believe this severing of perception from desire to be very peculiar and *ad hoc*, given the symmetry with which *De Motu* treats the two. Furthermore, the passage indicates that it has been talking about changes connected with the cognitive side of the animal's functioning, saving desire for more detailed discussion in ch. 10. *DA* 3. 12 tells us that the most essential function of perception in animal life is to present to the animal's awareness objects of pursuit and avoidance, so that it can survive (434^{b}9–27). So the fact that Aristotle does not spend much time talking about what happens when the animal gazes at a mountain or smells a rose or hears a symphony is hardly surprising: animals' perceiving is eminently practical, and their awareness of motivationally irrelevant parts of the world is bound to be limited. (This would presumably be true of humans too, except insofar as we have *nous* in addition.) So an account focused, like Burnyeat's, on the intentionality of awareness, and one that, like ours, combines an interest in intentionality with a concern for its physical embodiment, should be expected to focus on the very same cases, the cases that Aristotle himself stresses here: namely, cases in which animals become aware of motivationally salient features of their environment. The same things that are the objects of awareness in Burnyeat's view will be, in ours, both objects of awareness and occasions for material transition.

We conclude that the *De Motu* provides very powerful evidence that Aristotle conceives of both perceiving and desiring as thoroughly enmattered. Their activity is accompanied, of necessity, by a transition in matter.[25]

Exhibit B: De Sensu, *opening*   We have already mentioned the fact that the short treatises to which we give the title *Parva Naturalia* (together with *De Motu*) are referred to by Aristotle himself under the title, 'Functions shared by soul and body', *koina psuchēs kai sōmatos erga* (*DA* 433^{b}19–20). The opening of the first of these short works, which is of course the treatise *On Perception and Perceptibles*, gives reasons for thinking that the entire range of functions to be discussed in these treatises are 'shared' or 'common' in this way:

It is evident that the most important functions, both those shared by animals with other creatures and those peculiar to animals, are shared by the soul and the body, e.g. perception and memory, and emotion and appetite and in general desire, and in addition to these pleasure and pain...That all the enumerated items are shared by soul and body is not

---

[25] For further discussion of related passages, see Nussbaum (1978), commentary.

unclear. For all happen with perception: some as its corruptions and privations. That perception comes to be for the soul through body (*dia sōmatos*) is evident, both from argument and apart from argument.

Perception, then, is taken to be the clearest case of something that is a 'common' or 'shared' function. Can this passage be read as weakly as Burnyeat requires, so that perception is 'common to soul and body' just in case it has necessary conditions of receptivity in the sense-organs? We think not. To say that a function (*ergon*) is shared by (the 'common function' of) both soul and body must be to say that they both *do* it, are both active and acting together. Alexander takes it this very natural way: 'The activities (*energeiai*) of living beings are shown to be shared by soul and body', in that they are all linked to perception; and 'he takes it as evident that perception is an activity (*energeia*) that is shared by soul and body' (2. 16 ff. Wendland).[26] Soul and body are *active together*: we would say, not only together but indissolubly, as one thing. Similarly, a later passage (441ᵇ15 ff.) says of touching, construed as the activation of a potential, that it is a '*pathos* in the wet' as it is affected by the dry; we suppose that the dry affects the wet materially, producing a material change. We cannot see how to read this Burnyeat's way: that the only *pathos* present is just the becoming aware. As in the *De Motu*, Aristotle is saying that the matter undergoes something. And we note that, here as in *De Motu*, he seems to treat perception as an especially clear case of embodiment, not more problematic than desire, but less so.

Furthermore, if this passage is read in Burnyeat's way, an essential contrast disappears. If being a 'common function' means only that the function has some material necessary conditions, then everything, including thinking, is a common function. Thinking too, in the animal organisms that have it, has material necessary conditions: for it never takes place without *phantasia*, which is itself embodied (see Exhibit C below).[27] But we notice that Aristotle does not in fact include thinking among the functions that are said to be common to body and soul. It is perfectly clear that he means to distinguish it from all these—presumably because its activity is not the *activity of* a bodily organ or organs, an activity realized in suitable matter. (Aquinas reads the contrast this way, as we shall see.)

Exhibit C: DA *403*ᵃ5 ff. Our next passage takes up this very point. In the first chapter of *De Anima*, Aristotle says, 'It appears that the soul suffers and does most things not without body, like getting angry, being confident, desiring appetitively, in general perceiving, but thinking seems to be especially its own thing. But if this is *phantasia* or not without *phantasia*, then even this could not be without body.'

Here we have a dialectical passage, but none the less one that introduces a distinction that is developed and never effaced in the rest of the text. The way perceiving is 'not without matter' is different from the way thinking is. The latter turns out to have necessary conditions, but no organ and no correlated and

---

[26] See Alexander (1901).   [27] On *phantasia* and thinking, see Nussbaum (1978), Essay 5.

realizing change of the organ or organs. The former, as Aristotle will go on to say later in this passage, is a *logos enhulos*, a structure realized in matter.

In his paper Burnyeat grants something close to this (although it is difficult to tell exactly how much) for anger, the example that Aristotle goes on to discuss in detail, and for a range of similar examples. He makes, however (as we have already mentioned in discussing Exhibit A), a strong contrast between 'the emotional' and 'the cognitive side of our mental functioning'. Body may be involved in the former in something like the way we say; it is not involved in the latter. We find no such contrast, here or elsewhere; and we believe that the passage does not even permit this, for perception is explicitly named in the sentence we have quoted as one of the things in question that the soul 'suffers or does', *paschei* or *poiei*, 'not without body'. It is true that the passage (which is somewhat loosely structured) goes on to focus on a narrower group of cases—'anger, mildness, fear, pity, confidence, joy, love, hatred'—asserting of all of these that the body 'suffers something' along with them (403ᵃ16–18). But this is not because perception is not included in the conclusion of the general argument: the connection of perception with material change has been plainly asserted earlier, in the passage we cite. If anything, it is because perceiving is, here as in *De Sensu*, taken, along with *phantasia*, to be an especially clear and obvious case of bodily involvement, whereas desire is far less obvious: notice, for example, how Aristotle's remarks about thinking take the bodily status of *phantasia* for granted. (The need to devote special attention to desire stems, no doubt, from Aristotle's background in the Academy; for Plato persistently puts perception on the side of body, with no hesitation. But desire receives a variety of different treatments, being body in the *Phaedo*, soul in the *Republic*, immortal soul in the *Phaedrus* and *Laws*.) There is no reason, then, to suppose that the general conclusion of the passage applies only to the 'emotional' and not to the 'cognitive' side of the animal's psychology.[28]

In fact, we can go even further: neither here nor elsewhere does Aristotle even make Burnyeat's sharp distinction between the cognitive and the emotional. Desire and emotion are treated throughout the corpus as forms of selective intentional awareness. Even where appetite is concerned, he criticizes Plato's treatment of hunger, thirst, and so forth as blind urges impervious to conceptions and beliefs. Only the plant-like self-nutritive aspect of our make-up (*to phutikon*) is unaware and unreasoning, 'in no way partaking in *logos*'. But 'the appetitive and in general the desiderative partake in *logos* in some way'—as is shown, he says, by the success of moral advice and education (*EN* 1102ᵇ29–1103ᵃ1). And when he actually gives analyses of the emotions in the *Rhetoric*, it emerges that (presumably unlike appetites) they are, so to speak, less 'commonly animal' than perceiving is. For all require and rest upon belief, and a belief is actually one

---

[28] On some of the vicissitudes in Plato's position, see Nussbaum (1986), ch. 7. On the interpretation of *pathē* in this passage, see the arguments of Hicks, Rodier, and Hamlyn in favour of a broad interpretation. Rodier criticizes Simplicius for taking the narrower view. We note that Burnyeat himself produces evidence that Aristotle is prepared to call perceiving a *pathos*.

component of an emotion in each case.[29] The view that emotions are more animal, more bodily, than perceiving is actually a view unknown in the ancient world, though common enough in modern times.[30] If ancient thinkers make any distinction of the sort, it goes the other way: animals are always considered perceiving creatures, but frequently denied the emotions. So it would appear that an account of Aristotle's psychology that splits emotion off from perception, making one an activity of matter and the other immaterial, is both false to Aristotle's text and in a more general way anachronistic.

We can see the closeness of emotion and cognition in the very passage before us. For instead of making Burnyeat's distinction between cognition and emotion, Aristotle instead makes the emotions forms of cognitive awareness. For when Aristotle uses expressions of the form '*x, y, z,* and in general (*holōs*) *A*', what he means by this is that *A* is a genus of which *x, y,* and *z* are some of the species. (For three excellent examples, see *Metaph.* 1026ª2–3, quoted on p. 31 above, and *De Sensu*'s opening, Exhibit B.) So unless this passage is exceptional, Aristotle is actually treating emotion as a type of perception, a selective cognitive awareness of an object or objects in the world.[31]

The proper conclusion, Aristotle's conclusion, is that all these, perceiving, desiring, emotion, are formulae in matter (*logoi enhuloi*). Even though the structure of the passage moves from a broad class which explicitly includes (and subsumes other items under) perception to a narrower group of *pathē* whose members are all emotions, its conclusion is evidently what Aristotle has in other words asserted already about perception and *phantasia*—and it can be regarded as an expansion of that assertion, applying it to the more controversial case of desire. All these processes, then, are *logoi enhuloi*, formulae in matter, of which a proper sample definition would be, 'A certain movement of a body of such and such a sort—or of a part of it or of a particular faculty, caused by this for the sake of this' (403ª25 ff.).[32] The good natural scientist should, Aristotle concludes, treat the various psychological functions as common functions, giving priority to the formal account of (for example) anger as a form of intentional awareness, but also saying as much as possible about the physical doings involved.[33] (This, of course, is what Aristotle does for perception in the *De Sensu*, for both perception and desire in the *De Motu*.) The good scientist deals 'with everything that makes up the doings and affections of a body of this sort and matter of this sort'

[29] Cf. for example *Rh.* 1385ᵇ13 ff. on pity, 1386ª22 ff. on fear, both discussed in Nussbaum (1986), Interlude 2.

[30] On emotions in ancient thought, see Nussbaum (1987).

[31] Hicks in Aristotle (1907) reads the passage correctly, and finds the same view in the *De Sensu* commentary.

[32] The word used is *kinēsis*; but, as we have said, Aristotle does use the word generically, so this need not rule out his believing that the movement involved is an *energeia*; moreover, he is alluding to the immediate context, in which the example is desiring, which he does not characterize as *energeia*.

[33] Here we are sympathetic with the interpretation advanced in Modrak (1987a), though we would insist more strongly than she does that the material account is not on a par with the formal account, and cannot be given independently.

(403^b11-12). On Burnyeat's reading, perceiving is not the doing *of* any matter at all, since the matter is not active.

Exhibit D: De Anima *2. 1, 412^b4-25*

If it is necessary to say something general (*koinon*) about all soul, it would be the first actuality of a natural organic body. Therefore it is not appropriate to inquire whether the soul and the body are one—just as it is not appropriate in the case of the wax and its shape, and in general (*holōs*) the matter of each thing and that of which it is the matter...(The soul) is the what-it-is-to-be for a body of a certain sort: just as, if a tool were a natural body, for example an axe. For then its being an axe would be its being (*ousia*), and the soul is this. When this is separated from it, there would no longer be an axe except homonymously—but as things are it is an axe...And one can also examine what has been said by considering the parts. For if the eye were an animal, its soul would be the power of sight. For that is the being of an eye, according to the account (for the eye is the matter of sight)—in the absence of which there is no eye, except homonymously, as with the stone eye and the painted eye. One must then apply what has been said of the part to the whole of the living body. For there is an analogy: as the part to the part, so the whole of perception to the whole of the perceiving body, as such.

This is a central theoretical statement of Aristotle's hylomorphic view. We believe that it makes little sense on Burnyeat's reading, while on ours it is exactly what one would expect Aristotle to say. For on Burnyeat's reading, the relationship between soul and body is *not* that between the wax and its shape: matter merely supplies background conditions for transitions that are not carried out in and by the matter. The axe analogy, furthermore, would not be apt—for of course an axe cannot do anything without material transitions. And on Burnyeat's view, it of course makes a great deal of sense to ask whether soul and body are one; for if the body does not perform the soul's activities, there is an obvious sense in which they are not one, and the nature and extent of their unity is not at all evident. In fact, as we have said, the situation with perception, on Burnyeat's view, seems to be exactly the situation we have for *nous* alone, on our reading body providing necessary conditions without doing the functions. And where *nous* is concerned, Aristotle plainly thinks that the question about unity and separation not only makes sense, but is important. On our interpretation, on the other hand, the wax analogy and the axe analogy are apt; and the question about unity really *is* one that the Aristotelian ought to repudiate as ill formed. The soul is not a thing merely housed in the body; its doings are the doings of body. The only thing there is one natural thing.

To summarize: perception, desire, and the other 'very important things' mentioned by Aristotle in *De Sensu* 1 are activities of the soul realized in some suitable matter. There will be no explanatory independence to the material side, and yet a scientist may legitimately investigate it in the cases before him, as Aristotle does in the *De Motu* and the *Parva Naturalia*—provided that he does not present what he does as a reduction or a complete explanation.

In *Metaphysics* Z11, Aristotle mentions a philosopher known as Socrates the Younger, who wishes to argue that animals are just like the sphere: they may need to be realized in some materials or other whenever they exist, but this realization is not part of what they are, and need not enter into their definition. Aristotle accepts this move up to a point, apparently: for he seems to grant that in both cases there is a certain plasticity of composition. But he then distinguishes the cases. In the case of animals, to take away the matter is 'to go too far— for some things just are this in this, or these in such and such a condition' (1036ᵇ22 ff.). The point seems to be that although every actual sphere is embodied, the geometrical properties that make a sphere a sphere do not depend on the component materials' having any particular properties, except perhaps a certain rigidity. The functional essence of a living being like an animal (whose essence it is to be a perceiving creature) *does* require mention of material embodiment, in that its essential activities are embodied activities. Just as 'snub' directly imports a reference to material composition, so too does 'perceiving creature'—in a way that 'sphere' does not. We feel that Burnyeat's interpretation assimilates Aristotle to Socrates the younger, and does not allow sufficient room for the all-important distinction between sphere and animal that pervades Aristotle's thought about life.[34]

III. Why we Don't Have to 'Junk' Aristotle

Burnyeat goes wrong at the very beginning—wrong in a way that corrupts the way he sees contemporary issues, not just the way he reads Aristotle. It is because he is in the grip of what Husserl called the 'objectivist' picture, the picture according to which Newton (or, as Husserl would have it, Galileo) discovered for us what external objects really are (they are what is described, and, 'in themselves', no more than what is described, by the formulae of mathematical physics), that he sees no way of reading Aristotle but a Frank Baumian way, and no way in which Aristotle *could be* relevant to anything we are interested in today.

Who on earth is Frank Baum? You mean you've forgotten? The author of the Oz books, of course! You remember the Tin Man and the Scarecrow? In the world of Frank Baum, matter—the straw in the Scarecrow's head, or, perhaps, the sack that contains the straw—can have the property of 'seating', or being the location of, thoughts and feelings without having any other particularly relevant properties. Some scarecrows don't think thoughts and have feelings, and one scarecrow magically does, and that's all one can say about it. On Burnyeat's reading of Aristotle, we are *all* like the Scarecrow. We have already indicated why, in our view, this is a misreading of Aristotle. But our reply to Burnyeat would be incomplete if we did not indicate why his account of the present metaphysical situation, although a commonly accepted one, is not one *we* can accept.

The view that has ruled since the seventeenth century is that there is obviously such a thing as 'the mind–body problem as we face it today', in Burnyeat's

---

[34] To this extent our own use of an artefact example requires supplementation.

phrase. His conception of this problem is expressed in the statement; 'To be truly Aristotelian, we would have to stop believing that the emergence of life or mind requires explanation.' Putting aside 'life', the key idea here is that *of course* the 'emergence of mind' (as if it were clear what that is!) requires explanation, and, on Aristotle's view (the Frank Baum theory), it obviously doesn't. So let's forget that silly magical world that Aristotle lived in and get down to the real business of explaining the 'emergence of mind'.

If we may be forgiven for bombarding the reader with examples of great and near-great philosophers who have found this description of the present problem situation less than coercive (think of this as a softening-up bombardment in the artillery sense, rather than as an appeal to authority!), note that not only 'Continental' philosophers and phenomenologists have rejected the idea that 'matter' is such a clear notion, and also rejected the idea that tables and chairs and human bodies and such are obviously 'matter' in the sense of being *identical* with physicists' objects, but so, likewise, have such great 'analytic' philosophers as Wittgenstein and Austin. Coming to our own day, Kripke has pointed out (in conversation with Putnam) that if tables were 'space-time regions', as Quine claims, then such modal statements as 'this very table could have been in a different place now' would not be true, and similar arguments show that the relation between this table and its 'molecule slices' cannot be *identity* unless we are willing to abandon our commonsense modal beliefs (or reinterpret 'this would have been the same table' as meaning 'this would have been a *counterpart* of this table' in the David Lewis sense of 'counterpart'[35]). Reverting to Austin, we note that the burden of *Sense and Sensibilia*[36] was that the way philosophers use 'material object' is *senseless*. The Strawson of *Individuals*[37] certainly doubted that the relation between *me* as a bearer of 'P-predicates' (intentional states, and other attributes of a person) and my body can even be *stated* in the terms Descartes 'stuck' us with! So much for 'we are stuck with the mind–body problem as Descartes created it'! End of preliminary bombardment.

Now for the cavalry charge. If 'explaining the emergence of mind' means explaining how the brain works, how 'memory traces' are laid down, how the 'representations' from the right eye and the 'representations' from the left eye are processed to 'compute' the three-dimensional layout in front of the viewer (as in the work initiated by Hubel and Wiesel,[38] and extended and modified by David Marr[39] and others), how the various areas of the left lobe that collectively function as the 'speech centre' (in humans who have not developed speech in the right lobe as the result of massive and early damage to the left lobe), etc., then—as long as this work is not understood in a reductionist way, as telling one what 'seeing a chair', or 'remembering where Paris is', or 'thinking there are a lot of cats in the neighbourhood' *is*—why on earth should an 'Aristotelian' object to it? Does one still have to believe that integration takes place in the region of the heart to be an 'Aristotelian'? On the other hand, if 'explaining the emergence of mind'

[35] Cf. Lewis (1983), i. 26–54.   [36] Austin (1962).   [37] Strawson (1964).
[38] Hubel and Wiesel (1962) and (1974).   [39] Marr (1982).

means solving Brentano's problem, that is, saying in *reductive* terms what 'thinking there are a lot of cats in the neighbourhood' *is*, and what 'remembering where Paris is' *is*, etc., why should we now think that *that*'s possible?[40] If an Aristotelian is one who rejects that programme as an unreasonable programme for metaphysics, then yes, we *are* 'Aristotelians'.

The insight of Putnam's 'functionalism' was that thinking beings are *compositionally plastic*—that is, that there is no *one* physical state or event (no necessary and sufficient condition expressible by a finite formula in the language of first-order fundamental physics) for being even a *physically possible* (let alone 'logically possible' or 'metaphysically possible') occurrence of a thought with a given propositional content, or of a feeling of anger, or of a pain, etc. *A fortiori*, propositional attitudes, emotions, feelings, are not *identified* with brain states, or even with more broadly characterized first-order physical states.

When he advanced his account, Putnam pointed out that thinking of a being's mentality, affectivity, etc., as aspects of its *organization to function* allows one to recognize that all sorts of logically possible 'systems' or beings could be conscious, exhibit mentality and affect, etc., in exactly the same sense without having the same matter (without even consisting of 'matter' in the narrow sense of elementary particles and electromagnetic fields at all). For beings of many different physical (and even 'non-physical') constitutions could have the same functional organization. The thing we want insight into is the nature of human (and animal) functional organization. The question whether that organization is centrally located in the 'body' or in suitable stuff of some totally different kind loses the importance it was thought to have, in this way of thinking.

It was at this point that Putnam (and Nussbaum) cited Aristotle. Thinking of the *psuchē* as our organization to function permitted Aristotle to separate questions about specific material composition (which he at times discusses) from the main questions of psychology.

Putnam also proposed a theory of his own as to what our organization to function is, one he has now given up; but this theory we did not, of course, attribute to Aristotle. This is the theory that our functional organization is that of a Turing machine. Putnam has now given this up because he believes that there are good arguments to show that mental states are not only compositionally plastic but also *computationally plastic*, that is, reasons to believe that physically possible creatures which believe that there are a lot of cats in the neighbourhood, or whatever, may have an indefinite number of different 'programs', and that the hypothesis that there are necessary and sufficient conditions for the presence of such a belief in computational, or computational-cum-physical, terms is unrealistic in just the way the theory that there is a necessary and sufficient condition for the presence of a table stateable in phenomenalist terms is unrealistic: such a condition would be infinitely long, and not constructed according to any effective rule, or even according to a non-effective prescription that we can state without using the

---

[40] In this connection, see Putnam (1988).

very terms to be reduced.[41] Putnam does not believe that even all *humans* who have the same belief (in different cultures, or with different bodies of background knowledge and different conceptual resources) have in common a physical-cum-computational feature which could be 'identified with' that belief. The 'intentional level' is simply not reducible to the 'computational level' any more than it is to the 'physical level'.

What then becomes of Burnyeat's problem of 'the emergence of mind'? Some philosophers[42] now wave the word 'supervenience' around as if it were a magic wand. Materialists should never have claimed that propositional attitudes are reducible to physical attributes, they say, they should only have said they are *supervenient* on them. In one sense this is right, but in another sense it is simply papering over the collapse of the materialist world-view. For, after all, if Moore's theory of the Good in his *Principia Ethica* (he said the goodness of a thing is supervenient on its 'natural' characteristics) is a *materialist* view, then hasn't 'materialist' lost all meaning?

When the computer revolution burst upon the world, it was widely expected that computer models would clear up the nature of the various sorts of 'intentional' phenomena. In effect, people expected that a reductive account of the various subheadings included under the chapter-heading 'intentionality' would sooner or later be given. Now that this has not proved so easy, some thinkers (though not Burnyeat) are beginning to suggest that it is not so bad if this can't be done; intentionally is only a feature of 'folk psychology' anyway. If a first-class scientific account of intentional facts and phenomena can not be given, that is not because scientific reductionism is not the right line to take in metaphysics, but rather it is because there is, so to speak, nothing here to reduce. The 'Aristotelian' attitude, in the present context, is that both attitudes are mistaken; that intentionality won't be reduced and won't go away.

That claim—the claim that 'intentionality won't be reduced and won't go away'—has sometimes been called 'Brentano's thesis', after the philosopher who put it forward with vigour over a century ago. But Brentano himself did not only have a negative thesis; his positive view was that intentionality is, so to speak, a *primitive phenomenon*, in fact *the* phenomenon that relates thought and thing, minds and the external world.

This positive view may seem to follow immediately from the negative one; but there is a joker in the pack. The joker is the old philosophical problem about the One and the Many. If one assumes that whenever we have diverse phenomena gathered together under a single name, 'there must be something they all have in common', then indeed it will follow that there is a single phenomenon (and, if it is not reducible, it must be 'primitive') corresponding to intentionality. But this is not an assumption we wish to make. We want to follow Wittgenstein's advice and *look*: look to see if there *is* something all cases of, say, meaning something by a representation (or even all cases of meaning 'there are a lot of cats in the

---

[41] Putnam (1988), chs. 5–6.

[42] For a review (and searching criticism) of these views see Kim (1982, 1984).

neighbourhood') do have in common. If, as Putnam tries to show, there is not any isolable, independently 'accessible' thing that all cases of any particular intentional phenomenon have in common (let alone all cases of 'reference' in general, or of 'meaning' in general, or of 'intentionality' in general), and *still* these phenomena cannot be dismissed as mere 'folk psychology', then we are in a position which does not fit any of the standard philosophical pictures: not the picture of intentionality as a phenomenon to be reduced to physical (or, perhaps, computational) terms, not the picture of intentionality as 'primitive' (not if 'primitive' means '*simple and* irreducible'), and not the picture of intentionality as just a bit of 'folk psychology'.

Is such a philosophical attitude compatible with Aristotle, however? Many standard accounts of his methods certainly do not suggest a philosophical attitude that gives up many of the traditional assumptions about appearance and reality; that gives up, for example, the assumption that what is real is what is 'under' or 'behind' or 'more fundamental than' our everyday appearances, that gives up the assumptions underlying the conventional statement of the problem we referred to as the Problem of the One and the Many; or an attitude that gives up the assumption that every phenomenon has an 'ultimate nature' that we have to give a metaphysically reductive account of. Are we not assimilating Aristotle to Wittgenstein?

Nussbaum has in fact argued (developing further some seminal work by the late G. E. L. Owen) that the philosophical attitude we recommend *is* Aristotle's; that his recommendation to 'set down the appearances' and to preserve 'the greatest number and the most basic' announces a refusal of Eleatic and Platonist reality–appearance distinctions and a determination to found philosophy on attention to the variety of experience.[43] In her discussion she explicitly compares Aristotle's concerns with Wittgenstein's.[44] She has also tried to show in detail, for the case of the explanation of animal motion, how Aristotle's account succeeds in doing just this.[45] She argues that Aristotle preserves the non-reducibility and also the experienced complexity of intentional phenomena such as perception, belief, and desire, criticizing both materialist reductionism and Platonist intellectualism for their inability to offer a causal explanation of motion that captures the richness and relevance of ordinary discourse about motion and action. We have mentioned some of these arguments in Section II, and we shall not recapitulate further. But we wish to mention two issues on which the conclusions of these studies affect our argument here.

First, the position argued for in Nussbaum's 'The "Common Explanation"' makes it evident that our Aristotle is not guilty of the kind of reductionism with which Putnam now taxes functionalism. His opposition to materialist reductionism preserves the independence and irreducibility of the intentional and does not, as the modern functionalist would, seek to reduce these to independently

[43] Owen (1961, repr. in 1986), Nussbaum (1982b).
[44] In the longer version of Nussbaum (1982b) that is Nussbaum (1986), ch. 8.
[45] Nussbaum (1983), also Nussbaum (1986), ch. 9.

specifiable computational states. There is no hint of any such enterprise (or even a desire for such an enterprise) in Aristotle; this is one reason why we prefer the phrase 'organization to function' to the more common 'functional organization', as more suggestive of the irreducible character of the intentional activities in question.

Second, Aristotle's account also seems free of the difficulty we have just found in Brentano, namely the tendency to treat all intentionality as a unitary phenomenon. In Aristotle we find instead a subtle demarcation of numerous species of cognition and desire, and of their interrelationships.

In sum: *if* the 'emergence of mind' has to be 'explained', and the only possibilities are (i) the Frank Baum theory (some matter is just *like* that) and (ii) a reductionist account—or, possibly, (iii) an 'eliminationist' one—compatible with contemporary physics, and *if*, as Burnyeat claims, the Frank Baum account was Aristotle's (we are all like the Scarecrow), *then*, since modern physics has demolished the Frank Baum theory (in case anyone ever believed it), we are 'stuck' with 'our' problem—reductionism or 'supervenience' (redefine 'materialism' so *everything* counts as materialism) or 'eliminationism' (*à la* Dennett[46] or Quine[47] or the Churchlands[48]). But why should one believe the antecedent of this conditional?

IV. Aristotle and Theodicy: or, Aquinas' Separated Souls Change their Mind

If the interpretation of Aristotle defended by Burnyeat does indeed, as we have argued, force the text and neglect some unequivocal statements, if there is another interpretation that is both textually more sound and philosophically more powerful (we want you to believe the antecedent of *this* conditional!), then where does the rival interpretation come from, and why has it enjoyed such a long history? We find the history of this misreading so interesting that we cannot resist a brief digression.

In his earliest draft, Burnyeat called his view 'the Christian view'. Finding it in John Philoponus, St Thomas Aquinas, and Franz Brentano, he mentions as significant the fact that all three were 'committed Christians'. We agree with him that this fact is significant. For all three were not simply interpreters of the text of Aristotle; nor were they simply seekers after the best explanation of the functioning of living beings as we encounter them in this world. They were engaged in the delicate enterprise of Aristotelian theodicy—the attempt to use Aristotle's excellence and authority to bolster and flesh out a picture of the world that would be an acceptable foundation for Christian life and discourse. Such a thinker must give some story about the immortal life of the separated soul; this story will have to ascribe to it a cognitive functioning rich enough to support

[46] Cf. Dennett (1987).   [47] Cf. Quine (1960).
[48] Cf. Paul Churchland (1981), Patricia Churchland (1986).

Christian hopes and beliefs concerning the life after death. It will also need to insist upon the gulf between the human soul and the operations of animal souls that are not to be immortal. All this has obvious implications for what the thinker will say about the operations of perception and other forms of cognition in the human organism in this world. It will begin to look sensible to veer away from Aristotle's insistence on the seamless unity of form and matter, towards a picture that makes this relation more fortuitous, less organic, characterized by a certain degree of independence or even opposition. And if the aim is theodicy, this sensible course is also perfectly legitimate.[49]

Brentano makes the complexity of his relation to Aristotle's text explicit. In the remarkable monograph *Aristotle and his World View* (recently translated by Rolf George and Roderick Chisholm[50]), he candidly announces that his aim in presenting his account of Aristotle as a thinker about theodicy is 'to make this pessimistically inclined age aware of the resources of the optimistic world idea'. And he grants that the theodicy he sets forth, which makes much of the cognitive powers of the separated soul, goes beyond the text:

It is indeed true that this view is not set forth in Aristotle's writings as explicitly as I have described and defended it here, for Aristotle unfortunately did not find time to write the intended detailed exposition of his metaphysics.[51]

We reply with some astonishment that Aristotle surely found time to write quite a lot of detailed metaphysics, and that what he wrote simply does not agree with the picture mapped out by Brentano. When Brentano goes on to inform us that the 'eschatology' implied in Aristotle's view of soul yields the doctrine that 'In order that the number of those who inhabit the world beyond may increase to infinity, the human souls move one after the other from this world into the other' —*and* that this view has 'remarkable agreements' not only with Christianity but also 'with the religious doctrines of Judaism',[52] we reply that these 'agreements' are no accident, since that is where this allegedly Aristotelian view comes from. In the same passage Brentano defends the rapprochement with a reference to a statement by Theophrastus (*ap.* Porphyr. *De Abstinentia* 2. 26) admiring the Jews as an 'especially philosophical' people. We accept the compliment, but we deny the 'remarkable agreement'. If the concept of similarity is this elastic, it is about as useful as Nelson Goodman says it is.[53]

Theodicy, however, has its complexities. And the real point of this digression is to show how the greatest of the Christian interpreters of Aristotle, St Thomas Aquinas, was led by philosophy and theodicy together to reject Burnyeat's 'Christian interpretation' and to adopt one that is very close to ours. The committed Christian must indeed endow the soul with powers such that it can enjoy a cognitively rich afterlife. But he or she must also satisfy two further demands: and here the balancing act begins. First, she must explain why, if the body's capabilities are *not* perfectly suited to fit with, *act along with*, the functions of

[49] We do not discuss Philoponus in this paper; but see Sorabji's paper in this volume.
[50] Brentano (1976).   [51] Ibid.   [52] Ibid.   [53] Goodman (1972).

soul, God did *not* make the body less arbitrary and more organic. And she must also explain the point of the resurrection of the body, an element of doctrine that causes notorious difficulty for the more Platonistically inclined among Christian philosophers. If the soul in its separated condition is well equipped to perceive and imagine and think—if there are no material transitions necessary for its good activity—then this promised event will be at best superfluous, at worst a divine blunder.

Aquinas never, in fact, adopted the entirety of the Burnyeat position. For although in his commentary on *De Anima* he does interpret the reception of form without matter in much the way Burnyeat says he does—awareness of red being a non-reducible intentional item—he consistently holds that each act of perceiving has material necessary conditions, *and* that these conditions are *changes in the sense-organs.* 'For as things exist in sensation they are free indeed from matter, but not without their individuating material conditions, nor apart from a bodily organ' (*In II De Anima*, Lect. 5, n. 284).[54] Free from matter, in that I become aware of red without my sense-organ literally going red. But there is none the less some *concomitant necessary material change* in that organ. The *Summa Theologiae* asserts this repeatedly, and unequivocally:

But Aristotle insists that…sensing and the related operations of the sensitive soul evidently happen together with some change (*immutatio*) of the body, as in seeing the pupil is changed by the appearance of colour; and the same is manifest in other cases. And so it is evident that the sensitive soul has no operation that is proper to itself; but all the operation of the sensitive soul is the operation of the compound. (I, q. 75, a. 3; cf. I, q. 75, a. 4: 'sensing is not an operation of the soul by itself'; I, q. 76, a. 1, *et saepe*.)

Furthermore, Aquinas consistently contrasts perceiving with thinking in a way that brings him very close to our interpretation: for while he says of both that in the human organism they have necessary material conditions (thinking requires phantasms which themselves are realized in matter)—and both are for this reason to be called forms of the human body—sensing is *the act of* (an activity embodied or realized in) a corporeal organ, and thinking is not:

As the Philosopher says in *Physics* II, the ultimate of the natural forms, in which the investigation of natural philosophy terminates, namely the human soul, is indeed separate, but none the less in matter…It is separate according to the rational power, since the rational power is not the power of any corporeal organ, in the way that the power to see is the act of the eye: for to reason is an act that cannot be exercised through a corporeal organ, in the way that vision is exercised. But it is in matter, inasmuch as the soul itself, whose power it is, is the form of the body. (*Summa Theologiae* I, q. 76, a. 1, ad 1.)

He holds, furthermore, that each operation of intellect in a human being, both during the acquisition of knowledge and in using knowledge once acquired, requires that the intellect address itself to sensory phantasms, which he takes to be realized in matter, modifications constituted by matter (*ST* I, q. 84, aa. 7, 8;

---

[54] In this section we are indebted to John Carriero, and to his thesis, Carriero (1984).

q. 85, a. 1; q. 101, aa. 1. 2; q. 76, a. 1). This has the consequence that in its natural operation even the human intellect is firmly linked to matter and has very specific material necessary conditions. The main difference between intellection and sensing is that sensing is an act of a bodily organ, accompanied of necessity by a change in that organ; intellect is the form of the body in a different and looser sense. We think that Aquinas has correctly understood Aristotle's distinction between 'shared' functions (cf. 'the operation of the compound') and non-shared functions that none the less have material necessary conditions.

In some earlier works Aquinas did, however, hold that the separated human souls, once out of the body, would have a mode of cognition superior to that of the embodied soul. And it is here that further thought about theodicy has prompted, as we see it, a turning-back to the true Aristotelian position.[55] For in the *Summa Theologiae* he concludes that this cannot be so: that soul and body are so unified, so fitly and fully together in all their activity, that the separated soul has cognition only in a confused and unnatural way. With the death of the body, sensing and *phantasia* go; but then, he holds, all cognition of particulars and all modes of cognition built on this must go as well. But then the natural human way of cognizing must go: 'To be separated from the body is contrary to the principle of its nature, and similarly to cognize without turning to phantasms is contrary to its nature. So it is united to the body so that it should be and act according to its nature' (*ST* I, q. 89, a. 1). What remains is only an imperfect cognition, 'confusam in communi'.

We must, then, conclude, Aquinas continues, that the soul's natural and best home is in the body: 'The human soul remains in its being when it is separated from the body, having a natural fittedness and inclination towards union with the body' (*ST* I, q. 76, a. 1, ad 6). It is not in the body as in a prison; nor is it impeded by it from some better mode of cognition; nor, even, is it simply *housed*, Baum-like, in the body. The body's matter fits it, *does its actions*, through and through. Asking the question whether the soul is *convenienter*—appropriately, suitably, aptly—united with the organic human body, he retails several dualist objections, and then replies; 'Against this is what the Philosopher says in II of *De Anima*: "The soul is the act of a natural organic body potentially having life"' (I, q. 76, a. 5, *sed contra*).

This change was prompted by theodicy. First, as we have said, by concern with the resurrection of the body. Second, and much more stressed in the text, by the desire to show that God and nature did not do things arbitrarily and ill where human life is concerned. If the human mode of cognition is different, in its embodiment, from that of God and the angels, still it is exactly suited to human life, life in a world of changing perceptible particulars. Matter is suited to its function, and cognition's embodied modes to the nature of cognition's worldly objects (*ST* I, q. 84, a. 7). We note that it seems to be a consequence of this general principle that *if* a modern theory of matter had displaced Aristotle's in such a

---

[55] See Carriero (1984) and Pegis (1974); Carriero supplies refs. to *Summa Contra Gentiles*.

way as to make his particular sort of hylomorphism untenable (which we deny), Aquinas would then have had to show how the new matter itself was perfectly suited and united to *its* form (a *new* hylomorphism), in such a way that relevance and elegance are preserved in the universe as a whole.

Here theodicy converges with good philosophy. Aquinas' God would not have made us like Baum's Scarecrow, because, like the philosopher who is concerned with adequate explanations, God wants things to fit together in a suitable and coherent way. He wants a world that yields good explanations, not bad ones. If the body contributed so little, it could not be anything but a mistake that soul should be set up in one. And, we emphasize, not only a practical mistake: but a conceptual and philosophical mistake. For, having given the soul the sort of natural activity that, in its very nature, requires suitable matter for its fulfilment in activity, he would have failed to supply the suitable matter. So then, there just could not *be* those souls and those activities. The activities are forms in matter: take away matter and you cannot have *them*. The human soul would be a conceptually confused (not just physically handicapped) item. But God cares for conceptual fittedness, for explanatory relevance, for non-arbitrariness. He wants the function to be the reason why the matter is thus and so (*ST* I, q. 76, a. 5).

Of the Pythagorean view that 'any chance soul' can turn up animating 'any chance body', Aristotle writes:

Some people try only to say of what sort the soul is, but they determine nothing further about the body that is going to receive it... That is just like saying that one could do carpentry with flutes; for an art must have its appropriate tools, and the soul an appropriate body. (*DA* 408ª19 ff.)

(Notice how close Burnyeat's Frank Baum Aristotle is to the Pythagorean position.) This (religiously inspired) view, Aristotle says, is bad philosophy, since it makes the conceptual mistake of supposing you *could* have human life-activity without the embodiment of that activity in suitable matter. But you can't. It is an incoherent idea. If the person is banging around with a soft wooden musical instrument, then whatever she is doing, by definition it won't be carpentry. No more, by definition, can there be perceiving without *its* suitable embodiment. What these activities are in their nature is organically embodied forms: they require embodiment *to be themselves*. We think that Aquinas is taking this point, and attempting to save God from Pythagorean incoherence. The truly Christian view, says Aquinas, is one that makes God a good philosopher of nature, not a bad one, not one who tries to prise the activities apart from their constitutive matter. This view of embodied form he finds, as we do, in Aristotle.

V. Goodbye to Oz

We conclude: we can have non-reductionism and the explanatory priority of the intentional without losing that sense of the natural and organic unity of the intentional with its constitutive matter that is one of the great contributions of Aristotelian realism. We suggest that Aristotle's thought really is, properly understood, the fulfilment of Wittgenstein's desire to have a 'natural history of man'.[56] (It is also, in a different way, the fulfilment of Aquinas' desire to find that our truly natural being is the being that we live every day, and that God has not screened our real nature behind some arbitrary barrier.) As Aristotelians we do not discover something behind something else, a hidden reality behind the complex unity that we see and are. We find what we are in the appearances. And Aristotle tells us that if we attend properly to the appearances the dualist's questions never even get going. 'It is not appropriate to inquire whether the soul and the body are one—just as it is not appropriate in the case of the wax and its shape, and in general the matter of each thing and that of which it is the matter' (*DA* 412^{b}6–9). If you attend in the appropriate way to the complex materiality of living things, if you understand the common conception of what it is to be a living thing, you will not ask that question. The soul is not an 'it' housed in the body, but a functional structure in and of matter. Matter is, in its very nature, just the thing to constitute the functions of life. (It is *not* a thing to which the functions of life can be *reduced*.) 'Some things just are this in this, or these parts ordered in such and such a way' (*Metaph.* 1036^{b}22 ff.). Or, to quote Frank Baum's heroine, 'There's no place like home.'[57]

[56] Wittgenstein (1956), I. 141.

[57] We owe thanks above all to Burnyeat, for provoking this reply; we are sure it will not end the debate. We are also grateful to the participants in the Rochester conference (see above n. 2), and especially to Robert Cummins, our commentator, for stimulating comments; and to John Carriero and Jaegwon Kim for discussion of the issues.

4

HYLOMORPHISM AND FUNCTIONALISM[1]

S. MARC COHEN

WAS Aristotle's theory of the soul a prototype of contemporary functionalism? A growing number of scholars, including both philosophers of mind and historians of philosophy, would like to think so. To the former, the functionalist interpretation of Aristotle offers the security of a classical heritage. To the latter, its appeal is twofold; it promises both to illuminate and to revitalize Aristotle's thought. His contemporary students will be pleased to discover that although Aristotle's physiology of psychology may be antiquated, his philosophy of psychology is quite up to date.

Other scholars remain unconvinced by the functionalist interpretation. According to one influential line of criticism, functionalism is a live option in the philosophy of mind, while Aristotle's theory is too riddled with outmoded assumptions to be taken seriously any more. The spearhead of this critique, surprisingly, is not a functionalist philosopher of mind, but Myles Burnyeat, Laurence Professor of Ancient Philosophy at Cambridge University.

In a provocative paper,[2] Burnyeat has developed a powerful line of criticism of the views of Hilary Putnam[3] and Martha Nussbaum,[4] two of the leading functionalist interpreters of Aristotle. Although directed against their particular interpretation, his argument is quite general. If Burnyeat is right, not only Putnam and Nussbaum, but also Richard Sorabji (1974), Edwin Hartman (1977), and Kathleen Wilkes (1978) are all misguided in their more or less explicitly functionalist interpretations of Aristotle.

Burnyeat does more than dispute functionalist interpretations of Aristotle; he argues that when we correctly understand Aristotle's philosophy of mind, we will realize that the only thing to do with it is to junk it. So anyone who finds contemporary relevance in Aristotle's theory will have to come to terms with Burnyeat's argument. That is what I propose to do. I will try to show that Burnyeat has not

[1] An earlier version of this essay was presented at a conference at the University of Alberta in Edmonton in Mar. 1986 and was published (under the title 'The Credibility of Aristotle's Philosophy of Mind') in Matthen (1987). The results reached in the present essay are not significantly different from those of the earlier one, but there have been numerous alterations and improvements in both style and substance. Thanks are due to Paul Opperman and Christopher Shields for their help in eliminating various mistakes and confusions in the earlier version, and to Opperman (again) and David Keyt for similar assistance with the present version.

[2] Above, ch. 2.　　　[3] Cf. his 'Philosophy and our Mental Life', in Putnam (1975).

[4] Cf. Essay 1, 'Aristotle and Teleological Explanation', in Nussbaum (1978), 59–106.

succeeded in refuting either Aristotle or his functionalist interpreters. I will not, however, attempt to provide additional positive reasons for embracing a functionalist interpretation.

Functionalism is the theory that mental states are defined in terms of their relations to causal inputs, behavioural outputs, and other mental states.[5] It holds that the same mental state may be *realized* by several different physical states or processes. Mental states cannot, therefore, be reduced to physical states. They are, rather, functional states of the physical systems that realize them.

Aristotle had little to say about how mental states in general should be defined. His concern was to define the soul (*psuchē*). His theory—hylomorphism—holds that the relation of soul to body is that of form to matter. What are these two theories thought to have in common? We will begin with hylomorphism.

Aristotle's conception of the soul is biological: *psuchē* is that in virtue of which a body is a *living* body. As Aristotle puts it (*DA* 2. 1, 412ª20):

soul is the substance, in the sense of *form*, of a natural body potentially having life.

By 'substance' (*ousia*) he does not mean a Cartesian substance—an independently existing thing. In some sense *psuchē* for Aristotle is not a *thing* at all. He calls it a substance 'in the sense of form'. What sense is that?

Aristotle typically uses artefacts as examples to illustrate the distinction between form and matter.[6] A statue is some bronze with a certain shape; this house consists of these bricks and boards arranged and assembled in such and such a way; an axe is some iron that has the capacity to chop. In the simplest case, form is just shape; in more complex cases, it is more like functional organization. In each case, matter is compounded with form. Bronze, bricks, and iron are matter; shape, arrangement, and capacity are form. The matter and the form are *contingently* related: the matter might have had a different form, and the form might have been found in different matter.

Human *psuchē* is evidently a form of considerable complexity. Put simply, it comprises the capacities to be nourished, to take in sensory information about the environment, to move voluntarily, and to think. It is in terms of *psuchē* and its actions or movements that we explain these characteristic human activities and account for the bodily parts and systems on which they depend. These explanations and accounts are *teleological*. We explain movements in terms of the goals they are aimed at rather than in terms of the mechanical workings of the

[5] See Block, 'What is Functionalism?', in N. Block (1980) 171–84.
[6] Relying on the artefact model in explicating the form–matter distinction, as both Aristotle and most of his commentators do, makes for trouble in understanding his hylomorphic theory of mind. Critics such as Burnyeat and Ackrill (see below, pp. 68–9) see this as a flaw in the theory; but it might equally well be taken to be a shortcoming in the model. The problem with the artefact model is that it oversimplifies hylomorphism and ultimately misrepresents it in the cases that are most important to Aristotle. The crucial point of misrepresentation is the contingent connection between matter and form. In all but the simplest cases, matter already contains a great deal of form, and form carries with it many material requirements. (I am grateful to Montgomery Furth for his illuminating presentation of this point in discussion at the conference mentioned in n. 1. See Matthen (1987), 124.)

body which carries them out. We account for the eye or the heart not in terms of what it is made of but in terms of its function—what it *does*, what it is *for*.

Aristotle also applies the matter–form distinction to the 'actions' and 'passions' of the soul—what we would call mental (or emotional) states or psychological processes. In trying to say what *anger* is, for example (403ª29 ff.), a natural scientist and a philosopher will give different answers. The scientist will say that anger is the boiling of the blood in the vicinity of the heart. The philosopher will define anger as a desire for retaliation. One cites the matter; the other cites the form.

The form in this case is inseparable from matter: it must be realized in matter, Aristotle tells us, if it is to exist at all (403ᵇ3, ᵇ18). So anger cannot exist in a disembodied state. But neither can it be reduced to the boiling of the blood around the heart, for that is just its *matter*. Therefore, if we are correct in assuming that *this* form and *this* matter are only contingently related, then there is no essential connection between anger and the boiling of the blood around the heart. And in general, there will be no essential connection between a psychological state and any particular material realization of it.

Some psychic states are intimately associated with specific bodily parts, of course; sensation and the sense-organs are an obvious example. Aristotle discusses these in detail in *De Partibus Animalium*. His remarks strongly suggest a conviction that the same psychic state may have different material realizations. In animals made of flesh, for example, the organ of touch is the flesh; in other animals it is the part 'analogous to flesh' (*PA* 2. 1, 647ª21). Sensations of touch occur in the flesh of humans, but in different (although analogous) organs of other species. Such observations, which abound throughout the work, suggest a sympathy for the *compositional plasticity* that is characteristic of functionalism.

In a famous passage in *Metaph.* Z11, Aristotle considers whether there should be reference to matter in a definition: whether matter is, as he puts it, ever 'part of the form'. He points out that it is obvious that 'neither bronze nor stone belongs at all to the substance [i.e. form] of the circle' (1036ª33), for *circle* is a form that supervenes on different kinds of matter. He goes on to say that bronze would be no part of the form 'even if all the circles that had ever been seen were of bronze' (1036ᵇ1). In that case, he concedes, it would be hard—but correct—to abstract the bronze from the circle in thought. He then considers the case of the form *man*, which is always found in flesh and bones. 'Are these', he asks, 'parts of the form?' His answer (although clouded by a vexatious text) seems to be 'no'.[7] Here, too, he suggests, we simply fail to make the necessary abstraction.

Aristotle surely did not believe that the human form was likely to supervene on anything other than flesh-and-bones. At some abstract level, however, the possibility is at least conceivable to him. The reason it is conceivable is that he maintains that definitions must always be in terms of function, not matter. What

---

[7] See the appendix for a discussion of some problems in the interpretation of this passage.

makes something human is not what it is made of but what it *does*. Here again he seems sympathetic to compositional plasticity.

So the key elements of a materialistic variety of functionalism appear to be present in Aristotle's account. Psychical faculties and states require some material embodiment,[8] but not any particular kind of embodiment. Their definitions are always to be given in terms of form and function, never in terms of material composition. They are multiply realizable, in that the same faculty or state may be found in different kinds of creatures with significantly different physiological make-ups.

Burnyeat concedes that Aristotle's hylomorphism has the appearance of functionalism. But the appearance, he claims, is misleading. For contemporary functionalism was devised as a response to Descartes's mind–body problem. The problem arises because Descartes posits two fundamentally different kinds of substance: *matter*, whose nature is to be extended, and *mind*, whose nature is to think. The subject-matter of Cartesian psychology is entirely distinct from that of Cartesian physics. How, then, do we explain the interaction of mind and matter? Under what science could the laws of such interaction fall? That is Descartes's problem. For Aristotle, on the other hand, psychology is a part of physics, that is, of the general theory of nature; psychology therefore has an *Aristotelian* conception of matter built in. This conception of matter, Burnyeat argues, is not consistent with functionalism, or, indeed, with any plausible contemporary theory. It is thus Aristotle's physics that makes his philosophy of mind no longer credible.

In order to establish this mismatch between contemporary functionalism and the Aristotelian conception of matter, Burnyeat turns to Aristotle's theory of perception. His examination focuses on the mysterious Aristotelian doctrine that a 'sense is what is receptive of sensible forms without matter' (*aisthēsis esti to dektikon tōn aisthētōn eidōn aneu tēs hulēs*, 424[a]17 ff.). The received interpretation of this doctrine, as ably articulated by Richard Sorabji,[9] is one that a functionalist interpreter would find congenial. According to Sorabji, Aristotle means that sense-organs take on (come to be characterized by) the perceptible qualities of perceived objects. When one sees a tomato, for example, the transparent jelly composing the eyes goes red. In general, when one perceives a sensible object to be *F*, some part of one's sensory apparatus literally becomes *F*. (Aristotle describes the process as *without matter* in order to contrast his own theory with that of Empedocles and Democritus, who thought that in vision material particles emanate from the object seen and into the eye of the beholder.)

This account of the physiology of perception may strike us as embarrassingly naïve. Jonathan Barnes, for one, finds it 'open to devastatingly obvious empirical refutation'.[10] (He doubtless thought that anyone who looks into another's eyes can see that they do not turn red at the sight of a tomato.) However, its *naïveté* need

---

[8] With the notorious exception of *thought*. The difficulty of reconciling Aristotle's treatment of *nous* with the rest of his psychology is widely recognized.

[9] Sorabji (1974/1979), 49; see esp. n. 22.   [10] Barnes (1971–2), 109.

not disturb the functionalist interpreter. For Aristotle does not *identify* seeing red with the reddening of the eye-jelly (just as a contemporary functionalist would not identify pain with C-fibre stimulation). Rather, Aristotle maintains that the reddening of the eye-jelly is only the *matter* of which the perception of red is constituted (as a contemporary functionalist might concede that C-fibre stimulation is the material realization of pain in humans but would insist that other realizations are at least possible). A functionalist's philosophy need not be impugned because his physiology is unsound. If we discard the antiquated theory of the reddening eye-jelly and replace it with a more up-to-date physiology, we may still, it would seem, claim to be advancing an Aristotelian theory of perception.

Against the Sorabji interpretation of Aristotle's notion of a sense-organ's taking on form without matter, Burnyeat proposes an alternative that he credits to Philoponus, Aquinas, and Brentano. According to this rival interpretation, a sense-organ's taking on a sensible form is nothing more nor less than an *awareness* of that form. Taking *on* a form is to be thought of as taking *in* that form; the sense-organ's becoming *F* is to be thought of as the sense-faculty's becoming *aware* of *F*-ness.

If this account of Aristotle is correct, he cannot plausibly be interpreted to hold that perception *supervenes* on an underlying physiological process. The supervenience of the mental on the physical—the idea that in any two worlds where the physical facts are the same, the mental facts are the same—is a modern invention, and is alien to Aristotle, Burnyeat maintains. Of course Aristotle does believe that physiological states are psychologically relevant. But like Plato's Socrates in the *Phaedo*, Burnyeat's Aristotle regards these as necessary conditions only.

Burnyeat concludes that Aristotle's account of the physiology of perception is different from what the Sorabji interpretation supposes. A sense-organ's reception of sensible form, which is both necessary and sufficient for perception, is not a physiological process at all. Burnyeat even goes so far as to say that Aristotle's account allows there to be perceptual awareness without any corresponding physiological change. (The physiologically necessary conditions on his account are only *states* of receptivity, not *processes* or alterations.) This clinches his case against the functionalist interpretation, Burnyeat thinks. For it shows that Aristotle would have to hold that an organism's perceptual capacities are fundamental, not supervenient. They simply *are* the way they are, and do not require explanation in physiological terms. According to Burnyeat, Aristotle does not regard the emergence of the life-functions as a mysterious fact standing in need of explanation. Rather, Aristotle has the explanations going the other way around: we explain the physical properties of animals in terms of their contribution to the existence of animal life.

The linchpin of Burnyeat's argument is his understanding of the notion of receiving form without matter; it therefore demands careful scrutiny. He argues that receiving form *with* matter is not correctly construed as merely absorbing some matter which carries a form. If it were, then receiving form *without* matter would be receiving a form which is not carried by any material vehicle. But this, he rightly points out, is an absurd way to view the relation between form and matter. Form is not something that can leave one material vehicle (or exist without a material vehicle at all) and be taken on by another material vehicle. Rather, *x* receives the form of *y* just in case *y* causes *x* to become like *y* in form. Therefore, Burnyeat concludes, to receive the form of something *with* its matter is to become like it in both form and matter; and to receive the form of something *without* its matter is to become like it in form without becoming like it in matter.

When something is warmed by proximity to a hot stove, for example, its matter becomes like the matter of the stove: it gets hot. That is, its matter takes on the same form (heat) that the iron of the stove already has. It becomes like the stove in both form and matter. But when someone notices the warmth of the stove without being heated by it, he does not become like the stove in matter; for, unlike the iron of the stove, his flesh does not become hot. Rather, he becomes like the stove in form only. Or, as Burnyeat seems equally happy to put the point, he becomes warm without *really* becoming warm.

Burnyeat admits that one recalcitrant passage appears to favour Sorabji's interpretation over his own. In *DA* 2. 12, Aristotle raises the question whether sensible objects, such as colours or odours, can effect things that do not perceive; he offers arguments on both sides of the issue. On the one hand, he reasons, since the only effect an odour can produce is *smelling*, it follows that things which cannot smell cannot be affected by odours ($424^{b}8$). On the other hand, non-sentient bodies (like air) do seem to be affected by odours. He concludes his discussion with the following question ($424^{b}17$): what more (*para*) is smelling than being affected by something? The question is ambiguous. Is he asking what smelling is *over and above* a physiological process in which the sensible object, odour, affects the nose? Or is he asking what smelling is *as opposed to* what goes on when a non-sentient body is affected by an odour? The first reading has Aristotle explicitly drawing the distinction between physiological and psychological processes that is crucial to the functionalist interpretation. Burnyeat, of course, would prefer to adopt the second reading. The question, he says, is not what more there is to smelling an odour than having it affect the nose, but what more there is to odour's effect on the nose than there is to its effect on the air.

There is only one hitch for Burnyeat: Aristotle's answer, according to one influential edition of the text (Torstrik's), appears to block his reading of the question. Torstrik emended the text by adding the word *kai* ('also'), making the answer read: 'perhaps smelling is *also* perceiving' (*osmasthai kai aisthanesthai*). This response makes sense only on the first reading of the question: smelling, *in addition to* (*kai*) being affected, involves awareness (*aisthanesthai*). Without the *kai*, Burnyeat's reading is quite plausible. Why did Torstrik find it necessary to insert the *kai*?

The answer, along with a devastating refutation, is supplied by Kosman (1975), whom Burnyeat cites with approval. Kosman points out that Torstrik was following manuscript E (Parisinus graecus 1853), the one manuscript in which the *kai* occurs. E itself is written in two different hands; book 2 was written by the later of the two. Some fragments of the older recension of book 2 have survived, however, including a corrupt version of our passage. The older hand had written *osmasthai ai aisthanesthai*, which is meaningless. The later scribe presumably took the *ai* to be the remnant of an original *kai*, and corrected his text accordingly. (Torstrik also had philosophical motives, since he took Aristotle to be asking what perceiving is in addition to being affected, and preferred a text making that clear.) Kosman makes the much more plausible conjecture that the meaningless *ai* was the product of dittography. (*Ai ai ai!* The scribe should have written *osmasthai aisthanesthai*.) Once the *kai* is rejected, there is no reason to favour the first reading. Far from supporting the functionalist interpretation, Burnyeat concludes, this passage provides evidence against it.[11]

The idea that the effect of sensible form on a sense-organ is nothing *less* than a state of awareness has the consequence, Burnyeat notes, that the matter of which sense-organs are composed is *essentially* capable of awareness. For there is, according to Burnyeat's Aristotle, no physiological state of a sense-organ on which a state of awareness can supervene. Sensible form produces awareness in the sense-organ directly; there is no intervening or supervening involved.

What kind of matter is this that is essentially capable of awareness? It is nothing like Cartesian matter, whose essence is simply to be extended, and whose connection to mind and the mental is as tenuous and contingent as a connection can be. It is in terms of inanimate Cartesian matter that the mind–body problem is framed. But how can there be a mind–body problem if the 'animal matter' that composes the bodies of sentient beings has awareness built in at the ground level? And how can a theory be considered a version of functionalism if it denies the contingency of the connection between a psychological state and its physical realization?

According to Burnyeat, Aristotle's theory of perception is committed to both of the following claims:

(i) A sense-organ's taking on a sensible form is an act of awareness rather than a physiological change.
(ii) It is possible for perception to occur without any associated physiological change.

Burnyeat uses (i) as the leading premiss in his argument against the functionalist interpretation. It has solid (albeit disputed) textual credentials. (ii)'s credentials, however, are less clear, as is the relation Burnyeat supposes it bears to (i). He nowhere argues that (ii) follows from (i). His arguments are devoted to proving (i); then (ii) puts in a sudden appearance. This suggests that Burnyeat may have

---

[11] The fate of the *kai* in recent texts of *DA* has been curious. Hicks includes it, citing Torstrik, but Ross has vacillated. His OCT edition (1956) includes the *kai* (albeit with no mention of Torstrik in the apparatus) but his text with commentary (1961) omits it. Nevertheless, he glosses the passage as if the *kai* were there: 'What, then, is smelling, over and above a being affected? It is, besides a being affected, a *perceiving*…' (p. 297).

the following sort of argument in mind: perception is *nothing more nor less* than a sense-organ's reception of sensible form, and the reception of form is not a physiological process. So since there is nothing *more* to perception than the reception of form, it is possible for perception to occur without any corresponding physiological change.

This is not a convincing line of argument. The reception of sensible form may still require a physiological process, even if it cannot be identified with such a process. If the eye's taking on the visible form of an object is not a physiological process, it follows that vision cannot be identified with a physiological process. It does not follow that there is *no* physiological process that is essential to vision.

(ii) is certainly incompatible with token-physicalistic functionalism. But since (ii) does not follow from (i), Burnyeat has not shown that functionalists are obligated to deny (i). Still, they are not likely to be convinced by his argument for it. Nussbaum and Putnam,[12] for example, complain about the emphasis Burnyeat places on Sorabji's account of a sense-organ's taking on sensible form. They reply that even if he is right in his criticism of Sorabji (which they seem happy to grant), he will not have established that the reception of form is not a physiological process, but at most that it is not the particular physiological process Sorabji claimed it to be. There is no evidence, however, that Aristotle had some other physiological process in mind. I suggest, therefore, that functionalists should not be so quick to distance themselves from Sorabji's interpretation.

I shall argue that Burnyeat has not succeeded in refuting Sorabji. Nor, I contend, has he made a compelling case for his rival interpretation. My argument will consist primarily of a detailed examination of the passages in which Aristotle uses the enigmatic notion of a sense-organ's taking on sensible form without matter. A few preliminary observations will help to focus that examination.

Burnyeat makes a point of reminding us that it is absurd to suppose that receiving form without matter consists in receiving a form that is not carried by any material vehicle. But Sorabji would surely agree; on his account, 'without matter' is elliptical for 'without *receiving* matter'. And 'receiving matter' means: incorporating matter from the object. What is at issue is not whether the form existed somehow in an immaterial state during the process of transmission (of course it did not), but whether any of the object's matter was incorporated by the recipient of the form.

What may be bothering Burnyeat is a striking disanalogy in Sorabji's understanding of the notions of receiving matter and receiving form. Receiving (some of) an object's matter, on Sorabji's understanding, deprives the object of that matter; receiving its form deprives it not at all. Burnyeat's interpretation may at first appear to fare better in this respect: 'taking on the form of *x*' means 'becoming like *x* in form'; 'taking on the matter of *x*' means 'becoming like *x* in matter'. The analogy, however, is only superficial. For Burnyeat takes 'being like *x* in matter' to mean 'having matter that is like *x*'s matter', and 'being like *x* in form'

---

[12] Martha Nussbaum and Hilary Putnam, 'Changing Aristotle's Mind' (this volume, pp. 27–56).

to mean not, as we should expect, 'having a form that is like *x*'s form' but 'being aware of *x*'. Neither interpretation succeeds in preserving the analogy suggested by the labels 'receiving matter' and 'receiving form'. Sorabji's at least has the advantage of being more literal. The disanalogy in his reading is due to the metaphysical difference between matter and form; the disanalogy in Burnyeat's seems strictly *ad hoc*.

Burnyeat's understanding of these two notions, if correct, would devastate the Sorabji interpretation. For my matter becomes like your matter when my matter changes *qualitatively* and takes on the form that your matter already has. Taking on matter (or, perhaps, taking on form *with matter*) turns out to be a kind of qualitative change. So when Aristotle asserts that in perception a sense-organ receives form *without* matter, he is doing little more that denying that perception involves a qualitative change in the sense-organ. That is, he is doing little more than denying precisely what Sorabji interprets him to be asserting.

At this point Burnyeat seems to declare his own interpretation the winner by default. Sorabji's idea that 'receiving form without matter' describes a kind of qualitative change cannot be right, Burnyeat thinks, since Aristotle ought to describe qualitative change as taking on form *with* matter. Therefore, 'taking on for without matter' must mean something else: taking on the form of an object without one's matter being affected by it.

Note that on Burnyeat's theory, it is the *recipient's* matter that is at issue: the perceiver takes on the form of the object but the perceiver's matter is not affected. This creates two problems for Burnyeat, one philosophical, one textual. The first problem is that it seems incoherent to make the matter referred to in 'without matter' be that of the *perceiver*, and at the same time construe 'without matter' to be elliptical for 'without taking on matter' that is, without taking on any of the matter of the *object*. The second problem is that Aristotle's examples show that when he says 'without matter' he is thinking of the matter of the (donor) object, not the (recipient) perceiver.

The best place to begin is with Aristotle's wax analogy in *DA* 2. 12. A sense receives form without matter, he tells us, 'as wax receives the imprint of a signet-ring without the iron or gold; it takes the imprint of gold or of bronze, but not *qua* gold or bronze' (424^{a}19–22). In illustrating 'without matter' Aristotle says 'without the gold'. It is clearly the matter of the *donor* that is at issue rather than that of the recipient. The analogy would be a poor illustration of the theory Burnyeat attributes to Aristotle.[13]

In Aristotle's analogy, when the wax takes the imprint of gold (*to chrusoun sēmeion*) its shape is altered; it takes on the shape of the gold. It is clearly affected by the gold. But not, Aristotle says, *qua* gold. What is he ruling out? What would it have been like if the wax had received the imprint of the gold *qua* gold? It is hard to escape the conclusion that the wax would have received not just the

---

[13] Burnyeat sees in the analogy a polemical reference to the *Theaetetus*, where Plato used it as the model for a theory of judgement. He might therefore maintain that Aristotle had a good reason for using it here in spite of its failure to fit his own theory.

extrinsic, accidental features of the gold (its shape) but its intrinsic, essential ones as well (being gold). The wax would (at least in part) have come to *be* of gold (*chrusoun*). It would have done this, presumably, by incorporating some matter that carries the form of gold.

Other passages create similar difficulties for Burnyeat's interpretation. At 424^{a}1, Aristotle says that in perception the sense-organ is potentially such as the object of perception is actually. On the Sorabji interpretation, his point is quite clear, for in perception the sense-organ literally takes on the sensible form of the object: in perceiving the *F*-ness of something, the sense-organ itself literally becomes *F*. And of course the sense-organ cannot become *F* unless it is (*a*) already potentially *F* and (*b*) not yet actually *F*. One cannot feel warmth unless one's organ of touch is capable of becoming warm; and one cannot feel the warmth of something one's organ of touch is already as warm as. At 424^{a}7 Aristotle goes on to say that the organ which will perceive white and black must itself actually be neither white nor black, but potentially both. Again, his point seems quite straightforward: something which is already actually white cannot *become* white. To perceive is to take on sensible form, and a sense-organ cannot *take on* a form it has already assumed.

What is Aristotle's point on Burnyeat's interpretation? Why can't eye-jelly which is about to perceive white already actually *be* white? According to Burnyeat, for the eye-jelly to be (actually) white is just for the perceiver to be *noticing* whiteness. But why should Aristotle think that one who *will* be noticing whiteness cannot *already* be noticing whiteness? Whereas Sorabji takes perception to be, at least in part, a genuine process in which the sense-organ undergoes an alteration, Burnyeat understands it to be not a genuine alteration at all. In perception, according to Burnyeat's Aristotle, the sense-organ is merely brought into activity; perception is nothing more than the exercise of a capacity. This means that the simple logical point about genuine changes—that a thing which is already *F* cannot become *F*—is inapplicable. A thing which is already red cannot be about to *turn* red; but one who is already playing tennis may be about to play more tennis.

A crucial passage for Sorabji is 425^{b}22–6, where Aristotle argues that 'what sees' (*to horōn*) is itself 'in a way coloured' (*estin hōs kechrōmatistai*). This remark makes perfectly good sense on his interpretation. Aristotle is discussing the question of how, or whether, we perceive that we perceive. How can we see that we see, when all that we can see, properly speaking, is the proper object of sight, namely, colour? Aristotle's answer is that what sees is in a way coloured, 'for the sense-organ receives the sensible object without its matter'.

Aristotle goes on to say that this coloration of *to horōn* explains why perception and images (*phantasiai*) linger on after the object of perception has been removed. Since Sorabji understands this to be the literal coloration of the eye-jelly, the explanation is simple and plausible: we look at a tomato, and the eye-jelly goes red. Remove the tomato and the impression of redness persists. This is because the eye-jelly really *is* still red.

On Burnyeat's interpretation, however, Aristotle's explanation would beg the question. The reason the *impression* of redness persists can hardly be that the eye-jelly remains red. For the reddening of the eye-jelly, Burnyeat tells us, is nothing more nor less than an *awareness* of redness, and that is precisely what Aristotle is supposed to be explaining. To ask why the impression of redness persists is just to ask why we continue to be aware of redness. On Sorabji's interpretation Aristotle has a genuine explanation (albeit physiologically naïve); on Burnyeat's he has no explanation at all.

The only truly recalcitrant passage for the Sorabji interpretation now appears to be the discussion in *DA* 2. 12 of the fact that plants do not perceive. Clearly Aristotle is interested in the case of plants because they are apparent counter-examples to his theory of perception. A plant has a soul and it can take on sensible form—it can get warm, for example. So why, according to Aristotle's theory, does it not perceive warmth? In his answer, Aristotle must make clear that his theory can distinguish between the effect a sensible object has on a sense-organ and its effect on a non-sentient subject, such as air, or a plant. And Burnyeat's account takes Aristotle to be making just this distinction.

Sorabji agrees that Aristotle means to be drawing this distinction. He and Burnyeat also agree that Aristotle's reason for denying that plants perceive is that they take on sensible form only 'with matter'. Where they disagree is over the interpretation of this crucial phrase. Sorabji takes Aristotle to be asserting that plants can get warm only by (literally) taking in warm matter; Burnyeat takes him to mean that the only way plants can take in warmth is in a *material* way, by having their *matter* become warm.

One may be inclined to agree with Burnyeat here, if only because Sorabji attributes to Aristotle such an implausible theory of plant-warming. Surely Aristotle would have noticed that a plant can get warm by just sitting in the sun, without ingesting any material at all? But Sorabji and Burnyeat may both be wrong on this point. Aristotle says that the reason plants do not perceive warmth is that they do not have a mean (424^b2); that is, they do not have the right initial temperature, poised between warm and cold, to perceive these two qualities. Their matter can get warm, but that material change does not constitute the perception of warmth. The reason it does not constitute perception is not that it is only a material change, nor that it is only achieved by taking on external matter, but that it is the wrong kind of material change.

Burnyeat concedes that the requirement that the organ of touch be in a mean or intermediate state appears to support Sorabji's interpretation. His counter-proposal is that the intermediate state of the sense-organ is merely an initial condition required for perception to take place, and that Aristotle does not suppose there to be an actual physical change away from the mean—a warming or cooling, for example—in the sense-organ. Rather, the departure from the mean is what Aquinas called a 'spiritual' change, a becoming aware of warmth or cold. However, this proposal faces the same problem we encountered earlier at 425^b22–6. For Aristotle's explanation of our failure to perceive when our sense-organ is not in the right initial state becomes circular on Burnyeat's reading: an already warm sense-organ cannot perceive warmth because it cannot become warm, in other words because it cannot perceive warmth.

Burnyeat is surely right that a plant's inability to perceive warmth is bound up with the fact that its matter is not sensitive to warmth. But Sorabji is right on the larger issue. For it is still a physical difference between a plant's matter and ours that explains its insensitivity. Perceiving warmth does not involve getting warm in an immaterial way; it occurs when the right kind of matter—the kind that composes a sense-organ—gets warm in a straightforwardly material way.

But this talk of the right *kind* of matter, Burnyeat would surely say, smuggles in a notion that is antithetical to functionalism. For the right matter is matter that is *essentially* alive, *essentially* capable of awareness. And matter that is essentially alive cannot be only contingently related to the form—the soul—in virtue of which it is alive.

Burnyeat derives the conclusion that animal matter is essentially alive from two sources. One, which we have already examined, lies in the details of the theory of perception. The other is Aristotle's frequently enunciated *homonymy principle*, according to which a body that is not actually alive is a body in name only—is not really a body at all, just as an eye which cannot see is not really an eye. It is tempting to treat this principle as a mere linguistic ruling—that, for example, it is inappropriate or misleading to use the term 'body' for what is no longer alive—but Burnyeat understands it as a physical thesis that is incompatible with Aristotle's hylomorphic theory of mind. He refers us to John Ackrill's brilliant articulation of this tension in Aristotle's thought.

Aristotle's problem, as Ackrill presents it, emerges when he tries to specify the *matter* component of a living body, that is, of a hylomorphic compound whose form is its soul. On the one hand, the matter of any compound must *potentially* have that form; on the other hand, it must not have it *necessarily*. It might seem that there is no problem: the matter of an animal is its *body*. But this solution is blocked by the homonymy principle; if we try to pick out the matter without the form, the body without the soul that animates it, we must fail, for if what we pick out is not alive, then what we pick out is not a body. The homonymy principle prevents the fulfilment of the contingent specification requirement. As Ackrill (1972–3, 126) says:

The body we are told to pick out as the material 'constituent' of the animal depends for its very identity on its being alive, in-formed by *psuchē*.

Nor can we retreat to such candidates as flesh and bones, or other such bodily parts and organs, for the homonymy principle applies to them, as well. Here is the way Aristotle puts it (*GA* 734[b]24):

there is no such thing as face or flesh without soul in it; it is only homonymously that they will be called face or flesh if the life has gone out of them, just as if they had been made of stone or wood.

Yet if we descend to the level of the inanimate elements of which living things are ultimately composed—earth, air, fire, and water—we have gone too far. Although they satisfy the contingent specification requirement, since they are what they are independent of composing a living body, they fail in a different way. For the elements are too remote to be the matter of a living hylomorphic compound; they are not even *potentially* alive (cf. *Metaph.* Θ7). Ackrill (1972–3, 132) concludes:

Until there is a living thing...there is no 'body potentially alive'; and once there is, its body is necessarily actually alive.

This temporal language—'until', 'once'—distorts the homonymy principle. Ackrill makes it seem as if its point were to rule out a 'Frankensteinian' account of the generation of life: new animals do not come into being by having life installed in previously inanimate bodies. While I agree that Aristotle would find such an account incomprehensible, I do not take that to be the point of the homonymy principle. The point, rather, is to remind us of the crucial importance of function in the definition of a living creature or an organic system. The question is not whether there is a time before life begins at which what we have on our hands is a non-living body that is potentially alive; it is, rather, whether we can, in the case of a living animal, pick out something that now functions in certain characteristic ways although it will eventually cease to do so, which will continue to exist (at least for a while) after this happens, and whose functioning in those ways is definitive of the life and existence of that animal. What the homonymy principle tells us is that what we pick out for this role cannot be the body.

Yet there is something that looks, acts, and functions very much like the body, although it cannot, strictly speaking, be the body, since it will continue to exist after death, when the body no longer exists. Nor is this something the corpse, which only *begins* to exist at death. It is to this continuing something (which non-Aristotelians are inclined to call the 'body') that Aristotle needs to refer. Well, then, let him refer to it in some other way—say, as the BODY. The BODY has accidentally those properties the body has essentially, and in virtue of which the animal is alive. When the BODY functions, the body is alive; when the BODY ceases to function, the body, but not the BODY, ceases to exist.

The hylomorphist's appeal to the BODY does not just pay lip-service to the homonymy principle or treat it as a mere linguistic ruling. But it docs, as Bernard Williams[14] has pointed out, leave the hylomorphist with a pair of entities on his hands—the body and the BODY—which are the subjects of psychological and physiological investigation respectively. And so it seems that the hylomorphist has neatly sidestepped the mind–body problem only to be confronted with the

---

[14] Williams (1986). I am indebted on several points to Williams's discussion of Aristotle's hylomorphic theory; in particular, I have borrowed from him the distinction between the body and the BODY. I should point out, however, that Williams himself is less sanguine than I about the tenability of a hylomorphic theory.

perhaps equally intractable body–BODY problem. So the hylomorphist is by no means out of the woods.

Still, he is safe from Burnyeat's argument. For certainly the BODY is composed of ordinary matter, and there is no reason to think that the matter composing the body is any different. The difference between the body and the BODY, that is to say, need not be a difference in their matter. The homonymy principle need not be construed as the physical thesis that there is a kind of matter whose life and sensitivity are independent of and not explicable in terms of its physical properties. The principle tells us, for example, that a sightless EYE is not properly called an eye any more, and that this is because it has ceased to *be* an eye. This is not to say that the only difference between a functioning eye and a sightless EYE is that one can see and the other cannot. There is still room for a physical difference between the two to account for their functional difference.

Burnyeat has the idea that this is ruled out by the homonymy principle, which he sees as entailing an unbridgeable gap between the physiological and the psychological—between the non-living and the living. If this is how Aristotle intended the principle, we should expect to find him restricting its application to living things. Such a restriction would confirm Burnyeat's interpretation of homonymy and strengthen his conclusion that there is a kind of Aristotelian matter whose life and awareness are built in and are irreducible to anything physical.

On the contrary, Aristotle does not restrict the homonymy principle in this way. For one thing, he seems willing to apply it even to artefacts. Thus at 412^b14-15 he says that an axe no longer capable of performing its function 'would not be an axe, except homonymously'.[15] *Mete.* 4. 12 reiterates this point (the example is changed to a saw) and extends it even further into the inanimate realm. What we find is a systematic downward applicability of the homonymy principle, and, along with it, a systematically pervasive appeal to functional definitions. For the homonymy principle is now extended to natural bodies well below the threshold of life and consciousness, all the way down to the elements themselves (390^a7-19):

[E]ach of the elements has an end and is not water or fire in any and every condition of itself, just as flesh is not flesh.…What a thing is is always determined by its function: a

---

[15] The passage, unfortunately, is vexed. Aristotle suggests this analogy: as a living body is to its soul, so is an axe to its capacity to chop. If an axe were a living body, this capacity would be its soul, whose removal would render it no longer an axe, except homonymously. 'But in fact', Aristotle goes on, 'it is an axe' (*nun d' esti pelekus*). The most common reading of the quoted sentence takes it to withdraw the counterfactual assumption: an axe is not a living body, so it doesn't have a soul—it's just an axe. But on another reading, it refers back to the consequence derived from that assumption: since an axe is not a living body, it remains an axe even when it can't chop. On the second reading (but not the first), Aristotle refuses to apply the homonymy principle to the axe. The first reading is preferable, however, as becomes clear from Aristotle's justification: 'for it is not of this kind of body that the essence or formula is the soul, but of a certain kind of natural body having within itself a source of movement and rest' (*ou gar toioutou sōmatos to ti ēn einai kai ho logos hē psuchē, alla phusikou toioudi echontos archēn kinēseōs kai staseōs en heautōi*). Cf. Hicks in *Aristotle* (1907), 316–17. I wish to thank David Keyt for a helpful discussion of this passage and for convincing me that the favourable reading is in fact the right one.

thing really is itself when it can perform its function; an eye, for instance, when it can see. When a thing cannot do so it is that thing only in name, like a dead eye or one made of stone, just as a wooden saw is no more a saw than one in a picture. The same then is true of flesh, except that its function is less clear than that of the tongue. So, too, with fire; but its function is perhaps even harder to specify by physical inquiry than that of flesh. The parts of plants, and inanimate bodies like copper and silver, are in the same case. They all are what they are in virtue of a certain power of action or passion—just like flesh and sinew.

Aristotle thus insists on functional definitions even of copper and silver, of water and fire. His doctrine concerning inorganic compounds and their component elements, then, is not in principle different from that concerning animals and their parts. They are all given functional definitions; they all fit into a single hierarchical structure. All sublunary matter, even that of living things, is composed of the same four elements.

The fact that the proximate matter of a hylomorphic compound is itself ultimately composed of elemental matter does not, of course, entail that the properties of the compound, or even of its proximate matter, are reducible to properties of elemental matter. For matter at every level above the lowest (that of the elements or of prime matter) is itself a compound of matter and form, and its essential properties will be those of its form. What makes matter matter-of-a-certain-kind, such as animal-matter, is *form*.

Burnyeat's critique stresses differences between Aristotle's concept of matter and ours, and I have argued that the functionalist interpretation can survive it. The problem for the functionalist interpreter, as I see it, comes rather from the other side. It concerns the causal role of form in Aristotle's psychology.

The functionalist interpretation holds that *psuchē* is the form of a living body in the sense of an arrangement or functional organization of bodily components —a *formal* cause. Explanations that appeal to such a cause will explain the properties and behaviour of an organism in terms of functional properties of its material components. But Aristotle (perhaps unwisely) was working with a richer conception of form. For him, form or essence can also be an agent, an *efficient* cause. We know from *Ph.* 2. 7 (198ª25 ff.) that formal, efficient, and final causes often coincide, and *DA* 2. 4 leaves no doubt that *psuchē* is supposed to be a cause in all three senses. The passages in *De Anima* in which Aristotle uses the language of agency in speaking of *psuchē* are too numerous to mention.

It may well be replied that Aristotle's attribution of efficient causal efficacy to *psuchē* (and to form in general) should not be taken literally. His talk of *psuchē* as an agent may be just a manner of speaking. (A parallel case: you may know perfectly well that a computer program is a set of rules, an abstract characterization of behaviour in terms of inputs and outputs, and still say that the program 'runs' the computer, 'tells' it what to do, and 'causes' it to behave as it does. It is simply easier to talk that way.) As for his explicit identification of formal and efficient causes, Aristotle may mean no more than that the efficient cause must itself manifest the form it generates in another: a tiger begets a tiger, the source of life must itself be alive.

The success of the functionalist interpretation seems to me to depend on whether the apparent role of *psuchē* as efficient cause can be satisfactorily explained away. I am not convinced that it can be. Since the controversy over the interpretation shows no signs of abating, we may at least hope that its proponents will next turn their attention to this problem.

Appendix: Matter and Definitions in *Metaph.* Z 11

Although Aristotle makes it clear (1036^{b}1) that there can be no reference to bronze in the definition of *circle*, his treatment of the important biological case of flesh and bones and the form of *man* is obscure. He begins (1036^{b}5) with a question about the relation between matter and form in this case, but it is not clear where the question ends and the answer begins. Ross takes Aristotle to be answering his own question immediately: '...are [flesh and bones] then also parts of the form and the formula? No, they are matter; but because man is not found also in other matters we are unable to effect the severance.' Furth in *Aristotle* (1985), on the other hand, takes the mention of matter to be part of the question: '...are these then parts of the form and the formula? Or not, but *matter*...?' It would therefore be hasty to conclude on the basis of these lines that Aristotle disallows any reference to a specific kind of matter in the definition of a biological species.

Aristotle goes on to say (1036^{b}7) that although it 'seems to be possible' for a definition to contain reference to matter, it is 'unclear *when*' a definition is of this sort. That is why, he continues, some people raise doubts about the received definitions of *circle* and *triangle* in terms of *lines* and *continuous space* (1036^{b}8–9). (Their objection is presumably that lines and space are matter.) These people, Aristotle tells us, think that the relation of lines to circle is like that of flesh-and-bones to man and bronze to statue (1036^{b}10–12).

Flesh and bronze are lumped together here as examples of the kind of matter that is inadmissible in definitions. The question is: who lumps them together? Not the objectors; they would have relied on the clear case of bronze, which is definitely not part of the definition of *statue*, rather than appeal to the problematic case of flesh. The assimilation here, I think, is due to Aristotle.

A subsequent passage, however, raises problems for this interpretation. At 1036^{b}24 Aristotle says that 'the comparison which Socrates the younger used to make in the case of animal is not good; for it leads away from the truth and makes one suppose that man can exist without the parts, in the way that circle can without the bronze'. The comparison objected to is presumably the one mentioned at 1036^{b}11; Aristotle seems to be saying that man cannot exist without flesh-and-bones, and that Socrates' comparison of flesh to bronze (even if technically correct) is misleading in just this respect.

I am not convinced that this is what Aristotle is saying. His objection may simply be that whereas circles can be immaterial, *man* must be realized in matter (see Nussbaum (1984) 201). It will be instructive to examine his other reasons for objecting. *Animal*, he says, 'cannot be defined without reference to change' (1036^{b}29). In *Metaph.* E1 (1026^{a}3) he says that things that cannot be defined without reference to change 'always have matter', contrasting them with *concavity*, which can be defined, and presumably can exist, 'without perceptible matter' (1025^{b}33). He does not say merely that concavity can exist independently of any particular *kind* of matter. I take his point in Z11 to be the same: things which cannot be defined without reference to change must have *material* parts. Such a part, he says (1036^{b}30) must be 'in a certain state'. Does this mean 'made of a certain kind of matter'? Aristotle does not say so. Rather he continues: 'It is not a hand in *any* state that is a part of man, but the hand which can fulfil its work…' This remark, with its functionalist overtones, must seem slightly off-target to those who think that Aristotle requires a specific kind of matter. On their showing, shouldn't he have said: 'It is not a hand no matter what it is made of, but only if it is made of flesh-and-bones'?

5

LIVING BODIES

JENNIFER WHITING

THE *De Anima*'s commitment to the existence of essentially ensouled bodies has long been regarded as something of a problem for Aristotle. Because Aristotle says that such a body is the matter of an animal, the standard objection—at least since the publication of Ackrill's influential article[1]—is that this commitment conflicts with Aristotle's primary conception of matter as potentiality (to embody different forms) and as the substratum of generation and destruction (*GC* 320ª1– 4). For matter so conceived is supposed to persist through substantial change and to be what (in substantial change) loses and acquires form—in the case of living things, what loses and acquires soul. But if a body is essentially ensouled, then *it* cannot lose and acquire soul. So Aristotle seems to require of one thing both that it can, and that it cannot, lose and acquire soul.

Aristotle's commitment to the existence of essentially ensouled matter has more recently been taken by Burnyeat to show that Aristotle's philosophy of mind is no longer credible and must be 'junked' because he does not share our post-Cartesian conception of matter which leaves the emergence of life and mind in need of explanation.[2] According to Burnyeat, Aristotle takes as primitive the fact that certain kinds of matter, such as flesh and blood, are *essentially* alive and *essentially* capable of awareness and so takes the emergence of life and awareness as something for which no explanation can or need be given. Burnyeat takes this to debunk the increasingly popular portrait of Aristotle as the father of contemporary functionalism[3] because he takes functionalism to assume that the relation between matter and form is *contingent* in a way in which Aristotle's hylomorphism does not. Furthermore, Burnyeat thinks it would be a mistake for Aristotle (or his apologists) to try to solve Ackrill's problem by showing that there is a sense in which the matter of an animal *is* only contingently related to its form or soul. For then Aristotle would be 'abandoning his project of beating the

---

© Jennifer Whiting, 1992.

[1] Ackrill (1972–3).

[2] See Burnyeat, this volume. It is an oddity of Burnyeat's view that he seems to take Aristotle's Platonist and Democritean contemporaries as committed to the problematic post-Cartesian conception of matter (though this may not be so odd if, as Steve Strange suggests (pers. comm.), Descartes derives his account of the physical world from the *Timaeus*, which is itself indebted to Democritus on this point). In any case, Burnyeat's idea must be that Aristotle's reaction is distinct from the contemporary functionalist reaction because it is free from assumptions about matter that the contemporary functionalist cannot escape.

[3] See chs. 3 and 4; See also Putnam (1975), Nussbaum (1978), Essay 1, Modrak (1987a), chs. 1–2, Shields (forthcoming), and Irwin (1991).

Platonists and the Democriteans at one blow by stopping the question "What makes this a living thing?" before it can arise'.[4]

I doubt, however, that we need to take the concern to avoid having to explain the emergence of life and awareness as the dominant motivation for Aristotle's commitment to the existence of essentially ensouled matter. For it is also possible to interpret this commitment as part of Aristotle's solution to the problem of distinguishing generation and destruction *simpliciter* from alteration and other sorts of accidental change (such as growth and locomotion).[5] The main project of this paper is thus to argue that we can solve Ackrill's problem by allowing that there *is* a sense in which the matter of an animal is only contingently related to its form and that we can do so without undermining Aristotle's arguments for introducing essentially ensouled bodies in the first place. The plan is roughly as follows.

Section I solves Ackrill's problem by arguing that there are two distinct things Aristotle calls the 'matter' (*hulē*) of an animal: one (the organic body) is essentially ensouled, while the other (the quantity of elements constituting the organic body) is only accidentally ensouled. Since the relation between form (or soul) and the elements constituting the organic body is contingent in a way in which that between form (or soul) and the organic body itself is not, this allows for the sort of contingency required by functionalism without requiring us to reject Aristotle's commitment to the existence of essentially ensouled bodies.[6]

Section II argues that we can interpret Aristotle's commitment to the existence of essentially ensouled matter as part of his solution to the problem of distinguishing generation and destruction *simpliciter* from alteration and other sorts of accidental change, and so do not need to suppose that it is intended primarily to forestall Platonic and Democritean worries about the emergence of life and awareness.[7]

Finally, since Aristotle's commitment to the existence of essentially ensouled bodies has also been thought problematic because he says of such bodies that they are 'potentially alive'—thus suggesting that they are not necessarily alive—

---

[4] Burnyeat, p. 26.

[5] This view of defended in more detail in Whiting (1990) and (forthcoming).

[6] Here it is worth noting that I aim only to show that functionalist interpretations of Aristotle are not vulnerable to this objection. I do not pretend to provide positive arguments for such interpretations, references to which are provided in n. 3. Furthermore, I take the solution to Ackrill's problem in Section I to be self-contained and independent of my claims (in Section II) about Aristotle's reasons for introducing essentially ensouled bodies.

[7] I claim only that my story renders Burnyeat's hypothesis *unnecessary*. Someone could argue that my story about Aristotle's reasons for introducing organic bodies is compatible with Burnyeat's: it is possible that Aristotle is concerned both to defend the distinction between substantial and non-substantial change and to avoid having to explain the emergence of life and awareness, *and* that he takes essentially ensouled bodies to play an important role in the explanation of each. This is especially plausible if Aristotle takes the primary subjects of generation and destruction *simpliciter* to be living organisms, but the details of such an account would presumably differ from those of mine in so far as mine is intended to avoid the sort of mysteriousness Burnyeat ascribes to essentially ensouled matter.

Section III will explain briefly the sense in which Aristotle takes essentially ensouled bodies to be potentially alive.

I

It is relatively uncontroversial that Aristotle is committed to the existence of organic bodies which are essentially ensouled. For Aristotle says not only that the soul is the essence (*to ti ēn einai*) of a certain sort of body (*DA* 412ᵇ11–12), but also that this body is *organikon* (412ᵃ29–ᵇ1). This means that it has organs which are defined by their functions, and therefore that it cannot exist in the absence of soul, without which these organs could not perform their functions. For Aristotle says of all things defined by their functions that:

…each is in reality the thing capable of performing its function, such as an eye when it sees, while the one not capable <of performing its function> is *homonymously* <that thing>, such as one dead or one made of stone. (*Mete.* 390ᵃ10–12.)[8]

…there is no face not having soul, nor flesh, but when these have perished the one will be called <a> face and the other flesh *homonymously*, just as if they had been made of stone or wood. (*GA* 734ᵇ24–7.)[9]

And although Aristotle illustrates the homonymy principle with an eye (both here and at *DA* 412ᵇ21–3) and with a finger (at *Metaph.* 1035ᵇ24), his claim (at *DA* 412ᵇ22–3) that we should treat the whole body as we have treated its parts licenses applying this principle to the body as a whole. (So does his reference to natural bodies as the organs of the soul at *DA* 415ᵇ18–19.) So just as a dead or detached eye is only homonymously an eye, a 'body' having lost its soul is only homonymously a body.

But because of Aristotle's commitment to the homonymy principle and its application to the body (or matter) of a living organism as a whole, it is more controversial to claim that Aristotle takes each living organism to have some matter which is only accidentally ensouled. Part of the problem is that Aristotle seems to treat nearly all of the parts of animals—including homoiomerous parts such as flesh and blood—as defined by their functions and so as essentially

---

[8] For *some* defence of the authenticity of *Mete.* 4 see Furley (1983). Since the view expressed in this passage is also expressed elsewhere (as evidenced in the next note), my appeal to the *Meteorologica* here is relatively unproblematic.

[9] These passages (along with *PA* 640ᵇ34–641ᵃ34, *GA* 734ᵇ24–735ᵃ9, and *Pol.* 1253ᵃ19–25) illustrate what Ackrill calls the 'homonymy principle'. The idea (explained at *Cat.* 1ᵃ1–4) is that an '*F*' which is not (or no longer) capable of performing the function of an *F* is an *F* only in name: it does not satisfy the account of the being (or essence) of an *F*. For two alternative accounts of homonymy—an extreme account according to which the definitions of homonyms are unrelated, and a moderate account according to which the definitions may or may not be related—see Irwin (1981). As Shields (unpublished) notes, the moderate account allows Aristotle to treat corpses (along with detached organs and limbs) as extreme homonyms, but (*pace* Shields) this does not seem to me to be required by Aristotle's commitment to functional definitions. Nor does it seem *required* by my view. For clarification, see n. 20.

ensouled.[10] So if the anhomoiomerous parts (like eyes, limbs, and hearts) are
ultimately composed of functionally defined homoiomerous parts, then it seems
that organic bodies cannot be constituted by any matter which is only accidentally ensouled.

For this reason some commentators have denied that any of an animal's matter
can survive the loss of soul. On their view, Socrates' corpse is not composed of
any of the same matter as was its living ancestor: when Socrates dies, his matter
(namely the flesh and blood which constitute his bodily parts) is destroyed and
is immediately replaced by the matter of his corpse. This is presumably some
compound of the four elements, which these commentators believe can never
constitute a living organism or any of its parts.[11]

This interpretation rests on two common beliefs about Aristotle's account of
the matter of an animal. The first is that Aristotle takes the homoiomerous parts
(like flesh and blood) to be the *ultimate* matter of living organisms and so denies
that the four elements are part of the matter of a living thing. The second is that
Aristotle believes that the homoiomerous parts, being functionally defined, cannot survive the loss of soul. From these two beliefs it follows that the living body,
being composed of flesh and blood, cannot share any of its matter with its corpse,
which, given the homonymy principle, cannot be composed of flesh and blood.

Here, however, it is important to note what Aristotle says at *DA* 412ᵇ18–27:

If the eye were an animal, sight would be its soul. For this is the being (*ousia*) of an eye
according to its account (*logos*). But the eye is the matter of sight, which [sight] taking
leave it is no longer an eye, except homonymously, like the one made of stone or painted.
And it is necessary to take what is said of the part <to apply> to the whole living body, for
as part is to part so perception as a whole is to the whole perceptive body as such. But it is
not that <body>[12] having lost its soul (*to apobeblēkos tēn psuchēn*) which is potentially such
as to live, but the one having <soul>; and the seed and the fruit are potentially such a body
[i.e. the seed and the fruit are potentially bodies potentially such as to live].

This passage is important both because it suggests that Aristotle believes that
there is some matter which once was but is no longer (*ouket'*) an eye when sight
is removed and because Aristotle's use of the perfect participle in his reference to

---

[10] Homoiomerous parts are uniform parts (like flesh and blood) any proper part of which is the
same both in form and in name with the whole. This is not true of anhomoiomerous parts: the proper
parts of hands and hearts are not themselves hands and hearts. (See *HA* 486ª5–9.) Note, however, that
Aristotle recognizes (at *PA* 647ᵇ17–21) that in the case of some homoiomerous parts there is *a* sense
in which the proper parts are not the same both in form and name with the whole: while any proper
part of blood is itself blood, it is not true that any proper part of *a* vein (or *a* bone) composed entirely
of vein (or bone) is itself *a* vein (or *a* bone). This may escape notice more easily in Greek, where the
absence of an indefinite article complicates marking the distinction between mass- and count-nouns.

[11] Burnyeat expressed this view (while defending the views expressed in 'Is Aristotle's Philosophy
of Mind Still Credible?') in a lecture at Cornell University in 1982. See also Charlton (1970) 75–7;
and Jones (1974), many of whose claims about matter, criticized in Code (1976), are unobjectionable
if taken as claims about the organic body and its functionally defined parts rather than as claims about
the matter constituting the organic body and its parts.

[12] 'Body' is suggested (but not required) by the neuter, and supported by *to dunamei toiondi sōma* at
the end of the passage.

the thing having lost its soul shows that he takes *something* to survive the loss of soul. This suggests that there is something wrong with the interpretation according to which Aristotle holds the remarkable view that Socrates and his corpse have nothing in common except for their uncanny similarity. We can see what is wrong with this interpretation if we see how each of the two common beliefs on which it is based is open to challenge.

Against the second belief, *Mete*. 4. 12 seems to allow that flesh and blood survive (at least for a while) in a corpse. For although Aristotle says that flesh (and the other homoiomerous parts) have functions, he acknowledges that it is not always easy to tell what their functions are or when they are still capable of performing them. His example is instructive.

The function of it [flesh] is less clear than that of the tongue. Similarly also with fire, but <its function> is probably even less clear naturally than the function of flesh. And similarly also with plants and inanimate things such as bronze and silver. For all these are <what they are> by some potentiality to act or to be affected, just like flesh and sinew. But the accounts (*logoi*)[13] of these are not precise. So it is not easy to discern when they exist (*huparchei*) and when they do not,[14] unless a thing is very far gone and the shapes alone remain, as when the bodies of very old corpses suddenly turn to ashes in their coffins. (*Mete*. 390ᵃ14–24.)

This passage suggests that Aristotle takes the homoiomerous parts of animals (like flesh and blood) to differ from anhomoiomerous parts (like hands and eyes) in so far as the homoiomerous parts do not perish simultaneously with the animal itself. He seems to think that there is some indeterminacy about just when such parts perish: it is clear that they are no longer there in the case of very old corpses, but not so clear in the case of younger ones.[15] And this suggests that Aristotle thinks that it is possible that flesh survives (at least for a while) in a fresh corpse and is what decomposes. Furthermore, taking this as a serious expression of Aristotle's own view allows us to explain his otherwise curious remark (at *Metaph*. 1035ᵃ31–4) that Callias perishes into flesh and bones.[16]

But can we reconcile this with Aristotle's view that flesh and the other homoiomerous parts are functionally defined and so cannot survive the loss of soul? I think we can, *if* we recognize that Aristotle admits two accounts of flesh—one functional and the other compositional.[17]

---

[13] The *logoi* here may be the proportions of elements involved.

[14] This can also be translated as 'when they belong <to a subject> and when they do not'.

[15] Someone might object that Aristotle's point here is simply the epistemological point that it is not easy to tell when flesh and such parts still exist and when they do not, and so that we cannot take this passage as showing that he allows that flesh and such parts in fact survive the death of an animal. But the epistemological point is sufficient to show that Aristotle does not take it to follow simply from the fact that flesh and such parts are functionally defined that they perish simultaneously with animal itself. For a similar account, see Cohen (1984).

[16] See also *Metaph*. 1035ᵃ17–22. These passages provide some support for appealing to *Mete*. 390ᵃ14–24 (given the doubt cited in n. 8 about its authenticity).

[17] For my original account of the distinction between functional and compositional matter, there taken as equivalent to the distinction between proximate and non-proximate matter, see Whiting (1984), especially ch. 4, sect. III and ch. 5, sect. I. (I have since abandoned the terms 'proximate' and

Flesh plays an important functional role as the medium of touch and in this sense it perishes with the animal itself. This is reasonable since the ability of flesh to perform its function depends on its being related in certain ways to the other functionally defined parts of the organism as a whole—especially to the heart which Aristotle takes to be central not only to touch but also to the other senses. When flesh no longer stands in the right relation to a functioning heart it can no longer perform its function. And since death occurs when the heart ceases to function, flesh can no longer perform its function once death occurs.[18] The same applies to blood, which (by heating and cooling) contributes both to physiological processes (such as nourishment) and to psychophysical processes (such as anger). The important point here is that the ability of a part (whether homoiomerous or not) to perform its function depends on its standing in the right relations to the other functionally defined parts of the organism as a whole.

But immediately after pointing out that the homoiomerous parts have functions, Aristotle acknowledges that it is also possible to speak of the homoiomeries not as parts of a functional whole but rather in terms of differentiae (such as tension, ductility, brittleness, hardness, and softness) which are produced by hot and cold and their combined motions (*Mete.* 390^{b}2–10). And it is not clear that flesh and blood cease to exist simultaneously with the whole living organism when defined in this way. When Socrates dies, his corpse may still be constituted by flesh and blood in the sense that the contraries are still present in roughly those proportions causally necessary (but not sufficient) for the existence of functional flesh and blood. As the flesh decomposes and the proportions of these contraries change owing to the loss of heat and moisture, this gradually ceases to be true (*Mete.* 379^{a}17–26).[19]

There is further evidence of Aristotle's commitment to the distinction between functional and compositional flesh in *Generation and Corruption* where he says that 'flesh, bone, and each of the parts like these are twofold (*ditton*)...*for both the matter and the form are called flesh or bone*' (321^{b}19–22). Here Aristotle is talking about two things (the form and the matter) each of which is called 'flesh', and not about one thing capable of being considered or described in two different ways. This is clear not only from the fact that Aristotle goes on to ascribe different properties (and implicitly different criteria of identity) to the form and the matter—the form is what persists as matter flows in and out of the whole—

'non-proximate' because different commentators use them in so many different ways). I was pleased to find that my conclusions about matter, arrived at primarily through an investigation of form, were complemented by those reached by M. L. Gill (1989) in her investigation of matter, esp. ch. 4.

[18] See *Juv.* 469^{a}7–22, 469^{b}1–20.

[19] Just as we distinguish bronze as a certain kind of stuff from particular portions or pieces of bronze, we can also distinguish compositional flesh as a certain kind of stuff (e.g. that stuff composed of these elements standing in such-and-such proportions to one another) from particular portions or pieces of compositional flesh. Any particular bit of functional flesh must always be constituted by compositional flesh, but it may be constituted by different portions of compositional flesh at different times in so far as its compositional flesh can (as a result of material displacement) be constituted by different portions of the elements (in roughly the same proportions) at different times. For a further question about compositional flesh, see the next note.

but also from his claim that this phenomenon is clearer in the case of the anhomoiomerous parts because it is clearer there (than in the case of the homoiomerous parts) that the matter is different from the form (*GC* 321^{b}22–32).

Aristotle's view seems to be that functional flesh (the form) and compositional flesh (the matter) are homonyms; they share the same name, but the accounts of their being (or essence) are different.[20] Compositional flesh is only homonymous with functional flesh and so can survive the loss of soul. But that doesn't mean that compositional flesh can't *constitute* functional flesh. This is important because a proper account of compositional flesh will also help to show what is wrong with the first belief used to support the view that a living body cannot have any matter in common with its corpse—that is, the belief that Aristotle denies that the elements are part of the matter of a living organism.

This belief rests primarily on two passages. The first occurs in *Metaph*. H4, where Aristotle says that in stating the material cause of man, we must not name fire or earth but must state the peculiar matter (*tēn idion < hulēn >* 1044^{b}1–2). The second occurs in *Metaph*. Θ7, where Aristotle asks whether earth is potentially a man and then suggests that it is not earth, but rather the seed (or perhaps even the fertilized egg or embryo) which is potentially a man (1049^{a}1–3).

But neither of these passages shows that the elements are not the matter of a man, and the first actually suggests that the elements *are* in some sense the matter of a man. For it rules out earth on the ground that we ought to state the nearest or most proximate (*engutata*) causes. Aristotle's use of the superlative here suggests that he thinks that earth *is* in some sense the matter of a man and that his point is simply that it is not the most proximate matter of a man.

The second passage also fails to show that the elements are not the matter of a man. But this has gone unnoticed largely, I suspect, because commentators have not paid adequate attention to Aristotle's use of temporal adverbs.

---

[20] On homonymy, see n. 9. If we take 'compositional flesh' to refer to any portion of the elements standing in such-and-such proportions to one another, we can still distinguish two ways of specifying compositional flesh. We can specify it purely quantitatively—as in '4 parts of earth to 3 parts of water, etc.'—in which case it seems reasonable to say that the definition of compositional flesh, in so far as it has a definition, is not related to that of functional flesh. Or we can specify it causally—as in 'earth and water, etc., in whatever proportions are (hypothetically) necessary for functional flesh'—in which case it seems reasonable to say that the definition of compositional flesh, in so far as it has a definition, is related to that of functional flesh. Even in this case the relationship between compositional flesh and functional flesh will be contingent in so far as compositional flesh need not constitute functional flesh, since it must (if it is to constitute functional flesh) also stand in the right relation to the functionally defined organic body as a whole and it will be contingent whether or not any particular portion of compositional flesh does so. Our decision about which way to specify compositional flesh and bone, etc., will affect what we say about the issue of compositional plasticity, though the issue here is complicated by Aristotle's view that everything must (in some sense) ultimately be composed of the four elements. If we adopt the causal account, then functional flesh cannot be realized in anything except compositional flesh, though this still leaves open the possibility of variation in the proportions of elements capable of constituting functional flesh. If we adopt the quantitative account, then it seems at least logically (even if not physically) possible that functional flesh should be realized in something other than compositional flesh as we know it. But since these issues are not central to my argument I will leave them aside for now, noting only the relevance of *PA* 649^{b}22–8 (on the sense in which blood is hot) to their resolution.

Aristotle begins this chapter by asking whether earth is 'potentially a man or not, but rather only when it has already become sperm and not even then perhaps' (1049^a1-3). And Aristotle picks up this reservation again (at 1049^a14-16) where he says that 'the sperm is *not yet* (*oupō*) <potentially a man> for it needs to be in another and to change' and then concludes that the sperm is potentially a man 'whenever it is already on account of its own principle such'—that is, whenever it is able to develop into a man on its own.

I take this passage to show only that Aristotle thinks that sperm and earth, taken by themselves and before they are in developing embryos or ensouled bodies, are *not yet* potentially men.[21] But this leaves open the possibility that earth and sperm *are* potentially men when they are *already* in developing embryos or ensouled bodies. Note, however, that the sperm in an embryo and the earth in an ensouled body may be potentially men in different ways. The sperm is potentially a man in the sense that it *can become* a man, and Aristotle believes that this is true even though the sperm itself does not survive as a constituent of the final human product.[22] But there is evidence that Aristotle thinks that earth and the other elements are potentially men in a different way, one which allows them both to survive as constituents of the final human product and to have (in some sense) the characteristics belonging primarily to that product.

First, Aristotle argues in *GC* 1. 10 that the elements in a mixture can neither survive without being altered (for that is mere synthesis and not mixture) nor be destroyed. The elements are actually the new compound but potentially what they were before being mixed; their potentiality (*dunamis*) is preserved (327^b22-31). This point is confirmed by the following passage from *PA* 2. 3:

…earth and ashes and such things having been mixed with liquid are actually and accidentally liquid (*energeiai men hugra kai kata sumbebēkos*) but in themselves and potentially dry (*kath' hauta de kai dunamei xēra*). But when these have been separated, the watery, anaplestic <components> are both actually and potentially liquid (*kai energeiai kai dunamei hugra*) while the earthy <components> are dry… (649^b14-19.)

This passage is important for several reasons. First, it shows that earth dissolved in water somehow survives in that mixture. Second, it shows that this earth accidentally has characteristics (like that of being liquid) which belong to the mixture as a whole. And third, it says that the water (taken by itself) is both (at one and the same time) potentially and actually liquid. The importance of the third point will become clear in Section III. The important points for now are the first two. Since Aristotle believes that the homoiomerous parts of an organism are mixtures of the elements, this passage suggests first, that the elements somehow survive in the homoiomerous parts, and secondly, that these elements then

---

[21] The distinction between proximate and remote potentialities developed in Irwin (1988), ch. 11, § 124, shows how *x* can be the matter of *y* without being potentially *y* insofar as *x* can be the *non-proximate* matter of *y* without being *proximately* potentially *y*.

[22] See *GA* 1. 21.

have accidentally characteristics which belong primarily and essentially to the homoiomerous parts themselves.

The first suggestion is confirmed not only by the fact that Aristotle regularly appeals to the elements in order to explain the characteristics of animal parts, but also by his view that animals age and perish because they are composed of materials (namely, the elements) which differ with respect to their natural places and because the elements in living organisms are not in their natural places (*Cael.* 288^{b}15–19). The idea is that living bodies age and corpses decay because the elements which constitute them tend to move toward their natural places—fire up and earth down—with the result that the elements gradually become separated from one another and cease to be present in the proportions necessary for the existence of the homoiomerous parts.[23] Furthermore, the nature of nails, hoofs, horns, and beaks is explained by their earthy composition and man is said to have the smallest nails in proportion to his size because he has the least earthy residue (*PA* 655^{b}12–13; *GA* 745^{a}15–20). The coagulation of blood (which 651^{a}14 says is the matter of the whole body) is due to the presence of earthy fibres, and watery blood is associated with greater intellect (*PA* 2. 4). There are countless such claims scattered throughout the biological works, all of which suggest that the elements somehow persist in the organic body.

In these passages scattered throughout the corpus, Aristotle consistently uses adjectival or paronymous expressions derived from the names of the elements to characterize the parts of animals composed of these elements: parts composed of or dominated by earth (*hē gē*) are said to be 'earthy' (*geōdēs*) and parts composed of or dominated by water (*to hudōr*) are said to be 'watery' (*hudatōdēs*). Here Aristotle treats the animal parts (like nails and blood) as the subjects of which being earthy or being watery are predicated. This exemplifies his general view that whenever *y* comes to be from *x* (where *x* is matter which persists and comes to constitute *y*) we should say not that *y* is *x* but rather that *y* is *x*-en. For example, when a statue or a shield comes to be from bronze (where the bronze is matter which persists and comes to constitute the statue or the shield) we should say not that the statue or the shield is bronze, but rather that the statue or the shield is brazen. Similarly, when wood or flesh comes to be from earth (where the earth is matter which persists and comes to constitute the wood or flesh) we should say not that the wood or flesh is earth, but rather that the wood or flesh is earthen. The use of the paronymous expression '*x*-en' indicates *both* that the product is not strictly identical with its matter (but only composed of it) *and* that the matter of which it is composed must undergo change in the course of generation; its predicate position indicates that as a result of such change, the matter is now the matter *of* a different subject.[24]

[23] See *DA* 415^{b}28–416^{a}8.

[24] See *Metaph.* 1033^{a}5–23 (where Aristotle takes the expression '*x*-en' to indicate that the matter undergoes change in generation), 1049^{a}19–^{b}1, and *Ph.* 245^{b}7–17. The *Physics* passage shows that although generation and destruction *simpliciter* cannot (according to Aristotle) *be* alterations of matter,

Aristotle's reasons for treating constitutive matter as a predicate are complicated and will be explained more fully in Section II. At this point let me say simply that one of Aristotle's primary reasons is to avoid having to treat the apparent subjects of generation and destruction *simpliciter* merely as mere accidents of their constitutive matter and so to avoid having to treat generations and destructions *simpliciter* merely as alterations of the persisting matter. For this threatens to eliminate the distinction between generation and destruction *simpliciter* on the one hand, and alteration and other sorts of accidental change on the other. We will return to these issues shortly.

But first let me note that treating constitutive matter on a par with properties and other accidents such as size and location allows us to explain how Aristotle might come to say that the matter constituting a subject can have accidentally characteristics which belong primarily and essentially to the subject it constitutes —as in the foregoing example (from *PA* 2. 3) of the earth in a liquid mixture. For although Aristotle denies (at *Metaph.* $1007^{b}2-5$) that one accidental entity can serve as the proper subject of another, he allows that one accidental entity (e.g. the musical) can be treated as a subject to another (e.g. the white) insofar as both (the musical and the white) belong to one and the same subject (a man). And Aristotle may allow in a similar way that the matter which is predicated of some subject is itself a subject (albeit only coincidentally) of those properties belonging to the subject of which it is predicated, in so far as both (the matter and those properties) belong to one and the same subject. He may allow, for example, that the earth which is predicated of flesh is itself a subject (albeit only coincidentally) of whatever belongs to the flesh itself and so, for example, that the earth is accidentally alive (or ensouled) in so far as one and the same thing (the flesh or the organic body) is the proper subject to which both the earth and being alive (or being ensouled) belong.

This concludes my argument that Aristotle allows that the elements survive in the homoiomerous parts and that these elements have accidentally characteristics which belong primarily and essentially to the organic body and its functionally defined parts—in particular, the characteristic of being alive or ensouled. We are now in a position to see how Aristotle can consistently claim *both* that the matter of an animal is essentially ensouled *and* that the matter of an animal is only accidentally or contingently ensouled. For Aristotle is talking about different things, each with different criteria of identity and persistence—one, the organic body and its functionally defined parts (including the homoiomerous ones); the other, the elements constituting homoiomerous parts. And the organic body and its functionally defined parts (both homoiomerous and anhomoiomerous) are essentially ensouled but constituted by portions of the elements which (when they con-

they can *involve* alterations of matter: although the coming to be of a statue is not an alteration of some bronze in so far as the form of the statue and its privation are not strictly properties of the bronze, the coming to be of a statue may involve alterations (e.g. the heating and cooling) of that bronze as a result of which the bronze ceases to constitute (or belong to) one subject and comes to constitute (or belong to) another.

stitute an organic body) are (in virtue of constituting that body) accidentally ensouled. So there is (as the functionalist interpretation requires) a sense in which the matter of an animal *is* only contingently related to its form or soul, but not (*pace* Burnyeat) one which Aristotle takes to be incompatible with the sense in which the matter of an animal is essentially ensouled.

II

Here, however, we need to ask why Aristotle introduces essentially ensouled matter in the first place. In this section I will argue that Aristotle introduces essentially ensouled matter as part of his solution to the problem of distinguishing generation and destruction *simpliciter* from alteration and other sorts of accidental change, and so that we need not adopt Burnyeat's hypothesis that Aristotle takes such matter as primitive in order to avoid having to explain the emergence of life and awareness.

Note first that it is an important part of Aristotle's view that the elements can constitute different things at different times, some of which (e.g. organic bodies) are essentially ensouled and some of which (e.g. clay pots) are not. For this explains the sense in which the elements are matter and potentiality as well as the way in which matter can serve as the substratum of generation and destruction *simpliciter*, something Aristotle takes to be necessary if he is to avoid generation *ex nihilo* and destruction *in nihilum*. It also explains the continuity of certain properties throughout substantial change; it explains why, for example, Socrates' corpse has so much in common with his living body. But this raises a problem for Aristotle. For its suggests that all changes are simply alterations of the underlying elements and so threatens to do away with generation and destruction *simpliciter*.[25] For it suggests that being a man and being a corpse are simply accidents of the underlying matter and so that Socrates' death is simply an alteration of this matter which is first a man and then a corpse.

But Aristotle rejects this suggestion. For he believes (i) that generation and destruction *simpliciter* occur whenever the termini of a change are not properties or accidents of what persists throughout the change (*GC* 320ª1–2), and (ii) that the persisting matter is not the subject of which the things generated and destroyed (e.g. individual organisms) are properties; the matter is rather an accident of the things it comes and ceases to constitute (*GC* 322ª28–33).[26] Take, for example, the case in which some earth constitutes Socrates' flesh at t_1 and then

---

[25] See *GC* 314ª8–11, *Metaph.* 983ᵇ6–18.

[26] The claim that matter is not the subject of which the things generated and destroyed are properties is controversial and I defend it in more detail in Whiting (forthcoming). The general line of argument—sketched in Whiting (1990)—receives some support from the way in which Aristotle explains accidental differences as due to matter. On my view, these differences are differences in compositional and not functional matter. And functional matter, being the same for all members of a kind, is thus knowable and definable in a way in which compositional matter is not.

(when Socrates' flesh decomposes) a pot at t_2. In this case, Aristotle believes that we would say not that the earth is first flesh and then a pot, but rather that the flesh (which is earthen) is destroyed and a pot (which is earthen) comes to be. The case for treating matter as an accident is clearest with growth and decline, which Aristotle treats as processes in which a persisting subject changes by having matter added to or taken away from it (*GC* $321^b23-322^a4$; 322^a28-34).

We can see why it is important for Aristotle to take the persisting matter as an accident of the things that come to be and pass away if we recall that he takes generation and destruction *simpliciter* to consist in a form's coming to be embodied in some pre-existing matter. For since that matter can exist whether or not it embodies that form, it looks as though embodying that form is simply an accident of it, in which case the compound of form and matter seems to be an accidental unity on a par with a musical man. But if the compound is an accidental unity on a par with a musical man, then the dissolution of the compound (the matter's ceasing to embody that form) would no more constitute destruction *simpliciter* than would a man's ceasing to be musical.[27]

In order to solve this problem Aristotle needs to show how a form's coming to be embodied in some matter can yield a product which is not a property of what persists and which is itself an *intrinsic unity*—that is, a unity neither component of which is separable from the other *in a way such that it could serve as subject in some other unity*, as for example a man (in the unity pale-man) is separable from his paleness and so can stand as subject in the unity dark-man. This product, *qua* product of a form's coming to be embodied in some matter, is presumably a compound of form and matter neither of which is separable from the other: the form is essentially the form of this matter, and the matter essentially the matter of this form. Thus, when Socrates comes (or ceases) to be, there comes (or ceases) to be a compound which is an intrinsic unity of form and matter—the form (or soul) of *his* (as opposed to any other man's) body and the body of which *this* soul (and no other) is the form and the essence.

We are now in a position to see how Aristotle might have introduced functionally defined organic bodies (along with individual forms) as part of his solution to the problem of distinguishing generation and destruction *simpliciter* from alteration and other sorts of accidental change. The compound which comes (and ceases) to be when Socrates comes (and ceases) to be is a compound of his individual form or soul and his organic body. And although the organic body must be constituted by some compositional matter at any time at which it exists, it can, in so far as it is functionally defined, be constituted by different portions of compositional matter at different times. But in so far as it is functionally defined,

---

[27] But taking the persisting matter as an accident of the subjects of generation, destruction, and alteration will not by itself solve this problem. For a similar problem arises if Aristotle takes the form to be a species-form which pre-exists and (in generation and destruction) comes and ceases to be embodied in different portions of matter. For since the species-form can exist whether or not it is embodied in any particular portion of matter (as long as it is embodied in some portion of matter or other) it looks as though the compound of form and matter is still an accidental unity.

the organic body (unlike its constituent matter) cannot exist apart from the soul which is the set of capacities in virtue of which the organic body is capable of performing its defining functions; this body is *essentially* ensouled and so comes and ceases to exist simultaneously with the soul, which is its form and essence.[28]

Assuming that Aristotle takes the product of a form's coming to be embodied in some matter to be some sort of compound, we can see why Aristotle should take it to be a compound of form and an *organic* body if we examine the alternative. The distinction between the organic body and the matter constituting it at any given time yields a distinction between two kinds of compound. One, the 'thin compound', is a compound of form and an organic body. The other, the 'thick compound', is a compound of form and the portion of compositional matter constituting it at a given time.[29] This distinction is important for the following reason: if we take the subjects of generation, destruction, and alteration to be thick compounds, there will be generation and destruction every time what we would ordinarily call a man loses or acquires matter. Entire species of what we would ordinarily take to be accidental change (like growth and decline) will be assimilated to generation and destruction *simpliciter* if they involve any acquisition or loss of matter.

But Aristotle can save the appearances if he takes the subjects of generation, destruction, and alteration to be thin compounds. For the thin compound (of soul and an organic body) can be constituted by different portions of matter at different times and so can grow and decline without ceasing to exist. The thin compound will cease to exist if and only if its organic body ceases to embody the set of functionally defined capacities constituting its soul—that is, if and only if its soul, and hence its organic body, ceases to exist.

This concludes my argument that Aristotle's introduction of essentially ensouled bodies is not (as Ackrill claims) a problem, but rather part of Aristotle's solution to the problem of distinguishing generation and destruction *simpliciter* from alteration and other sorts of accidental change. If this is correct then there is no need to appeal to Burnyeat's hypothesis that Aristotle introduces such bodies in order to avoid having to explain the emergence of life and awareness. The non-contingency of the relation between a soul and its organic body (along with that body's functionally defined parts, both homoiomerous and anhomoiomerous) need not involve any sort of primitively or mysteriously alive or sentient matter. It is simply a matter of the functional relations among the (functionally defined) parts and the system as a whole.[30] Because the identity of each of these parts is

[28] I defend the view that individual form is the principle of individuation both of the compound and of its functionally defined organic body (or proximate matter, explained in n. 17) in Whiting (1986). See also M. L. Gill (1989), 4. 4. 1.

[29] See Irwin (1989), ch. 11, § 132 on the distinction between *formal* and *material* compounds. His material compounds differ from my thick compounds in so far as thick compounds cannot be constituted by different portions of matter at different times: they are compounds of forms and the particular portions of matter constituting them at particular times.

[30] On the relation to the whole, see *Pol.* 1253ª20 ff. The functioning of the whole need not depend on the functioning of each and every part, but the functioning of each of the parts will depend on that

dependent on its relation to the system as a whole in a way in which the identity of their constituent matter (which can survive in the absence of these functional relations) is not, these parts are essentially related to the system as a whole while their constituent matter is only contingently related to that system. Once again, the contingent relation between matter and form required by the functionalist interpetation is preserved, but not at the expense of essentially ensouled bodies.

III

I should like to conclude by considering a common objection to Aristotle's account of essentially ensouled bodies.[31] The problem arises because Aristotle says of such bodies that they are potentially (*dunamei*) alive (412^a19-21; $27-8$). But these bodies are, as we have seen, *essentially* alive. So they are necessarily actually alive. But this makes it difficult to understand the sense in which they are *potentially* alive. For we ordinarily say that something is potentially *F* only when it is not actually *F*. And even if we allow that something can at one time be both potentially and actually *F*, the distinction between potentiality and actuality seems to require that what is actually *F* might not have been *F*. But this is just what, in the case of the organic body, Aristotle denies: the organic body, unlike its constituent matter, could not have lacked soul.

The passage from *Parts of Animals* quoted in Section I (649^b14-19) shows clearly that Aristotle allows something to be at one and the same time both potentially and actually *F*: water in a liquid state is both potentially and actually liquid. But Ackrill, in pressing his objection, claims that this is possible only where the relevant potentiality is a capacity (like sight) which can be distinguished from its actualization (namely seeing) and not where the relevant potentiality is the matter of some object. The idea is apparently that although I am able to play squash (or am potentially a squash-player) even when I am actually playing, clay is not able to be (or potentially) a statue when it actually is (or constitutes) a statue. But this is not Aristotle's view.

First, Aristotle does not distinguish potentiality as capacity from potentiality as matter in the way that Ackrill suggests.[32] Because Aristotle takes actuality (*energeia*) to be prior to potentiality (*dunamis*), his distinction between two kinds

---

of the whole. Thus, the system as a whole might survive in the absence of functioning eyes, but the eyes cannot survive in the absence of the functioning whole (which is a matter of the functional relations between some critical subset of its parts).

[31] This objection is raised by Ackrill (1972–3), 124–7. He assimilates it to the objection raised in Section I because he accepts Aristotle's identification of matter with potentiality and form with actuality, and does not distinguish the organic body from its compositional matter in the way that I suggest. But someone might object that there is a problem here even if we accept this distinction. For it is clearly the organic body and not simply its compositional matter that Aristotle says to be potentially alive. And this seems odd if (as Ackrill suggests) the concept of potentiality depends on the idea that what is actually the case might not have been the case. For it is never true of the organic body at any time at which it exists that *it* (as opposed to its compositional matter) might not have been alive.

[32] See *Metaph.* 1048^a25-^b9.

of potentiality is based on a distinction between two types of actuality—one called *kinēsis* (or change) and the other called *energeia* in a strict sense. Here, as elsewhere, Aristotle uses the same term, in this case *energeia*, to refer to a genus and to one of its species. For the sake of clarity, I will use *energeia* only to refer to the species which is distinguished from that of *kinēsis*, and will use 'actuality' to refer to the genus which includes both *energeia* and *kinēsis*.

Aristotle explains the distinction between *energeiai* proper and *kinēseis* as follows:

> Of these, then, <it is necessary> to call some *kinēseis* and some *energeiai*. For every *kinēsis* is incomplete—reducing, learning, walking, building. These are changes and incomplete. For it is not the case that at the same time one walks and has walked, or builds and has built, nor that <something> comes to be and has come to be or is changed and has been changed, but these are different. But the same <subject> at the same time has seen and sees, and thinks and has thought. (*Metaph.* 1048^b28–35.)[33]

Part of the point of saying that a *kinēsis* is incomplete is that it is defined by an end the completion of which spells the end of the *kinēsis*: when the house has been built, the buildable no longer exists. For as Aristotle claims, 'the *energeia* of the buildable, *qua* buildable, is the <activity of> building' (*Metaph.* 1066^a2–3). In this case, the actualization of the sort of potentiality Aristotle associates with *kinēsis* cannot exist simultaneously with the potentiality itself. Here, actualization and potentiality are temporally incompatible.

This suggests that the sort of potentiality Aristotle associates with *energeia* proper can exist simultaneously with its own actualization. That this is at least part of Aristotle's point when he claims that 'the same <subject> at the same time sees and has seen' is confirmed by the fact that he goes on after listing several cases in which *x* at the same time *F*'s and has *F*-ed to say,

> if this were not the case, it would have been necessary to stop at some time, just as whenever <someone> reduces, but in fact <one does> not <stop> but rather one <at the same time> lives and has lived. (1048^b26–7).

In other words, if '*x* has lived' were not temporally compatible with '*x* lives', then just as one cannot be building a house which has already been built, '*x* lives' could not be true at any time at which '*x* has lived' was true. But as Ackrill himself recognizes, Aristotle is so far from thinking that '*x* lives' is temporally incompatible with '*x* has lived' that he thinks that '*x* lives (at *t*)' actually *entails* '*x* has lived (at *t*)'.[34] This suggests that Aristotle takes living and other *energeiai* not simply as compatible with, but as implying, the existence of the potentialities whose actualizations they are. And this would explain why he says that only a body that is actually alive is potentially alive: living is the actualization of one of the body's potentialities, an actualization which could not occur in the absence of that potentiality.

---

[33] Deleting (with Jaeger) *kai kinei kai kekinēken* (in l. 33) as an interpolation.
[34] Ackrill (1965), 120–5.

It should not surprise us if Aristotle claims that *energeiai* entail (and, as we shall see below, are entailed by) their correlative potentialities. For Aristotle introduces the distinction between two kinds of actualization immediately after claiming that taking form as actualization and matter as potentiality will solve the problem about the unity of substance by showing that 'the last matter and the form are the same and one, the one in potentiality, the other in actuality' (*Metaph.* 1045ᵇ18–19). And the point of introducing this distinction is to show that it is form as *energeia* (and not as *kinēsis*) which is in some way the same and one with the *dunamis* of which it is the actualization. The *dunamis* here is matter which is 'last' in the sense of being closest to the form: it is that of which the form (or soul) is the actualization—the organic body rather than its constituent matter.³⁵ The role played by the organic body here in Aristotle's account of the unity of substance supports Section II's claim that Aristotle takes the organic body (of which the soul is the actualization and essence) to play an important role in providing intrinsic unities of the sort required to distinguish generation and destruction *simpliciter* from alteration and other sorts of accidental change.

But Aristotle has reasons for saying not only that there is a sense of 'potentiality' in which any body that is actually alive is potentially alive, but also that there is a sense of 'potentiality' in which any body that is potentially alive is actually alive. The reasons lie in what Aristotle takes to be two important facts about living bodies. First, living bodies are natural rather than artificial. This means that they have internal sources of motion and rest (*Ph.* 192ᵇ8–15). Secondly, the soul is not only the formal and final cause of something's being an animal; it is also the efficient cause (i.e. an internal source of motion and rest: *DA* 415ᵇ8–28). These two facts work together in the following way: Aristotle argues that for any *natural* object *x*, the presence of an internal efficient cause of *x*'s being (or coming to be) *F* is a necessary condition for saying that *x* is potentially *F*. So if the soul is the efficient cause of a body's being (or coming to be) alive, then a body will be potentially alive only if and when it is ensouled.

The primary evidence for this interpretation appears in *Metaph.* Θ7, where Aristotle distinguishes natural from artificial generation in the following way: *x* is potentially some artefact (e.g. a house) whenever, *if* the agent has willed, then it comes to be <a house> if nothing internal or external prevents it (1049ᵃ5–12). But in the case of *natural* objects, *x* is potentially 'whatever it will be through itself (*di' hautou*) nothing external interfering' (1049ᵃ13–14).

There is some question here about whether Aristotle's account of artificial generation is merely conditional or whether the antecedent must be fulfilled—that is, about whether or not the external efficient cause (e.g. the willing agent) must be present (and active) if *x* is to be potentially some artefact. Aristotle's claim that matter is potentially a house whenever nothing must be added, removed, or changed might seem to suggest that the presence of an external efficient cause is necessary for some matter to be potentially a house. This would make the

³⁵ On the closeness of matter to form, see *Metaph.* 1035ᵃ11–14.

artificial case more like that natural case in which some matter is potentially alive (or an animal) only when it is actually alive (or an animal). But Aristotle's apparent belief that earth is potentially a statue when it has become bronze and whether or not a sculptor is present (1049ª17–18) suggests that he does not assimilate artificial to natural generation in this way. Furthermore, taking the contrast between artificial and natural potentiality as I have suggested is supported not only by Aristotle's claim that 'actuality is not said similarly of all things, but by analogy' (1048ᵇ6–7) but also by the fact that it helps to make sense of Aristotle's appeal to axes in *DA* 2. 1.

In that chapter, Aristotle asks us to imagine what would happen if an axe were a natural body. He then says that being-an-axe would be the substance and the soul of it and that if this were removed, it would no longer be an axe except homonymously. Now being-an-axe is presumably something like being-capable-of-chopping and it would seem that if this were removed, an axe would no longer be an axe and that this follows *whether or not an axe is a natural body*. What the hypothesis that the axe is a natural body adds is the requirement that the axe be capable of chopping *on its own*. This requirement is needed to explain why Aristotle thinks that his subsequent point about eyes is similar to the one about axes: if an eye were an animal, sight would be its soul and it would be able to see on its own rather than by depending (as in fact it must) on its relation to the soul of the whole living animal. This passage requires us to suppose that the relevant similarity between eyes and artificial objects like axes is that they do not have their own internal efficient causes of motion and rest: they cannot see or chop by themselves. This distinguishes them from living bodies, which have their own internal efficient causes of motion and rest.

It is important to notice this difference between natural and artificial potentiality because failure to do so will prevent us from seeing why Aristotle's view (that a natural body is potentially alive only if it is ensouled) is not as odd as it may initially sound. Aristotle believes that an axe is capable of chopping (or potentially chops) because it can chop *if* there is an external efficient cause around to chop with it. (The antecedent need not even be fulfilled.) But when Aristotle says that a body is capable of living (or potentially alive) he does not mean that it *can* live *if* there is some external efficient cause around to make it live: a natural body is potentially alive only given the presence of an *internal* efficient cause of its being alive—that is, only given the presence of its soul.[36]

---

[36] I would like to thank Paul Hoffman, Paul Matthewson, Philip Mitsis, Martha Nussbaum, Amelie Rorty, and Steve Strange for comments on an early draft of this paper, and Helen Cartwright, whose comments on another paper led to significant improvements here. Terry Irwin, as always, deserves special thanks.

6

ON ARISTOTLE'S CONCEPTION OF THE SOUL*

MICHAEL FREDE

THE study of Aristotle's conception of the soul, at least indirectly, has considerable bearing on modern philosophical concerns. It helps us to identify more clearly some of our preconceptions concerning both the mental and the physical. It also helps us to see the at times rather dubious historical or philosophical origins of these preconceptions.

Philosophers nowadays rarely talk about the soul. But they do talk about the mind. In fact, we are so used to talking about the mind, even ordinarily, that it is no longer readily apparent to us that to talk about the mind is to talk about the soul conceived of in a certain way. This becomes clear when we turn to the historical origins of our talk about the mind. One such origin is Descartes. If we look at Descartes we see that Descartes uses both the term 'mind' and the term 'soul' to talk about the same thing. If there is a preference for the term 'mind', it is because Descartes is rejecting a certain conception of the soul, that of the scholastic Aristotelians, which he wants to replace by another conception. And so he finds it convenient and appropriate to use the term 'mind', rather than the term 'soul', when he wants to talk about the soul as he himself conceives of it. In doing so he deviates from the established scholastic use of the term 'mind', and the fact that we follow Descartes in this deviation is one of the signs that he is an important source of our notion of the mind.

Now the notion of the soul which Descartes rejects, though not Aristotle's notion, is a historical descendant of it; and it shares with Aristotle's notion precisely the feature which Descartes rejects. Both Aristotle and the scholastic Aristotelians believe that the soul is that in virtue of which a living body is alive. Descartes, on the other hand, assumes that bodies, whether alive or not, form part of the physical world and can be explained in its terms without recourse to such entities as souls. To be more precise, Descartes has a certain conception of the physical world, or of the physical, according to which it, and hence also a body, whether it is animate or inanimate, can be explained in terms of matter and its properties. Accordingly he rejects an Aristotelian notion of the soul. All that is needed to explain a living organism and its vital functions is matter and its

© Michael Frede, 1992.

* An earlier version of this paper was given as the S. V. Keeling Lecture in University College London. I am grateful for the opportunity this gave me to discuss and clarify my views.

properties. But the relation between Aristotle's and Descartes's notion is a lot closer. It is not just that Descartes rejects an Aristotelian notion of the soul. Something like the converse is true, too. For the conception of the soul which Descartes adopts in place of an Aristotelian notion itself historically is a descendant of a conception Aristotle rejects; and Descartes' notion shares with the conception Aristotle rejects precisely the feature Aristotle is objecting to. The conception Aristotle rejects is a Platonist conception. According to the Platonists the soul not only is that in virtue of which a body is alive, it also is the proper subject of what we might call the mental functions, things like believing or desiring. On this Platonist conception it is, properly speaking, the soul which is thinking or feeling anger, and the living organism only derivatively can be said to do these things, namely in so far as its soul is doing them. Now later Platonists, under the influence of Stoicism, give up the assumption that our soul makes us alive. They, too, come to think that bodies, whether alive or not, are part of nature and can be explained in terms of it. But they retain the notion of the soul as the thinking self, distinct from the body, and the proper subject of the mental functions. It is in this way that the notion of the soul attacked by Aristotle is the historical ancestor of Descartes's notion of the mind: a Platonist notion of the soul freed of the role to have to animate a body. From Aristotle's point of view, then, Descartes's conception of the mind is fundamentally mistaken: (i) it does not even try to explain the life of an organism, since it rests on the assumption that the ordinary life-functions can be, and have to be, explained in terms of matter and its properties, and that, hence, a soul is not needed to account for them; and (ii) it presupposes that a natural body, however complex it may be, being a body, could not possibly be able to think, feel, or desire, and that, hence, an entity distinct from the natural body, namely the soul, has to be introduced to account for these mental functions. Thus, to the extent that our notion of the mind is a descendant of Descartes's notion, and in so far as an Aristotelian notion of the soul is diametrically opposed to the kind of notion Descartes has, Aristotle's view, indirectly, has considerable bearing on our notion of the mind.

What I have to say is very simple. We tend to underrate the physical to the extent that we tend to think of it as being determined by certain ultimate material constituents and a few basic properties of these material constituents. Such an impoverished view of the physical then creates a considerable pressure to introduce something non-physical to account for mental phenomena, as we can see in Descartes. Aristotle, in resisting such a narrow conception of the physical, is correspondingly also in a much better position when he tries to reject Platonist dualism. The remarks which follow will be little more than an attempt to elaborate and to elucidate this point.

Put systematically and in a nutshell, Aristotle's position, I take it, is the following. It ultimately turns on a certain conception of the physical or the natural, which is rather different from Descartes's and also rather different from the conception most of us are inclined to. Aristotle thinks that it is true of natural objects and their behaviour in general that they cannot be fully understood in terms of their material constituents and their properties, but have to be explained in terms of their essence or nature. But it would be a mistake to think of this difference in terms of the contrast between an antiquated, hopelessly inadequate Aristotelian science and modern science since Descartes. The crucial difference does not lie in the details of a theory of the material constituents of objects and their properties. The crucial difference rather lies in the answer to the question whether such a theory will provide us with a complete understanding of natural objects and their behaviour or not. And this, if we think, for example, of contemporary biology, remains as much a question nowadays as it was in Aristotle's time. Aristotle's introduction of essences or natures in the first place reflects the fact that he takes the anti-reductionist view that objects and their behaviour for the most part cannot be fully understood in terms of their material constituents and the properties of these. But to introduce essences or natures, at least in Aristotle, though perhaps not in scholastic Aristotelianism, is not to introduce new entities with a curious kind of agency and causal efficacy of their own. If this were Aristotle's view, then Aristotelian natural science in its scientific details would indeed be incompatible with modern natural science in principle. But this is not the way Aristotle thinks of essences or natures. When Aristotle is insisting on essences or natures, he is insisting that objects, natural objects, human beings, are not just configurations of more basic material constituents and hence should not just be conceived of in this way. They should not be conceived of just in this way, because essences or natures enter in a non-causal, but nevertheless crucial, way into their explanation and the explanation of their behaviour.

Since this is a point on which my account of Aristotle's conception of the soul crucially depends, let me at least try to explain it in some more detail. Essences, in Aristotle, enter explanations in various ways, for example as efficient causes. But this tends to be misunderstood. Efficient causes in Aristotle are not the nearest equivalent to what we might think of as a cause, something which in virtue of its agency enters into a causal explanation. This becomes particularly apparent when Aristotle explains that, strictly speaking, it is not the sculptor who is the efficient cause of the sculpture, the builder who is the efficient cause of the house, but the art of building and the art of sculpting. Essences, then, enter into an explanation somewhat in the way in which the art of building enters into an explanation of how a house is built or is being built. Nobody assumes that the art of building is an agent or has any causal efficacy, and nevertheless we readily see that it is quite crucial to an understanding of the details of a house how much art has gone into it. It is important, though, not to misconstrue the analogy. To refer to the art here is not to refer to the thoughts, beliefs, and intentions of the builder. We, of course, do assume that the builder had certain beliefs, thoughts, intentions when he built a house according to the art. But my point is that there are two different kinds of explanation here, one in terms of the art, the other in terms of the thoughts of the builder. To identify the two is to give in to the temptation to turn an explanation in terms of the art into another, familiar kind of causal explanation. The fact is, so at least I assume, that an explanation in terms of the art is a perfectly good explanation, though it is not a causal one. It does not involve any reference to episodes or dispositions in the builder's mind. And it seems that the latter kind of explanation in terms of what goes on in the builder's mind presupposes the former kind. For it seems that our assumptions about what goes on in the builder's mind already largely depend on our antecedent understanding of the art. And it also seems that we resort to an explanation in terms of the builder and what goes on in his mind precisely if there is something contrary to the art in the way he goes about building a house, if what he does cannot be explained any longer in terms of the art. So it is in this way, I submit, that Aristotle is thinking of an explanation in terms of the art of building. And the suggestion is that an essence or nature enters the explanation of natural objects and their behaviour somewhat in the way the art enters into the explanation of a house. I will return to this point later.

Forms, essences, or natures, then, are crucial explanatory factors of some kind without themselves being causal agents. And it is the insistence on this kind of explanation, rather than a peculiar, outdated, view of what happens causally, which distinguishes Aristotle's view of the physical, or the natural, from that of his Presocratic predecessors as much as from that of Descartes.

Now, for Aristotle, souls are just a particular kind of essences or natures, namely the essences or natures of animate bodies. A soul is what essentially distinguishes a living body from an inanimate body. To say that the soul is the essence of a certain, sufficiently complex, kind of natural body, again, then, is to say that the organism and its behaviour has to be understood in a certain way, if it is to be fully understood.

But once we grant ourselves such an essence or nature, Aristotle's view seems to be, we not only can understand the behaviour of natural objects in general as what it is, we also can understand the ordinary living functions of organisms. And not just that. Aristotle thinks that there is no reason to treat the so-called mental functions, things like desiring, thinking, and believing, any differently than the ordinary living functions. To put the matter differently: because Aristotle takes the position that the organism, in virtue of its form, is able to do all the things which a living thing of its kind can do, he also refuses to divide the things animate objects can do into two classes, namely into those things which the body is made to do by the soul and those things which the soul does itself. To explain: if we make a list of the things human beings (for example) might do, this list will include such items as these:

  (i)   they breathe in a certain way;
  (ii) they eat;
  (iii) they catch cold;
  (iv) they take walks;
  (v)   they write letters;
  (vi) they get upset;
  (vii) they think something over;
  (viii) they try to decide what to do.

Aristotle refuses to divide this list into two parts, a list of, as we might say, physical doings and a list of mental doings. He refuses to assume that the soul is the proper subject of the latter, that it has, as it were, a life of its own constituted by these mental doings, whereas the animate object is merely the subject of the physical doings. He rather thinks that there is just one subject, the animate object, which, in virtue of the particular kind of form or soul it has, is capable of all of these things, though it only is a natural body. Not any natural body can do these things, and only bodies which have complicated enough a nature can do all of them. Still, it is just a natural body which, in virtue of its nature or soul, is perfectly capable of doing all these things, a natural body which does not stand in need of a further thing, namely a soul, to do some of these things for it, because it itself, being just a body, would not be capable of doing this sort of thing.

Now a caveat is necessary here. When I say that Aristotle refuses to distinguish between mental doings, which are supposed to be doings of the soul or the mind, and physical doings, which are doings of the animate object, I do not mean to commit Aristotle to the view that there is no way in which a useful distinction might be drawn which extensionally comes reasonably close to the distinction between mental doings and physical doings. Aristotle might, for example, distinguish two senses of 'life': the sense in which any kind of organism has life, and that in which only some organisms, perhaps only human beings, have a life. And among the doings which constitute life in the second sense, the life which might be described in a biography, some clearly are more basic than others in such a way that we explain the latter in terms of the former. And it might turn out that these basic ones pretty much correspond to the mental predicates. But, what matters here is not whether such a distinction can be drawn at all. What rather matters is that Aristotle refuses to distinguish them as natural doings. On his view they all have to be explained alike as the kind of thing an organism which is complicated enough naturally will do in the appropriate circumstances.

A further caveat is needed. Actually it turns out that, on Aristotle's considered view, thinking, a very particular kind of thinking, namely intellectual intuition, the intellectual grasp of certain kinds of features, is unlike the other so-called mental functions. It is not related to the body in quite the same way as they are. Thus it needs a more complicated account. But even this more complicated account will make thinking something which a living body does in virtue of the soul, rather than something which the soul or the mind does for it. I shall return to this point.

This, very roughly, is the view which I want to attribute to Aristotle. One readily sees how it is diametrically opposed to the Cartesian view. And one also sees how this opposition turns on a very different conception of the natural or the physical. It is not first of all a disagreement about the status and explanation of mental items. It is, first of all, a disagreement about natural objects and their behaviour. Aristotle for natural objects in general insists on essences, in addition to matter and its properties. But, given these essences, Aristotle also thinks that no further kind of item, like a Cartesian mind, is needed to account for the so-called mental items. But this is a secondary disagreement.

Having provided a rough sketch of the position I would like to attribute to Aristotle, I now want to turn to some of the details. Here I necessarily have to be rather selective. The topic itself and the way I deal with it raise a great number of complicated questions. But I shall try to focus on a few selected problems the discussion of which might give a clearer intuitive content to the view I am trying to sketch.

One central point which we need to be as clear about as possible is why Aristotle insists on the assumption that there are essences or natures. One way to think about the matter is this: we might think of the form or nature of an object as its disposition or organization. There are certain material constituents, but they are disposed or organized in such a way that, thus disposed or organized, they can do things which—not thus disposed or organized—they could never do. But there are different ways in which we might think of this disposition or organization. Only a disposition or organization of a certain kind, and this only conceived of in a certain way, will count as an essence.

An example from Aristotle's own treatise on the soul may make the point clearer. Whereas most of Aristotle's predecessors had made the soul an entity distinct from the body it animates, there had been some who—like Aristotle— assumed that the soul was just a disposition of a body. There were, for example, those who claimed that the soul is the attunement of the body (cf. *DA* 407^{b}30 ff.). Now there are two ways in which one could construe the view referred to, and though Aristotle has only one of them in mind here, it is important to see why Aristotle would reject both of them. The view might be that the soul is a certain disposition of the body such that the body thus disposed can do things it otherwise could not do. Thus one might think of a living organism on the analogy of a stringed instrument. The instrument properly strung and tuned can do marvellous things which we would never have expected from a thing which just consists of some pieces of wood and some strings. According to Aristotle, though, this analogy is inappropriate. The crucial difference is that, whereas in the case of the stringed instrument there is an object there, namely the instrument, quite independently of whether it is appropriately disposed or not to be able to do what it is supposed to do, in the case of the organism there is no object there independently of its being disposed in such a way as to be alive. To be a living thing, and hence to be alive, is to be a kind of thing, and whatever makes it that kind of thing, its essential features or characteristics, is constitutive of its being an object in the first place; that is to say, there is no object there that is not alive, in the way in which one might have an instrument which is not tuned. There is no single object which sometimes is alive and sometimes is not, depending on how it is disposed.

The view Aristotle actually has in mind in the *De Anima*, though, when he talks about the soul as the attunement of the body is a different one. Moreover, it is different precisely in such a way that Aristotle's response to it relies on his particular conception of an essence or nature. On the view in question the soul is the harmony of the body in so far as the organism consists of certain material constituents which are blended harmoniously, such that a blend of this kind can do things the ingredients by themselves, or blended in some other way, could not do. What Aristotle has to say about this view will fit any view according to which an organism is just a certain appropriate configuration of the appropriate material constituents. Though such a view comes rather close to Aristotle's own, the crucial difference is the following: on the view criticized, we understand the configuration or organization in terms of the material constituents as a configuration these constituents, given their features, might enter into, such that, having entered into it, they constitute an organism. On such a view there is even a sense in which the configuration or organization is essential to the organism. For it would not be the kind of organism it is without this kind of organization. And yet the organization conceived of in this way does not yet count as an essence in Aristotle's sense. The reason is that thus conceived its relation to the materials thus organized is purely external, accidental, contingent. It is just one of the many ways these material constituents might be organized. It is not that we cannot understand how they might get organized this way. Given these constituents and their properties we can understand perfectly well that one way they might get organized is this. But Aristotle thinks that, though this is a way of looking at the matter, there is a more important way of looking at it, which is exactly the other way round: we do not try to understand the configuration in terms of the material constituents and their properties, but rather the other way round; we try to understand the material constituents and their properties in terms of the form or organization. It is materials of this kind with such properties we need if we want an organism which works in this way. Only if we give the organization this kind of priority over its constituents will it count as an essence.

But why should Aristotle insist on looking at the organization in this second way? Ultimately, I think, the answer is that Aristotle wants to hold on to the metaphysical primacy of objects, natural objects, living objects, human beings. He does not want these to be mere configurations of more basic entities, such that the real things turn out to be these more basic entities. But to look at an object just as the configuration the material constituents transiently happen to enter into is to look at the material constituents as the more basic entities. So since Aristotle, against the view of practically all his predecessors, wants to hold on to the ontological primacy of objects, he introduces essences which guarantee this status. This might be tied to, as we should put it, an epistemological point. What we try to understand when we do science are the ordinary objects around us. There might be something radically misguided about any view which interprets the scientific theories which we develop in order to understand these ordinary objects and their behaviour in such a way that these objects are no longer of any significance in our scientific view of things.

This may be the ultimate answer as to why Aristotle insists on essences. But a more concrete and less speculative answer is the one we already have alluded to: Aristotle thinks we need something like an essence for explanatory purposes. And this is what we need to get clearer about. Forms or essences, according to Aristotle, enter explanations in many ways, for example, as efficient or as final causes. What I want to pursue here is just one particular way in which nature seems to me to play an explanatory role, a way moreover which is particularly relevant to our subject.

Aristotle characterizes a nature as a principle of change and rest in the thing itself which is undergoing a change, as opposed to a principle of change external to the thing which is undergoing a change. It is easy to see the primitive intuition of which this is supposed to be a refinement. When an object hits me in such a way that I fall over, this has very little to do with my nature. But if I see an object coming my way and jump aside, to avoid being hit and falling over, this obviously has a lot to do with the kind of thing I am. Being this kind of thing I jump aside under the appropriate circumstances. An example Aristotle uses for an external principle of change is the art of building when a house gets built. I want to look at this example in some detail to see how what Aristotle has to say in this case might apply, *mutatis mutandis*, in the case of an internal principle of change like the soul.

The art of building is external to the building which is being built: it resides in the builder who is building a house. In what sense is this art a principle of the change which takes place when a house is being built? When a house is being built there are certain building materials, let us say bricks. These bricks can be put together in such a way as to form a house. In so far as it is true of them that, if they are put together in this way, they, thus put together, are a house, they are a potential house, to use Aristotle's phrase. And in so far as they are a potential house, they constitute the matter of a house in the strict Aristotelian sense of the term 'matter'. They are the matter of a house, a potential house, relative to a process, in this case an artificial process, namely an exercise of the art of building. Where there is no way to turn some stuff by some definite process into an actual something or other there also is no potentiality or matter, given Aristotle's notion of matter. I say 'Aristotle's notion of matter', because Aristotle's notion significantly differs from ours; for Aristotle to think of something as matter is already to think of it as the matter of some kind of thing or other which by some definite process could be turned into that sort of thing, if it has not already been so turned. Thus for Aristotle matter as such, by definition, presupposes a form or nature in terms of which it has to be understood.

But, of course, even on Aristotle's view something which, looked at in one way, is matter in this strict sense can also be looked at in another way. In fact, it seems that Aristotle is committed to the view that when something can be regarded as the matter of something, there also is another prior, more basic way of looking at it. Suppose we have bricks which are a potential house because nothing but an exercise of the art of building is required to turn them into a house. Looked at in this way they are matter, the matter of a house. But note that this presupposes something on the part of the bricks which might exist even if there were no such thing as the art of building, if there were no such things as houses. The bricks can be moved around in all sorts of ways. One of the many ways in which they can be moved around is such that they are put on top of each other and alongside each other in such a way as to form an object which is exactly like a house. If they could not be moved in this way, no art of building could turn them into a house. Just looking at the bricks, without thinking about houses or the art of building, just trying to think how these bricks could be moved, we could figure out that one way for them to be moved would be this. And we could describe this motion they are capable of in all detail without any reference, explicit or implicit, to houses or to the art of house-building. Would such a description be a description of house-building? Yes and no. But first of all no. There would be no way to tell from just this description that this was a case of house-building. And, in fact, it might not be a case of house-building. The bricks may have been moved this way by accident, however unlikely this is. Somebody may just have been trying to build a house, more or less successfully, or have practised building a house. What makes a case of house-building a case of house-building is that it is an exercise of the art of building. But this does not mean that there is something further to the building of the house than we mentioned in our first description. It just means that in the case of an actual house-building the process as a whole and its details have a certain explanation. We do not understand a case of house-building and the house except as respectively an exercise and the product of the art of building. On the other hand, the original description given is a precise description of what happens to the bricks when a house is being built. With some hesitation I will call it a material description of the building of the house. It is a description which makes no reference, explicit or implicit, to houses or the art of building. It is a description such that the process described this way is perfectly intelligible and explainable in terms of the mechanical properties of bricks and the mechanical properties of things which might move them this way. Nothing in Aristotle prevents us from saying that this process can be understood and explained in terms of physics or mechanics. But to understand the process this way is not yet to understand it as a case of house-building, if that is what it actually is. It is not that there are any details which have escaped description and explanation. It is rather that once we look at the process as a case of house-building we see that the details require, not a different, but a further explanation. After all, a house is a product of art, and one can see in its details the art which has gone into its building. But, to repeat what I already emphasized earlier: to say that the building of the house has to be explained in terms of the art is of course not to say that the art moves the bricks around. It rather is to say that the builder in virtue of his art moves the bricks around in a certain way which one also has to understand in terms of the art, the way the different moves contribute to the production of a house made according to the art, a house which serves its purpose in a certain way, etc. The art of building is not a mysterious force without whose agency we could not understand the house, or the building of it, at all. But we would not understand it as a house and as a case of building.

Let us, then, turn to the soul. One of the things a living thing might do is to digest food, which at least from a certain point onwards becomes part of the body. To say that the soul is the principle or even the efficient cause of this change is obviously not to say that the soul is doing anything to the food. It is rather to say that the living thing, in virtue of having the kind of soul or nature it has, is doing something to the food, or that the food is having something done to it in virtue of this nature. It is also to say that the food could not undergo this change unless it were the kind of stuff in the first place which could undergo this process described in material terms, in other words without any reference to processing of food by this kind of organism and to the state of the organism it is in as a result of this process. It is also to say that there will be a perfectly good explanation of this process, thus described. There, again, is nothing in Aristotle to prevent us from saying that this process can be understood and explained in terms of the appropriate kind of chemistry. And yet to understand the process this way is not to understand it as the natural process it is. Presumably the same process, as described in material terms, could be reproduced artificially. But if it were, it would not be a case of digestion. And this not because it lacked some details or some mysterious quality the natural process has, but because it, as a whole and its details, would have to be explained differently. What makes the digestion of food the process it is, and hence is essential to our understanding of it, is that it is the exercise of the capacity or ability of this kind of organism to digest food. And similarly for the other life-functions. In each case there is a material description in terms of material parts of the organism and of what happens to them in terms of their properties. But in each case the process is only the natural or physical process it is, rather than a materially equivalent, but formally different process, because it is the exercise of an ability the organism has in virtue of its form or soul. In fact Aristotle often talks as if the soul itself were a set of abilities the organism has to do the kinds of things which are characteristic of its kind. Thus to say that the soul is a principle of change is to say that these abilities are principles of change. It is their exercise which makes a physical or natural process the process it is, rather than a different, though materially equivalent one. Thus to say that an object has a certain nature is not to postulate a mysterious force or a mysterious kind of causation; it is to say something about how the object and its behaviour have to be understood and to be explained. The nature is supposed to make a real difference precisely in the way in which the art of building makes a real difference. It adds a further level of understanding to what happens. It is not that without it we would not understand at all what happens. But we would not understand it as what it really and most specifically is, namely a specific case of metabolism, tailored to the needs of a particular kind of organism.

It is in this way, then, that Aristotle can say that the soul, *qua* form, essence, or nature of the organism, is that in virtue of which it is alive. It is alive in so far as it does the kinds of things an organism of this kind characteristically does. But what it is doing would not count as these things unless it were exercising an ability which it had in virtue of its soul.

Now Aristotle's conception of the soul, as we said at the outset, is not only

determined by his particular version of the assumption that the soul is that in virtue of which an animate thing is alive; it is also characterized by his rejection of
the assumption that the soul is an entity distinct from the body it animates and
the proper subject of a subclass of the predicates we ascribe to living things,
namely the mental predicates. A lot more can be said about why Aristotle rejects
the notion of the soul as a distinct entity which is the proper subject of the mental
predicates, as that this notion raises the standard questions concerning the unity
of body and soul and their interaction, or that it threatens the substantiality of living objects. But I want to focus on Aristotle's rejection of the notion that the soul
is the proper subject of some of the doings we ascribe to living things.

At *DA* 408ᵇ11 ff. Aristotle says: 'To say, then, that the soul is angry is as if one
were to say that the soul is weaving or building a house. For it would seem to be
better not to say that the soul pities or learns or thinks, but that the human being
is doing this in virtue of the soul.' What is so absurd about saying that the soul is
weaving? Weaving clearly is something which the living body is doing; for it
clearly involves the use of the parts of the body. But if to say that the soul is
angry or is thinking is like saying that the soul is weaving, and the latter is
patently absurd because weaving involves the body in a certain way, then
Aristotle must also think that being angry and thinking and learning are like
weaving in that they involve the body in a similar way, and that hence their
proper subject, too, is the organism, rather than the soul. When Aristotle makes
these remarks in ch. 4 he is relying on a discussion of the so-called 'affections
of the soul'—the attributes which correspond to mental predicates—in ch. 1.
There he argues that these affections all involve the body and hence cannot be
affections peculiar to the soul, that is, having the soul, rather than the organism,
for their proper subject (403ª16 ff.). He concludes the argument by saying that it
thus would seem that the affections are 'enmattered formulae' (403ᵉ24–5). He
proceeds to explain this. All these so-called affections of the soul have two sides, a
material and a formal. And a full physical account or definition of them would
have to specify both (403ᵇ8–12). Thus to be angry or to be angered, Aristotle
says, is formally something like to desire revenge, whereas materially it might be
the boiling of the blood around the heart. There are considerable difficulties of
interpretation here. But the distinction between a formal aspect and a material
aspect of anger thus drawn does remind one of the distinction we drew earlier
between house-building regarded in purely material terms and house-building
regarded as an artificial process, an exercise of the art of building, between the
digestion of food regarded in purely material terms and the digestion viewed as a
natural process, an exercise of a natural capacity. Similarly if one is angered, what
happens in material terms is that something is making one's blood boil. A
material part of the organism undergoes a change described in terms of the
features of this material constituent, a change which thus described might happen
elsewhere and for a different cause (cf. 403ᵈ26–7). But to look at it just in this
way, as described materially, is not yet to understand it as anger. It is to understand it as one thing which can happen to stuff like blood and which does happen

to it if something does certain things to it. What makes it a case of being angered is something else. And this something else is not, as it were, something psychical or mental, a mental counterpart of the material process. For, on Aristotle's view, there is no independently existing material process; processes as materially described actually only exist as natural, artificial, or spontaneous processes. There is a natural process, which can be described in material terms, and this material description does not miss anything that is happening when somebody is angered. Nor do we lack an adequate explanation of anything which is happening. The appropriate kind of chemistry or physiology will supply us with a perfectly adequate explanation of what is happening as thus described. But what such a description does leave out is the fact that the process in fact is an exercise of the natural ability of the organism to have desires and more specifically to desire revenge.

If this is correct, then Aristotle seems to think that the so-called affections of the soul are just like all the other doings of living organisms. They are physical or natural the way he understands 'physical': they have a material side to be described in terms of the material constituents of the organism and their features, and a formal side to be specified in terms of the natural capacities of the organism. It is this formal side which makes them the natural processes which they are. So, given what we have said so far, we can see how Aristotle might think that, granted his notion of a nature, such a nature might account for all life-functions and hence for all anybody wants the soul to account for.

Two qualifications are needed here, on which I will be brief, though they deserve and need more detailed treatment. To say that a natural process is the natural process it is in so far as it is the exercise of an ability, is *not* to say that anger (for example) is functionally defined and that any functionally equivalent process would count as anger. For there to be anger there has to be a process as materially described. Something, on Aristotle's view, clearly would not count as a case of seeing, unless it satisfied a material description in terms of the material parts of the organism and their properties, specifically the eyes and their properties. Secondly, this claim that a natural process is the exercise of an ability of a certain kind needs to be understood in a certain way to avoid the objection that according to Aristotle an exercise of this sort of ability, such as the ability to see, is not a process in the first place. It does not take time, does not have a beginning, a middle, and an end, as a process does. But note that there are two ways of looking at one and the same activity, such as the activity of building a house. Looked at in one way it is a process, something that needs time to get done. Looked at in another way, namely as the exercise of the art of building, it does not take any time. The builder, in building a house, at each point already has fully exercised his art.

Thus we might end our brief account of Aristotle's conception of the affections of the soul, if there were not a formidable array of remarks in Aristotle's writings and in *De Anima* itself which threw all of this into doubt. All of these remarks ultimately concern the intellect (*nous*) and the characteristic activity Aristotle ascribes to it, a certain kind of intellectual intuition. They raise the question whether Aristotle himself in the end does not feel forced, after all, to reintroduce a separate subject in the form of the intellect to account for thought, or at least this kind of thought. They raise the question whether Aristotle is not all along wavering about his account of the soul as the nature of a certain kind of body. And, in any case, they are very confusing, so confusing that they have been the subject of debate since antiquity and have given rise to rather different interpretations and philosophical views.

I am in no position to solve these problems. But the following remarks may suffice to show that Aristotle, for all his remarks about intellectual intuition and the intellect, was at least strongly inclined to accept the view of the soul sketched above. To begin with, there is no doubt that Aristotle thinks that all human thought, properly speaking, presupposes the activity of an immaterial intellect which is not dependent on a body in any way. This is the notorious active intellect of *DA* 3. 5. Its activity clearly is not the exercise of a natural ability of a body, and thus its thought clearly cannot be explained in the way, I suggested earlier, Aristotle wants to explain the mental functions of human beings. But we can acknowledge this, without having to draw the conclusion that Aristotle's doctrine of the active intellect is incompatible with the view that the soul is just the form of a natural body. For it is open to us to assume, following in this a long tradition of interpreters, that this active intellect is not a human intellect, that it is not an integral part of the human soul. Thus there also is no need why Aristotle, given his view of the human soul as the form of a body, should be able to explain the activity of the active intellect along the lines he tries to explain the mental functions of human beings. I think that it is with reference to this kind of intellect that Aristotle sometimes says that not every kind of soul falls within the province of the study of the natural scientist. This kind of intellect or soul is not itself a natural object or the nature of such a natural object. Hence it does not fall within the province of natural science. But even if we can thus set aside the active intellect, there still is the activity of the human, passive intellect to worry about. Aristotle right from the beginning of the *De Anima* repeatedly raises the question whether intellectual intuition (*noein*) is like the other so-called affections of the mind. In these passages he clearly seems to be talking about our human intellectual intuitions, rather than about the intuitions of some superhuman mind. And since he is wavering on this question, one thinks, he must be wavering on the question whether the human soul may not be the proper subject of some affections, after all. To make matters worse, it becomes apparent that Aristotle's considered view is that our intellectual intuition does not involve the body the way the other mental functions do. So one easily comes to think that not even the passive intellect does fit the view of the soul outlined above. But this would be a mistake. Aristotle's view turns out to be this: the exercise of the intellect, Aristotle wants to say (cf. *DA* An. 429ª18 ff., esp. ª24–5), unlike the exercise of the other so-called mental faculties, does not involve the use of a bodily organ. For otherwise our cognitive abilities would be hampered by the restrictions the organ puts on them, the way the sense-organs limit what we can perceive. But this does not mean that the exercise of the intellect does not presuppose a body. It is Aristotle's view that we could not think the way we do unless, for example, we were capable of perception and could remember, and somehow process, what we perceive. Thus our ability to think presupposes a body. In fact, it presumably is Aristotle's view that the very exercise of this ability presuppose a body, if he does believe that thinking involves images of some kind (cf. 403^{a}8–9). How could this be? Aristotle's position might be the following. He might think that certain abilities developed to a certain degree, like the abilities to perceive, and to store, and to process what one has perceived, give rise to certain further abilities, such as the ability to think. But whereas the exercise of the former abilities directly involves the use of a bodily organ, the exercise of the latter abilities does not involve the use of a separate bodily organ, but rather the exercise of some of the former abilities and thus indirectly the use of their bodily organs. If this is the position Aristotle envisages, one easily understands some of the unclarity of his remarks. For the notion of an ability which is based on, or arises from, certain other abilities is a rather confused notion which Aristotle has not had occasion to develop and to clarify. If something like this is correct, the position which he comes to take on the human intellect and its activity does not pose a problem, either, for his view of the soul as the form of the body, let alone for our interpretation of this view. On Aristotle's considered view human intellectual intuitions importantly differ from the other so-called affections of the soul, but they do not differ from them in such a way as to justify our postulation of an intellect or a soul as the proper subject of these intuitions or thoughts.

Now, the reason why Aristotle, right from the beginning of the *De Anima* (cf. 402^{a}9), is so concerned with the question whether there are affections of the soul peculiar to it, as the Platonists maintain, is easy to see. If there were such affections peculiar to it, and if they really were affections—things which happen to the soul—the soul would be a distinct subject with a life and a history of its own. And given that this life of the soul clearly would explain a good deal of our external life, it would be tempting to think that it would explain our external life altogether; that it gives the body whatever life it has. So in order to be able to say that the soul is just the form or the nature of the living body, Aristotle has to show that there are no affections peculiar to the soul. And he tries to do this in the way we have seen, by assimilating, if this is the right word, these affections to the physical or natural affections of the organism as a whole, arguing that in the relevant details they are just like them. Moreover, in the course of book 1 of *De Anima* Aristotle is eager to show that the soul is absolutely changeless. Being a form or nature it is a principle of change, something one appeals to to explain change, which hence cannot itself be the kind of thing which is subject to change. Thus it cannot be the kind of thing which has a life of its own.

Aristotle's view, therefore, seems to be this. In order to do justice to physical or natural phenomena we need the notion of a form or nature anyway. But once we allow ourselves this notion, Aristotle thinks, this notion is strong enough to account for all that we would want a soul to account for, the life, the things living objects do, and even the so-called affections of the soul. Hence there is no need to introduce, in addition to the form or nature, a distinct soul, either to account for the life of an organism as a whole or for a mental part of it.

7

PSUCHĒ VERSUS THE MIND

K.V. WILKES

Introduction

THE Aristotelian *psuchē* is enjoying a revival. That is, many psychologists today are working in a theoretical framework that is recognizably Aristotelian. The irony, of course, is that they rarely if ever recognize this, and are likely to deny strenuously that Aristotle—whose theories in other scientific fields seem to have been throughly discredited by such as Galileo or Galen—has anything to say to them. But the case is clear, and easy to show. The reappearance of the *psuchē* is (or will be) at the expense of the mind; this too is a move in the right direction. So in this paper I shall sketch briefly the aspects of the *psuchē* that give it its contemporary appeal; then turn to remind the reader of the poverty of the notion of 'mind': and then, in what will be the main section, underline the manifest superiority of the latter over the former.

Before beginning on that, though, two preliminary but essential points of clarification.

First, I shall not translate *psuchē*. Evidently I could not translate it as 'mind', since my ambition is to contrast 'mind' and '*psuchē*'; but the commonly used 'soul' is just as misleading: stinging-nettles have *psuchē*.[1]

Secondly, whenever I talk of 'psychology' I am talking about theoretical and experimental scientific psychology: the pursuit of those in laboratories and white coats. I am not talking about commonsense psychology, whether that is considered as the domain of the man in the street or as 'philosophical psychology': armchair theories of action and perception, or 'sentential models' of cognition, and so forth. No doubt scientific psychology and commonsense (or 'philosophical') psychology differ only in degree—but degrees can be colossal.[2] Whenever I do need to mention commonsense psychology, I shall invariably preface the term 'psychology' by 'commonsense'. 'Psychology', alone, will stand for the scientists' work. This is of course true to Aristotle; the *De Anima* is a work in theoretical scientific psychology.

© K. V. Wilkes, 1992.

[1] Perhaps 'soul' would do if we were all Empedocleans; he, after all, claimed to have existed once as a bush.

[2] Some of these differences will emerge in the third section below, which should therefore help to justify this distinction.

I. The *Psuchē*

I shall rapidly run through the essentials of Aristotle's picture; rapidly, because they will be well known to readers of this volume. *Psuchai* are a subclass of forms; more precisely, they are forms of any living creature. Thus to have *psuchē* is to be alive, to be alive is to have a *psuchē*. So, 'if an instrument such as an axe were a natural body, then its substance (*ousia*) would be what it is to be an axe, and this would be its *psuchē*' *DA* 412ᵇ12–13; since not, not. Because they are forms, they tell us 'what it is to be' the thing in question. The matter of an organism is 'a natural body which has life potentially' (412ᵃ27–8). It is not easy to isolate in thought the material aspect of an organism, for good and sufficient reasons which we shall come to; but as a preliminary gesture towards it we could think of Adam on the Sistine ceiling, an instant before the finger of God touched him. Organisms, like any other substances, are in-formed matter, enmattered form, and not just any matter will do: just as you can't make a threshold out of a sponge, so you can't make a human being from earth (435ᵃ20–1). The matter of humans, and indeed of all organisms, must have a complex structure, which for Aristotle meant that they must have organs (412ᵇ5–6).

Psuchai can be thought of as pyramidal in structure, hierarchically organized in such a way that all the higher reaches of the pyramid presuppose the lower. At the simplest and lowest level we find plants; their *psuchē* consists in their capacities to grow, take nourishment, and reproduce themselves. These are capacities that all living things possess; the 'nutritive-reproductive' *psuchē* 'belongs to all other living creatures as well as to man, and is the first and most widely shared capacity (*dunamis*) of the *psuchē*, because of which they all have life (415ᵃ24–5). Of course the *manner* in which these capacities are exercised will differ from organism to organism; this depends on what other capacities they have and on the particular physical structure: on what (homoiomerous or anhomoiomerous) tissues or organs realize the *dunameis* in question. Next comes the most basic form of sensory perception, touch; and that goes along with a rudimentary capacity to desire. This is not an accidental coupling, but necessary 413ᵇ22–4: the capacities that constitute the *psuchē* interlock and help determine the nature of each other; they are not disjointed, like beads on a string.[3] There follow the senses in general, again essentially bound up with the ability to move; the higher the animal, the more diversity and range are found in its sensory, desiderative, and locomotive capacities—a dog has a wider range of ability than a mosquito. Again, the nature of the beast will determine the form that these activities take; not all animals smell by inhaling, for instance (*Sens.* 444ᵃ19–22), and the movement of a dog is very unlike that of a mosquito. Then comes imagination; then, with the human alone of the animal kingdom, reason and thought. (For a brief summary, see 414ᵇ33 ff., a passage which is, however, ambiguous about the status of the imagination. This he tries to clarify later, in *DA* 3.3.)

---

[3] Perhaps Aristotle was the first to take note of 'the holism of the psychological'—or more generally, of the *psuchē*-logical.

The hierarchical and 'pyramidal' organization of the *psuchē* may suggest that the lower capacities subserve the higher ones, making their exercise possible. This is of course true: if a dog does not eat it will not be fit to run or chase cats. But it is only part of the story, since there is essential feedback—the greyhound races to catch the hare that it sees, so that it may eat it. Thus the higher functions loop back on to the healthy regulation of the lower ones. Further: the more complex the organism, the more intricate the interlocking of its varied and numerous faculties. Take the human for instance. He is 'by nature [*phusei*—essentially] a social animal' (*EN* 1097^{b}11). Success in his 'environmental niche', which is a social niche, will then require essential reference to this fact; to the society in which he lives. It is not simply that he has to use his reason to deliberate how to obtain food, rest, and shelter, to work out that smoking may damage his ability to breathe by damaging his lungs; he has to use his reason to ensure that his social, material, economic, and political environments are well suited to his best flourishing, his *eudaimonia*. Thus we should form an image of numerous pyramids (each pyramid representing one human being) where the more basic ('lower') levels of the *psuchē* make the exercise of the higher ones possible; but where 'higher' functions not only loop back directly on to the lower ones, but often do so indirectly, as well, through other 'pyramids'. (Crude and simple example: A may need to *persuade* B to cook him a meal.)

There is also a hierarchical element along a different dimension. Nothing can exist without form and matter; that is as true for the eye as for the person whose eye it is. The form (function) of the eye is sight. The matter of the human eye, Aristotle thinks, consists of water (*Sens.* 438^{a}13–14). But an eyeful of water is a thing, even if of a somewhat unsophisticated kind; and so we need to discover how this new substance, water, contributes to the function of the eye. Part of the form of water is its capacity to take on any colour (cf. *DA* 424^{a}7–9). What are the constituent elements of the matter of water? Aristotle does not—presumably cannot—say: but they will themselves be low-level substances, and he ascribes to the form (functions) of these substances the powers of transparency and receptivity. But just how Aristotle analyses the eye is not wholly clear, and so perhaps this kind of hierarchical structure would be more clearly illustrated by a non-psychological example. A brick is 'form' relative to straw and mud (its matter—even so, straw and mud are themselves low-level substances); but the brick is 'matter' relative to a wall, which 'forms' the bricks but which is itself in turn 'matter' for the building: and the building, once it is used for occupation, is the matter which is 'formed' into a house. Whether something is considered *qua* form or *qua* matter is a function of the description under which it is put.

Dualism is out of the question in this picture. (Like everyone else, I am of course puzzled and embarrassed by *DA* 3. 5; I shall return to that in a final postscript.) The form–matter (*psuchē*–body) distinction gives no comfort to any form of dualism—indeed, quite the reverse. It is no accident that in order to get a grip on the 'body' side of the distinction we had to resort to the myth of Adam's creation. Ackrill (1972–3) finds it problematic for Aristotle that we cannot talk about the *psuchē* and the body as distinct from each other; he thinks that the contrast Aristotle needs between form and matter is in danger of becoming incoherent if we cannot do so. I would rather turn the tables: it is precisely *because* we cannot make sense either of the *psuchē* without the matter, nor the matter without the *psuchē*, that there is no toehold for dualism. This claim needs a little expansion.

Some forms, which are less intricate than are the *psuchē*-forms of organisms, can be separated in thought from the matter in which they inhere. 'As a circle may exist in bronze or stone or wood, it seems plain that these, the bronze or the stone, are no part of the essence [*ousia*] of the circle, since it is found apart from them' (*Metaph.* 1036ᵃ32–4). But as Furth (1978) notes, artefacts are poor examples of the form–matter relation when we are considering the most important and interesting substances: animals. The greater the intricacy and complexity of the form, the stronger the constraints imposed by it on its matter, and vice versa. As Aristotle continues, a few lines after the *Metaphysics* extract just quoted: 'for example, the form of man is always found in flesh and bones and parts of this kind: are these also parts of the form (*eidos*) and the formula (*logos*)? No: they are matter: but because man is not found also in matter other than these, *we are not able to perform the abstraction*' (*Metaph.* 1036ᵇ3–7). Aristotle thus recognized that some forms could be 'abstracted' from matter, and others could not; there will be grades of dependence here. Statues are 'independent' to a large extent: a statue of Socrates can be realized in numerous materials (but not by such things as water-vapour, note). Closer to our concerns: subordinate psychological functions, such as 'being angry', can be analysed into form and matter, which can then be treated 'independently'; cf. the well-known passage 403ᵃ29–ᵇ3:

But the student of nature (*phusikos*) and the dialectician would each give their own definitions of what anger is. The dialectician would describe it as a desire to retaliate, or something like not that; the student of nature would think of it as a boiling of the blood and hot stuff around the heart. Of these, the latter gives the matter, the former the form and principle.

This point can be linked to the claim made above, that the precise form that any specific capacity takes will be partly determined by the matter of the organ or organs that are the physically responsible basis. 'Seeing', like anger, can be studied by the 'student of nature' and by the 'dialectician'; and since different animals have different kinds of eyes, the dialectician's description will be, in the sense outlined above, 'independent' of that provided by the student of nature.

If an accurate description of the 'matter' side of the distinction provides sufficient conditions for the form, in other words for the thing in question being 'what it is to be' that thing, this is theoretically important—since it has implications for the sophistication of the substance with which we are dealing— but gives no cause for concern. There will be degrees of (mutual) form–matter implication, and degrees of conceptual entailment between them. It is for example necessary, but not sufficient, that the matter of a heap have some height:

that the matter of a threshold be solid: but these are minimal and non-specific constraints between form and matter, and the substances in question are unsophisticated, low-level ones. At the other extreme, Aristotle seems to think that the complex system of organs that make up 'a [human] natural body that has life potentially' is well-nigh sufficient for it to be a human individual; and there will be all sorts of shadings of constraints between these extremes: consider for instance a statue, or a corn-grinding machine. Sometimes one can consider an animal under its form-description, and at others under its matter description—just as we can consider someone *qua* son, or *qua* man. Being a man is a necessary and sufficient condition for being a son;[4] but we are none the less concerned with different aspects of the individual when we think of him under each description.

Moreover, if the form—matter distinction licenses dualism, it would license far too much. We would have to admit dualism for grass just as much as for Greeks; equally we would have to admit it for metabolism as well as mind. For the *psuchē* tells us 'what it is to be' an organism; and what it is to be a man is to have a *psuchē* which, *inter alia*, includes digestion and movement. (This is, incidentally, wholly compatible with the fact that the highest capacities should be accorded the greatest weight when we are studying any animal. What is distinctive about man is his capacity for reason—the other capacities, although essential to him, do not mark him out from animals. So evidently the highest capacities will be those of most interest to the investigator of *this* animal species.) The *psuchē* is the unity of the several capacities that make something a dog, or a human being. It is the 'actuality' (*energeia*) of the organism; and many of its consituent functions, such as sight, are actualities of specific bodily parts, as Aristotle says at 413^a5-6; see also *PA* 646^b11 ff. and 656^a2-3.

It is interesting to speculate what Aristotle would want to say about science-fiction robots or science-fiction Martians. 'The form of man is always found in flesh and bones': would he accept that it might be realized in other matter: that although the physical structure that in fact makes up human beings is sufficient for something to be a man, it might not be necessary? In such a case what would be necessary would be the right degree and the right nature of the complexity in the structure that underpins the individual interlocking capacities (rather as solidity, but not invariably being made of stone, is necessary for something to be a threshold). Speculation is of course idle; but the fact that he seems to be treating this truism as an empirical point (as of course it still is: science fantasy here is still far from fact) suggests that he could be flexible about this. A more down-to-earth speculation might concern what he would wish to say about individual capacities like 'sight': would he agree that a (sophisticated; complex) robot that could move about, pick things up, describe colours etc. could really 'see'?

We shall return to draw out the implications of all this in the third section. First, though, we should look at the successor-concept to *psuchē*: 'mind'.

---

[4] Here, evidently, I have to drop the example of Adam!

II. The Mind

Descartes's concerns in the *Meditations* were epistemological. Aristotle's, in the *De Anima*, were not; his view of the relation of epistemology to science is economically illustrated by a comment in *Metaph.* 1031^{b}6–7: 'there is knowledge of something only when we have grasped its essence'. Yet with Descartes epistemology came first, giving rise to ontology; and ever since then, philosophers (at least in the English-language traditions) have been saddled with a notion of 'mind' that stems directly from epistemological concerns.

Descartes needed a foundation of certainty wherefrom to combat the sceptic. He needed something which, as Hume was to put it, 'never deceives' *First Enquiry* (1748), § VII, pt. i, para. 52 = (1963), 66. This Descartes found in consciousness:

As to [the proposition]...*that nothing can be in me, that is, in my mind, of which I am not conscious*, I have proved it in the *Meditations*, and it follows from the fact that the soul is distinct from the body and that its essence is to think. (Descartes 1641 = Kenny 1970, 90.)

How he reached this conclusion is independently absorbing, of course; but just as intriguing is the sheer speed with which he moved from Aristotle's *psuchē* to the conscious *mens*. We begin the *Second Meditation* with a fairly accurate description of the individual: starting with the material body and then listing the *psuchē* functions in a roughly correct hierarchical order. This description of the human was, it is true, by the time Descartes wrote (1641) contaminated by the need felt by the Christian Fathers to inject into it a separable and immortal vehicle for the *psuchē*, a 'wind, flame, or ether'; and it also neglected the imagination (but then I would admit that Aristotle's discussion of the imagination is intricate and hard to follow[5]):

In the first place, then, I considered myself as having a face, arms, and all that system of bones and flesh as seen in a corpse which I designated by the name of body. In addition to this I considered that I was nourished, that I walked, that I felt, and that I thought, and I referred all these actions to the soul; but I did not stop to consider what the soul was, or if I did stop, I imagined that it was something extremely rare and subtle like a wind, a flame, or an ether, which was spread through my grosser parts. (Descartes 1637–41 = Haldane–Ross 1967, i. 151).

But after turning *one* page, we find:

But what then am I? A thing which thinks. What is a thing that thinks? It is a thing which doubts, understands, conceives, affirms, denies, wills, refuses, which also imagines and feels. (ibid 153.)

[5] This seems to me to be because Aristotle was himself somewhat confused about it. As just one example, consider his hesitation over whether non-human animals have imagination; contrast *de An.* 414^{b}16 and 415^{a}10 with 413^{b}22, and see also the uncertain 428^{a}8–11.

The equation of 'thinking thing' with 'conscious thing' is spelt out in the 'Arguments Concerning the Existence of God':

Thought is a word that covers everything that exists in us in such a way that we are immediately conscious of it. Thus all the operations of will, intellect, imagination, and of the senses are thoughts. (1637–41 = Haldane–Ross 1967, ii. 52.)

Finally, the transition from *psuchē* to mind and its contents is defended, on methodological grounds—using this extended notion of 'thought'—in the 'Reply to the Fifth Set of Objections':

...men in the earliest times did not distinguish in us that principle in virtue of which we are nourished, grow, and perform all those operations which we are common to us with the brutes apart from any thought, from that by which we think they called both by the single name *soul*...But I, perceiving that the principle by which we are nourished is wholly distinct from that by means of which we think, have declared that the name *soul* when used for both is equivocal; and I say that, when soul is taken to mean *the primary actuality* or *chief essence of man*, it must be understood to apply only to the principle by which we think, and I have called it by the name *mind*...in order to avoid ambiguity, D (37–41 = Haldane–Ross 1967, ii 210.)

Adopted and reinforced by the British Empiricists, this picture is one with which philosophers in the English-language tradition have been struggling ever since. By and large it did not impress writers and poets (recall Wordsworth or Coleridge; but there are countless more examples—see Whyte (1962), and was not supreme in philosophy in Continental Europe. But it drastically coloured the birth of scientific psychology: Wilhelm Wundt's 'new science' rested entirely on one methodology—conscious introspection. Anything which could not be introspected had to be consigned to his *Völkerpsychologie*.

The sheer novelty of this should not go unremarked. The verb 'being conscious of', in its present (range of) sense(s), dates in English from around 1620, and the noun 'consciousness' does not appear until 1678; 'self-consciousness' does not crop up until 1690. The *term* existed, of course, before then; but it still retained its etymological meaning of 'shared knowledge' (*cum* + *scire*). French and German display the same pattern. It took the challenge of scepticism to hoist consciousness—as we now have it—to the pedestal it still occupies today. (And then, alas, such pseudo-entities as impressions and ideas; qualia, sense-data, raw feels, and 'representations'; and a notion of 'sensations' that includes alleged 'visual sensations' on an equal footing with genuine sensations such as pain—all these came in to put their feet up on the pedestal.)

Descartes's restriction of psychology to the conscious *mens* was too restrictive to convince completely, or to convince completely for very long. Moreover, in the nineteenth century Brentano had been reviving the medieval intuition that 'the mental' tended to be *about* something; and so 'intentionality' became another candidate-criterion for what it was to be mental. But intensional states need not be conscious states; one of Brentano's pupils was, after all, Freud—the rediscoverer of non-conscious psychological states.

Since that time, in this century, philosophers of mind (and also any psychologists over-impressed by the philosophers) have been stuck with a concept 'mind' which purports to accomodate both the Cartesian emphasis on consciousness, and Brentano's stress on intentionality. The two do not fit well together. Phenomena that fit the 'Cartesian criteria' of consciousness, such as feeling pain, are not easily regarded as being intentional; whereas the battery of pre-, sub-, un-, or simply non-conscious phenomena, which the 'intentionality criterion' can easily absorb, fail the Cartesian criteria. The latter criteria (of immediacy, incorrigibility, privileged access) are epistemological; what makes a proposition intentional is a logical matter. In short, the mental, and with it the mind, are a mess.[6]

Dualism becomes almost unavoidable once consciousness is elevated to the pinnacle where Descartes and those after him put it. This is because it gave us the 'theatre' picture of the mind—see Hume, *Treatise* (1739), Book I, pt. IV, § vi = (1965), 253—there is an 'inner' realm, and an 'outer', and the task ever since has been how to put them back together again.

In my (1988a) I have enlarged on the birth of the mind, and the difficulties with the concept of consciousness, at much greater length. For our present purposes the above rapid and simplified run-through will do; further features of, and problems with, the concept of mind will emerge more clearly when we contrast it with the notion it supplanted, that of *psuchē*.

III. Some Comparisons

It will be simplest to enumerate some of the many dimensions along which—I believe—the *psuchē* is theoretically superior to the mind; 'superior', in the sense that it provides a better framework within which contemporary study should proceed.

(A) The single most striking thing about the notion of *psuchē* is the unity (upon which it insists) for all the brain and behavioural sciences; a unity which holds as much for the study of humans as for other animals; a unity which treats humans as just one species in the animal kingdom—albeit the one that may interest us most—linked more or less closely to the other species by common *psuchē*-capacities. Digestion, whether in mice or men, is just as much a *psuchē*-logical matter as is the faculty of imagination. This is best seen if we consider just one capacity, that of perception.

We saw above that for Aristotle sensory capacities and capacities to move were inseparable, neither fully intelligible without the other (except for some organisms which, he thought, might have *just* the sense of touch). In modern terms this would mean that neither the study of perception, nor that of movement, can be comprehensively conducted independently of each other; the heart

---

[6] Squires (1971) has an entertaining description of this mess.

of the matter would come from the study of sensori-motor control (although it would not be independent of the study of wanting, or of pain-perception, either). By contrast, the contemporary notion of mind detaches the tip of the iceberg of mentality that is *consciousness*, and draws a old line between conscious phenomena and everything else (whether inside the head or not). It is in fact highly instructive to see just how Descartes 'saves' perception for the mind, because common sense does not naturally regard seeing as a form of *thought*; moreover, at first he dismisses perception on the grounds that it is not incorrigible, and incorrigibility was essential: 'I have thought I perceived many things during sleep that I recognised in my waking moments as not having been experienced at all' (Descartes 1637–4 = Haldane–Ross 1967 151). Only two pages later, though, he continues:

But it will be said that these phenomena are false [seeing light, hearing noises, feeling heat] and that I am dreaming. Let it be so; still it is at least quite certain that *it seems to me that* I see light, that I hear noise, that I feel heat. That cannot be false; properly speaking it is what in me is called feeling [*sentire*]; and used in this precise sense that is no other thing than thinking. (Ibid. 153.)

It is a simple exercise to modify this passage, substituting 'walking' for 'seeing': 'it is at least quite certain that *it seems to me that* I am walking…That cannot be false; properly speaking it is what in me is called walking.' Now: all would jib at calling 'seeming to walk' the 'proper', or 'precise', sense of 'walking'. Equally, though, Aristotle, and common sense, would jib at calling 'seeming to see' the 'proper' sense of 'see'. But after Descartes's sleight-of-hand in this passage, 'seeing' becomes a *mental* function, and walking remains a *bodily* one; and the Aristotelian insight into the interlocking nature of these capacities was lost.

This point should, however, be generalized, since it does not concern only perception. Aristotle's insistence upon the inextricability of capacities and functions which we *now* call 'mental' or 'physical' was neglected; the brute fact, or fact about brutes, that there must be an interrelationship of the study of the human and of other animals was denied; and dualism became the main issue for all theories of the mind.

Aristotle's insight was lost or neglected, that is, by the philosophers. Never so by the scientists. This may not be surprising, since many of the first generation of scientific psychologists trained as physiologists (like Wilhelm Wundt) before turning to psychology; and were dominated by the giant figure of von Helmholtz, a physicist, physiologist, and scientific polymath. The scientists by and large have taken for granted the interaction of the psychological and the physiological—perhaps we should describe them as *psuchē*-ologists. The great figures in the history of psychology made great strides in psychophysics; took it for granted that perception, emotion, consciousness, attention, and thinking itself presupposed movement, either major movements of limbs, or hard-to-detect movements of muscles (such as those around the eye); argued for what was once called a 'muscle sense' concept, but which is now called kinaesthesia or proprioception; studied questions to do with the localization of psychological functioning; pursued and developed comparative psychology; and of course emphasized developmental and evolutionary conjectures and theories. (See Scheerer (1984, 1987) for full discussion of this.)

Essentially the same point can be made if we do indeed look at developmental psychology. 'Cartesian-based' psychology either neglects (Wundt) or mishandles (Locke) developmental considerations. But the form—matter doctrine presupposes the gradual articulation of a full-formed individual from more primitive low-level substances and capacities; this holds true whether we consider the theory as physiologists or as psychologists. The complete organism develops steadily out of the catamenial mass and the sperma, with progressive differentiation and articulation—first with homoiomerous stuffs, still very low-level substances, and then with anhomoiomerous organs such as the eye, the hand, or the respiratory or reproductive organs. See for instance PA 646^{b}5–24:

> ...it must necessarily be that the elementary material exists for the sake of the homogeneous parts, seeing that these are genetically posterior to it, just as the heterogeneous parts are posterior genetically to them. For these heterogeneous parts have reached the end and goal, having the third degree of composition, in which degree generation or development often attains its final term. Animals, then, are composed of homogeneous parts, and are also composed of heterogeneous parts. The former, however, exist for the sake of the latter. For the active functions and operations of the body are carried on by these; that is, by the heterogeneous parts.

As the physical organs come into being, so the *psuchē*-logical functions, activities, or capacities of the organism—which the 'parts' make possible—get developed, articulated, and refined.

(B) A second striking advantage of the *psuchē* over the mind (for contemporary psychology) is its insistence upon capacities or functions rather than upon individual mental events, and upon *types* rather than occasions of behaviour. Aristotle did not of course deny the existence of specific occasions of the exercise of capacities, indeed he presupposed them: 'perception is of particulars' (417^{b}22). But the 'particulars', the individual events and occasions, are not the phenomena with which the systematic study of organisms is concerned. This is a point that can scarcely be emphasized strongly enough, and its neglect lies at the heart of the present-day confusion between scientific and commonsense psychology. I have attempted in several places to argue for this, but will on this occasion borrow from a psychologist who is an ally in this matter:

> ...it is essential to recognise the fundamental divergence between the layman's and the psychologist's interest in explaining behaviour. The psychologist is not a layman who happens to know more facts in a more systematic way. Unlike the layman he explains on the level of the species, not on the level of individuals and individual behavioural episodes.
> ...Unlike the layman he is concerned with competence, not with what people do with their competences under normal circumstances. That human beings can do such things as road-crossing *at all* fascinates the psychologist, not that Jones happened to do it. (Russell 1984, 12-13.)

So it is the layman (or the philosopher who, misguidedly in my opinion, devises 'theories of action') who is concerned with how beliefs that p, or desires for *x*, explain actions such as 'A's cutting B dead in the street yesterday'. The psychologist attempts to find descriptions of behaviour which group it into patterns analogous to 'natural kind' categories in other sciences; then to identify the capacities ('competences') that can also be regarded as 'natural kind' capacities for the species in question; and then to show how the latter can help explain the former. And this is *exactly* what Aristotle is trying to do; except, of course, that he goes further and insists upon the necessary role of the study of the physiological structures and functions which underly these competences.

The picture deriving from Descartes lost this insight as well, because of the driving epistemological concern: the need to find some incorrigible foundation for human knowledge. That foundation seemed to lie in immediate conscious introspection of the *contents* of the mind—ideas. (Later: qualia, sense-date, sensations representations.) For: 'the perceptions of the mind are perfectly known' says Hume, *Treatise* (1739), Book II, pt. II, § vi = (1965) 346. These were the itemized building-blocks from which all the rest of our structure of knowledge was meant—somehow—to follow. Richard Rorty well expresses the contrast with the ancient Greek picture. In the Greek period there had not been

the conception of the human mind as an inner space in which both pains and clear and distinct ideas passed in review before a single Inner Eye. There were, to be sure, the notions of taking tacit thought, forming resolutions *in foro interno*, and the like. The novelty was the notion of a single inner space in which bodily and perceptual sensations ('confused ideas of sense and imagination' in Descartes' phrase), mathematical truths, moral rules, the idea of God, moods of depression, and all the rest of what we now call 'mental' were objects of quasi-observation.   (R. Rorty 1980, 50.)

The objects of internal gazings, and not the capacities of the mind (which might or might not include the capacity to gaze internally) bore the brunt of the epistemological burden; and ontology followed, since

[w]hat sets apart the ontologies of professional philosophers is that they are created in response to questions arising in other areas-specifically, epistemology, ethics, logic and semantics.   (R. Rorty 1970, 276.)

(Indeed—and this is in parenthesis—I have been tempted to take an implication of this point further, into the realm of ethics. If, with Aristotle, you emphasize capacities, traits, states of character, rather than individual items or events, then the contemporary distinction between 'moral'—roughly: 'other-regarding')—and 'prudential'—roughly: 'self-regarding'—becomes boring and secondary. For a character-*trait*, such as courageousness, can evidently be exercised both to save others and to save oneself (just as perception is the same capacity, no matter whether it is exercised to watch a pornographic film or a tiger-cub at play). Some of the excellences (*aretai*) are more often exercised in a way that is predominantly self-regarding, such as the excellence of temperance; others more often affect others (such as truth-telling, which none the less has its self-regarding aspects; justice at the other extreme is always other-regarding). But very many will be like courageousness—indifferently self- and other-regarding. The primary interest, for the writer on ethics ('ethics' is a better word than 'morals', since the latter strongly suggests a restriction to other-regarding behaviours), lies in the states of character, *however* they find their realization. Perhaps, however, some would think this a flaw in character-based ethical systems; it seems to me to be a most liberating advantage. Whatever the judgement, it stems directly from Aristotle's focus on the capacities and competences of the individual, rather than on the agent's occurrent mental acts and occasions of behaviour.)

(C) This leads directly into a third great merit of the Aristotelian account of the *psuchē*, when contrasted with the mind: its emphasis on activity, particularly social activity. This should not be surprising, when we recall that man's highest good, *eudaimonia*, is twice glossed in the *EN*—1095ᵃ19, and 1098ᵇ20–1—as 'living well and doing well' (*eu zēn, eu prattein*). In the same work, at 1112ᵇ31–2, Aristotle remarks 'a man seems to be a source of actions'; even more firmly, we get later a positive definition of a man in the following terms: 'choice is either desiderative reason or ratiocinative desire, *and such a source of actions is a man*' (ibid. 1139ᵇ4–5). Much of the work is concerned to emphasize that we become what we are by our actions and our choices, and 'living well and doing well' will essentially involve social activity, since 'man is a political creature, who by nature lives with others' (*EN* 1169ᵇ18–19).

Contrast the picture fostered by the Cartesian *mens*. We are locked into our solipsistic consciousness; bothered about how to establish that there is anything outside it, let alone whether there are other minds.[7] If the mind is an inner theatre, then if the 'I' exists at all—which Hume was the first to deny—this 'I' is passive, a spectator of the 'confused ideas of sense and imagination'. Activity must become uncertain; for, inasmuch as 'seeing' has been reduced to 'seeming to see', so we will be unable to distinguish between 'acting' and 'seeming to act'. In the end, if one follows the familiar arguments of such as Wittgenstein and Strawson, the position breaks down into incoherence: not only was Hume right in saying that we could not get a viable notion of what 'I' might be, but we cannot even get a viable notion of the immediate contents of the mind, prior to all else.

Few are now solipsists; and most believe that the Cartesian sceptic can be handled (although not all are sure just how to do so). But the legacy of the lonely ego crying in the wilderness is still with us, in the updated form of the thought-experiment that we might (all?) be brains in vats; or in the form of the thought that there is 'something that it is like' to be me, something that is in principle ineffable and incommunicable. (However these last few remarks are at present no more than notes for a longer essay.)

(D) The difference just drawn between the Aristotelian emphasis on *competences*, and the post-Cartesian emphasis on individual mental *items*, in turn leads in to a

---

[7] Contrast here *EN* 1169ᵇ33–5: 'we can contemplate our neighbours better than ourselves and their actions better than our own'.

fourth merit of the Aristotelian *psuchē*. That is, it insists upon the heterogeneity of the *psuchē*-logical. We saw, in the first quotation from Rorty above, that in the Cartesian *mens* ideas of God, moods of depression, moral rules, bodily and perceptual sensations, etc., are all on an equal footing, all actors on the theatre of the mind that is incorrigibly scrutinized by an Inner Eye. So long as some mental content is an object of the conscious introspective gaze, it is just another 'idea'— on all fours with any other mental content ('idea') that is equally so scrutable. (Once thinking is modelled on conscious perception, then the contents of the mind become as homogeneous as are the visible patterns of the external world. The paradox here is, of course, that Descartes only 'saved' perception for the mind by modelling it on thinking: 'see' had to be interpreted as 'seeming to [thinking that we] see'. This is a *thoroughly* vicious circle, incidentally.)

By contrast we find in Aristotle that 'there seem to be indefinitely many parts of the human *psuchē*' (*DA* 432^{a}24). And certainly, since metabolic and reproductive capacities are essentially included along with thinking and imagination, this of course must be so. Moreover, as we saw in the first section, 'the same' capacity takes on different shapes and forms depending upon its physical realization, and depending upon *psuchē*-logical holism—upon what other capacities surround and colour its exercise. But even if for whatever reason we wanted to expel the 'non-mental' capacities from the Aristotelian *psuchē*, and to forget the implicit holism, we ought *still* to prefer Aristotelian heterogeneity to Cartesian homogeneity. Consider just one mental occurrence, feeling pain. Some pains are the result of pinpricks; others of too much drinking the previous night; others of a recent bereavement—these are very different sorts of thing! 'Pain' picks out states that are not at all homogeneous; and yet this is but *one* psychological term. When we extend the point and consider the problems of calling 'mental' both the sensation of a pinprick, and an ascription to someone of a generous disposition or an Oedipal complex, then the absurdity of thinking that there is anything of importance that all mental phenomena have in common becomes manifest.

Part of the difficulty is the inheritance of the theatre model, with 'the mental' consisting of the element-like ideas illuminated by consciousness; that forced homogeneity on to conscious mental events. But when the notion of 'the mental' was enlarged by the use of intentionality as another criterion, the hold of the (Cartesian) idea that 'the mental' was somehow homogeneous did not disappear: 'the mental' was still thought to pick on a category of phenomena that was, in some special way, special. That is because 'the mental' is another way of talking of 'the contents of the mind'. If, as I have been arguing, 'the mind' is neither a coherent nor a useful notion, it would hardly be surprising if the category of 'the mental' is a failure too.

Psuchē includes everything 'mind' includes, and more besides: is it not therefore even *more* diffuse, unhelpful, incoherent? No; because the *psuchē* is highly structured—developmentally, in the sense that mature organs and capacities are refined and articulated out of more primitive stuff and function; 'vertically', in the sense that subordinate *psuchē*-capacities make possible the exercise of higher, more sophisticated, ones; and 'horizontally', in the sense that different animals have their own idiosyncratic ways of, and organs for, exercising capacities like reproducing, smelling, etc. It thus allows for and indeed requires a theoretical division of *psuchē*-capacities (and hence *inter alia* of the capacities we now call 'mental') into distinct or distinguishable kinds which become the objects of related and systematic investigations by the behavioural and brain sciences. The division, however, is based upon scientific-systematic considerations rather than upon epistemological ones.

(E) A related advantage of Aristotle's account, my fifth, is I know likely to attract even less agreement than the preceding ones. That is, that he paid absolutely no attention to consciousness *per se*. Hamlyn notes and deplores this:

…there is an almost total neglect of any problem arising from psycho-physical dualism and the facts of consciousness. Such problems do not seem to arise for him. The reason appears to be that concepts like that of consciousness do not figure in his conceptual scheme at all; they play no part in his analysis of perception, thought, etc. (Nor do they play any significant role in Greek thought in general.) It is this perhaps that gives his definition of the soul itself a certain inadequacy for the modern reader.   (Hamlyn 1968 p. xiii.)

We might set against this a nice comment by Joynt:

Consciousness is like the Trinity; if it is explained so that you understand it, it hasn't been explained correctly.   (Joynt 1981, 108.)

I cannot here defend what I realise to be a prima facie implausible position: that Aristotle did not need any such notion as that of consciousness. I have attempted to pursue this claim in my (1974) and (1988*b*). All I would wish to argue now is that we in the twentieth century have little difficulty in understanding the works of the ancient Greek 'psychological dramatists' such as Sophocles, Euripides, and Menander, and yet—as Hamlyn rightly notes—they had no concern with consciousness either; but the striking point is that nobody believes that these writers (I am deliberately avoiding mention of the philosophers) have 'left anything out'. The implication is that anything said in terms of consciousness could equally-well be said without it; and the conclusion to be drawn is that maybe— just maybe!—contemporary psychology would be better off describing its subject-matter without the notion too. I wish only to remind the reader of my earlier comment, the novelty of the term in its present sense; unheard-of before the seventeenth century.

(F) Finally, I would like to draw out some parallels between Aristotle's position and what I take to be the most promising form of the many psychological theories that fall under the umbrella-term of 'functionalism'.[8] As already

---

[8] I am well aware that it is anachronistic and misleading to attempt to force Aristotle into the pigeonholes provided by today's jargon of 'identity theories', 'materialism', 'central state identity theories', etc.; but there are unmistakeable echoes of Aristotle in contemporary scientific functionalism, giving us parallels we can exploit profitably.

mentioned (in the 'Introduction' on my first page) I am concerned with functionalism as it engages scientific psychologists; there are numerous brands of functionalism in philosophical psychology, and in common sense psychology, with which I am not—here—concerned. The most fruitful brand of functionalism, to my mind, links the study of psychology, neuropsychology, and neurophysiology in the following manner. We find numerous levels of description of activity: some at a level that is indubitably 'psychological' (feeling angry); others at a level that is just as obviously 'neurophysiological' (neuronal firings); but also at all sorts of levels in between (comparator functions in the amygdala; tecture-gradient detectors in the visual cortex; face-recognition capacities in the right hemisphere; and so on and so forth). Such a view conceives of the mind–brain relationship in a hierarchical manner that is perfectly mirrored by Aristotle's picture of the hierarchical form–matter relation. We lose little, and gain much, by comparing his terminology of 'form' and 'matter' with the contemporary jargon of 'function' and 'structure'.

Just as the form–matter distinction is relative to a level of description (a wall is a form for its constituent bricks; but in turn is also matter for a building) so is the function–structure distinction: the amygdala in the rat is the 'structure', the 'comparator' (which as it happens has the function of comparing incoming with expected stimuli); but one might rather study the function involved (which as it happens is performed by the amygdala). We can consider this complex phenomenon under either 'form/function' or 'matter/structure' description, just as we can regard Fido either as a dog, or as a herder of sheep. Aristotle would easily recognize the insight provided by contemporary computer science that whether something is considered to be 'hardware' or 'software' depends on the angle chosen. (Someone writing a programme in ADA—a very sophisticated programming language—will treat everything more subordinate as 'hardware'; but the 'hardware' concerned will presuppose many programs: BASIC, for instance, not to mention the assembly code and the machine code. All these are programs—software—relative to what lies beneath each of them, and are hardware relative to what lies above.)

Aristotle is in advance of many contemporary 'cognitive scientists' in understanding that both the 'dialectician' and the 'student of nature' can contribute to the study of human competences. He is not a 'top-down' theorist; at no point does he suggest that the dialectician gives the student of nature his marching-orders, and therefore he would deny, contrary to many contemporary theorists, that the direction of explanation must be only one-way. It is easy to read Aristotle as suggesting that each scientist can enter into the study of a capacity such as visual perception at any level he chooses: no priority. Nothing in Aristotle's biological writings says this explicitly, but I suggest that it is an inevitable implication of his picture of the form–matter relation, and of what it is to be a substance. It is surely evident that different people are interested in straw and mud; in bricks; in walls; in buildings; and in houses. In this I suggest he is entirely right, and that those who argue that the direction of explanation in

psychology must be one-way and 'top-down' are wholly wrong; the only support
I need for this claim is that in real scientific psychology the scientists are, and
always have been, operating on many levels simultaneously.

The fact that most of the time he got his physiology wrong (he thought that
the brain was there to cool the blood, and that the heart was the central organ for
sensation and cognition—(but he already suspected that the brain might be the
governing organ, see *Metaph.* 1035ᵇ26–7) is not particularly relevant. But one
could also say that it is highly relevant, and for the following reason. In the
section on the *psuchē* above I speculated about what Aristotle might say about
science-fictional robots or Martians. Contemporary writers often claim that the
'hardware' (neurons rather than silicon chips) is or ought to be irrelevant to contemporary psychology; it is claimed to be a fact that systems other than animal
organisms can perform many of the functions that we can perform too. So the
precise nature of the physical 'hardware' is irrelevant to *interesting* generalizations
about psychological competetence: these latter transcend the precise nature of
their actual 'matter'.[9]

This I suggest is something which a contemporary Aristotle could accept, but
which he would also wish to restrain. Not all complex systems can provide the
'matter' ('hardware') for a *psuchē*-competence. Form puts constraints on matter,
and vice versa. So we find real and actual variations in the ways in which different
organisms realize the same *psuchē*-logical functions. As we have seen, Aristotle
noted that different organisms breathed, and perceived, by different mechanisms
and physical structure. If silicon chips, Martian plasma, or—to cite some of the
wilder examples in the literature—sets of performing fleas, the banking system of
Bolivia, the population of China—could provide the physical realization of the
form/function...then fine. The brute fact is that most of them cannot, because
they will not have the right form-capacities: they will lack the necessary speed,
organization, or flexibility. The result is that Aristotle could admit the sheer
possibility of so-called 'multiple realizability'; but equally would insist that given
the facts at our disposal we will get at best 'variable realizability': form sets very
substantial constraints on matter, and on the organization of matter.

I propose that this too is the direction in which contemporary science is going.
It is no accident that the (serial) von Neumann machines which have attempted
to model human competence are increasingly giving way to parallel machines, the
PDP ('Parallel Distributed Processing') or 'connectionist' systems; and it is
equally no accident that PDP systems are very heavily biologically constrained.
That is, many of them are modelled very explicitly upon what we know or believe
to be true of animal brains. My point here is that the insight that comes (perhaps
indirectly, but certainly implicitly) from Aristotle is certainly right: maybe
chunks of stone, wood, and marble can act as a threshold; but not chunks of
butter, ants' nests, or soufflé. So also neural networks do indeed underpin our
various *pauchē*-competences; and systems other than ours, *by* modelling the

[9] For this see esp. Fodor (1981), 8.

structure, might also model the competences. But not bankers in Bolivia, performing fleas, nor even the population of China. Thus we have principled reasons for accepting 'variable' realizability of a macro competence by micro states. This is not problematic: why should it be? The variable realizability of 'macro' states by 'micro' states certainly holds true throughout physics, that superego of the sciences. But we can resist the step from 'variable' to 'multiple', simply for the reasons that Aristotle provides: matter puts constraints on form, and vice versa.

This, then, is my attempt to argue (*a*) that we *should* return from the mind to the *psuchē*; and (*b*) that indirectly and without realizing it we have in fact been doing so for some time.

Final Embarrassed Postscript

What to do with *DA* 3. 5? Here Aristotle—whom I have acclaimed so far as every physicalist's ideal role-model—seems to put himself very resoundingly in the dualists' camp. I cannot understand this chapter, and none of the secondary literature has so far helped me to do so. Thus I will end this paper with one or two comments which may help to mitigate the difficulty; all the same I have to say that I wish he had never written this chapter.

(A) If we have dualism here—and such a conclusion is hard to avoid, given e.g. 430ª23: 'this alone is immortal and eternal'—it is a dualism unlike any version of dualism with which we are now familiar. Certainly all periods and all cultures have tried to draw some line somewhere between what rots in the earth after death, and what somehow survives. *Where* the line is drawn varies from period to period and from culture to culture (contrast for instance Homer with the Old Testament; or indeed the Socrates who does or might survive death in Plato's *Apology* with Socrates' *psuchē* trapped by the body in Plato's *Phaedo*). With Aristotle (in the problematic chapter in question) we find the apparent survival of the 'active intellect'. Without the active intellect the so-called passive intellect 'thinks nothing' (*outhen noei*; 430ª25). The role of the active intellect is compared to that of light, which 'makes potential colours into actual colours' (430ª15–17). So presumably the passive intellect can no more think without the active intellect than the eye can see colours without light. But his makes it hard to consider the active intellect as being itself a form *of thought*; rather, it seems to be what makes thinking possible. If indeed this is what Aristotle says to be 'immortal and eternal', it is difficult to get personally engaged in, or excited by, its immortality: it would be nothing like *me* that survives bodily death. Perhaps the best comparison here would be with Heraclitus: the 'fiery' *psuchē*, after the death of the body, joins the cosmic bonfire, and enjoys the eternal circuit described in his cosmology; but the bit of flame or aether that was Heraclitus' *psuchē* is no longer *Heraclitus*.

(B) Aristotle believed that no physical stuff could take on the form of an object X unless it itself was non-X. Crudely: a blue eye would not be able to see blue things. Thus the stuff of the eye must be colourless (water), precisely because it can in fact see all colours. By parity of reasoning the organ of thinking cannot have a specific physical nature, because if so it could not contemplate that very nature. But the intellect can consider 'all things' (429^a18); therefore it cannot be physically realized in any of them. Therefore it cannot be physically realized at all. We can disagree with this—it is, to put it mildly, hard to understand Aristotle's insistence that perceiving and thinking is a matter of 'receiving the form' and becoming 'identical with its object' (*DA* 3. 4. *passim*)[10]—but equally we should understand the theoretical background that forced such a conclusion on him.

(C) We should also accept that Aristotle's background theories affect the *De Anima* in a manner which owes little to the systematic study of the *psuchē* in which he is engaged. (Remember in this context how far Descartes's epistemology determined his ontology.) All substances are in-formed matter—*except* God, the prime mover. He is 'in essence actuality'; pure and unadulerated form. In the *Nicomachean Ethics* we discover that man can, to some extent, aspire to godhood, inasmuch as he is capable of contemplation (*theōria*). But if it is possible for a man—temporarily, maybe, and perhaps not fully—to share in this divine activity, this cannot be due to his physical embodiment, for it must be due to his share in the divine...and gods are not physical.

I do not like this very much. But I suspect that the problem of understanding *EN* 10. 6–10, and that of understanding *DA* 3. 5, are two sides of the same coin. Theological overtones invariably confuse philosophical or scientific debates. When worried by *DA* 3. 5, it is illuminating to consider the difficulties we too have of reconciling Christian doctrines with what we get from scientific, and everyday, descriptions of the nature of the individual. Aristotle had a problem; but then so does everyone else. Aristotle's version of immortality is more like that of Heraclitus than that of contemporary Christianity; we (you, I, Heraclitus) do not survive as ourselves, but something else does: the Heraclitean fire, or the Aristotelian light of the intellect.

(D) All the above still leaves questions unanswered. Is the body a necessary condition for thinking in general, and the active intellect in particular? From the rest of the *De Anima* it would appear so. But in that case the active intellect becomes

---

[10] The idea that the eye 'takes on the form' of the object is said by Barnes to be 'open to devastatingly obvious attack on both empirical and logical grounds: when I see something square, there is simply no part of my eye which becomes square' ($1979b$, 38). I am not so sure that this empirically true fact is an objection. Why should the form of pinkness itself be pink? A clearer example is that of a circle: the form of a circle might be 'taken on' by something becoming circular, but also by something realizing in some 'language of thought' way the formula πr^2; or realizing some linguistic definition of circularity; or by a sequence of zeros and units, as indeed it would be in a digital computer. The plausibility of any of these alternatives is not at issue; what matters is that there could be an indeterminate numbers of ways in which the eye could 'take on the form' of shapes, colours etc. *Mutatis mutandis*, the same could hold true of the intellect.

an 'epiphenomenon', which is 'supervenient' on the human organism. I myself think that talk of 'epiphenomena' and of 'supervenience', are no more than high-sounding terms for carpets under which issues get swept. However that may be, though, Aristotle has told us nothing substantial about this form of imperishability and immortality. But *if* this is 'dualism', then committed dualists of today should want no part of it.

8

EXPLAINING VARIOUS FORMS OF LIVING

ALAN CODE
JULIUS MORAVCSIK

I. Introduction

'HUMANS have legs to help them with locomotion.' 'Our power to think enables us to grasp truths.' What kind of statements are these? Do they explain cognitive and physical phenomena? Are they consequences of definitions? Are they compatible with other kinds of definitions and explanations, and if so, do they call for supplementation by other types of explanations and definitions? These philosophical questions need to be answered in order to understand the frameworks within which philosophers of the past and thinkers of the present, be they social scientists or philosophers, define and explain human functioning in general and cognition in particular.

Since in her attempts to address such questions as these the contemporary philosopher of mind becomes centrally concerned with the relationship between mental phenomena and physical events or processes, one might suppose that in order to understand Aristotle's hylomorphic psychology we should try to determine how on his view the psychological and the physical are related, and consider what affinities that view may have with various contemporary anti-dualist positions such as materialism and physicalism. However, those undertaking this project often presuppose that the psychological and the physical can be distinguished in such a way as to form mutually exclusive classes, something that we are not in a position to do if we confine ourselves to an Aristotelian vocabulary. Aristotle himself does not have a sharp contrast between the psychological and the physical because, in so far as he has a conception of the physical, the physical is just the natural, and so he treats the psychological as a part of the physical. In this paper we explain briefly why this is so, and then make some remarks and observations about the framework he is using. Our way of looking at that framework involves attributing to Aristotle ideas and principles quite different from those employed in a theory in the contemporary philosophy of mind dubbed 'functionalism'—a view sometimes thought to bear striking similarities to Aristotelian hylomorphism. In this paper we try to clarify our own view by discussing the relation of hylomorphism to functionalism. As will emerge, our argument against functionalist interpretations of Aristotle is not in aid of the claim that some alternative solution to the problems to which functionalism is a response better captures the essence of his psychology, but rather stems from our belief that Aristotle was confronting a different set of concerns and issues.

We start by noting that in the very first chapter of the *De Anima* Aristotle argues that the study of the soul, or at least that part of it concerned with the emotions, is a task to be undertaken by the *phusikos* (403ᵃ27–8),[1] or natural scientist. The *phusikos* is somebody who investigates natural/physical things (*ta phusika*). It is important to see that for Aristotle plants, animals, and elemental bodies are 'physical', but artefacts such as tables and chairs are not. He contrasts *ta phusika* with artefacts by stating that only the former are endowed with a nature (*phusis*), where the nature of a natural thing is the internal source (*arche*) of change (*kinesis*) and resistance to change which belongs to that thing in its own right (*Ph.* 192ᵇ13–14, 32). A natural thing is a composite of matter and form, and although it is correct to apply the term 'nature' to both, strictly speaking and in the primary sense, the *ousia* of the thing is called its 'nature' (*Metaph.* 1015ᵃ13–16). The *ousia* of a thing is its form, or essence (*Metaph.* 1041ᵇ27–8 and ᵇ7–8), and hence the nature of a natural thing is its substantial form.

In the case of a living thing, its soul, and hence its form, is its nature, and its 'psychological' activity is the exercise (*energeia*) of the various capacities and potentialities (*dunameis*) assigned to its soul. Since the natural/physical activity of a thing just is the activity due to its nature, it follows that for a living thing its natural/physical activity just is its psychological activity. That is, on Aristotle's hylomorphic analysis the soul is 'physical' in the only sense of that term available to him.

Also in the introductory chapter, as a part of his argument that the soul is to be studied by the *phusikos*, Aristotle remarks that an emotion should be defined as a certain kind of *kinesis*—a *kinesis* that is (i) *of* such and such a body, or part of the body, or some *dunamis* (of the body), (ii) *by* the agency of something *X*, and (iii) *for* the sake of something *Y* (403ᵃ26–7). He is here engaged in the preliminary task of describing the general form that such definitions should take, and in this context is not concerned to provide us with a specific definition that fully conforms to this pattern. Such a definition would be an end-product of inquiry, not a guideline that structures inquiry. However, he does tell us that to say that anger is 'blood, or hot stuff boiling around the heart' is to give the matter, and to say that it is 'desire for retaliation' is to give the form. Without attempting to give full-scale interpretation of this passage, we wish to confine ourselves to the following observations. First, *kinesis* is not here to be construed as a physiological process as opposed to a psychological process. In the cases under consideration, a *kinesis* is simply the actuality of some potentiality possessed by the body, or one of its organs.[2] It is the anger itself that is the *kinesis*, not some underlying

---

[1] In this paper, all references starting with book and chapter are to the *De Anima*.

[2] We note that in this pre-theoretical passage Aristotle is not contrasting *kinesis* with *energeia*, and in this context even activities in which an end inheres fall under the rubric '*kinesis*'.

physiological state that can be specified independently of the other two factors (agent and purpose). Secondly, and in conformity with the general pattern of definition indicated above, the boiling of the blood is not matter for the anger; rather, the boiling is a *kinesis* of blood, the blood being a part of the body, and hence matter. Thus he is not indicating that creatures with very different physiologies could be in the same emotional state (anger) just so long as they have some physiological process that plays the right kind of functional role (loosely described as 'desire for retaliation').

Of course the term 'nature' does apply (though not in the primary way) to the matter, and Aristotle can draw a distinction within the natural between the material and the formal. Hence he also treats activity and behaviour that are due to the matter of a living thing as 'natural'. However, in his account of living things he does not simply equate the matter with the 'physical', or 'natural'. If 'materialism' is a view according to which principles governing the matter of a natural/physical entity are sufficient for all the behaviour and changes it undergoes *qua* natural/physical thing, then neither his psychology nor his physics is materialist.

Let us now see how this conception of nature is related to teleological notions. This will help place in perspective the relation between Aristotle's explanations and contemporary functionalism.

II. Teleological and Non-teleological Definitions and Explanations

There are at least three major families of teleological notions. The first is linked primarily to human, or human-like, purposive action. This family includes, but is not limited to, the concepts of aim, goal, what someone is after, plans, strategies, and the like. For example, in the right context, saying that Jones wants to get into medical school is to articulate his aim, and reference to this aim can explain some of his actions such as taking certain courses, studying hard, etc. According to some philosophers an adequate explanation of human action must always include more than merely teleological accounts in this sense.

A second group of teleological concepts characterizes *explanations* of what something accomplishes or how it functions—for example, explaining how someone works at her job, or explaining what something is for, or what it is supposed to do. For instance, in some contexts we explain our digestive system by showing how it enables the body to receive sustenance and hence help us to survive. As before, some philosophers think that such explanations always must be supplemented by non-teleological explanations.

Thirdly, there are concepts, primarily those pertaining to artefacts, that have a predominantly teleological content and are designated by words that themselves have *definitions* which explicitly mention or describe some function. For instance, a chair is something to sit on, a house provides shelter, etc. Looking ahead, our view contrasts with functionalist interpretations of Aristotle's psychology with respect to the use of this third type of teleological notion.

These families of notions can play roles in either theological or secular (natural) teleological theories. According to the theological version, the world is created and designed by God, and to give teleological definitions or explanations of things is to specify their place or role within God's intentional design. Although such accounts and their relationship to other types of definitions and explanations have figured prominently during various periods of Western philosophy, we shall lay them aside, since they are not relevant to the understanding of Aristotle's approach to human nature. Divine design and purpose, to be understood by an analogy with human purpose, presupposes a conception of deity similar to the Judaeo-Christian one. Aristotle's unmoved mover does not meet this condition, and no such account is invoked in the *De Anima*.

A natural teleological theory contains *both* functionally defined terms *and* teleological explanations, typically directed at biological and psychological phenomena. Such a theory can posit either general teleological processes or species-specific ones, and often posits both. For example, on the general level one might propose that members of living species propagate in order to maintain the species. On the level of the specific, one might propose that spiders have their unique web-weaving ability in order to catch food, and thus be capable of survival.

Although Aristotle is extremely interested in issues concerning human purposes or goals (in particular, in ethics and politics), this interest is not directly relevant to the topic at hand. Accordingly, we shall be ignoring it in order to concentrate instead upon the kinds of apparently teleological definitions and explanations that can be found in the *De Anima*, and to consider the sense in which they may be described as 'functional'. We know that teleological elements have important roles in Aristotelian explanations of nature, since they constitute one of the four factors that, according to Aristotle, need to be studied by anyone seeking an understanding of nature (e.g. *Ph.* 2. 198^{a}14–24). Our task here is to see precisely what role teleological notions play in his account of perceptual and cognitive phenomena.

In modern philosophical discussions the task of explaining cognition arises in the context of trying to determine what, if anything, makes cognition unique and different from mere physical or biological process. The rival theories compared are typically forms of materialism or physicalism, and forms of dualism. The Aristotelian context is quite different. At the core of his enterprise is the concern to characterize the explanatory principles that make living things different from non-living ones, and to exhibit the natures of different forms or manifestations of living. Thus the 'soul' is construed as that which enables a natural body to be a living thing (412^{a}19–21, 413^{a}20–31). The phenomena to be accounted for by the soul include nutrition, growth, appetite, perception, and thought. Aristotle sees all of these as having their sources within the organism, and consequently they show the living body to be a partially self-determining and self-maintaining entity.

For any one of the aspects of living mentioned, Aristotle wants to find some

form or definable structure, together with some power as the underlying explanatory configuration.[3] Perceiving, for instance, is the exercise of a certain power that
results from a definable structure in a bodily organ. The power in question is the
ability to receive a certain kind of sensible form without matter ($424^{a}17-19$); the
underlying structure is a mean state of the organ ($424^{b}1$). This explains why
Aristotle views the soul as both (i) structures in the living body ($424^{b}1-3$) and (ii)
ensuing powers (e.g. $413^{a}25-8$). This way of taking the notion of the soul as the
'form' of the living body seems strange only to those who think of 'form' as
necessarily to be analysed in terms of universals or properties of the sort familiar
to us from the philosophies of Moore and Russell. However, if one considers the
proposal from within a biological context, then the identification seems quite
natural. There must be something in the organism that makes certain kinds of
growth and development possible, and this is linked also to certain powers and
potentialities that the actual processes realize.

Such statements as these are not 'functional' in a contemporary philosophical
sense. They do not say that the soul, or its various aspects, are 'whatever it is that
performs for something (perhaps a human) a certain function'. Rather, they
attempt to characterize what it is that enables some elements of reality to have life
in them. In the course of this Aristotle appeals to certain powers and definable
structures. This is analogous to characterizing flexible materials in terms of various powers and structures that they need in order to be flexible. Such accounts
are not in any non-trivial sense 'functional'. At the same time, the accounts cited
do not imply materialism. There is nothing in the notion of structure, power,
and self-determination that would force one to take these either materialistically,
or for that matter, dualistically. Aristotle treats psychological activity as requiring definable structures, but does not hold that the elements that enter into the
specification of the form and structure are properties, features, powers, or
relations that belong to matter that can exist outside of the realization of some
enlivening potential. Thus although his hylomorphism is committed to the existence of physical/natural structures underlying perception and cognition, it is a
mistake to see these structures as arising from the powers of inanimate matter.

An account of an entity describing what it does need not be either 'functionalist' or materialist. Aristotle compares the living body to the seeing eye. The
seeing eye is simply an eye having sight ($412^{b}18-22$). This is hardly a 'functional'
account. Aristotle does not say that 'whatever (in all possible worlds) would
enable us to find our way around the world by recognition of colours, shapes,
etc., is what the seeing eye is'. We should not give Aristotle's 'What is *F*?'
questions anachronistic readings. Aristotle is not working with some conceptual
equivalent of the notion 'truth in *all* possible worlds', and here he is concerned
solely with the attempt to characterize the phenomena actually encountered in
nature. The characterization is supposed to show how nature works. He takes the

---

[3] The term 'structure' is here meant to correspond to Aristotle's notion of the *eidos*, or *logos*,
though it is not intended as a translation.

entity that is the eye for granted, and ascribes a certain natural structure and a certain natural power to it. Although the thought-experiment in which one considers counterfactual situations where something is the functional equivalent of an eye, but has a different material constituency, gives rise to fruitful contemporary questions, it none the less threatens to undermine Aristotle's own conception of bodily organs as *natural*. Being the functional equivalent of a natural organ does not make something natural. An artificial heart, regardless of how well it works, is none the less still an artefact, and not (in Aristotle's sense) *phusikē*, or 'physical'.

Aristotle does consider something like this kind of thought-experiment as part of the development of an *aporia* (puzzle) in *Metaph.* Z11 (1036ᵃ26–ᵇ20). The *aporia* concerns the question: 'which parts of a thing pertain to the form, and which are parts in the sense of matter?' Certain mathematical forms, such as *circle*, are observed sometimes made of bronze, sometimes of stone, sometimes of wood, etc. However, since the form can exist separately from bronze, stone, and so on, the bronze is simply matter, and is not a part of the form. In the *aporia* it is suggested that even in cases where some form is always observed embodied in the same way, none the less the situation is similar: nothing prevents the form from existing without that particular kind of embodiment. The example given is *man*. Although the form of man is always observed in flesh, bones, and the like, none the less we can (albeit with some difficulty) separate in thought the form from those particular materials. Since this example is given in the context of presenting an *aporia*, Aristotle is not here speaking in his own voice. It is clear, he writes, that this kind of thing is possible, although it is not clear in what cases it is possible (1036ᵃ7–8). Does he actually think that the case of man *is* like that of circle? After having stated the *aporia*, he answers that question in the negative— the case of man/flesh–bones is not like the circle/bronze case (1036ᵇ28). Therefore this passage should not be used to attribute to Aristotle the view that the form of man is 'compositionally plastic'.

We hasten to stress that there is plenty of evidence that when he deems it desirable, Aristotle can and does provide 'functional' definitions solely in terms of the contribution something makes either to something else, or to a larger element of which it is a component. For example, he characterizes a house as what gives us shelter against certain kinds of destruction such as wind, etc. (403ᵇ3–5). This is strongly functional, since it defines the entity in terms of what it can do for us. What would it be like for Aristotle to give this kind of functional account in his psychology? It would be to define seeing, for instance, as something like: 'whatever enables us to discriminate certain parts of the world (colours, shapes, etc.) in our daily interactions with the environment'. The general form of a functional definition of living would be: 'whatever enables us to continue to exist while exercising certain human capacities (themselves functionally defined)'. However, as we have seen, these are not definitions of *natures*.

We conclude this section by noting that there is a place where Aristotle does link the soul with functional organization. In *DA* 2. 4 (415ᵇ15–21) he says that the soul is that for the sake of which the bodily parts work, that for the sake of which they are organs. This, however, does not amount to a teleological definition of the soul, for as the passage shows, all that Aristotle wants to say here is that since it is the combination of the self-determining principles and other related powers that keep the body alive, the various parts of the body can be seen as working to maintain these very principles and powers. This certainly ascribes teleological roles to the various parts of the body, but does not define the soul itself, much less define it in 'functional terms'.

Having seen the limited way in which teleological elements enter Aristotle's analysis of what it is to live, let us now turn to consider explicitly a contemporary doctrine called 'functionalism', and see to what extent its patterns of analysis might resemble the Aristotelian ones.

III. Functionalism

There are many versions of functionalism current today. We shall be discussing only that version of functionalism which has its roots in analogies between computers and minds.[4] One analogy can be laid out in the following way. Accounts of computers distinguish between 'software' and 'hardware', between a program and the different material entities (machines and their actual processes) within which the program can be realized. On this view, our accounts of knowledge, belief, inference, etc., can be compared to accounts of 'software', and thus leave open the possibility that these phenomena can be realized in different ways by creatures, or even artefacts, having different material constituencies.

This contemporary kind of functionalism emerges as a response to two general philosophical concerns in the philosophy of mind.[5] First, there is the record of failure in the attempt to define mentalistic terms in either a behavioural or a materialist vocabulary. The second concern follows close upon the heels of the first. A philosopher who wants to be a materialist, but recognizes that mentalistic terms cannot simply be reduced to a materialist semantics, seeks a way both to eat his materialist cake and have an empirically adequate (and hence non-materialist) semantics for mentalistic terms.

The functionalist answer starts by interpreting mental and biological phenomena as sequences of states. This is supposed to be analogous to the workings of a computer, also as a sequence of states. In fact, we can characterize the workings of many things in this manner. As Ned Block shows,[6] one can think of the workings of Coke machines as sequences of states from the input of a dime (three quarters?) until the emission of a Coke bottle, with each state in the sequence determining its successor state.

States can be characterized at different levels of generality. Also, they can be

---

[4] Putnam (1966).
[5] For a good introduction to this view, see N. Block (1980), Introduction to Part III.
[6] Ibid. 173.

described in functional or in non-functional terms; non-functionally, by detailing the actual process, or functionally, by simply saying that a state *S* is whatever will take you from a non-functionally described state *S'* to *S"*.

Thinking of mental states as functional states gives the materialist a way out of the worries sketched above, for interpreting philosophical characterizations of belief, thought, feeling, etc., as *functional* descriptions allows the philosopher to remain absolutely non-committal as to how these states are realized. Functional states, and hence psychological states, are *compositionally plastic*. Our functionalist can be a materialist in her ontology, and none the less cheerfully admit that our talk about mental entities cannot be reduced to talk about matter. Her explanation of this fact is that mentalistic accounts are, one and all, functional accounts. She can embellish this story by allowing that we may link many functional states together, and (after having done so) see the entire chain of functional states as forming a bridge between non-functional states. Thus the functionalist can remain a materialist in her ontology, and yet accommodate the non-eliminative nature of our ordinary mentalistic talk.[7] Our present task is not to assess this analogy in terms of its alleged utility for the philosophy of mind, but rather to see to what extent it is useful for understanding what Aristotle says about the 'soul' and its parts. We have already shown that Aristotle's psychology, as a part of his natural science, is concerned solely with powers, structures, and activities found in nature. This still leaves open the possibility that his psychology is 'functionalist' at least in the sense that it allows functionally equivalent realizations of psychological phenomena in different kinds of *natural* physiological states or processes. In this section we argue that his definitions of important cognitive phenomena are not functionalist even in this more limited sense.

According to a functionalist interpretation of the mental, our account of belief, desire, knowledge, etc., is, in virtue of compositional plasticity, compatible with different physical—or even non-physical—realizations. How, and to what extent, does this translate into Aristotelian terms? Does Aristotle characterize perception and thought in such a way that in principle they could be constituted by different kinds of processes in different cases, just so long as the processes in question play the right functional role? This is the philosophical bite of the computer–human analogy. There is considerable evidence to show that the answer to this question is negative.

The fact that perception on Aristotle's view requires a medium (see 419^a11-21) immediately puts a heavy constraint on a functionalist interpretation. It places a strong non-functional condition on the characterization of the input,

---

[7] Here are two examples, provided by contemporary philosophers, of functional analyses of mental phenomena. 'In elementary cases, a belief state that represents a particular thing normally results from the perception of that thing and leads to behaviour involving that thing. What the thing is represented *as* depends on this behavior' (Harman 1973, 62). Ned Block gives as an example the interpretation of pain as a state caused typically by tissue damage, and having the tendency to cause efforts to get rid of whatever it is that causes the damage, as well as other behaviour (N. Block 1980, 172).

since the medium is construed by Aristotle as composed of various kinds of material. This of course does not show that he was a materialist. His views about the medium are compatible with theories of perception that fall altogether outside the materialist–dualist dichotomy.

We shall not attempt here to discuss all the details of the famous characterization of perception as the receiving of a perceptible form without matter (424^a17-19), but rather will concentrate on the explanatory force of this thesis and its relation to functionalism. In order for this definition to be functionalist, it would have to interpret perception as taking us from one non-functionally described state to another. It is difficult to see how one could interpret the Aristotelian definition in this way, for it specifies a process, but does not specify the non-functionally described states which the process is supposed to bridge. It does not say that perception is whatever takes us from sensible contact to having information about (say) 'secondary qualities' in order to find our way about.

Since Aristotle does not posit a unitary kind of matter for the different senses, but takes the (proximate) matter for each sense to be unique to it, this characterization is not in any interesting sense 'materialist'. Furthermore, the notion of 'becoming like the object in form but not in matter' is not to be understood simply as the perceiving subject (or relevant organ) coming to have the perceived quality in the way in which inanimate things have qualities. Even granting for the sake of argument that when, and only when, the eye-jelly turns red we see red, this biconditional would not explain how or why this kind of process constitutes *perception* of red. In the context of describing perception, 'receiving form without matter' remains a basic, primitive notion. It points in the direction of what we would call 'content' or 'information' today. Aristotle uses this notion in his definition of perception because he believes that perception has a certain 'content', and because this is the 'information' utilized by thought.

That Aristotle is left with an undefined basic notion in this context—that of receiving the form without matter—is no more surprising than similar results in modern so-called representational theories. Even today the problem of content still haunts the researcher. In an article describing one of the most influential current theories of vision,[8] we find the acknowledgement that a necessary condition for an adequate theory of vision is that it provide an answer to the question: 'what information does the visual system actually make available to the subject?'[9] Suggesting that the jelly turns red is hardly an answer to this question. Supposing matterless form of some sort to be preserved for thought is, although not particularly informative, a descriptive stab in the right direction.

Again, '[i]n his opening philosophical chapter, he [Marr] claims that the Computational Theory tells us the what and why of vision: the algorithmic and neurophysiological level tells us how these goals are accomplished.'[10] This is not the contrast between functional and materialist accounts. The neurophysiological corresponds roughly to what we find in Aristotle's account of activity through a

---

[8] Kitcher (1988).   [9] Ibid. 3.   [10] Ibid. 11.

medium, and the resulting information provided for thought and belief corresponds roughly to the computational. Needless to say, to draw this parallel is not to ascribe to Aristotle either the concept of a physiological level, or anything resembling computations. It is merely to show that his theory of perception and cognition—just as some of today's—runs up against the need to posit certain primitives to link describing the process with presenting the information contained.

To show that the materialist-functionalist dichotomy is not rich enough to capture Aristotle's thought on what living is, we turn very briefly to one more passage. At 429ª27–9 he refers approvingly (though not without qualifications) to the description of the soul as the 'place of forms'. This passage confronts us with many difficulties of interpretation. None the less, regardless of how they are solved, the whole tenor of this remark resists both functionalist and materialist readings.

We have now shown that Aristotle's account of perception and cognition is not couched in purely functional terms. It does not follow from this that there is a level of explanation at which—according to Aristotle—we find no teleological elements at all. None the less, our account does not involve the claim that inanimate homoiomerous stuff cannot be explained fully within an Aristotelian scheme without showing how it contributes to the functioning of living things. However, this does not mean that no telic notions of any sort are needed to explain the nature of the inanimate homoiomerous elements.

These observations lead to a consideration of Aristotelian matter. Even if it be granted that Aristotle's actual definitions in the *De Anima* are not easily construed along functionalist lines, it still could be urged that the spirit, at least, propelling his use of teleology in biology and psychology, is often 'functionalist', and that with some charity we might be able to see his definitions as gestures in that direction. Against this, we shall argue that his conception of matter precludes the possibility of a 'functionalist' interpretation of the psychological. Thus we now turn to that topic.

IV. Aristotelian Matter

The typical modern functionalist is driven by materialist sympathies, and functionalism as a doctrine about mental phenomena is logically compatible with materialism. In this section we shall show that Aristotle's conception of matter is *not* compatible with functionalism, and hence should not be congenial to these materialists.

An underlying thing, or substratum (*hupokeimenon*) is what underlies something in one of two ways: either (i) as a 'this' (for example, an animal) underlies its affections, or (ii) as matter underlies its correlative actuality (*entelecheia; Metaph.* Z13, 1038ᵇ5–6), an actuality being that which makes something what it actually is. Thus the matter of a thing, being something to which the term 'nature' applies, and being what underlies form, may be characterized as the 'underlying nature'. The matter of a natural substance is a potentiality (*dunamis*), and its form is the correlative actuality which it underlies (412ª9–10). In the case of a living thing, the matter (that is to say, the substratum for the actuality) is the *organic body*; the form (that is to say, the actuality which the body underlies) is the *soul* (412ª17–21, ᵇ5–6).

The sublunary perceptible substances are ultimately composed of the four elements earth, water, air, and fire, and much of their behaviour can be explained as due to the natures of these basic elemental constituents. In this sense one might say that there is one kind of matter for all plants and animals. None the less each kind of living thing has a unique kind of *proximate* matter that is idiosyncratic to just that kind of living thing. The powers and potentialities of the proximate matter are unique to it, and do not arise from the powers of the simple elements. The natural motions of the four elements are to four different natural places, and a living body would decompose and decay were it not for the fact that it possessed an internal principle, the soul, that counteracts the natural migrations of its material elements (415ᵇ28–416ª9).

Each non-elemental natural body has a nature that is unique to bodies of that kind, and its natural behaviour, including its resistance to disintegration and decay, is due to that nature, and not to the natures of the elements. There is for Aristotle no generic concept of physical matter, no one kind of matter for natural objects, but rather what counts as matter varies from case to case. The underlying nature must be understood by analogy—the matter for some kind of substance is what stands to that kind of substance in the way that bronze stands to the statue, or wood to the bed, or in general as that which has form stands to whatever it was that before accepting that form lacked it (*Ph.* 191ª7–12).

In *Metaph.* Θ6 we see that the concept of actuality (*energeia*) is also to be understood by way of analogy. An actuality *x* is something that stands to something *y* in the way that the one building a house stands to that which is able to build; or as that which is awake stands to that which is asleep; or as that which is seeing stands to that which can see; or as that which is shaped up out of matter stands with respect to the matter (1048ª35–ᵇ4). He sums this view up by saying that something is called an 'actuality' either (i) by being a *kinesis* with respect to some correlative *dunamis*, or (ii) by being an *ousia* with respect to some matter (1048ᵇ6–9). Just as there is no one kind of thing that counts as the *dunamis* in connection with all of the different cases of *kinesis*, so too what counts as matter will vary from case to case as the corresponding actuality, or substantial form, varies.

We have already seen that for Aristotle the soul of a living thing is its nature, and that his hylomorphic psychology is a part of a natural science according to which 'physical' bodies are endowed with natures that explain their natural behaviour. Such an account of soul is inconsistent with a physics that rejects the idea of specific natures serving as the internal principles of change for natural bodies. In particular, it is incompatible with Cartesian physics. Descartes does away with the idea that there are different kinds of physical bodies each endowed with a different kind of internal nature, and holds that body is a substance the nature of which is *extension*. Unlike Aristotle, who utilizes different kinds of matter for different kinds of natural body, Descartes argues for a single, uniform matter for everything in heaven and on earth. Cartesian bodies cannot have substantial forms as internal principles of change, and hence cannot have natures in an Aristotelian sense. For Descartes, then, the soul is not the nature of a physical body, nor is psychological activity the natural activity of a body.

For Aristotle all psychological activity, except for the contemplation of immaterial forms, is the activity of some bodily organ. Descartes regards all bodily organs as parts of extended substance and for him the body is a machine. The functioning of an organ is to be derived from the nature of body, and hence explained in terms of the mechanical principles governing inanimate, extended substance, not in terms of 'animal soul'. The mind is not, on his view, part of the nature or essence of any type of natural body, since the only nature for body is extension. For him, mental activity cannot be the exercise of some bodily organ. Thus the mechanical principles that Descartes uses to account for bodily functioning cannot account for thought, and thought cannot be derived from the nature of body. This new approach to natural science is not hospitable to a unified treatment of both mental and bodily phenomena.

None the less, while rejecting the idea that the soul is the nature of the body, Descartes does not simply give up the idea that thought is a natural activity. He still treats thinking as due to the nature of the subject that does the thinking, and argues that the soul, or mind, is a separate substance, the very nature of which is to think. The mind and the body are two distinct types of substance that causally interact, although each can exist without the other. The body is a subject the nature of which is extension, the mind is a subject the nature of which is thought, and just as the former is not a subject for mental properties, so the latter is not a subject for spatial properties. Once mental activity is no longer viewed as a natural activity of physical bodies, philosophy is confronted with a question that cannot arise for Aristotelian natural science: 'what is the connection between thought and the world investigated by the physical sciences?'

Functionalism is a post-Cartesian answer to this question—an answer which requires neither Cartesian mind–body dualism, nor a physicalistic reduction of mentalistic vocabulary. As such it is not committed to the ideas from Aristotelian physics that were repudiated in the seventeenth century, and does not treat mental phenomena as the operations of the essential nature of a certain kind of natural body. As we have seen, mental phenomena are, according to this contemporary view, compositionally plastic functional states. Although functionalism does not require physicalism, it is compatible with it. For instance, functional states can be realized in neurophysiological configurations, regardless of what other kinds of realizations they might, in principle, have. In this way functionalism provides a way of treating physical systems as the bearers of mental properties, and so for the functionalist, there is no need to introduce a separate

Cartesian *res cogitans* as the subject for these. A human being is a physical system that is itself the subject of such mental predicates as those expressing belief, desire, and so forth. Beliefs can be treated as neurophysiological states playing a certain functional role that could in principle have other than neurophysiological realizations. In general, the functionalist is able to construe mental properties as defined wholly by reference to (i) non-functionally defined input–output relations, and (ii) other mental predicates.

Functionalism is a way of avoiding Cartesian dualism after the Aristotelian conception of nature is abandoned, but like Cartesian dualism it too is incompatible with Aristotelian hylomorphism. The functionalist treats the mind as compositionally plastic, capable of realization in different types of material. Although we doubt that any contemporary functionalist would be tempted to embrace the Cartesian account of matter, any version of functionalism is none the less logically compatible with that account (although not compatible with a Cartesian psychology). That is, for the functionalist, the mind could (in principle) be a functional organization realized in non-Aristotelian, Cartesian matter. However, the Cartesian account of matter is incompatible with the Aristotelian conception of the soul as the *nature* of a certain kind of physical/natural body. Since a functionalist interpretation of the mental is compatible with a Cartesian view of matter, but a Cartesian view of matter as extended substance is not compatible with Aristotle's hylomorphic conception of soul, it follows that a functionalist interpretation of perception and cognition, far from providing an interpretation of Aristotle's definition of the soul as the form of the body, is not identical with, nor can contain as a species, an Aristotelian psychology. Since the acceptance of a functionalist interpretation of the mental implies the possibility (relative to one's psychology) of the Cartesian conception of matter, but Aristotle's hylomorphic account of soul implies the impossibility (again, relative to one's psychology) of a Cartesian view of matter as extended substance, it follows that a functionalist interpretation of perception and cognition, far from providing an interpretation of the soul as the form of the body, is actually incompatible with the acceptance of an Aristotelian psychology.

V. Final Remarks

In a recent article D. Charles writes: 'There are…two contrasting ways of understanding the essential role of the teleological, and its relation to material and efficient causation, in Aristotle's psychological and biological writings.'[11] Charles goes on to sketch what he takes to be the two types of account. According to one, Aristotle thinks that physical states may constitute a sufficient condition for a biological or psychological event. However, since the essences of biological and psychological phenomena also include telic factors, a full explanation of the

---

[11] Charles (1988), 1.

events in question would have to include teleological components as well, and could not be exhausted by mere physical analysis. This account interprets Aristotle as falling within the same genus as current non-reductionistic, materialist accounts, of which functionalism is one variety (though clearly not the only variety).

We take it that the essence of the other view is the denial of the claim that physical states are sufficient for biological and psychological events, together with an affirmation of the claim that sufficient conditions for such events must include telic factors. For the purposes of this section, we label this the 'strong teleological' view. Charles comments: 'If the second alternative successfully captures Aristotle's views, they would have proved outmoded when science developed to the point when it was rationally thought possible to find relevant physical sufficient conditions which could be understood independently of their role in the account of organisms.'[12] On the other hand, if the first version is correct, then 'Aristotle's views would remain of direct relevance for contemporary C20th discussions of non-reductionist versions of materialism.'[13]

Since we do not think that Aristotle is a non-reductionist materialist, but neither do we think that he is simply outmoded, we shall now try to locate our interpretation against the two sketched by Charles. Furthermore, we shall show how on our account important Aristotelian insights can be recovered. A full treatment would involve considering at least the following five questions.

   (i) Are the two alternatives mentioned by Charles the only viable ones?
  (ii) What assumptions about matter and causality are embodied in the descriptions of the two positions?
 (iii) What is the value of recovering the Aristotelian account?
  (iv) What is it for a form of explanation to become outmoded?
   (v) How do we interpret Aristotle's objections to earlier non-teleological, 'materialist' theorists such as Democritus or Empedocles?

To answer these questions one would have to compare possible philosophical accounts of ranges of fairly large-scale phenomena. Within such comparisons, three types of issues should be considered. First, what are the main questions to which the philosophical theory actually addresses itself? Secondly, what are the distinctive, key concepts and vocabulary of the theory? Finally, what are the proposed solutions?

With respect to the chief problems and concerns, our interpretation shows Aristotle to be different from both the modern non-reductionist materialist and the strong teleologist as characterized by Charles. One of the most influential versions of a non-reductionist account of the mental is functionalism, and as we have seen this is a view that is constructed in such a way as to be congenial to the contemporary materialist. The functionalist is able to maintain a materialism that presupposes a monolithic conception of matter while none the less answering the following semantic problem: 'how can one accommodate the semantic fact of the

---

[12] Ibid. 3.   [13] Ibid. 4.

non-reducibility of mentalistic terms, and yet not preclude the possibility of a materialist ontology?' According to our view, Aristotle's main interests are quite different. He is primarily concerned to differentiate the living from the non-living, and to explain the different forms of living that occur in nature. It is within this context that he develops his views about cognition. His account centres on the task of constructing a unified account that both (i) explains certain uniquely human powers and capacities, the natural and informational aspects of cognition and perception, and (ii) deals with the self-determining nature of many organic phenomena. Furthermore, the unified account he is seeking is intended to be a part of natural science, and as such provide analyses and explanations from within a general hylomorphic theory of nature—a theory which allots to each kind of natural substance a unique formal nature together with a correlative, and species-specific, material nature. Thus his chief tasks differ not only from the semantic concerns of the functionalist, but even from those of the strong teleologist whose focus is primarily on the question: 'what is needed, in addition to the physical, in order to generate biological and psychological phenomena?'

With regard to what we take to be Aristotle's key concepts, our interpretation differs from both of those mentioned by Charles. In our version the key notions include: nature, receiving the form without matter, potentiality and actuality, matter and form. These are the concepts Aristotle utilizes in his attempts to construct his own views about how perceptual processes are both natural and informative, and also about how various forms of living are parts of nature and yet crucially involve self-initiating processes. Once Aristotle's basic concerns and problems are formulated in terms of these notions, rather than in terms of sufficient physical conditions, we see Aristotle's enterprise as having aims and solutions that intersect with, but largely fall outside, the foci of the two views as formulated by Charles. Further, we think that for Aristotle the concept of matter is species-relative, and should itself be seen as including a teleological aspect—specific potentialities defined in terms of their exercise.[14]

We turn briefly to our second question concerning the presuppositions about matter and causation embodied in the two approaches mentioned by Charles. Both the strong teleologist and the modern functionalist presuppose a monolithic conception of matter according to which what we call 'matter' is uniform across living species (regardless of whether it does or does not have the nature of Cartesian 'extendedness'). The two modern interpretations disagree on how this uniform matter is linked to the teleological aspects of nature. We do not believe that this monolithic conception of matter is contained within Aristotle's ontology. Furthermore, the contrast between the two views Charles discusses centres on the notion of sufficient physical causes. This tends to assimilate Aristotle's views on causation both to a modern conception of the 'physical' and to a modern concept of 'efficient causation'. However, we do not believe that any of Aristotle's four '*aitia*-locating' factors coincide exactly with the modern notion of efficient

[14] See Code (1987), 54–8.

causation,[15] and as we have already indicated, Aristotle's conception of the natural/physical does not correspond to modern notions of the physical.

It is illuminating and rewarding, both for the history of science and the history of philosophy, to compare conceptions of matter proposed during different stages of historical development. For one thing, such comparisons give us a good perspective within which genuine achievement can be appreciated. Contemporary philosophical materialist or quasi-materialist theories of mind seem to assume that we have a more or less clear conception of what matter is. However, even putting Aristotle aside for the moment, this notion has changed radically in the period between Descartes and the physics of today. In our time there is widespread disagreement concerning the nature of the ultimate constituents of spatio-temporal reality. In this kind of situation, history can perform a useful function by showing just how different some of our past conceptions have been. We certainly do not wish to deny the existence of points of similarity between Aristotle and the twentieth century. None the less, we would urge that being presented with what is quite different from the conceptions of the recent past spurs the creative imagination considerably more than the attempt to interpret our heritage by emphasizing whatever similarities we can find between classical conceptions and the recently discarded assumptions about matter, potentiality, etc., found in contemporary science.

We noted that when faced with the deep problem of accounting for perceptual and cognitive processes that both are parts of nature and also can, somehow, carry information, Aristotle introduces a basic primitive notion of 'receiving form without matter'. This move, we submit, points to a problem that is still with us today. We here leave it to the reader to decide how much better the modern notions of 'perceptual content' or 'mental representation' fare than this primitive Aristotelian notion.

We also saw that, faced with the need to account for certain self-initiating processes, Aristotle invokes certain unique powers and potentialities for humans. The explanations of today are often couched in terms of such notions as instinct, or DNA. To be sure, progress has been made, but again we leave it to the reader to assess how much. Regardless of how one judges this matter, it should be noted that wrestling with these types of phenomena does not rely on any interesting thesis of materialism. To say the least, it would be strange to describe an account of species-specific instinct, or the informational aspect of DNA, in terms of the materialist–dualist dichotomy.

Perhaps some contemporary philosophers with materialist sympathies find it easier to regard Aristotle as a respectable ancestor if he can be seen as conforming to the pattern of non-reductionistic materialism. However, with respect to the evolution and changes of ideas it is often instructive to see differences in the various conceptions of cognition proposed in the course of the history of philosophy, and for this reason being different in the way in which our interpretation alleges

[15] Moravcsik (1974).

Aristotle to be different does not made him 'outmoded'. Furthermore, it should be obvious by now that we do not think that Aristotle's respectability has much to do with whether he did or did not happen to say some things in the course of his theorizing that coincide with what some scientists or philosophers happen to be saying in our own time.

We end with an observation about the way we understand the disagreement between Aristotle and the monolithic 'materialists' of ancient times—the likes of a Democritus or an Empedocles. The dispute does not centre on the possibility or impossibility of definitional reductionism, but rather (i) on the need to introduce strongly modal notions of potentiality and actuality to account for self-initiating processes, and (ii) on the prospects of success in explaining the information-carrying and -embodying aspects of cognitive processes within a purely monolithic 'materialist' framework.

The jury is still out on these issues. Meanwhile, we should attempt to reconstruct the conceptions of historically influential figures as faithfully as we can, resisting the temptation to set into high relief the lines of thought that happen to be suggestive of what is, for the time being, fashionable.[16]

---

[16] We would like to thank the members of our joint seminar in Stanford (Fall 1988) and Jim Bogen for lively exchanges on these issues.

9

ASPECTS OF THE RELATIONSHIP BETWEEN ARISTOTLE'S PSYCHOLOGY AND HIS ZOOLOGY

G. E. R. LLOYD

IN prominent texts in the *De Anima* and his zoological treatises Aristotle stresses the importance of the study of soul for the student of nature (*phusikos*). The aim of the present paper[1] is twofold: first, to investigate the extent to which his zoological researches were in fact guided or influenced by his general psychological[2] theory and by his specific psychological doctrines; and secondly, to explore the match or mismatch between the results of his zoological investigations and his general position on such questions as definition, essence, form, and matter. My thesis will be, on the first count, that the psychology does indeed provide what is, from some points of view, the major articulating framework for his zoology, though it is a framework that leaves plenty of scope for the introduction of supplementary material not immediately and maybe not even ultimately geared to resolving questions connected with his main psychological interests. Moreover, I shall argue that at certain key points in his zoology his specific psychological doctrines strongly influence his interpretation of the biological phenomena. Then on the second count I shall try to clarify what I take to be deep-seated tensions between his account of living creatures and his doctrines of definition and of form. For the issue of the credibility—for us—of his doctrine of *psuchē* it may be important to pose the prior question: was it credible even for Aristotle? The anti-functionalists are undeniably right to insist that, in the case of living creatures, there is no alternative to the matter they happen to possess. But the functionalists have a point, that the expectation generated by certain of his explicit statements on form and definition is that there should have been. There are problems here not just for our latter-day evaluation of Aristotelian philosophy of mind, but also internal to Aristotelianism itself. The hesitations I think we can detect on Aristotle's part can be seen as evidence of *his* realization of some of the problems. This is a case where we should resist trying

[1] Among important recent discussions of topics broached in this paper I may mention especially Balme (1961/1975), (1962), (1987a), (1987b), Sorabji (1974/1979), Barnes (1971–2/1979), Ackrill (1972–3/1979), Bolton (1978), Lennox (1980), (1987a), (1987b), Gotthelf (1985b), (1987), Frede (1985), Kosman (1987), Burnyeat, above, ch. 2.

[2] Throughout this paper I use the term 'psychological' not in our usual English sense, but in that of Aristotle's doctrine of *psuchē*.

to *unify* his doctrines beyond a certain point, though I am aware that that is always a difficult line of interpretation for which to argue.

First, however, some of the programmatic statements should be set out. In the opening chapter of *De Anima*, as he embarks on the inquiry concerning soul, he makes two important remarks. The first, 402ᵃ4 ff., reveals the strategic import-ance of psychology. It is agreed, he says, that knowledge of the soul contributes much to 'the truth as a whole', and especially to the understanding of nature, and this statement is immediately explained with the remark that soul is, as it were, a principle for animals. Secondly, he stresses that the inquiry should not be limited to *human* soul, though that is the way his predecessors had treated the problem (402ᵇ3 ff.). As is well known, that principle is repeatedly put into practice in the *De Anima* and the *Parva Naturalia*, not to speak of what we think of as the more purely zoological treatises themselves. Regular consideration is given to such questions as the different sense-faculties that different species of animals possess, whether they sleep, have imaginations, memory, and so on. This already gives a biological or zoological orientation to his psychological discussions. Conversely, when he considers zoological methods in the opening chapter of *De Partibus Animalium*, he notes at 641ᵃ17 ff. that the student of nature must treat of the soul as being the form and the substance (*ousia*) of the animal. However, *phusikē* is not concerned with the whole soul (including reason, *nous*), for if that had been the case—he adds in a further revealing remark, *PA* 641ᵃ34 ff.—then there would have been nothing to philosophy over and above *phusikē*, the study of nature.

One of the major themes of Aristotle's psychology, indeed its chief foundation, is, of course, that soul is to body as form is to matter, or more strictly as first actuality is to matter. This provides him with his answer to the question of how soul and body are related. Indeed he feels able to claim, notoriously, at 412ᵇ6 ff., that there is no need to inquire whether the soul and the body are one, just as there is no such need in the case of the wax and the shape made in it (e.g., by a seal), nor in general in relation to the matter of each thing and that of which it is the matter. But while this shows great apparent confidence in the unity of the living creature, aspects of which can be considered under the separate rubrics of 'soul' and 'body', it is nevertheless the case that Aristotle still insists rather sharply on the differences between these two, not least because the soul is, in a sense, that for which the body exists (e.g. *PA* 645ᵇ19). Repeatedly in *De Partibus Animalium* 1 especially Aristotle puts it that the chief topic of investigation for the student of nature is soul and the composite whole, rather than the body or the matter (e.g. *PA* 641ᵃ29 ff., 645ᵃ30 ff.). Yet while in the single case of the activity of reason we have a clear instance of an activity of the soul that does not involve the body (for reason, as is well known, is not the activity of any bodily organ on Aristotle's view), elsewhere the *distinction* between soul and body becomes more problematic the more Aristotle stresses their *interdependence*. Thus he recognizes that perception, for instance, is not an *idion* (property) of the soul, no more is it one of the body (*Somn. Vig* 454ᵃ7 ff.). But just as, in perception, the faculty of the soul involved does not operate on its own (as happens in the case of reasoning), so conversely on the body side of the equation it is not just any body, any inert physical stuff, that can see or hear: in particular, as he never tires of saying, a dead eye is an eye only in name.[3]

Aristotle's provisional resolution of those difficulties proceeds partly via his distinction between potentiality and actuality (the soul being the first actuality of a natural body that potentially has life, *DA* 412ᵃ27 f., or as he puts it at 412ᵇ5 f., of a natural instrumental body) and partly via his recognition that some faculties are 'common to soul and body', as at *Sens.* 436ᵃ6 ff. for instance, where he specifies quite a range of such items including perception, memory, anger, desire, pleasure, and pain. But while in principle a recommendation to study on the one hand the material or physical aspects of vital activities, and on the other what makes them the vital activities they are, may look unproblematic enough, in practice the correlativity of form and matter, actuality and potentiality, ensures that they cannot be treated independently of one another. How far that in turn threatens the crisp application, to zoological phenomena, of some of Aristotle's recommendations concerning definition (particularly when that is said to be of the form) is a question that will occupy us in Section II of this chapter.

I

The expectation generated by the programmatic statements that Aristotle makes in the *De Anima* and the *De Partibus Animalium* is that zoology will be largely, though to be sure not exclusively, devoted to a consideration of *psuchē*. Given that zoology is a study of living creatures and that what makes them the living creatures they are falls under the rubric of *psuchē*, that should occasion no surprise (however much later uses of the terms 'psychology' and 'biology' make it anything but obvious why the first should underpin the second). But if it is one thing for Aristotle to set out his programme for the correct method for studying animals, it is another for him to implement it. How far do the enormously rich and wide-ranging zoological treatises conform to a plan that tallies with his expression of a primary concern with *psuchē*? Do his particular psychological theories influence his zoological explanations, and if so how?

Part of the answer to the first question is straightforward enough. Obviously, whenever he is dealing with an instrumental part that is directly concerned with one of the major faculties of the soul identified in the *De Anima*, Aristotle cannot fail to bear in mind precisely that *that* is the function that the part serves, and he will indeed see the activities in question as the final causes of the parts. This is the case, for instance, of his various discussions of the organs of locomotion, especially of the detailed account, in the *De Incessu Animalium*, of the different modalities of locomotion, for example of the differences between birds' wings and

[3] See, e.g. *PA* 643ᵃ24 ff., *GA* 726ᵇ22 ff., 734ᵇ24 ff., 735ᵃ6 ff., 741ᵃ9 ff.

insects' wings and of the different ways in which the front and back legs of quadrupeds bend. Again perception has a fundamental role in his general definition of animal, being, of course, the faculty that, in Aristotle's view, distinguishes an animal from a plant; and, as already remarked, the questions of which animals have which senses, and the varieties in the sense-organs, naturally receive very careful discussion.

The various organs that serve the complex functions of the first faculty of soul, *threptikē*, covering both nutrition and reproduction, are a third clear example with interesting and complex ramifications. Among the instrumental parts that serve the function of nutrition are mouth, teeth, lips, tongue, stomach, liver, omentum, mesentery, and the whole digestive tract—though several of these parts have other functions as well, the tongue for taste, the teeth for defence, and tongue, teeth, and lips for voice and speech, for instance.[4] Moreover, since nutrition necessarily involves not just the intake of food but also the excretion of residues, the parts that serve the latter function too must be included, the kidneys and bladder for example. In general, as he often states in the *De Generatione Animalium*, there is no part of the living body that does not have soul.[5] But Aristotle is particularly exercised, in his account of reproduction, to specify *how* the soul is present in the *seed*, distinguishing the nutritive soul, which is present already potentially in the seed (and comes into operation as soon as the seed draws nourishment to itself, *GA* 736^{b}8 ff.), from the perceptive soul, which is supplied by the male parent and is present, again potentially, only at the point when a new animal is recognizable as such.[6] Again, his whole theory of the roles of male and female in generation revolves round his idea that the former provides the form and the moving cause, the latter the matter, a doctrine expressed at *GA* 738^{b}25 ff. in terms of the male supplying the *soul*, the female the body.[7]

Clearly, when dealing with the instrumental parts or the sense-organs Aristotle *must* pay due attention to the faculties of the soul that they serve. But one might suppose that the relevance of his general and particular psychological theories to his account of the simpler, uniform parts of living creatures would be only a very limited one. However, in several instances that is certainly very far from being the case. Two examples will serve to make the point, his accounts of flesh and of blood.

[4] See, e.g. *PA* 660^{a}19 ff., 22 ff., 35 ff. on the tongue, *PA* 659^{b}30 ff. on the lips, and *PA* 661^{b}1 ff., 13 ff. and *GA* 788^{b}3 ff. on the teeth.
[5] See, e.g. *GA* 726^{b}22 ff., 734^{b}24 ff., 735^{a}6 ff., 741^{a}23 ff. However the controlling principle is located in the heart or analogous part, e.g. *Juv.* 467^{b}14 ff., *MA* 703^{a}34 ff.
[6] See, e.g. *GA* 735^{a}4 ff., 16 ff., 736^{a}35 ff., ^{b}1 ff., 738^{b}25 ff., 757^{b}15 ff.: on how reason is acquired or transmitted, see *GA* 736^{b}5 ff., 737^{a}7 ff. See Code (1987).
[7] Cf. *GA* 737^{a}27 ff., where the female *katamēnia* are said to lack the *archē* of the soul. In *GA* 4. 3, however, when dealing with the likenesses of offspring to parents (to the mother as well as the father, and to grandparents on both sides) Aristotle talks of the movements in the seed that are derived from both parents (e.g. 768^{a}10 ff.: contrast, now, the interpretation of *GA* 4. 3 offered by Cooper 1988), and in general, while in some texts the differences between male and female contributions to reproduction are stressed, in others the emphasis is on the point that the female *katamēnia* are *analogous* to the semen in males (e.g. *GA* 727^{a}2 ff.) and are indeed seed, even if not pure, not fully concocted, and 'in need of elaboration', e.g. *GA* 728^{a}26 ff.

As already remarked, the faculty that distinguishes animals from plants, in Aristotle's view, is perception. To be more precise, what all animals possess is the primary mode of perception, namely touch.[8] However, what serves as the organ or more strictly the medium of touch is flesh, and in his account of flesh in *PA* 653^{b}19 ff., it is this that provides his initial and primary focus of interest. He is absolutely clear about the fundamental importance of flesh for every kind of living creature. Indeed, one of his ways of distinguishing between two of the main families of bloodless animals, the crustacea and the cephalopods, is on the question of whether their fleshy parts are on the inside or the outside of their bodies.[9] But instead of considering flesh from the point of view of the musculature, for instance, Aristotle deems its essential role to be as the medium of touch.

Moreover, this distinctive *cognitive* role of flesh has far-reaching repercussions on the account Aristotle offers of a wide variety of other uniform parts as well. At *PA* 653^{b}2 ff. he puts it that 'everything else' is for the sake of the flesh (or more strictly for the perceptive faculty of which it is the medium) and he specifies 'bones and skin and tendons and blood-vessels, and again hair and all kinds of nails and so on', explaining that, for example, the bones are devised for the preservation or protection of the soft, fleshy parts, and that in animals that have no bones some analogous part, such as spine or cartilage, plays a similar function.[10] Of course, Aristotle does not mean to suggest that there is no more to the function of the bones and the other parts he mentions than their being, in some sense, 'for the sake of' flesh. In particular he does not believe that mentioning that function absolves him from the obligation of giving detailed descriptions and explanations of those other uniform parts, the courses of the blood-vessels, the specific function of hair on different parts of the body, the different arrangements of bones in different species of animals, and much else beside. Yet evidently flesh, in his view, has a primacy, among the uniform parts, and the reason for that is clear, namely the role it plays in the primary mode of perception.[11]

While flesh is said to be an *archē* or principle for the body as a whole in virtue of its role in the faculty of touch, blood is described as in a sense the matter for the whole of the body.[12] At first sight that might make it appear that the role of blood would be limited to accounts where Aristotle has the material cause in view and so be of less importance where formal, final, and efficient causes are concerned, that is to say where the soul, acting in those capacities, is. Yet that is far from being the case. First the blood itself certainly serves a psychic end and a fundamental one: its final cause is nutrition, *PA* 650^{b}2 ff., 12 f.,[13] and it is, potentially, the body or flesh, *PA* 668^{a}25 ff. The network of blood-vessels serves other purposes as well, being compared to a framework for the rest of the body, *PA*

---

[8] See, e.g. *Sens.* 436^{b}10 ff., *Juv.* 467^{b}23 ff., and the other texts cited below at n. 69.

[9] See, e.g. *HA* 523^{b}2 ff., 5 ff., cf. *PA* 653^{b}36 ff.

[10] See, e.g. *PA* 653^{b}35 ff., and see also *PA* 654^{b}27 ff.

[11] See further *DA* 423^{a}13 ff., ^{b}26, 426^{b}15, *PA* 647^{a}19 ff., 656^{b}35 f.

[12] See e.g. *PA* 668^{a}5 f., 25 ff., *GA* 751^{a}34 ff.

[13] See further, e.g. *GA* 726^{b}1 f., 740^{a}21 f., ^{b}3, *Somn.* 456^{a}34 ff., *Resp.* 474^{b}3 ff., *PA* 652^{a}6 f., 678^{a}6 ff.

668^{b}24 ff., binding together the front and the back;[14] but their fundamental function is to nourish the body, and it is for that reason that they permeate every part of the body.[15]

But there is far more to the role of blood than just nutrition, since in Aristotle's view it contributes directly to a whole range of other functions of the soul. The nature of the blood, he says at *PA* 651^{a}12 ff., is responsible for many things both in respect of the *character* of animals and in respect of *perception*, in a chapter which has offered a variety of suggestions about how the intelligence, acuteness of perception, courage, and timidity of different species of animals are to be correlated with the quality of the blood they possess, its heat, purity, thinness, whether it contains fibres, and so on.[16] Again, as is the case with his theory of flesh, the account given of blood has far-reaching repercussions, since he treats a number of other uniform parts, lard, suet, marrow, and so on as kinds of blood or derivatives from it.[17]

The two cases we have considered, flesh and blood, illustrate how, even at the level of the fundamental uniform parts that form the material of the living body, Aristotle's account is concerned with far more than just their role as stuff and in each case he develops distinctive theories of the vital functions that these parts serve. But we can go further still. The primary simple bodies in Aristotle's element theory are, of course, earth, water, air, and fire, considered as combinations of the primary pairs of opposites, hot and cold, wet and dry. But when he comes to consider those opposites in *PA* 2 he leaves us in no doubt that it is not just as inert material that they are important. The very reason why it is essential to get clear about hot and cold, wet and dry—topics on which there had been so much dispute and confusion in the past—is that 'it seems clear that these are responsible practically for death and life, and again for sleep and waking, for maturity and old age, and disease and health'.[18] They are responsible, of course, in the first instance as material causes.[19] However, we have to be clear that these primary qualities are not treated in the zoology as merely physical in our sense, where that is contrasted with biological.

Thus of the pair wet and dry he tells us at *GA* 733^{a}11 f. that wet is particularly associated with, or productive of, life (*zōtikon*), while the dry is 'furthest from what has soul' (*to empsuchon*).[20] More strikingly still, the kind of heat that he refers to repeatedly in his explanation of generation in *GA* is explicitly described

---

[14] Cf. *GA* 743^{a}1 ff.: yet at *PA* 670^{a}8 ff. he suggests that the lower viscera serve to anchor the blood-vessels.

[15] See, e.g. *PA* 668^{a}4 ff., 11 f. At *PA* 668^{a}13 ff. the blood-vessels are compared with a network of irrigation channels, and at 668^{a}16 ff. with material laid out along the foundations of a house.

[16] See esp. *PA* 647^{b}31 ff., 648^{a}2 ff., 650^{b}18 ff., *Somn.* 458^{a}13 ff., *Resp.* 477^{a}18 ff. At *PA* 667^{a}11 ff. Aristotle further suggests that differences in the size and texture of the heart contribute also to character, *ēthē*.

[17] See, e.g. *PA* 651^{a}20 ff., ^{b}20 ff., and cf. *GA* 726^{b}9 ff. on seed. Furthermore, at *PA* 673^{b}26 ff. he suggests that the liver's *telos* resides chiefly in the blood, and cf. *PA* 674^{a}6 ff., on viscera that are for the sake of the blood-vessels.

[18] *PA* 648^{b}4 ff., cf. *GA* 784^{a}32 ff. on ageing.   [19] See e.g. *Long.* 466^{a}18 ff.

[20] Cf. also *Long.* 466^{b}21 f., *HA* 489^{a}20 f., *PA* 647^{b}26 f.

not just as what is appropriate to living creatures, their proper or own (*oikeion*), heat,[21] but as the vital (*psuchikon*), heat.[22] Of course the relation between vital heat and just ordinary heat raises plenty of difficult questions, some of which the Aristotelian discussions leave rather unresolved, as for example whether we are to think of vital heat as indeed a separate kind of hot or as the hot working in a particular fashion.[23] But whatever answer we offer to that question, it is abundantly clear from the very characterization of it as *vital* that in this context Aristotle has in mind far more than a merely physical quality (again, in *our* sense). What little Aristotle has to say on the subject of *pneuma* is notoriously obscure and has occasioned protracted scholarly debate:[24] yet some of the perplexing features of that doctrine—the role of *pneuma* as the material instrument of psychic activities—are shared, to a greater or less degree, by the primary qualities. On the one hand Aristotle is aware of the dangers of hylozoism and explicitly criticizes some of his predecessors for their failure to pay due attention to the differences between the animate and the inanimate.[25] On the other, his own view of the material substrate of animate beings incorporates the crucial assumption that the matter in question is not just inert stuff: as the definition of soul at *DA* 412ᵃ20 f. puts it, what the soul is a first actuality *of* must itself possess the potentiality for life—a potentiality exemplified not just by the instrumental parts, but to a lesser degree by the uniform parts of which they consist, and indeed by *their* material components, even when these are analysed in such apparently purely physicalist terms as the hot, the cold, the wet, and the dry:[26] that appearance, we may say, is rather deceptive.

Of course the extent to which Aristotle's account of parts of the body proceeds by reference to the faculties of the soul varies a great deal. That feature of his approach is at its most prominent in such a case as the heart, seen by Aristotle as the controlling principle of the living creature,[27] and in particular as the centre of the faculties of locomotion, of perception, and of nutrition/generation—a set of theses for which he argues in some detail, and in the case of perception, at least,

---

[21] See, for example, *GA* 784ᵃ35 f., ᵇ5, 786ᵃ20 f.

[22] See, for example, *GA* 732ᵃ18 f., 739ᵃ11, 752ᵃ2 f., 755ᵃ20, 762ᵃ20, cf *zōtikē thermotēs* at *Resp.* 473ᵃ9 f. and the frequent references to natural (*phusikē*) heat, e.g. *GA* 732ᵇ32, 766ᵃ35, ᵇ34, 783ᵇ30, 784ᵇ26, 786ᵃ11, *PA* 650ᵃ14, *Juv.* 469ᵇ8 ff., 470ᵃ19 ff.

[23] At *GA* 736ᵇ34 ff. the 'so-called hot' is contrasted with fire and said to have the nature of *pneuma* in it, which in turn is said to be 'analogous to the element of the stars'. Again at *PA* 652ᵇ7 ff. Aristotle criticizes as crude the notion that the soul of an animal is fire or some such *dunamis*, though he allows that it might be said to subsist in some such body, and at *GA* 762ᵃ18 ff., discussing how animals and plants are formed in earth and the moist, he says that there is water in earth, and *pneuma* in water, and vital heat in all *pneuma*, concluding that 'in a way' (*tropon tina*) everything is full of soul.

[24] See, e.g. Rüsche (1930), Peck in Aristotle (1943), 576 ff., Verbeke (1945, 1978), Nussbaum (1978).

[25] See, esp. *DA* 411ᵃ7 ff., 14 ff. As is well known, however, Aristotle himself admits that the dividing line between what does, and what does not, have *psuchē* is hard to determine and that nature passes in continuous sequence from the inanimate to the animate, *HA* 588ᵇ4 ff., *PA* 681ᵃ12 ff.

[26] Value-judgements are also in play in some of Aristotle's uses of these four primary opposites, most notably in the frequent association of what is hotter with what is nobler; see e.g. *Resp.* 477ᵃ16 ff., *GA* 732ᵇ 31 ff., 733ᵃ33 ff.

[27] See e.g. *Juv.* 469ᵃ10 ff., *PA* 647ᵃ24 ff.

in the face of some difficult anatomical facts.[28] But even when a part is not directly linked to a specific faculty of the soul it may, and generally does, serve such faculties indirectly or the general well-being of the living creature as a whole. Thus his view of the brain and the lungs is that in different ways they both act primarily to balance the heat in the region round the heart, and so indirectly help to ensure its activities and the life of the animal as a whole.[29] To be sure, some parts, he explicitly insists, have no final causes. The useless residues (unlike the useful ones, such as semen) are just that, the end-products of such processes as digestion. One example is bile, where interestingly enough he expressly contradicts the view of those who had ascribed a role to it in perception,[30] and where he states the general doctrine that while some parts have a purpose, others arise of necessity as a consequence of these, *PA* 677ª15 ff. Yet even here though the useless residues serve no good, the account he offers of how they arise, of necessity, in the body, refers to those processes of which they are the by-product; and those processes themselves, digestion for example, take one inevitably back to the functions of the soul.

Two final examples may be given to illustrate the pervasiveness of psychological considerations in Aristotle's zoological theories. In the seemingly unpromising case of the diaphragm, which acts as a membrane separating the upper from the lower viscera, the particular function that Aristotle sees it as serving is to ensure that the perceptive soul (in the heart) is not affected too rapidly by the exhalations that arise from the processes of digestion.[31] Nature likes to keep the nobler parts apart from the less noble, when she can, but 'nobler' in this case is the perceptive faculty of soul and the 'less noble' (by implication) the nutritive function.

Then it is particularly remarkable that even in the case of the three pairs of dimensions, up–down, right–left, and front–back, in living creatures, Aristotle's account is essentially psychological in orientation. These three pairs are not just spatial differentiations, nor are they value-neutral. They are each defined, so far as the animal body goes, in terms of a particular faculty of the soul: thus up is the direction of growth and that from which nourishment is taken in,[32] right is the principle or beginning of movement,[33] and front the principle of perception.[34] These theories incorporate value-judgements—for the three terms that are prin-

---

[28] I detailed these in my (1978), 222 ff., especially those connected with Aristotle's claims that the senses of taste and touch evidently extend to the heart and so the other senses necessarily do so too, *Juv.* 469ª12 ff.

[29] See esp. *PA* 652ª24 ff., ᵇ6 ff., 656ª19 ff., *GA* 743ᵇ29 ff. on the brain and *PA* 668ᵇ33 ff. on the lungs.

[30] See *PA* 676ᵇ22 ff., where Aristotle appears to have Plato, *Timaeus* 71 A ff. in mind. Cf. Aristotle's criticisms of the view that the brain is the seat of perception at *PA* 656ª15 ff., though certain senses are located in the head, 686ª8 ff.

[31] See *PA* 672ᵇ14 ff.: but he denies the view that the *phrenes* participate in thinking, *PA* 672ᵇ31 ff.

[32] See e.g. *IA* 705ª32 ff. This doctrine leads Aristotle to the conclusion that plants are—functionally—'upside-down' since they take in their nourishment through their roots, *PA* 686ᵇ31 ff., *IA* 705ᵇ6, cf. *PA* 683ᵇ18 ff. on the Testacea.

[33] See e.g. *IA* 705ᵇ29 ff.   [34] See e.g. *IA* 705ᵇ8 ff.

ciples are superior to their contraries[35]—and they are invoked in a whole series of detailed explanations of anatomical and zoological facts, such as the relative positions of the windpipe and oesophagus, those of the two kidneys, and the position of the heart, down to such questions as why in general the right claw of crabs and crawfish is bigger than the left.[36]

Thus far we have been concerned mainly with the theories and explanations advanced in *PA*, *IA*, and *GA*, and the question that now arises is how far similar considerations are at work also in the more purely descriptive inquiry in *HA*.[37] *HA* has often been thought of as a fairly unsystematic, diffuse, and at points repetitive presentation of primary data. Yet, as has been argued most recently by Lennox and was indeed already clearly shown in Peck's analytic table of contents,[38] the overall plan for the study of the differentiae of animals that is set out in *HA* 1 is adhered to—on the whole—quite closely, at least so far as *HA* 1–9 go.[39]

At *HA* 487ª11 ff. Aristotle identifies four modes of differentiation—in respect, namely, of lives (*bioi*), activities (*praxeis*), characters (*ēthē*), and parts (*moria*)— and after the preliminary sketch (*tupōi*) of these in *HA* 1. 1–6, the whole of *HA* 1. 7–4. 7 deals with parts, books 5–8 discuss activities and lives, and book 9 considers characters, though of course there are digressions, within each of these main sections, that do not conform to this simplified schema. But the first point that may strike one concerning the particular differentiae that Aristotle uses to organize his material is that three of the four relate directly and primarily to the soul. It may appear to some modern commentators to be rather strange that his zoology should extend to the study of animal *characters*, though I have already remarked on the references to the intelligence and courage of different species in Aristotle's theory correlating these with the qualities of their blood.[40] Moreover, the nutritive and locomotive faculties of the soul bulk large in his account of *activities* and *lives*, when he discusses, for example, where different species of animals feed, whether they are swimmers or fliers or go on land, though there is, of course, much else to his discussion of those differentiae, including other primarily psychological factors such as whether a species is social (*politikon*) and whether it lives in groups or is solitary.[41]

Moreover, in his preliminary account of the fourth main type of differentia, the parts, at *HA* 488ᵇ29 ff., he focuses first on the 'most necessary' parts of an animal —namely, first those to do with nutrition, the intake and storing of food, and the

---

[35] See esp. *IA* 706ᵇ12 f., *PA* 665ᵇ22 ff., and cf. Lloyd (1966), 52 ff.

[36] See Lloyd (1966), 52 ff. which discusses also the particular difficulty (recognized by Aristotle) presented by the fact that the human heart is on the left, *PA* 665ᵇ18 ff., 666ᵇ6 ff.: cf. Byl (1968, 1980), who stresses rather the symbolic importance of the heart's being in the centre.

[37] This is not to deny that *HA* has its theoretical concerns and assumptions: cf. Balme (1987*a*), 88 f., Lennox (forthcoming).

[38] See Lennox (forthcoming), and cf. Peck in Aristotle (1965), xci ff., xciv ff.

[39] *HA* 10 is anomalous and its authenticity (as also that of the other later books, 1–9) has been doubted: see, however, Balme (1985).

[40] See above on *PA* 651ª12 ff., the conclusion of the discussion in *PA* 2. 2 ff. I discussed aspects of Aristotle's views on the characters of animals (e.g. *HA* 488ᵇ13 ff.) in my (1983), 18 ff.

[41] See especially *HA* 487ᵇ34 ff.

excretion of residues, and then again those to do with reproduction—whereas perception, especially touch, and differences in the organs of locomotion figure prominently (though not exclusively) in the subsequent preliminary list. This doctrine of the necessary parts of an animal (that is, those that correspond to various essential vital functions), plays, as I tried to show some years ago, an important heuristic role.[42] At least in the detailed analysis of the internal parts of the bloodless animals, in *HA* 4. 1–7, Aristotle is particularly concerned to identify what serves the three basic functions, (i) the intake of food, (ii) the excretion of residue, and (iii) the control of the vital functions as a whole—which he expects to find and usually does find in the centre of the animal.[43]

Thus he regularly considers such questions as the position of the mouth, the presence or absence of teeth and tongue or analogous organs, the position and nature of the stomach and gut, as also the reproductive organs and the differences between males and females.[44] A series of passages shows that he actively considered whether or not certain lower groups of animals produce residue and attempted to identify and trace the excretory vent. But while the whole course of the alimentary canal is thoroughly discussed in connection with each of the bloodless groups, he has little or nothing to say about the brain or about the respiratory (he would say refrigeratory) system. He has of course no idea of the nervous system, though his conception of the role of the heart as the controlling principle of the major vital functions answers the question of where the ruling principle of the animal is located. But although he recognizes that some creatures continue to live, even when divided—and they have *several* principles of life[45]— his expectation is that normally there will be just one such centre and indeed that it will be (as the heart is) in the middle of the body. Naturally, then, interpreting the function of the brain in the larger, blooded animals as one of refrigeration, he also misses the true role of the analogous parts in such creatures as the cephalopods, where the influence of his expectations concerning the function of the heart dominates his account of the central internal parts.

We may now attempt to take stock of this first section of our analysis. Given that Aristotle's doctrine of *psuchē* is a doctrine of the vital faculties of living creatures, and given further his explicit insistence on the importance of *psuchē* for the student of nature as a whole, we should expect—and we actually find—that both his general doctrine of soul and his specific theories distinguishing its various faculties exercise a profound influence throughout the zoological treatises. Of course those psychological theories are not the sole preoccupation of his work in zoology: other concerns, some of a strategic nature, can be identified. One that I have discussed elsewhere is his use of human beings as a model for other animals, a model to which they aspire and from which they deviate to a greater or lesser degree.[46] The framework provided by his schema of causation, formal, final,

[42] See Lloyd (1979), 213 ff., on *PA* 655ᵇ29 ff., *Juv.* 468ᵃ13 ff. especially.
[43] See esp. *PA* 681ᵇ33 ff., *Juv.* 467ᵇ28 ff.
[44] The evidence is set out in detail in Lloyd (1979), 213 f., nn. 438–41.
[45] See e.g. *PA* 682ᵃ1 ff.
[46] See Lloyd (1983), pt. 1, §3, pp. 26 ff. with references to previous discussions in p. 26 n. 56.

efficient, and material causes, or more simply the contrast between what is for the sake of something and the necessary, broadly coincides with his distinction between soul and body, but enables questions to be raised that a mere dichotomy between soul and body might obscure. The notion that Aristotle is further particularly concerned to establish correlations in order eventually to provide demonstrations of zoological propositions, has been argued with some force in recent years,[47] and other strategic and tactical aims for stretches of his zoology could be suggested. Moreover, many detailed descriptions of the parts of animals, and of animal behaviour, exhibit no specific direct influence from his particular psychological theories, whatever may be the indirect effects of his overall concern with soul.

On the other hand those theories are clearly invoked in contexts that extend far beyond his discussion of the instrumental parts or sense-organs that directly serve the main faculties of the soul—nutrition/generation, perception, locomotion. His account of two particularly important uniform parts, flesh and blood, ascribes to them a role in more than just the processes of nutrition, in cognition in the one case, and in character and intelligence in the other. The doctrine that the matter of the living creature has a potentiality for life applies not just to instrumental, not just to uniform, parts, for it also extends as far as the primary qualities, at least when he invokes vital heat and the connection between wet and life. Even spatial dimensions, in the animal kingdom, are defined in terms of faculties of soul. The theory of the essential parts of the animal, corresponding to vital faculties, provides an important heuristic tool and an articulating schema for much of his zoological work. In such contexts we may talk not just of a general background of psychological interests—provided by the doctrine that soul is the form and final cause of the living creature—but also of specific influences from the detailed application to zoology of his particular psychological theories.

II

Having considered aspects of the relevance of the psychology to the zoology, we may now turn to discuss how the points we have made may relate to the interpretation of Aristotle's general theories on such topics as definition, essence, form, and matter. Of course what is said on those topics outside the zoology is highly complex and disputed: my aim here is to tackle some applications of those notions in the zoology, which provides, after all, our most extensive evidence of Aristotle at work in natural philosophy.

On the question of definition, first, some further preliminaries are necessary. Outside the zoology, as is well known, we may distinguish between what we may call a narrower view of definition and a broader one. According to the broader one, to give an account of a composite *sunholon*, both matter and form must be included. When something is a 'this in a this' (*tode en tōide*), then just to give

[47] See esp. Lennox (1987*b*).

an account of the form or essence is inadequate, for the account[48] of such an item should include matter as well. This is, moreover, regularly illustrated with reference to natural objects, *ta phusika*, including the parts of living creatures.[49] Indeed, since the *dia ti* question can be asked in respect to all four causes, the account of what a thing is may include all four.[50]

On the other hand there is also a narrower view of definition according to which it relates to form or essence and matter is excluded. We should be careful to distinguish, as Michael Frede has recently done in a useful discussion,[51] between two possible ways of taking the general dictum that definition is of the form (or essence). This might correspond either to the (strong) view that no definition of a *sunholon* is possible: the only legitimate objects of definition are forms or essences. Or it could be the weaker view that the only way in which a definition of a *sunholon* can be given is *by specifying* its form/essence: but it is perfectly possible to do that and so in that sense a definition of a *sunholon* is not ruled out. But on both the weak and the strong view the definitions that are given do not include any reference to matter.

What the *Metaphysics* has to say about the definitions of animal and man is controversial, and I shall have to be brief on the undeniably complex questions of the interpretation of Z10–11 in particular, for the sake of getting to evaluate the actual practice in the zoology. Those two chapters introduce, famously, remarks to the effect that while the soul of animals is the essence, 'if one is to define each part well, one will not define it without its function (*ergon*), which does not belong without perception' (1035ᵇ16 ff.); and again that one should not 'do away with matter' (1036ᵇ22 ff.); and 'for an animal is something capable of perceiving[52] and it is not possible to define it without movement[53] and so not without the parts' being disposed in a certain way' (1036ᵇ28 ff.). Quite *what* concessions are being made in those passages is untransparent, but it is essential to notice that

---

[48] Aristotle often uses the term *logos*, but sometimes *horismos/horizesthai*, when such an account is in question: see e.g. *Metaph.* 1025ᵇ30 ff., cf. 1064ᵃ21 ff.

[49] See esp. *Metaph.* 1025ᵇ24 ff., *DA* 429ᵇ13 f., see Balme (1987ᵇ) 306 ff.

[50] See esp. *Ph.* 194ᵇ16 ff., where the four causes correspond to four types of *dia ti* question.

[51] Frede (forthcoming).

[52] At *Metaph.* 1036ᵇ28 the MSS and editions have *aistheton*, perceptible, but Frede–Patzig (1988), ii, 210 f., plausibly conjecture that we should read *aisthetikon*, capable of perceiving, which certainly gives a better sense.

[53] As Frede (forthcoming) points out (cf. Frede–Patzig (1988), ii. 211 ff.), this could be taken in two ways, either that it is not possible to define animal without reference to motion, or that it is not possible to do so without making it clear that the animal is in motion. Cf. Balme (1987ᵇ), 302 ff., who has recently argued that the earlier chapters of *Metaph.* Z (esp. 5–6, 10–11) state an *aporia* that is only resolved in *Metaph.* Z17 and H 6. However those two chapters address the problem of the unity of the genus and differentiae. Z10–11 mainly address a rather different issue, namely the unity of the constituents of the composite whole, where the parts in question are form or essence, and matter. Moreover, *after* a brief allusion to the problem of the unity of the parts of the definition at 1037ᵃ18–20, Aristotle *goes on*, at 1037ᵃ21–ᵇ7, to state firm if no doubt provisional conclusions on the topics under discussion in Z10–11 (how there is a *logos* of the composite whole). One may contrast the end of Z13, where after the new beginning signalled at 1038ᵇ1 ff., Aristotle does point to the difficulties that stem from the denial of universal as substance for definition and does explicitly refer forward to a later discussion, 1039ᵃ14 ff., 20 ff.

when Aristotle comes to sum up the arguments of those two chapters, as he does at 1037ᵃ21 ff., he is quite firm. There he claims to have explained the way in which there is, and the way in which there is not, a *logos* of the composite whole, where it is clear that by *logos* he means definition, not merely account, and where his recommendation corresponds to the narrow definition according to which matter is excluded. 'With the matter', he says at 1037ᵃ27 ff., 'there is no (*logos*)— for it is indeterminate: but according to the primary substance there is one, for example of man the *logos* of soul...But in the composite substance, such as snub nose or Callias, matter too will be present.' To recapitulate Frede's point, Aristotle might be saying that no definition of a *sunholon* is possible (the only things you can define are forms) or he might be saying that the only way in which a definition of a *sunholon* is possible is by specifying its form or essence. But *either way* matter is excluded.

Full weight should be given to the fact that there is something of a discrepancy within the *Metaphysics* itself on the kind of definitions of animals and their parts that are to be given. Some texts treat them as a *tode en tōide* and point to the broader notion of definition, while others clearly recommend the narrower—not just in general but in relation to such items as animal and man in particular. It is obviously tempting to resolve this discrepancy by privileging one set of texts and treating it as canonical, the other as deviant, or otherwise by constructing arguments that Aristotle might have used to square his apparently divergent recommendations. However, to the latter point it has to be said that that would have to *be* a *construction*. Moreover, so far as privileging one group of texts goes, there is not just no clear indication as to which to take as canonical, but no indication whatsoever. In these circumstances we should rather contemplate the possibility of genuine hesitations on the subject on Aristotle's part.

However, since my principal task in this section is to review Aristotle's actual practice in the zoological treatises, the first issue that must be addressed is the extent to which they exhibit a concern with definition at all, and if so what the focus of that concern is. Pierre Pellegrin, for instance, has recently argued that the zoology is essentially a 'moriology', and that whatever may be true of Aristotle's analysis of the differentiae of parts, he should not be seen as intent on giving definitions of animal species. Good examples of such definitions— Pellegrin points out with some justice[54]—are not to be found in the zoological works. Without entering into detailed debate on yet another controversial issue,[55] three remarks may be in order. First, in Aristotle's apologia for zoology in *PA* 1. 5, even if it is expressly said that the student of nature is chiefly interested in form rather than in matter, it is also stressed that he should study the whole nature (*PA* 645ᵃ30 ff.). Secondly, the attack on the dichotomists in *PA* 1. 2–4 is an attack on their incorrect procedures in obtaining their account of animals (*PA* 642ᵇ30 ff., 643ᵃ7 ff., 17, ᵇ10 ff., 644ᵃ10 f.); they are criticized for mistakes in obtaining the animal kinds (a point conceded by Pellegrin), and that would be

---

[54] See Pellegrin (1982/1986) and (1985), esp. 99.   [55] Cf. further Lloyd (forthcoming).

strange if Aristotle were not concerned to do better in the same regard. Thirdly, the absence of good complete examples of definitions of animal species might be as much a sign of his realizing the difficulty of the task as of his not wanting to undertake it.[56]

Those difficulties take us to the heart of the matter. He has plenty of criticisms to offer of the dichotomists' incorrect procedures.[57] By implication, certain points about the procedures he would appear to approve emerge, though problems certainly arise concerning how he sought to apply those procedures in practice.

It is clear, for instance, that an animal kind is not to be defined in terms of a genus plus a single differentia arrived at by a single line of division: rather it should be defined by a conjunction of a plurality of differentiae (e.g. *PA* 643[b]12). Again certain natural kinds, such as birds and fish, picked out in ordinary Greek, should not be split up, that is they should not be put into different divisions (*PA* 642[b]10 ff.). Again division should be by items in the *ousia* and not by essential or *per se* accidents (*sumbebēkota kath' hauto, PA* 643[a]27 f.);[58] for this he offers a geometrical illustration: one should not define a triangle by saying that its internal angles sum to two right angles (though the application of this principle to zoological kinds is not as clear as it might be). Nevertheless all this shows, as Balme has put it,[59] that Aristotle's 'aim is not simply to make out and identify but to grasp the substantial being of the object'. Some of his remarks clearly indicate that every species of animal should figure somewhere in the eventual division and indeed only once (*PA* 642[b]31 ff., 643[a]13 ff.). I have always thought that that goes to show that he did indeed have in mind, as his goal, a comprehensive and exclusive system, not merely a description of non-exclusive groupings (though many modern commentators deny that he ever even sought a comprehensive classification of animals).[60]

The rules of correct division, stated in general terms, may be clear enough. The difficulties arise, as I remarked, in their application. Two interlocking questions that prove remarkably recalcitrant are:

(i) Does Aristotle operate with, or presuppose, what I have called the narrow, or the broad, view of definition?

(ii) Granted the equation 'soul is to body as form is to matter', how, in practice, in defining (whether of the broad or the narrow variety) is that to be cashed out?

[56] Those difficulties did not, however, deter him from making a series of remarks concerning the being and essence of certain animal kinds, and indeed of offering certain definitional accounts, see further below, pp. 163–4. Cf. further Gotthelf (1985) on what he calls partial definitions (though it should be observed that it is only *complete* definitions that will meet *all* the requirements on indemonstrable primary premisses in the *Posterior Analytics*).
[57] There is a particularly clear and incisive analysis of Aristotle's critique of the incorrect use of *dihairesis* in Balme (1987a) 69 ff., setting out the implied positive recommendations at 74 ff.
[58] Cf. *PA* 645[a]36 ff., *HA* 491[a]9 f. See Kullmann (1974), 63 ff.
[59] Balme (1987a), 75.
[60] See e.g. Lennox (1987a), (1987b) Pellegrin (1982/1986)—though contrast Pellegrin's rejection of a taxonomic interest in Aristotle with his chapter on Aristotle's classification of animals. In Balme ((1961), 212 = (1975), 192) allowance is made for the possibility of an eventual classification of animals, though in the revised version of the paper, (1987a), all reference to such an idea is omitted.

Here the application of some of the results of the first part of this paper raises some far-reaching questions that can be brought to bear on current controversies on the viability or credibility of Aristotle's philosophy of mind in general.

On the first question it might seem that the answer must be obvious. It must be the broad view, it might be thought, since if the narrow is adopted (where matter is excluded) there is a very obvious objection. If definition is in terms of soul alone, this would seem to provide a totally inadequate means of differentiating animals. Of course the differences between plants, (other) animals, and humans can be and are grasped through the faculties of soul (as when he says that 'we define animal by the possession of perception', *PA* 653ᵇ22 ff.), but this will not be enough to secure the differences *within* animal kinds that Aristotle needs. After all, all animals possess the faculties of nutrition/generation and the sense of touch, and most also have all the other senses and the faculty of locomotion, even though only one has reason in addition. Rather it is, of course, at the very least the *modalities* of those faculties in the different kinds of animals that will enable us to differentiate them. Those modalities will include, for instance, their methods of reproduction (viviparous, ovoviviparous, oviparous, larviparous, etc.), their modes of locomotion (walkers, flyers, swimmers, corresponding to their organs of locomotion and whether they are biped, quadruped, footless, polypod) and their modes and organs of nutrition.[61] Those types of differentiae evidently do receive much attention and at *GA* 732ᵇ15 ff. he is particularly concerned to point out the lack of correlation between organs of locomotion and modes of reproduction, insisting that the latter cannot be held to depend on the former.

So if we take into account, as we surely should, the diverse modalities of the faculties of soul, that provides a far less impoverished basis for differentiating the chief groups of animals that Aristotle recognized.[62] However, a further difficulty for the narrow view of definition is presented by his apparent endorsement of the point that the major groups identified by common usage[63] have been marked out, in general, by the *shapes* of their parts and of their whole body, while within each group the differences are ones of degree, of the more and the less, for example of bigger–smaller, softer–harder, smoother–rougher.[64] Here too, however, caution

[61] See e.g. the differentiation by modes of locomotion at *PA* 639ᵇ1 ff. and at *MA* 698ᵃ5 ff., and reference to the modes and organs of nutrition in the account of bloodless kinds in *PA* 678ᵃ26 ff.

[62] When in the *Politics* Aristotle compares classifying constitutions with classifying animals, he envisages a procedure that first identifies the essential parts of an animal and then considers all the possible permutations of these, *Pol.* 1290ᵇ25 ff.: here the essential parts are specified as the sense-organs, the parts responsible for receiving and elaborating the nourishment, and the organs of loco-motion, a specification that keeps close to his usual view of the principal faculties of the soul.

[63] However, he recognized that some important groups had *not* been named before him, specifying in particular that this was the case with the major division between the blooded and the bloodless, *PA* 642ᵇ15.

[64] See Lennox (1987*b*). I would agree with Balme (1987*a*), 79, however, that the reference to morphology in *PA* 1, e.g. 644ᵇ7 ff. (cf. *HA* 491ᵃ14 ff.) is to be taken to relate to popular criteria, not to Aristotle's own. At *Metaph.* 1044ᵃ9 ff. he specifies that differences in the 'more and the less' relate to differences in the composite whole, not to differences in the 'substance according to the form': this would suggest that it is differences in the *sunhola*, rather than in the forms or essences as such, that are in question when he gives an account of the different kinds of beak that birds have or the different lengths of their legs, while such differences have to be related to, and may be explained in terms of,

is needed. In practice differences in shape are cited often enough:[65] but we have to bear in mind that Aristotle's explicit doctrine is that the parts are in general for the sake of their functions. Every organ or tool, and every part of the body, is for the sake of something, and *that* is specified by some activity (*praxis tis*): and so the whole body is for the sake of some complex activity[66] and so in a way the whole body is for the sake of soul and the parts of the body for the sake of the function (*ergon*) towards which each is naturally directed (*PA* 645ᵇ14 ff.).[67] On this basis it would appear that while, naturally enough, morphology is often used to distinguish animal kinds, it is primarily the *activities* of the parts that have the shape they have that interests Aristotle—a viewpoint that is compatible with the narrow as well as with the broad sense of definition. That shape by itself is *not* a sufficient defining characteristic is clear from what is said at *PA* 641ᵃ18 ff., where he points out that once the soul has left the animal, none of the parts remains the same *except in shape*.

The best way to test how much, in practice, Aristotle was willing to include in animal definitions is to review the limited number of texts that use the vocabulary of definition, essence, and substance; though since, notoriously, *ousia* is said in many ways, and *logos* too, these texts provide evidence that has to be used with the greatest circumspection.[68] One such group of passages does not take us very far, although it does confirm that Aristotle uses the usual, *De Anima*, definitions of plant, animal, and human based on the faculties of soul they possess.[69] Again, when he says at *PA* 693ᵇ13 that flying belongs to the *ousia* of a bird, and at *PA* 695ᵇ18 f. that the nature of fish, according to the *logos* of their *ousia*, is to be swimmers, this too fits the narrow view of definition well enough, where it is limited to the faculties of soul, in that both these cases refer to the modalities of the faculty of locomotion.

However, a test case for how much might be included in definition is provided by references to such factors as *being blooded* or *bloodless*, mentioned in both the bird (*PA* 693ᵇ6) and fish (695ᵇ20) examples, and said more generally to belong to the account that marks out (*horizonti*) the *ousia* of the blooded and the bloodless animals at *PA* 678ᵃ33 ff. How are these texts to be interpreted? One view takes it first that when being blooded or bloodless is said to belong to the 'account that marks out the being' of certain animals, it is indeed a *definition*, not just some

differences in activities, life-styles, and feeding-habits, see e.g. *PA* 692ᵇ22 ff., 693ᵃ10 ff., 694ᵃ1 ff., ᵇ12 ff., *IA* 714ᵃ21 ff.

[65] See e.g. *PA* 692ᵇ8 ff.

[66] Reading *polumerous* with Peck at *PA* 645ᵇ17.

[67] Cf. *PA* 641ᵃ1 ff., 642ᵃ9 ff., 646ᵇ10 ff., 655ᵇ20 ff., 687ᵃ7 ff. and especially 694ᵇ13 ff. (nature makes instruments for the work and not vice versa).

[68] There is a partial collection of texts from *PA* 2–4 and *IA* in Gotthelf (1985), a survey from which he has, as he says, p. 28, omitted some 'methodological or otherwise theoretical' statements.

[69] At *PA* 653ᵇ22 ff., for instance, he says 'we define animal by the possession of perception, and first of all by the primary one, that is touch', a point repeatedly made elsewhere, e.g. *Sens.* 436ᵇ10 ff., *Somn. Vig.* 454ᵇ24 f., *Juv.* 467ᵃ24 f., 469ᵃ18 ff., ᵇ3 ff., *PA* 666ᵃ34, *GA* 731ᵇ4 f., 736ᵃ30 f., 741ᵃ9 f., 778ᵇ32 ff. Cf. *PA* 686ᵃ27 ff. on humans and *GA* 731ᵃ24 ff. on plants (with *GA* 715ᵇ16 ff., where the *ousia* of testacea is said to resemble that of plants).

weaker sense of 'account' that Aristotle has in mind. But given that the blood is said to be the matter of the whole body,[70] the conclusion we should draw, on this line of interpretation, is that we have strong evidence here for the broad sense of definition,[71] with Aristotle appearing to insist that a definition of an animal kind should include reference to the matter as well as to the form. The *ousia* thus marked out is the composite whole, *sunholon*, and—despite the recommendation of *Metaph.* Z11, 1037ᵃ26 ff.—it is to be defined by both components, not by the form alone.

However, that line of interpretation may be less secure than appears at first sight, and not just because of the conflict with *Metaph* Z11. Passing over some minor difficulties,[72] I turn to one that arises from consideration of a text in the criticism of the dichotomists, *PA* 643ᵃ1 ff. There Aristotle puts it that it is not possible for a single indivisible *eidos* of being to belong to animals that differ *eidei*: rather it (the supposed indivisible *eidos* of being) will always admit of differentiation. His particular concern is to undermine the use of privative terms as differentiae, and quite how he can rescue his own use of such terms (e.g. bloodless) is itself controversial.[73] However, his argument proceeds by taking two positive examples, bipedality and bloodedness. Bipedality in a bird and bipedality in a human are to be differentiated (643ᵃ3 f.), and there is no doubt at all that he does indeed endorse this differentiation; when he comes to consider the question at *PA* 693ᵇ2 ff., for instance, he distinguishes between the inward-bending two-leggedness of birds and the outward-bending two-leggedness of humans. But his remark about bloodedness is that if they (the kinds that are blooded) are blooded, the blood is different, or else the blood is not to be included in the *ousia* (*PA* 643ᵃ4 f.)—where we should observe that he says not that bloodedness is a genus represented in different species, but that the blood itself is different.

Of the two options mentioned, I think it is clear that Aristotle himself takes the first: the blood is indeed to be differentiated, and as we have already seen in Section I, he offers a careful and detailed account of the differences in the quality of the blood of different-blooded animals and insists on the importance of doing so since the blood is responsible for many characteristics both of the character and of the perception of animals.[74] Moreover, if that is the option he favours, the one

---

[70] See above n. 12.

[71] In the sense 'define' the verb *horizesthai* is usually used in the middle, not in the active, as at *PA* 678ᵃ34 in our passage, where the sense may be looser, 'mark out'. However, even in the middle the verb is used of different kinds of definition, notably at *DA* 403ᵃ29 ff. where Aristotle first describes and then criticizes the definitions of 'anger' that on the one hand the *phusikos*, and on the other the *dialektikos*, would give.

[72] One such is that in the discussion of fish, Aristotle first says that their nature is to be swimmers according to the *logos* of their *ousia*, where *ousia* can be taken as essence or primary substance in the *Metaph.* Z sense: but then two lines later he remarks that fish are 'blooded according to their *ousia*', where, on the line of interpretation suggested, this should be glossed as the *sunholon*, *PA* 695ᵇ17 ff. (cf. *PA* 693ᵇ6 ff., 13 on birds). But if this is a somewhat harsh transition, one may note that it is no more so than many in the *Metaphysics* itself.

[73] See e.g. Balme in Aristotle (1972ᵃ), 110, 120 f., Gotthelf (1985), 34 f.

[74] See above, p. 152 and n. 16, and cf. e.g. *PA* 679ᵃ25 f. on bloodless animals.

he *rejects* (on this interpretation) is that blood is no part of the *ousia* (*PA* 643ᵃ4 f.) —where he can hardly be rejecting the idea that blood is part of the composite whole and presumably has in mind that it is no part of the essence.

What this might be taken to suggest is that although blood is said to be matter, it has a role in the being of certain animals that that by itself does not capture. Rather, bloodedness has to be differentiated and the differentiations that will mark out the blood of one species from that of another contribute to the activities of each[75]—and *mutatis mutandis* the same will apply also to what is analogous to blood in the bloodless groups. But if that might suggest a line of argument that would go to save the principle suggested in *Metaph.* Z11, that definition is of the *form*, it would do so only at the cost of highlighting the problem that may be said to emerge as one of the by-products of our analysis in Section I. If *bloodedness* belongs to the being as essence (and not just to the *sunholon* as the composite of form and matter) how far does the essence or the form extend? What I have called the narrow view of definition threatens to become indistinguishable from the broad: or in other words the threat is to the very application of the form–matter dichotomy in the case of living creatures.

There is no doubt that the form–matter dichotomy is needed in the zoology, and not just for any definition of an animal kind or animal part that Aristotle might wish to attempt; nor just for the sake of the standard analysis of substances as *sunhola* of form plus matter (and, after all, living creatures are the paradigmatic and primary examples of substances in the *Metaphysics*). Aristotle also needs that dichotomy in zoology in, for example, his theory of reproduction, where the form is contributed by the male parent, the matter by the female.[76] However, the problem is clear from a consideration of the differences in the way in which the dichotomy applies in the two main spheres to which it is applied, to living creatures on the one hand, artefacts on the other—difficulties that Ackrill, among others, has remarked.[77] Of course, even in the case of artefacts, the matter of which a house is built is not just matter, certainly not 'prime matter' (if, as is controversial, that corresponds to an idea that can be reached by abstraction; though all are agreed that it is nowhere encountered in the world). Rather, the matter is bricks or stone or wood, each of which has certain characteristics that differentiate it from other kinds of thing. But in the case of artefacts the bricks or stone have the characteristics they have (as bricks or stones) whether or not they are incorporated in a house.

But that is not true of the material parts of living creatures, neither the uniform parts, flesh, bones, blood, and so on, nor the non-uniform ones. As Aristotle says in so many words at *PA* 645ᵃ35 ff., the material the biologist has to deal with are things 'that do not even occur separated from the being itself'. *All* the parts of the body have soul:[78] all (with the exception of the useless residues) contribute

---

[75] At *PA* 647ᵇ29 ff. Aristotle remarks generally that there are differences in the uniform parts that are 'for the sake of what is better', exemplifying this with the variations in the blood: cf. *PA* 648ᵃ13 ff.

[76] See above, p. 150 and n. 7 and cf. Code (1987).

[77] Ackrill (1972–3/1979). Cf., however, e.g. Williams (1986), Lear (1988), ch. 4.

[78] See above, n. 5.

in one way or another to the vital faculties of the living creature. In practice, in zoology, as he says at *PA* 643ª25, no part is *just* matter. Unlike what is true of the analysis of artefacts, the zoologist has to study composite wholes whose constituent *material* parts cannot be said to have the characteristics they do as the material parts they are *outside* the composite whole: their characteristics cannot be properly specified independently of the form, that is the vital faculties.

We are used to the notion of the correlativity of form and matter; what will count as form, what as matter, will depend on the *whole* under consideration. But in the case of living creatures, the fact that their (proximate) matter is not independently identifiable as the matter it is outside living creatures (dead flesh is no flesh) introduces a fundamental difference. For Aristotle to talk as he does of a man being decomposed into bones, tendons, and flesh (e.g. *Metaph.* 1035ª18 ff.) is from one point of view to talk loosely: for the man is not destroyed into flesh and bones but into what is only homonymously flesh and bones (and even if he had specified blood as the matter, the same point would apply).

From the vantage-point of the issues we have considered, some final remarks may be ventured on the current debate between functionalists and anti-functionalists on the question of Aristotle's philosophy of mind and its credibility. First, a series of texts demonstrate, I should have thought conclusively, that the anti-functionalists must be right on the basic point: there can be no question of the souls/forms of living creatures being realizable in matter other than the matter in which they are found, and what has been called the 'compositional plasticity' of *psuchē* is minimal, if not zero.[79] On the other hand, that is certainly not ruled out, indeed it is emphasized, in the case of artefacts—within limits of course: the same form of a house can be realized in either bricks or stone or cement (even if not in pure sand or in water: the saw, as Aristotle put it, not in wood nor wool[80]), and that shows that the expectations that the functionalists entertain are expectations that have a genuine Aristotelian basis, even if not one in his psychology or biology.

Burnyeat argues that since the Aristotelian theory of matter has been exploded by science since Descartes, we cannot consider his theory of mind credible. But that seems both too hard and too soft. Too hard, maybe, because it is not everything about Aristotle's theory of matter that is at fault. (One might add that as between Aristotle and Descartes's own view of matter, there may not be too much to choose between them from the point of view of *modern physics*, whatever we say about modern philosophy of mind: a philosophy of mind that aimed to take modern physics fully into account could not afford to start from a Cartesian mind–matter contrast any more that from an Aristotelian one.) But too soft, because even for Aristotle there is a problem. This is not the quasi-evolutionary problem of the emergence of life. But a problem exists, none the less, in reconciling the artefact model of *sunholon* with the vitalist one, of

---

[79] When the possibility of the eye being constituted by air (rather than, as he believes, water) is mentioned at *Sens.* 438ª13 ff., ᵇ3 ff., this is not in the spirit of investigating 'plasticity' but part of a complex argument from exhaustion to show that it *must* be of water. Contrast Code (forthcoming).

[80] *Metaph.* 1044ª29.

reconciling one view that has it that matter is independently identifiable (in the sense that what counts as the matter has the properties it has independently of the whole of which it is the matter) and one that has it that it is not. Of course *sunhola* come at different levels of complexity, and so correspondingly do forms and matters. But the difference between the artefact model and the vitalist one is not one simply of grades of complexity (after all, there is nothing to choose between houses and dogs, or between bricks and blood, on that score) but one of the nature of the analysis of matter to be given: is it, or is it not, dependent on the *sunholon* or the form? The problem is the more acute in that there is a perfectly well-unified theory of matter on offer from Aristotle's rivals, the atomists. Indeed, Aristotle himself up to a point offers a unified theory of compounds, the homoiomerous substances that consist of compounds of the simple bodies. They have all undergone *alloiōsis*, qualitative change, and this allows him to claim that, as the homoiomerous substances they are, they acquire new properties. Yet what that theory still fails to provide for are the differences we have remarked between flesh and bones on the one hand, and the inanimate homoiomerous substances such as gold on the other.

Whether or not we find Aristotle's theory of mind credible, the unity of his theory of matter, both of his theory of the elements and that of the homoio-merous parts, is under extreme strain in Aristotle himself. The difficulties we have identified lead back to the issues we raised in relation to the ultimate constituents of material objects: the problem of reconciling what is true of earth, water, air, and fire *haplōs*, in an unqualified sense, and what is true of them as the constituent elements of living uniform parts: or again of reconciling what is true generally of hot, cold, wet, and dry, and of hot, cold, wet, and dry as what is 'responsible practically for death and life, and again for sleep and waking, for maturity and old age, and disease and health'. It is all very well to say that Aristotle has (as indeed he has) a top-down theory of life, but the problem when he *gets down* to the bottom level, to the general theory of material elements, is severe. He cannot afford two theories of the material elements, one for living things, the other for the inert. But to resist that conclusion he needs to explicate the relationship between the two, the relationship between, for example, vital heat, and heat, or between pneuma and air, or between pneuma in oil and pneuma in semen.[81]

These are problems, indeed, in his theory of matter. Burnyeat's paper focuses most usefully on that as the locus of important difficulties. But they were not problems that needed Descartes to discover, for some emerge already from a comparison with ancient atomism. Indeed, the hesitation in many of Aristotle's own pronouncements on just these issues can be taken to suggest that he already had a sense of the difficulties. To my mind the hesitations or the vacillations that we detect point to that conclusion, to a realization on Aristotle's own part of some

[81] See the texts cited above, nn. 22–3. For *pneuma* in semen, see e.g. *GA* 735^{b}33, 736^{a}1, 9, cf. 737^{b}26 ff.: for *pneuma* in various inanimate substances, see e.g. *Mete.* 383^{b}20 ff., *GA* 735^{b}19 ff., 761^{b}11, 762^{a}18 ff. (the last two passages in connection with spontaneous generation).

of the difficulties the complex of theories we have been discussing presented. I have focused in particular on the problem that arises in attempting to resolve the question of what is to be included in the definitions of living creatures—where both narrower and broader views are to be found both inside and outside the zoological treatises. Again I remarked on the problem of demarcating the living from the non-living. Any erosion of the firm distinctions between non-living and living, and between plants and animals (distinctions that correspond to the clearly demarcated differences in the faculties of soul that they possess), would be a major source of embarrassment for Aristotle's theory: and yet in practice he clearly allows that there are problematic cases.[82] Again, although he says less on the problem of the nature of vital heat, quite how far he has resolved to his own satisfaction its role in spontaneous generation, for instance, is not clear.

It is undeniably one of Aristotle's great originalities to have introduced matter as the correlative to form. But to win his point against Plato (as well as against the atomists) he has both to distinguish clearly between form and matter and to insist on the unity constituted by the two, the unity of the *sunholon*. Of his two main models, the artefact model does an excellent job illustrating the *distinction* (especially where the matter can be identified by the properties it has independently of the *sunholon* in which it figures). Conversely, the *unity* of form and matter is seen most clearly in the case where the form is the soul, the matter the living body of which it is the actuality.[83] Yet the greater the confidence Aristotle expresses in the unity, the greater the tensions that arise in the application, in practice, of the very idea of the distinction between form and matter. The more the vitalist model dominates, the more hylozoism threatens. But the more the contrast between the vitalist and the artefact model emerges, the more difficult it is to dismiss the competition provided by atomism. That he still works with the form/matter distinction in the zoology is abundantly clear: that there are difficulties in his so doing I have tried to show: that some of these are such that he himself was aware of them (in a way quite close to the form in which I have presented them) is I think likely.[84]

---

[82] Cf. the texts cited above, n. 25.

[83] The problem of the unity of form and matter in the composite whole is related to, but importantly distinct from, the problem of the unity of genus and differentia discussed at *Metaph.* Z12, 1037^{b}10 ff., H6, 1045^{a}7 ff. It is striking that to resolve the latter he appeals at 1045^{a}23 ff. to the relationship between form and matter, actuality and potentiality, *as if* their constituting a unity were less problematic.

[84] An earlier draft of this chapter was read to the Southern Association for Ancient Philosophy meeting at Cambridge in Sept. 1988. I would like to thank all these who participated in the discussion, and Myles Burnyeat, Malcolm Schofield, and Robert Wardy for subsequent further detailed comments.

10

DIALECTIC, MOTION, AND PERCEPTION: *DE ANIMA* BOOK 1

CHARLOTTE WITT

THE fact that *De Anima* is frequently read and taught omitting book 1 suggests a widespread acceptance of the idea that it has nothing important to tell us about Aristotle's views on the soul. To be sure, Aristotle's critical analysis of his predecessors' views of the nature of soul in 1. 2–5 is a goldmine of fascinating information concerning the ideas of soul held by important Presocratics, like Empedocles and Democritus, and by Plato. In discussing these figures Aristotle is an incisive and witty critic and, like most historians who are also philosophers, he is not always entirely fair to his elders.[1] Aristotle's purpose is not primarily historical, however, since a discussion of earlier views on a given topic is an integral and important part of his philosophical method, dialectic. In other words, the first book of the *De Anima* is as intrinsic a part of Aristotle's project in the treatise as the second two books. For Aristotle does not collect alternative views on the soul merely in order to refute them outright, but rather he is canvassing the opinions of the wise 'in order that we may profit by whatever is sound in their suggestions and avoid their errors' (403^b23–4). The method of dialectic collects and evaluates *endoxa*—common opinions and the opinions of the wise—in order to shape and direct the inquiry that follows. Book 1 of the *De Anima*, therefore, is also an important source for our understanding of Aristotle's views on the nature of soul.

Two characteristics of soul receive extensive discussion in book 1: the soul as the source or origin of motion of the living being and the soul as the seat of perception and cognition. Living or ensouled entities differ from non-living entities by virtue of these two characteristics, and, Aristotle tells us, earlier philosophers held that soul is responsible for them (403^b24–8). In the chapters which follow Aristotle presents criticisms of particular explanations of how soul accomplishes these tasks, and what soul must be like in order to do so, but he does not criticize the two characteristics themselves nor their attribution to soul. Not surprisingly then, both topics, perception and motion, receive extensive discussion later in the *De Anima* and elsewhere.[2] As we shall see, a careful look at Aristotle's discussions

---

[1] For a critical assessment of Aristotle's treatment of the Presocratics see Cherniss (1935).

[2] Perception is also discussed in *De Sensu*, and motion receives extended analysis in *De Motu Animalium*. For a fresh translation, commentary, and interpretation of the latter text see Nussbaum (1978).

of his predecessors' views in book 1 reveals several interesting and perhaps sur-prising commitments which have direct consequences for our understanding of Aristotle's own theories concerning the nature of soul, and how the soul is the source or origin of motion and perception.

I. Aristotelian Dialectic

There are many reasons a philosopher might find value in a critical discussion of the views of earlier philosophers on a given topic. Today, for example, the refu-tation of theories other than one's own is customarily included in the theory's presentation and defence, and the theories to be refuted may include the views of historical figures as well as contemporaries. Or one might think it important to survey earlier attempts in order to avoid potential mistakes and pitfalls. Or one might include a historical survey simply as a pedagogical device, as a way of introducing the contours of a philosophical problem to students or readers.

Aristotle has a richer conception of the value of the opinions of the wise for his own philosophical inquiry than the three alternatives listed above. It is stated clearly in his description of the philosophical purpose of dialectic in the *Topics*:

For the study of the philosophical sciences it [dialectic] is useful, because the ability to puzzle on both sides of a subject will make us detect more easily the truth and error about the several points that arise.   (101ᵃ35–7.)[3]

A dialectical treatment of the opinions of the wise has a negative purpose ('detect error') and a positive purpose ('detect truth'). The sentence from *DA* I quoted above states the dual purpose of dialectic even more clearly; it is 'to profit from what is sound and to avoid errors'. Dialectic, when it is used in a philosophical investigation, is aimed at ascertaining truth, and the sorting-out of what is true and what is false in the opinions of the wise is an integral part of that process for Aristotle. If this is so, then it follows that Aristotle believed that some of what his philosophical predecessors thought concerning the soul was true, and so we can profitably read book 1 of *De Anima* as explaining what Aristotle thought was right in earlier views, as well as explaining what he thought was wrong. Further, we can expect to glean information concerning Aristotle's views from his criticisms of earlier philosophers.

Before we turn to the issues discussed in book 1, however, it is important to have in hand a clearer grasp of what dialectic is for Aristotle. Dialectic is a form of argument or reasoning, according to Aristotle, which uses opinions (or *endoxa*) as its premisses. Which are the relevant opinions? Opinions which are accepted 'by everyone or by the majority or by the wise—that is, by all, or by the majority, or by the most notable and reputable of them' (*Top.* 100ᵇ20–2). The first step in a dialectical argument is to collect and organize the *endoxa* on a given topic; the relevant beliefs are of two basic sorts—common opinions and the

---

[3] Translations from the *Topics* are adapted from Aristotle (1960).

beliefs of the wise.[4] Aristotle never tells us directly why these two sorts of opinions, as opposed to my eccentric cousin Tom's beliefs, are a good starting point for an investigation. Two reasons come to mind: (i) they are opinions which will have to be addressed by our theory since they are either very widespread or very influential; (ii) they are more likely than other opinions, those of a crackpot or the stupid, to be true or partly true or enlightening.

Step two in a dialectical argument is to develop the puzzles or difficulties (*aporiai*) surrounding the *endoxa* we have collected. It is clear from the following passage from the *Metaphysics* that Aristotle thinks that this is a crucial step towards an adequate theory:

For those who wish to get clear of difficulties it is advantageous to state the difficulties well; for the subsequent free play of thought implies the solution of the previous difficulties, and it is not possible to untie a knot which one does not know. But the difficulty of our thinking points to a knot in the object; for in so far as our thought is in difficulties, it is in like case with those who are tied up; for in either case it is impossible to go forward. Therefore one should have surveyed all the difficulties beforehand, both for the reasons we have stated and because people who inquire without first stating the difficulties are like those who do not know where they have to go; besides, a person does not otherwise know even whether he has found what he is looking for or not; for the end is not clear to such a person, while to him who has first discussed the difficulties it is clear. Further, he who has heard all the contending arguments, as if they were the parties to the case, must be in a better position for judging. (995³27–ᵇ4.)[5]

The survey of difficulties or puzzles concerning a given topic consists in part of a statement of difficulties concerning the *endoxa* (the beliefs of the wise or the many), and in part in the development of any additional difficulties surrounding the issue whether they directly involve the *endoxa* or not.[6] The purpose of the critical phase of dialectic is twofold: it offers a glimpse of the end or goal of the investigation just as the negative of a photograph outlines a positive image, and it also helps one decide which theory is adequate or most adequate in relation to the array of puzzles and problems.

II. The Soul as Origin of Motion

Aristotle's most sustained and complex dialectical treatment of his predecessors' views concerns their idea that the soul is the origin of the animal's motion by

[4] Aristotle's description of *endoxa* in the *Topics* lists both common beliefs and the opinions of the wise, but the *endoxa* in *DA* 1. 2–5 consist of the opinions of the wise alone. This is consistent with Aristotle's definition of dialectical premisses in the *Topics*, however, since the definition is stated in the form of a disjunction; the premisses of a dialectical argument need not include *endoxa* of both sorts.

[5] Translations from the *Metaphysics* are adapted from Aristotle (1984).

[6] In *DA* 1 Aristotle develops *aporiai* of both sorts: in ch. 1 he presents a series of puzzles concerning soul in his own terminology, and in chs. 2–5 he develops the puzzles which arise from a consideration of the *endoxa* concerning soul.

itself moving. Near the beginning of *DA* 1. 2, Aristotle states very succinctly the position that he will criticize in the following chapter:

Some say that what originates movement is both pre-eminently and primarily soul; believing that what is not itself moved cannot originate movement in another, they arrived at the view that soul belongs to the class of things in movement.   (403ᵇ28–31.)[7]

He attributes this view to a heterogeneous group of thinkers: the atomists Democritus and Leucippus, who identified soul with spherical, fiery atoms; the Pythagoreans, who apparently considered the swirling, tiny particles sometimes visible in a sunbeam to be soul; the Platonists, who defined soul as a self-mover; and Anaxagoras, who said that mind (*nous*) moves the whole (403ᵇ31–404ᵇ6). Given that this list includes philosophers with clearly materialist theories of soul, like Democritus, and philosophers with clearly dualist theories, like Anaxagoras, who sharply distinguished mind from everything else in the cosmos, and some thinkers whose views are more difficult to classify in these terms, like Plato and the Pythagoreans, we need to determine exactly what the view is which Aristotle attributes to them all.[8]

The argument which these diverse thinkers share runs as follows:

(i) the soul is the primary origin of motion of the animal;
(ii) only something in motion can originate motion in another; therefore,
(iii) the soul moves.

Aristotle portrays his predecessors as believing (i) and (ii) and therefore accepting (iii) (403ᵇ29–30). His position, in contrast, is to accept (i) but to reject (ii) and hence the inference to (iii). Aristotle's acceptance of (i), the idea that the soul is the origin of motion of the animal, is clear from the fact that he never challenges it in his criticisms of earlier philosophers, and from the fact that it is mentioned prominently in his own account of animal motion later in *De Anima* (432ᵃ15–19). Additional evidence of Aristotle's acceptance of (i) can be found in his criticism of the theory that the soul is a *harmonia* of the body: 'the power of originating movement cannot belong to a *harmonia*, while all concur in regarding this pretty well as a principal attribute of soul' (407ᵇ34–408ᵃ1). In addition to rejecting the argument just outlined, Aristotle also argues vigorously against the plausibility of (iii), the position that it makes sense to attribute motion to the soul.

Why does Aristotle reject premiss (ii) of the argument to the conclusion that the soul moves? His rejection of (ii) is easy to miss since it is accomplished in a sentence: 'We have already pointed out that there is no necessity that what originates movement should itself be moved' (406ᵃ3–4). Most commentators take

---

[7] Translations from *De Anima* are adapted from Aristotle (1984).

[8] Aristotle here attributes a materialist account of soul to both the Pythagoreans and Plato, whom we would tend to identify as early dualists. Whether or not Aristotle thought of a particular theory of soul as materialist or not is difficult to determine from *DA* 1, since he uses the word 'incorporeal' as a comparative term, and it seems to refer to more or less refined matter rather than to contrast a material with an immaterial notion of soul. See 409ᵇ20 ff. and Hicks's note ad loc. in Aristotle (1907).

Aristotle's reference to be to a section of his argument for the prime mover, an unmoved origin of all motion, in *Ph.* 8. 5. There Aristotle argues that it is not necessary that everything that causes motion should itself be moving (256^b27–257^a32). He considers two possibilities. Either the cause x moves in the same way as the motion it causes y, or cause x moves in a different way from the motion it causes. Suppose that x is heating y. All that is required in order for x to heat y is that x be hot; it need not be undergoing the motion of becoming hot. Nor is it a necessary condition of the possibility of x heating y that x be undergoing some other type of motion (e.g. locomotion) or even that x be *capable* of undergoing some other type of motion. There is no logical requirement that x move or be capable of undergoing motion for x to be the cause of y's motion. So the fact that the soul is the origin or cause of the animal's motion does not warrant the inference that the soul moves.

In the *Physics* Aristotle argued that there is no requirement in principle that a cause or origin of motion itself move. But thus far he has given us no reason to question the idea, which he attributes to several pre-Socratics and Plato, that the soul in fact does move when it causes the animal to move. He has given us no reason to question the truth of the conclusion of the argument we have been considering. Aristotle's criticisms of this idea can be divided into two sorts: he objects in general terms drawn from his own theory of motion to the coherence of the idea that the soul moves (406^a12–406^b15), and he also objects in detail to the particular theories of Democritus and Plato (406^b15–407^b26).

Aristotle begins his criticism of the idea that the soul moves, or that movement is an attribute of soul, by making an important distinction between two ways in which an entity is moved: by virtue of itself and by virtue of something else. For example, a ship under sail moves by virtue of itself, but the crew moves by virtue of the ship's motion. Of course, a member of the crew could also walk about the ship, and in this case he would be moving in virtue of himself, or by virtue of a movement proper to himself. Aristotle's position is that the soul does not move by virtue of itself, in contrast to both the ship and the crew, each of which is capable of moving by virtue of itself. By drawing this distinction, he leaves open the possibility that the soul could move by virtue of the movement of something else, namely the body. More importantly, however, he uses the distinction to pave the way for another point concerning the question of what motion is natural for the soul.

As we saw in Aristotle's example of ship and sailor, there is a close connection between the idea that an entity moves by virtue of itself, and the idea that there is a kind of motion proper or natural to it. Ships sail and humans walk. What kind of motion is proper or natural to soul? In order to understand the way that Aristotle approaches this question it is helpful to remember that he construes the term 'motion' broadly; it covers locomotion, alteration, diminution, and growth (406^a12–13). Now each of these species of motion involves place (*topos*). Locomotion, alteration, diminution, or growth all occur somewhere, at some location. But, if one of these forms of motion is proper to the soul, then soul must have a location or place, and Aristotle thinks that this idea is implausible. He does not tell us explicitly why it is implausible, but he does provide an explanation of his point by means of the example of a colour, an attribute. The attribute does not have location, he says, but rather the body in which the attribute inheres has location. So the attribute does not move by virtue of itself but rather by virtue of the body, which, having a location, can undergo locomotion or one of the other species of motion. There is no motion proper to colours, although there is to coloured bodies. Similarly, soul does not have a location in virtue of itself, although it may have one by virtue of the body with which it is associated.

Aristotle denies that the soul can move in virtue of itself, and that it has a distinctive location of its own. The illustration of the first point, ship and sailor, suggests that he thinks of the soul as a part of, or contained within the body; the soul is carried along when the body moves just as the sailor is carried along by the ship. He does not explain here why the soul cannot move in virtue of itself. The imagery of parts and containment suggests that the soul is a material entity transported like cargo in the body. On the other hand, since, as we shall see below, Aristotelian matter by definition has a natural tendency to move we might take Aristotle's point to be that the soul just is not the sort of thing that can move by virtue of itself, that is to say, it is not matter or material. But if the latter is the case, then how are we to think of the soul as being carried along by the body?

The soul does not have a location, and hence is not capable of motion by virtue of itself by analogy with an attribute like colour. This comparison suggests that Aristotle does think of the soul as just not being the sort of thing that can move, that is, as not being a material thing. For a colour does not have a location, and so does not move by virtue of itself because of the sort of thing it is, because it is not a material body. The colour has a location and moves only in virtue of something else, namely the location and movement of the body in which it inheres. Here the relationship is not one of parts to wholes, or contents to container, but rather of inherent to subject (*Cat.* 1ᵃ24–5). The analogy between soul and an attribute is helpful because it suggests that Aristotle is not thinking of soul in terms of a special sort of matter, itself incapable of motion, that resides within an ordinary material body and is carried about by it. The comparison suggests instead that souls, like attributes, just are not beings capable of motion, and that the location and motion of soul is entirely dependent upon that of a material body or a material organism. But this dialectical move also raises questions. Are we to think of soul as an attribute of the body, as a colour is an attribute of it? And if not, how are we to understand the relationship between soul and body? I return to these questions below.

Aristotle's following two arguments against the idea that the soul moves also involve concepts drawn from his theory of motion, in particular his contrast between natural and unnatural motions. For Aristotle, all bodies are composed out of four basic kinds of stuff—earth, air, fire, and water—and each of these stuffs has a natural motion, a motion towards its natural resting-place. Earth, for example, naturally moves downwards towards the centre of the earth. That is earth's natural motion. If we throw a clod of earth up in the air, we are using force to divert earth from its natural path; it is an unnatural motion. For every natural motion, there is an opposite motion which is unnatural to the entity in question. But, Aristotle asks, what sense does it make to talk about the unnatural motion of soul (406^a21-7)? Can we conceptualize a soul diverted from its goal by some intervening force, as we can in the case of earth?

And, if we simply concentrate on the natural motion of soul, additional questions arise. For example, supposing the soul to undergo a form of locomotion causes difficulties, for Aristotle's theory identifies motion in any direction with a particular kind of stuff. If soul were naturally to move up, it would be fire. If it were naturally to move down, it would be earth. But, Aristotle assumes, we should not want to identify soul with any particular kind of stuff. There is an additional problem if we hold that the soul moves with the very same kind of motion that it imparts to the body, namely locomotion. For, if the soul *did* loco-mote just as the body does, then it is possible that the soul could leave the body and then re-enter it. And if the soul could stroll out of the body and back again, then animals could revivify. As Hicks states in his commentary, Aristotle considers this last point to be a *reductio ad absurdum* of the idea that the soul engages in locomotion.[9]

These three arguments taken together have a single purpose, which is to show that souls do not undergo the same kind of motion that material substances (or organisms) do. While it makes perfectly good sense to think of the earthy material which composes the body being deflected from its natural downward direction by a tornado, it is quite difficult to imagine the soul's motions being blown off course by some entirely independent force. Further, since natural motions are defined in terms of the natural places of the four elements in the cosmos, soul could not be assigned a natural place without at the same time being identified with one of the elements, apparently a very implausible idea for Aristotle. For if the soul does move in the same way as each of the four elements, in other words is capable of change with regard to place or locomotion, then it would be possible for souls to leave and re-enter bodies—an absurdity. One possibility which Aristotle leaves open at this point is the idea that the soul is a composite or blend of the four material substances—earth, air, fire, and water.

From these considerations Aristotle invites us to conclude that once we try to specify the kind of motion in question, we shall see that it makes no sense to attribute motion to soul. We might rather be inclined to think that what Aristotle has shown is that *given his analysis of motion* (in particular, the distinction between natural and unnatural motion) it makes no sense to say that the soul moves.[10] It

---

[9] See Hicks in Aristotle (1907), 249.

[10] Hicks comments: 'The same method is pursued throughout cc. 3–5: A. deduces absurd and inconsistent conclusions by combining the doctrines of his own system with the propositions which he undertakes to refute. He does not stop to enquire whether those who maintain these propositions would have accepted the doctrines of his own system' (ibid. 239). In contrast, I see Aristotle proceeding in two steps; first, he criticizes the view that the soul moves in terms of his own theory of motion, and then he criticizes the theories for their internal inadequacies.

remains to be seen whether or not some other philosopher can make better sense of the claim. And, as if to respond to this unvoiced criticism, Aristotle now turns to consider two of the most important contemporary accounts of the soul in motion—those of Democritus and Plato.

Democritus, as Aristotle portrays him, thought that the soul itself moved with the very same kind of motion with which it moves the body. His spherical, fiery atoms move continuously, and pull the body along:

> An example of this is Democritus, who uses language like that of the comic poet Philippus, who accounts for the movements that Daedalus imparted to his wooden Aphrodite by saying that he poured quicksilver into it; similarly Democritus says that the spherical atoms owing to their own ceaseless movements draw the whole body after them and so produce its movements. (406^{b}17–20.)

Aristotle makes two criticisms of this account of animal motion. First, he asks how this account could explain an animal resting. After all, if the atoms are constantly bouncing around, and so moving the body, why is the body sometimes in motion and sometimes at rest? Secondly, Democritus' explanation makes no mention of intention or thought, which clearly play a role in animal motion. These two points are related in that an important part of the explanation for why an animal is at rest at a given moment, and in motion at the next, is the animal's intention (*prohairesis*) or purpose. A lion chases a stag in order to obtain food; it rests under a tree in order to avoid the heat of the day. Democritus' crude materialist account of motion, by omitting the causal role of the animal's intention, cannot explain even this simple range of phenomena.

Aristotle's criticisms of Plato are numerous, and some are quite difficult to understand and evaluate, in large part because understanding Plato's account of soul in the *Timaeus* is no easy matter. As Aristotle understands it, in the *Timaeus* Plato explains how the soul was created out of the four material elements. The soul is self-moved and, like the heavens, it moves in a circle; the soul is in contact with the body and moves it (*Timaeus* 34 B ff.). There have been many interpretations of Plato's *Timaeus* and the account of soul found there; some of these differ from Aristotle's account.[11] None the less Aristotle's interpretation is a reasonable one, and should not be dismissed as a self-serving distortion of Plato's views.

Aristotle's first criticism of Plato is very interesting because it rules out the idea that the soul is material: 'it is a mistake to say that the soul is a magnitude' (407^{a}2–3). He explains his point by contrasting two sorts of unity: the unity of a series like the number series, and the unity of a magnitude. The unity of a magnitude requires the continuity of its material parts (*Metaph.* Z1030^{b}9–10; *Ph.* 227^{a}10–13). But this notion of unity does not apply to soul and its characteristic processes, like thinking. There is a unity to thinking, but it seems more like the serial unity of numbers than the unity by continuity of a material substance; it is a temporal rather than a spatial unity. Further, it is implausible to attribute

---

[11] One key point is whether the account of the genesis of the soul in the *Timaeus* should be taken literally (as Aristotle takes it) or metaphorically. See Hicks in Aristotle (1907), 252.

thought to a magnitude (407ª10–11). Plato was wrong to conceive of soul as a magnitude, and if so, he was wrong to conceive of it as material. From this section of the text it is clear that the issue of the unity of the soul—how it is unified —is an important one for Aristotle, and it is equally clear that he rejects the idea that it is one by continuity, a kind of unity characteristic of material substances.

Aristotle also makes a series of criticisms of the Platonic notion that thinking is circular motion. If circular motion is eternal then thinking must also be eternal; but we know that it stops and starts. Circular motion is repetitive, but we think about a variety of objects. Thinking seems to be more like resting than it is like movement. In short Plato's attempt to compare thinking to the regular, circular motion of the heavens is a failure.

Neither Democritus nor Plato has provided an adequate account of the soul's motion. The mechanistic, rectilinear motion of Democritean soul-atoms is not adequate to the phenomena to be explained. And the celestial, circular motion of Platonic soul engaged in thinking is equally flawed. Furthermore, Plato's depiction of the soul as a magnitude in the *Timaeus* is mistaken, for the soul is not a magnitude or material body. Since it is not a magnitude or material body it does not have any natural motion, and indeed, the ideas of natural and unnatural motion do not even apply to it. The only possible kind of motion for the soul is indirect; we could say that it is moved by virtue of the body being moved. But there is no movement which is proper to it.

We began this section with Aristotle's distinction between an entity which moves by virtue of itself, and an entity which moves by virtue of another thing. Aristotle's position that the soul is not a magnitude can help us to understand the distinction as it applies to soul. For, if soul is not a magnitude then it is just not the sort of thing that could move, and, like an attribute, it moves by virtue of a body moving. But it is still not clear whether or not Aristotle wants us to push the analogy to the point of thinking of soul as an attribute of the body. If the soul is an attribute of the body, then the model of a colour inhering in a body provides us with an understanding of the way in which the soul can be said to move indirectly when the body does. But if the soul is not an attribute of the body, then it is still unclear how the soul moves indirectly when the body does, for we have already eliminated the possibility of thinking of the body as containing the soul.

Another loose end from the discussion thus far is the possibility that the soul, while not to be identified with any one of the four elements, is some combination or arrangement of them. If soul were an arrangement of the four, then it would also be an attribute of them, that is, of the body. And if it were an attribute of the body, then, as I explained above, we could understand how the soul moves by virtue of the body moving on the model of how an attribute like a colour moves when the body in which it inheres moves. The discussion thus far has left open two possibilities: either the soul is some combination of the four elements and hence an attribute of the body or it is an attribute of the body in some other way. Aristotle rejects both these ideas in the following chapter; the first in the course of his critical discussion of the idea that the soul is a harmony, and the second in connection with his discussion of mind or *nous*.

III. Soul as a *Harmonia*

The position Aristotle considers next, the definition of soul as a *harmonia*, is one which is also critically examined in Plato's *Phaedo* (85 E ff.). It seems to be a fairly popular account of soul, although Aristotle only mentions Empedocles by name in connection with it (408ª19–28). Aristotle distinguishes two possible versions of the view: the soul is a composition (*sunthesis*) of the parts of the body or the soul is the ratio of the mixture (*logos tēs meixeōs*, 408ª5–15). The distinction reflects Aristotle's view that stuffs can be mixed in two ways; a combination of sand and sugar is a composition (*sunthesis*) in which the ingredients retain their identity, a combination of sugar in water is a mixture (*meixis*) in which the ingredients are transformed or can be transformed. The proportion of sugar to water is the ratio of the mixture.

Aristotle's first criticism of the *harmonia* view is that a *harmonia*, whether a composition or a ratio of ingredients, cannot be a source of motion. A composition or a ratio is not the sort of thing which could be an agent or which could be the origin of motion of the animal. The ratio of eggs to milk in a cake does not cause it to rise. Further, it is equally absurd to attribute the soul's functions— perception, desire, thought, and so on—to a *harmonia*. Aristotle's general point is that if we think about what the soul does, or what it is responsible for, then it is very implausible to think that soul is either the composition of the parts of the body or the ratio of the mixture of the ingredients of the parts.

Aristotle's second criticism of the view of soul as a *harmonia* of the bodily parts concerns the issue of the unity of soul. If the soul is a composition of the parts of the body, and there are many such compositions corresponding to the various parts, the unity of soul is shattered. The same is true if soul is identified with the ratio of the mixture, for one ratio corresponds to flesh and another to blood, and so there will be many souls in the body, one for each ratio. The idea that the soul is a composition or a ratio of bodily parts generates numerous souls corresponding to the different compositions or ratios which constitute the parts. One ratio of material elements constitutes flesh and a different ratio constitutes bone, and so an organism with flesh *and* bone will have two ratios, two souls. But, as we have seen, the unity of soul is an important issue for Aristotle, and any theory which appears to make it impossible should be rejected.

In rejecting the *harmonia* theory, Aristotle is rejecting the idea that the soul could be defined as being a composition of the four elements or a ratio of their mixture. One of the two possibilities left open at the end of the last chapter is closed; not only is soul not to be identified with any one of the four material substances, but it is also not to be identified with a combination of all four. The idea of soul as a *harmonia* of the body is one kind of attribute theory of soul, and evidently it is to be rejected. But there is still the possibility that the soul is an attribute of the body in some other sense.

The idea that the soul is an attribute of the body is questioned in principle later in this chapter in the course of a discussion of thought (*nous*): 'But thought seems to be a substance implanted within us and to be incapable of being destroyed' (408^{b}18–19). If thought is an important capacity of the soul, and thought is a substance, then soul cannot be an attribute of the body, because it is not an attribute at all. There is a clear categorical divide in Aristotle's ontology between substances and attributes; if something is a substance then it is not an attribute and vice versa. By characterizing one part of soul as a substance, Aristotle is casting doubt upon the idea that soul is an attribute. So not only is soul not an attribute of the body or the organism in the sense that it is not a *harmonia*, but it is not an attribute at all.

Earlier I suggested that Aristotle models the soul's motion—that it moves not by itself but by virtue of the organism's motion—on the case of an attribute and the subject in which it inheres. A colour moves when the body it qualifies moves; colours just are not capable of motion by virtue of themselves. Even though in this chapter Aristotle doubts that soul is an attribute of the body or organism, he can still use the model of an attribute to illustrate how and why something can be incapable of motion by virtue of itself, and yet move by virtue of its relationship to an entity which is capable of motion. So in questioning the view that soul is an attribute, Aristotle is not endangering the comparison he drew earlier between soul and an attribute.

It might seem, then, that Aristotle's point is that soul, being a substance, is not an attribute, and further, that it is itself the subject of attributes, namely psychological properties like emotions, pains and pleasures, thoughts, and so on. As we shall see, however, this Cartesian conception of soul—as a substance and subject of psychological attributes—is problematic for Aristotle.

IV. An *Aporia* for Aristotle

Aristotle's dialectical treatment of his predecessors' views has reached a critical point because it has generated requirements for a theory of soul which appear to be incompatible (408^{a}34 ff.). On the one hand there is the requirement that the soul shall not be capable of motion in itself. On the other hand there is the requirement that the soul shall be not an attribute but a substance, and the subject of psychological attributes. But if the psychological attributes—being pleased, being fearful, thinking—are motions that affect the soul, it would follow that the soul is moved when it is pleased, fearful, etc. In order to break this impasse or *aporia*, it seems that Aristotle must reject one of the following:

(i) the soul is not capable of motion in itself;
(ii) the soul is the subject of psychic attributes/motions;
(iii) psychic attributes are motions.

Before discussing Aristotle's solution to this *aporia*, it is important to see that it is a puzzle generated by Aristotle's own views articulated in the course of criticizing earlier philosophers. It serves as a concrete example of how a dialectical examination of the views of the wise can help Aristotle to sharpen and explore the difficulties surrounding his own views.

Given that Aristotle has just restated his view that the soul is not capable of motion in itself (408^{a}30–4), his only option for resolving the *aporia* is to reject either (ii) or (iii). Either it is a mistake to think of the soul as the subject of psychological properties or it is a mistake to think of psychological properties as motions which move or affect the soul. Although Aristotle clearly rejects (ii) in the text under consideration, there is some evidence in his later discussion of perception (for example, his reluctance to call it an 'alteration') that he might later settle on the alternative strategy and reject (iii).[12] In any case, this dilemma opens up the question of how we are to understand psychological processes if they are both originated by soul and soul is not affected or changed by them. Thus far, Aristotle has been chiefly concerned to refute the idea that the soul must move if it is the cause or origin of motion. In the next chapter, Aristotle turns to consider those psychological processes which seem to imply that the soul is changed or moved from outside, for example, perception and the acquisition of knowledge.

Let us postpone Aristotle's discussion of perception and return for the moment to his resolution of the *aporia*. Since he here accepts the idea that emoting and thinking are motions, Aristotle's only option is to reject (ii), the idea that the soul is the subject of psychic properties that involve motion:

Yet to say that it is the soul which is angry is as if we were to say that it is the soul that weaves or builds houses. It is doubtless better to avoid saying that the soul pities or learns or thinks, and rather to say that it is the man who does this with his soul.   (408^{b}11–15.)

Aristotle's position is that the man rather than the soul is the subject of psychic attributes involving motion, and so it is the man rather than the soul that is moved by these psychological happenings.

The soul is not affected or moved in itself when the person's blood boils in a fit of rage or when the person learns something. None the less, the soul is the cause of the anger or the learning in that these motions originate or end in the soul. To understand Aristotle's point it is helpful to consider the way in which the soul is the cause of an activity like building, which Aristotle here compares with psychological processes. At first sight the comparison seems to be no help at all; for surely the Aristotelian moving cause of an activity like building is the builder, and not the builder's soul. In fact Aristotle tends to think of the art of building in the soul as the origin of the activity of building: 'Of productions and movements one part is called thinking and the other making—that which proceeds from the starting-point and form is thinking, and that which proceeds from the final point of thinking is making' (*Metaph.* 1032^{b}15–17). The 'starting-point and form' in

[12] For a discussion of this possibility see Shields (1988).

question is the art of building in the soul (*Metaph.* 1032^{a}32–^{b}14). The art of building both originates the actual building, and does so without moving or changing itself. Similarly the knowledge that a person has concerning justice might be the cause of her anger in certain circumstances without necessitating that either her soul or her knowledge is itself moved in causing her anger.

These Aristotelian examples are meant to show how it possible for the soul to originate a motion without itself moving or changing. Yet they also contain a problem for Aristotle. For one might ask about how, in the first place, the soul acquires the knowledge or skill that is the origin of the motion in question. For surely the art of a builder is acquired, as is the knowledge of justice, and it seems that these acquisitions are most plausibly described as alterations of soul. But if so, they seem to run counter to Aristotle's prohibition against viewing the soul as capable of motion in virtue of itself. Aristotle does not discuss this sort of issue in book 1, however, and so we must simply mention it in passing.

IV. Like is Known by Like: Perception and Motion

We might be able to explain how the soul causes some psychological processes without itself moving in the way sketched above, but others, like perception, seem more problematic. For perception seems inherently to involve the notion that the soul receives an impression from outside and is changed. Perception seems to be a prime example of an alteration of the soul. And indeed the theory of perception, based on the principle that 'like is known by like', which Aristotle criticizes, is one which analyses perception in terms of a chain of motions between object and soul.

Before we consider Aristotle's criticisms of the 'like is known by like' theory of perception, it is important to explore further the connection between this kind of theory of perception and the earlier question of whether or not the soul moves or changes. It turns out that Aristotle is not simply changing the subject from the issue of the soul's motion to an entirely unrelated issue of the soul as the origin of perception. Rather, as is clear from the most prominent version of the 'like knows like' theory of perception, which Aristotle attributes to Empedocles and to Plato in the *Timaeus*, the soul is moved or affected during perception (*DA* 1. 2, 404^{b}11–18). On this view the eyes are stimulated by daylight to emit light-rays which strike external objects, and a series of motions begins:

So the whole, because of its homogeneity, is similarly affected and passes on the motions of anything it comes into contact with or that comes into contact with it, throughout the whole body, to the soul, and thus causes the sensation we call seeing. (*Timaeus* 45 D.)

That there is a close connection for Aristotle between the question of whether or not the soul is altered in perception, and the 'like is known by like' principle, is also evident later in *DA* 2. 5 where the two issues are raised together (417^{a}14–^{b}16). So the idea that the soul is altered or changed during perception is a basic assumption of the 'like is known by like' theory. And that is why it makes perfect sense for Aristotle to attack this theory in particular at this point.

Although I have claimed that Aristotle is worried about the 'like is known by like' theory of perception because it implies that the soul moves or changes, he criticizes it on other grounds. He does not beg the question of the motion of the soul in his own favour. Rather, he shows that the theory fails on its own terms, quite apart from any of its implications. In his criticisms Aristotle concentrates his fire upon the idea that the soul should be defined as constituted by the four elements on the grounds that soul can know and perceive everything:

It remains now to examine the doctrine that soul is composed of the elements. The reason assigned for this doctrine is that thus the soul may perceive and come to know everything that is; but the theory necessarily involves itself in many impossibilities. (409ᵇ24–7.)

Aristotle attributes this view to Empedocles, and describes him as holding that the soul is constituted by earth, air, fire, and water, the principles of all things; given its constitution the soul can know everything because 'like is known by like' (404ᵇ7–15).

For Aristotle, the central difficulty with this view is that it tries to explain how perception of everything is possible by holding that both soul and world are made up of the same material stuffs. But this fact, even if it were true, would not explain how we can perceive objects, which are something over and above their material constituents. Even if the soul were able to perceive earth, air, fire, and water because of its constitution, this would not explain how it perceives 'god, man, flesh, bone' (409ᵇ32). In other words, this theory of perception fails because it does not explain how the organism can perceive the full range of objects it does perceive. So the theory fails to explain the phenomena, and hence it poses no threat for Aristotle's thesis that the soul is not changed or altered by psychic processes.

V. Conclusion

From Aristotle's discussion of rival and earlier views of soul and psychological processes we can extract several positions which should guide Aristotle's own explorations:

 (i) *With regard to the nature of soul*: it is not a magnitude and not material; it is a substance and not an attribute; it is a unity, and the principle of its unity is not material continuity.

 (ii) *With regard to the function of soul*: soul is the origin of perception and motion, as well as psychological processes like emotions and desires; an adequate account of how soul causes perception, motion and the like must not attribute motion to soul.

It is certainly possible to read the *De Anima* as presenting a theory of soul which adheres to these rather general guidelines; indeed it is likely that there is more than one interpretation which is consistent with them. It should be noted that they do cast doubt upon two currently popular interpretations of Aristotle's conception of soul: the materialist interpretation (in either its reductionist or non-reductionist versions) and the view that soul is an attribute of the body or person.[13] The evidence from book 1 does not settle the question of the correct interpretation of the nature of soul in the *De Anima* as a whole, however, and it is important to note that Aristotle does not even directly raise the general issue of the ontological status of soul (e.g. the question of materialism) in 1. 2–5.

But Aristotle's express topic in book 1, namely the issue of whether or not the soul moves, does pose a very interesting question for our interpretation of the two subsequent books. Do Aristotle's own definition of soul and his explanation of psychological processes honour his own idea that the soul does not move in itself? Does his definition of soul make plausible the idea that the soul only moves by virtue of the animal moving? And does his explanation of psychological processes assign the primary causal role to soul, while at the same time leaving soul unaffected by them? The most striking and peculiar legacy of Aristotle's dialectical treatment of earlier philosophers in *DA* 1 is the idea that the soul does not move and is not affected by psychological processes, and it is this idea which we should bear in mind as we read the subsequent books of the treatise.[14]

[13] For an argument in favour of the attribute interpretation see Barnes (1971–2). Shields (1988) discusses the implications of *DA* 1 for materialist interpretations of Aristotle.

[14] I should like to thank Cynthia Freeland, Mark Okrent, Amélie Rorty, and Christopher Shields for their helpful comments.

DE ANIMA 2. 2–4 AND THE MEANING OF LIFE

GARETH B. MATTHEWS

A CHECK of almost any standard encyclopaedia will reveal how problematic the concept of life remains for us today. Sometimes the experts try to disguise the problems; sometimes they make them completely obvious. The entry under 'Life' in a recent edition of *The World Book Encyclopedia* makes the problems obvious:

Nearly all living things share certain basic characteristics. These characteristics include (1) reproduction; (2) growth; (3) metabolism; (4) movement; (5) responsiveness; and (6) adaptation. Not every organism exhibits all these features, and even nonliving things may show some of them. However, these characteristics as a group outline the basic nature of living things.[1]

One doesn't have to be much of a Platonist to become concerned and puzzled about discussions like this. How can it be that only 'nearly all', and not simply 'all', living things share the characteristics that 'outline the basic nature of living things'? And how can a list of characteristics such that only 'nearly all' living things have those characteristics and some non-living things also have them be a list that outlines 'the basic nature of living things'? Why doesn't the admitted failure to find a set of characteristics necessary and sufficient for being alive lead to the conclusion that perhaps there really is no such thing as 'the basic nature of living things'?

Aristotle seems to have been the first thinker to try to understand what it is to be a living thing by reference to a list of characteristic 'life-functions' (or, as he called them, 'psychic powers' or 'soul-powers'—*dunameis tēs psuchēs*). The list Aristotle gives varies from place to place in his texts, but it is usually a selection from among the following: self-nutrition, growth, decay, reproduction, appetite, sensation or perception, self-motion, thinking.

From our modern point of view, the strangest item on Aristotle's list of life-functions is thinking. Descartes convinced us moderns that thinking has nothing essential to do with life.[2] So it is surprising to us to find Aristotle including

---

[1] (Chicago: World Book, 1986), xii. 242.

[2] '...because probably men in the earliest times did not distinguish in us that principle in virtue of which we are nourished, grow, and perform all those operations which are common to us with the brutes apart from any thought, from that by which we think, they called both by the single name *soul*...But I, perceiving that the principle by which we are nourished is wholly distinct from that by

it. Otherwise Aristotle's list is not out of line with modern efforts to say what a living thing is by reference to a list of characteristic life functions.

Some modern writers give a list of such functions and then say that (i) anything that can perform them all is alive; (ii) anything that cannot perform any of them is not alive; and (iii) anything that can perform some, but not all, may be alive or not. Aristotle's approach is bolder. He says it is sufficient for being living that a thing can perform *one* of these functions. 'Provided any one alone of these is found in a thing', he writes in *DA* 2. at 413ª22−5, 'we say that thing is living— viz. thinking or perception or local movement and rest, or movement in the sense of nutrition, decay and growth' (1982, i. 658). And at the beginning of the next chapter he makes much the same point:

> Of the psychic powers above enumerated some kinds of living things, as we have said, possess all, some less then all, others one only. Those we have mentioned are the nutritive, the appetitive, the sensory, the locomotive, and the power of thinking. (414ª29−32, trans. J. A. Smith in Aristotle (1910−52))

Aristotle's claim that 'provided any one alone of these [psychic or life-functions] is found in a thing we say that thing is living' invites two different questions. First, we may ask, is it empirically true? That is, is it true as a matter of empirical fact that we count whatever, and only whatever, can perform at least one of the functions on Aristotle's list as a living thing. Let us call that question 'the Empirical Question'.

The Empirical Question asks whether a biconditional along the following lines is materially adequate as an account of what we include in the class of living things:

x is a living thing iff x can think or x can perceive something or x can move itself or… (1)

By contrast, the Definitional Question asks whether a definition of the following sort is satisfactory:

x is a living thing $=_{df} x$ can think or x can perceive something or x can move itself or… (2)

Let us consider the Definitional Question first. Certainly Aristotle himself is not given to offering disjunctive definitions. His favoured form of definition belongs to the genus−differentia type. (2) can hardly be a good candidate for what Aristotle wants to say about the Greek equivalent for 'is alive', unless some special story can be told to show that its disjunctive form is accidental to the claim being made and that (2) is really equivalent to some other, nondisjunctive, way of putting things.

This sort of objection to (2) has real force. What it is for something to be alive ought to be something more unitary than the disjunctive form of (2) suggests. One wants to know what being able to think, being able to perceive something,

means of which we think, have declared that the name *soul* when used for both is equivocal….I consider the mind not as part of the soul, but as the whole of that soul which thinks' (*Reply to Objections V* in Descartes 1637−41 = Haldane−Ross 1967, ii. 210).

being able to move oneself, etc., have in common that makes them *life*-functions, that is, functions such that being able to perform a single one of them qualifies a thing for the appellation 'living thing'. Thus even if (1) is correct and Aristotle's list of psychic functions is materially adequate in picking out all and only living things, (2) seems unsatisfactory.

Let's turn now to the Empirical Question. Is (1) adequate?

I have left (1) in open-ended form. A good first thing to do in evaluating (1) would be to try to get a complete list of Aristotelian psychic, or life, powers, or functions. I think this is a complete list from *DA* 2, anyway:

(i) thinking (*nous, dianoētikon*);
(ii) perception or sensation (*aisthēsis*);
(iii) local (*kata topon*) movement (*kinēsis*) and rest (*stasis*);
(iv) movement (*kinēses*) with respect to nutrition (*kata trophēn*) and decay (*phthsis*) and growth (*auxēsis*) or self-nutrition (*threptikon*);
(v) touch (*haphē*);
(vi) appetite (*orexis*) or desire (*epithumia*) and passion (*thumos*) and wishing (*boulēsis*);
(vii) reproduction (*gennēsis*).

There could well be disagreement on how these powers are to be counted. Thus to some readers it may seem that growth ought to be considered a separate power in Aristotle's list; that may be correct. And perhaps the appetitive powers referred to in (vi) should be listed separately. Finally, touch is, of course, a mode of perception, or sensation. It gets discussed separately because, according to Aristotle, some animals have no other sense modality than touch (413^{b}4–9). But then, perhaps, we should list non-tactile perception as a distinct power.

In general, however, this seems to be the list of psychic powers Aristotle has in mind in *DA* 2.

Let us consider first the last item on the list, reproduction. Obviously some individual organisms, though certainly alive, are too immature to reproduce; others are too old. Still others are sterile throughout their full lives, either because of an individual defect, or because, as is the case with mules, their very kind is sterile. So being able to reproduce is necessary neither for an individual organism to be a living thing, nor even for a kind of organism to be a kind of living thing.

Let us recall, though, that Aristotle's claim is not that every living thing has every psychic or life power; rather, it is that everything with a psychic power is alive (and, presumably, only such things). Might something be able to reproduce itself without being alive? Well, sounds reproduce themselves in echo-chambers and visual appearances reproduce themselves in mirrors, though neither sounds nor visual appearances are alive, at least not in the way, or perhaps in the sense or senses of 'alive', we are interested in. Even more troubling are viruses, which were, of course, unknown to Aristotle.

Let us dismiss worries about sounds and appearances and viruses and suppose that a suitable sense of 'reproduction' can be spelt out in an appropriate way so that everything with the power of reproduction (in *that* sense of 'reproduction') is alive. Are there difficulties with other items on Aristotle's list?

No doubt there will be similar problems with specifying the sense or senses of, say, 'appetite' and 'local movement and rest' we are interested in, so that having the power picked out by the expression in the suitable sense will definitely guarantee that the entity that has it is alive.

Suppose, however, that all such problems can be solved. Would it then be plausible to say that the Empirical Question can be answered affirmatively? Apparently so.

The Definitional Question, though, will still be difficult to handle. There are two main sorts of problem with it. The first is that in finding appropriate senses of 'reproduction', 'appetite', etc., so that the definiens will cover just the right cases, no more and no less, we may well have to make implicit or explicit appeal to the notion of life. For example, in specifying the required sense of 'reproduction' to apply to, say, the division of an amoeba but not to the echoing of a sound, we may have to make at least implicit reference to the notion of life. If this turns out to be so, the definition will be circular. Circularity is not a problem with the Empirical Question; our only demand on (1) is that it state truly necessary and sufficient conditions for something's being a living thing. But circularity is a serious problem for the Definitional Question.

The second problem, as I have already suggested, is that it is not clear what these psychic powers have in common that makes the possession of one of them sufficient for an entity to count as a living thing. This problem is one familiar to readers of Aristotle as a problem in the unity of the definition.

At this point it is worth taking into account Aristotle's ideas about how the psychic powers are related to each other. Aristotle does not suppose that a given living thing might have, say, the power of reproduction and nothing else. Rather he thinks of the psychic powers, either all of them or at least many of them, as 'nested' in an order or sequence of decreasing extension (or increasing, depending on which way you look at the sequence). The idea is that everything with power p_3 has p_2 (though not the other way around), and everything with p_2 has p_1 (though not the other way around).

Now how does this nesting idea help us deal with the Definitional Question? Well, it might be Aristotle's view that what gives the disjunctive definition, (2), its unity are supplementary connections like these:

> If *x* can think then x can perceive something (though not vice versa).   (2*a*)
> If *x* can perceive something then x has the power of touch (though not vice versa).   (2*b*)
> If *x* has the power of touch then x can nourish itself.   (2*c*)

So far the powers seem to be appropriately nested. But we have left out appetite, local motion, and reproduction. Aristotle does not seem to suppose that these powers expand the nesting by simply adding steps of increasing, or decreasing, extension; however, he does seem to think these relationships hold:

x has appetite iff. x has the power of touch. (2d)

x can move itself iff. x has non-tactile powers of perception. (2e)

If x can reproduce itself, then x can nourish itself. (2f)

If we then break up the power of perception, or sensation, into touch and non-tactile perception, we come up with the following set of relationships:

[x can think]→

  [x has non-tactile perception and x can move itself]→

    [x has touch and x has appetite]→

     x *can nourish itself*

                      ←[x can reproduce itself]

One implication of all this is that everything that has any one of the psychic powers has the power of self-nutrition. Should we conclude that what it means to say of something that it is alive is simply that it can nourish itself? Sometimes Aristotle talks that way. Consider this passage from *DA* 2. 4.

> It follows that first of all we must treat of nutrition and reproduction, for the nutritive soul is found along with all the others and is the most primitive and widely distributed power of soul, being indeed that one in virtue of which all are said to have life (*kath' hēn huparchei to zēn hapasin*). (415ª22 5, trans. Smith.)

It seems to follow that the other psychic powers are not really in or of themselves life-functions; rather, they are life-*presupposing* functions, that is, functions such that nothing has them without being alive.

On this reading, Aristotle's statement, 'Provided any one alone of these [powers] is found in a thing we say that thing is living', means something like this: 'Provided any one alone of these powers is found in a thing it *will be right* to say that that thing is alive [even if "is alive" means only "can nourish and reproduce itself"].'

There are other passages, however, in which Aristotle suggests something different. Consider this passage, immediately preceding that quoted twice above:

> We resume our inquiry from a fresh starting-point by calling attention to the fact that what has soul in it differs from what has not in that the former displays life. Now this word ['life', *zēn*] has more than one sense [*pleonachōs de tou zēn legomenou*], and provided any one alone of these [powers]... (413ª20–3, trans. Smith.)

If we take this idea seriously we might suppose that the nesting relation among 'can think', 'has non-tactile powers of perception', 'has the power of touch', and 'can nourish itself', plus the relationships given in (2a–f), are all relationships of meaning and that together they yield a series of broader and broader senses for 'is alive' or 'is a living thing'. In the narrowest sense, 'x is a living thing' would mean: 'x can think and x has power of non-tactile perception and...x can nourish itself.' In the broadest sense, 'x is a living thing' would mean simply 'x can nourish itself.'

Other passages in Aristotle seem to mesh with this idea. Consider this passage from book 1 of the *Nicomachean Ethics*:

Let us exclude, therefore, the life of nutrition and growth. Next there would be a life of perception, but it also seems to be common even to the horse, the ox, and every animal. There remains, then, an active life of the element that has a rational principle... ($1098^{a}1-3$, trans. W. D. Ross in Aristotle (1910–52))

We can understand Aristotle here to be using 'life' first in the sense of 'nutrition and growth', then in the richer sense that includes the idea of having perception, and finally in a sense that includes also the idea of having a rational principle.

There is, however, one major problem with the suggestion that, according to Aristotle, 'is a living thing' (or 'is alive') is homonymous in this way. At $415^{a}7$ ff. Aristotle says, 'Lastly, certain living beings—a small minority—possess calculation and thought, for (among mortal beings) those which possess calculation have all the other powers above mentioned, while the converse does not hold...' The qualification, 'among mortal beings [*tōn phthartōn*]', makes it clear that, according to Aristotle, there can be non-mortal beings that think, and are therefore alive, but do not nourish themselves, or grow. Indeed, that seems to be Aristotle's view.

If this is right, then 'x can think' does not after all guarantee 'x can nourish itself'; at most 'x can think and x is a mortal being' provides that guarantee.

We might try saying that there is simply a further sense of 'alive' and 'living thing' such that 'x can think and x is not a mortal being' yields 'x is a living thing' in that new sense. But where, now, is the unity in these definitions? If the nesting story was supposed to avoid the unwelcome conclusion that 'living thing' is a case of mere chance homonomy and it was supposed to do so by providing some unity, some common focus, to its various senses—namely, the idea of self-nutrition—that reference point is no longer available.

I think we need to try a very different approach.

Perhaps it would be well to remind ourselves at this point that, as Aristotle supposes, individuals of a given species naturally act so as to preserve their species. Here in *DA* 2. 4, within a discussion of nutrition and reproduction, Aristotle makes that point:

...for any living thing that has reached its normal development and which is unmutilated, and whose mode of generation is not spontaneous, the most natural act is the production of another like itself, an animal producing an animal, a plant a plant, in order that, as far as its nature allows, it may partake in the eternal and the divine. That is the goal towards which all things strive, that for the sake of which they do whatsoever their nature renders possible [or 'whatever they do naturally'—*hosa prattei kata phusin*]. ($415^{a}27-^{b}2$, trans. Smith.)

Aristotle goes on to say that the soul is, among other things, 'the essence of the whole living body' ($415^{b}11$). He adds that 'in everything the essence is identical with the cause of its being, and here, in the case of living things, their being is to live, and of their being and their living the soul in them is the cause or source' ($415^{b}12-14$).

Now if the soul of a living thing is the cause of its living, and its living is naturally directed towards the preservation of its species, then the soul's powers (the 'psychic powers' we have been talking about) are presumably powers naturally directed toward the preservation of the species of that particular thing.

My suggestion, then, is that the list of psychic powers can be seen as a list of the general sorts of possibilities that individual organisms have to act so as to preserve, or to contribute to the preservation of, their species. For a plant this will be simply the movements of metabolism—nutrition, growth, and decay—plus, of course, reproduction. Animals, most of them, are capable of changing place. They act according to desire or appetite and perception—most rudimentarily through touch, but, in higher animal species, through non-tactile modes of perception as well. As for human beings, they need to exercise their capacity to reason and calculate to be able to act so as to preserve their species.

If we pull this point about species-preservation out of Aristotle's discussion and make it the key to our understanding of what a psychic power is supposed to be, we can offer the following as a definition of 'psychic power':

x is a psychic power $=_{df}$ there is a species s, such that, for x to be preserved, individual organisms that belong to s must, in general, exercise x.

Relativized to a species the definition would look like this:

x is a psychic power for species $s =_{df}$ for s to be preserved individual organisms that belong to s must, in general, exercise x.[3]

It is plausible to suppose that psychic powers, following this definition, will turn out to be, or at least to include, reason, sense-perception (tactile and non-tactile), local motion, appetite, metabolism (including food-intake, growth, and decay), and reproduction. It is also natural to suppose that these powers are co-exemplified in complex patterns that produce the nested sequence discussed above. Now we can say (going beyond any claim explicitly stated in Aristotle, though I think something like this is suggested by what he says) that what it means to say that an organism is alive is that it can exercise at least one psychic power; that is, at least one of the powers that organisms of its species must, in general, be able to exercise for the species to survive.

x is alive $=_{df}$ there is a species s, and a psychic power p, such that x belongs to s, p is a psychic power for species s, and x can exercise p.

Because of nesting it will turn out that any mortal organism that is alive will have the power of self-nutrition. Still, 'is alive' does not *mean* (on this

---

[3] Fred Feldman has made clear to me how important, and how difficult, it will be to understand 'exercise' in the right way here. Perhaps many animals, such as rabbits, need to be able to exercise their power to remain motionless in the presence of predators for their species to survive. Yet such a power should not count as a psychic power lest (see the next definition) a dead rabbit count as being alive.

A first thing to say is that psychic powers are powers to act, not purely passive powers. So exercising such a power will have to be doing something, not simply failing to do something. Relevant to the rabbit case will then be the power to *keep itself* motionless, which will be part of the capacity for local movement and rest. Irrelevant will be the capacity to lie inert.

This response is only a first move, however. Much more discussion would be required to gain justified confidence that we know how to pick out the relevant powers.

reconstruction of Aristotle) 'is capable of self-nutrition'. What it does mean is 'can exercise a power such that members of the organism's species need to be able, in general, to exercise that power in order that the species may survive'.

Monsters (*terata*) might be thought to present a problem here. They are not regular members of any species, yet they can certainly be alive.

What Aristotle should do to accommodate monsters, I think, is simply to broaden the understanding of '*x* belongs to [species] *s*' to include monsters. The idea would be that each monster is a *failed* or maimed or deformed member of one or more species. (That seems to be what Aristotle does say at, e.g. *GA* 769ᵇ30.) So long as the monster can exercise at least one psychic power of a species it is a failed member of, it is alive.

This is perhaps a good point at which to address the question of circularity in the proposal I am presenting here.[4] 'Clara is alive', according to this proposal, means that there is a species, say, cat, and a psychic power, say, touch, such that Clara belongs to the species mentioned, touch is a psychic power for that species, and Clara can exercise the power. What 'touch is a psychic power for the species, cat', means is that, for the species cat to be preserved, individual cats must, in general, be able to exercise tactile perception. Although I haven't tried to say what it is for a species, such as cat, to be preserved, presumably it is, or includes, keeping in existence individual organisms, in this case individual cats. But, as Aristotle says in *DA* 2. 4, 'for living things, to be is to be alive' (415ᵇ13). So keeping individual cats in existence is keeping them alive and we have, it seems, a circle.

Though, I agree, there is a certain circularity in the proposal, it is not, I think, a vicious circularity. The idea is that for Clara to be alive is for her to be able to exercise one of what is, for her species, a cluster of, so to speak, 'self-perpetuating powers'. More carefully, it is for her to be able to exercise one power in a list such that it is necessary for individuals of her species, in general, to be able to exercise those powers for there to go on being individuals in that species that can exercise one or more of those powers. If we are justified in supposing that dead cats, dead trees, and dead human beings can't exercise any powers at all, then the circularity in the proposal is not, I think, objectionable.

The account I am offering can help us reconcile these three apparently incompatible claims, each of which we seem to find in Aristotle:

(i) Being a living thing amounts to nothing more than having the power of self-nutrition.

(ii) There are (something like) distinct senses of 'living thing' to go with each of the following: (*a*) plants, (*b*) animals whose only sense modality is touch, (*c*) other non-human animals, and (*d*) human beings.

(iii) There is at least one non-mortal being that thinks and is therefore alive, even though it has no power of self-nutrition.

---

[4] Both the worry about monsters and the question of circularity are matters that Fred Feldman brought to my attention after he read an early draft of this paper.

As for (i), it is true that among *mortal*, living things, the common and funda-mental species-preserving power is self-nutrition, plus the associated power of reproduction. When Aristotle makes a claim like (i), he must be taken to be focusing on mortal beings.

Still, what exactly having species-preserving, or psychic, powers amounts to varies from species to species. And in this way something like (ii) is also true.

As for (iii), Aristotle's complicated nesting story guarantees that as long as a mortal being has at least one psychic power, it will also have the psychic powers, if any, that, so to speak, enfold it, including, of course, self-nutrition. Non-mortal beings are usually left out of Aristotle's discussion. But they can easily be included. To preserve their species they need only preserve their existence by continuing to engage in whatever activity is essentially theirs. That may just be thinking; it does not, presumably, include either self-nutrition or reproduction.

In his book, *The Selfish Gene* (Oxford, 1976), Richard Dawkins locates the origin of life in the chance formation of the first 'replicator' molecules. As Dawkins puts the matter, plants and animals, including human beings, have become the 'sur-vival machines' for the currently successful replicator molecules, which we call 'genes'.

In many ways Dawkins's story is quite un-Aristotelian. Aristotle knew nothing of DNA and he was not what one would call an evolutionist. Still, it distorts things only a little bit to say, mimicking Dawkins, that, in Aristotle's view, indi-vidual plants and animals, including human beings, are survival machines for plant and animal *forms*. The functions that individual plants and animals need to perform to play their role in this survival process are the *dunameis tēs psuchēs*, the psychic or life functions. These functions are nested in ways that Aristotle tries to bring out. And for any given individual organism to be alive is just for it to be able to perform at least one such function (plus, of course, any functions presupposed by it in that species of organism).

Whether the notion of life that rests on the idea of life functions is really very important for modern biology I am not competent to say. But if, for whatever scientific or non-scientific reasons, we want to deal with the threats to incoher-ence posed by encyclopaedia entries under 'life' of the sort I began this dis-cussion with, the best way to do so, I think, is to appeal to the picture I have constructed from *DA* 2. 2–4. According to that picture there are organisms that tend to preserve their form through the exercise of identifiable functions. For a given individual to be of the sort, living thing, is just for it to be one of these nat-urally species-preserving organisms. And for a given individual living thing to be actually living–that is, alive—is just for it to be able to perform one of the psychic, or living, functions appropriate to its species (though, of course, since the functions are nested in certain ways, being able to perform a given psychic function may presuppose being able to perform one or more others).[5]

[5] I wish to thank Michael Frede and Fred Feldman for their comments on an earlier version of this chapter.

12

INTENTIONALITY AND PHYSIOLOGICAL PROCESSES: ARISTOTLE'S THEORY OF SENSE-PERCEPTION

RICHARD SORABJI

I

THE most valuable aspect of Aristotle's theory of sense-perception is, I believe, one which has been relatively neglected. It lies in his redrawing the map in which perception is located in a debate which is still being conducted in contemporary controversy on perceptual content. I shall discuss this in Section I of this chapter. It has to do with the formal cause of perception. What has been most discussed recently is what I believe to be the material cause. I shall turn to that in Section II, because the formal cause and material cause together complete the definition of perception, as explained at the opening of the *De Anima*.[1]

Perception for Aristotle is not to be viewed as a rudimentary reaction with little content, as is suggested by Plato. Nor on the other hand is it the work of reason and thought (*dianoia, noein, nous*), as was claimed by Aristotle's rebellious successor Strato.[2] It is a half-way house between the two.

Plato's position has been very well described by others: he argues in the *Theaetetus* that the soul uses the senses as channels to perceive sense qualities like whiteness, but cannot use them for distinguishing and comparing qualities, or for hitting on something's being the case (*ousia*) or the truth (*alētheia*); for that requires reasoning (*sullogismos*) and belief (*doxazein*).[3] Reasoning is described in turn as the silent dialectical debate of the soul with itself, and belief either as the conclusion of this debate, or as a silent affirmation, negation, or answer in the debate.[4] Plato's distinction of reasoning and belief from perception reflects Alcmaeon's earlier distinction of perception from understanding and thought

---

[1] *DA*, 403ª25–39. I shall be returning to the subject of the first section in Sorabji, *Mind and Morals, Man and Beast*, in preparation.

[2] Strato *ap.* Plut. *De Sollertia Animalium* 961 A; *ap.* SE. *M.* 7. 350; *ap.* Porph. *Abst.* 3. 21; *ap.* Epiphan. *Against Heresies* in *Dox.Gr.* p. 592, 16–18.

[3] Plato, *Theaetetus* 184 D–187 B. See the illuminating accounts by Burnyeat (1976) and Frede (1987*b*) and before that Cooper (1970).

[4] Plato, *Theaetetus* 189 E–190 A, *Sophist* 263 E ff., *Philebus* 38 C–E.

(*xunhienai, phronein*).[5] But Plato greatly narrows the role of perception. This narrowing only becomes critical when Aristotle revives the other half of what Alcmaeon says by denying reasoning and belief (*logos, dianoia, nous, logismos, doxa*, in Aristotle) to animals other than man.[6] Aristotle is then obliged enormously to expand the content of perception beyond the rudimentary level to which Plato had reduced it. Typically, an animal that follows a scent does not merely perceive the scent in isolation, but perceives it as lying in a certain direction, and otherwise would not go in the right direction for it. But this already involves *predication*: the scent is *connected* with a direction. We can put this by saying that the animal perceives that the scent comes from that direction, or perceives it as coming from there. If animals lack reason and belief, these predications must be something that their perception can carry out.

Plato did not have to face this problem. For even when he is tempted to deny the reasoning part of the soul to animals (and this is a subject on which he wavers to the end),[7] he is still not obliged to deny them belief (*doxa*), since he is perfectly ready to associate belief with the lower, non-reasoning parts of the soul.[8] I know of only two exceptions. One occurs in the *Theaetetus* and related dialogues, where one (not the only) definition of *doxa* makes it the outcome of *reasoning* (references above).[9] The other occurs also in the *Theaetetus*, where the denial of reasoning to some (not all) animals may in the context imply a denial to those same animals of belief.[10] But the *Laws*, written later, does not take any of this as settled.

Aristotle does three things. First, he tidies up the concept of reason (*logos*) in the direction of the *Theaetetus*, by bringing all of *doxa* (belief) under it (*DA* 428ᵃ19–24, see below). Secondly, he gives to perceptual content one of the most massive expansions in the history of Greek philosophy. Thirdly, despite expanding the role of perception, he maintains Plato's denial that perception involves belief or is a function of reason.

As regards the expansion of perceptual content, not only does he incorporate in perception the one function recognized by Plato, perception of whiteness and other sense-qualities perceptible by only one sense, but he adds perception of the common qualities (*koina*) perceptible by more than one sense: movement, rest, shape, extension, number, unity.[11] These are overlooked by Plato when he says

[5] Alcmaeon *ap.* Theophr. *De Sensibus* 25. Alcmaeon also distinguishes belief (*doxa*) from perception, if it is his theory that Plato reports at *Phaedo* 95 B, as the reference to the brain has been taken to suggest.

[6] See *DA* 414ᵇ18–19, 428ᵃ19–24, 434ᵃ5–11, *PA*, 641ᵇ7; *EE* 1224ᵃ27, *Pol.* 1332ᵇ5: Alcmaeon *ap.* Theophrast. loc. cit.

[7] Contrast Plato, *Timaeus* 77 A–C, 91 D–92 C, *Statesman* 263 D, *Republic* 620 A–D, *Phaedo* 81 D–82 B, *Phaedrus* 249 B, *Laws* 961 D with *Republic* 441 A–B, *Symposium* 207 A–C, *Laws* 963 E (cf. *Theaetetus* 186 B–C, discussed below).

[8] e.g. Plato *Republic* 442 B–D, 574 D, 603 A, *Phaedrus* 255 E–256 A, *Timaeus* 69 D, *Laws* 644 C–D, 645 A. In *Timaeus* 77 A–C it is plants, not animals, which are distinguished as lacking *doxa*.

[9] Another account of belief, which fits some but not all of the cases, is that it results not from reasoning, but from fitting a memory imprint to a current perception, *Theaetetus* 193 B–195 E.

[10] Plato *Theaetetus* 186 B–C. I thank Myles Burnyeat for the reference.

[11] *DA* 418ᵃ17–18, 425ᵃ16, *Sens.* 442ᵇ5.

that you cannot perceive through one sense what you perceive through another.[12] Moreover, the common properties (*koina*) which Plato does recognize, such as likeness and difference, and which he (Plato) assigns to the province of reason,[13] are assigned by Aristotle to that of perception.[14] This already involves perceiving a proposition, in other words, *that* something is the case—that the qualities differ. It has been shown by Stanford Cashdollar how much propositional perceiving Aristotle recognizes. One can perceive that the approaching thing is a man and is white, that the white thing is this or something else, whether the white thing is a man or not, what the coloured or sounding thing is, or where, that one is perceiving, walking, thinking, living, existing, that one is sleeping, that something is pleasant, whether this is bread, whether it is baked, 'this is sweet' and 'this is drink'. The lion perceives that the ox is near.[15]

It would be wrong to suppose that this propositional perception really involves an inference of reason[16] merely on the ground that sense-qualities, like colour, are said to be essential (*kath' hauto*) objects of perception, whereas the son of Diares and the son of Cleon, who enter into propositions, are said to be coincidental sense-objects (*kata sumbebēkos*). Coincidental does not mean inferential. I have argued elsewhere that the reason why colour is said to be essential to sight is that sight is *defined* as the perception of light, shade, and colour.[17] By contrast the son of Diares is not essentially related to colours seen, and hence not to sight. It is this that accounts for his being called a coincidental object of perception. There is no suggestion that he is perceived only indirectly by way of inference.

Propositions are also involved in *phantasia*, which in Aristotle's *De Anima* is perceptual and post-perceptual appearance.[18] Examples of post-perceptual appearances would be imagination, dreams, and memory, all due to prior perception. An example of perceptual appearance given by Aristotle is the appearance that the sun is quite small, only a foot across. This appearance too is due to (*hupo*) the perceiving.[19] The word *phantasia* is used in connection with perception, propositional or otherwise, just so long as we want to talk of things appearing. Plato and Aristotle in their discussions explicitly connect *phantasia* with the verb 'to appear' (*phainesthai*).[20] To mark the connection of *phantasia* with appearing, and to bring out the continuity between different texts, I shall use the translation 'appearance', although readers should be aware that some translators will render the same word as 'imagination' or as 'impression'. A perceptual appearance is typically an appearance *that* something is the case, or, as we would sometimes prefer to say, an appearance *as of* something's being the case. I shall

---

[12] Plato, *Theaetetus* 184 E–185 A.   [13] Ibid. 184 D–187 B.

[14] Arist. *DA*, 426ᵇ12–427ᵃ14, 431ᵃ20–4ᵇ1, *Somn. Vig.* 455ᵃ17–18.

[15] Arist. *DA* 418ᵃ16, 428ᵇ21–2, 430ᵇ29–30, *EN* 1113ᵃ1, 1147ᵃ25–30, 1149ᵃ35, *MA* 701ᵃ32–3, cit. Cashdollar (1973). Also *EN* 1118ᵃ20–3, 1170ᵃ29–ᵇ1; *DA* 425ᵇ12, *Insomn.* 1, 458ᵇ14–15, 462ᵃ3. I am not quite convinced by Cashdollar's examples from *DA* 418ᵃ21–3, 425ᵃ25–7.

[16] This view is rejected by Hamlyn in Aristotle (1968) and Cashdollar (1973), who cites J. I. Beare, W. D. Ross, Irving Block, and Charles Kahn.

[17] Sorabji (1971).   [18] *DA* 3. 3.   [19] *DA* 428ᵇ26.

[20] Plato, *Sophist* 264 A–B; Arist. *DA* 3. 3, 428ᵃ13–14.

call both of these appearances propositional, meaning by that no more than that something is a *predicated* of something. There is not merely an appearance of whiteness, but of whiteness as belonging to something or as being located some-where. Aristotle grants perceptual appearance to animals, even though he seems uncertain whether it belongs to all animals,[21] as the Stoics were to insist.

It cannot detract from the clear example of a propositional appearance that the sun is only one foot across that Aristotle later goes on to contrast appearance with affirming or denying as not being true or false, because it involves no combina-tion of concepts (*sumplokē noēmatōn*, 432ª10–12; cf. 431ª8–16). We are free to assume that Aristotle is talking here of another kind of appearance, that involved in imaging (431ª15). We need not therefore resort to the interesting device suggested by Irwin (1988), who concedes that for Aristotle a dog cannot have an appearance with the structure 'that it's red', but urges that we can still describe its appearance that way, because the unstructured appearance explains the dog's behaviour in the same way as would a structured belief.

The propositional content of perception and appearance answers another prob-lem. It has been thought that Aristotle oscillates wildly on the mental capacities he allows to animals. Having distinguished animals from men as lacking reason in the *De Anima*, he none the less allows the lion to entertain propositions about the ox he is going to eat in the *Nicomachean Ethics*. Moreover, there and in the biological works he allows animals emotions, which are elsewhere treated as involving belief (*doxa*) in past or future harm or benefit.[22] I think it can now be seen that this suggested oscillation is apparent rather than real. Perception was all along treated in the *De Anima* as admitting a propositional content. As for emotions, Aristotle (admittedly not out of any concern for animals) defines anger and fear as involving an *appearance* (*phantasia*) of past or future harm, as often as he mentions belief (*doxa*).[23] And the Aristotelian Aspasius (again for independ-ent reasons) later recommends that this become the preferred definition of emotions.[24] Admittedly, *post*-perceptual appearance, mere *imaging* of terrible things, does not provoke fear, according to Aristotle.[25] But there is no reason why *perceptual* appearance should not. There need, then, be no change in the concept of emotion when this is ascribed to animals who lack belief. Had there really been an oscillation, I do not think that Aristotle could have been protected from the charge of confusion by saying that he used different explanatory frameworks in different places. For he is not an anti-realist, who believes that explanations are helpful devices which need not correspond to the real nature of things.

We can now see how generous a content Aristotle gives to sense-perception

[21] Contrast *DA* 415ª11, 428ª10, 22, 24 with 433ᵇ28, 434ª1–5.
[22] Fortenbaugh (1971). He has quite correctly put to me that some of the beliefs involve a *moral* judgement that the harm is unjustified. Even so, that is not true of fear, while pity is not ascribed to animals and anger is defined in terms of a moral belief only in the legal context of the *Rhetoric*, not in the biological context of *DA* 403ª25–ᵇ9, nor yet in that of the *Topics*.
[23] A. *Rh.* 1378ª31, 1382ª21–2, *Top.* 156ª32–3.
[24] Aspasius, *in EN* 44. 33–45, 10 (Heylbut). So also, for different reasons again, Posidonius in Galen, *PHP* (De Lacy).
[25] A. *DA* 427ᵇ21–4.

compared with most other Greek philosophers. I have already commented on Plato's parsimony. The Platonist author of the *Didaskalikos* sharpens Plato's point when he says that even sense-qualities like whiteness are discriminated (*krinein*) not without a certain empirically based type of reason associated with belief (*ouk aneu doxastikou logou*).[26] The Cyrenaics hold that one can only be aware of one's own experiences.[27] The Epicureans allow all perceptual appearances to be true, but all true only the films of atoms impinging on the sense-organs, which may not faithfully represent the external causes.[28] The Pyrrhonian sceptics express perceptual appearances as propositions: 'honey is sweet'. But on one interpretation this is no more than a statement of, on another a mere reaction to, how the perceiver is himself perceptually affected.[29] As for the Stoics, although they allow a generous content to perceptual appearances in humans, I shall have to return to the question how much content they allow to perceptual appearances in animals or infants.

Having expanded perceptual content, Aristotle is faced with his remaining task. He needs to show that this expansion does not after all turn perception into belief, or make it a function of reason. For he agrees with Plato that this would be wrong. One of Aristotle's devices for distinguishing perception from belief (*doxa*) is to call it a kind of discriminating (*krinein, kritikē*). It has been argued by Theo Ebert that *krinein* does not in the Greek of Aristotle's time yet mean judgement.[30] If not, there should be no danger of confusing it with *doxa* (belief). But it can cover a wide range of activities short of belief, from the perception of colour to the perception of propositions. It can cover, for example, the kind of activity in which a bird engages in selecting some feathers for its nest while discarding others.

Aristotle has a further device for making perception fall short of belief, but this one commits him to disagreeing with Plato. Plato had defined perceptual appearance (*phantasia*) as a belief formed through sense perception (*doxa di' aisthēseōs*).[31] Aristotle denies that perceptual appearance is belief, and he produces an excellent argument for his denial: we can have the perceptual appearance that the sun is quite small, only a foot across, but we may believe that it is very large.[32] The argument enables Aristotle to treat perception and perceptual appearance as only a half-way house on the way to *doxa*. His argument has been much repeated in the modern literature against the view that perception is some function of belief.[33] Plato by contrast had classified illusion as a case of *doxa*.[34]

---

[26] Albinus (?), *Didaskalikos* 156. 2–10 Hermann. In requiring this type of reason (which is described as a set of acquired, as opposed to innate conceptions), the author diverges from Plato, but in a way that sharpens Plato's view of how little perception can achieve on its own.

[27] Plut. *Col.* 1120 C; cf. Eusebius, *PE* 14. 19. 2–3.

[28] S. E. *M.* 7. 206–10, Plut. *Col.* 1121 A–B.   [29] S. E. *PH* 1. 13, 1. 19–24.

[30] Ebert (1983): except in the sense of a legal judgment.

[31] Plato, *Sophist* 263 E–264 D.   [32] *DA* 428^{b}3–10.

[33] It is recognized as a difficulty by Armstrong (1968, relevant section reprinted in Dancy 1988), and it is urged as a difficulty against theories such as those of Armstrong and Pitcher (1971) by Jackson (1977), Fodor (1983) and Crane (1988, 1989).

[34] Plato, *Republic* 603 A.

Aristotle has two more arguments, separated by a 'furthermore' (*eti*), to show that what animals possess does not amount to belief (*doxa*).[35] First, belief involves being convinced (*pistis, pisteuein*), which animals cannot be. Conviction is more passive than the assent (*sunkatathesis*) later required by the Stoics, but it plays a similar role in the argument that animals cannot be said to have beliefs. Aristotle's other claim involves something slightly closer to assent: belief involves being open to persuasion (*pepeisthai, peithō*), which in turn implies possessing reason (*logos*). This has been called a 'rhetorical' criterion for belief, on the grounds that persuasion involves dialogue with *others*.[36] But I think that what Aristotle actually has in mind is Plato's definition of belief in the *Theaetetus* and *Sophist* as the outcome of a silent dialectical conversation (*logos*) within the soul.[37] Plato says explicitly that others are not involved, and I assume that correspondingly Aristotle would allow his persuasion to be self-persuasion, while complaining that animals are not capable even of this.

So much for Aristotle's distinction of perception from belief. But a difficulty may be felt about his idea that sense-perception enables animals to make predications, for example, to perceive sweetness as belonging to something. How can they perceive anything so complex, if they do not have concepts? To this Aristotle might find two answers. First, some animals may perhaps have concepts. Secondly, Aristotle might take comfort from certain modern discussions which purport to show that perceptual content can be predicational without the use of concepts being implied.

To take the second point first, a number of discussions have urged that perception requires no conception.[38] A person can perceive a building as eight-sided, for example, and generally be able to recognize eight-sided buildings, without having the concept of eight, or other relevant concepts. He may not even be able to count. It may be a controversial claim that his recognitional capacity would not itself amount to his having a concept of eight-sidedness.[39] But there is a more formal argument for perceptual predication without concepts, which can be expressed in terms of an example of Aristotle's already mentioned. The argument is that if you can rationally wonder with regard to the perceived length of a foot-rule and the perceived diameter of the sun whether these two lengths are really the same, you must be conceptualizing them differently—even if you are conceptualizing each as 'that length'. For after all no one can rationally wonder whether A is A, where A is one and the same concept, but only whether A is B. None the less, even though you are conceptualizing the two lengths differently, you may be perceiving them in exactly the *same* way and (*inter alia*) as the same length, which implies that your *perceiving* them does not involve conceptualizing.[40]

---

[35] *DA* 428ª19–24.   [36] Labarrière 31–4.

[37] Plato, *Theaetetus* 189 E–190 A, *Sophist* 263 E ff.

[38] See Evans (1982), Peacocke (1986 and forthcoming), Crane (1988), Millar (1985–6); Irwin (1988).

[39] See Geach (1957) and contrast Peacocke (1989), Irwin (1988).

[40] Example adapted from Peacocke (1986 and forthcoming).

There are other modern arguments too of the same general type.[41] The upshot of these arguments is that, although perceiving the sun as a foot across doubtless involves the use of concepts, perceiving it as matching something else in size, or as small, does not necessarily do so. The argument is like Aristotle's in attempting to locate perception on the map somewhere short of belief.

Aristotle's other recourse might be to argue that some animals do in any case have concepts. He does discuss the issue of whether perception involves concepts, in a passage, *APo*. 2. 19, which may again be in the tradition of Alcmaeon.[42] The passage is sometimes taken as a treatment of our acquisition of universal concepts and sometimes as a treatment of our acquisition of universal truths. In fact there is no conflict: to acquire one is to acquire the other, as a preceding discussion in *APo*. 2. 8–11 shows. To acquire the universal truth that lunar eclipse is some kind of lunar loss of light, or that it is a lunar loss of light due to the earth's screening of the sun, *is* to acquire an (increasingly scientific) concept of lunar eclipse. Aristotle firmly argues that sense-perception must chronologically pre-cede (so that it does not presuppose) the formation of universal concepts. On this both Stoics and Epicureans would agree. Perception for them precedes, and cannot pre-suppose, the formation of conceptions (*ennoiai*) and preconceptions (*prolēpseis*).[43]

Aristotle does not deny, however, that those who do have concepts may bring them to bear in perception. Does this include animals? That depends on how we take his remarks on experience (*empeiria*: compare our 'empirical'). Although he says that animals have little experience,[44] this presumably implies *some*, rather than, as the commentator Alexander followed by Asclepius half suspects, none. And does experience involve having universal concepts? This may seem the easiest way to read Aristotle's words, 'experience or the whole universal stabilized in the soul', since it is difficult (not impossible) to take the second of these two descriptions ('the whole universal') as referring to something *distinct* from the

---

[41] Crane (1988) appeals to the possibility of conflicting appearances within sense-perception. An analogous argument applied to the case of a conflict between sense-perception and belief might say that the same subject (the sun) cannot rationally be simultaneously believed to be large and believed to be not large, so long as it is conceived in terms of the same concepts (conceived as the sun) and largeness is conceived in the same way. When therefore we simultaneously believe that the sun is large and *perceive* it as small, this suggests that perception differs from belief in not *conceptualizing* the sun or largeness at all. The simplest reply, as Crane's retraction (1989) makes clear, is that it is per-fectly rational simultaneously to *believe* that my bank balance is small and to *wish* that it were large, employing concepts in both cases. So whatever may be the case about two opposite *beliefs*, it remains to be shown what is irrational about an opposition between belief and such *different* states as wishing or perceiving (Cf. Plato, *Republic* 436 A–439 E, 602 E).

[42] The passage is in the tradition of the developmental psychology which is described by Plato at *Phaedo* 95 B, and often attributed to Alcmaeon on the basis of the reference to the brain.

[43] See for the Stoics e.g. Cic. *Acad*. 2. 30–1, 'Plut.' (Aët.) 4. 11. 1–4 (*Dox. Gr.* 400 = *SVF* 2. 83), and for the Epicureans e.g. Diog. Laert. 10. 31, and Philodemus, *On the Gods*, col. 12, 10 (Diels): animals lack *hupolēpseis*. I doubt Diels's view in his edition (p. 63) that in Polystratus, *On Irrational Contempt*, col. 1, the words 'each of these' refer to concepts possessed by animals.

[44] Arist. *Metaph*. A1, 980ᵇ26–7, with Alexander, *In Meta*. 4. 15, (Hayduck); Asclepius, *In Meta*. 7. 24 (Hayduck).

first ('experience').[45] Moreover, when an illustration is offered of experience in humans, the man of experience is described as knowing that eating fowl is good for health, a truth which seems general enough. If he is said to know only the particular (*kath' hekasta*) rather than the universal (*katholou*), this is only because he is ignorant of the more universal and explanatory truth that light meat is easy to digest.[46] On the other hand, there is evidence on the other side. For one thing, Aristotle denies that animals (*thēria*) have any universal concept (*katholou hupolēpsis*)—they have only memory and perceptual appearance (*phantasia*) of particulars.[47] Moreover, in the very passage where he allows animals a little experience, he treats experience in humans rather cautiously. It seems to be a conjunctive apprehension (*hupolēpsis*), or set of thoughts (*polla ennoēmata*) about particular cases (*kath' hekaston*), which guides action in the next case, but which does not yet involve a single universal (*mia katholou*). The man of experience knows that this remedy helped Callias when he had this illness, and similarly for Socrates and each of many others. But he has not marked off these people as belonging to a single kind, so that he can say the remedy helps all phlegmatic, or bilious, or feverish people when they have this illness. There is then some universal concept which he has not got.[48]

We may protest that he has other universal concepts, 'this remedy', 'this illness'; why does Aristotle not draw attention to this? Perhaps the answer is that he is here interested only in the universal concepts of *technology* and *science*. But it would be odd if those who lacked these special qualifications had no universal concepts at all. In fact, we have noticed Aristotle granting to laymen a pre-scientific concept, based on prior observation, of lunar eclipse as *some* kind of lunar loss of light. The present passage, then, is not denying the man of experience some pre-scientific and pre-technological universal concepts. And if universal concepts are in another text denied to animals, this is perhaps because that text overlooks the modest concession offered here, that animals do have a *small* share of experience.

It is not quite excluded, then, that Aristotle might grant some animals universal concepts. What is clear is that he grants them predicational perception and a little experience, and these two concessions represent two ways in which he compensates them for their lack of beliefs (*doxai*). But how, it may be wondered, does he distinguish their experiential information from belief? He tries to do so by defining experience as consisting of many memories,[49] and he is peculiarly insistent that memory belongs to the perceptual part of the soul to which percep-

---

[45] Aristotle *APo.* 100ᵃ6–8. The expression might instead refer, as Myles Burnyeat has pointed out to me, to technological skill (*technē*). This is uneasy, because the end of the sentence then startles us, saying as it does that what has been referred to is merely that from which comes the origin (*archē*) of technological skill. It would need to be reinterpreted as meaning that experience (*empeiria*) provides the origin of technological skill, and technological skill the origin of scientific understanding (*epistēmē*).

[46] Arist. *EN* 1141ᵇ14–21.   [47] *EN* 1147ᵇ5, stressed by Irwin (1988).
[48] Arist. *Metaph.* 981ᵃ5–30.   [49] Arist. *APo.* 100ᵃ5–6, *Metaph.* 980ᵇ29–30.

tual appearance (*phantasia*) also belongs.[50] More exactly, memory is the having of a mental image (*phantasma*, a cognate word) taken (*hōs*) as a copy of that of which it is an image.[51] We can see how concerned Aristotle is to classify states of mind on one side or other of the perception–belief frontier. And we need not think that he has transferred memory to the wrong side of the frontier when he remarks that it involves *saying* in one's soul that one has encountered the thing before,[52] for such metaphorical references to saying are common enough to be discounted.[53]

The Stoics, some of them, would agree with Aristotle, for they too analyse experience and memory in terms of perceptual appearance (*phantasia*). Experience for them is a multiplicity (*plēthos*) of similar appearances from many memories,[54] while memory is a storing of appearances.[55] Despite that, there are differences. For in humans perceptual appearance is, for the Stoics, tantamount to rational thought.[56] Moreover, some Stoics deny animals learning by experience (*experisci, experimentum, usus*) in contexts where others might have ascribed it,[57] and some of them deny animals memory except in the sense of recognition of what is perceptually present, and treat memory proper as requiring rational reflection (*deliberatio, consideratio*).[58]

In another respect the Stoics are very like Aristotle. For they deny to animals reason and belief (although reason is slightly redefined),[59] and so they ought, like Aristotle, to expand perceptual content, if they are to account for the ability of animals to get around in the world. Yet this time the orthodox interpretation creates a problem, since it drastically narrows the perceptual content of animals. On this interpretation, which has attracted the ablest scholars,[60] perceptual appearance (*phantasia*) has propositional content not in animals, but only in humans. I have therefore attempted elsewhere[61] to raise a doubt about the orthodox interpretation, and to suggest that the Stoics allow animal perception as much content as does Aristotle. Here I will only indicate the main lines of that counter-proposal.

One argument for the orthodox interpretation of the Stoics is that neither

---

[50] Arist. *Mem.* 450ᵃ16–17, 22–3.

[51] Ibid. 451ᵃ15. My understanding of *phantasma* as a mental image in Aristotle, which I take to be confirmed by the very pictorial account of it throughout the *De Memoria* (see Sorabji in Aristotle 1972, *passim*), has been defended by Huby (1975).

[52] Arist. *Mem.* 449ᵇ22–3.   [53] A list is given by Cashdollar (1973), 162.

[54] 'Plut.' (Aët.) 4. 11. 1–4 (*Dox. Gr.* 400 = *SVF* 2. 83).   [55] S. E. *M.* 7. 372 (*SVF* 2. 56).

[56] 'Plut.' (Aët.) 4. 11. 1–4 (*Dox. Gr.* 400 = *SVF* 2. 83); Diog. Laert. 7. 51, 7. 61; Stobaeus 1, p. 136. 21 Wachsmuth (both in *SVF* 1. 165); pseudo-Galen, *Def. Med.* xix. 381 Kühn (*SVF* 2. 89).

[57] Sen. *Ep.* 121. 19–23; Hierocles 1. 51–3. 52 (von Arnim and Schubart).

[58] Only recognition: Sen. *Ep.* 124. 16, Plut. *De Sollertia Animalium* 961 C; Porph., *Abst.* 3. 22. Rational reflection: Calcidius, *In Tim.* 220. Cf. the Antiochan Lucullus in Cic. *Acad.* 2. 38: memory requires assent.

[59] Reason is a collection of conceptions, Galen, *PHP* 5. 3, p. 421 M (*SVF* 2. 841) and as such can by the Middle Platonists be distinguished from the intellect as being its tool, 'Albinus', *Didaskalikos*, ch. 4.

[60] Frede (1983); Inwood (1985), 73–4; Long–Sedley (1987), 240; Labarrière (forthcoming). I thank all of them for friendly and helpful discussion.

[61] Sorabji (1990). Further objections are addressed there.

animals nor infants have concepts.[62] The infant's mind, in a passage already cited,[63] is compared to blank paper. But we have now seen that the lack of concepts would not, at least in the opinion of various modern philosophers, rob animal perception of propositional (that is, predicational) content. And we cannot assume that the lack of concepts would weigh with the Stoics either.

I am also not convinced by the argument that a *lekton* (a sayable, or, roughly speaking, a proposition) is defined as corresponding only to a rational appearance,[64] that is,[65] to the appearance enjoyed by a rational being, as opposed to an animal. It would be wrong to infer from this that what appears to an animal cannot have corresponding to it a proposition, or sayable. For propositions are here being defined—and it is quite legitimate to define things this way—by reference to a sufficient, not a necessary, condition. What subsists in accordance with the appearance enjoyed by a rational being will be a star example of a proposition (*lekton*). But there may be other *lekta* too, and indeed we know there are. The ones that would interest us would subsist in accordance with the appearance enjoyed by an animal. But we know that there must be *lekta* which correspond to no appearances at all. For the effects of causes are all *lekta*,[66] whether they have ever been noticed and appeared to anyone, or not.

The interpretation for which I have argued is that in Stoicism the perceptual appearances (*phantasiai*) enjoyed by animals are (at least in many cases) verbalizable and conceptualizable by us, even though not by the animals themselves. What has not, I think, been noticed is that appearances that something is the case are repeatedly described, not as verbalized and conceptualized, but as verbalizable and conceptualizable.[67] The point is that it is not said by whom. Evidence already cited suggests that in humans perceptual appearances are always conceptualized, whereas in animals they never are, which is why the *phantasiai* of humans are distinguished as rational (*logikai*) and as thoughts (*noēseis*). But that does not mean that we cannot verbalize and conceptualize how things appear to animals, and do so in propositional form.

The Stoics themselves seem very ready to do so. Chrysippus describes a hunting dog that comes to a crossroads where its quarry might have gone in any of three directions. The dog sniffs the first two, perceives no scent, and takes the third *without* sniffing. It is said 'virtually' (*dunamei*) to go through a syllogism about its quarry: 'The animal went either this way, or that way, or the other way. But not this way, or that way. So that way.'[68] Chrysippus is not conceding that the dog really reasons, or forms *doxai*, beliefs. It is only doing something analogous (*dunamei*). But how could there be an analogy, if its sense-perception

[62] Frede (1983); Long–Sedley (1987), 240.

[63] 'Plut.' (Aët.) 4. 11. 1–4 (*Dox. Gr.* 400 = *SVF* 2. 83).

[64] S. E. *M.* 8. 70; Diog. Laert. 7. 63.   [65] Diog. Laert. 7. 51.

[66] S. E. *M.* 9. 211. The point is well made by Long–Sedley (1987), 201–2.

[67] Diog. Laert. 7. 49; 'Plut.' (Aët. 4. 12. 1) (*Dox. Gr.* 401 = *SVF* 2. 54); S. E. *M.* 7. 244, 8. 70 (*SVF* 2. 187), 8. 10 (*SVF* 2. 195).

[68] S. E. *PH* 1. 69; Plut. *De Sollertia Animalium* 969 A–B; Philo, *De Animalibus* 45; Porph. *Abst.* 3. 6; Aelian, *Nat. An.* 6. 59.

allows it only to grasp a scent? At the least, it must perceive the *absence* of a scent and perceive it as pertaining to one direction rather than another. And this implies that its perceptual appearance involves predication.

Also important is what the Stoics Chrysippus, Seneca, and Hierocles say about the self-preservation of animals depending on their awareness of their own persons, in relation to the surrounding environment.[69] It would not be enough to secure preservation that an animal's body should appear to it without further characterization. The richest set of examples is supplied by Hierocles. Admittedly, neither he nor the others use the verb 'to appear' (*phainesthai*). But he repeatedly speaks of animals grasping (*antilambanesthai*; *katalambanein*), or being conscious (*[sun]aisthanesthai*). The frog, for example, is conscious (*sunaisthanetai*) of how far the distance for a leap should be.[70]

A similar view of animals is put in the mouth of a non-Stoic character, but with the standard Stoic example of a syllogistic premise, by Plutarch:

Wolves, dogs, and birds surely perceive (*aisthanesthai*) that it is day and light. But that if it is day, it is light, nothing other than man understands.[71]

This passage, though not explicitly about the Stoics, gains significance from a closely related one which is. The Stoics hold that inference from signs is peculiar to man. Such inference involves syllogistic premises of an 'if...then' variety, like those discussed in the Plutarch passage. In reserving it for man, the Stoics concede that non-rational animals receive perceptual appearances. What then do they deny? Not, it turns out, that these appearances are propositional, although that would have clinched the case, but only that these animals have appearances arising from inference and combination (*metabatikē, sunthetikē*), appearances which explain (*dioper*) our having the concepts of logical implication (*akolouthia*) and sign.[72]

Further, in their efforts to deny reason to animals, the Stoics redefine the kinds of mental capacity available to them. Animals cannot, for example, remember what is absent, but only recognise what is perceptually present.[73] Their memory therefore is merely the apprehension of a proposition (*katalēpsis axiōmatos*) in the past tense of which the present tense has been apprehended from perception.[74] Here in the very act of downgrading animal capacities, the Stoics evidently concede to them the apprehension of propositions.

Exactly the same happens with one of the other Stoic redefinitions. Seneca denies that animals are capable of anger, because they are not rational,[75] whereas anger involves rational assent to the appearance of injustice (*species iniuriae*).[76]

[69] Chrysippus *ap*. Diog. Laert. 7. 85; Sen. *Ep*. 121, 7–10; Hierocles, ed. H. von Arnim, *Berliner Klassikertexte* 4 (Berlin, 1906), 1. 39–5–7.

[70] Hierocles 2. 37–8.

[71] Plut. *On the E at Delphi* 386 F–387 A. I thank Brad Inwood for the reference.

[72] S. E. *M*. 8. 276.   [73] Sen. *Ep*. 124, 16.

[74] Plut. *Sollertia* 961 C; repeated by Porph. *Abst*. 3. 22.

[75] Sen. *De Ira* 1. 3. 3–8, esp. 1. 3. 4.   [76] Ibid. 2. 3–4.

They merely seem to be angry because they have an appearance, albeit a muddled and confused one,[77] and an involuntary reaction (*impetus*), which is not, however, a rational one. Once again, in downgrading their capacities, a Stoic none the less concedes that animals entertain at least a muddled appearance. And that muddled appearance is presumably a propositional one—the appearance that injustice has occurred.

On the orthodox interpretation, the Stoics will have been inconsistent in allowing such consciousness to animals. Their official view should have led them to reject Aristotle's expansion of perceptual content. On the interpretation I have offered, they will have endorsed it. Equally, I would give an opposite answer to the interesting question that has been raised by C. Gill (1991), whether we should compare the Stoics with Donald Davidson or Daniel Dennett. Davidson (1982) would be the orthodox choice, because he denies propositional attitudes to animals. But I would prefer Dennett (1976), if a selection is to be made, because he allows the ascription of propositional attitudes to animals, provided their behaviour can be analysed *by us* in intentional terms.

Before returning to Aristotle, I should like just to consider whether the Epicurean school had any alternative strategy to enable animals to get around in the world. The Epicureans fall into two camps. Some, notably Lucretius, allow animals to have a mind or thought, whereas others deny them reason, reasoning, thinking, and belief.[78] Illustrating the first tendency, Lucretius goes to some length to say that animals dream,[79] while arguing that in dreams the mind (*mens*, *animus*, *mens animi*), the equivalent of Epicurus' thought (*dianoia*), is at work, selecting for close attention some of the many configurations of atoms that reach the dreamer.[80] In fact he explicitly ascribes a mind (*mens*, *animus*) to horse, lion, and deer.[81] So he need have no problem about how animals cope.

Other Epicureans deny to animals reason and reasoning (*logos*, *logismos*, *epilogismos*).[82] One denies them not only reason, but also thinking (*noēsis*—the terms are not sharply distinguished) and belief, including false belief (*doxa*, *pseudodoxia*).[83] His method of compensating them for the loss of belief and thought is to say that they have *analogues* of belief.[84]

Another strategy for the Epicureans might be extrapolated from the sugges-

---

[77] Ibid. 1. 3. 7.

[78] For the contrasting views see H. Diels (ed.) Philodemus *Über die Götter* 1, p. 63; Annas, (forthcoming) in J. Brunschwig and M. Nussbaum (eds.), *Passions and Perceptions*.

[79] Lucr. 4. 984–1010.

[80] Epicurus, *Letter to Herodotus*, ap. Diog. Laert. 10. 51; Lucr. 4. 728–31, 747–8, 750–61, 767, 803–15, 975–7.

[81] Lucr. 2. 265, 268, 270, 3. 299.

[82] Hermarchus *ap.* Porph. *Abst.* 1. 12 (*logos*); Polystratus, *On Irrational Contempt* col. 6 (*logismos*), col. 7 (*logismos*, at least such as ours) Indelli; Philodemus, *On the Gods*, col. 13, line 2 (*epilogismos*), 15. 28 (*logismos*) Diels.

[83] Philodemus 12. 17, 13. 39 (*noēsis*), 13. 6–7 (*doxa*), 14. 34 (*pseudodoxia*).

[84] Philodemus 13. 17–18 (analogue of *prosdokia*: belief about the future). 14. 6–8 may even go further and contemplate their having analogous beliefs, rather than analogues of belief.

tion[85] that they belong to the same tradition as those empiricist doctors who were called memorists. On the memorists' view, even human beings do not need reason. Thinking is a function of memory, and neither memory nor thinking is a function of reason. Reason is very narrowly conceived as performing certain deductive operations postulated by logicians. Interesting as this view is, I doubt if any of it attracted the Epicureans. For to humans they allow reason,[86] while to animals one, we have seen, denies not only reason, but also thinking and belief. In another author, memory is subordinated to thought (*dianoia*), because in memory thought receives likenesses of what was formerly perceived.[87] Similarly, in yet another, memory is said to be in abeyance during dreams,[88] even while, as we have seen, thought (*dianoia*), or equivalently the mind (*mens, animus, mens animi*) is at work. I believe we find a larger role assigned to memory in such Platonist treatises as the *Didaskalikos* than we do in the empiricist treatises of the Epicureans.

If there is another strategy open to the Epicureans for compensating animals, it would lie in expanding perceptual content, like Aristotle and, I believe, the Stoics. In this some help might be provided by Epicurus. He speaks of perceptual appearances as being true,[89] and he gives a causal analysis of truth not unlike the subsequent Stoic analysis of what it is for a perceptual appearance to be 'cognitive' or warranted,[90] and not unlike certain modern accounts of what it is for primitive perceptual states to have an informational content.[91] Unfortunately there are complications, for Epicurus holds that perceptual appearances are all true, but true only of the films of atoms that impinge on the sense-organs. As regards the physical objects which transmit those films, there is something that can be true or false of these, but that is *opinions* based on the appearances, not the appearances themselves.[92] Nonetheless, he does not seem to deny that perceptual appearances are about the transmitting physical objects, even if they are not true or false of them. Vision sees a tower as small and round or as large and square.[93] It sees not only colour, but the *distance* to the coloured thing, not only light and shade, but *where* they are.[94] There is therefore predication, and the content of vision is propositional in the sense I have been using. It looks as if a perceptual appearance which is true of the impinging film is also true of how the physical

---

[85] Frede (1989). I thank Stephen Everson for drawing my attention to his fascinating account of the memorists.

[86] *Logos* in Hermarchus *ap*. Porph. *Abst*. 1. 12; animals are given the conventional description contrasting them with man as irrational, *aloga*.

[87] Diogenes of Oenoanda, new frag. 5. 3. 3–14, Smith. Admittedly, some memory at least is treated by Hermarchus as irrational (*alogos*) and contrasted with reasoning (*epilogismos*) *ap*. Porph. *Abst*. 1. 10.

[88] Lucr. 4. 765.   [89] S. E. *M*. 7. 205, 8. 63.

[90] Diog. Laert. 7. 46; Cic. *Acad*. 2. 77; S. E. *M*. 7. 248–51; 11. 183.

[91] Dretske (1981); Burge (1986). The debate on the viability of such analyses continues.

[92] S. E. *M*. 7. 208, 8. 63; Epicurus, *Letter to Herodotus*, in Diog. Laert., *Lives* 10. 50–1.

[93] S. E. *M*. 7. 208–9; Lucr. 4. 353–63.

[94] Lucr. 4. 379–86; anonymous Epicurean treatise on the senses Herc. Pap. 19/698, col. 25, fr. 21 Scott, translated Long–Sedley (1987), 80.

object appears, though neither true nor false of how it really is. Given that the appearances are propositional, that appearance is not always a bad guide to future experience, and that memory should enable an animal to act on those appearances which are good guides, our Epicureans may be able to give animals enough perceptual content to manage in the world.

I have presented Aristotle as a catalyst in the debate on how perception relates to other capacities of mind, particularly belief and reason, a debate which was made urgent by his denial of these last capacities to animals. This denial necessitated an expansion of the content of perception and its differentiation from belief—a discussion which is still continuing today.

I can now draw a general conclusion about Aristotle's Philosophy of Mind. He does not try to reduce perception to things at a *different* level, such as physiological states, or behaviour, or the performance of functions. Rather he relates it to capacities at the *same* level, such as belief, reason, appearance, memory, experience, and concept formation. Yet many commentators have seen Aristotle as a reductionist, that is a materialist,[95] at a time when materialistic theories were dominant, and as a functionalist,[96] when theories of that kind prevailed. Some of my own earlier ideas were careless enough to suggest that I too favoured, or at least gave comfort to, a functionalist interpretation.[97] But if I were now to compare Aristotle with any contemporary philosophers, I would compare him with those who are distinguishing the content of perception and thought, thus relating capacities at the same level, rather than reducing them to physiology, behaviour, or function.

I would add more: I think Aristotle's relation of sense-perception to other capacities would be seen by him as throwing light on the *formal* cause of perception, not the *material* cause. The same happens with anger, whose material cause is specified as a physiological process, but whose formal cause relates it to another capacity: desire. For the formal cause of anger is the desire to retaliate.[98] Thus I do not agree with the view that Aristotle's account of perception and anger as each composed of a material and formal aspect really boils down to a polite form of materialism, in which there is nothing more than a physiological process.[99] Rather, the specification of the formal cause by reference to other capacities is meant to tell us something about what we should call the intentional aspect of anger and perception, even if he does not himself characterize it as intentional.

This brings me to the second part of the chapter. For many commentators have picked out a group of phrases (becoming like, being potentially such, receiving form without matter) which I believe describe the physiological process in sense-perception, in other words its material cause. But others have construed

---

[95] Slakey (1961), 470; Matson (1966).

[96] Hartman (1977); Wilkes (1978), ch. 7; Nussbaum (1978), 61–74, drawing on Putnam (1975); Nussbaum–Putnam, 'Changing Aristotle's Mind', pre-publication version of ch. 3 above.

[97] Wilkes (1978); Burnyeat pre-publication version of ch. 2 (hereafter 'Burnyeat'). I argued that Aristotle supplied the materials for defining anger by reference to behaviour. But he did not do this as part of a general programme, and I think it no accident that I found no further similar examples.

[98] *DA* 403^{a}3–^{b}19.   [99] Williams (1986).

them as referring to some cognitive representation. One recent writer, finding this implausible, has suggested that Aristotle had not yet distinguished physiological process from cognitive representation, since he lacked understanding of the intentional character of representation.[100] But I believe that these commentators have been looking in the wrong place. What we should call the intentional aspect of perception is handled in the passages we have already looked at. The passages to which I shall now turn are concerned with its physiological aspect. But the conviction has been so strong that they are concerned with something else that it will take me a little time to put the case.

II

Controversy has centred on an interconnected group of phrases. Aristotle says that in perception the sense-organ becomes like the thing perceived, is potentially such as the thing perceived is already, and receives the form of the thing perceived without matter. Some (myself included) have taken these phrases, despite the mention of form, to refer to the material cause of perception, its physiological process. Others have taken them or at least the last phrase, to refer to the formal cause. There are two corresponding ways of construing the last phrase grammatically. I have followed the oldest interpretation according to which it means that the organ receives form without *receiving* matter. On Philoponus' rival interpretation, the reference is to receiving form without *standing to it as* matter.

My present conviction is that at least two of the phrases, and probably all three, refer to the physiological process, although the case of the 'reception of form' is slightly less certain. Moreover, I still take the physiological process to occur as follows. In vision, for example, the eye-jelly (*korē*) does not receive particles or other bits of *matter* from the scene observed. It simply takes on colour patches (perceptible *forms*) to match it.[101] One advantage of understanding a literal taking on of colour is that this explains how shapes and sizes can be received: the coloured patches in the eye-jelly have shapes and (small-scale) sizes corresponding to those of the scene. The reception of shape and size had previously been thought to constitute a difficulty for any such literal interpretation, and it had also been thought that the literal interpretation would be 'open to devastatingly obvious attack', since we don't find people's eyes going coloured, or their ears noisy.[102] But the relevant organ is deep within, as I argued. For it is the *korē* which takes on colour patches,[103] and the *korē* is not the pupil, as all recent

---

[100] Glidden (1984), 128–9.   [101] Sorabji (1974/1979).

[102] For both points see Barnes (1971–2) 109, repr. (1979*b*) 38 and for the second, Hamlyn in Aristotle (1968), 104 and 113; and (1959), 9 and 11. A related objection concerning size and shape is found in Galen, *On the doctrines of Hippocrates and Plato* VII 7. 4–15, translated by Philip De Lacy in *Corpus Medicorum Graecorum*, V 4. 1–2.

[103] *DA* 431ª17–18, *HA* 491ᵇ21, *PA* 653ᵇ25.

English translators of the psychological works suggest,[104] but the eye-jelly within the eye.[105] It would not have been obvious, with the instruments then available, that the eye-jelly did not go coloured, or the inside of the ear noisy.

Reactions to this literal physiological interpretation have been varied. It has been sometimes accepted and sometimes rejected,[106] the latter in one case on the ground that it would give essential support to the functionalist interpretation,[107] which I have sometimes been taken as upholding.[108] Among those who disagree, one interpretation of the reception of form without matter is that the organ receives a coded message, a vibration for example, not literal coloration.[109] This view still takes the reception of form to be physiological. Others dissent, saying, for example, that to receive form without matter is simply to *become aware of colour*.[110] Brentano adds that it is to become aware of an intentional object.[111] Another writer finds it difficult to attach any very precise meaning to the reception of form,[112] while another offers a non-physiological gloss, but agrees that a literal coloration process *underlies* the reception of form.[113] A final variant is that the reception of form is *both* an awareness *and* a change in the organ which is not, however, a literal coloration process.[114] Evidently disagreement is widespread.

I shall try to show that all these interpretations are mistaken, but one in particular deserves attention, Myles Burnyeat's, because it is the most daring and the most fully argued. It is also the most discussed, even though it has a status like that assigned by Averroës to some of Aristotle's received forms: it is between corporeal and spiritual, because it has never appeared in print, and yet it has been the subject of at least four discussions.[115] Many of the authors concerned with this particular interpretation state their latest views in the present book. My knowledge is necessarily based on a pre-publication version, and I must beg forgiveness for not being able to take account of any changes that may have been made.

In his earlier version, Burnyeat endorsed an interpretation of Aristotle which he called the Christian interpretation, because he found it in three Christians, Philoponus, Thomas Aquinas, and Brentano. This is the interpretation according

---

[104] Beare, Hamlyn, Hammond, Hett, Hicks, G. R. T. Ross, Smith. Philoponus also explains that 'pupil' is only the everyday, not the technical, meaning *In DA* 366, ll. 11–14, 368, 1–3, Hayduck. His own technical meaning differs from Aristotle's.

[105] Arist. *Sens.* 438ᵃ16, 438ᵇ5–16, *HA* 491ᵇ21, *DA* 425ᵃ4, *GA* 780ᵇ23.

[106] Agreement is expressed by M. Cohen (1987) and Charlton (1980). Nussbaum agreed on the need for a physiological process (1978), 147–8, but later pointed out that it would suit the functionalist interpretation if the process was variable (Nussbaum–Putnam pre-publication version of ch. 3). Robinson initially disagreed (1978), but appears not to in (1983). Disagreement is manifested by Hamlyn (1968), 104 and 113; and (1959), 9 and 11; Burnyeat; Glidden (1984); Bernard (1988); Lear (1988).

[107] Burnyeat.   [108] M. Cohen (1987) and perhaps Wilkes (1978).

[109] Glidden (1984), 20–1. This is also one half of Lear's interpretation, I think (1988), 116.

[110] Burnyeat, Robinson (1978); Lear (1988).   [111] Brentano (1874/1959), translated (1973).

[112] Barnes (1971–2).

[113] Bernard has described his interpretation as being that the sense receives the definiteness of the thing perceived.

[114] Lear (1988), 116.

[115] Burnyeat; M. Cohen (1987); Nussbaum–Putnam, Charles (1988), 36–7; Lear (1988), 110–16.

to which to receive form without matter is simply to become aware, but Burnyeat added something of his own which was not in any of these authors. For Aristotle, he held, no physiological process at all is needed for the eye to see, and *a fortiori* not the coloration of the eye-jelly. It is just a basic fact, not requiring further explanation, that animal matter is capable of awareness. And this is why Aristotle's philosophy of mind is no longer credible. For it turns the matter of animal bodies into something pregnant with consciousness, whereas we are wedded to Descartes's conception of matter, which makes it something quite distinct from awareness, so that awareness is something whose occurrence calls for explanation.

I have three initial disagreements with this particular interpretation, the first of merely historical interest—the interpretation advocated is not particularly Christian, as we shall see. Secondly, I do not think that Aristotle can be making a physiological process unnecessary to sense-perception. For the theory of the opening chapter of the *De Anima*, a theory already referred to, is that *every* mental process, with the possible exception of intellectual thought, requires a physiological process. We have already encountered the illustrative example that anger requires the boiling of the blood around the heart. And perception is explicitly included in the theory.[116] Thirdly, on my interpretation, Aristotle's theory comes out prosaic and commonsensical. There is nothing bizarre about the coloration of the eye-jelly. If we want a bizarre theory of matter, we should rather look to Descartes, not, admittedly, to his distinction between matter and awareness, but to his claim that matter is merely three-dimensional extension. We need to go to the further shores of physics, not to common sense, to find anything comparable with this.[117]

To explain my disagreement with the whole range of interpretations, I shall need to go into some exegetical detail,[118] and some readers may prefer to skip to the final section, where I say what I take the significance of my interpretation to be. Roughly speaking, I think it necessary to establish that Aristotle's original doctrine involved literal coloration, if we are to understand the process through which Brentano came to take the opposite interpretation, and to read into the doctrine his own idea of an intentional object.

As a preliminary, we need to note the phrases with which Aristotle expresses his theory of the perceptual process and how they are connected. He says that the organ receives form,[119] receives perceptible form,[120] receives or is affected by forms of perceptibles;[121] and he adds that it does so without matter.[122] In several places, instead of talking of reception (*dechesthai, dektikon*), Aristotle talks of being affected (*paschein*) by form, as if that were a more general description of the same thing.[123] He also says that the sense-organ is potentially such as the

---

[116] Aristotle *DA* 1. 1, 403ª3–ᵇ19. Sense-perception is included, 403ª7.

[117] Sorabji (1988), chs. 1–3.

[118] I previously confined the case to two footnotes: Sorabji (1974), 22 and 28 of the 1979 version.

[119] *DA* 429ª15–16, 434ª29–30.   [120] *DA* 424ª18.   [121] *DA* 424ᵇ2, 427ª8–9.

[122] *DA* 424ª18–19, 424ᵇ2–3, 434ª30.   [123] *DA* 427ª8–9, 424ª23, cf. 424ª34, ᵇ3.

sense-object is actually.[124] He says further that it starts off unlike the sense-object, but becomes like it.[125]

These phrases are all linked together. For two are combined with an 'and' at 429ª15–16, where it is said that if thinking is like perceiving, the thinking part of the soul must be able to receive form and be potentially such as its object. The rest are connected at 418ª3–5, where the sentence, 'the organ is potentially such as the sense-object is already, *as has been said*', refers back to the other form of words at 417ª20: 'it is while unlike that it is acted on, but once acted on, it is like.'

So far it is still a little unclear what kind of likeness is involved. But there is a significant variant at 425ᵇ23, when Aristotle says that what the organ receives is *perceptibles*. These perceptibles are specified elsewhere. For when he says at 423ᵇ30–1 that the sense organ is potentially such, the 'such' refers to the 'hot, cold, dry, and fluid' at 423ᵇ28–9. A little lower at 424ª7–10, he says that the organ is potentially, but not actually, white, black, hot, or cold. And this informative description is intertwined with some of the others, because it immediately follows the explanation that the organ is potentially such (i.e. hot, cold, dry, or fluid, 423ᵇ31), and that being potentially such, it is then made such as the object is in actuality (424ª1–2). There may be a claim of the same kind at 3. 13, 435ª23, where it is said that the organ receives hot, cold, and all the other objects of touch, but the text there is ambiguous, as we shall see.

Except perhaps for the last, all the foregoing expressions are most easily taken as referring to the same process, and they are connected with becoming black, white, hot, cold, dry, or fluid. There are two further references to a process of coloration, both of them linked to the idea of receiving form. The exact meaning is admittedly more disputable this time, but the references are most naturally understood in the same way as the others. At 425ᵇ22–4, Aristotle says that what sees is coloured in a way, and he explains this by saying that the organ receives perceptibles without matter. As I understand it, he says 'in a way', because the transparent fluid in the eye is colourless in itself,[126] but receives *borrowed* colour during the sensory process. At 427ª8, he says that something indivisible cannot at the same time be white and black, and so cannot receive the forms of these qualities either. I take it that 'and so not either' (*hôste oude*) is not introducing a second process for which becoming white or black is prerequisite (although that would already give a significant enough role to coloration), but is rather supplying a more relevant description of the same process.

I have said that it is the sense-organ that undergoes the process described. This is explicit in five passages where Aristotle refers to the organ with the word *aisthêtêrion*.[127] In three other passages, he uses an ambiguous expression, which can, however, refer to the organ: 'that which sees' (*to horôn*, immediately glossed by reference to the organ),[128] 'what is going to perceive' (*to mellon aisthêsesthai*),[129]

---

[124] *DA* 418ª3, 422ª7, 423ᵇ31–424ª2, 429ª16.
[125] *DA* 417ª20.   [126] *DA* 418ᵇ26–30, 429ª15–26.
[127] *DA* 422ª7, 422ᵇ1, 423ᵇ30, 425ᵇ23, and the ambiguous 435ª22.
[128] *DA* 425ᵇ22.   [129] *DA* 424ª7–8.

'what can perceive' (*to aisthētikon*).[130] In a final passage, he starts off by saying that the *sense* receives the forms of perceptibles without matter,[131] but he qualifies this by saying the organ *aisthētērion* is the primary thing in which a power of that kind resides.[132]

It is necessary to distinguish a different doctrine, which does apply to the sense, not the organ, and which concerns not mere becoming like, but actual identity. This turns on Aristotle's general theory of causation, explained in *Ph.* 3. 3. It is there illustrated by saying that when somebody teaches a pupil, there are not two activities going on, one of teaching and one of learning, but a single activity, which is equally one of teaching and one of learning, and which is located in the learner. The application to sense-perception of this causal theory is that the activity of a sound in working on one's hearing and the activity of hearing it are not two activities, but one and the same activity,[133] and located not in the organ but in the sense (*en tēi kata dunamin*).[134] This doctrine about the activity of the *sense* tells us nothing about whether the *organ* takes on sounds.

A further preliminary point to notice is that Aristotle normally postulates only that we *receive* forms in our sense-organs, not that we *perceive* them there. The only exceptions come in the course of a dialectical argument at *DA* 425ᵃ22–5, in an argument whose conclusion is rejected at *Sens.* 447ᵃ23–7, and in a non-psychological work at *GA* 780ᵇ32.

The foregoing provides the preliminary evidence that for Aristotle sense-perception involves the sense-organ's becoming white, black, hot, cold, wet, or dry. It is not essential to my case whether 'receiving form without matter' refers, like the other phrases, to this physiological process, or, as one interpretation holds,[135] to some further process dependent on it. But as a matter of fact, I think the following is what actually happens. initially, the reception of form is something in which the sense-*organ* (*aisthētērion*) engages[136] and is connected with being 'potentially such'.[137] In other words, it involves the literal coloration of the organ of sight. But when Aristotle compares perception with *thought*, he realizes that the desired analogy is only partial. Certainly, when a person thinks of a stone, matter is left behind, because the stone is not in his or her soul, only its form.[138] But Aristotle refrains, when he gets beyond the first tentative comparison in *DA* 3. 4, from repeating the standard expressions. The stone is not described as 'matter', and its form is not spoken of as being 'received', probably because these words had expressed a doctrine about the sense-*organ*, and thinking does not in the same way involve an organ, in his view. Instead, the comparison is with the doctrine which concerns not the organ but the sense, that the activity of sound is in the sense and is not merely such as, but identical with, the activity of hearing.

---

[130] *DA* 418ᵃ3.   [131] *DA* 424ᵃ18–19.   [132] *DA* 424ᵃ24–5.

[133] *DA* 425ᵇ26–426ᵃ26.   [134] *DA* 426ᵃ4.

[135] Bernard (1988). The best candidate for this further process might be not Bernard's, but Lear's action of sound on the sense (425ᵇ26–426ᵃ26), which, however, I would construe somewhat differently from Lear (1988).

[136] *DA* 425ᵇ23.   [137] *DA* 429ᵃ15–16.   [138] *DA* 431ᵇ28–432ᵃ1.

In this roundabout way, the idea of form, though not in so many words the idea of reception of form, gets connected with a second, non-physiological, doctrine, but only in the case of thought, not in the case of perception. It is this second, non-physiological application of the word 'form', confined to the case of thought, which has in at least one case absorbed attention and led (mistakenly, I think) to a rejection of the physiological interpretation of the reception of form for the case of perception.[139]

So much for preliminaries. That a literal coloration process is involved in (visual) perception can be made undeniable, I believe, by examining a virtually continuous passage, *DA* 423[b]27–424[b]18. Here Aristotle finds that there is a problem affecting the organ of touch, but no other sense. For the eye-jelly is colourless and the interior of the ear soundless. Otherwise they would obtrude their own character and interfere with the reception of form.[140] But the organ of touch cannot equally be free of the qualities of heat, cold, fluidity, and dryness, for these, as explained in *On Generation and Corruption*, are the defining characteristics of the four sublunary elements (423[b]27–9). This creates a problem: the organ of touch cannot afford to possess already the degree of heat, cold, fluidity, or dryness which it is to perceive, since the perceptual process involves starting off merely potentially such as the sense-object, and being subsequently made such as it. The organ cannot be made to acquire in this way the temperature it already possesses (423[b]30–424[a]4). The conclusion must be that we have a blind spot for that particular temperature. And indeed that is why (*diho*, 424[a]2) we do in fact have a blind spot for what is as hot, cold, hard, or soft as we are (*diho tou homoiōs thermou kai psuchrou ē sklērou kai malakou ouk aisthanometha*, 424[a]2–3). The empirical fact is that we notice only extremes (*alla tōn huperbolōn*, 424[a]4). And this shows, by inference to the best explanation, that the sense organ is somewhere in the middle range of temperatures, etc., and that derivatively the sense is as it were a mid-point (*hōs tēs aisthēseōs hoion mesotētos tinos ousēs tēs en tois aisthētois enantiōseōs*, 424[a]4–5). Just as what is going to perceive white and black must be neither of these in actuality, but both in potentiality, so in the case of touch it must be neither hot nor cold in actuality, though both, presumably, in potentiality (424[a]7–10).

There are three reasons why I think this first part of the passage cannot be handled by those who deny that Aristotle is referring to a literal taking on of temperatures and other qualities. First, a relevance must be supplied for the sudden reference in the middle of the *De Anima* to *On Generation and Corruption* and its doctrine that hot, cold, fluid, and dry are the defining characteristics of the four elements. Secondly, and most crucially of all, the *diho* ('that is why') at 424[a]2 appears to become unintelligible on other interpretations. *Diho* offers to explain why there is a *barrier* to our perceiving certain temperatures. No barrier would have been presented to our perceiving medium temperatures, if the organ

---

[139] Lear (1988).

[140] *DA* 418[b]26–30, 429[a]15–26. No exception is provided by the fact that the ear produces an echo, for this is said to be a foreign (*allotrios*) sound, not its own (*idios*), 420[a]17–18.

merely had to receive a coded message, for example a vibration, or if we were merely being told that the organ becomes aware of temperature. The barrier arises because the organ needs to acquire the temperature to be perceived, and is debarred from acquiring the temperature it possesses already. The inability of coded messages, or of references to awareness, to supply a barrier, affects not only the present passage in 2. 11, but also the statement in 3. 4 that what is to receive forms must obtrude no interfering characteristics of its own. My case could very well rest on the single word *diho*. The third question is why Aristotle says that what is going to perceive black and white must be potentially both, and similarly for what is going to perceive hot and cold. This cannot be brushed aside as if it were the merely negative point that the thing must not be actually black or white. It means more to say that it is potentially these.

I would add a fourth point, although it is not decisive, that the meaning of the word *mesotēs* (424ᵃ4) must be respected. Literally, it means something in the middle. Of course, sense is only said to be *as it were* a *sort of* mid-point, but some connection with the literal meaning must be retained. Admittedly, this constraint is probably no harder for others than for me, since I too must explain how senses other than touch are to be viewed as mid-points: the eye-jelly does not have a medium colour.[141] But it is a constraint that is seldom at present observed. Let me now give a translation of the passage:

It is the differentiating characteristics of body *qua* body which are the objects of touch. By differentiating characteristics I mean those which define the elements, namely, hot, cold, dry and fluid, about which we have spoken earlier in the work on the elements. And their organ (*aisthētērion*), which can exercise touch and in which first of all the sense called touch resides, is the part that is potentially such (*dunamei toiouton*). For perceiving is being affected in some way. So what makes a thing such (*hoion*) as it itself is in actuality makes it such (*toiouton*) because it is potentially (*dunamei*) so. And that is why (*diho*) we do not perceive what is similarly hot or cold, hard or soft, but perceive the extremes, which suggests that sense is as it were a sort of mid-point (*mesotēs*) between opposites in perceptibles. And it is for this reason that sense discriminates (*krinei*) perceptibles, for the middle is discriminating (*kritikon*), since it comes to be to each of the two extremes its opposite. And just as what is going to perceive white or black must be neither of them in actuality, but potentially both (*dunamei d' amphō*), and similarly too in the other cases, so also in the case of touch it must be neither hot nor cold.[142]

Shortly afterwards, Aristotle concludes his chapter on touch, 2. 11, and begins his survey of all five senses in 2. 12. Whereas the previous chapter had talked about being 'potentially such', the new chapter brings in another of the interlinked phrases and affirms that with all five senses the organ receives the perceptible forms without matter. It then offers to explain various phenomena on the basis of what precedes. One thing to be explained (424ᵃ32–ᵇ3) is the fact that plants do not perceive, even though they are alive and are affected (*paschein*) by

---

[141] Different evidence for the sense of sight being an intermediate blend (*logos*) is that extremes of dazzle or darkness impair its functioning, 424ᵃ27–32.

[142] *DA* 423ᵇ27–424ᵃ10.

heat and cold, as shown by their being warmed or cooled. The explanation is twofold: plants do not have a mid-point (*mesotēs*), and they cannot receive the forms of perceptibles, but are acted on in company with matter. The first part of this explanation, the lack of a *mesotēs*, has on some interpretations been found unintelligible,[143] but it is elucidated in 435ᵃ20–ᵇ3. Plants are made predominantly of earth, and the characteristic properties of earth are cold and dryness. But touch needs to be a sort of mid-point (*mesotēs*) among all the tangible qualities, and its organ has to be able to receive (*dektikon*, 435ᵃ22) not only the characteristics of earth (cold and dryness), but heat and cold and all the other tangible qualities.

If 'receive' here refers as usual to the perceptual process, there will have been some carelessness, because cold and dryness are precisely what plants, being already cold and dry, could *not* receive. If such carelessness is accepted, there will be further confirmation of my claim that the reception of perceptible form is the literal taking on of heat, cold, fluidity, and dryness, etc. Alternatively, Aristotle may be using the idea of qualities received in a less usual way to refer to the organ's standard qualities, not to those which it temporarily assumes during perception. He will be saying that the organ is standardly characterized by an intermediate blend of hot and cold, of fluid and dry, etc., and cannot just be cold and dry. That too would confirm part of what was said above, but would throw no light on what happens to the organ at the very moment of perception. The conclusion of the argument is that plants could not have the sense of touch, and without touch no other sense is possible.

There is an underlying assumption, rather contrary to the spirit of functionalism, if that is taken at its broadest to be the idea that mental processes can be defined by functions that can be realized in various different types of matter. For Aristotle is here assuming that sense-perception can only be realized in an organism with a mean temperature not too far from our own. Admittedly, Aristotle does elsewhere allow for certain other variations of mechanism. For smelling, fish use their gills, dolphins their blowhole, and insects the middle part of their body,[144] the first two of which contain water, not air.[145] Indeed, it is a major theme of Aristotle's biological groupings that, in different genera, parts can be analogous in function but different in structure, and a case in point is the nostrils, the gills of fish, and the middles of insects. He also entertains what we should call the conceptual possibility that colours, sounds, and odours might have been perceived through direct application of a balloon-like membrane to the thing perceived.[146] Even when he argues that there could be no sixth organ to create a sixth sense, he still recognizes the epistemic possibility that there might be some unknown substance or property not possessed by anything on earth, but capable of constituting a sixth organ.[147] The anti-functionalist restriction to mean temperatures is then perhaps the exception, rather than the rule.

[143] Slakey (1961).
[144] *PA* 659ᵇ14–19. For further details, see Sorabji (1971), 57–8, repr. (1979), 77–8.
[145] *DA* 425ᵃ5.   [146] *DA* 423ᵃ2–12.   [147] *DA* 425ᵃ11–13.

The second explanation in 2. 12 of why plants do not perceive is that they cannot receive (*dechesthai*) the forms of perceptibles, but are affected (*paschein*) in company with (*meta*) matter. The word for being affected here, as elsewhere,[148] stands in as a more general description of receiving. I prefer the oldest interpretation, according to which plants become warm by letting warm air or other warm matter into their systems, instead of leaving the matter behind. It has been objected that this is plainly false,[149] but I do not think so. Nor is there any need that it should be *plainly* true, for it is not an observation, but a hypothesis constructed to help explain the insensitivity of plants, and it would again have been difficult with the instruments available to discover whether it was true or false. The main rival interpretation takes the point to concern the matter of the plants themselves, not the matter they receive. On this view, for the plants to receive form in company with matter is for their matter to take on heat and cold, while for them to receive form without matter would be for them not to stand as matter to, but simply to become aware of, heat and cold.[150] But this reading gives us a tautology, instead of an explanation, because it merely tells us that plants do not become aware of heat, but grow hot instead. This does not *explain* why they don't perceive. Of course, it is part of this interpretation that Aristotle does not think it appropriate to explain such a thing. But in fact he purports to be offering an explanation (*dia ti, dia touto, aition*)[151] in both of the chapters where he discusses the question. The passage in 2. 12 reads:

And [it is clear from the preceding] why (*dia ti*) ever it is that plants do not perceive, although they have some part of the soul and are affected (*paschein*) in some way by the tactile qualities themselves. For they are heated and cooled. The explanation (*aition*) is that they do not have a mid-point (*mesotēs*), nor a principle of a sort to receive (*dechesthai*) the forms of perceptibles. Rather they are affected in company with matter (*paschein meta tēs hulēs*).[152]

It is difficult to see how this can fail to be offering an explanation, or how it could instead be saying that no explanation is needed, because the ability or inability to perceive is a basic fact which needs no explanation.

But there is more to come, and the point that follows has not, I think, received attention. I am not referring merely to the fact that it would be historically appropriate for Aristotle to insist that sensory reception involves leaving matter behind—although it is relevant that that would be appropriate, because so many of his predecessors had made sense-perception depend on receiving matter from the object perceived. But far more important is the little-considered question of the relevance of the rest of the chapter. Aristotle devotes the remainder to a puzzle which he finds so obviously relevant that he does not even think it necessary to state what the relevance is, merely saying: 'But someone might be puzzled.' As I see it, the relevance is in fact immediate. I have taken Aristotle's point to be

---

[148] *DA* 424ᵃ23, 427ᵃ8–9.   [149] Burnyeat.   [150] Ibid.
[151] *DA* 424ᵃ32–3, 435ᵇ1.   [152] *DA* 424ᵃ32–424ᵃ32ᵇ3.

that being acted on by heat without receiving air or other matter is a *necessary* prerequisite for perceiving heat, odour, etc. This at once makes relevant the question: is it also *sufficient* for perceiving heat and odour? Or, equivalently, could something that didn't perceive still be acted on by heat or odour—that is, without receiving air or other matter?

It may be thought an obstacle that Aristotle does not explicitly add the words 'without receiving air or other matter'. All he says is:

Rather they are affected in company with matter. But someone might be puzzled whether something incapable of exercising smell would be affected at all (*paschein ti*) by odour, or something incapable of seeing by colour, and similarly for the other cases.[153]

So far my ground is only that the necessary relevance is provided, if we understand Aristotle still to have in mind what he has just been discussing: the possibility of being affected by perceptible qualities *without* receiving matter. But in fact this interpretation is strikingly confirmed. For Aristotle goes on to consider the case of something insentient, timber, being split in a thunderstorm, and he insists that this is not a case of sound acting on a body. Why not? Because it is the air accompanying the thunder that acts. The word for accompaniment is *meta*, the same word that was used when Aristotle complained that plants are affected in company with (*meta*, 424b3) matter. Evidently the subject of his puzzle is whether insentient things can be affected by perceptible qualities, rather than by the *matter* accompanying those qualities. On the alternative interpretation, no particular relevance is apparent either for Aristotle's puzzle, or for his example of air entering the timber:

And it is at the same time clear in the following way too: it is neither light and darkness, nor sound, nor odour that acts (*poiein*) at all on bodies, but rather that in which they reside. It is the air, for example, accompanying (*meta*) thunder that splits the timber.[154]

It is important that the entire discussion down to the end of the chapter should be shown to be relevant, and in particular the question that Aristotle goes on to ask at 424b16–17:

What, then (*oun*), is exercising smell (*osmasthai*) besides (*para*) being affected in some way?

Let us see how the alternative interpretations fare in providing relevance. Aristotle goes backwards and forwards on whether the various perceptible qualities, as opposed to the matter accompanying them, can act on something insentient. He first puts the case on the other side, but finally decides (*alla* = 'but', 424b12) that the tactile qualities, hot, cold, fluid, and dry, and flavours can so act, and that odour and sound can so act on stuff like air, which is free-flowing. Air, for example, can be made smelly (424b12–16), and he means, I am sure, without taking on cheesy matter. This, of course, shows that being affected by odour without receiving matter is *not* sufficient for exercising the sense of smell

---

[153] *DA* 424b2–5.   [154] *DA* 2. 12, 424b9–12.

(*osmasthai*). His question now is not merely relevant: it cries out for an answer (424ᵇ16–17):

What, then, is exercising smell besides (*para*) being affected in some way?

The implication is that exercising smell is partly a matter of being affected by odour, but is also something else besides (*para*).

It is not only relevance that is decisive here, but also the word *para* (besides). This word implies that exercising smell has two aspects. If no physiological process were needed, as maintained by the alternative interpretation, there would be no room for two aspects. So that interpretation must reconstrue the *para* sentence. It might do so by taking the sentence in effect to be asking, 'What is exercising smell as opposed to being acted on in the way the air is?' But *para* does not mean 'as opposed to'; it means 'besides'. Furthermore, the proposed question would rob the second half of the chapter from 424ᵇ3 to 424ᵇ18 of relevance and connection of thought. The question of relevance has come up three times. First, why does Aristotle raise the puzzle whether something insentient can be acted on by perceptible qualities? Secondly, why in discussing the question does he make so much of the air accompanying the thunder as the agent that splits the timber? Thirdly, why after answering the question does he think it relevant ('what, *then* (*oun*),...?') to ask what exercising smell is besides being acted on? I have tried to show how one point flows naturally from another.

Aristotle's answer to the question, 'what is exercising smell besides?' may be to us disappointing. He is only able to say that it is perceiving (*aisthanesthai*), thereby supplying the genus, since the sense of smell is defined by genus and differentia as one kind of perception, the perception of odour. But his silence cannot lend any support to the rival interpretation, because the *para* sentence has told us that exercising smell is partly a matter of being affected by odour and partly something else. It is not in any case surprising if he does not, at the tail end of his discussion of the five special senses, and before his discussion of the generic functions of sense-perception, give us a formula to tell us more about what perceiving is. For though he has a great deal more to say about what it is, that more does not take the shape of a formula. Some of it was said in 2. 6, ch. but much is reserved for book 3 of the *De Anima*, after the discussion of the five special senses is concluded, and I have tried to bring out what it is in Section I above.

Much has been made of the fact that there is no manuscript warrant for reading *kai* (also) into Aristotle's answer, so that it tells us that exercising smell is *also* perceiving. But my interpretation rests not on Torstrik's conjecture of *kai*, but on the word *para*, 'besides'. The passage in its entirety reads as follows:

(424ᵃ32) And [it is clear from the preceding] why (*dia ti*) ever it is that plants do not perceive, although they have some part of the soul and are affected (*paschein*) in some way by the tactile [qualities] themselves. For they are heated and cooled. The explanation (*aition*) is that they do not have a mid-point (*mesotēs*), nor a principle of a sort to receive (*dechesthai*) the forms of perceptibles. Rather they are affected in company with matter (*paschein meta tēs hulēs*).

(424^{b}3) But someone might be puzzled whether something incapable of exercising smell would be affected (*paschein*) at all by odour, or something incapable of seeing by colour, and similarly for the other cases.

(424^{b}5) But if the object of smell is odour, if it produces anything at all, odour produces an exercise of smelling, so that none of the things which cannot exercise smell can be affected (*paschein*) by odour, and the same story goes for the other cases too. Nor can any of the things which can exercise smell be affected by odour except in their capacity as perceivers. And it is at the same time clear in the following way too: it is neither light and darkness, nor sound, nor odour that acts (*poiein*) at all on bodies, but rather that in which they reside. It is the air, for example, accompanying (*meta*) thunder that splits the timber.

(424^{b}12) But (*alla*) the objects of touch and flavours do act (*poiein*). For otherwise by what would inanimate things be affected (*paschein*) and qualitatively changed? So do the other sense-objects also act on things (*empoiein*)? Or rather not every body can be affected (*pathētikon*) by odour and sound, and the ones which are affected (*paschein*) lack definite boundaries and do not stay put, for example, air, for this is smelly as if it had been affected (*paschein*) in some way.

(424^{b}16) What then (*oun*), is exercising smell besides (*para*) being affected (*paschein*) in some way? Rather, exercising smell is perceiving (*aisthanesthai*), whereas the air on being affected (*paschein*) quickly becomes perceptible (*aisthētos*).

I have now surveyed the evidence that Aristotle thinks perception requires a physiological process, that that process is one of the organ's taking on colour, temperature, and other qualities, and that that is what he is referring to by a group of interlinked phrases. I think it highly probable, although it is not essential to my case, that one of those phrases is 'receiving form without matter'. It is now necessary to consider the evidence on the other side for the view that what is being described is only a becoming aware of sense-qualities, and for the further view that no physiological process is needed. I am aware of three pieces of positive evidence.

One piece of evidence, *DA* 2. 5, has, I believe, often been misunderstood. It was used by Brentano to prepare the ground for his view that in Aristotle the sense-objects, colour and temperature for example, are not, or not only, physically present in the observer, but present as objects of perception.[155] It has been used as one of the arguments against the materialist interpretation of Aristotle as holding that perceiving is nothing but a physiological process.[156] It has been used to show that the change involved in perception cannot be anything like becoming red or smelly,[157] and finally to show that no physical change at all is needed in perception.[158]

The relevant passage is not discussing perceiving so much as the *switch to* perceiving after one has not been using one's senses. This should either not be called being affected (*paschein*) and qualitatively changed (*alloiousthai*), or should be recognized as a distinct way of being affected or qualitatively changed. But the

[155] Brentano (1867), 79–80, translated (1977), 54.

[156] Barnes (1971–2) 109 = (1979) 38. Barnes also cites *Ph.* 244^{b}7–15. But I think that says only that perceptual alterations are noticed, not that they are non-physical.

[157] Burnyeat; Lear (1988), 111–12.   [158] Burnyeat.

point is not, as supposed, that the switch is not a physical one, nor even that it is not wholly physical. The point is put in terms entirely different from that, by reference to a series of Aristotelian concepts.[159] First, the change should not be called *alloiousthai*, because the literal meaning of *allo-iousthai* is 'becoming other', whereas the being who switches to using his sense or intellect is rather developing more into himself (reading *eis hauto*, 417^{b}6) and finding fulfilment (*entelecheia*, 417^{b}7). Again, nothing has been subjected to destruction (*phthora*); rather that which was in a potential state before is preserved (*sōtēria*) by the switch to perception (417^{b}3). The same is true, in the case of the intellect, with regard to an earlier stage of development. The learner who switches from not knowing to knowing is not switching to a privative phase (*sterētikai diatheseis*), but to a stable possession (*hexeis*), and to his real nature (*phusis*, 417^{b}15–16). None of this is couched in terms of the switch being wholly or partly non-physical. And indeed it could not be wholly non-physical, because one of the examples given is that of a builder switching to actually building (417^{b}9). I presume that the point could even be extended to a purely physical switch, such as a rock's switching from its perch on a ledge to falling in the direction of its natural position, just so long as that could be viewed as a switch towards its true nature.

The second piece of positive evidence adduced comes from the opening of *DA* 2. 12, briefly discussed above, where Aristotle first states that the sense-organ receives perceptible forms without matter. In doing so, he uses the analogy of a signet-ring imprinted in wax. Plato had used the model of imprints in a wax block, it is said, to illustrate the wide gap between perception and judgement. In perception there is no awareness, just a causal interaction with sensible qualities in the environment. To judge what these qualities are, or that 'this is Theodorus', one needs to go beyond one's present perception and compare it with the imprints one has retained as if in wax. Only then do awareness and judgement come in. If Aristotle believes instead that wax imprints are an appropriate model for perception itself, he must be denying Plato's view of perception. Two inferences are drawn, the first that the reception of sensible forms must be understood in terms of *becoming aware of* colours, sounds, smells, and other sensible qualities, not as a literal physiological change of quality in the organ. The second inference is that no physiological change is needed at all.[160] I do not believe that these inferences are justifiable. Aristotle uses the signet-ring model in his treatise *On Memory*, where he clearly intends a physiological interpretation, explaining various different forms of memory failure by the surface imprinted being too hard, too fluid like running water, or too worn like the old parts of buildings.[161]

A third reason for holding that there is no *physical* difference which accounts for our perceiving, while plants do not, draws on a difficulty in Aristotle's thought, which is not particularly tied to the theory of perception. Aristotle holds that an eye is *essentially* sighted and flesh *essentially* alive, so that a dead eye and

---

[159] This is very well explained by Van Riet (1953).   [160] Burnyeat.   [161] *Mem.* 450^{a}27–^{b}11.

dead flesh do not even have the same definition. There is then no specifiable physiological difference which accounts for our advantage over plants, because in specifying the difference we should be forced to presuppose the very perception we wanted to explain. This difficulty has been much discussed,[162] and I would agree it is a real one. But I am not convinced that Aristotle's idea of the eye as *essentially* alive is part and parcel of his whole approach to perception, rather than an idea whose relation to the rest of his theory he has insufficiently considered. In any case, it has been pointed out that strictly speaking there is no disharmony with the theory of perception as I have explained it.[163] For Aristotle believes that the concept of an eye can be used in different, though related, senses. An eye that is at one time alive and at another time dead can still be referred to as an eye all right, even though it is not an eye in the fullest sense. It is an eye in this second-ary sense to which we need to refer in explaining the perceptual advantage which we have over plants.

I have called these three pieces of evidence positive, because I believe the remaining evidence consists in, or depends on, objections to the alternative account which I have given. Consequently, much of it has been addressed already. But I need to consider two outstanding types of objection. One set of difficulties concerns the implausibility of the view I ascribe to Aristotle. Does my heart go hard as concrete, for example, when I feel concrete?[164] I think Aristotle could answer this by reference to the idea of small-scale models which he uses in his treatise *On Memory*. We think about the relative sizes of two or more objects by having images which serve as small-scale models.[165] Similarly a small-scale hardening within the heart might serve as the basis for feeling the hardness of concrete. I say that Aristotle *could* answer this way, because I do not think he did in fact think much in this context about the tactile qualities other than hot, cold, fluid, and dry. These are the four that define the four elements, and many of the others can, in his view, be reduced to them.[166] What is more difficult is Aristotle's inference (and I have treated it as an inference, not an observation) that the organ in our hearts (perhaps some of the blood in it) has a medium temperature. This would not necessarily be contradicted by observation, since blood heat might be thought of as medium. But it does seem to be in conflict with Aristotle's theory in *Juv.* and *Resp.* that the heart is the centre of vital heat and needs to be cooled by incoming air. I doubt if such a conflict of theories, however, is sufficiently improbable to discredit the interpretation. It has been overlooked by modern critics, and could have been overlooked by Aristotle.

A final objection appears to me to be mistaken. It is complained that form is not the sort of thing that could pass into my organ, or anywhere else, without being carried by a material vehicle.[167] What is true is that sensible forms cannot exist without being embedded in some matter or other at every moment, and also that the transfer or spread of sensible forms is not to be viewed as a genuine case

[162] Ackrill (1972–3); Williams (1986); Burnyeat; Cohen (1987).
[163] Cohen (1987), drawing on Williams (1986).
[164] Burnyeat.   [165] *Mem.* 452^{b}8–15.
[166] *GC* 2. 2.   [167] Burnyeat.

of motion (*phora*).[168] That said, however, Aristotle allows all sorts of possibilities to sensible forms. We have noticed him allowing that a thing's odour can float off into the air, however much difficulty that may give the ancient commentators, when they think about the doctrine that particular qualities are inseparable from what they inhere in.[169] In the *De Sensu* he describes the instantaneous spread of heat from one block of material to another.[170] The transmission of effects through an intervening medium to an observer is different from either of these two cases, and different, as the commentators will stress, for each of the three long-distance senses, sight, hearing, and smell. Most obviously in the case of sight the intervening medium does not become coloured. But the same principle applies, that a sensible form, or its effect, located in one piece of matter can cause another instance of the same form to appear in an adjacent piece of matter.

Such are the objections to the literal physiological interpretation. Although not accepting them, I ought to qualify what I said in my original publication.[171] Aristotle sometimes says that physiological explanations play a subordinate role, when there is a purposive explanation available, and tell us only how, not why (*dia ti*) something happens: they tell us only the instrument (*organon*).[172] He is by no means consistent about this, and frequently allows throughout his biological works that physiology is straightforwardly explanatory (*dia, aition, aitia, diho, dihoper, gar, men oun, dihoti, hoti, hōste*), not only where purposive explanations are missing,[173] but also where they are available.[174] However, there is one mood in which he confines them to telling how. Equally, he holds that the powers which constitute the soul, powers of growing, perceiving, and desiring, and indeed the soul itself, can *explain* growing, perceiving, and desiring.[175] One way in which he thinks them explanatory is that he treats it as a *basic* fact about the universe that such powers exist. Appeal to basic facts is explanatory in a way: it can be used to explain the occurrence of the requisite physiological processes. They are only to be expected as necessary for the operation of the powers which are taken as basic. But this is not to treat the powers as basic in the sense that their operation has no explanation in terms of physiological processes. At most, it implies that the physiological processes tell us how, rather than why, the basic powers can operate. And even this perspective is, as I say, not consistently maintained in the biological works. On my interpretation, it is not maintained here in the *De Anima* either, because he cites the physiological process to explain why (*dia ti*) plants do not perceive.[176]

---

[168] *Sens.* 446ᵇ28–447ᵃ1.

[169] *Cat.* 1ᵃ25. I shall discuss the commentators' treatment of this in my (1991).

[170] *Sens.* 446ᵇ28–447ᵃ6.

[171] The original article was my (1974). The reasons for qualification are explained in my (1980), 166–74.

[172] *GA* 789ᵇ3–22.   [173] *PA* 677ᵃ18, *GA* 778ᵃ35–ᵇ1, ᵇ14, ᵇ18, 782ᵃ20–783ᵇ8, 789ᵇ20.

[174] *PA* 658ᵇ2–5; 663ᵇ14; 677ᵇ25–30; 679ᵃ28; 694ᵇ6; *GA* 738ᵃ33–4; 743ᵇ7–18; 755ᵃ21–4; 766ᵃ16–30; 767ᵇ10–23; 776ᵃ25–ᵇ3; 788ᵇ33–789ᵃ4; 789ᵃ12–14.

[175] *DA* 415ᵇ8–12; ᵇ21–8; 416ᵃ8–9; ᵇ21–2; *GA* 740ᵇ25–741ᵃ2; cf. 726ᵇ18–21; 729ᵇ27; 739ᵃ17; *PA* 640ᵃ23.

[176] *DA* 424ᵃ32–3.

III

With the idea of a literal coloration process defended, I can now bring out its his-' torical significance. It was seen in Section I that Aristotle had plenty to say about what *we* should call the intentional objects of perception. But Franz Brentano thought that Aristotle had actually himself framed the concept of an intentional object. This seminal notion was introduced by Brentano into modern philosophy in 1874. His idea was that if I inherit a fortune, the fortune must exist, in order to be the object I inherit. But if I hope for a fortune, the fortune need not exist outside my mind, in order to be the object of my hopes. This feature—not having to exist outside the mind in order to serve as an object—is called by Brentano intentional inexistence. Furthermore, he proposes it as the distinguishing feature of mental, as opposed to physical, phenomena, that they are one and all directed to objects of this kind. Even in sense-perception, the square shapes I may represent some scene as containing need not really exist in the external scene, in order to be the objects my sense-perception represents as being there. Descartes's earlier distinction between the mental and the physical, according to which we have infallible awareness of our own mental states, is hard to accept in the age of Freud, and so the completely different criterion proposed by Brentano has merited attention.

But where did he find the idea of an intentional object expressed in Aristotle? Curiously enough, in the doctrine, which I have interpreted as physiological, of form received without matter. In *Die Psychologie des Aristoteles* (1867), Brentano interpreted that doctrine as meaning that the object of sense-perception (colour or temperature, for example) is not, or not only, physically present in the observer, but present as an object (*objectiv*), that is, as an object of perception.[177] In *Psychologie vom empirischen Standpunkt* (1874), he went further: in his doctrine that the senses receive form without matter, Aristotle was already referring to intentional inexistence. The forms received without matter were intentionally inexistent objects.[178] Throughout, Brentano claimed to be following the medieval scholastics, and his earlier interpretation at least would have been readily suggested by Thomas Aquinas' insistence on the intentional status of what is received.

In fact, however, Brentano's interpretation was only made possible by a long history of distortions, a history which I shall be telling elsewhere,[179] and which here I will only sketch. First, the Greek commentators, Alexander, Themistius, and Philoponus, dephysiologized Aristotle's theory of the reception of form without matter. Their motive was not to give the most straightforward reading of the text, but to rescue Aristotle from certain particular problems in physics and logic. If literal coloration was transmitted to the eye, we might get different colours colliding in the same place. Again, if Socrates' fragrance was transmitted to the

---

[177] Brentano (1867), 79–81, 86, 120 n. 23, translated (1977), 54, 58, 229 n. 23.
[178] Brentano (1874/1959), 125, translated (1973), 88.   [179] Sorabji (1991).

observer's nostrils, we might violate the logical requirement in Aristotle's *Categories*, which was taken to mean that Socrates' particular fragrance cannot exist separately from him. The commentators' interpretations were designed to give Aristotle the most defensible view.

The result was a theory in which, except for the case of the tactile qualities, hot, cold, fluid, and dry, the reception of form was no longer to be understood as a physiological process. By Philoponus it is called a cognitive (*gnōstikos*) reception. The Islamic philosopher Avicenna added in the idea of an intention or meaning (*maᶜnā*, in the Arabic), giving as examples shape, colour, quantity, quality, where (*pou*) and posture. Sense-perception does not abstract from these. In the medieval Latin translations of Avicenna and Averroës available to Albert and his pupil Thomas Aquinas, the Arabic word was translated *intentio*, and *intentio* in perception now appears to be a kind of message which is physically housed. It is the information housed, not the physical housing. It can still in these authors exist in mid-air between perceiver and perceived, and so it is not a message of which anyone is inevitably aware, but Brentano was to change this. For him an intentional object is the object of a mental attitude.

The irony in all at this will now be apparent. Brentano's idea of intentionality was lent the authority of Aristotle, but only through the distortions of successive commentators. We can also see the value of getting clear on the physiological interpretation which I have argued Aristotle originally intended. Only so can the distortions be detected. The purpose of the best commentators is not simply to reflect Aristotle, but to reconstruct him, and that invites originality. The reinterpretation of Aristotle was not perfectly uniform—Philoponus, Aquinas, and Brentano had different versions—much less was it specifically Christian. It was the work of commentators, whether Christian, pagan, or Muslim. It was the commentators who made possible Brentano's interpretation and who lent authority to his important new proposal for the philosophy of mind. Brentano's interpretation should not be taken at face value, but seen for what it is, the culmination of a series of distortions. The moral is that in the history of philosophy the distortions of commentators can be more fruitful than fidelity.[180]

[180] I am extremely grateful to Myles Burnyeat for ammunition both for and against my suggestions in Section I, as well as for pressing the issue in Section II. Further acknowledgements for my discussion of the Stoics in Section I are given in my (1990) and in n. 60, and for Section II will be given in my (1991), but I should like here to acknowledge John Ellis's work on the inseparability of Socrates' fragrance (1990 and London Ph.D. Diss. 1991).

13
ARISTOTLE ON THE SENSE OF TOUCH

CYNTHIA FREELAND

Introduction

IN Aristotle's classic catalogue of the five senses, the sense of touch is special for several reasons. It is the most basic of all the senses, the only one common to all animals (*DA* 413^{b}4–10). Certain primitive animals, such as sponges and ascidians, possess touch alone of all the senses, and this is enough to distinguish them from the plants which they otherwise closely resemble (*HA* 588^{b}4–22, *PA* 4. 5). Without touch, he tells us in *DA* 3. 13, it is impossible for an animal to exist, whereas the other senses exist for an animal's 'well-being' (*to eu*; 434^{b}23–5, 435^{b}18–21).[1] Perhaps because of its pervasiveness, Aristotle links touch closely to fundamental biological processes such as sleeping, aging and dying, disease and health (*Somn. Vig.* 455^{a}12–^{b}2, *DA* 435^{b}4–5, *PA* 648^{b}2–10). He also sees it even in primitive animals as providing a basis for certain higher-order cognitive capacities involving imagination (*phantasia*) (*DA* 433^{b}31–434^{a}10).

In this chapter I propose to examine the central place of Aristotle's account of touch within his empiricist epistemology and general physical theory. In Section I I shall review certain puzzles Aristotle himself raises about the objects, organ, and medium of this sense. I will consider whether Aristotle held a 'literalist' account of the nature of sensory representation, according to which an organ becomes literally 'like' the sensed object. Though some commentators seem to find the literalist view more plausible for the sense of touch than for distal senses like hearing and sight,[2] I will argue that this view is equally absurd for touch and that Aristotle was not committed to it.

© Cynthia Freeland, 1992.

[1] I take all translations from Aristotle (1984) except for *Meteoralogica* (1952) and *Parts of Animals* (1961*b*).

[2] See for example Bynum (1987), 169: 'If the organ of touch is midway between hot and cold, then something hotter can make the organ hotter too, while something colder can make it colder. Touch, therefore, can discriminate a whole range of temperatures between hot and cold.' For criticisms, see Modrak (1987*a*), 59: 'Were the literalist interpretation right, the organ of touch would literally become as hot as the object sensed or as solid, for the object is said to make the organ such as it is (424^{a}2). But this is absurd.' In part what I go on to say here can be seen as an explication of Modrak's claim about the absurdity involved in a literalist construal of touch perception, as well as of her proposal that Aristotle's doctrine that each sense is a 'mean'—what she calls 'the *logos* doctrine'—must be interpreted in some alternative way; see Modrak (1987*a*), 56–62.

In Section II I shall consider why, although he recorded an extraordinary variety of tactual organs throughout the animal kingdom, Aristotle never directly responded to certain obvious sceptical temptations. One such sceptical problem concerns (species) *intersubjectivity*: I argue that we must go beyond the *De Anima* account of tangibles, and understand the broader role of touch in animals' behavioural economies, in order to grasp his justification for making interspecies comparisons.

A second major sceptical problem concerns *objectivity*: In Section III I shall examine Aristotle's justification for maintaining that touch is a pre-eminent source of information about the physical/material world. He says in $423^{b}27$ that the differentiae (*diaphorai*) of body as body are tangible (*haptai*), and he proceeds on just this basis to classify and explain the fundamental principles of sensible bodies in *GC* $329^{b}7-16$ ff. In a recent commentary on the *De Generatione et Corruptione*, C. J. F. Williams has interpreted Aristotle's argument in the *De Anima* as moving from the universality of touch among animals to its role as an index of material reality:

From the alleged fact that the sense of touch can exist in animals without the other senses, but not they without it, he infers that the qualities detected by touch are the distinctive qualities of body, qua body.   (Williams 1982, 157.)

Williams faults this argument as 'over-hasty'. I believe that Williams is wrong in his interpretation of this key argument as well as in his criticism, but it is not simple to explain why. Aristotle rejected the most viable then-current rival physical theory—atomism—on the grounds that it reduced all sensory modalities to touch; we should not attribute to him a reductionist analysis which makes this same mistake. I will suggest an interpretation of Aristotle's defence of the objectivity of tactile representation which reveals a deeper and more complex link between his theory of sense-knowledge and his project of scientific explanation than has previously been recognized.

I. The Sense of Touch: Organ and Objects

Touch is the last of the five senses Aristotle discusses in book 2 of the *De Anima*. In a remark prefatory to his general discussion of the senses in ch. 6 of that book, Aristotle announces that each sense must be dealt with and described in relation to its objects ($418^{a}7-8$); this accords with his treatment of the senses as capacities (*dunameis*), which are typically defined through their actualizations (*energeiai*). This approach leads Aristotle into a general puzzle at the start of his account of touch in ch. 11: since this sense appears to perceive several pairs of contraries (he lists hot–cold, dry–moist, and hard–soft), Aristotle finds it unclear whether touch is a single sense or a group of senses. He appears to resolve the puzzle by reminding himself and us that the other senses too may perceive more than one basic pair of contraries (thus sounds may be both sharp or flat and loud or soft); yet he admits even so that tangible objects seem unusual in not falling into a natural named group as sounds, colours, tastes, or smells do.

Now, because this admission is made, and because it appears in conjunction with a second major puzzle about this sense—namely, what its organ is and where it is located—it may seem that Aristotle really should have regarded touch as a *group* of senses, or even that he has here made an exception to his general rule about how to define and characterize a sense. The latter claim is defended by Sorabji (1971), who actually praises Aristotle for substituting another definitional criterion in place of the proposed one referring to sense-objects. He thinks it would be 'unsatisfactory to rely heavily on the objects of touch in defining the sense' (Sorabji 1971, 85): their variety would make such objects 'laborious' to count, and their diversity would make them hard to unify. Sorabji's critical observations may be well taken, but the fact remains that Aristotle clearly thinks he is pursuing the line of procedure laid out back in ch. 6; and indeed, if he were not, then he would be making nonsense of his own metaphysical views. Additionally, since Aristotle compares touch to the other senses in admitting both a variety and diversity of objects, then Sorabji's critical points would have to apply across the board and not to touch alone. In general, Aristotle seems not to regard it as a tremendous obstacle in characterizing a *dunamis* that that *dunamis* is capable of quite a variety of actualizations under different circumstances— such variety would simply have to be factored into any proposed account of the *dunamis* in question.[3]

To be sure, Aristotle offers differing lists of tangible objects in various texts; to the list given in *DA* 2. 11 we might add heavy–light (or weight) from *Sens.* 445^{b}3–7, and three new pairs mentioned in *GC* 329^{b}7–16: viscous–brittle, rough–smooth, and coarse–fine. Sorabji thinks that Aristotle cites all of these pairs by reference to what he calls the 'contact criterion': anything that can be contacted can be touched, and vice versa. As a point in his favour, he notes Aristotle's treatment of taste as a sort of touch—based on the fact that *in* tasting, animals must contact their food. This line of reasoning seems perverse. Aristotle does think that touching occurs through contact, but this is due to his analysis of touch, its objects, and its organ. The very fact that there is a kind of touching/ contacting which can be singled out and differentiated as taste indicates that the contact criterion alone does not suffice to pinpoint the sense of touch. Aristotle distinguishes the sensory modalities of taste and touch on the basis of their objects (all of which are experienced via contact)—rather than because they involve contact alone. In other words, the tongue is equipped to distinguish the tactile qualities (such as temperatures and textures) of foodstuffs through contacting them; but additionally, and importantly, it is the sense-organ for certain other qualities in foods—their tastes.

Now, as I mentioned earlier, Aristotle's discussion of touch begins with two major puzzles, the one we have just been considering, about its involvement with a diversity of objects, and a second one, concerning the nature of the organ and medium of touch. Aristotle argues in the *De Anima* against the natural viewpoint

---

[3] I have sketched such a proposal in interpreting *Metaph.* Θ's account of *dunameis* in Freeland (1987*b*).

that flesh (or skin) is the organ of touch. He offers two key arguments here. The first involves a somewhat dubious and obscure comparison between touch and vision. Aristotle reasons as follows: since we don't perceive visually when a visible object is placed directly upon our organ (the eye), but do have touch perception when an object is placed directly upon our flesh/skin, then the flesh itself cannot be the organ of touch; instead it must be some unnamed organ 'inside'. This argument is faulty; it relies upon a parallel between vision and touch which itself begs the very question at issue. The second argument seems more persuasive. Aristotle observes that we can experience touch sensations through external and inanimate objects—such as pressure applied to a membrane held across the skin, or blows to a shield held in front of us. He considers that it is implausible to refer to such detachable accoutrements as 'our' sense-organs, but that they serve as parallels to our own flesh; thus it makes more sense to call both flesh and such external things media for the sense of touch.[4]

Aristotle's exclusive concentration on passive rather than active touching has much to do with his conclusion that the organ for this sense is something 'inside' the animal which perceives objects directly upon or in contact with its flesh (now understood as the organ's medium). Contemporary scientists have criticized the Aristotelian picture of touch as a contact sense. Thus James J. Gibson remarks, 'The old idea that touch is strictly a proximity sense, as vision has been taken at the beginning of infancy, is based on a narrow conception of the sense of touch' (Gibson 1966, 102). Gibson emphasizes that we perceive tactually not just through our skin but via small hairs and hair follicles. Other animals, by comparison, may feel things through antennae, whiskers, or even hard hooves and horns —just as a blind person manœuvres through space by 'feeling' objects at the end of a cane. Given Aristotle's fascination with the construction, shape, and opera-

---

[4] My aim here is to explicate rather than to criticize Aristotle's argument; however, we should notice that contemporary scientific accounts might weigh in favour of the conclusion Aristotle rejects —that in certain instances we do use external objects as a sort of extension of our organs of touch. Think, for example, of the way a blind person perceives bodies, their locations, and their dimensions through a cane. Major 20th-c. studies which have contributed to our knowledge of the sense of touch, including Katz (1925) and James J. Gibson (1966), are particularly critical of the Aristotelian concentration on *passive* touch, i.e. on sensations of touch which are experienced when an area of the skin is held in place and subjected to stimulation. These and other researchers following them distinguish such perception from what has come to be designated as 'haptic' or *active* touch, i.e. *tactual scanning* by an organ, usually a hand (Gibson 1966, 123 ff.; Schiff–Foulke 1982, 19 f., 71–3). Now Aristotle may have wished to rule out the inputs achieved by such scanning, since they could involve including such common sensibles as shape rather than the specific sensibles he is attempting to uncover. True, research has revealed that when permitted active scanning, the hand is much more acute at registering and discriminating among shapes (especially three-dimensional ones); but, interestingly, such scanning is also a better source of information about such 'purely' tactile qualities as texture (Gibson 1966, 122–9). Contemporary psychologists and neurologists have produced reasonably detailed maps of the types and locations of touch sensory receptors along the body, and they have paid special attention to the most 'loaded' regions, which occur in the hands (especially on the fingertips) and also in the tongue and lips (Sherrick–Craig 1982, 55–81 in Schiff–Foulke 1982). It does seem astonishing that Aristotle never comments on the acute touch sensitivity of these regions; nor does he even once mention the special role played by the hands in (what he considers to be) humans' superior abilities at tactile perception.

tion of a wide diversity of animal appendages (such as the crab's claws, octopus's feelers, insect's antennae, or elephant's trunk), it is remarkable and surprising that he never once discusses any special role such appendages might play in the animals' sensory/perceptual systems—especially their tactual systems (this is not to say he ignores their performatory roles). Implications of Aristotle's apparently anthropocentric concentration upon human flesh/skin will be taken up further in Section III below.

Actually, Aristotle's conclusion in *DA* 2. 11 that flesh is not the organ of the sense of touch cannot quite be made to square with what he maintains in his detailed discussion of flesh in *PA* 2, 8. There he writes, '…Flesh is either its [the sense of touch's] primary organ (comparable to the pupil in the case of sight), or else it is the organ and the medium of sensation combined in one (comparable to the pupil *plus* the whole of the transparent medium in the case of sight)' (653^b24– 7). Elsewhere Aristotle maintains that the heart plays a key role in sensations of touch, as in sensory perception generally; this has led some commentators to identify it with the unnamed 'organ within' mentioned by *DA* 2. 11 (so Hamlyn in Aristotle 1968, 111).

Without deciding between the two candidates—the flesh or the heart—we can proceed to review some related claims Aristotle makes about the operation and physical constitution of the organ of touch. His view is that a sense and its organ can coincide in fact although they differ in essence (*einai*: 424^a24–5). The sense is the capacity to perceive (*NB*: it is not what has the capacity to perceive—that is the animal), while the organ is something material or physical which is affected during perception. More precisely, Aristotle maintains that it is actualized by receiving the sensible form of the sensed object without its matter; in this process, the organ is said to become *like* the object. This general account of the processes of sense-perception is explicitly said to apply to touch in *DA* 2. 11, 423^b30 ff. Each sense is held to be 'a sort of mean' (*mesotēs tis*) between extremes (424^a4–5); more precisely, neither the sense nor the sense-organ is a 'magnitude' (*megethos*), but rather 'a certain form or power in a magnitude' (*alla logos tis kai dunamis ekeinou*; 424^a26–8).

How does this schematic description actually apply to instances of tactual perceiving? Certain claims Aristotle makes support a 'literalist' interpretation (see Barker 1981, Slakey 1961, and Bynum 1987; for criticisms, see Modrak 1987*a*, 56–62). On this interpretation, flesh consists of a certain given ratio of elemental principles: a certain balance of hotness and coolness, solidity and fluidity, hardness and softness, and so on. Then, when it comes into contact with perceptible objects, it is literally and actually affected in the relevant ways—perceiving warm objects it becomes warmer, etc. Much of what Aristotle writes from *DA* 423^b30– 424^a10 can be taken to support this interpretation, especially the concluding lines:

As what is to perceive white and black must, to begin with, be actually neither but potentially either (and so with all the other sense-organs), so the organ of touch must be neither hot nor cold. (424^a7–10.)

Though we might think that flesh has a temperature and so is actually hot or cold, at various times, a supporter of the literalist reading can argue that what Aristotle means is that things perceived at flesh (body) temperature seem neither hot nor cold because temperatures like our own seem neutral. Furthermore, Aristotle also maintains that excesses in sense-objects may affect the organ to the extent of damaging it; this causal process is said, in the case of touch alone, to damage not just the organ but the entire organism: '...excess in tangible qualities, e.g. heat, cold, or hardness, destroys the animal itself'. This suggests that the sense-organ is (for example) heated during sensation, perhaps so much so that it is harmed.

Whether we say that the sense-organ for touch is flesh or is an internal organ like the heart, the literalist interpretation accords an absurd view to Aristotle. Keep in mind that through touch we perceive such qualities as brittleness and viscosity, as well as certain common sensibles like shape and number (see Graeser 1978). Do my fingertips actually become more dry and brittle when I pick up a bunch of dead twigs to start a fire? Does the flesh in my back become more cold and slippery if some prankster slips an ice-cube down my neck? (Mere effects upon the surface should not count, since the organ is 'inside'.) Part of the absurdity here involves the details of Aristotle's theory of anatomical composition: he insists that each body part and organ, of any type of creature, exists as the combination in a certain ratio of various of the four elements. (Flesh is said to be primarily 'earthy'; *Sens.* 438^{b}30.) It would be impossible for these crucial ratios to be maintained if the body were literally altered when the organism perceived tangible objects. Further important considerations against the literalist view will emerge in Section II below.

Aristotle really needs some way to distinguish between two fundamentally different ways of being affected by 'tangibles'. One way would be to sense or 'feel' them, the other would be to be causally (or literally) altered by them. I have read, for example, that after a certain point people who freeze to death or who experience prolonged exposure to cold no longer perceive coldness ('feel cold'). Aristotle seems to struggle to come up with the distinction I have just recommended in *DA* 424^{a}32 ff. when he tries to explain why plants don't perceive tactually even though they have souls and are affected by tangibles. He says: 'The explanation is that they have no mean, and so no principle in them capable of taking on the forms of sensible objects but are affected together with their matter' (424^{a}32–^{b}3; see Modrak 1987a, 59). Now plants *have* a certain temperature, texture, liquidity or solidity, etc., and so they clearly have organic parts whose constitution involves definite ratios of the elemental principles. Aristotle must mean that when the 'special' mean of a tactual organ is affected, the actual ratio of elements in the flesh is not affected, as it would be in the case of a plant. Some alteration occurs when I feel the coldness of an ice-cube on my back, but this alteration must be understood to be different in kind and not merely in degree from the more serious, indeed devastating, alteration that occurs when my flesh is frozen if I become lost in a blizzard (*contra* Tracy 1969, 207).

A re-examination of the literalist interpretation will in fact reveal that Aristotle consistently hedges all talk of the causal processes of sense- and touch-perception with qualifiers. Thus in 417^b2-7 he describes an actualization which is 'another sort of alteration'. As I mentioned above, in 424^a25-8 he describes what can perceive as being not a size (*megethos*)—that is, not something physical—but a certain ratio (*logos tis*) or capacity. In 424^a1 he refers to perceiving as 'some kind of suffering' (*paschein ti*). The real problem for Aristotle probably stems from the fact that animals and their perceiving organs really can be affected by tangible objects in two quite distinct ways, which can sometimes be confused. In English the confusion is reflected by an ambiguity in 'feeling hot' or 'feeling dry'. I could say 'I feel dry' when I've been walking somewhere in the desert and would like a drink; in fact, my tongue may literally be more dry than usual, but I'm not claiming to be feeling something dry, as I do when I pick up a handful of dead leaves. This ambiguity is reflected in Aristotle's Greek by sentences using the verb *haptesthai* or 'to touch': my tongue, say, and skin have been literally affected by what is touching them, the dry air, but nevertheless my resulting feeling of being 'dried-out' is not what I sense when I touch dry objects. The latter sort of the phenomenon is the one Aristotle intends to address, and should focus on, in giving his account of sense-perception as a 'kind of being affected by' tangible objects (in parallel with other modalities of sense-perception).

Aristotle never provides a clearly satisfactory non-literalist account of the physical nature and operation of the senses. In part this is due to problems in his conceptualization of the nature of conscious awareness, apperception, and psycho-physical links. But even beyond these, he is obviously limited by his primitive understanding of anatomy, and in particular, by his ignorance of facts about the nervous system and its components. Aristotle's attempt to differentiate plants from animals by referring to the latter's possession of a special sort of 'mean' would make more sense to us if we redescribed it as the claim that animal bodies include neural cells. For the sense of touch, these cells today are designated 'mechanoreceptors' (in contrast, say, to the photoreceptors or chemoreceptors activated in visual or olfactory perception, or in taste; Alpern–Lawrence–Wolsk 1967, 133–9; Schiff–Foulke 1982, 55–81.) Such cells are indeed 'actualized' or stimulated by tangible aspects of external objects—certain ones by temperature, others by texture or pressure. But the best description Aristotle has to offer is that the components of the flesh of various animals exist within special ratios enabling those animals to respond behaviourally to tactile (or other sensory) stimuli.

The limitations on Aristotle's physical theory here are interestingly parallel to those which concern his effects to explain sexual reproduction in the *De Generatione Animalium*. There too he must struggle to account for the extraordinary complexity of reproductive processes in terms of a very primitive and simple set of explanatory factors, the foamy hotness and incorporated 'motions' of the semen. Just as this is no ordinary hotness, but a hotness which 'encodes', as we would say, the genetic formula for reproduction true to type, so also will the combination hotness—coldness and dryness—moistness of the sense-organs, and especially of the flesh, somehow 'encode' transmission of a variety of complex and variable inputs to the central processor of the animal.[5]

II. Animal Variations and Intersubjectivity

A. *The Problem*

In the *De Anima*'s treatment of sensation Aristotle tends to use general terms (like 'the sense of touch' or 'tangible objects'), but in his biological works it is clear that he recognizes a wide diversity in sensory (tactile) capacities among members of the animal kingdom. About the lower end of the spectrum, for example, Aristotle maintains that the distinction between plant and animal is hard to draw. In *HA* 8. 1 he writes 'In regard to sensibility, some animals give no indication whatsoever of it, whilst others indicate it but indistinctly' (588^{b}18). He uses two sorts of information about an animal's sensory capacities: first, anatomical observations—as when he tries to resolve the status of certain doubtful creatures, the ascidians, which are rooted, 'but yet they have some fleshy substance and therefore probably are capable of sensation of a kind' (681^{a}25–8); and secondly, behavioural evidence—as when he adds to his remarks about the ascidians that they discharge a residue, something plants are not known to do (681^{a}29–35). At the higher end of the spectrum of touch sensitivity Aristotle locates human beings (*DA* 421^{a}20–3; *PA* 660^{a}11–14). He even goes so far as to maintain that it is *because of* our superior touch sensitivity that we humans are the most intelligent of all the animals (421^{a}22–3). He adds:

This is confirmed by the fact that it is to differences in the organ of touch and to nothing else that the differences between man and man in respect of natural endowment are due; men whose flesh is hard are ill-endowed with intellect, men whose flesh is soft, well-endowed.   (421^{a}23–6.)

This should be taken with a grain of salt because Aristotle offers several alternative explanations for humans' superior intelligence, most notably our standing upright (*PA* 4. 10), having a large brain (for cooling, to balance our sensitive sense-organs in the head; *PA* 2. 7); having acute hearing, which is incidentally relevant because of its role in understanding voiced signs, or language (*HA* 608^{a}17–21); and having the finest, most supple tongue (which also plays a role in language; *PA* 660^{a}15–28).

Aristotle's belief that it is possible to provide rank-orderings of animals' various types of sensory abilities—as well as, in his *Ethics*, of their diverse sensory pleasures—reflects a conviction that he is in a position to acquire an accurate and objective picture of the perceptions of radically different kinds of beings. Why is

---

[5] See interpretative discussions in Balme (1987*b*) and Furth (1987). See also Modrak (1987*a*), 55–62.

Aristotle unconcerned that intersubjectivity might be endangered by the great diversity among various animals' perceptual *phainomena*? What justifies his view that the sense of touch encased in a crab's hard claw or an octopus's sinewy feelers represents the same tangible features of reality encountered by our own flesh?

I do not mean to press Aristotle for any deeper examination of 'extra-human' animal senses or feats.[6] Of course, he was unaware of animals' sensory modalities in relation to parts of the spectrum we are unable to perceive—for example, the dog's capacity to hear extremely high-pitched sounds, or the bee's infra-red vision. There are other aspects of animal behaviour he was familiar with which could well have prompted more speculation about modes of sensory experience beyond our knowledge—directional awareness exhibited in migratory patterns of birds and of some fish, for example (described in *HA* 8. 12). I am asking a simpler question: on what basis does he maintain that the same set of tangibles is experienced through a variety of differentially equipped perceivers, who might be expected to perceive them in radically distinct ways?

Later on, in confronting similar—though far less detailed—evidence of animal variations, Sextus Empiricus asked,

How could it be said that touch produces similar effects in animals with shells, animals with fleshy exteriors, animals with prickles, and animals with feathers or scales? (*PH* 1. 50, cited from Annas–Barnes 1985, p. 32)

Aristotle would himself have been familiar with this sort of sceptical move (Annas–Barnes cite a parallel from *Theaetetus* 154 A),[7] and also with relativist versions (in Xenophanes, Protagoras, or Heraclitus) tending toward the conclusion that each type of animal perceiver senses differently. Aristotle's assessments of *comparative* accuracy presuppose that there is some intersubjectively valid scale of comparison; but why does Aristotle think this?

One might simply respond that indeed Aristotle has no justification for supposing that there is species intersubjectivity, that his claims about our knowledge of other animals involve anthropocentric projection, and his convictions about our own excellence of touch reflect anthropocentric prejudice. Aristotle has claimed that soft flesh accounts for intelligence and accurate discrimination among men. Why not in women—and beyond this, what about those delightfully soft, squishy—and unintelligent—beings, the oyster and the clam? Although in his exhaustive studies of animals and their parts Aristotle may attend to their peculiar features and functions, he nevertheless seems compelled to describe such features in terms of their human analogues. Thus, although he spends a considerable amount of time studying the fascinating nose of the elephant, he describes it

---

[6] Aristotle presents what seems to be an argument for the claim that his listing of the five senses is complete and exhaustive in *DA* 424^{b}22–25^{a}14; whether this is in fact his aim has been doubted by Maudlin (1986). While I think it is an interesting question why Aristotle did not envision other animals' possession of senses alien to our own—or even of human possession of some 'sixth sense' such as ESP, or even the less controversial sense of balance—this is not my question here.

[7] Annas–Barnes (1985), 40.

as a combination nose *and hand*; or again, insects' antennae are viewed similarly as a sort of combination of *hands* and eyes (see *PA* 658^{b}33–659^{a}36).

Geoffrey Lloyd in his (1983) has presented a serious and sustained critical examination of Aristotle's anthropocentric presuppositions and their role in his zoological studies.[8] Lloyd surveys a number of Aristotle's claims about man's superiority to the other animals, most of which are dubious or just plain false. Though Lloyd does not address either Aristotle's remarks about human excellence at touch perception or the supposedly superior softness of human flesh, these are just the sorts of claims that his book is concerned to criticize (he discusses such similar Aristotelian dicta as the remark that our tongue is the softest and most flexible, that our blood is thinnest and purest, or that our upright position is best; see Lloyd (1983), 27–43, 'Man as Model'.). Before seconding Lloyd's conclusion, however, and admitting that Aristotle's 'criterion' is simply anthropocentric (not that the *motives* operating behind anthropocentrism are themselves simple; see Lloyd, pp. 41–2), I would like to examine a further set of texts. These prove relevant to understanding Aristotle's views on interspecies comparisons between human sensory capacities and those of the other animals, and also on the relative accuracy of the various sensory modalities themselves.

B. *Touch in Animals' Behavioural Economies*

Up to this point I have concentrated on the conception of the sense of touch presented by Aristotle in *DA* 2. 11. Characteristic of his treatment of this sense here is, as I have said, an emphasis on its passivity. Furthermore, Aristotle treats tangibles by analysing sensory experience into single and simple, momentary stimuli. A better and fuller picture of Aristotle's views on this sense, however, must include a study of the ties between sensation and other characteristic animal capacities: desire, pleasure, and movement. We need to explore the biological (as against the sensory) functions of touch, in order to reach a better assessment of Aristotle's views on interspecies comparisons between various animals' senses.

Though Aristotle does not emphasize the fact in his *De Anima* discussion, he believes that an animal's sense of touch functions in quite complex behavioural processes. In most instances the relevant sort of touch would be what contemporary scientists term 'haptic', active or exploratory touch: the digging and rooting performed by the pig's snout, the collecting of pollen and honey by the bees' legs, etc. Animals are equipped to perceive and interact with the environment in which they live on a day-to-day basis. Since this environment includes very diverse relations to food and water, hot, dry, cold, or moist weather, friend and foe, potential mates, parents and young, etc., in practice it is very difficult to assess and compare animals' various kinds of sensory capacities—what need does the

---

[8] James G. Lennox has provided persuasive defences of Aristotle against many of Lloyd's criticisms in Lennox (1985), esp. 311–15.

heron have of the woodpecker's superior ability to detect vibrations beneath tree bark, for example?

In the *De Anima*, and to an extent in his *Ethics*, but even more in the zoological works, Aristotle acknowledges and comments upon the intricate connections between sensation, pleasure and desire, and behaviour. At the most primitive level, he maintains, animals' possession of the sense of touch is purposive; it is linked to rudimentary approach–avoidance behaviours:

An animal is a body with soul in it: every body is tangible, i.e. perceptible by touch; hence necessarily, if an animal is to survive, its body must have tactual sensation. All the other senses, e.g. smell, sight, hearing, apprehend through media; but where there is immediate contact the animal, if it has no sensation, will be unable to avoid some things and take others, and so will find it impossible to survive. (*DA* 434^{b}12–19.)

The connection between sensation and desire, even at the most primitive level, is explicitly formulated at 414^{b}1–6:

If any order of living things has the sensory, it must also have the appetitive (viz. psychic power or *dunamis*); for appetite is the genus of which desire, passion, and wish are the species; now all animals have one sense at least, viz. touch, and whatever has a sense has the capacity for pleasure and pain and therefore has pleasant and painful objects present to it, and wherever these are present, there is desire, for desire is appetition of what is pleasant.[9]

The integral connections between perception and desire prompt Aristotle to move in several directions in assessing the comparative accuracy of animals' various sensory abilities. On the one hand, he holds that it is possible to distinguish better from worse sensory capacities on the basis of the scope of things discriminated. Thus at 421^{a}9–16 he acknowledges that we humans have a relatively poor sense of smell, comparing our limits in this modality to those faced by the 'hard-eyed' animals—each group perceiving poorly because it only recognizes the objects as 'to be feared' or not. This passage suggests that primitive

---

[9] Having laid out this fundamental relation between touch and desire, Aristotle can proceed to elaborate several other points about the roles of the various senses in animals' behavioural economies. For example, though touch is so basic as to be essential to all animals' very being, Aristotle tells us in ch. 1 of the *De Sensu* that higher animals which have the capacity for locomotion are also equipped with the distal senses, smelling, seeing, and hearing (436^{b}18–437^{a}1). He actually holds that taste too is essential to all animals, defining it as perception of flavours, including the sweet, and claiming that food or nutriment is sweet (421^{a}1–^{b}44), whereas touch is said to detect food only *qua* incremental addition to the animal body. Also, scent is called the middle among the five senses, presumably because even though it is a distal sense, it functions closely with taste and touch, the food-detecting senses. See 445^{a}4–16. The higher senses are said to be essential for the being of the locomotive animals, but in certain 'higher' animals *among* these, '...they serve for the attainment of a higher perfection. They bring in tidings of many distinctive qualities of things, from which knowledge of things both speculative and practical is generated in the soul' (437^{a}1–3). Aristotle further rank-orders the senses, calling sight 'in its own right' the best source of knowledge, but saying that hearing is 'incidentally' superior since it plays a key role in the use of language, hence in articulate thought. Much this same point about the connections between hearing, language, and intelligence is made in the discussion of types of animal 'voices' and 'languages' in *HA*. 608^{a}17–21.

creatures such as the clam or oyster perceive tangible objects around them only as things 'to be feared' or 'to be eaten'.[10]

A second method for assessing and comparing the senses' accuracy, based on keenness instead of scope, is mentioned in *GA* 5. 2, in a discussion of sight, scent, and hearing. Aristotle says here that accuracy means 'in one sense to perceive as accurately as possible all the distinctions of the objects of perception, in another sense to hear and smell far off' (781ᵃ14–16). Of course, animals with long nostrils (such as the Laconian hound) or long ears perceive things that are far off much better than men do. In fact, 'In respect of sense-perception at a distance, man is, one may say, the worst of all animals in proportion to his size…' (781ᵇ18–19). Nevertheless, Aristotle hastens to say, we are the best at *discriminations*.[11]

Aristotle once again discusses the contrast between humans' and animals' sense of smell in the *De Sensu*; his discussion here introduces complications involving *appetite* and *pleasure*. Smells are divided into two species (443ᵇ17 ff.). All animals perceive smells among the first species, ones related to food (and to the appetite for food.) These smells are classified as pleasant or unpleasant incidentally (*kata sumbebēkos*, 443ᵇ25). By contrast, Aristotle maintains that there is a second species of odours perceptible to man alone. These odours are classifiable in and of themselves (*kath' hauta*, 443ᵇ27) as pleasant or unpleasant, without reference to our appetites. He mentions, for example, the scent of flowers. This *De Sensu* passage not only contradicts what the *De Anima* passage said about humans' relatively poor and limited sense of smell, but it leaves the status of animals' superior sense of smell a little unclear. Aristotle recognizes that dogs, for example Laconian hounds, have extremely keen senses of smell, but does he want to maintain that they nevertheless only 'classify' smells as pleasant or unpleasant? What might 'classifying' in such a case mean? Behavioural discrimination would seem to indicate a more refined classificational scheme, unless we make the artificial move of saying that anything the dog follows a trail of, it scents *as* pleasant.

Aristotle seems to maintain that human perceptual capacities are superior to those of other animals because they are often less directly connected to appetite. This in turn leaves room for them to be experienced 'for themselves', in other words as sources of information leading to experience and knowledge. This point

---

[10] There is an important issue of translation here. In discussing the human sense of smell Aristotle first says that we smell nothing of odours *without* either pain or pleasure (*kai outhenos aisthanetai tōn osphrantōn aneu tou lupērou ē tou hēdeos…*; 421ᵃ10–12). Next he says that the hard-eyed creatures don't differentiate among colours except with respect to the fearful and the not-to-be-feared (*kai mē diadēlous autois einai tas diaphoras tōn chromatōn plēn tōi phoberōi kai aphobōi…*; 421ᵃ14–16). Here he adds that 'this is how it is with the human race with respect to smells' (421ᵃ16). Does Aristotle mean to say that we humans may distinguish and classify smells into various categories always accompanied by 'pleasant' or 'unpleasant', or that we only classify them as 'pleasant' or 'unpleasant'? The first remark suggests the former; the second, the latter.

[11] As to just what sense, Aristotle is not very clear; he means at the very least to be focusing on the three distal senses here. The explanation he gives is not too helpful: 'The reason is that the sense-organ is pure and least earthy and material, and he is by nature the thinnest-skinned of the animals his size' (781ᵇ20–1).

is stressed in what he says about our superior vision, for example, in *Sens.* 437ᵃI ff. Even in the problematic example of scent, we could interpret his reasoning as follows: in many cases human discriminations among odours are less clear than those concerning sights or colours, because scents affect our appetites more directly—they seem to fall more naturally into categories such as 'delightful' and 'appetizing' or 'disgusting' and 'repellent'. Nevertheless, and despite our inferiority at distance scenting as compared with, say, dogs, we do have the superior capacity for what could be termed 'aesthetic' pleasures of scent, namely pleasures involving accurate observation and discrimination, with no correlative appetite. (We can delight in the scent of a rose without wanting to eat it.) Animals' perceptions, no matter how accurate, are typically tied to their appetitive behaviour in more direct ways—the hound which accurately scents the rabbit or fox is better able to follow, kill, and eat it. In regard to touch, too, we are supposedly superior because our soft flesh gives us greater discriminatory powers. This would seem to imply that the touch modality also allows for a wide variety of 'aesthetic' pleasures, at least for humans. But most of what Aristotle says about the value of pleasures of touch in his *Ethics* indicates otherwise.

Aristotle's rank-ordering of sensory *pleasures* in *EN* 10. 5 reflects his ordering of the sense themselves in the *De Sensu*. Pleasures of sight are at the top, superior 'in purity' to those of touch. Aristotle also maintains that hearing and smell are purer than taste, so that these pleasures too are 'similarly superior' (1176ᵃ1–2). This ordering, which occurs in the context of consideration of diverse animal experiences and pleasures, seems rather oddly unqualified; in other words, Aristotle seems to be talking about each sense in general rather than, say, the relative importance of hearing and smell to bees. Nevertheless, he asserts a kind of hedonic relativism, remarking that:

...the pleasures of creatures different in kind differ in kind, and it is plausible to suppose that those of a single species do not differ. But they vary to no small extent, in the case of men at least... (1176ᵃ8–10.)

In this same paragraph Aristotle cites with approval Heraclitus' saying that 'Asses would prefer sweepings to gold' (1176ᵃ6–7).[12]

Aristotle's idea that some pleasures are higher because they are 'purer' probably involves his conviction that pleasures, like sense-perceptions themselves, in those modalities are less tied to appetite and desire. This becomes clear in his account of incontinence in book 3 of the *Ethics*. There Aristotle argues that, although one could pursue pleasures of sight, hearing, or smell to an excessive

---

[12] Such claims must be understood in the light of the general point made in this chapter: that pleasure is a supervenient actualization which occurs when a psychic power is activated (actualized) by an object. Good or better pleasures involve better or more excellent sense-capacities, as well as better objects. The excellent sight of the eagle, then, would provide it with its own proper pleasure when it pursues the mouse fleeing beneath it, whereas the woodpecker enjoys detecting vibrations that indicate larvae for it to eat. In this sense pleasures tend to be objective, i.e. agreed upon, between members of a species. However, it is still not clear why Aristotle holds that certain pleasures (e.g. those of sight) are *in general* superior to others (e.g. those of touch).

degree, these are nevertheless not the sorts of bodily pleasures with which temperance or incontinence are concerned. Smell comes closest to allowing for the right range, but this is because it is more closely related to appetite: '…Self-indulgent people delight in these (the odour of unguents or of dainty dishes) because these remind them of the objects of their appetite' (1118ª10–12). Incontinence mostly concerns lower, more 'bestial' pleasures or desires, those of taste and *especially* those of touch.[13] These sorts of sensory pleasures are characteristic of animals, who do not, according to Aristotle, take any real pleasures in objects of the three 'higher' senses. For example, 'the lion does not delight because he sees "a stag or a wild goat", but because he is going to make a meal of it' (1118ª22–3). In fact, even taste seems to have less to do with incontinence than does touch:

Temperance and self-indulgence…are concerned with the kind of pleasures that the other animals share in, which therefore appear slavish and brutish; these are touch and taste. But even of taste they appear to make little or no use; for the business of taste is the discriminating of flavours, which is done by wine-tasters and people who season dishes; but they hardly take pleasure in making these discriminations, or at least self-indulgent people do not, but in the actual enjoyment, which in all cases comes through touch, both in the case of food and in that of drink and in that of sexual intercourse. (1118ª24–33.)[14]

It is worth pointing out that by calling the pleasures of eating, drinking, and sex pleasures *of touch* in the *Ethics* Aristotle vastly complicates the account of tangible *perception* given in the *De Anima*. Although sometimes I suspect that Aristotle denigrates the sense of touch simply because he sees it as being fundamentally more passive (as a contact sense) in its operation than the other senses, it is hardly true that tactual perception of edible, potable, or sexually arousing objects is a matter of passive registering—or at least in each case, passive stimulation is quickly followed by active tactual scanning. Tactual scanning

[13] For discussion of this claim, see Young (1988).

[14] Aristotle alludes, by way of evidence, to 'a certain gourmand who prayed that his throat might become longer than a crane's, implying that it was the contact he took pleasure in' (1118ª33–ᵇ2). Such pleasures of swallowing are mentioned also in Aristotle's discussion of tongues and throats in *PA* 4. 11, where he describes lizards, serpents, and seals as 'greedy in their food' (*lichna*) (691ª8–9). Peck in Aristotle (1961) mistakenly translates *lichna* as 'dainty in their food'; Ogle in Aristotle (1872b) as 'fond of dainty food'. At the same time, Peck translates Aristotle's remark that serpents have fine, hairy, and forked tongues *dia tēn lichneian tēs phuseōs* at 660ᵇ8–11 as 'owing to their having such inordinate appetites'. Ogle translates 'because of their great liking for food'. Anyone who has ever watched a snake or alligator swallow food, if only on a television nature programme, will agree that they are not 'dainty' but 'greedy'. Interestingly, however, Aristotle's discussion of long-necked birds in *PA* 4. 12 focuses solely on their necks' usefulness in water environments; he comments: 'Their neck is to these birds what his fishing-rod is to the angler, while their beak is like a line and hook' (693ª21–2), and no mention is made of the crane's potential for voluptuous swallowing. Aristotle actually does mention one creature with a sort of parallel capacity, when he discusses the forked tongues of lizards or serpents in *PA* 2. 17. These long forked tongues afford their possessors unusually acute capacities of taste, and Aristotle comments, 'They are also forked, and the tips of them are fine and hairy, owing to their having such inordinate appetites (*dia tēn lichneian tēs phuseōs*); by this means the serpents get a double pleasure out of what they taste, owing to their possessing as it were a double organ for this sense' (660ᵇ8–11).

with the lips and tongue, for instance, seem essential to human pleasures of eating; it seems simply false that the gourmand's chief pleasures are those of passive touch. And it is very odd to consider sexual pleasure to be a pleasure *of touch*, especially passive touch, since so much has to with activity, and with alternative sensory modalities, even cognition—even, perhaps especially, in the case of a self-indulgent person, someone we think of as deriving self-esteem from a sense of conquest, etc.[15]

What emerges from this discussion of perception and desire, and the role of touch in animals' behavioural economies? Aristotle associates superior sensory capacities both with a higher intelligence and a greater capacity for incontinence (bestiality). Animals with more refined sensory capacities are not necessarily those possessing keener senses, but those capable of making more subtle distinctions among sensory stimuli—that is, of using classifications other than a simple two-category division of objects into the pleasant and the unpleasant. When such higher animals fail to exhibit their discriminatory capacities to the fullest, they pervert their abilities, using them only to distinguish those aspects of reality relevant to their appetites, not those which can become the basis for learning and reflection.[16]

The various passages I have just surveyed, from the *Ethics* and biological writings, have great relevance for the study of Aristotle's epistemology in the *De Anima* and other works. However, it is never altogether clear just how an animal's experience of the *pleasure* connected to any sensation is linked to its

---

[15] In fact, Aristotle's views on the possibility of incontinence with respect to sexual desire have other puzzling aspects. *HA* 6. 18 makes it clear that in the natural course of things all animals get excited by sexual appetites; there Aristotle describes a variety of modes of excitement as well as of behavioural responses to the excitement (we think here of his *Ethics* remark that each animal has its own proper pleasure). But a bit further along in this book, which is a general study of animals' sexual habits, Aristotle appears to moralize about various species. He is particularly hard on the horse, which he calls—in both sexes—'the most salacious of animals next after the human species' (575^b30–1). Or again, the cow is called 'sexually wanton'—most especially so, following only the mare (and presumably the human female) in the animal kingdom (572^a10–11). This is, by the way, in contrast to the bull, seen by Aristotle as the 'least salacious of male animals'—a most odd observation, in the light of the fact Aristotle has just commented that a bull can mount several cows in a day, and, if young and vigorous, can mount the same cow more than once, 'and a good many cows besides' (575^a20–1). (Living in Texas, I had the opportunity to ask a rancher what he made of these remarks of Aristotle's. His response: 'Those heifers do get kind of frisky, but all I've got to say is that there's one bull for thirty-seven cows; what more do you need to know?') Obviously Aristotle must be applying his moral terminology to various animals not in virtue of the actual frequency of their sexual behaviour but rather in the light of certain attitudes they display toward such behaviour; perhaps the bull is more business-like about his duties than the stallion. Moral terminology applies to a human's sexual behaviour because he or she has the capacity to hit the mean and behave rationally with respect to sexual appetite; does Aristotle mean to say that the same is true of the horse? If each animal has its own proper pleasure, why does he seem to regard the horse's pleasure as so improper? Aristotle may regard cows and bulls as domesticated animals, animals having some amount of intelligence equipping them to 'behave better' than they in fact do. Thus they would be placed in a comparison class with, say elephants and camels, which actually do manifest higher standards in relation to their sexuality—at least, if we are to believe stories reported about the elephant in *HA* 546^b8–11, or the camel in 630^b32–631^a8.

[16] For an extremely interesting and detailed study of animals' intelligence, in particular of Aristotle's application of the term *phronēsis* to animals, see Labarrière (1984, 1987).

sense-perceptions themselves. Commentators have considered questions about the objects of perceptual faculties, such as how each sense perceives common as against proper sensibles or proper as against incidental objects (see e.g. Hamlyn in Aristotle 1968, 117–21; Modrak 1987*a*, 55–80), and yet certain of the passages just surveyed indicate that perception itself may have as its objects such simples as 'the pleasant' and 'the unpleasant'—or slightly more qualified versions, such as 'not to be eaten' or 'to be mated with'. Typically in analyses of animal behaviour these sorts of interpretative classifications of sensory inputs are attributed to *phantasia* or imagination (Bynum 1987, 170–2; Labarrière 1984). Indeed, Aristotle says that the two faculties (sensation and imagination) are one in fact, though not in being (*einai*) (see Nussbaum 1978, 255). The co-ordinated operation of these two faculties suggests that the perceptual world inhabited by many animals, especially the lower animals, is quite limited by comparison with the human perceptual world. Recall that Aristotle maintains that although we do not excel over all other animals in keenness of the distal senses, we are superior in our ability to discriminate stimuli (objects) in these three modalities. For example our sense of smell equips us to perceive 'the truth' about pleasant or unpleasant smells 'in themselves', and supposedly without relation to our appetites. Aristotle maintains that humans possess the finest tactile discriminatory capacities, and, in part because of this fact, the finest sense of taste. This means that from his standpoint humans may not exactly be living in a different perceptible world from that of the other animals, but that they experience the same world of perceptible objects in clearer, less subjectively loaded, ways. We can classify things and regard them as pleasant in and of themselves, not merely in relation to us.

The human experience of such aspects of the physical world as its tangible qualities may, then, reasonably be taken as the starting-point for an intensive scientific examination of these qualities, not from simple anthropocentrism, but because humans are the best witnesses when it comes to testimony about sensory experience. Aristotle's recommendations about the use of dialectic in launching a scientific investigation involve studying the *phainomena* as reported by the majority, or by the most qualified of the experts.[17] It should not be surprising then that he thinks he is pursuing a reasonable procedure in hypothesizing about the natural world, its causes and its principles, on the basis of human experiences of this world—and primarily of its tangible qualities. Although in fact such primitive animals as sponges may *not* experience 'our' realm of sensory qualities (including such basic tangible contrarieties as light–heavy, hot–cold, etc.), their testimony—as poor witnesses—is not relevant. Aristotle does not have to concern himself with the perceptions of the sponge—or of the elephant, crab, or bee —when proposing a scientific explanation of how tangibles 'really are' any more than he would have to take into account a child's primitive theories about the moon in trying to explain the nature and causes of lunar eclipses.

---

[17] For a new interpretation of the role of dialectic in gathering first principles for a science, see Bolton (1987).

III. Touch and Tangible Reality

In their recent commentary on Sextus' modes, Annas and Barnes construe Sextus' argument from animal variation, quoted above, as follows: Sextus first collects diverse appearances (or at least suggests the likelihood that there are conflicting appearances); next he adds in the sceptical reservation about being unable to prefer one of the appearances; the result is supposed to be a suspension of judgement about the nature of reality (and here, more specifically, tangible reality).[18] In other words Sextus extends the sceptical argument from doubts about *intersubjectivity* to doubts about the *objectivity* of sensible (here tangible) impressions.

One classic move that has been made to avoid being drawn into scepticism of this sort involves invoking a distinction between primary and secondary qualities. We are familiar with deployment of this move in the British empiricist tradition, by Locke, for example. Speaking quite generally, through this move the empiricist (more or less) concedes the sceptic's or relativist's points concerning the problem of intersubjectivity. However, some favoured form of knowledge— usually, scientific knowledge—is held to guarantee 'objectivity' or to provide access to substances as they 'really are'—material things characterized by primary qualities. Aristotle was acquainted with a version of the Lockian program in the form of the atomistic explanations of sense-perception proposed by Democritus. Certainly he had metaphysical objections to the atomist program. But he also was independently critical of the atomist account of sense-knowledge. Interestingly, he rejected atomist explanations of sensation in the *De Sensu* not on principle, but on the grounds that they are too reductionistic: Democritus proposed to treat all the modalities of sense-perception as forms of touch ($442^a29^{-b}3$).

This criticism seems strange, because we might think it could be turned against Aristotle himself. By treating touch as the one sensory modality that provides information about the nature of the physical elements, Aristotle appears to commit himself to a reductionist analysis of the other four sensory modalities; like the atomists, he seems to invoke some privileged form of access to (scientific knowledge of) the 'real' underlying qualities of bodies. Is there an important difference here between touch and the other modalities, or did Aristotle endorse some form of primary–secondary quality distinction that carried across *all five* modalities?

In her recent study of the *De Anima* entitled *Aristotle: The Power of Perception* (Modrak 1987*a*), Deborah Modrak suggests that Aristotle does have an across-the-board parallel to our familiar distinction between primary and secondary qualities, in his distinction between common and proper sensibles. Modrak explains,

---

[18] See Annas–Barnes (1985) 39–41.

Colors, sounds, flavors, odors and tactile qualities are proper objects for Aristotle, secondary qualities for us; motion, figure, extension and number are common objects for him and
proper objects for us.   (Modrak 1987*a*, 78.)

However, in contrast to the usual (e.g. atomist or British empiricist) outlook on
this distinction, Aristotle does not suppose that proper sensibles are any less
indicative of features of the 'real' (physical) world than common ones. Indeed, as
Modrak emphasizes,

Not only are the proper objects more basic both in perception and in the world than the
common or incidental objects, they are apprehended with considerably more accuracy.
The senses seldom make mistakes about their proper objects (*De An.* 428^{b}18–19).
Aristotle sometimes makes the stronger claim that mistakes about proper objects never
occur (*De An.* 418^{a}12, 418^{a}15, 427^{b}11, 430^{b}29; *De Sens.* 442^{b}9).   (Modrak 1987*a*, 79.)

Here, then, we have a puzzle. Supposedly each sensory modality equips its user
with accurate information about the nature of the external world; yet somehow
the sensory modality of touch is prior, as it reveals the nature of the physical
elements. How can this puzzle be resolved?

There *is* undoubtedly a close, yet complex, link between Aristotle's view of the
physico-chemical world and his account of the 'proper objects' of the sense of
touch. In the *De Anima* he explains:

What can be touched are the distinctive qualities of body *qua* body; by such differences I
mean those which characterize the elements, viz. hot cold, dry moist, of which we have
spoken earlier in our treatise on elements.   (423^{b}27–9.)

The relevant passage on the elements comes in *GC* 2. 2; there Aristotle writes:

Since, then, we are looking for principles of perceptible body, and since perceptible is
equivalent to tangible, and tangible is that of which the perception is touch (*hapton d' hou
hē aisthēsis haphē*), it is clear that not all the contrarieties constitute forms and principles of
body, but only those which correspond to touch. For it is in accordance with a contrariety
—a contrariety, moreover, of tangible qualities—that the primary bodies are differentiated.
(329^{b}7–11.)

As noted in my introduction above, C. J. F. Williams has called Aristotle's
argument an 'over-hasty' bit of reasoning from the mere universality of this
sense-modality to its priority in reporting on the physical elements in the external
world (Williams 1982, 157). A further *De Anima* passage Williams considers
relevant is 434^b. Here Aristotle explains a claim he has made about the
indispensability of touch to animals. He says, 'An animal is a body with soul in it;
every body is tangible, i.e. perceptible by touch (*hapton de to aisthēton haphēi*);
hence necessarily, if an animal is to survive, its body must have tactual sensation
(*haptikon einai*)' (434^{b}11–14).

Now it seems to me that Aristotle is reasoning from a certain conception of
fundamental interactions among bodies as such to the claim that animals need,
for their survival, to be equipped with some basic sensory capacity that will regis-
ter these bodily interactions. Bodies as bodies are described as 'tangible' (*hapton*)

because they are the sorts of things that interact with one another by touching. Animal bodies, like all physical bodies, are tangible and will come into physical contact with ('touch') other bodies. Certain of these other bodies are crucially relevant to the animal—as food, potential mates or threats, etc. Fortunately, nature has designed animals so as to enable them to discriminate/perceive these relevant bodies through the sense of touch. This is one of Nature's admirably constructed effects. Nature works from the given circumstance of universal contact to the hypothesized goal of survival, via the means of sense- (particularly touch-) perception.

In other words, I don't see Aristotle arguing as Williams claims he does from what is given in sense-knowledge to restrictive conclusions about the elements. Even if he does so, I suggest it may be only *in a sense*. Recall that for Aristotle the order of knowing often is the reverse of the order of being: through the data immediately given to sense-observation, which are in this case the *phainomena*, we glean access to the facts as they really are. (See Owen 1961, Nussbaum 1982*a*, and Bolton 1987). However, genuine knowledge of these facts 'in themselves' involves a scientifically accurate grasp of their explanatory interconnections and relations. What may seem prior 'to us' may not be prior in the order of scientific explanation. This means that in the *De Anima* it is reasonable for Aristotle to attempt to explain animals' possession of the sense of touch teleologically, as a sort of adaptation or purposive suitability to the world as it is, namely a tangible world. The tangible world is a world filled with bodies which are characterized by a variety of tangible properties; in his scientific study of such bodies, Aristotle must proceed to theorize about the true nature and ordering of such properties. This is in fact precisely what he does do in *GC* 2. 2. When he begins that theoretical examination of the elements by citing a variety of perceived characteristics of tangible things, I take him to be listing the *phainomena*, not all of which will be permitted to count as equally significant in the developed explanatory scheme of things.

Aristotle's procedure in *De Generatione et Corruptione* bears out my point, for he seeks to identify certain among his initial list of tangible qualities as explanatorily fundamental. Thus he outlines certain criteria that the *archai* for this science must meet; they must be active or passive, for example, enabling him to rule out the pair heavy–light from his initial list. In addition, they must not be explicable in terms of other, more basic principles. Aristotle supposes that he can account for the distinctive characteristics of some pairs in his preliminary list in terms of characteristics of other, more fundamental pairs, the hot–cold and the moist–dry. In fact, all his explanations or reductions involve only the latter pair, the moist–dry; the exact nature of the proposed derivations is unclear. He writes, for example, about the pair viscous–brittle as follows:

Again the viscous derives from the moist; for the viscous (e.g. oil) is a moist thing modified in a certain way. The brittle, on the other hand, derives from the dry; for brittle is that which is completely dry—so completely, it has actually solidified due to failure of moisture. (330ª4–8.)

The nature and structure of these and other purported reductions in this chapter show that Aristotle is discussing intrinsic qualities of bodies, namely features they possess 'in themselves' rather than in relation to us and our senses. That is, he is not claiming that sensations of viscousness are in some special way compounded from, or reducible to, sensations of moistness. (To make this point clearer, by contrast, contemporary studies show that under special conditions certain tactile sensations are experienced as a result of compound application of other tactile stimuli: thus, for example, a combination of warmth and pressure produces an experience of oiliness, whereas pressure plus coldness is experienced as wetness. These and similar experiences are discussed as cases of 'touch blends'; see Schiff–Foulke 1982, 10–11, 141.[19])

Two further sorts of evidence show that Aristotle would draw a significant distinction between the realm of tangible experiences of things and the scientifically explainable ordering among tangible objects. The first evidence is in an important passage of *PA* 2. 2; in this chapter Aristotle is trying to get clear about the nature of blood, and in particular about the proper way to describe its essential hotness. He digresses into a complex theoretical examination of various meanings and applications of the term 'the hot'. Eventually he distinguishes five different ways in which things may be hotter than other things, as an answer to his initial question: '...we must find out what is the particular effect which a body has in virtue of being hotter than another, or, if there are several such effects, how many there are' ($648^b12–13$). Only one of the five ways listed involves sensation: in some cases a body is called hotter 'if it produces a more violent sensation when touched, and especially if the sensation is accompanied by pain' ($648^b15–16$). Having made this point about the multivocity of 'hot' Aristotle assures us at the end of ch. 2 that 'there will be an equal variety of senses attaching to "cold"' ($649^b5–7$); then he asserts at the start of ch. 3 that the same point will apply to the other fundamental pair of opposites, the moist and the dry. Unfortunately Aristotle says nothing more to amplify these last points, and so we are left feeling a bit puzzled about how a thing can be in various ways more moist, dry, or cold than something else without *feeling* any more moist, dry, or cold. (We can take a stab at this by noting that certain extremely cold things, such as liquefied gases, might seem to burn the skin if we were exposed to them. And so on.)

I consider this passage from *De Partibus Animalium* to be very important because here Aristotle explicitly allows that sensing hotness involves a kind of being affected by hot things that is distinctive and *sui generis*, and that should not be assimilated to being heated, burned, or cooked. This recognition would

[19] In certain cases touch blends give rise to experiences of what could be termed 'touch illusions'. One example of this is discussed in Alpern–Lawrence–Wolsk (1967), 136; because of increased neural firing that occurs with even slight changes of temperature, 'If alternating thin strips of slightly warm and slightly cool temperature stimulate the forearm, one will experience a sensation of intense heat. In this situation, both types of temperature fibers will increase their firing rate—one type in the warm strips, one type in the cool strips.... Since most people have never before been subjected to an alternating temperature stimulus, the feeling of intense heat is an understandable outcome.'

seem to be inconsistent with a literalist interpretation of Aristotle's view of sense-perception. A second sort of consideration based upon certain claims in Aristotle's physical treatises also militates against the literalist interpretation. The point I have in mind is put most clearly in a passage from the *Meteorology*:

All these [homoiomerous] bodies differ from each other, firstly, in the particular ways in which they can act on the senses (for a thing is white, fragrant, resonant, sweet, hot or cold in virtue of the way it acts on sensation), and, secondly, in other more intrinsic qualities commonly classed as passive—I mean solubility, solidification, flexibility, and the like, all of which, like moist and dry, are passive qualities. It is by these passive qualities that bone, flesh, sinew, wood, bark, stone and all the other natural homoiomerous bodies are differentiated. (385^{a}1–11.)

Now, whatever one makes of the authenticity of *Mete.* 4 (and the intimations of a primary–secondary quality split in this passage might raise doubts in one's mind), the distinction between hot and cold as *active* and moist and dry as *passive* principles is *bona fide* Aristotelian doctrine also insisted upon in *De Generatione et Corruptione*. In fact, it will be recalled that Aristotle 'reduces' and explains all the various other tangible qualities of bodies in terms of the moist and dry, a move suggesting that these other properties too—e.g. the fine–coarse or brittle–viscous—should be considered to be *passive* qualities of bodies. Now the *Meteorology* passage I have just quoted does raise a serious problem for Aristotle's account of sensation: if sensation is a process in which active external agents somehow affect and alter passive sense-organs, how can any of the *passive* tangible features of bodies ever make themselves felt? Since, quite obviously, they do, then I consider that there is another reason to reject the literalist interpretation, which would render such perception impossible. Thus although Aristotle begins his inquiry into the physical elements in *GC* 2. 2 by stating that it concerns perceptible, and more narrowly tangible, body, he soon departs from any narrow consideration of *phainomena* about such bodies, or of their appearances to us (or to other animals). By emphasizing certain ambiguities in the English verb 'to feel' or in the Greek verb 'to touch' (*haptesthai*) I have tried to pave the way for an appreciation that even within the realm of *sensible things* there is a distinction between what appears (or what we sense) and what is. *De Generatione et Corruptione* focuses on the realm of tangibles as it is, in itself; the *De Anima* sometimes confuses the two realms, and does not confine itself as we might expect to the realm of tangibles *as* experienced. (I must emphasize that I do *not* mean by this a realm of tangible sense-data, but rather the perceived world of tangible features, aspects or qualities of things: the world of smooth skin, soft fur, warm sun, cool wet puddles, etc.)

We are now in a position to resolve the puzzle mentioned above concerning the priority of touch over the other senses. Aristotle holds that there are certain physical elements which enter into all complex natural bodies as primitives, and he thinks that these physical elements can be characterized in terms of their tangible properties. However, this does not mean that more complex bodies and

their properties are any less 'real' than the physical elements. Aristotle has a complicated picture in which complex natural bodies are defined in terms of their
characteristic functions or *dunameis*, which in turn result from but are not reducible to the *dunameis* of their physical components. The complex *dunameis* of a
flower, for example, depend upon but are not reducible to the *dunameis* of its
material constituents. Presumably these more complex and higher-order *dunameis*
are various sensory features of the flower, such as its colour or scent; these too are
not reducible to the (tangible) features of the flower's material constituents. This
is why Aristotle can differentiate his view from that of the atomists: visual or
olfactory perception would not occur without touch and tangible objects, but
they are perceptions of higher-order aspects of those objects which are real, *sui
generis*, and non-reducible to touch perceptions. Of course, numerous questions
could be raised concerning the complex layerings characteristic of Aristotle's
metaphysics (see e.g. Waterlow 1982, Furth 1987, Freeland 1987*b*, and Kosman
1987), but these would take us far afield from his account of sensation in general,
and of the sense of touch in particular.[20]

[20] I am grateful to Gail Fine and Don Morrison for comments on an earlier version.

14

ARISTOTLE ON THE IMAGINATION

MALCOLM SCHOFIELD

Introduction

EVERY educated man knows that Aristotle invented logic. It is not so widely known that he contests with Plato[1] the distinction of having discovered the imagination. Men imagined things, just as they argued correctly and incorrectly, before the birth of the Old Academy; but it was Aristotle who gave the first extended analytical description of imagining as a distinct faculty of the soul, and who first drew attention, not least by the ambiguities and strains of his own account of the matter, to the difficulty of achieving an adequate philosophical understanding of imagination. I shall not in this essay attempt a survey of all Aristotle's uses of and pronouncements about *phantasia*.[2] I shall restrict myself to a set of fundamental problems in the interpretation of his official and principal discussion of it in *DA* 3. 3. In that chapter lurk most of the pleasures and puzzles which the student of Aristotle's views on imagination will want to savour.

It has been doubted whether Aristotle's *phantasia* should be rendered as 'imagination' at all. Plato in the *Theaetetus* (152 A–C) and *Sophist* (264 A–B) introduces *phantasia* into philosophical discourse about mental states as the noun corresponding to the verb *phainesthai*, 'appear'; and it is his doctrine that any belief which a man forms because of what he perceives with his senses is an instance of *phantasia*.[3] Now a clear connection with the verb is preserved by Aristotle in talking of *phantasia* in *DA* 3. 3 and elsewhere. Moreover, it has been noticed that the range of 'appearances' which Aristotle allocates to the faculty includes cases which are not obviously instances of mental imagery, but seem

---

© Faculty of Classics, University of Cambridge 1978. Originally published in G. E. R. Lloyd and G. E. L. Owen (eds.), *Aristotle on Mind and the Senses: Proceedings of the Seventh Symposium Aristotelicum* (Cambridge: Cambridge University Press, 1978), 99–130; reprinted with minor changes of presentation in J. Barnes, M. Schofield, and R. Sorabji (eds.), *Articles on Aristotle*, iv: *Psychology and Aesthetics* (London: Duckworth, 1979), 103–32.

[1] See in particular *Phil.* 38 A–40 E, *Soph.* 263 D–264 B. In the former passage, it seems hard to deny that Plato, in talking of the work of the painter in the soul, is identifying imagination (so e.g. Hackforth 1945, 72); the latter passage is too brief for very sure appraisal, but its account of *phantasia* is not dissimilar enough from that of the painter's work in the *Philebus* nor from Aristotle's treatment in *DA* 3. 3 for one to be able to share Cornford's brisk confidence in asserting that *phantasia* is not here imagination (1935, 319). But these are both late dialogues, which may owe something at this point to discussions in the Academy to which Aristotle contributed.

[2] Useful surveys are offered by Freudenthal (1863), Beare (1906), 290 ff.; Ross (1923), 142–5; Rees (1971).

[3] So at least he seems to say at 264 A 4–6; but no doubt he would allow that 'because' (*dia*) requires elaboration and restriction.

more like examples of direct sensory experience; and again, that in his causal explanation of *phantasia* Aristotle allows that a man may have *phantasia* of what he is at the moment actually perceiving (428ᵇ25–30), yet (as Wittgenstein remarked) 'while I am looking at an object I cannot imagine it'.[4] Some scholars have accordingly inferred that *phantasia* is for Aristotle, at least in some moods, a comprehensive faculty by which we apprehend sensory and quasi-sensory presentations generally.[5] Thus his view of *phantasia* is equated[6] *pro tanto* with a view of sensory activity (or rather passivity) more typically associated with phenomenalists and sceptics; or else he is taken to have succumbed temporarily to a Kantian conception, according to which 'sensation [i.e. sense-perception] would...be reduced to the level of a mere passive affection which has to be interpreted by *phantasia* before it can give any information or misinformation about objects' (Ross 1923, 142).

Its Kantian associations might justify continuing to call the *phantasia* of this latter interpretation 'imagination'. But it is recognised that to admit such a comprehensive role for *phantasia* as either interpretation envisages is hard to reconcile with Aristotle's treatment of the senses in book 2 of *De Anima*. It is widely allowed, although not universally nor by me, that Aristotle's official designation of *phantasia* in *DA* 3. 3 as 'that in virtue of which we say that a *phantasma* occurs to us' (428ᵃ1–2) implies that it is a faculty more narrowly but more usually named 'imagination', viz. one in virtue of which we can have mental images.[7] And we find Ross, for example, portraying Aristotle's usual view of *phantasia*, both in *De Anima* and in *Parva Naturalia*, in terms which call to mind Hobbes's 'decaying sense' and Hume's 'faint and languid perception': its characteristic sphere, on Ross's reading, is mental imagery (Ross 1923, 143–4).

One conclusion one might draw from this apparently conflicting evidence of Aristotle's meaning is summed up in Hamlyn's glum verdict (on 427ᵇ27): 'There is clearly little consistency here [sc. in *DA* 3. 3].' My view is that the conflict in the evidence is in good part merely apparent. For it is a bit artificial to divide the work Aristotle assigns to *phantasia* between mental imagery and the reception of sensory or quasi-sensory presentations. If we are to attribute to him a concept of imagination, then without endowing it with a Kantian scope we can permit it to range beyond the confines of mental imagery, as several modern authors, writing in the wake of Ryle and Wittgenstein, would urge.[8] And although we must recognise a proprietary connection between *phantasia* and the verb *phainesthai*, 'appear', we need not suppose that the use of the word Aristotle wishes to exploit is the phenomenalist appropriation of it as the universal, basic, neutral term to

---

[4] Wittgenstein (1967), no. 621.

[5] So e.g. Beare (1906), 290; Ross (1923), 142–3; Lycos (1964), 496 and n. 1; Hamlyn in Aristotle (1968), 129, 131, 133–4.

[6] e.g. by Hamlyn and Lycos.

[7] See e.g. Hicks in Aristotle (1907) on 428ᵃ1; Hamlyn in Aristotle (1968), 129 (although it was Professor Hamlyn who in discussion sowed the seeds of doubt in my mind about this interpretation).

[8] See e.g. Ishiguro (1967); Strawson (1970), 31–54; R. Scruton (1974), 91–120. The basic texts in Ryle and Wittgenstein are Ryle (1949/1963), ch. 8; Wittgenstein (1958), II. xi (cf. 1967, nos. 62 ff.).

report on one's any and every sensory or quasi-sensory experience without ever yet committing oneself to a claim about how things are in the external world. Commentators who have supposed just this have been too little sensitive to the protean character of 'appears' and cognate expressions, so irresistibly exhibited by Austin.[9] I shall argue that in the contexts which concern us Aristotle has his eye on the more everyday use of *phainesthai* to express scepticism, caution, or non-committal about the veridical character of sensory or quasi-sensory experiences, on those comparatively infrequent occasions when for one special reason or another it seems inappropriate in a remark about one's own or another's experience to claim that things are as they seem: 'it *looks* thus and so [—but is it really?]'. This usage is not unnaturally associated with the imagination, for 'imagination involves thought which is unasserted, and hence which goes beyond what is believed'.[10]

According to the view which I shall advance, then, we need not charge Aristotle with the radical inconsistency in his treatment of *phantasia* diagnosed by Hamlyn. None the less, we should be wary about assimilating *phantasia* and imagination. Grant that a conceptual link between imagination and a use of 'appears' can be forged: even so, the link is not nearly as close as the morphologically grounded connection between *phantasia* and *phainesthai*, nor does 'appears' supply the obvious, natural entrée to the study of the imagination which *phainetai* provides to that of *phantasia*. A little lexicography will show that the syntactic behaviour and the semantic range of *phantasia* (not to mention *phantasma* and *phainesthai*) are markedly different from those of 'imagination'.[11]

---

[9] See Austin (1962), esp. chs. 3 and 4; also Chisholm (1957), esp. ch. 4.

[10] Scruton (1974), 97.

[11] *Phantasia*, like *phantasma*, derives from the verb *phantazō* (found only in its middle and passive forms before the Hellenistic period), which means 'to make apparent', 'to cause to *phainesthai*'. Now nouns of the *-sia* type formed from *-zō* verbs tend in the first instance to connote the action signified by the verb; nouns of the *-sma* type so formed regularly connote the result of the action, or what is done by doing the action. On might therefore expect that *phantasia*, in its primitive sense, would signify just that action which consists in producing *phantasmata*: that if *phantasmata* are (say) 'presentations' (in the sense 'what is presented'), *phantasia* will be 'presenting' (or 'presentation' in an active sense) and likely to behave syntactically not unlike 'imagining' or 'imagination'. But this expectation is largely disappointed in Greek before Aristotle: and the reason is not far to seek. We have noted the absence of active forms of the verb *phantazō* in pre-Hellenistic texts. What this means in practice is that we read not of persons *making* things appear thus and so, but of sights, dreams, etc. being presented or presenting themselves to persons. This fact no doubt explains both the relative rarity of *phantasia* compared with *phantasma* (cf. LSJ s.vv.) and the near absence of an active force in *phantasia* when it does occur in writers before Aristotle. If human agents do not *phantazousin*, actively make apparent or present things, if *phantasmata* are rather made to appear by the chances of life, then there will not be much scope for the action-noun *phantasia* as 'presenting', 'making apparent', although *phantasma* will find a place naturally enough. Contrast other pairs of nouns similarly formed from *-zō* verbs whose active voices are, however, employed: *diadikasia*, *diadikasma*; *eikasia*, *eikasma*; *skeuasia*, *skeuasma*. Here it is invariably the latter member of the pair which is the rarer. When *phantasia* does gain what one might call a natural toehold in the language, it does so in a secondary sense, 'presentation' as corresponding not to the active but the passive of the verb—a frequent use in Aristotle (cf. Bonitz, *Index Aristotelicus* 811ᵃ38–ᵇ11).

Not only *phantasma* and *phantazō*, then, but *phantasia* too has a natural passive tendency in the language as we find it, at odds with the active force of 'imagination'. This certainly leaves its mark on Aristotle's treatment of the faculty of *phantasia* in *DA* 3. 3, notably in his predilection for *phainetai*,

And if for a moment we banish the rendering 'imagination' from our minds, then in one section of *DA* 3. 3, at any rate (the discussion whether *phantasia* is a faculty of judgment, 428^{a}1–^{b}9), reflection on the range of phenomena Aristotle assigns to *phantasia* and on the way he introduces them into his argument suggests a rather different physiognomy for the concept from that conveyed by 'imagination'. Aristotle seems to be concerned with a capacity for having what I shall compendiously call non-paradigmatic sensory experiences[12]—experiences so diverse as dreams and the interpreting of indistinct or puzzling sense-data, which may be held to resemble the paradigm of successful sense-perception in one way or another, yet patently lack one or more of its central features, and so give rise to the sceptical, cautious, or non-committal *phainetai*. One merit of this interpretation of *phantasia* is that it makes immediately intelligible Aristotle's ensuing causal analysis of the faculty, which takes as its crucial premiss the fundamentally sensory character of *phantasiai*, and proceeds to define them in terms of sense perception proper, as causal traces of actual perceptions (428^{b}10–429^{a}2). Nor is the immediate intelligibility of that analysis all that is salvaged. For if we read it as an account not of imagination but of non-paradigmatic sensory experiences, it is readily taken as a not implausible attempt to give a single general explanation of an extremely interesting feature of human psychology, namely the operation of our sensory equipment in a variety of non-standard ways. As a theory of the imagination, on the other hand, its very generality renders it disappointingly jejune, aside from its pre-echoes of the unilluminating view of imagination familiar to readers of the British empiricists. This is not, of course, to deny that mental imagery would be reckoned by Aristotle as one type of non-paradigmatic sensory experience. It is simply to argue that the focus of his attention, in these sections of *DA* 3. 3, is not imagery or imagination as such.

These considerations should not lead us to abandon altogether a direct equivalence between *phantasia* and imagination. For in a passage from the opening section of his discussion of *phantasia* in *DA* 3. 3 (427^{b}16–24), Aristotle offers two criteria to distinguish it from belief (*doxa*) which fit the concept of imagination so perfectly, and are so fundamental to it, that it would be perverse to take the topic to be anything other than imagination. He tells us that *phantasia*, unlike belief, is up to us when we wish, or, in modern parlance, is subject to the will;[13] and that,

---

'appears', as an index to the operation of *phantasia*, a predilection which suggests that he thinks of the mind in *phantasia* as the passive recipient of experiences, not as actively imagining. Nonetheless, the very fact that Aristotle (like Plato before him) presses *phantasia* into service as the name for a mental disposition or act, comparable with thinking and perceiving, reveals a philosophical impulse to force the word into a more active sense (latent, of course, within it). Again, he occasionally refers to *phantasia* the faculty as *to phantastikon* (*DA* 432^{a}31, *Insomn.* 458^{b}30, 459^{a}16), which must be either (following Plato in the *Sophist* 236 C) the capacity for producing *phantasmata*, or the capacity for *phantazesthai* in the novel Aristotelian sense, attested (though in the passive) in two places at least (*Ph.* 192^{a}15, *DA* 433^{b}12), of 'making (something) appear for oneself'—i.e. a middle usage predicable of persons, with a force approximating to that of 'imagining'.

[12] On this notion see further n. 20 below.

[13] Cf. e.g. Ryle, *The Concept of Mind* (1949/1963), 233; Wittgenstein, (1958), 213; (1967), nos. 621, 626–8, etc.

whereas we are immediately affected by fear if we believe we are confronted by something alarming, in the case of *phantasia* it is merely as if we saw something alarming in a picture.[14] I do not say that these marks of imagination are not true also of some non-paradigmatic sensory experiences (if not of others, such as after-images or hallucinations). But it seems pointless to invoke the latter notion here unless the context demands it. And in the immediate context there is no trace of the concerns characteristic of the sections we considered briefly in the previous paragraph: the use of *phainetai* as signally appropriate to cases of *phantasia*, its emphatically sensory character (certainly *phantasia* is treated at 427^b16-24 as rather like seeing,[15] but the criteria employed to distinguish it from belief make it analogous to thinking rather than to perception). Moreover, the whole section 427^b6-26 bears signs of being composed separately from the sections which follow.[16] So they cannot be held to constitute a wider context sufficiently intimately connected with 427^b6-26 to require our importing the idea of non-paradigmatic sensory experience into the section. Here at least, then, there seems every reason to identify *phantasia* with imagination.

But it was no doubt Aristotle himself who was responsible for putting together ch. 3 of *DA* 3 in the form in which we have it. He gives no sign that he is aware of changing subjects in the course of the chapter. We owe it to him, therefore, to try to understand how the concept of imagination which figures pretty clearly at the beginning of the discussion of *phantasia* could reasonably be treated as one and the same concept as the rather different notion which seems to be in question from 428^a1 onwards. I shall suggest (and have already hinted) that Aristotle can be fairly interpreted as adopting different but complementary vantage-points on a more or less coherent family of psychological phenomena. But it would be a triumph of generosity over justice to pretend that he manages to combine his different approaches to *phantasia* with an absolutely clear head.

In the body of the essay I shall devote most of my space to the themes broached in this introduction. But first a word or two on my method and its limitations. In seeking to establish what Aristotle understands by *phantasia* we shall have to try to build up a picture chiefly from relatively isolated remarks tossed off in the course of the argument of *DA* 3. 3, which must then in turn be tested against them. In the chapter Aristotle makes many distinctions between

[14] Cf. Ryle's construction of imagining as a sort of pretending (1949/1963), 244–57 (criticized by Ishiguro (1966) 161 ff.); Scruton (1974), 97, etc., who treats imagination as unasserted thought (and will, no doubt, come under fire for doing so). In mentioning Ryle and Scruton, I do not mean to subscribe to their views on imagination, only to point up parallels between Aristotle and some of the best contemporary work.

[15] This is because Aristotle thinks of imagination first and foremost as visualising, on which see Williams (1973), ch. 3; Scruton (1974), 100–6.

[16] The principal ground for this claim is that the discussion of the relation of *doxa* and *phantasia* at 428^a18-24 makes no reference to the arguments already offered at 427^b14-24 (cf. Hicks in Aristotle 1907, 456). Freudenthal thought the passage 427^b14-24 was not only hard to relate to what preceded and followed, but also in contradiction with Aristotle's usual views on the topics it discusses (1863, 9 ff.); but he received a magisterial (if not entirely convincing) rebuke from Rodier in Aristote (1907) ii. 408–13.

phantasia and other dispositions of the soul, sometimes (but not often enough) with clearly articulated examples. What he fails to do is to draw the threads of his discussion together, to provide a synoptic view of *phantasia* as he interprets it. This tempts one to examine other texts in the hope of achieving a more definitive impression of his conception, particularly from *Parva Naturalia* and elsewhere in *De Anima*. But these require cautious employment. For *DA* 3. 3 remains Aristotle's one concentrated, extended theoretical discussion of *phantasia*;[17] elsewhere he is mainly concerned with its role in particular mental operations— dreaming, remembering, thinking, and so on. An account of his view of *phantasia* which relies too heavily on his treatment of these related phenomena runs the risk of distortion, the risk either of taking the way *phantasia* works in memory, dreams, and so on as its mode of operation *tout court*, or more insidiously of putting the emphases of the description in the wrong places. Ross fell into this trap, so much so that he was forced to doubt whether some of the more important things Aristotle says in *DA* 3. 3 really 'represent his deliberate view' (1961, 143). If that chapter does not give us Aristotle's considered opinion, it is doubtful whether he had a considered opinion and certain that we could not with any confidence reconstruct it.

Of course, the persuasiveness of the account of *phantasia* in *DA* 3. 3 which I am offering would be much weakened if it seemed not to correspond with what Aristotle has in mind when he talks of *phantasia* in other contexts. In this essay I have not attempted to show that my account will work for his handling of *phantasia* elsewhere. And it may consequently be objected, for example, that in Aristotle's theory of animal movement *phantasia* cannot be associated with sceptical, cautious, or non-committal *phainetai*, since the point of making *phantasia* a necessary condition of movement is to require that the moving animal positively fix upon some object of desire.[18] Or, more generally, it might be thought implausible that Aristotle should wish to specify a faculty of the soul in such negative terms, in view of the constructive work he puts *phantasia* to do not only in action but in remembering, thinking, etc., too.[19]

I offer some general considerations in reply, in lieu of the detailed investigation which a proper answer would entail. It will be evident from what I say in the main body of the paper, and particularly from its third section, that I take Aristotle's chief problem in *DA* 3. 3 to be that of providing conceptual room for an independent notion of *phantasia*, between thinking on the one side and sense-perception on the other. If this is so, then we might reasonably expect two things: first, that Aristotle will take as fundamental to *phantasia* in *DA* 3. 3 features which will not necessarily receive much emphasis in other contexts

---

[17] Notice the references to the chapter as Aristotle's official account at *Mem.* 449[b]30–1 (where 7–8 is also in Aristotle's mind), *Insomn.* 459[a]15 (possibly an editorial addition), *MA* 700[b]21–2.

[18] This objection I owe to Professors D. J. Allan and D. J. Furley.

[19] This point was put to me by Fr. E. de Stryker.

where he is not particularly concerned with the demarcation problem of that chapter; secondly, that Aristotle will elsewhere, when concerned with other problems, be likely to emphasize features of *phantasia* not given much prominence in *DA* 3. 3, or even to blur distinctions made or implied there. Thus, to take the first point, it is principally in connection with his attempt in *DA* 3. 3 to distinguish *phantasia* from sense-perception as faculties of judgement that he links *phantasia* so closely with the particular use of *phainetai* which I have tried to isolate. This aspect of *phantasia* continues to attract Aristotle's attention in contexts where he is concerned with perceptual or quasi-perceptual judgements, as in *De Insomniis*. But—and here I move to the second point—in other contexts, notably in his accounts of thinking and remembering, he is not concerned with *phantasia* as a faculty of judgement at all. When he introduces *phantasia* or *phantasmata* here, he has in mind our capacity for visualizing, just as he does in that section ($427^{b}6-26$) of *DA* 3. 3 where I interpret him as discussing the active power of imagination.[20] I am inclined to believe[21] that much the same aspect of *phantasia* is what Aristotle chiefly had in mind when he claims that *phantasia* is a necessary condition of animal movement, although here he is certainly concerned with judgement (even if only as assent to what one visualizes). This at any rate is suggested by the way he develops his view in *DA* 3. 9–11. For he seems to think that movement and the desire which is its principal cause require either the thought of a desirable object or at least something like thought (*noēsin tina*, 'a sort of thinking'), namely *phantasia* (*DA* $433^{a}9-12$). What he says elsewhere about the connection of thought and *phantasia* makes it very likely that it is mainly imagination or visualization that he is thinking of (see especially *DA* $403^{a}8-9$, $431^{a}14-17$, $432^{a}3-14$, *Mem.* $449^{b}31-450^{a}7$). Here, as in *DA* 3. 3, he first suggests that *phantasia*, as opposed to *noēsis*, is the prerequisite of desire in non-rational animals and in what prompts the fevered or the weak-willed man to act (here we catch an echo of sceptical, cautious *phainetai*: 'it seems good [but

---

[20] In a memorable intervention in the discussion of this paper at the 1975 Symposium Aristotelicum (whose text she kindly showed me subsequently), Professor C. J. de Vogel took my interpretation of *phantasia* in *DA* 3. 3 as *non-paradigmatic* sensory experience to be in conflict with the evident fact that Aristotle elsewhere treats *phantasia* as indispensable to thinking and as playing a *normal* part in the acquisition of knowledge. But let us take the case where the *phantasia* we are concerned with is a piece of visualizing: I do not mean to deny that, according to Aristotle, all thinking involves visualizing or that that is the norm; what I mean is rather that visualizing is not normal sensory experience (for normal sensory experience requires, as it does not, that we keep our eyes and ears open, etc.), but is sufficiently like and sufficiently closely connected with normal sensory experience to be thought of as a non-standard form of it. Of course, one is not very often going to use sceptical, cautious, or non-committal *phainetai* in commenting on the visualization one does in the course of thinking, just because one is interested principally in the thought, not in its accompanying imagery. But (as Mr Sorabji pointed out in the discussion) if one did reflect on it one would certainly wish to report on it in terms which (as *phainetai* does) make it clear that one is not necessarily making a claim about how one confidently sees the world. The same would not be true of animal imagination; but animal imagination is an obscure corner of Aristotelian doctrine (cf. nn. 35, 41, 55).

[21] *Contra* the interesting interpretation advanced by Nussbaum (1978); I am grateful to Professor Nussbaum for allowing me to discuss a draft of her material on *phantasia* with her.

principle forbids it]').[22] But later in the same discussion Aristotle simplifies his account by making *phantasia* the crucial factor in all desire, explaining that it can be prompted either by thought or by sense-perception—evidently recalling his doctrine that all thinking involves visualizing.[23]

I have slipped into discussion of particular issues of interpretation willy-nilly. But my chief point remains this: investigation of *DA* 3. 3 indicates that Aristotle's *phantasia* is a loose-knit, family concept. So we should expect that in its appearances elsewhere in his psychology its different elements are variously picked out or woven into fresh patterns. And that, I contend, is just what we would find if we carried out a detailed investigation of those contexts.

I. *Phantasia* and *Phainetai*

Ross states: '*Phantasia* is in its original meaning closely related to *phainesthai*, "to appear", and stands for either the appearance of an object or the mental act [or, we might add, disposition] which is to appearing as hearing is to sounding' (1961, 142). He goes on to cite a number of passages in Aristotle where *phantasia* seems to him to be used in this way. They and others like them constitute the evidence for holding that Aristotle at least sometimes conceives of *phantasia* as a comprehensive faculty in virtue of which we apprehend sensory and quasi-sensory presentations in general. I shall argue that this evidence can and should be given an alternative interpretation.

The most promising text for a broad conception of the faculty of *phantasia* might be thought to be a passage not in the psychological treatises but in the *Metaphysics*. For in *Metaph.* 1010ᵇ1–14, Aristotle introduces the notion of *phantasia* in a context where the verb *phainesthai* is not merely used but used in a phenomenalist style to express sensory and quasi-sensory 'appearing' in general. The passage constitutes part of his argument against Protagoras' view that all *phainomena*, appearances, are true.

It is perfectly plain that here, as indeed in the rationale of Protagoras' doctrine offered at 1009ᵃ38–ᵇ9, Aristotle is including under *phainomena* any sensory or quasi-sensory appearances whatever. Witness the beginning of his second objection in the passage, at 1010ᵇ3–9:[24]

---

[22] Cf. *DA* 429ᵃ4–8; 433ᵃ10–12 (with 433ᵃ1–8). *Phainetai* bulks large in the discussion of pathological conditions in *Insomn.* 460ᵇ3–16, used with its sensory connotation. The *phainetai* appropriate to mention of *to phainomenon agathon* (cf. *DA* 433ᵃ26–30 with e.g. *EE* 1235ᵇ25–9, *EN* 1114ᵃ31 ff.) need not, of course, of itself suggest a *sensory* appearance; but no doubt Aristotle would say that any thought of the form 'this *seems* a good plan' must involve visualization. (I owe an awareness of the importance of Aristotle's remarks about *to phainomenon agathon* in this connection to Professor Furley's paper in Lloyd and Owen (1978).)

[23] *DA* 433ᵇ28–9; *MA* 702ᵃ17–19. As Professor Nussbaum suggests, Aristotle may put such stress on *phantasia* partly because it (unlike thinking) has a material basis which renders it an appropriate component in a physiological account of movement.

[24] Translation adapted from Kirwan in Aristotle (1971), whose version and interpretation (p. 110) are, however, spoilt by the assumption that *phainetai* is to be rendered 'is imagined'.

Next, one may legitimately be surprised that they should find perplexing the question whether magnitudes and colours are such as they appear (*phainetai*) to those at a distance or to those nearby, to the healthy or to the sick; or whether it is what [appears so] to the weak or to the strong that is heavier; or whether it is what [appears so] to those asleep or to those awake that is true.

What directly concern us, however, is Aristotle's first objection to the thesis that every *phainomenon* is true (1010^{b}2–3). The text is corrupt, but runs thus in Bonitz's widely accepted and plausible reconstruction: 'Even if perception, at least of what is special, is not false, still *phantasia* is not the same as perception.' A proponent of the idea that a broad conception of *phantasia* is to be found in Aristotle might argue that this objection is naturally read as implying such a conception, as follows: Aristotle is in effect accusing the Protagoreans of fallaciously inferring from the true premiss:[25] 'All perception (or, all perception of proper objects, the fundamental sort of perception) is true' the false conclusion 'Every *phainomenon* is true'. And it is clear enough that he means to challenge the inference by pointing out that it depends on an additional tacit premiss (which is false) to the effect that every *phainomenon* is a case of perception. But what he actually says is that *phantasia* is not the same thing as perception. The natural explanation of his putting the point this way is that he thinks of *phantasia* as the faculty in virtue of which any *phainomenon* is experienced, and speaks here of *phantasia* rather than *phainomenon* simply because he wants to refer to the mental disposition or act involved, and so to make the appropriate contrast with perception. Moreover, the evident influence of Plato's *Theaetetus* in this paragraph (Plato is actually mentioned at 1010^{b}12) and elsewhere in the chapter makes it unsurprising that Aristotle should have used *phantasia* in this broad manner. For that is just how Plato uses the word in introducing Protagorean relativism (*Theaet.* 152 A–C).

Despite its plausibility, this interpretation of *phantasia* is not the only one possible for an unforced reading of the text. This can be made clear by an example. Aristotle is prepared to grant to Protagoras that hearing is always of sound; his point is presumably that it is not true that wherever there is the appearance of a sound in our ears we are actually hearing (we may be dreaming, for example: cf. 1010^{b}8–11), and even if we are hearing a real sound, it may appear to us other than as it really is (as coming from the right, for example, when it actually comes from the left: cf. 1010^{b}4–8). Now in saying that *phantasia* is not the same as perception, Aristotle might mean (as someone who held the interpretation sketched above would probably argue) that perception (that is, of proper objects) is only one sort of *phantasia*, to be compared with interpretation of perception, dreaming, and further sorts of *phantasia*. He would then be suggesting that, while the *phainomena* experienced in perception may always be true, those experienced in other sorts of *phantasia* need not be. But observe that he may equally well mean that some *phainomena* are indeed cases of perception

---

[25] On the interpretation of this premiss (and on its text), see the excellent discussion by Kirwan (1971), ibid. 110–11.

of proper objects, and as such true, but that others (such as those we experience in dreams) involve the *co-ordinate* faculty of *phantasia*, imagination or non-paradigmatic sensory experience, which of course admits of falsehood. In other words, Aristotle's objection to Protagoras will be no less forcefully and naturally expressed if *phantasia* is not the genus of which perception is a species, but a species, co-ordinate with perception, involved like it in the apprehension of just a part of the whole field of *phainomena*. Nor does the comparison with the *Theaetetus* give the former alternative unequivocal support. For Aristotle is denying precisely what Plato makes Protagoras affirm, namely that perception and *phantasia* are one and the same. If his concept of perceiving has a different scope from Protagoras', then his concept of *phantasia* may very well do so too.[26]

We must conclude that it is hard to know how to understand the denial that *phantasia* and perception are identical without further evidence of Aristotle's teaching about them. For that we have to turn (as Aristotle would surely expect us to turn) to *De Anima*, and in particular to the passage in which he elaborates his reasons for distinguishing between *phantasia* and perception (*DA* 3. 3, 428ª5–16). I consider first such indications as it contains that the word *phainetai* ('appears') is a specially appropriate and significant vehicle for describing what we experience in virtue of *phantasia*.

There are three occurrences of the word in the passage. In one of these Aristotle's argument explicitly turns on the bearing of its use on the character of *phantasia*; and in consequence the other two, although less important in themselves, gain in interest and significance. Here is the telling example, in the fourth argument of the set (428ª12 15):[27]

Further, it is not when we are exercising [our senses] with precision on the object of perception that we *say* that this appears (*phainetai*) to us [to be] a man, but rather when we do not perceive it distinctly.

Hamlyn complains that this argument 'is concerned with imagination in the sense of appearances only and as these are perceptual phenomena they do not serve to mark a distinction from perception' (1968, 131). But if an interpretation makes an Aristotelian point as irrelevant as that, the fault may very well lie in the interpretation. And it is not difficult to find a genuine contrast between perception and *phantasia* expressed in Aristotle's sentence. Aristotle is surely pointing out that if we clearly *see* a man, we do not say: 'It looks like a man', since the caution, doubt, or non-committal implied by that form of words is out of place. It is when our eyes let us down that *phainetai* becomes an appropriate location; and the judgement we make by employing it is not straightforwardly a report of what we perceive, but a more guarded statement of how what we perceive looks to us, how we interpret it. 'How it looks to us', 'how we interpret it': Aristotle puts it the first way, in the language of what I am calling non-paradigmatic sensory

---

[26] We should observe how *very* much wider the concept of *aisthēsis* ascribed to Protagoras in the *Theaetetus* is than Aristotle's perception of proper objects. It includes feeling cold or hot, pleasures, pains, desires, fears (156 B2 ff.).

[27] With most editors and commentators I reject the words *tote ē alēthēs ē pseudēs* (428ª15) as a gloss.

experience, in essentially passive terms. But the appearance of 'to us' in his formulation reveals his awareness of the subjectivity of the judgement, and so suggests that he would not object to the idea that in *phantasia* we consciously or unconsciously interpret the data of our senses. It is natural to assign such interpretative activity to the imagination. This is particularly the case where the interpreting is conscious. Suppose you and I are looking at a distant object in murky light: we may have to exercise our imaginations, comparing and contrasting what we *can* see with the way familiar middle-sized things of our everyday acquaintance look, before we are able to conclude that it looks like a man; we may have to try seeing it under different aspects before we succeed in seeing it as a man.

Whatever is placed beyond the reach of sense and knowledge, whatever is imperfectly discerned, the fancy pieces out at its leisure; and all but the present moment, but the present spot, passion claims for its own, and brooding over it with wings outspread, stamps it with an image of itself.[28]

But even if the indistinctly perceived object immediately and irresistibly looks to me like a man, even if I have not consciously engaged in a moment's *reflection* about what it is that I see, there is still reason to account my judgement the product of imagination. For as in the earlier case I do not just perceive a man, but see something as a man,[29] and if I say 'it looks like a man', I employ a form of words which indicates an appreciation that I am going beyond what I actually perceive.[30] If I am wrong, I may reasonably be accused of merely imagining that it was a man;[31] right or wrong, I may be held to have *decided* what it looked like no less than if I had had to make my mind up slowly. The instantaneous character of my verdict does not tell against my having actively engaged in imagination: imaginative leaps may notoriously occur in the twinkling of an eye. Notice, too, that the two criteria of imagination proposed by Aristotle at 427^b16-24 are satisfied in the relevant way in this case as in the one where imagining takes time. Just because imagination is here employed as an aid to perception, not in free fantasy, one's attitude to the appearance in question is not likely to resemble much one's attitude to a picture; but neither is it probable that someone to whom it merely looks as if there is an enemy soldier in the distance will be immediately affected by the spontaneous emotion appropriate to perceiving an enemy clearly —the caution, doubt, or non-committal signalled by *phainetai* will tend to act as a brake. Again, imagination remains subject to the will in these cases, inasmuch as it makes perfect sense to ask a person to exercise his imagination upon what he imperfectly sees.[32] The fact that he has no psychological option but to see what he

[28] W. Hazlitt, *Why Distant Objects Please* (from *Table Talk*).

[29] For discussion, after Wittgenstein, of the close relation between imagining and 'seeing as', see e.g. Strawson (1970), 44–52; Scruton (1974), ch. 8.

[30] On going beyond the evidence as a criterion of imagination, see Scruton (1974), ch. 7.

[31] For some remarks on this use of 'imagine', see Strawson (1970), 53–4; also Ryle (1949/1963), 244–5.

[32] For this interpretation of what it is for imagination to be subject to the will, see Scruton (1974), 94–5.

sees as a man no more counts against this being an instance of imagination than the obsessive, haunting character which mental images may exhibit, pleasantly or unpleasantly, debars them from being products of the imagination.

Aristotle in his argument at 428ᵃ12–15 alerts us to a use of *phainetai* which is appropriate only in special perceptual circumstances. He takes it to show that men exercise *phantasia* precisely where sense-perception fails them. It would be perverse to read him as tacitly allowing³³ (indeed insisting) that none the less *phantasia* has a broad Protagorean scope, and is in fact present in all sense-perception. If Aristotle had meant us to make this inference, he should have phrased his argument differently; and he should have introduced the concept of *phantasia* as an essential tool of his analysis of sense-perception, instead of omitting virtually all mention of it throughout book 2 of *De Anima*.

Phainetai occurs, probably as an index of *phantasia*, in the first and fifth arguments of the set designed to show that it cannot be identical with sense-perception (428ᵃ6–8, 15–16). In the latter case Aristotle has in mind a special phenomenon (after-images seem the likely candidate, cf. Hicks, ad loc.); this suggests a sceptical as much as a Protagorean use of the verb. The same is true of its use in his first argument, which is more general in scope: 'Perception is either a capacity (e.g. sight) or an activity (e.g. seeing); but something can appear (*phainetai*) even if neither of these is in question³⁴ (e.g. dreams).' I submit that we should be guided by the results of our examination of the fourth argument, and take it that in both these further arguments Aristotle means to point to *phantasia* conceived as a faculty for non-paradigmatic sensory experiences.

His other arguments at 428ᵃ5–16, in which *phainetai* does not occur, are best interpreted upon the same assumption. Certainly they are hard to marry with a broad Protagorean conception of *phantasia*. Consider the rather opaque second argument (428ᵃ8–11). Aristotle there claims (ᵃ10–11) that all animals have perception, but apparently not all *phantasia*. But on a Protagorean or typically phenomenalist view of 'appearances', these are the raw materials of which all perception, in however lowly an animal, is constructed.³⁵ The third argument is likewise easy to square with the interpretation of *phantasia* I am advancing, difficult with the broader interpretation. Aristotle says (428ᵃ11–12): 'Next, perceptions [sc. in the strict sense, of proper objects] are always true, but most *phantasiai* turn out false.' Aristotle's point is perhaps best expanded in terms of imagining:

³³ Perhaps in something resembling the manner of Grice (1961).

³⁴ *Huparchontos* is usually translated not 'in question', but 'present', which is perhaps an easier rendering of the Greek. But the idea that the faculty of perception is not present in sleep is not only not Aristotelian doctrine, but in direct contradiction with what Aristotle is most naturally taken as saying in the next sentence (428ᵃ8–9), when he states: 'sense perception is always present'. My translation attempts to capture what Aristotle (as the Greek commentators saw) must have been meaning to say: see Rodier and Hicks ad loc. I suspect a similar use of the word at *PA* 642ᵃ5.

³⁵ At the same time it is difficult to be confident of just what conception of *phantasia* does lie behind Aristotle's denial of it to some animals. Is it that only more sophisticated organisms like the ant and the bee have the capacity for interpreting and misinterpreting the world, but not the worm or grub (I follow Torstrik's reading at 428ᵃ11–12)? Aristotle's whole treatment of *phantasia* in the non-rational animals is puzzling. See further nn. 41, 55 below.

if someone has an image of an F thing, or sees x as F, what he imagines—an F thing—may not and probably will not exist (be a real contemporaneous F thing) at all. '*Probably* will not?' Perhaps Aristotle had run his mind over some of the main sorts of non-paradigmatic sensory experience—such as dreams, memory-images, after-images, fantasy, hallucinations, the seeing of aspects—and reckoned that correspondence to truth was on the whole a rarity among these phenomena; perhaps his trust in common forms of speech suggested to him that the scepticism or caution or non-committal implied by the use of *phainetai* he associated with *phantasia* was usually likely to be justified. In any event, the claim that most *phantasiai* are false is not implausible, so construed. Yet if *phantasiai* were here in effect a mere synonym for Protagorean *phainomena*, it would surely be a highly improbable, if not indeed in the end unintelligible, thesis.[36]

But if those who believe that Aristotle sometimes gives *phantasia* a broad Protagorean scope cannot sustain their interpretation relative to these arguments for the non-identity of sense-perception and *phantasia*, they may yet turn for support to his attack on Plato's view that *phantasia* is a blend of perception and belief. Aristotle's argument there ($428^a24-{}^b9$) has recently been well analysed by Lycos (1964), whose account is lucidly summarized by Hamlyn ad loc.; and since I am concerned simply with the scope *phantasia* is allowed by Aristotle to have, I refer the reader for a detailed treatment of the reasoning to these authors.

Aristotle first expounds Plato's view of *phantasia*, according to which 'appearing (*phainesthai*) will be believing what one perceives (and that not just coincidentally)' (428^b1-2). He then offers a counter-example to this thesis, a case where one experiences a false 'appearance' about what is before one which conflicts with the true belief one holds about it (428^b2-4): 'But things also appear (*phainetai*) falsely, when one has at the same time a true supposition about them (e.g. the sun appears (*phainetai*) a foot across, but is believed to be bigger than the inhabited world).' Now as we have remarked, Plato, in the passage of the *Sophist* to which Aristotle's discussion relates (264 A–B), holds that any belief which is formed as a result of perception is a case of *phantasia* and can properly be expressed by a form of words which includes *phainetai*. He seems to opt for a generously Protagorean range for *phantasia* and *phainetai*, even if he does not identify perception and *phantasia*. But in producing his single counter-example to Plato's thesis, Aristotle does not commit himself to accepting a similarly broad conception of *phantasia*. All he needs to do is to produce a case which he himself accepts as a case of *phantasia* and which Plato too might reasonably be expected to accept as such. So if the particular use of *phainetai* involved in the statement of the counter-example is one which is indicative of *phantasia* for both Plato and himself, that is sufficient for Aristotle.

I submit that Aristotle accepts the sun example as a case of *phantasia* just because it involves a use of *phainetai* which is naturally read ('appears...but is believed') as implying scepticism. This accords not only with the results of our

---

[36] Cf. Bennett (n.d.), 104–18; (1971), 89–102.

examination of 428^a5-16, but also with the context in *De Insomniis* in which this example is used a second time. Aristotle argues at 460^b3 ff. that we are easily deceived with respect to our senses when we are in pathological conditions—in emotional states like love and fear or physiological disturbances like fevers. He points out that the coward in his fear thinks on the basis of a slight resemblance that he sees the enemy, the amorous man in his passion that he sees his beloved; and he comments that the greater the sway of the emotional state, the more tenuous the resemblance needed to make these things appear so (*phainetai*: the word is used four more times of deceptive appearances in the next sixteen lines). This, then, is the context in which Aristotle produces the sun example to show that in a normal frame of mind we are well able to resist and contradict a false appearance, exercising another faculty besides *phantasia*.[37] Notice the company which *phainetai*, used of the sun's misleading appearance, and in consequence *phantasia*, are made to keep—sceptical employments of *phainetai*, non-paradigmatic sensory experiences which we may think of as hallucinations, or as the seeing of unreal aspects.

The sun's looking a foot across would in truth be a rather unconvincing example of a Protagorean *phainomenon*. Someone who pronounces that the sun looks to him a foot across may be endeavouring to offer a report of his perceptual field sufficiently cautious to satisfy a sceptic or a phenomenalist that no illegitimate inferences from the perceived to the real are being made. It is one thing to aver that the sun looks small in comparison with the other items in one's perceptual field. It is quite another to make an estimate of *how* small it appears to be. For judgements of size take into account perspective, yet the very problem with the sun is that one's normal procedures for coping with perspective break down. So the assertion that the sun looks a foot across seems to presuppose some tacit, and no doubt highly questionable, assumption about how far the sun looks to be from the earth. It in fact embodies an imaginative comparison such as: the sun looks like a foot-wide beach ball kicked high in the air (but not *very* like—for the sun looks much higher than that). Compare Austin's observation on 'The moon looks no bigger than a sixpence':[38] 'It doesn't look as if it *is* no bigger than a sixpence, or as a sixpence would look if it were as far away as the moon; it looks, of course, somewhat as a sixpence looks if you look at it at about arm's length.' There is no sign in the text either of the *De Anima* passage or of the *De Insomniis* passage that Aristotle had reflected on the oddity of his example or on its non-paradigmatic perceptual circumstances. But it helps to make the texture of the analysis of *phantasia* in *DA* 3. 3 the richer; and it does something to reinforce the

---

[37] Beare, the Oxford translator, takes the actual word *phantasia*, used here at 460^b19-20, to refer not to the faculty but to the presentation of the sun as a foot across. This may be right; but there is no doubt that the faculty to which Aristotle does refer is *phantasia*, as is shown e.g. by the mention of *to phantastikon* as the faculty involved in cases of this sort at *Insomn.* 458^b30, and by *DA* 429^a7-8, where Aristotle says that men act in accordance with their *phantasiai* (again, the translation is doubtful) because their reason is sometimes clouded by emotion or sickness or sleep.

[38] Austin (1962) 41; cf. S. R. L. Clark (1975), 75–6.

identity of *phantasia* and imagination, albeit beneath the surface of the argument.

A final passage in *DA* 3. 3, at the end of the causal analysis of *phantasia*, helped to persuade Ross that Aristotle in this chapter construes the faculty in the broad manner I have been denying. He states that at 428ᵇ18–30 Aristotle

distinguishes between *phantasia* with respect to the special sensibles, the incidentals, and the common sensibles, and points out that while in the first case *phantasia* is infallible so long as the sensation is present, in the other two it is fallible even in the presence of sensation. This amounts to throwing on to *phantasia* the work of apprehending the incidentals and even the special sensibles as well as the common sensibles; and sensation would accordingly be reduced to the level of a mere passive affection which has to be interpreted by *phantasia* before it can give any information or misinformation about objects. (1923, 142–3).

Ross's statement of Aristotle's doctrine is seriously misleading, and his gloss on it the product of oversight and faulty inference. He omits to mention that in the first part of the passage to which he refers, Aristotle has restated his view (cf. *DA* 2. 6) that there is sense perception not merely of special or proper objects (e.g. white) but of incidentals (e.g. that this white thing is Coriscus) and common objects (e.g. movement and magnitude). This view of perception is offered in book 2 of *De Anima* as an adequate account of the matter; and even if sense-perception, *aisthēsis*, is there treated very much as a passive affection, in the present chapter Aristotle is keen to stress that it is a capacity in virtue of which we *judge* (cf. Hamlyn 1959). Nor does there appear to be a general need for a special interpretative faculty performing the job Ross assigns to it; for however bare Aristotle's conception of perception of incidentals may be, it is (I take it)[39] an interpretative sort of perception. It would therefore be surprising if in his causal analysis of *phantasia* Aristotle meant to abandon the relatively self-sufficient theory of perception reiterated in the course of his argument at 428ᵇ18–25. The only evidence Ross appears to rely on in believing that he is committed in the passage to a new theory is that cited in his first sentence—the distinctions made between sorts of *phantasia* (428ᵇ25–30). Yet those remarks could suggest that the work of apprehending sensibles is now assigned to *phantasia* only if what Aristotle has said in the immediately preceding lines about perception is forgotten, as of course it is forgotten in Ross's description of the passage; as it is, we can only understand Aristotle's doctrine here about *phantasia* by reference to his reasserted doctrine about *aisthēsis*.

None the less, the account of *phantasia* at 428ᵇ25–30 reported by Ross does present an embarrassment for my own interpretation. If *phantasia* is imagination or non-paradigmatic sensory experience, it is easy enough to see how it is possible to have *phantasia* of incidentals or common sensibles while one is still engaged in the relevant sort of perception. Aristotle's examples of an indistinctly perceived thing looking like a man and of the sun appearing a foot across are respectively

---

[39] Following Hamlyn in his commentary, pp. 107–8, 119; and see now the excellent discussion of Cashdollar (1973), 156–75.

cases in point—and cases which illustrate the fallibility of *phantasia*.[40] But what of the notion that while someone is perceiving a special object, e.g. seeing something white, he may also enjoy an infallible kind of *phantasia* of the self same object? It will not do to suppose (for example) that the perception in question is indistinct, leaving interpretative work for *phantasia* to do. For interpretation carries with it the possibility of error, especially if one cannot clearly *see* what colour one is looking at; it may look white, but be some other colour. I have no answer to this puzzle. All I can suggest is that Aristotle has here been overwhelmed by the scholasticism of this attempt to distinguish three sorts of *phantasia* corresponding to his three kinds of sense-perception, which strikes most readers as a baroque extravagance. That is, he is so intent on constructing parallel subdivisions that he fails to notice that the idea of an infallible type of *phantasia* cannot bear scrutiny.[41]

II. *Phantasia* and *Phantasma*

In *DA* 3. 3 Aristotle specifies the faculty of *phantasia* as 'that in virtue of which we say that a *phantasma* occurs to us', and contrasts this usage with 'saying something with a metaphorical use (sc. of *phantasia*)' (428^a1-2).[42] In the previous section we examined some texts which have suggested to some (wrongly, in my view) that *phantasia* is sometimes given an extremely broad Protagorean scope by

[40] I take it that these count as cases of *phantasia* just because the perception involved is non-paradigmatic: if in the first example one's perception was distinct, then it would be a straightforward instance of incidental *aisthēsis* (which might still, of course, be mistaken in its apprehension of the object in question); if in the second example the distance of the sun from the earth were such as our normal perceptual adjustments for perspective could accommodate, we should be dealing with a normal case of *aisthēsis* of a common object. Notice Aristotle's observation that *phantasia* goes wrong especially when the perceived object is a long way off (428^b29-30).

[41] Some members of the Symposium seemed in the discussion to feel that the schematism involved in Aristotle's distinctions between (for example) perception and *phantasia* of incidentals was so artificial that it might well break down in other contexts. We might then find Aristotle using the terms *aisthēsis* or *phantasia* indifferently to refer to any perception involving interpretation of the proper objects of perception, without any hint of the unreliability of *phantasia*. This would certainly suggest one explanation of why he treats now *aisthēsis*, now *aisthētikē phantasia* as the condition of movement in the lower animals. Cf. e.g. *DA* 431^a8-10 (*aisthēsis*); *MA* 701^a29-36 (*aisthēsis* or *phantasia* indifferently); *DA* $433^b31-434^a7$ (*phantasia*).

[42] I take the metaphorical use of *phantasia* which Aristotle has in mind to be what Simplicius thought: he wrote (ad loc.) that Aristotle distinguished the use of *phantasia* he was concerned with from that derived metaphorically from it 'when we use [the expression] *phantasia* for *to phainomenon* (what appears [to be the case]), both in sense perception and in belief' (cf. the common use of the word recorded by LSJ s.v.1, Bonitz, *Index* 811^a38-^b11). In short, Aristotle is concerned with the employment of 'appears' peculiarly appropriate to imagination or non-paradigmatic sensory experience, and treats its applications in ordinary perceptual reports or in statements of belief ('that seems to me a dangerous course of action') as extensions of that usage. His justification would presumably be that it is pre-eminently in cases of non-paradigmatic sensory experience that *phainetai* (and so *phantasia*) has distinctive force: it is most especially in these cases that one really needs an expression whereby one can convey that it *looks* so; in ordinary perceptual reports one can as well say: 'It's a dog' as: 'It appears to me to be a dog,' and in voicing one's beliefs: 'That is a dangerous course of action.' Contrast the way Grice (1961) would handle the question of basic sense and metaphor.

Aristotle. Here, by contrast, is a considered statement prominently placed in his official treatment of *phantasia* which has often been taken to restrict the faculty to experience of mental images (for *phantasma* is standardly translated 'image'). If the text really does mean this, it will require considerable ingenuity to explain on Aristotle's behalf why examples such as those of the sun appearing to be a foot across or of an indistinctly perceived thing looking like a man are pertinent to a discussion of *phantasia*. In neither of these examples does it seem plausible to suppose that the contemplation of mental images is involved; nor does Aristotle in presenting them suggest that it is.

I hold that it is a mistake to interpret *phantasma* at 428[a]1 as meaning 'mental image'.[43] 'Image' is not the root meaning of the word, nor is it a very frequent meaning in Plato; and there are strong contextual reasons, supported by a crucial piece of evidence in the passage of *De Insomniis* to which I have already alluded, for taking it otherwise here. I do not deny that in many Aristotelian contexts the *phantasmata* of which he speaks *are* what we would call mental images, nor that the word *phantasma* may conveniently and apply be translated and understood as 'image' (as e.g. in *De Memoria*); only that that translation is inappropriate in *DA* 3. 3.

Phantazō, the verb from which *phantasma* derives, means 'make apparent', 'make show', 'present'. Only passive and middle forms (in particular contexts it is often hard to tell which) occur in pre-Hellenistic literature;[44] we find these used both absolutely and with a complement or predicate. Thus in Herodotus Artabanus reminds Xerxes that God smites with his thunderbolt not the small animals but the 'excessive' ones, and does not allow them to 'make a show of themselves' (*phantazesthai*); the Scythians 'made themselves no longer apparent' to Darius (*ouketi ephantazonto sphi*); a dream 'is presented' to Xerxes (*oneiron phantazetai moi*) (7. 10; 4. 124; 7. 15). Plato supplies numerous examples of the verb with a complement. God is not a magician who presents himself or makes himself appear in different guises on different occasions (*phantazesthai allote en allais ideais*) (*Rep.* 380 D); the beautiful will not present itself to the philosophic lover as beautiful in the way that a face is (*oud' au phantasthēsetai auto to kalon hoion prosōpon ti*) (*Symp.* 211 A); some pleasures 'present themselves as great and numerous, but are in fact jumbled up with pains' (*megalas...tinas hama kai pollas phantastheisas, einai d' autas sumpephurmenas homou lupais*) (*Phil.* 51 A); and so on cf. Ast, *Lexicon Platonicum* s.v.). Notice how in these Platonic examples the guises described by means of the verb are all deceptive guises, guises which are at odds with reality.

We should consequently expect *phantasma* to mean 'appearance', 'apparition',

---

[43] In addition to the considerations I adduce in the text, I might add that it would be hard for anyone to maintain that the basic sense of *phantasia* had to do with mental images, when its commonest meaning in Greek is 'presentation', in the sense of 'what is presented'. If, on the other hand, Aristotle means to claim that the word is used in its basic sense in connection with just a particular sort of presentation, viz. non-paradigmatic sensory presentations, then his position is a very much more plausible one.

[44] LSJ s.v. II say 'in early writers only in Pass.'; but this is clearly wrong.

'guise', 'presentation', often with the strong implication of unreality. The pre-Aristotelian evidence in general bears out this expectation, although the range of the noun is narrower than that of the verb: I have not met with an instance of *phantasma* as 'guise', and 'presentation' never seems a very apt translation. In its earlier extant uses in the tragedians the word is used of ghosts or apparitions in dreams; and both Plato and Aristotle so use it on occasion (see LSJ, s.v. 1a). Plato, however, more often employs *phantasma* to talk of unreal appearances more generally; he treats it as the abstract noun corresponding to *phainesthai*, 'appear' (which perhaps helps to explain why in him, at least, the meanings 'guise' and 'presentation' available from *phantazō* are not exploited). Examples of this usage are particularly frequent in contexts where Plato is developing his metaphysics of copies and paradigms or where he is concerned with artificial representations.[45] It certainly hardens on occasion in such a way that *phantasma* can almost be said to *mean* 'image' or 'representation' in context. A notable psychological instance, which is very like Aristotle's favourite usage, occurs in the *Philebus* (40 A). But Plato himself makes the basis of his own usage quite plain in the *Sophist*. He there defines sophistry as a species of image-making, viz. *phantastikē*, appearance-making (or as Cornford translates, semblance-making); and he is naturally concerned with *phantasmata* that are images. But his word for image is *eidōlon*, not *phantasma*, and he explains why he calls one species of *eidōlon phantasma*—because there are some *eidōla* which *appear* to be faithful likenesses or copies (*eikones*) of an original, but are not really: *ar' ouk, epeiper phainetai men, eoike de ou, phantasma?* (236 B). And elsewhere (e.g. in the seventh deduction of the *Parmenides*) Plato uses *phantasma* as the noun corresponding to *phainesthai* when he has no concern with images: if you approach nearer to *the others*, then contrary to your first impression they appear many and different, and because of this appearance of difference (*tōi tou heterou phantasmati*), different in character and unlike.[46] Again, in the *Cratylus* Socrates insists against Protagoras and Euthydemus that things have a fixed being of their own, and are 'not dragged up and down relative to us or by us through private appearance' (*tōi hēmeterōi phantasmati*) (386 E).

It is with these last two examples of *phantasma* in Plato that one in our *De Insomniis* passage (460b3 ff.) is most closely comparable. In view of the Protagorean reference of the *Cratylus* text this might suggest once again a broad Protagorean conception of *phantasia* in Aristotle. But what disposes Plato to use *phantasma* in these contexts is the unreality or unreliability of the appearances in question; and it is with just such appearances that Aristotle too is concerned at 460b3 ff., as my earlier references to the passage showed. After giving his examples of the way in which persons in pathological conditions are liable to be deceived by false appearances, Aristotle adds a qualification: if a man is not gravely ill (Aristotle is thinking of fever), he can sometimes realize that what appears to him is false; but if his affliction is greater, he may be so deceived that

---

[45] e.g. *Rep.* 510 A, 532 C, 598 B, 599 A; *Soph.* 234 E, 236 C, 240 D.
[46] *Parm.* 165 D (cf. 166 A); see in general LSJ s.v. II.

(for example) he actually recoils from the animals he thinks he sees. Then comes the crucial couple of sentences (460^b16-20):

The reason for these things happening is that the governing element (*to kurion*) and that to which the *phantasmata* occur do not judge in respect of the same faculty. An indication of this is that the sun appears (*phainetai*) a foot across, but often something else contradicts *phantasia*.

Here *phantasma* is plainly used simply as the noun corresponding to *phainesthai*, one of the verbs Aristotle employs in presenting and discussing his examples of false appearances throughout the passage, as well as in the sun example. For the frequent employment of *phainetai* to indicate unreal appearances is the only feature of the passage which adequately and naturally accounts for the mention of a part of the soul concerned with *phantasmata*. The most striking support for this reading of *phantasmata* is Aristotle's immediate employment of the sun example to illustrate and justify his distinction between *to kurion* and 'that to which the *phantasmata* occur'. But that distinction is, of course, introduced to help explain how it is that false appearances deceive some but not others—as we learn in ch. 3 of *De Insomniis*, it is when *to kurion* is enfeebled or incapacitated that deception is most likely to take place. There is no hint, on the other hand, that Aristotle is at all preoccupied with mental images in the passage. The topic is 'being deceived with respect to our senses' (460^b3-4). And although the phenomena Aristotle mentions are pathological in character, and might be dismissed as hallucinations, and so as mere mental imagery, by a modern writer, that is not how he describes them. In the sun example, there is even less room for imagery; the same is true of the example known as 'Aristotle's experiment' which follows it in the text.[47] Could Aristotle, however, be using *phantasmata* to mean '*sense* images', what Hume would have called 'impressions'? That seems highly unlikely. Aristotle has a technical term, *aisthēma*, which at least in some contexts seems to denote an image-like sense datum.[48] But I do not know any text where it is very plausible to suppose that *phantasma* is used in this way; indeed, *phantasma* is sometimes contrasted with *aisthēma*, as being a term appropriate to occasions where there may be no actual perceiving going on.[49]

The similarities between this *De Insomniis* passage and *DA* 3. 428^a1-^b9, make

---

[47] *Insomn.* 2, 460^b20-2; cf. Ross's note on the passage in Aristotle (1955), 273–4.

[48] For a good discussion of the evidence, see Sorabji in Aristotle (1972*b*), 82–3.

[49] Cf. *DA* 431^a14-15; 432^a9-10; *Insomn.* 462^a29-30. In the second of these passages Aristotle says that '*phantasmata* are as *aisthēmata*, except without matter'. 'Without matter' has caused difficulty. Rodier said (ad loc.): 'En réalité, les *aisthēmata* n'ont pas plus de matière que les *phantasmata*, puisque la sensation ne saisit que la forme sans la matière. Seulement la sensation se produit en présence d'un objet matériel, tandis que l'imagination peut avoir lieu même en l'absence de cet objet.' I take Aristotle to mean that in imagining it is as if one were actually perceiving, but of course the physical basis of the sense image of actual perception, viz. the coloration of the *korē*, is not present— or at least, if it *is* present (as in the case of genuinely perceptual appearances, like seeing an indistinct object as a man), it is not the physical basis of *phantasia*: the matter of a *phantasma* even of a perceptual sort is a change or motion in the sense organ caused by the perception itself (cf. *DA* 428^b25-30; *Insomn.* 460^b22-5). On the matter of *aisthēmata*, see Sorabji in Aristotle (1972*b*), 83; Sorabji (1974/1979), 19 n. 22.

it hard to resist the conclusion that when Aristotle specifies *phantasia* as 'that in virtue of which we say that a *phantasma* occurs to us' (428ᵃ1−2), *phantasma* again does duty simply as the noun corresponding to cautious, sceptical, and non-committal *phainetai*. Here, too, Aristotle illustrates his arguments with examples employing the verb, twice as an explicit pointer to the nature of *phantasia*; he uses the same sun example, which we know from *De Insomniis* to constitute an instance of a *phantasma* in this sense of 'appearance'. Moreover, to read *phantasma* in this way allows us to see in the analyses which follow the fulfilment of a methodological promise held out by the formula at 428ᵃ1−2. For notice that *phantasia* is not stated to be the faculty in virtue of which *phantasmata* occur to us, but that in virtue of which *we say that* a *phantasma* occurs to us. I take Aristotle to be intending by this formula to distinguish cases of *phantasia* by the linguistic behaviour they prompt. Now the linguistic behaviour in question must surely be the utterance of factual statements about what is perceived (or as it were perceived) which include and rely significantly on *phainetai*, used in the cautious, disbelieving, or non-committal way I have attempted to specify. That, at least, is the one type of locution which is prominent and is implied by Aristotle to be an important clue to the character of *phantasia* in the body of the section of the chapter that begins with the formula about *phantasma*.

Aristotle's choice of this linguistic criterion as the working guideline for his investigation of the connection or want of connection between *phantasia* and other faculties of the soul, perception, belief, knowledge, etc., is one of the most impressive features of his treatment of the imagination. It provides a particularly clear and arresting testimony to his enthusiasm for philosophizing on the basis of *endoxa*, of course.[50] But it is also evidence of deep insight into the problems of characterizing a psychological phenomenon such as imagination. For in attempting to say what makes imagination different from sense-perception or belief Aristotle steers clear of two opposite but equally fruitless modes of differentiation, with which he was none the less familiar. He does not make the distinction between imagination and perception in physical or physiological terms; he employs those terms in his causal analysis, at 428ᵇ10 ff., but only after he has sought to clarify in quite different terms what the two phenomena are that he wants to relate in a causal connection. Nor, on the other hand, does Aristotle adopt the procedure associated with Hume, of reflecting on the presence of sensory features in imagining, and then attempting to give an account, based on introspection, of the difference in sensory quality between imagining and perception. He had once defined *phantasia* as a sort of weak perception, in the early *Rhetoric* (1370ᵃ28); but that approach has been abandoned by the time of *De Anima*. Instead he opts firmly for behavioural criteria. Thus at 427ᵇ16−24 he asks: is believing a voluntary activity like imagining? Are the emotional consequences of imagining the same as those of belief?[51] And he divines that

[50] Cf. Owen (1961), 83−92.
[51] At *Metaph.* 1010ᵇ9−11 he distinguishes between the action appropriate to perception and that appropriate to *phantasia*, unfortunately too briefly and obscurely: cf. Kirwan (1971), 109−10.

linguistic behaviour is of fundamental importance. Not only does he advert to it as a means of differentiating imagination from perception, as when he notices that the language a man characteristically uses when imagining—'appears'—is not what one would expect if he were reporting what he could see without difficulty (428^a12-15). He also hits on the propensity to say *phainetai* as giving a way of *identifying* instances of imagination or *phantasia*. Imagining is not the sort of thing one can in any interesting sense observe; and its intentional, thought-dependent aspects make language a peculiarly appropriate vehicle for its realization, not only its communication.

It is true that within the section 428^a1-^b9, it is only at 428^a12-15, in the example of an indistinctly perceived thing looking like a man, that Aristotle explicitly draws attention to the use of the *word 'phainetai'*. But it is hard to see any more immediate reason for his taking the sun example to be a case of *phantasia* than that he has observed that people say: 'The sun looks a foot across', when they believe its size to be very much larger (cf. 428^b2-3). The sceptical, cautious, or non-committal implications of using the word may, as I have suggested, have led him to assert that 'most *phantasiai* turn out false' (428^a12). And when he remarks that things appear (e.g. dreams) although sense-perception is not involved (428^a7-8), it may be the disposition people have to employ *phainetai* in their dream-reports which is again for Aristotle the most immediate pointer to the presence of *phantasia*—or at least what governs his approach to *phantasia* in dreaming.

This last point deserves elaboration. Dreaming is a particularly interesting sort of *phantasia*, not least because with dreaming neither of the criteria for imagination laid down by Aristotle at 427^b16-24 is satisfied: dreaming is not subject to the will, except in Freudian ways which Aristotle shows no sign of anticipating; nor is one always as emotionally detached from the horrors of a dream as from a horrific picture—sometimes it is much more as if belief were involved, as Aristotle recognizes in ch. 3 of *De Insomniis*. Consequently dreaming presents a challenge to my thesis that there is a unity to Aristotle's treatment of *phantasia* which is compatible with identifying *phantasia* with imagination.

One might perhaps suppose that, if a philosopher is going to associate dreams with imagination at all, he will do so on the basis of the consideration that dreams involve mental imagery. That is at any rate the sort of interpretation a reading of Ross's account of Aristotle's treatment of *phantasia* might suggest (1923, 144); and certainly Aristotle's use of *phantasma* with respect to dreams in e.g. ch. 1 of *De Insomniis* is compatible with such an interpretation. But in fact between dreams and cases of *phantasia* which do satisfy the criteria for imagination spelt out at 427^b16-24 Aristotle forges a different link. What he exploits in *De Insomniis*, and indeed makes central to his account of dreaming, is the appropriateness of *phainetai*, 'appears', both to descriptions of the content of dreams and to the seeing of aspects.

He takes as the starting-point for his analysis of dreams the phenomenon of pathological appearances—the way marks on the wall look like animals to the sick man, or the way that, from the slightest resemblance, the amorous man takes a boy he sees in the distance or with back turned to be his beloved (*Insomn.* 460^{b}3 ff.). This is not just the point from which Aristotle happens to begin; in ch. 1 of *De Insomniis*, after puzzling over the relation of dreaming to sense-perception and judgement, he seems to despair of finding any other mode of attack on the problem of the nature of dreaming (458^{b}25–8):

With respect to this whole matter, so much at least is clear, that the very same thing which is responsible for our being deceived while suffering from fever causes this phenomenon [sc. being deceived] in sleep.

The similarity between the two cases which leads Aristotle to suppose their causal analysis must be the same is evidently that, as with the pathological seeing of aspects, so in dreaming things appear to be what they are not, and are often mistakenly taken to be what they appear. This is borne out not only by his explicit concentration on the phenomenon of deception here and throughout much of the treatise, but by the thoroughgoing character of the parallelism he endeavours to establish in ch. 3 between dreaming and pathological 'appearances'. He goes so far as to construe the *phainetai* of dream-reports as the *phainetai* appropriate to the appearance of an aspect. What happens in a dream, according to him, is that *something* looks, in virtue of some small resemblance, like something else (*Insomn.* 461^{b}10–21): it is not just that Coriscus appears to me, but that a trace of my sense-datum of Coriscus appears to me as Coriscus (ibid. 461^{b}21–30). Coleridge was wittingly or unwittingly a pretty faithful Aristotelian when he described dreams as devices 'by which the blind fancy would fain interpret to the mind the painful sensations of distempered sleep'.[52]

Now the pathological seeing of aspects shares with dreaming an important difference from cases like seeing an indistinct object as a man, or (to take an instance from *De Insomniis*) seeing the shifting shapes made by clouds now as a man, now as a centaur (461^{b}19–21). The difference in question is that very failure to satisfy the criteria of imagination proposed at *DA* 3. 3, 427^{b}16–24, which we noted with respect to dreams: the fevered man's appearances are *not* subject to his will; and if his affliction is bad enough, not only his emotions but his actions will resemble those appropriate to belief (cf. *Insomn.* 460^{b}15–16). But Aristotle's own unitary explanation of dreams and such pathological phenomena, on the one hand, and the similarity between pathological and normal seeing of aspects, on the other, put us in a position in which we can now exhibit the unity in Aristotle's conception of *phantasia* while retaining our characterization of it as imagination. For the causal explanation of dreaming and of pathological appearances accounts for just those features of these phenomena which make them unlike cases of *phantasia* which satisfy the criteria of 427^{b}16–24. It is evidently because sleep and fever impair the operation of our faculties in general, leaving *phantasia* alone efficacious, that the will has no control over what appears

---

[52] *Biographia Literaria*, p. 5 of the Everyman Edition.

to us in such conditions (see *Insomn.* 460ᵇ28–461ᵇ5)—or to put it in a more Aristotelian way, we cannot *act* when asleep (cf. *EN* 1098ᵇ31–1099ᵃ3). And as Aristotle himself labours to show, it is for the same reason that the 'governing element', the faculty we have for making judgements on the basis of what our senses tell us, is also stifled, so that appearances are taken as veridical by default (see *Insomn.* 460ᵇ13–16; 461ᵇ5–462ᵃ8); and consequently *phainetai* can be employed to refer to the appearances in a sceptical manner only by an observer (or the patient himself upon recovery, the dreamer when he has woken). Should these differences incline us to withhold the name 'imagination' from dreaming and the pathological seeing of aspects? The question has by this stage, I hope, an artificial air. We could appeal to 427ᵇ16–24 and refuse the name if we wished: but we could also agree to be impressed more by the similarity between these phenomena and the central cases of imagination, and rule that the criteria of 427ᵇ16–24 apply to *normal* imagination, reflecting that in *De Insomniis* Aristotle has provided both a description and a causal explanation of the abnormality of what we might call *abnormal* imagination.[53]

III. *In Confinio Intellectus et Sensus*

It is instructive to notice what occasions Aristotle's introduction of the topic of *phantasia* in *DA* 3. By the beginning of that chapter he has completed his account of sense perception, and he now turns to consider thinking, reminding us of what his investigation of the opinions of his philosophical predecessors in 1. 2 had revealed: that soul in animals is defined by them in one of two ways above all, by reference to the capacity for movement or to the capacity for judgement (criteria accepted by Aristotle himself: 3. 9, 432ᵃ15–17; cf. 1. 2, 403ᵇ25–7 *et passim*, 3. 3,

---

[53] Here I am attracted by the argument of Ryle (1949/1963), 244–5: 'Make-believe is compatible with all degrees of scepticism and credulity, a fact which is relevant to the supposed problem, "How can a person fancy that he sees something, without realizing that he is not seeing it?"...The fact that people can fancy that they see things, are pursued by bears, or have a grumbling appendix, without realizing that it is nothing but fancy, is simply a part of the unsurprising general fact that not all people are, all the time, at all ages and in all conditions, as judicious or critical as could be wished.' Ryle has been criticized for 'lumping together', as conditions in which people are particularly prone to be uncritical of their fancies, 'dreams, delirium, extreme thirst, hypnosis, and conjuring-shows' (p. 233): see Ishiguro (1966), 160–1, and more fully Shorter (1971), 138–9, 142–3. And no doubt it is indeed dangerous to suppose that, just because in all these conditions one can be said to have imagined things (no less than if one visualized Helvellyn knowing perfectly well that one was doing so), a genuinely unitary concept of imagination is applicable to all the different cases. But where we apply a single word without evident ambiguity to different phenomena, there is a case for assuming that there are important conceptual connections and affinities between them (why else should the same word be used? and how is one to be sure that in differentiating distinct senses of a word one is not merely extrapolating illegitimately from different contexts of its use?). At any rate, it is plain that Aristotle thought that a single faculty of imagination was involved in the very various phenomena he treats as cases of *phantasia*; and I have endeavoured, in the manner of more recent students of the imagination such as Strawson (1970) and Scruton (1974) to trace the similarities between the different phenomena noticed by Aristotle which might have fortified him in this belief.

$427^{a}17-21$). The fact that both in thought and in perception the soul judges and is acquainted with things that are led the ancients, Aristotle tells us, to identify the two faculties. And so in his attempt to determine the nature of thinking he takes for his first task the demonstration that this identification is a mistake. He observes that all animals have sense-perception, but not all think; and he moves immediately to forestall a possible counter-argument based on the idea that animals *do* think in a way, because they have *phantasia*, which is also a sort of perception.[54] The equation cannot be thus circuitously reinstated. *Phantasia* (which, Aristotle agrees, nearly all animals[55] do have) is different both from sense-perception and from thinking, although sense-perception is indispensable to it as it is itself to *hupolēpsis* ($427^{b}6-16$). This thesis about *phantasia* evidently requires defence; and in a way the whole of the rest of the chapter is just that defence, a digression necessary for Aristotle's justification of his treatment of thinking as a genuinely independent faculty in the chapters which follow (3. 4–8). The first sections of the discussion of *phantasia* ($427^{b}16-428^{b}9$) show that it cannot be the same as perception or thinking (at least in the sense of *noein* which most interests Aristotle and which he studies at 3. 4–8). The final section ($428^{b}10-429^{a}9$) shows how sense-perception is indispensable to it (argument for the contention that thinking requires *phantasia* is reserved until 3. 8, $432^{a}3-10$).

Aristotle shows himself aware, then, of a real temptation to assimilate *phantasia* to perception on the one hand and thinking on the other (cf. also 3. 9, $432^{a}31-^{b}3$). But he was intent on demonstrating why these temptations must be resisted rather than on exploring them. This preoccupation with refutation, as so often in Aristotle, has unfortunate consequences. His combative instincts give him a predilection for single short knock-down arguments which can leave the hungry reader unsatisfied. In stressing non-identities he does not pause to reflect on the equally important affinities between *phantasia* and the other faculties which incidentally come to light in the course of his arguments. Nor does he appear to have tried to formulate in his own mind a single statement about what *phantasia* is like (as distinct from what it is not like), free from the inconsistencies which at least apparently result when we lay side by side observations he finds it natural to make in one context with opposed observations or ways of speaking which seem to come naturally to him in other contexts. For us these features of his treatment of *phantasia* are as interesting as his avowed aims and intended achievements.

Although at $427^{b}14-15$ and in a number of other places Aristotle states or implies that *phantasia* is not the same as thinking (*dianoia, noein*), it is perhaps significant that in his official account of *phantasia* in *DA* 3. 3 he seems to waver on this point—as though when he came to consider *phantasia* at length on its

---

[54] For this interpretation of the connection of $427^{b}14-16$ with what precedes, see Rodier ad loc.

[55] 'Nearly all animals': the doctrine of this chapter (cf. $428^{a}9-11$, 21, 23), and elsewhere ($415^{a}10$). At the end of the day he allows, notwithstanding his *aporia* on the matter, that even 'incomplete' animals have an indeterminate sort of *phantasia* (cf. 2. 3, $414^{b}16$, 3. 11, $433^{b}31-434^{a}5$, with Rodier on $413^{b}22$, $433^{b}31$, $434^{a}4$; Hicks on $434^{a}1$); or at least, those of them that move: presumably the stationary animals (cf. 1. 5, $410^{b}19-20$, with Hicks ad loc.) do not.

own account, not briefly in the course of comments on thinking, he had found it more like thinking than his usual characterization[56] of it as a *sine qua non* of thinking suggests. At any rate, he there states his favourite thesis about the indispensability of *phantasia* to thinking in the more restricted formulation: 'there is no *hupolēpsis* without *phantasia*' (427^{b}16); his argument for the non-identity of *phantasia* and *dianoia* is billed as proof that *phantasia* and *hupolēpsis* are not the same (427^{b}16–17), and actually confines itself to differences between *phantasia* and *doxazein*, believing (427^{b}17–24); and he moves on to the next section of the chapter with the cautious observation 'thinking...seems[57] to include on the one hand *phantasia* and on the other *hupolēpsis*' (427^{b}27–8).

Hupolēpsis is 'taking something to be the case' or (in that sense) 'judgement', a general notion here including as its species *epistēmē* (knowledge), *doxa* (belief), *phronēsis* (practical understanding), and their opposites (427^{b}24–6). The illustration of *phantasia* Aristotle gives is of someone producing things before his eyes like the mnemonists (427^{b}18–19). It might seem natural to infer that Aristotle here supposes the relation of *hupolēpsis* and *phantasia* as species of *noein* to be that of the disposition or act of judgement and the piece of thinking from which the disposition or act results.

But it would be rash to attribute to him the view that the activity of thinking is *phantasia* on the basis of this evidence. He has not stated that *phantasia* and *hupolēpsis* are the only forms of thought; and elsewhere he shows himself ready to distinguish between *phantasia* and the process of thinking. A passage from *De Memoria* (449^{b}31–450^{a}5) is particularly instructive, employing as it does language similar to that Aristotle uses when speaking of *phantasia* at 427^{b}16 ff.:

It is not possible to think without *phantasma*. For the same effect occurs in thinking as in drawing a diagram. For in the latter case, though we do not make any use of the fact that the size of the triangle is determinate, we none the less draw it with a determinate size. And similarly someone who is thinking, even if he is not thinking of something with a size, places something with a size before his eyes, but thinks of it not as having a size.[58]

This passage makes it plain that not merely the *hupolēpsis* which results from thinking, but the process of thinking itself is distinct from *phantasia*, which it nevertheless requires. Aristotle, exploiting a point made by Plato in the *Republic* (510 D–511 A), recognizes that what one engages in thinking about and what one imagines in so thinking may be distinct in the sense he hints at.

---

[56] Cf. 403^{a}9; 431^{a}17; *Mem.* 449^{b}31–450^{a}1. Imagination seems to be regaining some of the credit as handmaid to thought which it lost in the heyday of Oxford philosophy: see e.g. Vendler (1972), 73–80; Kaplan (1969), 225–31, with Quine (1969), 342–3.

[57] Rodier (ad loc.) took *dokei* here to mark an 'opinion courante' (i.e. an *endoxon*), not a view of Aristotle's own. This may be right; but (as we shall see) there is reason to think Aristotle found something tempting in the opinion. I have not put any weight on 427^{b}16–17 in this connection, since the text is doubtful and obscure. But emboldened by Professor W. J. Verdenius, I would retain *noēsis*, and translate (with Professor D. J. Allan): 'It is clear that *phantasia* is not the same sort of thinking as *hupolēpsis*.'

[58] Translated after Sorabji in Aristotle (1972b); cf. his comments ad loc., and pp. 5–7 of his ch. 1.

It is perhaps not possible to demonstrate that the distinction between *phantasia* and the activity of thinking adumbrated in this *De Memoria* passage is pre-supposed in the treatment of thinking in *De Anima* (although it is perfectly consistent with the doctrine of 3. 4–8).[59] But the fact that Aristotle in 3. 3 makes his distinction merely between *phantasia* and *hupolēpsis* is not enough to suggest that he has not yet seen that distinction between thinking and *phantasia*. For we should recall that a principal concern of 3. 3 is to show that *phantasia* is not any of the more familiar capacities in virtue of which we *judge* and are acquainted with what is. It is enough for him to demonstrate that *phantasia* is not *hupolēpsis* or any of its species. And if he guardedly allows that *phantasia* may be reckoned a species of thinking, that may in part be due to this overriding concern with judgement: he may be prepared for the sake of argument to concede to the man who equates *phantasia* and thinking *tout court* that *phantasia* is a sort of thinking, so long as it is distinguished from thought in the sense of judgement, *hupolēpsis*.

At the same time, Aristotle may have been the readier to make the concession because of a feature of the arguments by which he distinguishes *phantasia* from *hupolēpsis*. He notes that *phantasia*, unlike belief, is up to us when we wish; and that the emotional responses appropriate to belief and *phantasia* are different—in the former case 'we are immediately affected', in the latter it is 'as if we were looking at terrible or enheartening things in a picture' (427ᵇ17–24). These criteria of *phantasia* do not distinguish it from the activity of thinking: that, too, is in our power when we wish (cf. 417ᵇ24); nor does the thought of disaster or success automatically inspire immediate gloom or cheer. Aristotle may well have been persuaded by these features common to *phantasia* and thinking to allow the claim of *phantasia* to be a sort of thinking at 427ᵇ28. Nor is that claim without plausibility. A mnemonist instructing his pupil might well ask him to *think* of a set of places in which mental images may be put.

So Aristotle is tempted to view *phantasia* as a form of thinking, or at least as a thought-like component of thinking. But as we saw earlier, he also speaks of *phantasia* in ways which suggest that, if pressed, he would have had to agree that the thought-like features which he takes to be characteristic of *phantasia* at 427ᵇ16–24 are not invariable features of it. Thus it seems unlikely that he would wish to allow that the persons in the grip of fevers or strong emotion described in *De Insomniis* are able to engage in *phantasia* or not as and when they wish: what appears to them is patently not under their control. And he obviously does not think such persons capable of maintaining the emotional detachment from their *phantasmata* seen as typical of *phantasia* at 427ᵇ23–4: they, like dreamers, are often helplessly deceived, even to the point of moving bodily towards or away from what appears to them. Moreover, in just this context in *De Insomniis* Aristotle permits himself to speak of *phantasia* as a faculty in virtue of which we

---

[59] For in *DA* Aristotle seems to be concerned with judgements, not with the process of thinking, in passages in which the relation of thought and *phantasmata* is in question.

judge (460ᵇ16–18). Here, evidently, *phantasia* is much more like perception (one might think of its as *mis*perception)[60] than thought.

So, too, in the remaining part of the discussion in *DA* 3. 3, from 428ᵃ1 to the end of the chapter. It is, for example, striking that, for his causal analysis of *phantasia*, Aristotle draws from the considerations which have filled the preceding pages the single idea that it is thought 'not to occur without sense-perception, but only in things which perceive and with respect to those things of which there is perception' (428ᵇ11–13); and the chief conclusion of the analysis is that the change resulting from actual sense-perception which he argues is *phantasia* 'must be like perception' (428ᵇ14). When he goes on to infer that it, too, must be capable of truth and falsehood, working out an elaborate comparison between the propensities of sense-perception and *phantasia* for the one or the other (428ᵇ17–30), it looks as though, having begun by treating *phantasia* as a form of thinking, he ends by taking sense-perception to be the key to its nature.[61] In particular, in concentrating on its propensity to give true or false views of facts, Aristotle seems clearly to count *phantasia*, like sense-perception, as a faculty of judgement— contrary to what the discussion at 427ᵇ16–24 might have led one to expect. It is worth stressing this point, since some scholars, adopting Ross's emendation at 428ᵃ3 (which turns the statement of the manuscripts that *phantasia* is a faculty or disposition for judgement into a question), suppose that in rejecting at 428ᵃ5–ᵇ9 any identification of *phantasia* with other faculties of judgement, Aristotle means to deny that it is itself such a faculty (so e.g. Rees 1971). As Rodier saw (1900, ii. 412–13; 416) emendation at this point is unnecessary; and the associated interpretation is impossible. For Aristotle glosses 'faculties in accordance with which we judge' by the words 'and take things truly or falsely' (*alētheuomen ē pseudometha*, 428ᵃ4). And his strategy throughout the section 428ᵃ5–ᵇ9 is not to

---

[60] An interpretation given further licence by *Insomn.* 458ᵇ31–3. There, having referred in a general way to the *phantasmata* discussed at 460ᵇ3–27, Aristotle remarks that whether the faculties of sense-perception and *phantasia* are the same or different, it is clear that sense-perception is a *sine qua non* of *phantasia*: 'For mis-seeing and mis-hearing belong to the man who sees and hears something which is truly there, but not what he takes it to be'.

[61] We need not suppose that the original association with thinking is abandoned. It is certainly significant that Aristotle relates *phantasia* to perception rather than to thinking in his definition at 429ᵃ1–2. But the significance lies in the evidence his treatment of *phantasia* affords of the consistency of his approach to psychology. The fact that Aristotle's definition is a *causal* definition suggests that he is characteristically concerned, in his discussion at 428ᵇ10 ff., with the question what it is in our psychological nature which makes us able to exercise *phantasia* in the way we do. And his answer 'prior perception' characteristically relates *phantasia* first and foremost to the hierarchy of faculties distinguished in book 2. It does not greatly illuminate the specific psychological character of *phantasia*. The definition is presumably supposed to be true equally of dreams and memory, where the prior perception must be a thing of the past, and of the 'seeing as' cases, phenomenologically quite distinct, in which the prior perception has to be contemporaneous (I take it that Aristotle insists on the priority here simply because it is a precondition of one's seeing *x* as *y* that one should see *x*). And the definition leaves it quite open what further conditions besides prior perception must be satisfied if the change that is *phantasia* is to occur. Do I have to activate *phantasmata*—and if so what governs my success? Or if *phantasmata* just happen to me, why those particular *phantasmata* at that precise moment? It is not even clear that the definition could not apply as well to Aristotle's conception of discursive thinking (*dianoeisthai*) as to his notion of *phantasia* (cf. 432ᵃ3–8; 408ᵇ1–29).

argue that the dimension of truth and falsehood is inhabited by sense-perception, knowledge, belief, etc., but not by *phantasia*. It is rather to maintain that, although *phantasia* is properly to be assessed for truth and falsehood no less than perception or belief, the assessment has or can have different results in the case of *phantasia* from those obtained in the other cases. This is the point of the sun example (428^{b}2–9); and besides remarking that perceptions are always true, but some *phantasiai* false (428^{a}11–12), Aristotle distinguishes *phantasia* from knowledge and understanding (*nous*) on the very same ground (428^{a}16–18), and is prepared to concede an initial plausibility to the identification of *phantasia* and belief precisely because they cannot be differentiated in this way (428^{a}18–19).

So the unity of Aristotle's conception of *phantasia* begins to look somewhat fragile. One might argue on his behalf that in different parts of *DA* 3. 3 Aristotle endows *phantasia* with such very different features just because he has different sorts of exercise of the imagination in view. Seeing a distant object as a man (cf. 428^{a}12–15) *is* very like seeing, while imagining a set of places for mnemonic purposes (cf. 427^{b}18–20) *is* very like thinking; and in the former case one does—albeit hesitantly—take something truly or falsely (viz. the distant object to be a man), but not in the latter case. It would perhaps be possible to place Aristotle's examples and his remarks about them on a complex, but consistent and unified, conceptual map of the imagination, in the style I have adopted in the two preceding sections of this paper. But profitable and charitable though the exercise might be, it is time to notice that Aristotle himself shows no sign of being aware of the tensions within his account of *phantasia*; nor, consequently, of the importance and difficulty of the philosophical task of saying just how thinking and sensing both contribute to the imagination. Moreover, some of the inconsistencies of Aristotle's account seem more than merely apparent. Doubtless the fact that in belief, unlike *phantasia*, one *necessarily* takes something truly or falsely (cf. 427^{b}20–1)^{62} does serve to differentiate *phantasia* and belief. Yet it does not follow (as he evidently thinks) that *phantasia* is not sometimes a sort of *hupolēpsis* closer to belief than to knowledge or practical understanding. As commentators have noticed, it is difficult to report or discuss such examples as the sun looking a foot across without introducing words like 'suppose', 'conjecture', etc., which connote precisely the sort of thinking involved in *hupolēpsis*; and Aristotle himself, in an unguarded moment, once uses *dokei* in presenting the example (*Insomn.* 1, 458^{b}29).^{63}

---

[62] 'Takes something truly or falsely' is the sense *ē pseudesthai ē alētheuein* must have if this observation is to supply a reason for differentiating belief and *phantasia*. It does not prove the difference Aristotle alleges, viz. that believing, unlike *phantasia*, is not in our power. Hamlyn (ad loc.) notes: 'The real point is that beliefs are determined at least by *our view of the facts*; this is not true of imagining something.' Cf. Scruton (1974), 94–7. This construction of the Greek is in agreement with Greek usage (cf. LSJ s.vv.); and it is supported by the fact that Aristotle at 428^{a}4 glosses *krinomen*, 'judge', by *alētheuomen ē pseudometha*.

[63] But although Aristotle does appear to be committed to an inconsistency here, it is perhaps not a very serious one. For he could simply withdraw his claim that *phantasia* is quite distinct from *hupolēpsis*, while insisting that it is to be differentiated from the particular sort of *hupolēpsis* he has in mind at 427^{b}17–24, viz. *doxa* (belief).

Conclusion

My intention, however, has been to show reason to celebrate Aristotle's pioneering treatment of the imagination. The great virtue of his account is its recognition of the range of psychological phenomena which deserve to be associated in this familial concept. His attempt to generalize from them about the logical peculiarities of the imagination is not carried through with a clear and steady view of the whole topic. But it remains seminal for anyone who seeks a better understanding. For Aristotle reminds us of the variety of the phenomena we need to consider, and compels us to find ways of connecting them; he puts in our hands, even if he himself does not exploit them very fully, many of the contrasts and comparisons which seem fundamental for the conceptual mapping of imagination; and his very inconsistencies suggest crucial problems in its comparative anatomy.[64]

Additional Note 1991

Since this article and its principal theses have attracted a fair amount of comment, while its author has moved on to other concerns, it seemed best to leave the piece unchanged for its appearance in the present volume. Discussions of the article are included in Watson (1982), Labarrière (1984), Modrak (1986, cf. also 1987), Watson (1988), Wedin (1988).

[64] In writing this essay I have incurred numerous debts of gratitude: to Professor J. I. Ackrill, who proposed the topic to me; to the members of the Southern Association for Ancient Philosophy (and particularly Professor D. W. Hamlyn), who heard and discussed an ancestor of the present paper at their meeting in Cambridge in 1973; and to Messrs J. Barnes, M. F. Burnyeat and R. R. K. Sorabji, each of whom sent me valuable comments on a penultimate draft. I hope I have made profitable use of their generous help. The paper was read to the 1975 Symposium Aristotelicum; and it has been revised in the light of the discussion at the Symposium, and of comments made to me privately by its members, particularly (once more) Richard Sorabji and my chairman, Michael Woods.

15
THE COGNITIVE ROLE OF
PHANTASIA IN ARISTOTLE

DOROTHEA FREDE

I. Problems with a Unified Concept of *Phantasia*

THE difficulties with the concept of *phantasia* start with the translation. One problem is that *phantasia* does triple duty. It designates the capacity, the activity or process, and the product or result. It is, of course, not alone in having so many chores. 'Sight', for example, in English has as many functions: it signifies the capacity to see, the seeing, and what is seen. This multiplicity need not by itself create any confusions. We usually know quite well whether we mean the capacity of sight or the seeing or the thing seen. Even grammatically it is usually clear what we mean: 'you are a terrible sight' is quite unequivocal, as is 'my sight is getting worse and worse'.

What makes *phantasia* more troublesome than 'vision' is partly that we have no single word in English that would do all three jobs. But, unfortunately, that is not the major problem in Aristotle. We are also unsure what capacity, what process, and what product the word denotes in each case. In order to provide a preliminary clarification I want, as other commentators have done before me, to refer to the etymological derivation of *phantasia* from *phainesthai* or *phantazesthai*[1] and claim that 'appearance' in a wider sense should be regarded as the central meaning to which all functions of the term are related. It would then be (i) the capacity to experience an appearance, (ii) the on-going appearance itself, and (iii) what appears.

Sometimes, however, this does not seem appropriate; rather something like our 'imagination' would be more adequate. The latter sense is not unrelated to 'appearance', since it means something like the *creation* of an appearance, so that it is related to the former like active to passive (or medium).[2] Unfortunately this is still not all, there is yet another distinction to be observed. Just as we do in

---

© Dorothea Frede, 1992.

[1] Cf. Schofield (1979), 105 n. 11. Aristotle often treats *phantasia* as the noun corresponding to *phainesthai* (cf. *DA*, 428ª7, 14; 428ᵇ1, 3; 433ª28). Where there is no question of simple appearance but intentional imagining is meant he uses *phantasthēnai* (433ᵇ12).

[2] In its active sense it also has those three functions, and 'imagination' covers all three meanings: the capacity to create appearances, the creating itself ('imagining') and the created appearance itself, what is imagined. Aristotle does not use *phantasia* for poetic creativity but calls the poet an *eikōnopoios* (*Po.* 1460ᵇ9). For an interesting overview of the history of the 'creative' sense of phantasia cf. Rosenmeyer (1986).

English, so one distinguishes in Greek between a 'mere appearance', a phantom, and a 'real appearance', a phenomenon.

Aristotle uses *phantasia* in all those meanings, although he most frequently seems to presuppose the passive or medial meaning of 'having an appearance'; but the active use in the sense of *eidōlopoiein* (*DA* 427ᵇ18–20) also occurs.[3] Aristotle's often displayed insouciance about the different meanings does not imply any confusion, however. Throughout his psychological writings he not only distinguishes very carefully between capacity, activity, and product, but in the case of *phantasia* he also often switches to *phantasma* to designate the product, and occasionally uses *phantastikon* for the capacity (432ᵃ31).[4]

But even granted that Aristotle himself does not suffer from confusion about the many meanings, the crucial question remains: what kinds of 'appearances' does Aristotle have in mind and why should there be a special capacity for them? The treatment of *phantasia* in 3. 3, the only place where it is discussed extensively, is confusing, at least at first sight. On the one hand, *phantasia* is regarded as a necessary condition of thought ('there is no supposition without it', 427ᵇ15); on the other hand its definition suggests that *phantasiai* are mere after-images of sense-perception, often false ones (428ᵃ11–16), which guide animals since they do not have reason, and human beings when they are disturbed by passion or disease, or are asleep (429ᵃ4–8).

Because of such seeming inconsistencies there has been quite some discussion of this subject in the last years, especially about the cognitive value that Aristotle attributes to *phantasia*.[5] It is not possible to do justice to all these attempts here, let alone to go into the philosophical intricacies of the different interpretations that have been suggested. I will confine myself here to a 'minimal account' of the role that Aristotle ascribes to *phantasia* in 3. 3 and then try to show how this is borne out in the rest of the book and in other relevant texts. I call my account minimal since I do not pretend to deal adequately with all the problems the compressed text contains.

Let us first take a brief look at the problems with 3. 3 itself. Although the overall intention of the chapter is clear, namely to distinguish *phantasia* from the other capacities of the soul,[6] Aristotle seems here to display the untidy-genius

[3] Without wanting to be over-confident on this much debated question, my suspicion is that this active use of imagination, the *eidōlopoiein* in 427ᵇ20 (that is up to us and is *neither true nor false*) is the sense of *phantasia* that is ruled out in 428ᵃ2 as *kata metaphoran*, since it never recurs in *De Anima* and does not suit the *cognitive use* which Aristotle wants to ascribe to *phantasia*: i.e. as a capacity according to which we judge and are right or wrong (*kath' has krinomen kai alētheuomen ē pseudometha*, 428ᵃ3), and which does affect us emotionally (cf. 432ᵇ8 as against 427ᵇ24). Most importantly, free phantasizing does not fit the definition of *phantasia* that is soon to follow: a motion in the soul caused by sense-perception.

[4] At that point Aristotle expresses doubt whether it is a separate faculty of the soul or whether only its being is different (*tōi men einai—pantōn heteron*). When discussing the soul's capacities themselves Aristotle never includes a *phantastikon* (413ᵃ23–5; ᵇ12–13, 414ᵇ31–2). In *Somn. Vig.* 459ᵃ16, 458ᵇ30, 462ᵃ8 it is clear that it is the same faculty as *aisthēsis*, only the activity is different.

[5] Cf. Nussbaum (1978), 221–69; Schofield (1979); Watson (1982); Modrak (1986, 1987a).

[6] Leaving aside the criticism of the pre-Socratics' identification of thinking and perceiving (427ᵃ19–ᵇ6)

syndrome to an unusual degree. Repetitions and inconsistencies abound. The definition of *phantasia* itself is postponed till the last section of the chapter (428^{b}10 ff.); criteria that are at first introduced to distinguish between sense-perception, thought, and *phantasia* are circumstantial, and most of them are soon modified, if not contradicted. Sense-perception, for instance, is at first differentiated from *phantasia* because it is always true while the latter is usually false (428^{a}11). Later on it turns out that only 'specific' perceptions are almost (!) always true while the perceptions of common and accidental objects may be false (428^{b}18 ff.). *Phantasia* is initially separated from both sense-perception and thought (427^{b}14), but then it is subsumed under *noein* and regarded as the counterpart of *hupolēpsis* or supposition (427^{b}27). Furthermore, at first *phantasia* is said to be 'up to us', since we can imagine what we please while suppositions depend on the external circumstances since they are true or false (427^{b}18). Soon afterwards it is clear that not all *phantasiai* are up to us (dreams clearly are not) and that *phantasiai* can also be true or false, otherwise they would not mislead us. Finally, not all animals are said to have *phantasiai* but all have perception (428^{a}9–11): this claim is also modified later.[7]

What surprises one more than these inconsistencies (which can partly be resolved and partly brushed aside as mere negligence)[8] is the fact that Aristotle uses so many arguments from indirect evidence: that is to say, that he spends so much time to point out what sense-perception, *phantasia*, and thought do *not* have in common rather than distinguishing them by their specific objects. That is what one would have expected after his careful description of the senses and his insistence that the *object* defines the faculty in book 2.[9]

A closer look at the final definition of *phantasia* itself explains, however, why Aristotle is so roundabout in his procedure. He seems to want to prepare the ground beforehand and to lead us into agreeing that *phantasia* and sense-perception must be *different*, precisely because according to his final definition there is no separate capacity in the soul and there are no separate objects for *phantasia*: '*Phantasia* is a motion that does not happen without sense-perception but comes to be as the result of the activity of sense-perception and is *like* the perception' (428^{b}11–15; 429^{a}1; *Somn. Vig.* 459^{a}17 f.). *Phantasia*, thus, does not have a faculty of its own but is 'parasitic' on sense-perception.

The truth or falsity of *phantasia* depends likewise on the character of the corresponding sense-perception: the *phantasia* that follows the perception of the special object (*idion*) of the sense (like colour of vision) is true while the perception lasts, but it can become false once the perception is over. The *phantasiai* following the perception of common objects (as that something is in motion) and

---

[7] On the 'indefinite' possession of *phantasia* in 3. 11 by animals that have only tactile perception cf. further below.

[8] It will, for instance, become clear that *phantasia* is here subsumed under *noein* because it fulfils some cognitive function for animals that do not have reason (10, 433^{a}10). Watson defends the coherence of the chapter by pointing out its anti-Platonic stance but does not straighten out all wrinkles.

[9] Cf. 415^{a}20; 418^{a}7 ff.; cf. *EN* 1139^{a}8–11. For a discussion of the 'physiology' of *phantasia* cf. Watson (1982), 103–4. Cf. also Sorabji (1974), 76–92.

of accidentals (that the white thing is a book), can be false both with and without the perception (428^{b}25–30).[10] What precisely the status of the different kinds of *phantasiai* is supposed to be is difficult to say at this point, since Aristotle does not give any further depiction of the *causal* connection between sense-perception and *phantasiai*; nor, even more deplorably, does he give anything like a phenomenological description of the different kinds of *phantasiai* that would illustrate what distinguishes them from the corresponding sense-perceptions. It looks as if *phantasiai* here have been degraded to mere epiphenomena, the lingering after-images of sensations.[11]

This impression squares well with Aristotle's assertion earlier in the chapter that we speak of appearance when we do not have clear perception (428^{a}12–15) and, still earlier, that *phantasiai* are somehow non-committing, in that we look at them 'as in a picture' (427^{b}23–4). The impression does not square well, however, with the assertion that without *phantasiai* there can be no thought (427^{b}16) and with the attempt to assign a cognitive function and value to *phantasia* that prompts Aristotle to subsume it under the title of *noein* (427^{b}27 ff.). What kind of *noēsis* and *krisis* can we expect *phantasia* to perform if it is utterly dependent on perception, a mere after-image or an unclear appearance?

To answer the question of a positive cognitive function of *phantasia* we have to look beyond 3. 3 and determine what kinds of mental activities, though not performed by perception and reason, are nevertheless necessary for cognition. For it will turn out that there is a wide *gap* between the two, and that at least one of the functions of imagination is to fill that gap. This is not to deny that some *phantasiai* are 'mere appearance'; it is just to show that not all are. I will confine myself to a depiction of two main functions of *phantasia* in Aristotle's psychology: its role in the *synthesis* and retention of sense-perceptions, and its role in applying *thought* to objects of sense-perception.

II. *Phantasia* as Synthesizer

Aristotle's 'anatomy' of sense-perception gives us a relatively clear picture: perception is conceived of as the interaction between the object of perception and

[10] Modrak (1986) tries to establish a unified concept of *phantasia* as 'awareness of a sensory content under conditions that are not conducive to veridical perceptions' (p. 48). The latter seems to be untenable, for she maintains that *aisthēsis* is then 'limited to cases of veridical perceptions' (p. 52) and suggests at least tentatively that '... all cases of false perceptions are, strictly speaking, cases of *phantasia*' (p. 65 n. 44 also p. 52 n. 16). She does not, however, discuss 428^{b}18–25, which contradicts such assumptions and admits false perceptions on all levels. She puts too much emphasis on Aristotle's statement in 428^{a}13–15 that we 'never say something appears to us when we perceive it clearly but only when unclearly', and plays down the importance of the distinction made on the physiological level: that *phantasiai* are caused by sense-perceptions.

[11] Aristotle describes in *Somn. Vig.* 459^{b}12 ff. with great precision how the after-images of the sun change character and decay: at first it looks yellow, then crimson, then purple, then black until it disappears. He there gives an explanation for the reoccurrence of images: there is a continued motion, both in the inner sense and in the sense-organs of which we are sometimes not aware because we are concentrating on something else (459^{b}9). This suggests that we are always full of such unperceived motions.

the actualized capacity. The sense-organ is affected by the *perceptible form* of the object without the matter (*tōn aisthētōn eidōn aneu tēs hulēs*, 2. 424ᵃ17). Aristotle compares it to the wax that receives the imprint of a seal without its matter (gold or iron). In other words, the soul receives the colour without the paint (coloured surface).

Yet perception is not the mere passive reception of such immaterial imprints. It is also treated as a critical faculty, for it is supposed to 'judge' (*krinei*) what it receives. This translation might be too strong, however, for Aristotle seems to have in mind merely the discernment of the specific objects of the sense.[12] Although he does say that the soul enunciates what it sees (*legei*, 426ᵇ20 cf. 427ᵃ1, 9), this cannot mean explicit predication, since animals have sense-perception but not opinions or convictions. This must mean that a dog surely recognizes its master, but that he does so without saying to himself 'this is the master'.[13]

It is difficult to be dogmatic about the extent of the 'diagnostic power' of sense-perception. But, to cut a long story short, to judge from the great pains Aristotle takes to explain how vision, for example, discerns its own immediate objects like black and white, or how the soul can conceive simultaneously that something is white and sweet, the cognitive power of sense-perception is narrowly limited to what is immediately perceived, the *energeia* itself (417ᵇ24–8; 425ᵇ6 ff.; *APo.* 87ᵇ28 39).[14] Because of the emphasis on the singleness of each act of perception and on the need for the presence of its object, it is doubtful that for Aristotle we can have something like a 'panoramic' view of a whole situation, for he does not seem to include anything like a 'field of vision' in his explanations. This would suggest that when I let my eyes glide over the different books on my bookshelves there is always just the piecemeal vision of this or that coloured object; the *overall impression* of all the different books (including those behind my back) would then be already a *phantasia*, a synthesis of what I perceive right now and what I have perceived a second ago and so on.[15] Kant describes very nicely how such a synthesis of a manifold takes place when he describes how we look up and down a house.[16]

Scholars have in recent years drawn attention to the integrative role of the 'common sense', which is also called by Aristotle the 'inner sense' or the 'first sense'. It seems that it fulfils most functions that we ascribe to consciousness,

---

[12] Like the cognitive power of *phantasia*, the cognitive power of *aisthēsis* has been rather controversial. On the relative self-sufficiency of the senses cf. Schofield, above, ch. 14, p. 249.

[13] Sensory interpretation need not be 'propositional' but can be mere 'noticing'. The same holds for *phantasiai*. Cf. *Somn. Vig.* 458ᵇ1, where *doxa* says that something is a man or a horse but *aisthēsis* notices colour or beauty. A 'perceptive predication' is defended by Cashdollar (1973), 161, 167.

[14] *DA* 426ᵇ8–14 (*hoti diapherei*) (cf. 431ᵃ20–ᵇ1). Aristotle is rather circumlocutive here: from the comparison of perception with a geometrical point that is numerically identical but used twice (as beginning and end-point of a line) one gets the impression that the soul discerns black and white 'back-to-back', as it were, in contiguous acts. In *Sens.* 7 Aristotle allows the inner sense simultaneous perception of different senses but still insists that one sense cannot perform opposite motions at the same time (447ᵇ20).

[15] Cf. *APo.* 1. 87ᵇ28–39. Sorabji in Aristotle (1972*b*) introduces the possibility of a 'specious present' (p. 66), but that would not be what Aristotle means by 'hama', which suggests strict simultaneity (cf. *Sens.* 448ᵇ22 'tōi atomōi').

[16] *Critique of Pure Reason*, A 190 ff.

since it receives all the sensory information and has a kind of 'authority' over the different senses.[17] The dominant role of the common sense is only indicated in the *De Anima* (426^b17-29) but further elaborated in the *Parva Naturalia*. As a result, one might ask why not assign the 'synthesizing' role to the inner sense rather than to *phantasia*?

Aristotle does indeed ascribe to the inner sense the ability to receive and discern different sensations and perceptions at the same time (*Sens.* 7), so that in principle we can see, hear, taste, or smell an object all at once. Thus the inner sense is responsible for the *koina aisthēta*, the motion we both see and feel, or for the objects of accidental perception, as when we perceive the white thing as the son of Diares.[18]

We should remember here, however, that the inner sense is not a faculty above the different senses but only their centre, where all the different perceptions converge. It may be permitted to speak of 'consciousness' here, but with the proviso that the inner sense *qua* sense contains not more than the imprints of the different sense-perceptions at any moment. Since even in the inner sense the imprints of the perceptible forms last only as long as the perception itself, what lingers on in it when I avert my eye is then already a *phantasia*, an after-image. This would explain why Aristotle at one point calls these imprints 'perceptions *and* imaginations' (425^b23) and why he claims that we already have *phantasiai* while sense-perception is still in operation and the object is present (428^b27).[19]

A much simpler explanation for the simultaneity of perceptions and their after-images would be that unclear perceptions can thus be classified as appearances. But there must be more to it than that. There would be an unbridgeable causal gap if the *phantasma* or image were not produced while the sense-perception was still in operation.[20] Once the perception itself is gone, what should give rise to the ensuing *phantasma*, the kind of after-image that we can see 'with closed eyes'? Once in existence the residual motion has a life of its own, it can change in character and truth-value in the way that Aristotle suggests. He is, unfortunately, not very explicit about when and where those changes take place, and when a perception turns into a *phantasia*; indeed, his account of dreams and the motions that occur in sleep between the inner sense and the external sense-

---

[17] Cf. Kahn (1966). Kahn points out the continuity between *De Anima* and the other psychological writings (esp. *Sens.* 7), where the 'common sense' is depicted as a co-ordinator (pp. 52, 57 ff.). In *Somn. Vig.* the inner sense is depicted as *to epikrinon kai kurion* (461^b25) that says 'what something is like' (461^b6).

[18] Cashdollar has defended accidental perception as a real perception against Kahn's claim that it falls partly outside perception. Cashdollar has to introduce 'habit' as part of the mechanism that allows us to identify the seen object. One might feel tempted rather to use *phantasia* to explain the association with past experiences.

[19] The remark in 425^a17 that we perceive the common objects *kinēsei* can be taken to support this interpretation, for it seems to suggest that some compound activity is already necessary to grasp the size or shape of an object, or the number of different objects. Hamlyn in Aristotle (1968), comments somewhat cryptically: 'A plurality of the senses or a plurality of occasions on which the sense is exercised gives perception of a plurality of number' (118).

[20] Cf. *Ph.* 202^a6-9, 242^a57-62, *APo.* 95^a24-36.

organs suggests that the history of the residual motions may vary in complexity and duration. His claim that we are often unaware of those residual motions because of stronger immediate impressions shows that he assumes their continued existence.[21]

One might wonder at this point why Aristotle does not ascribe all after-images to memory, except perhaps the immediately 'decaying' ones that simply seem to linger in the retina for moments after we have seen (like the sun's changing after-images, *Mem.* 449[b]22–30) or that ring in the ears after we have heard. Instead, he explains memory in terms of images. The answer to this question is relatively simple: memory, according to Aristotle in the *De Memoria*, is always the act of remembering a past experience *qua* past. Thus I would have a memory of a sunset only if it were a particular sunset that I had experienced. Free-floating items that come to my mind when I contemplate, say, sunsets in general, are mere images, while memories are images that are likenesses of something retained from the past with the association of the time-lapse.[22]

Image-theories as explanations of representations have been criticized by various philosophers for various reasons.[23] These criticisms need not particularly concern us as long as it is understood that for Aristotle there is no need to assume any precise *correspondence* between a *phantasma* and that which it is a *phantasma* of.[24] Nor need the *phantasmata* be confined to *visual* images: any kind of retained sensory impression would be a *phantasma*, according to Aristotle; vision is just the sense that gets most attention (429[a]2–4). Unfortunately we do not even have a verb that would express how we 'hear' a melody that haunts us, or experience a smell, touch, or taste. 'Recall' might be the best if we keep in mind that it need not be done intentionally.

Phantasiai can thus be separated from their origin, while perceptions cannot, and this means that they can give us a coherent picture of a situation that transcends the immediate perception. Imagination can give us the impression of a change over a certain time, as when my eyes glide over different objects in this room or my ears follow a melody. Strictly speaking, the eyes or ears perceive only one object at a time; thus animals without *phantasia* would only get a sequence of incoherent imprints. That *phantasiai*, once they are separated from their origin, may change in quality and the object may change as well explains why Aristotle declares at times that most of them are false and misleading. Since there is no control, no special faculty in the soul, that 'keeps them in order', *phantasiai* can become mere appearances that drift in and out of our consciousness, reappear in

---

[21] Cf. above, n. 11. As *Somn. Vig.* 459[b]5 ff. shows, Aristotle is clearly aware that it is difficult to draw a line between perception and *phantasiai* and that there is a great variety of after-images (*en bathei kai epipolēs* [b]7).

[22] *Mem.* 450[a]21 ff.: '… *prosaisthanesthai hoti proteron*.

[23] Nussbaum discusses the problems of an 'image-theory' extensively and with reference to present philosophical criticism of such theories (1978, 224 ff.). Cf. also Schofield above, ch. 14 n. 8. For a brief review of the present-day discussion cf. von Eckardt (1988).

[24] According to *Insomn.* 460[b]6 a small resemblance of the *pathē* is sufficient. Problems like that of 'density' or exactness of correspondence therefore need not arise in Aristotle.

dreams, or delude us in a state of fever. For that very reason Aristotle does not treat the *phantastike* as a separate faculty of the soul, but regards it as a phenomenon that supervenes on sense-perception. Since there is no faculty that is in charge of the images as such, one can do no more when the quality of the images decays or their truth-status is doubtful than to go back to sense-experience itself. Where the senses themselves are not decisive, as in the case of 'incorrigible' appearances like that of the size of the sun, reason itself has to find other means of deciding (428ᵇ3).[25]

There is very little direct evidence for my claim that Aristotle designed *phantasia*, amongst other things, to constitute something like a 'field of vision' or to furnish us with coherent trains of events. I have, so far, given only reasons why Aristotle should hold this view. What speaks for it, besides the narrow limitation of actual sense-perception itself? There is, first, the perseverance assigned to *phantasiai* (*to emmenein* 429ᵃ4; *Insomn.* 460ᵇ1–3) which makes them fit to supply us with after-images, memory of past events, and more or less coherent dreams (*Insomn.* 460ᵇ27). Secondly, we can, on this hypothesis, explain the remark that *phantasia* provides us with the cognition of the attributes of things (*DA* 402ᵇ23 *sumbebēkota*), without which science would be empty dialectic. I suggest that he is speaking of the collection of overall impression of sensory objects arrived at by experience. There is, thirdly, the vexatious duplication of sense-perceptions and *phantasiai* in the presence of the object, a puzzle that has prompted the criticism that Aristotle had simply been overwhelmed by his own baroque scholasticism.[26] If imagination is responsible for the 'wider picture of things' then the simultaneity is not only the result of the need for causal continuity, as mentioned above, but necessary for the coherence and continuity of our perceptions as such.

Thanks to imagination, then, we get a fuller picture of a situation or a sequence of situations. If Aristotle regards this as one of the functions of *phantasia*, we can make sense of his claim in *De Sensu* (448ᵇ13) that 'one sees the sun or a four-cubit rod, but it is not apparent how large they are' (*all' ou phainetai hosa estin*). For there is no question here of an unclear perception as it was in *DA* 3. 3; the explanation seems rather that estimating the size of something is what one might expect from *phantasia* as a kind of comparative seeing, perhaps by comparing the size of the sun with that of tree-tops or chimney-pots. If *phantasia* renders a fuller picture than the different senses themselves, then it is clear why it is often depicted as the counterpart of *doxa* (*Insomn.* 462ᵃ1: *ou monon phaneitai alla kai dokei*; cf. 461ᵇ1). It gives us the sensory representation of a state of affairs that goes beyond the mere simultaneous reports by the different senses.

---

[25] On the incorrigibility of this appearance cf. *Insomn.* 458ᵇ28. Aristotle there also discusses the control of *phantasiai*, 461ᵃ30 ff.

[26] The uncontrolled status of *phantasiai* as after-images justifies Schofield's contention that *phantasia* should be understood as corresponding to a sceptical, cautious, and non-committing *phainetai* (ch. 14, pp. 251–2, 253–4, 267–8). This is a rather one-sided depiction that does not do justice to the role of *phantasia* in memory, thinking, or decision-making; nor is the causal account of *phantasia* that explains differences in trustworthiness taken into consideration (cf. p. 269).

One might wonder why, except in connection with practical reason, few traces of such a wider use of *phantasia* can be found in Aristotle. The most plausible explanation is perhaps that Aristotle is not usually interested in describing observations of trains of events but rather in things and their properties (cf. *DA* 402^{b}27).

III. Thought and the Objects of Sense-Perception

The role of *phantasia* is, however, not limited to the rendering of after-images and (if I am right) general impressions of present situations and sequences of events. All *thinking*, so Aristotle says repeatedly, depends on them as well. This is the second point we have to turn to. That there can be no thought without *phantasia* is at first claimed without further elaboration (*DA* 427^{b}16; cf. 403^{a}8–9). But in the following chapters Aristotle explains what his reasons are at greater length.

Something has already been said about the possible 'interpretative' or diagnostic function of both sense-perception and *phantasia*. Since the senses are not confined to the special sense-objects but include also the common objects (size, number, motion, rest, shape) and the accidental objects (e.g. what the underlying object is), it might seem as if both the senses and *phantasiai* already presented the mind with 'finished products', that is, with 'matters of fact' or 'states of affairs': I see the pale thing as the son of Cleon...[27] But one has to be careful not to jump to such conclusions too soon. Seeing something may indeed be always seeing 'something as something'.[28] But this seeing-as need not be explicit and it should not be, since sense-perception and imagination are common both to man and animals and therefore the seeing-as cannot be explicitly predicative or propositional, as mentioned before. This is, presumably, also the reason why Aristotle claims that animals have *phantasiai* but not opinions or convictions, no *pisteis* (428^{a}21).

But if *phantasiai* are not *per se* diagnostic what is their relationship to the intellect? In 3. 3 Aristotle only mentions that without *phantasia* there could be no suppositions, but shortly afterwards he specifies the different kinds of suppositions as *epistēmē kai doxa kai phronēsis kai tanantia toutōn* (427^{b}25), in other words any kind of thinking that assumes a state of affairs. Given this broad range of intellectual activities, it is surprising to see that the intellect (*nous*) itself is defined in 3. 4 quite narrowly and confined to the intelligible forms: the intellect is related to the intelligible as perception is to the sensibles; it receives their forms, the intelligible forms, without matter. The intellect as such has nothing to do with the body: it thinks by itself (429^{b}9) once it has grasped those immaterial forms. Is the intellect

---

[27] The *nous* in so far as it thinks the intelligible is '*chōristos*' (4, 429^{b}5), cf. 430^{a}4–5 '*hē epistēmē hē theōrētikē*'. Aristotle sees no difficulty, however, in applying the nous to sensible objects (430^{a}7).

[28] Sometimes *aisthēsis* seems to performs 'predicative' functions as well, cf. 431^{a}8, but this may be just the implicit recognition that animals have as well.

then strictly confined to the intelligible forms? And how is it related to the material objects given in sense-perceptions?

At first sight it looks as if we have a rigid dichotomy here, for Aristotle seems to limit the intellect exclusively to the thinking of essences, even in material entities like water or flesh, while sense-perception is confined to the material aspect of the same entity ($429^{b}10$ ff.). He concludes: 'Quite generally, then, just as things are separable from matter, so are the objects of the intellect' ($^{b}21$). Such dualism allows Aristotle to claim that with respect to immaterial objects the *nous* is nothing but those objects, since it has no nature of its own but is like a clean slate ($429^{a}21-3$; $430^{a}1$).[29] So when I think 'man is a rational animal', that is all my mind *is* at that moment. Similarly with perception: when I see something red that *is* my perception. The strict separation of the sensual and the intellectual capacities of the soul is asserted time and again: the *nous* is the form of the (intelligible) forms, while sense-perception is the form of the perceptibles ($432^{a}2$).[30]

But in spite of such assertions the autonomy of the intellect, its separation from the body and the senses, is not complete. Aristotle later concedes ($432^{a}3$ ff.) that we only get to know the intelligible forms of all material entities (which means virtually everything except the mind)[31] through knowledge of the sensibles. Sense-perception is thus indispensable at least for learning, and that seems to hold even for abstract sciences such as geometry. Furthermore, as a closer look at the text shows, the function of the intellect in the *De Anima* is not limited to the contemplation of essences, whatever that may mean. It thinks about quite different subject-matters as well (cf. $429^{a}23$ 'what it thinks and assumes'). As we can conclude from Aristotle's own example, the intellect's activity includes discursive thinking about concrete sensible items ($430^{a}31$ ff. 'e.g. Cleon is pale or was or will be', cf. $426^{b}22$, 31; $427^{a}9$). And this is the point where imagination comes in. It establishes the connection between the intellect and its sensible objects.[32]

That there is the need for such a connection is explained by Aristotle somewhat cryptically so far as the details are concerned, but is clear in the overall intention. The need for images comes from two sides; they are necessary both for practical and for theoretical reasoning. That we need images for practical reasoning is more easily intelligible and also stands more in the foreground in Aristotle's discussion in *DA* 3 (especially chs. 7–9). All activities, whether based on non-rational or on rational desire, presuppose that I envisage something as good or

---

[29] *nous* is supposedly free from all influence by the state of the body ($429^{a}24$); it is *apathēs* ($429^{a}15$) and affected by its objects in a way that differs from the senses ($429^{a}29$, $^{b}29$).

[30] Cf. $430^{a}3$; this leads on to the topic of the notorious ch. 5 and the active intellect.

[31] In *Insomn.* $458^{b}10$ Aristotle argues that dreams cannot be a matter of *doxa* since we 'not only assert that some object approaching is a man or a horse, but that the object is white or beautiful, points on which opinion without sense-perception would say nothing ...' This suggests that asserting a universal predicate is a matter of *doxa* alone, even if the subject-matter is a sensible object (*to prosion*).

[32] The necessity of *phantasia* to supply information about the sensible objects, their *pathē enhula as logoi enhuloi*, is anticipated in *DA* $402^{b}16$ ff. where Aristotle calls mere formal definitions a matter of empty dialectic.

bad for me, to be pursued or avoided. The necessary condition of my thinking that something is good or bad, according to Aristotle, is that the soul shall have certain *phantasmata* (431ᵃ14–17): I have to have the image of a future good or bad (433ᵇ12; 28).

But why should not the intellect suffice for figuring out what is good or bad, and, furthermore, why is not sense-perception sufficient to establish the connection with sensible objects where they are needed? We have to remember here, once again, the narrow confinement of intellect and sense-perception to their respective objects.[33] The intellect by itself can only think what is non-sensible, the intelligible forms; but the intellect needs sensible images to decide whether something is desirable or not; it has to envisage concrete situations containing material objects to decide that something is worthwhile or should be avoided.[34] Sense-perception, on the other hand, is strictly limited to what is before the senses at the time when it is. Sense-perceptions in the wider sense (as we would say) are always already *phantasmata* for Aristotle, at least where he uses precise speech.[35] There can, of course, be no sense-perceptions of future goods and evils. All sensible projections are due to imagination. Such images are *based* on sense-perceptions and function like them, but they are not themselves sense-perceptions: 'to the rational soul images serve as perceptions' (431ᵃ14). In order to make a decision I have to create for myself the appearance of a future good, a worthwhile aim (cf. 433ᵃ14).

Unfortunately, Aristotle is not over-concerned with providing us with clear examples to clarify the meaning of the already very compressed text. He mentions one case, however, that illustrates his model: when one sees that a beacon is fire and that it moves, one realizes that it is the enemy (so far sense-perception and calculation do the job). But the soul also calculates through images and thoughts 'as if seeing' (*hosper horōn* 431ᵇ7) and deliberates about what should happen in the future with relation to the present. The soul would not be moved towards anything if it could not envisage it under a concrete aspect. As Aristotle

[33] Aristotle's language is sometimes imprecise, e.g. when he speaks of 'seeing the future' (433ᵇ10); his comment that he means that the things in question are either thought or imagined shows that he was aware of the wider use of *aisthēsis*.

[34] *Phantasia* has to envisage that *tode toionde* (434ᵃ19) where the matter in question is not present. Cf. Aristotle's insistence on the particularity of the minor premiss in the practical syllogism (*EN* 1147ᵃ3, 1147ᵃ24). The recognition of the minor premiss is a matter of *aisthēsis* (as the faculty). Nussbaum's interpretation of *phantasia* tries as far as possible to sever the ties to 'envisaging' and to broaden *phantasia* so that it comprises all kinds of phenomena that would include 'views' in a wider sense (cf. 1978, 263, 'envisaging the good'). Her interpretation does not provide an adequate answer to the question why Aristotle assigns *phantasia* to *aisthēsis* alone and why he seems to insist that there are always sense-impressions involved. Though Nussbaum asserts that *phantasia* is just another aspect of sense-perception (pp. 234 ff., 255 ff.), she does not explain how the function of interpreting in the wider sense that she ascribes to *phantasia* (so that it 'endows the object of perception with a formal content', p. 265) can be fulfilled by a psychological process that is nothing but a secondary motion ensuing upon sense-perception.

[35] Sense-perception is also used in the wider sense elsewhere in Aristotle (cf. *APo.* 2. 99ᵇ35), when he is concerned with the genus of the faculties that make up experience. It is only when he is concerned with the exact analysis of the act itself that he confines himself to the narrow sense (cf. also *Sens.* 7).

at one point puts it: thinking of something terrible alone does not move us (432^{b}29). We have to envisage the phenomenon itself to be stirred to action. My geometric mind, for example, will tell me that I can pass along any path wide enough for my two feet; yet the depiction of walking over a plank from one of the towers of the World Trade Center to the other will tell me that this is an absolute *pheukton*, a thing to avoid.

Most of the attention in the relevant chapters of *De Anima* that deal with *phantasia* is devoted to its importance for practical reason or desire. That it has an important function to fulfil here is confirmed by the fact that Aristotle even provides a subdivision to distinguish between the calculative or deliberative imagination as it functions in human decision-making, and the non-rational imagination that is shared by the animals.[36] Without *phantasia* the desire would be without direction, hence even primitive animals have to have imagination at least 'indefinitely'; they have to aim at something (433^{b}31 ff.). Even a worm has to have a kind of notion of its aim in its search for food.[37]

Besides this important function of imagination in practical reasoning, Aristotle also concedes that *theoretical reasoning* cannot do without 'images' (431^{b}2; 432^{a}3 ff.). It has been mentioned earlier that, given his understanding of how learning takes place, we could never attain the essences of things without starting from their appearances. But not just learning; all thinking depends on the sensible images. For in spite of his initial insistence on a rigid dichotomy of the soul's faculties into *aisthēsis* and *nous* in accordance with its different objects (431^{b}20–432^{a}2), he later concedes that the intelligible objects of all thought, even in the abstract sciences, are contained in sensible objects.[38] He thus arrives at the general conclusion that one could not get to know them nor understand them without sense-perception (*oute mē aisthanomenos mēthen outhen an mathoi oude xunheiē*). More importantly still, one cannot even think (contemplate) without images: *hotan te theōrēi, anankē hama phantasma ti theōrein* (432^{a}8–9). Images, which are 'like sense-perceptions except without matter' (i.e. sensible matter), provide the substrate of all thought, so that reason 'thinks the forms in the images' (431^{b}2). It seems that Aristotle, like Kant, wants to say that we cannot think of a line without drawing one in our mind.[39] Even when he denies the identity of the objects of thought and the objects of imagination (432^{a}12–14), he still insists that whenever we think of the form of something we have something like a *Gestalt* of it in mind.

---

[36] This does not imply that we all of a sudden have two separate capacities, the one based on perception, the other on reason. The *bouleutikē* or *logistikē phantasia* (433^{b}29, 434^{a}5–7) must supply the necessary vision that illustrates concretely what is desirable as a good for practical reason.

[37] *Phantasia*, thus plays a crucial role in *MA*. Cf. 701^{b}18: '*phantasia* and thinking have the power of the actual thing.'

[38] Cf. 8, 432^{a}3–9: *ta te en aphairesei legomena kai hosa tōn aisthētōn hexeis kai pathē.* This seems to suggest that the essences of sensible things are not intelligible without observation of their dispositions (functions?). This fits well with the claim in 402^{b}21–403^{a}2 that *phantasia* gives us the information of the *sumbebēkota* that it is necessary to obtain for the knowledge of the essence of things.

[39] Cf. *Critique of Pure Reason*, B 154.

I do not want to turn Aristotle into a *Gestalt* psychologist, but his basic idea must be that the comprehension of the formal definition of material entities (and that includes those things that have only extension, as in geometry, cf. 431^{b}12–17; 432^{a}2–6) is not enough. The explanation must be that when, for example, one thinks of a house, it is not enough to think 'a shelter against destruction', or in the case of a circle that it is 'the common *locus* of all points having the same distance from a central point'. If we had only the formal definition we would have no way of recognizing an exemplar when we met one, since we should have no *Gestalt* that told us what they looked like. Nor could we do constructions in geometry, of course, since it depends on seeing the relevant relationships.

This would mean that the objects of imagination in Aristotle's epistemology have the function of rendering an object for knowledge when there is no direct perception. But there is more to it than that, I suspect. For sense-perception is not only confined to the moment of actual perception, it is also always narrowly limited to the *particular* object directly under inspection (417^{b}22–8). The scientist, however, has to have not just a view of this or that leopard in front of him, spotted in this or that way; he has to form a picture of 'leopards' and, among other things, their specific spottedness before he can go into the more abstract business of his science. It seems that *phantasia* is supposed to render us that service as well, for *phantasmata* are flexible and can be enriched by repeated observations, while immediate sense-perceptions cannot.

Phantasmata are often depicted as inaccurate impressions. And sometimes that is all there is to them. But it is that less detailed but more general picture that we need for our generalizations; the disadvantage of inaccuracy turns then into an advantage.[40] The example of the sun's appearing a foot in diameter can, once again, illustrate this claim. When I reflect on the real size of the sun I do not reflect on this particular vision of the sun, I reflect on the 'overall vision' of the sun and why it must be a delusion. Thus, although the images are less vivid, and mostly less accurate and direct than sense-perceptions themselves, they not only are longer-lasting and supply us with an image when the perception is gone, but they are also more fruitful because they give us something like a standardized picture of a state of affairs in general.[41]

Such pictures are necessary in decision-making, where Aristotle actually mentions a kind of 'merger' of different *phantasiai* into one image that allows us to compare the relative goodness (or badness) of several possible ends (434^{a}9). They are also necessary in science: the scientist who wonders why a stick looks bent in water does not ask himself why this stick does but why straight objects in general do. Because of the brevity of Aristotle's remarks in the discussion of *phantasia* it must remain somewhat speculative that they are supposed to perform this service for the intellect. But it seems clear that *epagōgē*, induction, could not

---

[40] Ross in Aristotle (1961*a*), 39 even claims that Aristotle 'In the main...does not regard it as a valuable faculty but as a disability.'

[41] Similarly Freudenthal (1863) ascribes to *phantasia* 'kein sinnliches Einzelbild sondern Verallgemeinerung durch Denkthätigkeit' (p. 31).

work without such *phantasiai*; there must be a 'collection' of sensory impressions that presents the mind with the phenomena that are to be explained and preserved.[42]

The *locus classicus* discussing the connection between the sensual and the intellectual in the formation of science, *APo*. 2. 19, does not make any mention of *phantasia*, but it is clear that the kind of *aisthēsis* that leads to memory, experience and, finally, to *nous* of the first principles really consists in *phantasiai*. Only retained perceptions (for those animals which have a *monē* of their perceptions) lead to memory and experience (99ᵇ36–100ᵇ9). That Aristotle uses *aisthēsis* here in its wider sense is clear, for he emphasizes that it is not the particular perception that leads to *empeiria* but the perception of the universal. Taken in the strict sense, sense-perceptions cannot do this (cf. *DA* 417ᵇ15); only the collected *phantasiai* of many sense-perceptions can lead to the sight of the universal feature in the particular. In *APo*. 2. 19 Aristotle may have found it too cumbersome to introduce *phantasia*, and in a way also unnecessary, since he is not interested in a detailed account of how the *aisthēmata* are gained and processed. It is sufficient to know that the basic information comes through the senses.[43]

The upshot of this interpretation of *phantasia* is that it plays a crucial cognitive role both in practical and in theoretical thinking in Aristotle by supplying the necessary link between the sensible and the intelligible. Such a link is necessary not only in view of the fact that most objects of science are 'enmattered' but also because of Aristotle's insight that our thinking cannot be entirely abstract but always needs a kind of *Gestalt*. This result is, of course, not new, but the reasons given here may add to the plausibility of Aristotle's conception.

A final question should here at least be addressed briefly: does the integrative function of *phantasia* permit us to ascribe to Aristotle's psychology something like a conception of the unity of consciousness that comprises both the senses and the intellect, as some commentators have assumed?[44] I would want to be rather cautious at this point. It is undeniable that Aristotle displays scientific optimism when he describes how the mind progresses from sense-perception to knowledge. He seems to presuppose that sufficient empirical study of particulars will result in the recognition of the relevant general features. In *APo*. 2. 19 Aristotle even

[42] For a review of the discussion of *epagōgē* in *APo*. 2. 19 cf. Modrak (1987a), 161 ff. Modrak, however, for reasons that are unclear, denies the need for a plurality of experiences (1987a, 175, 224 n. 44).

[43] Cf. *APo*. 2. 19. *Phantasia* is not mentioned there; but cf. Barnes in Aristotle (1975), 252; sense-perception and memory together bring about the '*monē*' (99ᵇ36) of impressions that is necessary for experience. The individual act of perception gives us the particular cognition (100ᵃ17); *aisthēsis* (in the wider sense) is then charged with the deliverance of the universal (*kai gar hē aisthēsis houtō to katholou empoiei* 100ᵇ4–5).

[44] The establishment of a full integration of rational and perceptual faculties in something approaching the modern sense of consciousness is the main contention in Modrak (1987a); see pp. 113 ff. Even if one agrees with her that Aristotle tried to avoid Platonic dualism, her attempts to downplay Aristotelian dualism too often make her gloss over difficulties; the interpretation relies on unifying metaphors as, e.g., *phantasmata* being 'vehicles for associations' (p. 139) or the '*noēton* is a representation of an occurrent *phantasma*' (p. 125). If there is a unity of consciousness in Aristotle, then one should confine it, with Kahn (cf. n. 17 above), to the inner sense.

suggests that this is only to be expected: 'And when many such things (i.e. perceptions) come about, then a difference (*diaphora*) comes about, so that some come to have an account from the retention of such things, and others do not' ($100^{a}1$; cf. $87^{b}28$ ff.). Thus, it looks as if Aristotle sees a continuous progress from sense-perception to knowledge. And, indeed, what else should one expect? Since most sciences study natural material objects their form and characteristic properties can only be found in these objects themselves.

To characterize the gaining of knowledge from sense-perception Aristotle introduced the famous simile of a routed army gradually reduced to calm order; the simile suggests that from scattered impressions a sufficiently broad orderly picture of the relevant distinctions will gradually emerge that warrants the formation of general concepts necessary for *dianoia* ($100^{a}12$ ff.). Does it guarantee the secure capturing of the first principles? While this is at least insinuated in *APo.* 2. 19, the relevant chs. 1 and 2 of *Metaph.* A are not so optimistic: while everybody has perceptions (*rhadion kai ouden sophon*, $982^{a}12$) so Aristotle there states —the highest knowledge, the knowledge of the reasons, is the privilege of the *sophoi*, and a most difficult thing to achieve. It does not look as if any amount of empirical knowledge through *phantasia* by itself will lead securely from the knowledge of the 'fact that' to that of the 'reason why'.[45]

But even apart from the question of a continuous path from what is better known to us to what is better known as such, there are indications that Aristotle himself quite consciously wanted to preserve the separation of the sensible and the intelligible, of *aisthēta* and *noēta*, in spite of the mediation by *phantasia*.[46] This separation would forbid us to assume anything like a unified concept of consciousness based on perception for Aristotle's psychology. The reasons cannot be fully discussed or documented here; a few reminders have to suffice. The definition of memory as well as of dreams assigns these mental events exclusively to the 'sensible' side, a fact that has often been regarded as rather curious. Though Aristotle grants that we have opinions in dreams ($458^{b}10$), he attributes dreams exclusively to the *aisthētikon*, 'in so far as it is *phantastikon*' ($459^{a}8$). This decision on Aristotle's part leaves the opinions that occur in dreams curiously unexplained, but it suggests that he saw a need to assign psychic phenomena either to the sensible or to the intelligible domain: no real fusion seemed conceivable to him.

The same is true for memory: memories are only revivals of *phantasiai* of past experiences. Knowledge is 'remembered' only accidentally (*Mem.* $450^{a}12-14$), i.e. we only remember when and how we first learned Pythagoras' theorem, but not the theorem itself. This is not as strange as it may sound at first, given Aristotle's presuppositions: I do not recall a past *phantasia* in the case of theoretical knowledge; the question is rather whether I still know it, that is understand it. Once again, it seems as if for Aristotle the decision to locate memory with the

---

[45] On the 'intellectual habituation' of handling first principles cf. Burnyeat (1981), 114.

[46] The problematic status of *nous* is discussed by Barnes (1979*b*), 39–41; a more integrative reading is suggested by Sorabji (1971/1979).

sensible faculties forbids him to admit also a kind of intellectual memory. This means that just as in the case of dreams, the status of beliefs embedded in sensory memories remains unaccounted for.[47]

If Aristotle wants to keep the two faculties separate and regards *phantasia* only as a necessary link between sensory and non-sensory mental activities, a link, however, that remains firmly confined to the sensory side, then he must have seen good reasons for doing this, for the difficulties entailed by his dualism can have hardly escaped his notice. One of his reasons must certainly have been that he did not want to accept any physical impact on the functioning of the intellect *per se*, which would be implied if there were more than an accidental connection. Furthermore, he may not have wanted to give up the link between the best part in us and the only divinity that he recognizes: the pure active mind (cf. 408^{b}18–29; *Metaph.* 983^{a}6–7).

The dualism that I maintain for Aristotle does not make his philosophy of mind incoherent. It imports some awkwardnesses that seem to be unavoidable for any metaphysics that distinguishes between the corporeal and the incorporeal in a strong sense, since the question of their connection and interaction necessarily arises. Aristotle must have hoped that his conception of *phantasia* would help to overcome that awkwardness.

The relationship between *phantasia* (or *aisthēsis* in the wider sense) and *nous* has recently been likened to that between matter and form.[48] As a metaphor this is perhaps not unacceptable since the senses do deliver the material that reason works on. The metaphor has its dangers, however, since it suggests a necessary relationship between them. In opposition, however, to matter in its usual sense, *phantasiai* can and do exist by themselves; they need not be 'informed' by thought. And, more importantly, *phantasiai* are sometimes quite recalcitrant and resist 'information'. As Aristotle asserts in *Insomn.* 458^{b}28, 'so even when persons are in excellent health, and know the facts of the case perfectly well, the sun, nevertheless, appears to them to be a foot wide'. Thus, *phantasiai*, even though they often function as incentives for thought, as substrates of thought, and the anchor of thought in the physical world, remain phenomena in their own right.

I have largely treated *phantasia* as a unified concept in Aristotle; but is that justified, or is there not rather only a 'more or less coherent family of psychic phenomena, a loose-knit family concept?[49] If one excludes the metaphoric meaning of 'phantasizing', then at least the *causal* account for all imagination is the same: all *phantasiai* are motions in the soul caused by sense-perceptions. They are sensory images or imprints that can exist independently from their original source. Their history may be quite different, depending on whether they are due to immediate awareness or have undergone a long-term storage, as may be their

---

[47] Esp. in *Insomn.* the difficulty is obvious since Aristotle distinguishes between opinions that are part of dreams and opinions we have in sleep besides the dreams (458^{b}15). Nevertheless he defines dreams as *phantasmata* in sleep (459^{a}19).

[48] Cf. Modrak (1987*a*), 123–4, 215 n. 29.

[49] Cf. Schofield (1979), 108; 110. ch. 14, pp. 253, 256.

function and the occasion of their occurrence in dreams, hallucinations, memory, thoughts, or decisions. Most of all, their character and value may vary: they may be clear or confused, simple or complex, true or false. In spite of this range and flexibility it seems that Aristotle's insistence on their sensory nature indicates that he regarded them, with good reasons, as a unitary phenomenon in the soul, as sensory appearances.[50]

[50] For an interpretation that reaches similar results but is much more extensive and technically refined cf. Wedin (1988). A discussion of his very rich investigations would exceed the limits of this article.

16

ARISTOTLE ON MEMORY AND
THE SELF

JULIA ANNAS

ARISTOTLE'S treatise *On the Soul* and the attached essays which we call the *Parva Naturalia* are rightly regarded as the first systematic philosophy of mind. But we risk distorting or impoverishing our interpretation of Aristotle if we forget that for him the 'study of the soul' is not divided as we divide it, between on the one hand philosophy of mind, and on the other psychology, which uses other methods and goes on in another building. This matters most where philosophers and psychologists now have rather different approaches to an issue; and one such issue is that of memory. Philosophers treat *memory* as a unitary phenomenon which raises several deep philosophical problems about the past and the self. Psychologists, on the other hand, study long- or short-term memory, our abilities to retain images, language, or numbers; they regard 'memory' as an ordinary-language catch-all term which covers a variety of very distinct abilities. For a philosopher, long-term memory is not interestingly different from the short-term kind; the same philosophical problems arise for both—how do they relate to the past? and so on. From the psychologist's point of view the differences are what matters; the proper object of scientific study will be a specific ability, while memory as such is too vague a notion for useful scientific investigation.

Aristotle's attitude to memory is, I suggest, more like that of the modern psychologist than that of the modern philosopher; he is more interested in accurately delineating different kinds of memory than he is in discussing philosophical problems that arise for memory in general. This does not diminish the philosophical interest of his discussion, for the distinctions he draws are philosophically significant, as well as being pioneering steps towards an empirical psychology.[1]

The short treatise *On Memory and Recollection*[2] is often regarded as a treatise on memory and also on a loosely associated phenomenon, recollection, of which the former is of obvious philosophical interest to us, the latter only doubtfully so, especially since it involves discussion of details like the 'place' systems of

---

© Julia Annas, 1992.

[1] Cf. his attitude to a definition of 'soul' in general (*DA* 414^{b}20–33); his main concern is to get down to investigating the various different types of ability (perceiving, thinking, etc.) which constitute being a soul.

[2] I shall refer to Ross's text (1955).

mnemonic techniques.[3] But a closer look at the work suggests rather that it is better regarded as a treatise on two kinds of memory.

Officially, ch. 1 of the work is about memory, and ch. 2 about recollection; so it may appear that we have two separate, co-ordinated topics. The division, however, is not sustained. For one thing, after the main discussion of recollecting in ch. 2, we return without any warning at 452^{b}7 to the question of how one estimates time-lapses, a question arising for both memory and recollection. Some points are made which apparently concern memory alone (452^{b}26–8, 28–453^{a}4). The chapter then concludes with a series of points which both compare and contrast memory and recollection. So Aristotle does not hold the two sharply apart. And, more significantly, memory has invaded even the official account of recollection. Aristotle is handily equipped with two quite distinct sets of words for memory (*mnēmē* and associated verb) and for recollection (*anamnēsis* and associated verb). Yet after an opening in which the two are contrasted by means of these two sets of words (450^{b}18–451^{b}10) we find Aristotle giving an account of what distinguishes recollecting from relearning which freely uses 'memory' words to refer to recollecting.[4] The conclusion seems inescapable that for Aristotle there is a broad acceptable usage of 'memory' which covers two phenomena which the natural scientist (the psychologist, we should say) needs to distinguish as memory proper and as recollection. No confusion need arise as long as it is clear on each occasion what is being referred to.[5] When in ordinary life we talk about memory and remembering, we are in fact referring to two rather different kinds of ability which, when we are studying the soul scientifically, it is also important to distinguish.

It thus seems preferable to say that in his treatise Aristotle is discussing two kinds of memory, not memory plus the 'specialized' subject[6] of recollection. This is not a trivial point, for, as we shall see, many scholars have attributed to Aristotle a theory of memory as a whole which is too narrow in that it focuses only on memory in the narrow sense; if his account of memory as a whole includes recollection, it turns out to be more plausible and interesting than often thought.

If Aristotle's memory and recollection are two kinds of memory as we, and he, ordinarily use the word, can we compare his distinction with any more familiar

---

[3] The problematic passages discussing these techniques have been brilliantly elucidated by Sorabji in Aristotle (1972*b*).

[4] 451^{b}10–452^{b}7; the conclusion is: *to men oun anamimnēskesthai touton sumbainei ton tropon* (452^{b}6–7) and the main point of it is to show how one can distinguish recollecting from relearning (452^{a}4–6, answering the problem raised at 451^{b}6–10). 'Memory' words (*mnēmē, mnēmoneuein*, etc.) occur in this passage at: 451^{b}16, 26, 452^{a}3, 7, 10, 18, 20 (*bis*), 22–3, 24, 452^{b}5. (Both verbs, *mnēmoneuein* and *memnēsthai*, occur.) In all these occurrences the reference is to recollecting, not memory in the narrower sense in which it is distinguished from recollecting.

[5] In fact this is so clear that commentators have not even expressed surprise at the way recollection is explained by the use of memory words.

[6] Sorabji in Aristotle (1972*b*), 35–6 provides reasons deriving from Plato for Aristotle's devoting part of his treatise 'to this apparently specialized subject'. He does not regard it as an everyday kind of memory.

distinction of two kinds of memory? I think that we can, and in this paper I propose to follow through the suggestion that Aristotle's distinction between memory and recollection can be illuminated by a distinction between what I shall call
personal and non-personal memory. I shall of course have to begin by explaining
this distinction.[7]

We often say things like, 'I remember Paris', 'I remember that Caesar invaded
Britain' and the like. In general our claims come in either the form

> I remember that *p*   (1*a*)

where 'that *p*' stand for some item with propositional content—that Caesar
invaded Britain, for instance; or the form

> I remember *a*   (1*b*)

where '*a*' stands for some item which does not have propositional content—
Paris, that party, my cat, and so forth.

There are two ways of regarding claims like 1*a* and 1*b*, and these ways define
the difference between personal and non-personal memory.

Suppose I am wondering whether it is true that I remember that Caesar
invaded Britain. I may think that it is *not* true unless something else is also true,
namely that I remember *learning* that Caesar invaded Britain. For what makes
Caesar's invading Britain something I *remember*, as opposed to something I have,
for instance, just learnt? Surely not just the fact that I once learnt it, but the
further fact that I can now regard it as something I *once learnt*. If I have absolutely no memory of having learnt it, if I have, so to speak, no way of relating the
fact not only to my present self but also to my past self, how can it belong in my
memory, as well as being part of what I *now* think to be true?

This line of thought has often been attacked, on the grounds that it relies on
a confusion between what constitutes memory and what is evidence for it. Still,
what matters here is that it is a very common way of thinking about memory, and
it is one which many reflective people and many philosophers have found plausible. If it is confused, the confusion is not a trivial one.

On this view, claims of the form (1*a*) and (1*b*) will imply the truth of claims of
the form

> I remember (my) *F*ing that *p*   (2*a*)

and

> I remember (my) *F*ing *a*   (2*b*)

where '*F*ing' stands for some experience of mine. Thus 'I remember that Caesar
invaded Britain' will imply that I remember learning (reading, hearing, etc.) that
Caesar invaded Britain, and 'I remember that party' will imply that I remember

---

[7] I omit consideration of remembering *how* to do things, which, while of interest, is not relevant to
present purposes. It is also worth noting that as I use 'personal memory' it does not imply (as the
term does in the work of some modern philosophers who have used it) that the remembered item, as
well as the remembering, was part of the agent's past experience.

being at (hearing about, reading about) that party. If (1*a*) and (1*b*) are thought to imply (2*a*) and (2*b*) then the memory-claim is one of personal memory.

Non-personal memory is easily defined by contrast; it is memory where (1*a*) and (1*b*) are *not* thought to imply (2*a*) and (2*b*). Thus, I may claim to remember that Caesar invaded Britain even though I cannot now remember learning that fact. This is a non-personal memory of mine because I now remember the fact because I did learn it before, even though I now may not be able to remember the learning.

The difference between these two kinds of memory need not lie on the surface; we often say things like 'I remember that party' without going into the question of whether this is meant as a claim of personal or of non-personal memory. Still, we are usually prepared on reflection to classify it as one or the other. The distinction is of course rough and ready, but I think adequate for present purposes, since my present claim is that the distinction itself is not only simple but available to common sense; it can be made without taking a stand on other issues concerning memory, and it is common sense that we do have both these kinds of memory. In some cases I will retract a claim of the form (1*a*) or (1*b*) unless I can come up with some (2*a*) or (2*b*); in other cases not; it depends on the circumstances.

Philosophers who have dealt with memory have had a tendency to neglect one of these kinds of memory, or reduce it to the other. Traditional empiricist theories have neglected non-personal memory; modern theories tend to neglect personal memory. As often, we find that Aristotle does not neglect relevant facts, and has no reductive impulses about them. He describes both these kinds of memory without the urge to a higher theory that would explain away one of them in terms of the other. For I shall argue that Aristotle's memory is best understood as personal memory, and his recollection as a kind of non-personal memory (though there are kinds of non-personal memory that do not have the special features of recollection).

My hypothesis that Aristotle's memory is personal memory, and that his recollection is a kind of non-personal memory, is a bold one. For Aristotle himself does not discuss the matter in these terms, or make claims about the relation of memory and the self. This is partly because his interest lies in distinguishing kinds of memory rather than in treating it as a unitary philosophical phenomenon, and also partly because he does not treat the self as a topic of explicit reflection in the psychological works, though much of what he says has implications about it. However, I think it worthwhile to see whether the hypothesis can be sustained that Aristotelian memory is personal memory and recollection a kind of non-personal memory. If it can, this will help clarify Aristotle's distinction to us; and will also show that Aristotle does have, even if potential rather than actual, an interesting account of the relation of memory and the self.

I shall test my hypothesis by seeing whether it can be sustained as an interpretation of what Aristotle says memory is, what he says recollection is, and what he says and implies about the relation of the two.

Aristotle begins by considering memory, and makes the claim, repeatedly and with emphasis, that memory is of the past.[8] There is one very obvious objection to this, namely that if this is so Aristotle can give no account of memory of timeless truths, such as that $2 + 2 = 4$, or that the interior angles of a triangle add up to two right angles, or of memories of my cat, or that noise, items which are not timeless but do not seem to be past either. This obvious objection is at once brought to mind by the examples Aristotle brings in. I can't, he says, remember 'this white thing here' (*todi to leukon*) when I'm seeing it, only later (449^b15-16); and I can remember that the interior angles of a triangle add up to two right angles (499^b20)—just the kind of examples that seem hardest for a claim that memory is of the past.[9]

These apparent difficulties all vanish, however, if what Aristotle is here thinking of is personal memory. For if so, the claim that I remember that the interior angles of a triangle add up to two right angles, and the claim that I remember this white thing here, will be in an important sense incomplete as they stand. It won't be true that I remember the theorem unless I remember *learning* the theorem, and it won't be true that I remember the white thing unless I remember *seeing* the white thing. If this is how Aristotle is thinking, it is easy to see why he says that memory is only of the past: on this view, I shan't remember the theorem unless I remember learning the theorem, and learning the theorem is something in my past, so that memory of the theorem will involve a past experience of mine. The past experience of learning the theorem is easily thought of as part of what is remembered when the theorem is remembered—indeed as the distinguishing part.[10] Aristotle's statement that memory is of the past, coupled with his use of examples that have no apparent reference to the past, causes no problems if what he has in mind is personal memory; personal memory is just the kind of memory that does essentially involve something in the past, namely the past learning, seeing, or whatever of the object of memory.

Later in the chapter on recollection Aristotle distinguishes it from memory by reference to the past, in ways which confirm the present suggestion. Recollection, he says, is recovering past knowledge or experience—and not only is this not recovering memory (since you are recovering knowledge, not recovering

---

[8] He says that people often go wrong on this (499^b9-10). One obvious way in which this could occur would be by their failing to distinguish personal memory (memory) from non-personal (recollection)—since, as we shall see, recollection is not of the past in the same way. Indeed, if we do not assume that this is what the mistake is, we are hard put to make sense of the comment. Sorabji in Aristotle (1972*b*), 65, says, 'The reference is presumably not merely to mistakes about the object of memory, but to mistakes about the object of whatever activity one is analysing'; but there has been no reference to objects and activities in general, other than memory.

[9] Freudenthal, followed by Ross, deletes the phrase *tas tou trigōnou hoti duo orthais isai*. They are certainly awkward where they are, and Ross *may* be right in inclining to Gohlke's suggestion that they be transposed to $^b17$, after *to theōroumenon*. It seems arbitrary simply to omit them, though on some readings of this passage they are very awkward.

[10] I say 'part', since obviously personal memory is not the same as memory of one's past experience *tout court*. There is such a thing as remembering *learning* the theorem which need not involve remembering the theorem (remembering the learning experience, we might say), but this is not what is meant by personal memory.

memory), it is not acquiring memory either. The reason given here is that memory requires a lapse of time. Whether we regard memory as a state or as an experience, it does not come into being along with the experience it is a memory of. 'There is no memory proper (*kath' hauto*) until there is a lapse of time (*prin chronisthēnai*); for a person remembers now (*nun*) what he knew or experienced before, and does not now remember what he experienced now (*ouch ho nun epathe, nun mnēmoneuei*)' (451ᵃ29–31). Here 'now' seems to be 'only just now'—the specious present, we might say; if I have only just had an experience, then although it is strictly in the past, since I refer to it in the past tense (cf. *ho nun epathe*) it counts as being in the earlier part of the specious present, and so not as something I can remember.

Is it true that I can't remember something I have only just found out or experienced? It doesn't seem to be true of non-personal memory. For I can learn that 2 + 2 = 4, and then at once recall it; however instantaneously I do this, there seems to be no good reason for denying that I remember it. But if we are thinking of personal memory, it does seem to be true. For then remembering that *p* will involve remembering learning that *p*. And there is something odd in saying that I remember learning that *p* where learning that *p* is still in my specious present. There has to be some lapse of time before we readily say that learning that *p* is something in my past, and so something that I remember. And so there has to be some lapse of time before there is personal memory. My suggestion is, then, quite strongly reinforced by this passage, since it is precisely this difference about lapse of time which Aristotle takes to mark one of the distinctions between memory and recollection.

In ch. 1 Aristotle explicates the thought that memory is of the past in a very famous passage. Memory, he says, is different from perceiving or thinking of something in the present, in that one remembers that one perceived, or thought of the thing. 'For whenever someone is actually remembering, he always in this way says in his soul that he heard or perceived or thought of this before' (449ᵇ22–3). This is echoed in later passages (450ᵃ19–21, 451ᵃ5–7). It is surely wrong to read Aristotle's claim here, as Sorabji does, as being that if I can 'say in my soul' that I perceived, etc. then I can be sure that I have a memory.[11] If so, Aristotle would be saddled with the consequence that I could turn an apparent memory into a real one by deciding to say the right things in my soul about it; and we have no reason to saddle Aristotle with such a consequence. Rather, the 'saying in one's soul' is just part of the analysis of what memory is: if one remembers, then one says in one's soul, etc.; but saying things in one's soul is no kind of test for or way of finding out whether I am remembering.

What is it to say in one's soul? We would naturally take it to mean at least this: memory is a kind of thought which includes in some way thought of the past experience, learning, etc. The idea that thought is a kind of internal speech is a

---

[11] Sorabji in Aristotle (1972*b*), 9–10, 86. He uncharitably takes Aristotle to be unwillingly burdened with the absurd consequences this leads to.

common enough one. However, Aristotle later says that memory belongs to the primary perceptive part of the soul, and to thinking only incidentally. Further, he ascribes memory to animals as well as to humans (450ª15–16, cf. *HA* 488ᵇ24–6) and even contrasts it with the more intellectual recollection, which only humans have. Surely Aristotle does not mean to ascribe to animals the kind of rational thought that can in humans be described as inner speech. This remains an unsolved problem, but perhaps is not very important: Aristotle's main point is that animals do something which is relevantly like what in humans is remembering, even though they do not have the more elaborate intellectual performance which is recollection. However, we are left with a feeling of dissatisfaction: memory seems to involve thought in some ways and not in others, and, as with *phantasia* or 'imagination', Aristotle combines interest in the phenomenon with inability to place it convincingly in terms of his perception/ thought distinction.

It is obviously false of non-personal memory that it involves saying in one's soul that one perceived or thought of the thing before: I can remember that 2 + 2 = 4, or that Caesar invaded Britain, without anything which could be described as saying in my soul that I learnt this before. But with personal memory the thought seems actually required. If remembering that Caesar invaded Britain involves remembering learning that Caesar invaded Britain, then it is plausible to hold that when I remember that Caesar invaded Britain I say in my soul that I learnt this before. Indeed, this is just what personal memory *is*, and Aristotle's definition can be regarded as a definition of personal memory. The frequent charge that the definition is too narrow fails if he is here in fact only intending to define what we would call personal memory, rather than memory in general.

Two other points connected with saying in one's soul are also relevant here. Firstly, Aristotle adds (449ᵇ28–30) that only those animals have memory that have a sense of time. Like the need for a time-lapse, a sense of time (by which he presumably means a sense that time has passed) is required only for personal memory; to remember that I saw or learnt something before, I do need to have a sense of myself as a continuing entity which carries on through lapse of time.

Secondly, at the end of the chapter, after giving his analysis of memory in terms of a representative image, Aristotle cites as a contrasting phenomenon to memory the experience of 'Antipheron of Oreus and other lunatics', who 'spoke of their images as though they were things that had occurred and as though they were remembering them' (451ª8–11). We know nothing about Antipheron, and possibly he was just someone who was massively deluded about what he had learnt in the past; but the preceding passage (451ª2–8) in which Aristotle says that sometimes we are unsure whether we remember or not, because we aren't certain whether or not past perception is responsible for seeming memory, suggests that Antipheron was someone who mistakenly thought that he remembered *doing, seeing*, etc. various things. We may compare George IV of Britain, who at the end of his life came, as the result of too much brandy and opium, to believe that he had been present at the battle of Waterloo. He would tell people about Waterloo at length, and doubtless most of his stories would be perfectly good non-personal memories ('I remember that the infantry then charged'); where he went wrong was in taking them for personal memories ('I'll never forget seeing the infantry charge...'). Again, what Aristotle says fits personal but not non-personal memory.

The bulk of ch. 1 is taken up by Aristotle's account of how memory is related to *phantasia* and how it involves *phantasmata* or images. He regards it as obvious that memory involves having an image, since he argues on the basis of this that memory belongs to the primary *perceptive* faculty, and to thinking only incidentally.[12] However, if memory is to be thought of on the lines of perceiving rather than as essentially a kind of thinking, we get a problem. The thing remembered is in the past, no longer there to hand. What we have to hand is the image. But how can perceiving the image constitute remembering the past item which is no longer there? What we want to remember is the past item, and that is no longer available. What is available is the present image, but that seems to be irrelevant. Aristotle's answer is that, indeed, all we have is the present image, but that we can regard it not only as an image but as an *eikōn*, a likeness or representation; remembering something just is my treating my image of it as a representation of something which is itself in the past and no longer available.

Aristotle talks about the images in a very literal way—the memory-images are impressions or pictures in us.[13] We would be wrong, however, to think that he is describing the pictorial content of sense-data or mental images, as more recent analytical and phenomenologist philosophers have done. Rather, Aristotle's crudely literal talk of images seems due to the fact that he has what he finds a plausible physiological underlying picture.[14] The images result from previous sense-experiences we have had. An *aisthēma* or sense-impression has a certain effect on us, not only at the time, but by way of leaving a trace (hence the apt label 'decaying-sense theory'). Depending on our physical constitution, the trace is retained more or less well. What makes such a trace a *memory*-trace is that, as well as having representational content which becomes available to us in certain states (like dream-images) it has a content which is representational of some past state. I regard my memory-image as an image of something which it represents, which is no longer available, but was so in the past.

If we abstract from the crudity due to Aristotle's underlying physiological model, we can sketch his analysis of memory in outline as follows: memory involves having an image which is the effect of a past experience, and regarding it as representing something in the past. Aristotle is not very explicit, but it is surely clear that what the image represents is one's past experience of the object,

---

[12] The argument here is not at all clear, but fortunately I do not need to go into it in detail for present purposes.

[13] 450ᵃ5, 29–32, 450ᵇ15–16, and cf. the extended comparison with seeing a picture as an object and as a representation at 450ᵇ20–451ᵃ2.

[14] Thus as soon as the idea of impressions in the soul is introduced at 450ᵃ30–2, we get a long discussion of the physical differences between 'hard' and 'soft' people which explain their possession or lack of retentiveness. Aristotle stresses this elsewhere (449ᵇ6–8, 453ᵃ14–ᵇ7.)

not just the object. The memory-images are said to result from our perceivings of things, not from the things themselves ($450^{a}31-2$, $451^{a}4$). And after all Aristotle is giving an account of saying in one's soul that one saw, heard, etc. the thing before.[15]

So Aristotle's account of memory in terms of a representational image also points towards personal memory: a memory of Paris, on this view, is having a image which is a causal result of having seen Paris in the past, and which now represents to me my past seeing of Paris. This is the story which Aristotle tells to explain how it is that, when I remember Paris, I say in my soul that I saw it before. It need hardly be said that this account is built for personal memory, and does not fit non-personal memory at all. When I remember that $2 + 2 = 4$, and this is not personal memory, there is no need to assume images of any kind, still less images which represent a past experience of mine.

Not all scholars would accept the account I have given, in which the memory-image represents the experience which is its causal antecedent. Many would follow Sorabji in holding that the image represents, not one's past experience of the remembered item, but just the remembered item.[16] On this view, my memory-image represents Coriscus, not my past seeing of Coriscus. If this is right, Aristotle's talk of representational images will not fit personal memory quite so closely. However, if it is right, then Aristotle's story of images will also not fit closely his view that memory involves saying in one's soul that one saw, etc. this before. One reason for preferring the idea that the memory images represent one's past experience of the object rather than just the object is that Aristotle then has a unified account of memory.

Aristotle's image-theory has on the whole been seen as a liability. Often this results from carelessly conflating his theory with the rather different mental-image theories of later empiricists like Hume. However, there is one rather powerful objection. On this view, memory essentially involves an image, and even if we do not regard this too crudely, memory is made extremely dependent on the perceptive and imaginative faculty. As Aristotle himself points out, things that are remembered in their own right are things of which we have *phantasia*— things which we can represent to ourselves. Things that are not grasped without *phantasia*, he adds, are remembered incidentally, *kata sumbebēkos* ($450^{a}23-5$). The most plausible interpretation of this compressed passage is that we can remember in their own right things which we can sense and thus have *phantasia* of, represent to ourselves. Objects of thought (as explained earlier, $449^{b}31$ ff.) can only

---

[15] The chief reason for taking the memory-image to represent the remembered object, rather than one's experience of it, is the passage $450^{a}20$ ff., where the representational nature of the image is explained by the way we can regard a painting as a painting or as a picture of Coriscus. But throughout this passage the representation of an object is clearly the *analogue* for memory, not memory itself, and the analogue of the portrait is a *noēma* ($451^{a}1$), not just a picture itself. The earlier passage $449^{b}30$ ff., which concerns an image of a triangle (a passage much used by Sorabji) is not explicitly about memory, but about the relation of thinking to images in general.

[16] Sorabji does note the alternative view (1972, 7A. 1) and ascribes it to G. E. M. Anscombe. It is urged by Cooper (1975), 68–9, in which he cites *DA* $428^{b}10-14$, $429^{a}1-2$.

be remembered in so far as we can represent them to ourselves, that is, have some image of them which is the result of sense–experience. This sounds outrageous. Aristotle appears to be claiming that I can only remember a geometrical theorem in so far as I can remember learning it from a diagram. Worse—it seems to be the diagram which is intrinsically memorable. The theorem is only memorable incidentally, because the diagram is.

If Aristotle's account of memory here were his sole account of memory as a whole, he would indeed be saddled with this outrageous consequence. But his ideas about memory as a whole look more reasonable if the analysis here is an analysis of personal memory, and if he also allows recollection to be a kind of memory; for none of the outrageous consequences follow from the account of recollection. On the usual view, Aristotle holds that the only thoughts that can be remembered are thoughts for which we can in some way have an associated image (with resulting embarrassment for his theories of mathematical and other abstract thinking.) On the view I am suggesting, Aristotle is not committed to this. He is in this passage not talking about all thoughts, only thoughts that we can remember acquiring through some kind of sense-experience. Thus the diagram is intrinsically, the theorem only incidentally, memorable, as *what I remember seeing*. But the theorem might be intrinsically memorable some other way: as we shall see, it might be recollected, and if so it would be remembered in its own right, and not through some associated image.

Recollection is the recovery of knowledge or perception that one previously had (451^{b}2–5). (Aristotle adds 'or of what we said memory was the state (disposition) of' (451^{b}3–4); we shall return to this.) However, it won't do, as Aristotle at once realizes, to define it as *any* recovery of past knowledge or perception. For one can relearn something. If I know that *p*, what distinguishes the case where I have recollected it from the case where I have learnt it again? Aristotle says (451^{b}8–10) that recollection is marked by there being in the person some principle (*archē*) over and above relearning; and his account spells this out. In recollection there are two features. One is what we might call association of ideas. I go from one idea to another; Aristotle discusses at length the way in which these connections can be improved and systematized by habit; there are mnemonic systems and techniques (like the 'place' system) for improving one's ability to recollect. But more important in distinguishing recollection (452^{a}4–7) is the fact that the person who is recollecting can do it himself—'he can in some way move by himself on to what follows his starting-point' (*di' hautou kinēthēnai*). He is not recollecting, but relearning, if he cannot do this, but has to do it *di' allou*—through somebody or something else.

Sorabji criticizes this feature of Aristotle's account.[17] Moving by one's own agency does not, he claims, distinguish recollecting from relearning; for one can relearn through one's own agency, and one can recollect even if one is dependent on external memory-jogging. I do not think that these points overturn Aristotle's

---

[17] Sorabji, in Aristotle (1972*b*), 37–40, 103.

account, however. It may be true that I can be said to relearn some things through my own agency, but I cannot relearn entirely through my own agency in the sense of renewing what I know from within myself—or at least, if I do, this is surely a case of recollecting.

As for the other point, Aristotle need not exclude memory-jogging. His point is that recollection requires me to do it through (*dia*) myself, and this does not exclude external aids. If I can't do it without the external aids at all, then the performance is through (*dia*) them, and is relearning, not recollecting; but then this is more than memory-jogging. Of course it is hard to draw the line here; how much memory-jogging shows that I could not have remembered without it to the extent that the achievement is 'through' it rather than 'through' me? But the distinction is clear even if the means of drawing it are not always clear.

What distinguishes recollection, then, is that it is done 'through' me; it is more of an active, deliberate performance on my part than memory is. Aristotle repeatedly calls it an investigation (*zētēsis*) or a hunting-down, and in this active rather than passive role it resembles thinking a great deal more than it does perceiving.[18] He even says that it is like a kind of inferring (453ª9–14) and hence belongs only to rational animals which can deliberate and make inferences—unlike memory, which requires only a sense of time. Only humans deliberate, he says at *HA* 488ᵇ24–6, and only they recollect, although many other animals share in memory and learning.

Of course recollection is not *entirely* up to me; however actively I search, I shall not recollect unless I have in fact retained what I want to recollect; and my retentiveness is not up to me, but is largely determined by my physiological make-up. However, I can improve my retentiveness by practising mnemonic techniques, thus helping the development, by means of habituation, of a natural tendency. Thus while it is the active searching and inferential ability which is definitive of recollection, it also requires a suitably prepared 'matter' of retentiveness. In this respect it is somewhat like a virtue—a disposition which I am naturally fitted to acquire, but shall not do so unless I by my deliberate choices and actions transform, by habituation, the material of my disposition.[19]

Because recollection, as a more intellectual process of searching and investigation, is more up to me than memory is, it turns out to be a kind of memory which I can improve. Indeed large sections of ch. 2 are about precisely what we would call improving one's memory. This is one indication that recollection is a kind of non-personal memory; for when we talk of improving one's memory it is

---

[18] At 451ᵇ22–3 Aristotle appears to allow recollection without search, but I follow Sorabji (note ad loc.) in holding that the passage need not be read this way, and that Aristotle nowhere else in *De Memoria* countenances recollection without search.

[19] Cf. 452ª29–30. Sorabji in Aristotle (1972*b*), notes the comparison with a virtue, but makes little of it; his account gives more emphasis to the mechanics of retention. It is interesting that Hume takes seriously the question whether having a good memory is a virtue. (I owe this point to Annette Baier.) In the *Treatise* (III, ɪɪɪ, iv) he concludes that it is not, because its exercise is not specially agreeable to oneself or others; in the *Second Enquiry* he gives an alternative reason, which would not hold in the ancient world, namely that it is not very useful to oneself or others.

non-personal memory that we have in mind. Personal memory does not fit, for two reasons. One is that it would usually be pointless to improve our memory of our own past experiences. What we need to remember are usually the facts, not our past learning of them; before an examination what I work on is my memory of Caesar's invading Britain, not my learning of that fact. For the examiner is interested in my memory of the facts, not—unless from some irrelevant Proustian concern—in my memory of my learning the facts. Secondly, it is dubious that one *can* do much to improve one's personal memory. One can of course go over one's past experiences; Aristotle seems to be referring to this at 451ᵃ12–14—'exercises preserve memory by reminding; and this is nothing other than often contemplating [the image] as a representation, not as itself.' But it is not clear how much one can 'exercise' in this way; notoriously one 'improves' one's past experience and memory becomes entangled with imagination. At any rate, these limited forms of exercise are nothing like the extensive mnemonic techniques which one can use in recollection.

One can, then, improve and extend one's recollection in striking and powerful ways; but one's memory can at best be preserved by exercise. Again the distinction seems to fall neatly between non-personal and personal memory.

Given Aristotle's characterization of recollection, most of the major differences between it and memory can be characterized as what recollection is *not*. We have already seen that, unlike memory, it does not belong to the perceptive faculty and is not shared with other animals. It is not of the past in the way that memory is. Aristotle never says that it is and it has no characteristics that make it likely that it is. It is recovery of past knowledge, but it lacks those features of memory which make the past acquiring of knowledge part of what is remembered. Unlike memory it does not involve saying in one's soul that one saw, etc., this before. Indeed, at 453ᵃ8–10 recollection is said to be a kind of inferring; 'the person who recollects infers (*sullogizetai*) that he saw or heard or in some way experienced such a thing before.' What I have to infer is obviously no part of the thought I already have; recollection seems actually to exclude the saying in the soul that memory involves.

Further, while recollection involves images, their role is rather different from the role they play in memory. In recollection nothing is said about any representation of their source in perception. They are never referred to in pictorial language; Aristotle talks of *kinēseis* rather than of *eikones* or even of *phantasmata*. His interest lies in the way they are connected with one another rather than the way each one is connected to my experience of it. Thus he points out that mathematics is easy to remember because our *kinēseis* of it are ordered, and this is because they are produced from items that are themselves ordered (452ᵃ1–4). If I remember one of two connected geometrical theorems, it is easy to go on to remember the other, because *the theorems* are connected; my learning of them, and my retention of the image of the diagram, is neither here nor there. It might be that I learnt them at widely separated intervals and have a clear image of one diagram and a dim one of the other; that is irrelevant to ease of recollecting the two theorems together.

Despite all these differences between memory and recollection, Aristotle is still happy to use 'memory' words for recollection—at 452ª10–12, for example, he says, in a passage which is unmistakably about recollection, that 'Remembering is the existence within the person of the power of getting [the changes] moving, and this in such a way that he can move from himself and from the changes he has, as we said.' There is nothing odd in Aristotle's being prepared to call recollection memory, if he regards these as two kinds of memory as a whole. And, since memory turned out to fit personal memory so well, it is no surprise that the differences between it and recollecting all turn out to be respects in which recollecting fits non-personal memory. Recollection and non-personal memory can both be well described as a recovery of knowledge that one previously had, but without essential reference to one's previous acquiring of that knowledge, and so without one's own past experience being represented to one, in images or not.

Obviously recollection cannot simply be identified with non-personal memory. For that was defined simply by contrast with personal memory, and it is easy enough to find cases which we commonsensically assign to non-personal memory, but which do not involve the rather special features of recollection, such as actively searching for the recovered knowledge. It is enough for my hypothesis that recollection is clearly one kind of non-personal memory; the personal—non-personal distinction illuminates Aristotle's distinction for us, even though we lack a distinction which is exactly the same as his.

However, is there more that we can say about the area of memory-claims which lack the active features of recollection but are not personal memory either? We might think, after all, that this is rather an extensive area. We cannot do more than conjecture what kind of response Aristotle would be able to make, but we can easily construct two Aristotelian responses. One is that such cases will always turn out, if pressed, to be in fact cases either of memory or of recollection; an unspecific claim that I remember *a*, or remember that *p*, must ultimately involve either a memory of some previous learning experience of mine, or involve some active search to recover the past knowledge. The other response would be to admit freely that there are other kinds of memory not covered by the concepts of memory and of recollection, and not to be reduced to or analysed in terms of those concepts. In terms of the distinction with which I opened this paper, the first response would be more characteristic of the philosopher, the second of the psychologist; and since Aristotle has precisely not had to choose between these as distinct callings we have really no way of deciding how likely he would have been to choose one over the other.

How are memory and recollection related? Aristotle says a puzzling thing at 451ᵇ4–6. When one recollects, he says, remembering results and memory follows —*to de mnēmoneuein sumbainei kai mnēmē akolouthei*. The manuscript tradition is divided here, and I am inclined to follow Ross in reading *tōi de mnēmoneuein sumbainei kai mnēmēn akolouthein*—'it results that memory follows when one does remember'. But this remark has no very obvious point in context.[20] It is not clear what this passage does claim, and in any case it is not decisive, since 'memory' could quite well here be being used in the broad sense.

More helpful is the statement at 453ª10–12, that in recollecting one *infers* that one saw, etc., the thing before; for memory includes this thought. What this suggests is that what one recollects must be a possible object of memory. For, after all, if one recollects something, one *did* learn it before, and in recollecting one infers this. But if one learnt something, then in theory one can have memory of that experience of learning. Of course, for many reasons one may have forgotten the experience, so one can have recollection without memory. But what one recollects is an appropriate object of memory, and normally one will be able to remember it. This is, I think, how we should understand the passage 451ᵇ3–4, referred to above (p. 306): recollection is the recovery of knowledge or perception one had before—'or of what we said memory was the state (disposition) of'. What one recollects is, in a perfectly good sense, the object of memory: it is the kind of thing which memory is a disposition to remember. This does not, nor should it, imply that when I recollect something I thereby have memory of that thing. Recollection, then, will result in non-personal memory, not personal.[21]

Thus the relationship here between recollection and memory also fits my hypothesis. If I remember that Caesar invaded Britain, then not only do I know it now, I knew it before. And I cannot have known it before without learning it at some point.[22] I can remember it, if we are concerned with non-personal memory, without bringing my previous learning to mind. But that previous learning is just what personal memory would bring to mind. Non-personal memory is possible without personal memory, but non-personal memory requires the past experience which personal memory is of, although memory of that experience is not part of non-personal memory.[23]

I conclude that the suggestion that Aristotle's memory is personal memory, and his recollection a kind of non-personal memory, stands up well against what we find in the text on memory, on recollection, and on their relation. Thus we

---

[20] Sorabji's note ad loc. includes a suggestion by J. L. Ackrill which may ease the difficulty somewhat.

[21] But recollection is a *search*; how can one search for some item of knowledge unless one knows one remembers it? I try to recollect your telephone-number; this is pointless unless I already know that it is something I remember, rather than imagine. Aristotle can meet this point: recollection is a search for what I remember in the broad sense; if I successfully recollect, then I know that I now know it because I knew it before. I *infer* that I *learnt* it before; and I may then remember learning it before (in which case it is also an object of memory in the narrow sense).

[22] Given very weak assumptions of an empiricist kind. In the *Phaedo* Plato excludes previous learning by means of his claim that the relevant items are not the kind of thing that can be learnt by an embodied person, since only the mind, taken to be sharply separate from the senses, can grasp them.

[23] I suspect that it is just this requirement which has encouraged philosophers who think that memory as a whole must be a unitary phenomenon to attempt to reduce non-personal to personal memory.

can regard memory and recollection as being two kinds of memory in general; and I have argued that we can ascribe the same thought to Aristotle too.

The implications of this have been made clear already: if Aristotle's notion of memory in general includes recollection as well as memory, then he is not committed to a narrow theory of memory which ties all memory to the having of images, or the remembering of one's own past experience.[24] As often, Aristotle is not interested in producing a striking and revisionary theory which will be false of certain obvious phenomena, which must then be explained away. If we have two kinds of memory which are rather different, then these must be separately discussed without trying to force a common pattern on them.

We may still feel disappointed that Aristotle remains at the point that he does, and does not further discuss the problems in recognizing both personal and non-personal memory. What kind of account do we give of the way that both these kinds of memory occur in one and the same person? For memory relates me to my past self in involving a memory of my past experience. Recollection recovers the knowledge I had in the past, but not through my having it then, and so does not relate me to my past self. Is it just a brute fact that one kind of memory involves the self in this way while the other does not? For, as we have seen, they are closely related in that what I recollect —that is, remember without relating it to my past self—is something I can in principle have memory of, and so relate it to my past self. Perhaps Aristotle is wise to leave these questions alone, especially in view of the generally unsatisfactory account he gives of the relation between the perceptual faculty, to which memory is assigned, and the thinking faculty, to which recollection is assigned. But a large part must be played in this by his disinclination to pursue problems about the self, at least in the psychological works. This is perhaps a failure in Aristotle's philosophy of mind; but we are back with the conclusion that we should not demand from Aristotle a philosophy of mind rigidly demarcated as we would see it. Instead we should be ready to respect the self-imposed limitations of his work; in this case a work which raises issues relevant to philosophy of mind, but which also marks the boundaries for a developing empirical psychology.[25]

---

[24] It is interesting that Aristotle has often been criticized for his account of memory taken as an account of memory in general, on the grounds that it is too restrictive; it has been overlooked that his account of recollection is extremely like modern accounts of memory.

[25] This is a revised version of an article which originally appeared in *Oxford Studies in Ancient Philosophy*, iv (1986), as a contribution to a Festschrift for John Ackrill. Earlier versions were read at Pittsburgh, Cambridge, and Oxford. I am very grateful for helpful comments on these occasions, and to Thomas Baldwin, Jonathan Barnes, James Lennox, and Michael Woods for written comments. John Ackrill's careful and illuminating study of Aristotle's psychological works has been a model and inspiration.

17

NOUS POIĒTIKOS: SURVEY OF EARLIER INTERPRETATIONS

† FRANZ BRENTANO

I. Earliest Interpretations

1. It seems that not even Aristotle's immediate disciples agreed in their conception of the active intellect [*nous poiētikos*]. When Theophrastus[1]* speaks of it, he leaves no doubt that he takes the *nous poiētikos* to be something belonging to the human nature.[2] The *Ethics* of Eudemus, on the other hand, has been cited in support of the opposite opinion: this philosopher, who is said to have followed his teacher's path most faithfully,[3] seems to identify the active intellect with God.[4] If this were true, then Aristotle's greatest disciples, who received the doctrine directly from the master, would have been divided on the very issue which to this day accounts for the deepest division between interpretations. It would also be certain that we must for ever give up hope for a well-founded exegesis. But such a contradiction does not exist. We shall see later how the passages from Eudemus and Theophrastus can brought into perfect agreement.

2. The fragment from the fifth book of Theophrastus' *Physics*, which Themistius has preserved for us in the second book of his *Treatise on the Soul*, discloses three points even to the casual reader.

(*a*) In Theophrastus' view Aristotle took not only the active but also the receptive intellect, which becomes all intelligible things, to be immaterial.[5]

(*b*) He took both intellects to be capacities of one and the same subject.[6]

(*c*) He took this subject to be an essential constituent of man.[7]

We cannot determine from this passage whether Theophrastus himself agreed with this doctrine of his master, and it is here of no importance for us. But it is more likely that he did in fact agree.[8] The objections he raises are no proof of actual doubt; they are merely difficulties put forward in accordance with a method that was as customary with him as it had been with his teacher. He wants to clarify the problem and develop guidelines for the scientific investigation that is to commence.[9]

Translation © 1977 by The Regents of the University of California. Originally published as Franz Brentano, *Die Psychologie des Aristoteles* (Mainz: Franz Kirchheim, 1867, repr. Darmstadt: Wissenschaftliche Buchgesellschaft, 1967), 5–36. Translation by Rolf George, sponsored by the Brentano Foundation (Dir. Roderick Chisholm), *The Psychology of Aristotle* (Berkeley: University of California Press, 1977), 4–24, 182–97; revised for present work by translator, 1990. Insertions and comments by the translator are enclosed in [ ].

* For notes to this chapter see pp. 328–41.

3. History has preserved for us only very few reports of other Peripatetics of this early period. They are too sparse to yield clear and firm views even concerning their own philosophical opinions; even less do they allow us to discern how they might have interpreted Aristotle's doctrines, from which they deviated without much hesitation, as is well known. Strato, the head of the school after Theophrastus, already denied all intellectual cognition, and indeed the entire domain of the intellect,[10] and we have similar reports about Aristoxenus and Dicaearchus, fellow students of Theophrastus.[11]

4. By contrast, the Peripatetic school of the first and second centuries AD had more respect for the statements of their founder. They took it to be almost their exclusive task to explain and defend the works of Aristotle. We possess a few writings from that school, all by Alexander Aphrodisiensis, of which some are concerned with the doctrine of the soul. Alexander does indeed interpret Aristotle's doctrine as saying that the *nous poiētikos* is a purely spiritual substance, separate from the nature of man and acting upon him, the first ground of all things, the divine intelligence itself.[12] Through its influence man acquires actual knowledge, while the capacity for receiving this influence[13] depends upon a certain mixture of elements in the human body. Hence he claims that the human soul is wholly dependent upon the body in its thinking and being, and is mortal.[14] Given the great reputation of Alexander, which earned him the name of an exemplary exegete, many must have followed his interpretation; we must suppose that they are the ones Themistius had in mind when he tells us[15] that there were some who took the *nous poiētikos* to be the deity.

5. There were others who thought that the *nous poiētikos* should be identified with immediately known propositions and the truths that follow from them; they were thus opposed to both Alexander and Theophrastus. This last interpretation probably connects some passages in the last chapter of the *Posterior Analytics* and the *Nicomachean Ethics* with the *nous poiētikos*.[16] Themistius criticized both this interpretation as well as that of Alexander by drawing upon Theophrastus' testimony.[17]

II. Medieval Conceptions

6. These were the controversies in antiquity; and there was no more unanimity in the Middle Ages. It is obvious that the Arabic philosophers, who through the Syrians had a connecting tradition with the Peripatetic school of Alexandria,[18] were influenced by Alexander Aphrodisiensis, though they were by no means in complete agreement with him.[19] In particular, the views of the two most famous teachers among the Arabs, Avicenna (Ibn Sina) and Averroës (Ibn Rushd), differed from those of Alexander in that they, like Themistius and Theophrastus, supposed that not only the *nous poiētikos*, but also the *nous* that receives thought and that, to begin with, is potentially all things, is something

immaterial. We briefly want to put forth their views, especially since the available accounts do not seem suited to give a completely clear and correct picture of them. It will become clear from the resulting conclusions how alien to the spirit of Aristotelian philosophy was the element that Alexander introduced into psychology through the separation of the *nous poiētikos* from human individuality.

7.   Like Alexander Aphrodisiensis, Avicenna teaches that of the two intellects that Aristotle distinguishes in *DA* 3. 5, i.e. the intellect that becomes all things and the intellect that produces all things, the former, but not the latter, is found in man as its subject.

In outline, his doctrine is as follows:

(*a*) Avicenna uses the term 'material intellect' (*intellectus*[20] *materialis*) to describe the Aristotelian potential intellect [*nous dunamei*]; he followed Alexander in this.[21] The term is not meant to describe this intellect as corporeal, but merely as a passive substratum of the ideas, as capacity for thought. This material intellect is a cognitive faculty peculiar to human nature, with which intelligible forms are apprehended.

(*b*) Its subject is not some bodily organ, but the soul. For with man, the highest part of the soul is spiritual and not mixed with the body.[22] Therefore it does not perish even when the body dies (this holds of the individual human soul);[23] in one of its parts it is independent of body in its existence, and immortal.[24]

(*c*) Initially the material intellect knows only potentially. In order for it to know actually, ideas have to be imparted to it from some other substance, which is purely intellectual and separate from human nature.[25]

(*d*) The reason for this is that all intelligible forms pre-exist immaterially in the pure intellects [*Geister*], the intelligences, the highest of which[26] moves the uppermost sphere, and the others the remaining heavenly spheres. From the highest intelligence they flow into the second, from the second into the third, and so forth to the last, which is the so-called active intelligence (*intelligentia agens*).[27]

(*e*) Finally, from this active intelligence the intelligible forms flow into our soul, as do also the sublunary substantial forms into corporeal matter. For only the active intelligence gives natural things their forms, while the agency of the lower causes is everywhere merely preparatory and is limited to making matter suitable for the reception of the form. The reception of the intelligible form into the material intellect is analogous to this. Here, too, it is only the active intelligence that imparts the form; the images are capable of nothing but preparing the material intellect for the reception of the emanation.[28]

(*f*) This preparation, to be sure, is an essential precondition of knowledge in the material intellect.[29] The material intellect is illuminated by the light of the active intelligence and recognizes the general only if it looks upon the particular representations, which are in the imagination. The activities of the imagination and of the sensory thought-faculty (*virtus cogitativa*) are needed to put it in a position to combine with the active intelligence and receive the intelligible forms that emanate from the latter.[30]

(*g*) But what does the material intellect do after receiving the forms? Does it retain the ideas, once grasped, for all future? By no means; rather, the ideas remain in it only as long as it actually cognizes them; thus in this respect it does not differ from other cognitive faculties. For the sensible forms, if they too continue to exist within us after actual perception, are retained not within the apprehensive faculties themselves, but in other faculties, which might be called the storehouses of the apprehensive powers. Thus the imagination is the storehouse for the common sense or the fantasy[31] (storehouse of forms), and memory is the storehouse for the estimative and sensory thought-faculty (storehouse of the intentions). Hence the apprehensive powers must turn to these whenever a representation received earlier is to be renewed.[32]

(*h*) But for the ideas of the material intellect such a storehouse cannot exist, for it would have to be the faculty of a bodily organ. (The reason for this is that every intellectual subject actually cognizes all forms that it contains; in such a case the expressions 'to contain a form' and 'to recognize a form' are equivalent.) But this is impossible since no form that exists in a faculty that uses a bodily organ for its operation is more than potentially intelligible.

(*i*) Hence nothing remains[33] but to assume that whenever we intellectually cognize something, the intelligible form flows anew from the active intelligence into our material intellect so that learning is nothing but the acquisition of a perfect ability to combine with the active intelligence in order to receive the intelligible forms.

Thus Avicenna. Anyone even moderately familiar with Aristotle's doctrine sees clearly how strange a transformation it has suffered. The sensory ceases to be the source of intellectual cognition; in a manner evidently approaching Plato, sensory representations are to constitute merely an occasion for our intellectual knowledge.

8. The doctrine of Averroës is quite different from that of Avicenna. Averroës, an excessive enthusiast of Aristotle,[34] is concerned to develop the latter's pure doctrine. We shall see with what success.

The two principles that Aristotle distinguishes in *DA* 3. 5, namely the intellect that becomes all things and the intellect that brings forth all things, Averroës takes to be two purely intellectual substances which are by nature distinct from man as sensitive being, and teaches the following concerning their nature and their mode of integration with man as sensitive being:

(*a*) The newborn child is devoid not only of all *actual* intellectual cognition, it also does not yet possess a *faculty* of intellectual cognition, and in general there is nothing in it which is not corporeal and corruptible. Only insofar as the child is by nature constituted so that the power of intellectual cognition can later on unite with it, and insofar as it contains sensory pictures (images) within it, which are potentially intelligible, can one say that it is capable of intellectual cognition.[35]

(*b*) None the less, the child is already human and different in kind from irrational animals. For the specific difference of man is not an intellectual but a sensory power, which Aristotle[36] calls the passible intellect (*intellectus passibilis*),[37] and which has its seat in the middlemost cell of the head.[38] Through this faculty we distinguish individual representations and compare them with each other. None of the animals can do this, since in its place they have only a kind of judgement by natural instinct (*virtus aestimativa naturalis*), by virtue of which, for example, the lamb views the wolf as its enemy. We have already encountered both of them in Avicenna as *virtus cogitativa* and *virtus aestimativa* or *existimativa*.[39]

(*c*) Depending on the disposition of the passible intellect persons differ with respect to their talent for intellectual cognition.[40] Through its activity in connection with the activities of the imagination and of memory they acquire habitual knowledge, whose subject is not something immaterial [*geistig*], but precisely the passible intellect.[41]

(*d*) The same is not true of actual intellectual knowledge. It can only be found in an intellectual faculty, and man achieves it by merging with two immaterial substances which are in their nature separate from the human body as well as from each other. They are the material intellect (*intellectus materialis*),[42] so called because it is by its nature merely the capacity for intelligible forms,[43] and the active intellect (*intellectus agens*), which is called active because it makes actually intelligible the sensory pictures in man that are potentially intelligible (the images), and which thus moves the material intellect.[44] The material intellect takes up the concepts which have become intelligible and which are in the images; the active intellect does not receive them, it does not even have knowledge of them,[45] but it makes them knowable to the material intellect. But this does not mean that it is not itself also a cognizing being; it means only that the objects of its thought all belong to another, higher domain; it knows the world of spirits.

(*e*) Each of the two immaterial beings to which we owe our knowledge is a single substance which does not multiply with the number of knowing subjects.[46] All who were, are, and will be, know whatever they know intellectually by the same cognizing faculty and through the activity of the same active power. These two alone are what is eternal in man, while everything that is peculiar to an individual perishes with the death of the body, as it came about with the generation of the body.[47]

(*f*) The union with them takes place in the following way. In their real essence the intelligible forms are in the images. At first the faculty of sensory thought (the passible intellect), in combination with imagination and memory, prepares the images to receive the influence of the active intellect; through it they become actually intelligible.[48] Thus we can compare them with certain subordinate arts which prepare the instruments for the work of some higher art; as, for example, the art of tool-sharpening for the art of sculpting, and the art of military drill for the art of the general.

(*g*) Once they have done this, and once the activity of the active intellect has made the images intelligible,[49] the material intellect, which stands to all intelligible forms in the relation of potentiality, receives from the images the concepts of sensible things.[50] Hence the recognized intelligible forms have two subjects: (i) the images and (ii) the material intellect;[51] just as the sensible forms, e.g. the colours, have two subjects: (i) one that lies outside the sensing subject and (ii) the faculty of sight.

But if in this way both our image and the material intellect are united with the same intelligible form, then obviously, by means of the image a form of the material intellect is united with us. And if a form of the material intellect is so united, then since every form forms a unity with its subject, the material intellect itself must be united with us; and now we have knowledge by means of the material intellect, as if it were an innate faculty of knowledge.[52]

(*h*) We all, it was said, have knowledge through one and the same material intellect; does it not follow from this that we all know the same things? By no means. We merely need to consider how we recognize something by means of the material intellect. We do this only in so far as it has been connected with us through the images, which must be appropriately disposed. But we do not all have the same images, and even those who do, do not have the images disposed in the same way. Hence one of us is united with the material intellect in one way, another in a different way; for this reason it is not true that each knows what the other does.[53]

(*i*) Thus this objection has been removed; but our assertions appear to lead at once to another inconsistency. We said that the material intellect receives the intelligible forms from the images within us; must there then not be a change in it, in that one and the same intelligible form is sometimes actual in it, and then ceases to be actual? By no means. The material intellect does not receive the intelligible forms merely from a single person, but from all persons living on the surface of the earth; and among these were found, and are found, and will be found at all times, some that have the required disposition for images of every intelligible form. It is a natural necessity that a philosopher be found in the human race.[54] And so the intelligible forms are at the same time eternal and always new. Their eternity derives from one of the two subjects in which they are, namely the material intellect, and their novelty from the other, namely the image. The sciences can neither come into being nor perish, except *per accidens*, i.e. in so far as they are combined with Socrates or with Plato.[55]

(*j*) We have seen in what way our union with the material intellect takes place; let us now consider in what way we are united with the active intellect. It is through this union, if it is perfected, that we come to know the pure intellects and thus to achieve the highest bliss. For we must not hope to achieve this in another life[56] since, as we said, our individual being ceases with our death. But we can partake of it in this life, though only when life is drawing to a close.

(*k*) For the union with the active intellect becomes more perfect as our knowledge of the material world, which is mediated through images, becomes more complete. This can be shown as follows. It is evident that we know conclusions because we know their premisses. But the active intellect is also the cause of all our knowledge; hence it is clear that we must here envisage one and the same thing as the effect of two different entities. But one and the same effect can be ascribed to two different things only in the following two cases: first, when one of them is the instrument of the other (as one can attribute the recovery to the physician as well as to the medicine),[57] and secondly, when one of them is related to the other as the form to its subject (e.g. as warmth is related to fire; here one can say that the fire, or the warmth of the fire, produces heat). Hence the active intellect must be related to the propositions that in us become the premisses of new knowledge, either as form to matter or as the original cause to its tool. (The second relation is very similar to the first, for here, too, the active intellect appears in a sense as the perfection, while the premisses that are immediately known appear as that which is made perfect through it.)[58] But wherever that which is made perfect is absorbed, the perfection itself is at the same time also absorbed. For example, the pupil takes in at the same time the colour which is actually seen and the light which makes it visible.[59] The same holds for our case: the material intellect receives the active intellect together with the truths that become known. The more thoughts someone receives into the material intellect, the more he merges with the active intellect, until finally, when he has attained all knowledge of the corporeal world, he is wholly united with the active intellect. Perfection is fully united with him since he has received the totality of the perfectible.[60]

(*l*) This opens to him knowledge of the entire domain of intellects. For by nature the active intellect has knowledge of all spiritual substances. Whoever has received the active intellect wholly into the material intellect knows through the active intellect whatever the latter knows.[61] In this exalted contemplation he finds highest happiness and perfect bliss; he has achieved the last and ultimate goal that a person can obtain.[62]

This is the doctrine of the Arab, a doctrine of which the level-headed philosopher from Stagira had certainly never dreamt. But in spite of its eccentric mysticism and its sophistical turns of phrase it found much favour with the Arabs, and also attracted many adherents in the Christian West. The great Scholastics, in particular Thomas Aquinas, thought it therefore necessary to inveigh against it with all their might. In view of such profound misinterpretations, which no longer allow us to recognize even the outlines of the Aristotelian doctrine, the Doctor Angelicus calls out indignantly that Averroës ought not so much to be called a Peripatetic as a despoiler of Peripatetic philosophy: 'Non tam peripateticus quam Peripateticae philosophiae depravator!'[63]

9. But how did he, the greatest thinker of the Middle Ages, interpret the words of the Philosopher? His sympathetic spirit allowed him to sense more than he could read of this most difficult doctrine of Aristotle's in the often corrupt text. His explanation coincides to a remarkable extent in all the above-stated points with the fragment of Theophrastus, which has come to us in the paraphrase of Themistius.

Aquinas, too, takes not only the active intellect [*intellectus agens*] to be immaterial, but also the potential intellect [*intellectus possibilis*] (for, in contrast to the

expression of the Arabs, this is what he calls the intellect that is all things potentially).⁶⁴ Secondly, he too takes not only the potential intellect but also the active
intellect to belong to human nature and does not think of it as a purely spiritual
substance outside the person; both are faculties of the human soul. In saying that
they are separate from the body,⁶⁵ Aristotle merely means that they do not have
an organ like the faculties of the vegetative and sensitive part, but are found only
in the soul as their subject. For the human soul stands on the boundary between
the world of bodies and intellects; because of the sublimity of its nature it exceeds
the receptive power of matter and cannot be wholly included in it. Thus it
possesses powers that are not faculties of the ensouled body but belong exclusively to it; there remain for it some activities in which corporeal matter does not
participate. In this way the potential and the active intellect are incorporeal in
their activity and existence, unmixed with matter.⁶⁶

The potential intellect is the proper cognitive faculty of the intellectual part; all
our ideas are found in it. But they are not actually in it from the beginning;
rather, it is initially the mere capacity for thought and is like an empty tablet
upon which nothing is written. It receives the intelligible forms through a kind of
affection and this is the reason why Aristotle⁶⁷ says that thinking is an affection.⁶⁸

But in addition to the affected entity in which it exists, each affection
presupposes an active principle. What then is the active principle that brings
forth the intelligible forms in our intellect? Aristotle says that the origin of our
knowledge is in the senses.⁶⁹ This agrees with what he teaches elsewhere, namely,
that the soul cognizes nothing without images.⁷⁰ But no corporeal thing can call
forth an impression in something incorporeal; thus, according to Aristotle, the
mere power of sensory bodies does not suffice for the generation of our thoughts,
but something higher is required. In the third book of *De Anima* he says, 'the
active surpasses the affected in dignity.'⁷¹

This higher agent is another intellectual faculty of the soul, the so-called active
intellect. The images which are received from the senses are only potentially
intelligible since particular matter still adheres to them. It makes them actually
intelligible through abstraction and for this reason it is the proper and pre-
eminent (active) cause of intellectual knowledge, while the images are only the
accompanying cause and, in a sense, the matter of the cause.⁷²

The active intellect illuminates the images and abstracts the intelligible species
from the images. It *illuminates* [*erleuchtet*] them; the images are to the intellect as
colours are to the sense of sight. The influence of the active intellect prepares the
images so that intellectual concepts can be abstracted from them, just as the
sensitive part is raised to a higher power through its union with the intellective
part. The active intellect *abstracts* the intelligible species from the images, i.e.
through the power of the active intellect we can grasp and consider the general
nature of things without their individual determinations; the representations of
this nature are received into the potential intellect as forms.⁷³

   10.   We have already said that this conception, which differs so entirely from

the views of Alexander and the Arabs, recommends itself by its agreement with what we have gathered from the statements of Theophrastus.

But here again objections arise which appear difficult to overcome. Some of them have already been urged by Durandus,[74] who for his part decided to give up the active intellect altogether. Thomas said that the active intellect acts upon the images; otherwise the images could not generate thoughts in the intellect, since nothing corporeal can act upon an intellectual thing. But if this were so then the active intellect could give the required help only if it created through its activity something intellectual. However, in a sensory faculty which is tied to an organ no intellectual accident can possibly be found. Hence the effect which has been attributed to the active intellect is evidently impossible.

But let us assume, even, that the active intellect could transform the images into something intellectual: they would in any case not be the same after the transformation as before; they would no longer be images. But Aristotle says that we can never think anything without at the same time having the corresponding image within us.[75] Hence, according to him, the image has evidently not been transformed into a higher, intelligible, thing at the moment of cognition.

11. Thus here, too, we find ourselves entangled in difficulties. This explains the restructuring of the Thomistic doctrine by Suárez.[76] Suárez himself, of course, did not think that he had departed from the views of St Thomas.[77]

Suárez claimed that

the abstracting activity should not be viewed as an influence of the intellectual cognitive power [*Erkenntnißkraft*] (of the active intellect) upon sensory representations, but as an activity that is immanent in reason [*Vernunft*] itself. Since it is the same soul that knows through sense and through the intellect, the presence of the sensory representations suffices to stimulate the intellect into activity, and this activity is directed toward the object of sensibility. But no sensory representation can have any further influence upon the origin of an intellectual representation; for one must stricly maintain that no material thing can influence and change anything immaterial.

Hence one should not believe that

the intellect (the active intellect) purifies the sensory representation, eliminating, as it were, the material element, in order to transfer it thus transformed and spiritualized from the imagination into itself (the potential intellect). The activity of abstraction does not produce any change at all in the sensory representation; it consists only in the intellect generating within itself the intelligible picture of the object of which the imagination possesses a sensory picture.[78]

12. A mere stimulation by the sensory image could perhaps have sufficed for Plato, but never for Aristotle. For Plato took all higher knowledge to be present in us from birth, acquired in an earlier life, so that after birth the soul merely requires a stimulus in order to recollect. But Aristotle is concerned with the original acquisition of our thoughts. According to his doctrine the intellectual part is entirely devoid of ideas; thus even the active intellect, if it belongs to the soul, has

no thought in it; how can it then be in a position to impart concepts to the potential intellect? It is indeed correct that the intelligible is in a way contained in the sensory representations of imagination, since the general is concretely contained in the particular; but the images, being material, do not in any way act upon the intellect; thus it is evident that we now entirely lack a sufficient active principle which would lead the potential thoughts to actuality.

Furthermore, suppose that the active intellect has enough power at once to generate ideas in the intellect whenever it is stimulated by a sensory representation. It is obvious that if this is the case the ideas must be potentially contained in the active intellect from the beginning, since the images can produce no change in it. But then we would have to object against Aristotle, as he himself does against Plato,[79] that it is inexplicable why a lack of sensation should always lead to a lack of cognition; even less could one understand why Aristotle claims that even after knowledge has been achieved, actual cognition is possible only so long as one can retain the corresponding particular representation in the imagination.[80] This view, then, is obviously a departure from the Aristotelian view concerning the relation between sensory cognition and intellectual cognition.

Furthermore, Aristotle teaches that there is no activity without a striving towards activity.[81] Hence, if the active intellect through its activity is to produce intellectual cognition, we must attribute to man a striving for knowledge. This striving, which leads to the operation of the active intellect, must be thought of in either of two ways. On the one hand, it may be an unconscious drive, like that from which the vegetative activity of plants and the workings of inanimate nature result. But obviously, if this is the case, then sensory cognition can play no role, for the only precondition for such activity is the presence and correct disposition of that which is capable of receiving the effect.[82] But according to this conception the potential intellect is by nature disposed to receive the influence of the active intellect, and is most intimately united with it. Hence the intellectual part would have to produce thoughts within itself from the beginning, even without all sensation. On the other hand, the striving from which the operation of the active intellect results might be thought of as conscious. Then it must be a sensory or intellectual desire. But it is not a sensory desire, for how could the sensitive part desire truth? And how could the desire of the sensitive part govern the movement of the active intellect, especially in a theory that does not allow the sensory to act upon the intellectual at all? But it can also not be an intellectual desire, for any intellectual desire presupposes intellectual thought, as Aristotle teaches us in the twelfth book of *Metaphysics*,[83] and we are here concerned with the problem of how thought arises in the intellective soul in the first place. Even after the intellective soul begins to think, the first thing it knows is not the truth of the thought towards which the desire (from which the activity of the active intellect is said to originate) would have to be directed; rather, the first thing it knows is the nature of external things.[84] Hence such a view of the *nous poiētikos* is altogether incompatible with the remaining Aristotelian doctrine.

And so we must leave the medieval commentators, too, without having found

anything that seemed altogether satisfactory, and must turn to more recent
interpreters. Here, too, we would be prolix if we surveyed all individual opinions.[85] Thus, as in our treatment of the older periods, we shall restrict ourselves
to consideration of the views of some of the most eminent German and French
experts on Aristotelian philosophy.

III. Most Recent Interpretations

13.   Above all, we encounter here Trendelenburg, who has discussed the doctrine of the *nous poiētikos* in his meritorious commentary upon the three books of
De Anima (Jena, 1833). We summarize his remarks as follows:

(*a*) The difficulty of the Aristotelian doctrine lies mainly in the following:
the *nous* is sometimes said to be so intimately connected with the other faculties
of the soul that it does not appear capable of existence without them (*nous
pathētikos*). On other occasions, when it is envisaged as the highest *nous*, as *nous
poiētikos*, it is separated from the rest of human nature and contrasted with it
is as something higher and its ruler.[86]

(*b*) What then are we to understand by these two? We believe that Aristotle
used the expression *nous pathētikos* to designate all lower powers that are required
for the thinking of things, tying them together, as it were, in one knot. He calls
these powers passible intellect [*pathētikos nous*] partly because they are led to
completion by the *nous poiētikos*, partly because they are affected by their
objects.[87] If one attends to the contribution of the senses, then the acquisition of
general concepts through the comparison of individual sensations is the work of
the passible intellect.[88]

(*c*) Different from it and more noble is the *nous poiētikos*, even if we must
not take it to be the divine intellect itself, as some have done who have already
been refuted by Themistius. It belongs to the human soul[89] and thus is not the
same for everyone.[90]

(*d*) But Aristotle nowhere indicates what it actually is, what the limits of its
domain are, and how it uses its power to generate knowledge.[91] Only one thing is
clear, namely, that it comprehends the first and last principles of knowledge and
that it is ultimately its testimony in which we trust when we accept the truth.[92]
Without it we should have no warrant, for there is no knowledge of principles,
since they are unprovable; on the other hand, the passible intellect can also not be
the guarantor since it depends upon the comparison of sensations. Thus if we
appealed to it we should likewise commit the fallacy of begging the question.
Thus there remains only the *nous poiētikos* that grasps the first principles through
its own power.[93] The following words from the eleventh book of the *Metaphysics*
refer to these supersensible principles: 'Some (of the sciences) get the "what"
through perception, others by hypothesis.'[94] But whence do they derive this basis,
if not from their own intellect?[95]

(*e*) We said that our *nous poiētikos* is not the divine intellect; none the less, it is something akin to the deity. The divine intellect, too, is a *nous poiētikos*; for to one who does not deny God's existence it can be nothing other than that *nous* from which the truth of things flows. Aristotle has intimated this kinship between the divine and the human intellect in the twelfth book of the *Metaphysics*[96] without, of course, determining here or elsewhere anything concerning the way in which the human intellect partakes of the divine.[97]

(*f*) By taking it to be something divine he was consistently led to suppose that it did not develop from matter but was added to the other powers from outside. He derives it from the deity;[98] from there it enters into the foetus; all this is in full agreement with his entire doctrine of the intellect.[99]

14.   This explanation carefully tries to avoid going beyond what Aristotle clearly maintains. None the less, it seems to us to contain several points which, when compared with the words of the Philosopher, show that here, too, the doctrine of the *nous* is not represented in a way that wholly conforms to Aristotle's sense.

We must make this point in particular concerning the *nous* that in *DA* 3. 5 is contrasted with the *nous poiētikos*, i.e. the *nous* that becomes all things. According to Aristotle it is not something sensual, but something intellectual, as is shown in particular by the fourth chapter; this entire chapter deals with this *nous* and describes it as belonging to the intellectual soul [*psychē noētike*] (429ᵃ29 ff.), as unmixed with the body (429ᵃ24), as separate from the body (429ᵇ4), as simple (429ᵇ22), and as without matter (430ᵃ1 ff.). There is not the slightest intimation anywhere that the discussion has shifted to some other faculty,[100] and the *nous poiētikos* is not introduced until the beginning of ch. 5.

15.   Brandis, if we understand him correctly, also departs on this point from Trendelenburg,[101] with whose conception he otherwise fully agrees. He, too, decided in his *Geschichte der griechisch-römischen Philosophie* (1857) that the *nous poiētikos* belongs to the individual person. In opposition to other interpretations he has more recently maintained this view even more definitely in his *Entwickelung der griechischen Philosophie*. Brandis also agrees with Trendelenburg in attributing knowledge of principles which are in themselves true and certain to the *nous poiētikos*,[102] while mediating thought is attributed to the passible intellect.[103] Brandis's view is best clarified by a passage quoted verbatim from the last-mentioned work.

After noting that the human intellect is not attached to matter, he continues:

In its connection with [the faculty of] representation it is to be described as passible intellect, in that it borrows from it and from sensory perception the stuff for mediating thought, and requires images (Schemata): in this respect it is neither simple nor eternal. To put it otherwise: it has neither simplicity nor eternity in so far as it acts as mediating thought. Only intellect in the narrower sense of the word, the theoretical or active [*energetische*] intellect, is said to be (and truly is) immortal and eternal when it is separated from the body, and upon it rests the actual ego or human self. It was imparted to us from outside and is said to be itself divine, or the most divine within us. This is meant to indicate its independence from the organic body, not that the universal world spirit is temporarily conferred upon us.[104]

16.   This altered conception of the *nous* that becomes all things does indeed remove one difficulty; but now it is no longer quite comprehensible why it should perish with the body and yet belong to the intellectual part. It could perhaps be impeded in its operation, but why should its existence be impaired?

Aside from this there is another difficulty that immediately concerns the conception of the *nous poiētikos*. For if the *nous poiētikos* is not a higher, divine intellect, but a power peculiar to the individual soul, then it seems impossible to construe it as a thinking faculty. For one could neither say that it thinks from the outset and always, nor that it receives fresh thoughts. We could not say the former, for such an assertion would offend equally against experience and against Aristotle's doctrine in *De Anima* and the logical writings that refer to precisely these experiences.[105] And we could not maintain the latter, for the reception of thought is precisely a coming into being of thinkables [*noēta*], an affection which is attributed to the *nous* that is potentially, and that is contrasted with the *nous poiētikos*. And of that *nous* it is said, not that it becomes the 'mediating thoughts', but that it becomes *all things*,[106] namely all intelligible things, as Aristotle explains in the eighth chapter.[107]

Thus even our respect for the judgement of two such distinguished experts on Aristotelian philosophy cannot move us to adopt a view which cannot possibly be reconciled with Aristotle's clear and important characterizations.

17.   These explanations approach the view of Theophrastus at least in that they attribute the *nous poiētikos* to individual persons. But there are other recent interpretations which turn out to be more closely related to the views of Alexander and the Arab commentators. Among them we mention first of all that of Ravaisson.

In the first volume of his *Essai sur la métaphysique d'Aristote*, he proclaims[108] that according to Aristotle man has only a passive intellect which comprehends all forms, receives all ideas and, analogously to prime matter, can become all things. 'It is', he says, 'universal potentiality in the world of ideas, as prime matter is in the world of things.' By contrast the *nous poiētikos* is said to be 'the absolute intelligence, the creative activity that leads all possible forms to actuality and brings forth all thoughts'.

This is reminiscent of the doctrine of Avicenna, but the latter holds that every form and every thought emanates immediately from the active intellect. By contrast, Ravaisson thinks that Aristotle does not deny that corporeal beings, as secondary causes, bring forth other corporeal beings, and that he assumes, correspondingly, that thoughts are secondary principles which awaken other thoughts in us, so that only occasionally need a higher substance be invoked as a first mover. This higher substance, the deity itself, directly dispenses the principles from whose power all knowledge and all discursive thought proceeds. What holds for the theoretical domain also holds for the practical; the divine wisdom gives the primitive light for the distinction between good and evil and gives the first impulse to the will, so that virtue appears merely as a tool of absolute thought.[109]

In the more detailed characterization of the *nous* which is potentially all things Ravaisson nearly agrees with Alexander. The sensitive principle is basically the same as the intellective and rational; hence the intellect distinguishes and compares the abstract form, which is its own object, with the sensible form. It could not do so if it did not comprise both of them in *one* consciousness. Thus the entire difference between sense and intellect is reduced to two modes of being of one and the same thing. Hence it is natural that the intellect in its existence is tied to the body; nothing peculiar to an individual person is immortal.

18.   Ravaisson thinks that only through this conception can Aristotle's doctrine of the intellect be made consistent not only with itself but also with Aristotle's *Metaphysics*. This interpretation alone, he thinks, conforms to the spirit of the Aristotelian system. It appears that he places greatest emphasis upon the analogy of potential intellect and prime matter, both of which, he thinks, require God as prime mover.

None the less, we have already shown that the conception of the intellect that becomes all things as an organic faculty is incompatible with Aristotle's statements. But even if we assume that this account does not on this point contradict the Philosopher's clear statements, precisely this would deprive it of all merit. For if the intellect that becomes all things had an organ as its subject, then the power of the prime mover, as governing the corporeal world, would extend to it just as much as it extends to the senses. This power would in any case be incapable of generating anything intellectual [*Geistiges*] in such an intellect, which would be a faculty that is mixed with matter.

Furthermore, let us suppose that the intellect that becomes all things is one and the same with sense, and differs from it only in state. Now since sensory perception must already be present if this intellect is to grasp the first general representation, it would not be a faculty devoid of all actuality that now apprehends its first form. Thus Aristotle would have had more reason to assume a new and immediate intercession of the deity for the generation of the first sensory representation than for the awakening of the first general thought. Even though Avicenna departs considerably from Aristotle, he is nonetheless closer to him in so far as he does not deny the intellectuality of the receptive intellect; also he is better able to maintain his analogy between it and prime matter.

19.   There are others who likewise want to construe the *nous poiētikos* as an intellect separate from human nature. They depart from Ravaisson on important points, but their attempts are not therefore happier, nor are they themselves more satisfied with them.

Renan wants to see in the doctrine of the *nous poiētikos* a theory rather like the view of Malebranche.[110] Since he cannot deny that this doctrine has little agreement with the general spirit of Peripatetic philosophy, he alleges that Aristotle frequently embodied fragments of older schools in his system without bothering to reconcile them with his own views. Thus the entire theory of the *nous* is said to have been borrowed from Anaxagoras.[111] Renan himself admits that the doctrine of the generation of our intellectual knowledge in the *Analytics* and a great many statements in *De Anima* itself stand in glaring contradiction to his conception of the doctrine of *nous*; but, he thinks, this should not in the least sway us. The attempt to make Aristotle consistent would be childish since he himself had so little concern with such things.[112]

20. Renan's own words make further criticism unnecessary. One can perhaps admit that some thinkers of the immature period of Greek philosophy, as, for example, the older Pythagoreans or Empedocles, often failed to concern themselves both with the compatibility of certain doctrines they had borrowed from elsewhere, and with the principles of their own systems. But Aristotle was extremely circumspect; it was his custom always to point out apparent contradictions and even to make them his motivation for extending an inquiry; hence, for him, more than for any other philosopher, Renan's assumption is most unjustified. Thus we now turn to another recent commentator.

21. Zeller likewise takes the *nous poiētikos* to be a universal intellect, the absolute thought of the deity; but he neither agrees with Ravaisson nor tries to make Aristotle a Greek Malebranche; rather, he comes to adopt a view according to which we should have to attribute to our philosopher an even more curious theory, which would contain the same absurdities that made Averroës famous in the Middle Ages.

Zeller understands Aristotle as follows. The highest thought rests consummately in its object.[113] Man thinks this thought in the universal intellect, so that all human intellectual activity, except where it develops from experience, is identically one and, indeed, identical with the intellectual activity of God. According to this view Averroës departed from Aristotle only in reposing not only some, but all intellectual thoughts of man in a separate substance united with him through just this thought; thus Averroës would be guilty only of a multiplication of this absurdity, but by no means of an enlargement of it.

22. The curious and absurd aspects of this theory suffice to make us doubt the correctness of such results; but nothing remains to recommend this conception once one sees that not a few of Aristotle's statements stand in blatant contradiction to it. Even Zeller admits this and refers to several passages where we find the *nous poiētikos* described as something belonging to the individual soul.[114] Nor can he make anything of the *nous* that becomes all things; he cannot bring it into a closer connection with the *nous poiētikos*, since the latter supposedly is not a part of human nature but the absolute world spirit. Thus he finds himself forced to attribute it to the human body, together with the senses.[115] On the other hand, he admits that it can in no way be counted among the corporeal, and for this reason he objects that Trendelenburg's interpretation evidently changes Aristotle's doctrine on this point.[116]

23. Other variations of the view that separates the *nous poiētikos* from the human individual could be cited. But those already mentioned, having been

advanced by such eminent scholars, suffice to disclose the contradictions necessarily imported into the Aristotelian doctrine by any such attempt, engendering a
confusion that becomes greater the more one attends to particular passages. One
must say in praise of Zeller that he has done this more than anyone; but this is
the very reason why precisely in his representation more than in any other this
part of Aristotelian psychology appears as a wad of confused notions and a heap
of contradictory statements.

If this were indeed Aristotle's theory, then the epithet of a sensualist, which
has been applied to him, would be flattering rather than an insult to his
philosophical honour. For sensualism is at least a point of view, whatever its
shortcomings; but such prattle is without all sense and reason.

Notes

1. Themistius (1899), 107–8.
2. Brandis (1862–4), 572.
3. Simplicius (1882), 411: 'Eudemus, Aristotle's most faithful companion, also agrees with this.'
4. *EE* 1248^{a}25. [In the 19th c. this work was commonly attributed to Eudemus.]
5. With respect to potential intellect he advances, Themistius (1899), 107–8, the follow-ing query among others: 'What is the effect of the body on the incorporeal? Or of what kind is the change?' And later on he says of it, 'The sensations cannot be without body, but the intellect is separate.'
6. There can be no question that potential intellect [*nous dunamei*] has the nature of an accident; for otherwise, being a potentiality, it would have to be identical with substan-tial matter. That the *nous poiētikos* also has the nature of an accident is shown by the question, 'What is the subject of the productive agent?' This subject is the same as that of the potential intellect. This is shown (setting aside a remark of which it is doubtful that it really stems from Theophrastus, rather than from Themistius) by the query raised shortly afterward, why the active intellect does not move the receptive from the beginning and always: 'If moving were part of its nature, then it should have to (move) now and always.' [Brentano states his reasons for doubting Themistius' reliability in a later chapter, not included in this selection: Bk. II, Pt. IV, n. 338 (Brentano 1867, 222).]
7. He raises the question: 'How is the intellect ever assimilated, given that it is from the outside and, as it were, imposed?' Later on he remarks, opening the way for a solution, 'But "from the outside" does not mean something that is, as it were, imposed, but something that is in a way part of the initial generation.' [Cf. Brentano (1867), 217.]
8. Torstrik in Aristotle (1862), 189 thinks the opposite.
9. For some of these difficulties, we find solutions in the extant fragments themselves. It seems to me that the following words of Themistius indicate that solutions were also given for the others: 'It would be too cumbersome to list them one after the other (although they were not stated in a complex way, but tersely and briefly), for the sub-ject is replete with many queries, objections, *and solutions*' (1899, 108, ll. 8 ff.). Simi-larly he remarks at the end: 'It would perhaps be hasty to assert that someone could understand the theory of Aristotle and Theophrastus…concerning these matters on

the basis of the quotations we have adduced' (1899, 108, ll. 36 ff.). Themistius would certainly not have spoken in this way if Theophrastus had contradicted Aristotle.

10. Cic. *Acad.* 2. 121, *ND* 1. 35; S. E. *M.* 7. 350.

11. Cic. *Tusc.* 1. 19, 51.

12. Alexander (1887), 89. '(The active intellect) is impassible, unmixed with any matter and incorruptible....Such an entity was shown by Aristotle to be the first cause, which is also intellect in the proper sense.' Ibid. 108: 'By virtue of its [the active intellect's] nature the intelligible becomes actual mind. It becomes the cause for the material intellect, because it is so related to this kind of form, to separate, imitate, recognize, and make intelligible each of the forms that are embodied in matter. It comes from outside and is the so-called *nous poiētikos*, which is neither a part nor a faculty of our soul but comes from outside whenever we recognize it [the form]....If it is of this nature, then it is evidently separate from us.'

13. He calls this capacity 'material intellect' [*nous hulikos*], an expression based on Aristotle's words (*DA* 430ª10, 13, 19) and retained by the Arabs.

14. Alexander (1887), 211.

15. Themistius (1899), 102, ll. 30 ff.: 'One must be astonished that on the basis of these words (of Theophrastus) some have come to the conclusion that according to Aristotle the *nous poiētikos* is either the first god or the premisses together with the sciences that result from them, of which we shall treat later.'

16. See *APo* 89ª1, 89ᵇ7, 100ᵇ8; *EN* 1139ᵇ17, 1141ª5.

17. Cf. above, n. 15.

18. Renan (1852*a*), 73.

19. But there were also many who followed him blindly, for Averroës complains that at his time no one was considered a true Aristotelian if he did not subscribe to Alexander's opinions. Cf. Averroës (1953), 433.

20. The Latin translation we have before us always uses the expression *intellectus* for *nous dunamei* [potential intellect], while *nous poiētikos* is usually rendered as *intelligentia*. Evidently this is to indicate the different natures of the two intellects in the doctrine of Avicenna; for in translations of Arabic writings (at least the earlier translations), *intelligentia* is the expression for incorporeal spirits. Thomas Aquinas remarks about this, *ST* I, q. 79, a. 10.: 'The word *intelligentia* in the proper sense signifies the activity of the intellect, i.e., understanding [*intelligere*]. But in some books translated from the Arabic, separate substances, which we call angels, are called intelligences, perhaps because substances of this kind are always engaged in the act of understanding [*intelligunt*].' We had conjectured that the difference between the use of *intellectus* and *intelligentia* is based upon an analogous distinction in the Arabic original. However, a learned friend has informed us that this is not the case.

21. See above, n. 13.

22. Avicenna (1968), 81–2: 'There is no doubt of this: that in man there is some substance that apprehends the intelligible by receiving it. Thus we shall say that the substance that is the subject of the intelligibles is not body nor does it in any way have being because of body, it being the power [*virtus*] in the body, or its form.' There follow a number of proofs; some of them taken from Aristotle, others peculiar to Avicenna.

23. Avicenna thinks indeed that a plurality of human souls is not conceivable without relation to the bodies animated by them; he therefore disputes the possibility of the soul existing before the body (1968), 105: 'Thus, we shall say that the human soul did

not exist antecedently as a separate being, entering the body later on: for the human souls are one and the same in species and in definition; thus if we had maintained that they have separate existence and do not come into being with the bodies, then it would be impossible that the souls should of themselves form a plurality.' Hence in all the human bodies there would be only one soul, an idea which, as Avicenna justly says, does not need refutation. Ibid. 107: 'numerically one soul would be in two bodies, which is patently false in itself.' Ibid. 110: 'We also know that there is not just one soul in all bodies.' But this does not keep him from assuming that the souls continue to exist in their multiplicity after the death of the body, hence after the former union has been dissolved. He tries to show that the two claims are not inconsistent, as follows: although there can be no doubt that the souls are incorporeal after death, the consequences of their erstwhile union with the body have not been obliterated. They had then different being and essence because of the differences between their matters, the times of their creation, the affections corresponding to their various bodies—and they still do. To this must be added that the various theoretical and moral activities upon which they were engaged during life might well have left permanent traces in them, and there is also the possibility of individualizing qualities unknown to us.

24. Avicenna (1968), 113 ff.

25. Ibid. 126–7: 'We shall say that the human soul at first understands potentially, and later understands actually. But no thing goes from potency to actuality except through a cause that has it as an effect and bestows that actuality upon it. Hence there is a cause through which our soul goes from potency to actuality where intelligibles are concerned. But the cause for giving intelligible form is nothing but the active intellect, in whose power are the principles of abstract intelligible forms. Its [the active intellect's] relation to our souls is like that of the sun to our sense of sight; for just as the sun is actually seen through itself [i.e. by its own light], and what before was not actually visible becomes actually visible through its light, so also the disposition of that intellect [the active intellect] is in relation to our souls.' In pt. 1, ch. 5, he had distinguished three senses of potency, namely, 'first potency, called *material*, second potency, called *potential*, and a third, called *completion*.' Correspondingly he distinguishes three intellects: (i) material intellect; (ii) actual preparedness for intellection [*intellectus in habitu*] ('and it is possible to call this the actual intellect when it is compared to the first...although it could also be called potential intellect compared with that which follows after it', cf. Aristotle, *DA* 429^{b}5); (iii) actual intellection [*intellectus accommodatus*], 'which is called actual intellection because, as we shall learn, preparedness for intellection would not lead to actuality unless through the intellect that is always actual' (this is the active intellect, which always cognizes actually because it is pure spirit; see above, n. 20), 'and because, when potential intellect becomes united with active intellect in some way, then is imprinted upon it (by giving it in a certain way a form) that which is acquired from outside.'

26. The highest here means the highest of created intelligences, not the deity. Avicenna thinks of the latter that, because of the perfect unity and simplicity of its being, it is impossible that it should be immediate cause of more than one thing. That [highest created] intelligence he thought to be the first intelligence from which a multiplicity of effects could emanate since, having received its being from another entity, it was a mixture of potentiality and actuality and thus not devoid of all multiplicity. He thought that in so far as this intelligence recognizes that it partakes in potentiality, it generates the substance of the sphere that it moves; in so far as it recognizes that it partakes in

actuality, it generates the soul of that sphere. Finally, in so far as it recognizes its principle, it generates a second intelligence which moves the next-following, lower sphere;
this continues down to the sphere of the moon (*Metaph. tract.* 9. 4 [= (1907), 558]).
Alfarabi already had a similar doctrine. *Fontes Questionum*, ch. 8; for a modern translation, cf. [= (1892), 97].

27. Avicenna calls it the giver of forms; this designation is easily explained through the
efficacy that he attributed to it, as we shall presently see. Cf. also al-Shahrastani
(1846), ii. 383, 426.

28. Avicenna (1968), 128: 'Thus the rational soul, being in a certain kind of union with
the forms, is capable of having present in it free from all admixture the forms that
come from the light of the active intellect itself.'

29. I.e. so long as the human soul is united with its body. Once it is free from body it no
longer requires the preparatory sensory powers. Avicenna (1968), 150: 'But when the
soul is once freed from body and from the accidents of body, it will be capable of
union with the active intellect, and in this intellect it shall find intelligible beauty and
eternal delight.'

30. Ibid. 127–8: 'The rational faculty, illuminated in us by the light of the active intellect,
considers the particulars that are in the imagination, as we have said; in this way they
are rendered free from matter and its appendages and are imprinted in the rational
soul. They do not move by themselves from imagination toward our intellect [from
images to intelligibles]. It is also not the case that the universal [*intentio*], strictly by
itself, creates on its own a likeness of itself. Rather, the consideration [of the
particulars] prepares the soul, so that it can receive the abstraction from the active
intellect. For thinking and considering are motions that make the soul capable of
receiving the emanation, just as the middle terms prepare of necessity for the reception of the conclusion, though these two things take place in different ways, as we shall
see later. But when it occurs that the rational soul is ready for the pure form through
the mediation of the active intellect, then something is contained in the soul which
stems from the form, which in one respect is *sui generis*, in another respect not *sui
generis*, just as light falling upon coloured objects produces in the sense of sight a process that is not similar to it in every respect.'

31. According to Avicenna, both appear identical. In (1972), 87 ff. he enumerates the
powers of the soul as follows. (*a*) Sensory powers: (i) common sense or sensory representation [*sensus communis seu phantasia*]; (ii) imagination; (iii) the capacity for sensual judgement [*vis existimationis*; Avicenna takes this power to be located at the back
of the precentral gyrus of the brain. It perceives the non-sensory meaning, which is
contained in the sensible particulars; for example, in the sheep, it is the capacity of
perceiving that this wolf is to be avoided while its own lamb is something to be cared
for, loc. cit.] (elsewhere he calls it *aestimativa*, and in the case of man *cogitativa*); (iv)
memory and reminiscence. (*b*) Intellectual powers: the capacity for action, which is
the principle that moves the body toward action; the capacity for knowledge.

32. Avicenna (1968), 8: 'That which receives is not the same as that which preserves. The
storehouse of that which is apprehended by sense is the faculty of imagination, while
the storehouse for that which apprehends intentions is memory.' Ibid. 145: 'The
image, and whatever adheres to it is preserved in its preserving faculty whenever the
soul averts its attention from it; these preserving faculties do not apprehend (for if
they did, they would apprehend and preserve at the same time); rather, they are a
storehouse; if the apprehending or judging faculty (estimative faculty) of either the

intellect or the soul turns toward it, then they encounter that which is already in possession....But the soul of the animal has discrete faculties, and each faculty has attached to it special instruments. A storehouse is assigned to those *forms* that at certain times are not contemplated by the estimative faculty, and a storehouse is also assigned to those *intentions* that, at certain times, are not considered by the estimative faculty. Therefore the estimative faculty is not the place in which these are preserved; it merely judges. Therefore we say that the estimative faculty sometimes attends to the forms and intentions reposed in these two faculties, and sometimes averts itself from them.'

33. Avicenna conducts his proof by considering four possible assumptions. According to the first of these, the storehouse of the intelligible forms would be in a bodily organ; according to the second, in the intellectual part of the soul; according to the third, no such storehouse exists, but the ideas, existing independently outside the mind, mirror themselves anew in the soul, as it were, whenever the soul turns toward them. Finally, according to the fourth assumption, the soul is thought to unite, again and again, not with ideas that exist as independent entities, but with the active intellect, in order that it may pour the intelligible forms into the soul. He finds that the first three assumptions must be rejected and thus indirectly infers the truth of the fourth; (1968), 146: 'We shall now speak of human souls which perceive intelligibles in that (active) intellect, and thereupon turn away from these toward others, so that the former intelligibles are not wholly actual in those souls, hence are not known in complete actuality by them. Perhaps they have a storehouse in which they preserve them? But this storehouse either belongs to their own essence (second assumption) or to their body (first assumption) or to something corporeal belonging to them. But we have already said (against the first assumption) that their body and what depends upon it is not worthy of this, and not worthy of being a subject of intelligibles; for it is not fitting that the intellectual forms should have a location, but their conjunction with body would make them have a location; but if they had a location, they would not be intelligibles. Or we say (third assumption) that those intelligible forms are things that exist by themselves, so that each of them is a species and a thing that exists by itself; now the intellect sometimes looks upon them, then it turns away from them, and then turns toward them again; and the soul is like a mirror, while they (the intelligible forms) are like external things which are sometimes apparent in it and sometimes not apparent; and this takes place according to the relations between them and the soul. Or else (fourth assumption) form after form flows from the active principle into the soul according to the soul's demands [*secundum petitionem*]; this emanation from the principle ceases when the soul turns away. If this were so, then, necessarily, each case of learning would take place as if it were for the first time. (This is an objection against the fourth assumption which will be resolved later.) Now we shall say that the last member of this alternative is true. For it is impossible to say that this form is in the soul with full actuality and is not cognized by the soul with full actuality. For to say that the soul cognizes something means nothing but that the form exists in it.' (Similarly he says, further down, '[to say] that the intelligible form is in the soul is the same as [to say] that it is apprehended'.) Hence it is impossible that it is a storehouse for them, and it is also impossible that the essence of the soul is their storehouse. 'For [to say] that it is its storehouse is the same as [to say] that the form exists in it. (This is the refutation of the second assumption.)...Also it will be explained later in first philosophy (in *Metaphysics*) that this form does not have independent existence (refutation

of third assumption). Hence it remains that the last alternative is true and that *learning
is nothing but the attainment of a perfect disposition for uniting oneself with the active
intellect* until this [disposition] becomes a cognition that is simple, and from which
emanate ordered forms by virtue of the thought-activity of the soul (these are the
truths inferred from those simple cognitions). The disposition that precedes learning
is imperfect, but after learning it is perfect....Hence learning for the first time is like
the healing of an eye, which, having been made healthy, can, when it wants to, apprehend a form by looking upon some individual. When it now looks away from the
object it transforms the object into a potentiality relative to itself, indeed the kind of
potentiality that is nearest to actuality. For if one says that Plato knows intelligible
objects, this means that if he wanted he could recall these forms to his mind. Of this,
too, the meaning is that *if he wanted he could be conjoined with the active intellect*, so
that the latter forms in him that thought [*ipsum intellectum*]; it does not mean that that
thought is present to his mind and always actually formed in his intellect; and it also
does not mean (as the above objection intended) that he was capable of this prior to
learning; for this mode of potential cognition is a capacity that allows the soul to
conjoin itself with the [active] intellect whenever it wants to think. From the active
intellect the intellectual form flows into the soul; this form is the truly acquired
(attained) cognition [*intellectus adeptus*], and this capacity is actual intellect, and to
that extent is consummation [i.e. actual cognition].' (What he here calls *intellectus
adeptus* is the same as what he called *intellectus accommodatus*—above, n. 25. It would
be wrong to identify it with what he there called 'preparedness for intellection'
[*intellectus in habitu*], even though one might at first be inclined to do so, since the
expression *intellectus adeptus* appears to be an adaptation of *nous epiktētos* [acquired
intellect], and *intellectus in habitu* an adaptation of *nous kath' hexin* [intellect as a state],
both of which mean the same in Alexander Aphrodisiensis.)

34. Numerous passages testify to this boundless veneration of Aristotle. Thus he says,
(1953), 433: 'All those who hold this view believe nothing except when they have
Aristotle's word; for a subject is difficult to the extent in which no Aristotelian
statements exist about it; for it is very difficult to find something on one's own, or even
impossible, unless one should find something similar in Aristotle. For I believe that
this man was the measure in nature and the example that nature introduced to demonstrate ultimate human perfection in the material world.' He sees all perfection of
science in the imitation of Aristotle; therefore he criticizes Avicenna, who was a much
clearer head than himself, for his greater freedom of movement. Ibid. 470: 'Avicenna
did not imitate Aristotle except in dialectics; but in other matters he blundered,
especially in metaphysics, and this because he began virtually on his own.'

[A few words need to be said about Brentano's lengthy quotations from Averroës.
The Arabic originals of this philosopher's commentaries on Aristotle are lost; extant
are merely Latin and Hebrew translations. This led the editor of the edition of
Averroës (1550) to give two versions of many crucial passages. One of them is the old
13th-c. Latin translation of Michael Scot, the other a Latin translation of the Hebrew
version by Mantino (around 1549). These are printed in adjacent columns. Brentano
produced his own text by picking suitable sentences from one or the other column;
for example, the point of n. 39 below could not have been made had he stuck with
one or the other version. I have translated Brentano's mixture; hence this is not an
authentic rendition of Averroës.]

35. Averroës (1953), 405: 'Thus when we say that a child knows potentially, this can be

understood in two ways. One way is that the imagined forms that exist in him are potential intelligibles. But it can be understood in a second way: it is obvious that the material intellect, which is capable of receiving the intelligible itself which belongs to the above-mentioned imagined form, is both potentially receptive and potentially connected with us.'

36. *DA* 430ᵃ24: 'passible intellect'.

37. Averroës (1953), 454: 'And it is through that intellect [which Aristotle calls passible] that man differs from other animals.'

38. Ibid. 476.

39. See above, n. 31. Averroës does indeed occasionally say that the passible intellect is the imagination: e.g. (1953), 452, where he distinguishes four senses in which Aristotle uses the word 'intellect' in *DA*: 'Here Aristotle means by passible intellect the same as the human faculty of imagination....Hence the expression "intellect" is used in four senses in that book. For he speaks about material intellect, potential intellect, active intellect, and the faculty of imagination.' But this is not a very precise statement, and he seems to use the name 'faculty of imagination' in the more vague sense of a sensory faculty. Elsewhere the says that the passible intellect is the same as the faculty of thinking [*virtus cogitativa*] (e.g. p. 476 'By passible intellect Aristotle means the faculty of thinking'), which he distinguishes as a higher faculty from imagination. Ibid. 415: 'The faculty of thinking belongs to the kind of faculties that exist in the body. Aristotle says this clearly in that book [i.e. *Sens.*] when he places the individual distinguishable capacities in four orders: he puts the common sense into the first, then the faculty of imagination, then the thinking faculty, and finally memory. And he holds that memory is more spiritual, followed by the power of thinking, the imagination, and finally sense. Hence only man can have the cogitative faculty; but this does not make this faculty one that distinguishes intelligibles; for such a faculty would have to distinguish universal intentions and not particulars.'

40. Averroës (1953), 453.

41. Ibid. 'And you must know that use and exercise are the cause of that [part] of the power of active intellect which becomes apparent, the active intellect being in us for the purpose of abstraction, while the material intellect is there for reception. The causes, I say, why states [habits] come about through use and exercise lie in the passible and corruptible intellect, which Aristotle called passible, and of which he says that is obviously perishes.'

42. Averroës says most clearly that the *intellectus materialis*, too, is spiritual, e.g. (1953), 18: 'And this is his (i.e. Aristotle's) statement concerning the material intellect, namely, that it is separate from body.' Ibid. 384: 'Aristotle says the following two things about the (material) intellect, namely, that it belongs to the genus "passive faculty", and that it is not changeable since it is neither a body nor the faculty of a body; for these two belong to the principles that hold of the intellect.' Ibid. 454: 'No one can conclude from this (i.e. from the fact that Aristotle speaks of a corruptible intellect) that the material intellect is an admixture of the body.' Cf. also n. 39 above, where Averroës distinguishes between the passible and the material intellects, and the subsequent notes.

43. Ibid. 387: 'The definition of that material intellect is, of course, that it is that which is a potency relative to all material universal forms and in no kind of actual being before it recognizes them.' By this, Averroës does not want to say that the material intellect does not also recognize intellectual things; for he says, ibid. 410: 'Moreover, it is

necessary for the receptive intellect that it recognize that intellect which exists in actuality. For if it recognizes the material forms it is all the more necessary that it recognize immaterial forms; and the fact that it has cognizance of the separate forms, i.e., of the active intellect, does not stand in the way of its recognizing material forms.' Likewise, ibid. 451: 'The material intellect is actualized by the active intellect and perceives it.' And ibid. 499: 'The material intellect recognizes both, the material forms and the separate [*abstractus*] forms.'

44. Ibid. 406: 'It is consistent [with what has preceded] to believe that there are formed in the human soul two parts of the intellect, one being that which *receives*—and what it is has here been established—and another being that which *acts*; and it is the latter that makes it the case that the intentions and concepts existing in the faculty of imagination actually move the material intellect, while previously they moved it only potentially...and [it is consistent to believe] that those two parts are neither generated nor corruptible, and that the relation of the active to the receptive intellect is just like the relation of form to matter.' (Some of the expressions here used would seem to suggest that Averroës took the *intellectus materialis* and *agens* to belong to human nature, which is of course not the case. This can be explained from the fact that Averroës retains Aristotle's mode of expression, even where he connects with it altogether different conceptions.) Ibid. 495: 'Now the intellect in us has two modes of action—depending on the way in which it relates to us—one of which belongs to the genus of *affections* and consists in recognizing it [the intellect?], while the other belongs to the genus of *actions* whose function it is to abstract the forms and to strip them of matter, which is nothing other than making them into actual intelligibles, while previously they were only potential intelligibles. This being so, let us therefore say that it is obvious that...'

45. Ibid. 441: 'The active intelligence recognizes none of the things that are here.'

46. To be sure, so far as the *intellectus materialis* is concerned, with which we are said to receive our thoughts, this is a most remarkable and altogether ridiculous claim; none the less, Averroës states it very clearly, e.g. ibid. 399: 'Not a few doubts arise against Aristotle's claim, the second...of which, which is more difficult than the rest, is that the final entelechy (the *intellectus speculativus*, cf. p. 392) in man exists in as many numbers as there are individual persons while the first entelechy, (the *intellectus materialis*, ibid.) presumably is *numerically one in all persons*.' Ibid. 401: 'That second problem that he advanced, namely, in what way the material intellect is *numerically one in all individual persons*, indeed ungenerated and incorruptible, while the intelligibles that actually exist in it and are identical with the speculative intellect are as many as there are persons, and come about and pass away through their generation and corruption—this problem, I say, is most difficult and arduous.' Ibid. 406: 'From this statement we can see that the *material intellect is one and the same in all individuals*.' Averroës (1550), ix, fo. 62vb: (1961), 448: 'It is necessary that the soul does not divide corresponding to the division into individuals.'

47. Averroës (1953), 161: 'This (i.e. that the intellect is separated from the body as the eternal from the corruptible) will be the case, since it is sometimes united with body and sometimes not.'

48. Ibid. 419: 'The cogitative faculty belongs to the genus of sensible faculties. But the imaginative and the cogitative and the recollective [faculties]...all co-operate in producing the image of the sensible thing, so that the separate rational faculty can perceive it and extract the universal intention, and finally receive, i.e. comprehend, it.'

If animals had a passible intellect, then they, too, would be connected with the active and material intellect. Ibid. 454: 'And through this intellect humans differ from the other animals. If this were not so, then it would be necessary that the connection between active and receptive intellects occur in the same way in the other living things.'

49. The activity of the *intellectus agens* must precede that of the *intellectus materialis*. Ibid. 495: 'But this sort of action, which consists in generating intelligibles and actualizing them, exists in us prior to the action of the intellect.' Cf. also the preceding note.

50. Ibid. 438–9: 'Given that it is as we have said, namely, that the relation of the intentions in imagination to the material intellect is the same as the relation of the sensible to the senses, as Aristotle says, it is necessary to assume another mover (i.e. the *intellectus agens*) which makes them actually move the material intellect, and this simply means that it makes actual thoughts [*intellectas*] by separating them from matter.'

51. Ibid. 400: 'It is necessary to assign two subjects to these actually existing intelligibles, one of which is the subject due to which the intelligibles are true, i.e. forms, which are truthful images; the other, the subject due to which the intelligibles are only a single one of the entities in the world, and this is the material intellect itself.' Cf. below, n. 55.

52. Ibid. 404: 'Let us then say that man manifestly does not actually cognize unless that intellect actually unites with him....And since it has already been shown that the intellect cannot unite with all individuals by multiplying according to their number with respect to that part that is the opposite of intellect *qua* form, i.e. with respect to the material intellect, the only thing that remains is that this intellect unites with all of us through the union with us of concepts or intelligible intentions, which themselves are concepts or intentions present to the mind, that is, through that part of them that exists in us and that in a certain way behaves like a form.' (It is obvious that the material intellect, which is united with us in this way, cannot be called a form or entelechy of us in the same sense as other cognizing faculties. Hence Averroës says, ibid.: 'Hence on the basis of what has been said it is manifest that the first entelechy (*prōtēn entelecheian*, cf. Aristotle, *DA* 412^{a}22) of the intellect differs from the first entelechy of the remaining faculties, and that this term "entelechy" [*perfectio*] applies to them only equivocally.' Averroës (1953), 500: 'Man...recognizes all things through the *intellectus adeptus* [actual intellection] whenever it is united with the imagined forms, by means of appropriate intellection.'

53. Averroës derives the difference between practical and theoretical knowledge from different stages of preparedness of the passible intellect. Averroës (1953), 454: 'The operative intellect at any rate differs from the speculative through the difference in preparation which exists in that intellect.'

54. Averroës (1550), ix, fo. 64^b: 'Thus of necessity there must be a philosopher in the human race.'

55. Averroës (1953), 401: 'And since all this is as we have said, it cannot be that the intelligibles that are actual, i.e. the speculative ones, are generable and corruptible only by virtue of the object that makes them true (of which Averroës has just remarked that it is that which "in a certain way moves the intellect"), and not by virtue of the subject due to which they are one of the existing things, i.e., the material intellect.' Ibid. 406: 'It must therefore be supposed that there are three parts of the intellect in the soul; the first is the receptive intellect, the second, the active intellect,

and the third is actual intellection or factual intellect (actual thought); and of the three, two are eternal, namely, the active and receptive intellects; the third, however, is partly generable and corruptible, partly eternal. The preceding justifies the claim that the material intellect is one and the same in all individuals; furthermore, we are of the opinion that the human species is eternal, as we have proclaimed elsewhere: therefore it is inescapable that the material intellect cannot be deprived of the universal principles which are by nature familiar to the whole human species—by this I mean the first principles and particular pervasive concepts common to all things—since intelligibles of this kind are always one as far as the recipient is concerned, though many as regards the received concept. Hence according to the way in which they are one they are undoubtedly eternal, since their being does not simply result from the reception of the object, which is the moving force, but consists in attention to, or perception of, the represented forms, and there is nothing on the part of the receptive intellect which would prevent this. Hence they [the intelligibles] have generation and corruption only so far as their multiplicity is concerned, which is accidental to them, but not in so far as they are contained in it [the receptive intellect] as units. And thus if one of the first intelligibles or primary notions passes away because its object passes away—i.e. the object through which it is joined and connected with us and true— then this intelligible cannot be corruptible absolutely speaking, but corruptible only with respect to a single individual.' Ibid. 407–8: 'And if intelligibles of this kind are considered, in so far as they have being *simpliciter* and not in respect of some individual, then it must truly be said of them that they have eternal being, and that they are not sometimes intelligibles and sometimes not, but that they always exist in the same manner....It is held that the inhabited universe cannot be without some abode for philosophy, just as one must suppose that the inhabited universe cannot be without an abode for the natural crafts. Because, even if those arts are not present in some parts, for example, the northern quarter of the world, it does not follow that the remaining parts are also deprived of them; for it has already been proved that habitation is possible in the north just as much as the south. Thus perhaps the major part of philosophy exists at all times, [being transmitted in the same way] as man comes from man and horse from horse. Therefore the speculative intellect is ungenerated and incorruptible.' Ibid. 448: 'It is not the case that the so-called material intellect sometimes understands and sometimes does not, excepting the forms of representation which exist in particular individuals; it is not the case that it sometimes understands and sometimes does not if you take the species into account. For example, it does not happen to the material intellect that it sometimes has the concept of a horse and sometimes not, except in so far as Socrates or Plato are concerned; considered absolutely, however, and in relation to the species, the material intellect always grasps this universal [i.e. horse] unless the human species disappears altogether, which is impossible....If potential intellect is not viewed in respect of some individual, but absolutely and in respect of any individual whatever, it is not found to be sometimes thinking [cognizing] and sometimes not, but it is found to be always thinking'. Averroës (1550), ix. fo. 62^{va-b} = (1961), 448: 'The sciences [knowledge] are eternal and neither generable nor corruptible except *per accidens*, for example, owing to their union with Socrates and Plato;...for no part of the individuality [of a person] belongs to the intellect.' (From this passage Renan unjustly draws the conclusion that Averroës thought of the material intellect as a universal; our preceding discussion and earlier quotations will have made it sufficiently clear that this is false. Averroës simply denies here that the intellect belongs to that which constitutes the individuality of this or that person. See above, n. 46.)

56. As Avicenna had thought. See above, n. 29.

57. Arist. *GC* 324ª29.

58. Averroës (1953), 496: 'The intellect that exists in us has two kinds of activity, namely, knowing the intelligibles and forming them' (cf. above, n. 44). 'But the intelligibles in us are formed in two ways, namely, either *naturally*—this holds for the first principles of which we do not know when and whence and by what reason they come to us, or *voluntarily*—this holds for the intelligibles that are derived from those first propositions or principle. But it has already been proved that it is necessary that those intelligibles that we have by nature should come from that thing which is intellect devoid and freed from matter, namely, the active intellect itself. This having been established, it follows that the intelligibles derived in us from those first propositions or principles should be formed by the *combination of known propositions* and *the active intellect*. For we can say neither that the first principles contribute nothing toward the discovery of those acquired intelligibles, nor that those principles bring forth these intelligibles on their own. For we have already shown that the active intellect is one and eternal....Hence the speculative intellect [derived propositions?] must be something that is formed out of the active intellect and the first principles, and this genus of intelligibles must be voluntary in contrast to the first natural intelligibles. But in every action resulting from the combination of two diverse things, one of these two things must in any case fulfil the function of *matter and tool*, and the other, that of *form or agent*. Hence the intellect in us is in every case composed of the acquired intellect and the active intellect, and either the principles are comparable to matter and the active intellect to form, or else the principles are comparable to the instrument and the active intellect to the agent. The arrangement is nearly the same in the two cases.' (Cf. Arist. *DA* 413ª8, where the moving principle, too, is called an entelechy [*entelecheia*].) Averroës now raises an objection against the doctrine he has just developed; by removing this objection he arrives at the conclusion which states, more precisely, that the relation between the active intellect and immediately recognized truths is not literally a relation between form and matter, or main cause and instrument, but merely analogous to such a relation: 'It is claimed that whenever we arrive at conclusions by means of the active intellect and by means of principles, the principles must be related to the active intellect as genuine matter and genuine instrument. But I say that there is no necessity to this claim. What *is* necessary is merely that there should be a *proportion and relation* which makes the received intelligibles [*intellectus adeptus*] comparable to matter, and the active intellect comparable to form.' Later on (ibid. 499), he explains this as follows: 'For of any two things, of which one is the subject, and one is more perfect than the other, the more perfect must be related to the less perfect as form is to matter.' He says that the active intellect and the speculative principles have one and the same subject, i.e., the material intellect, inasmuch as the material intellect recognizes them both.

59. Ibid. 499: 'The case is similar to that of transparent bodies (such as air, water, glass, pupil, etc.), which receive light and colours at the same time; the light, however, brings forth the colours.'

60. Ibid.: 'Thus we have now ascertained how it is possible that this intellect (i.e. the active) in the end combines with us. The reason why it is not combined with us from

the beginning is that the active intellect combines with us through conjoining the speculative intelligibles. But clearly it is combined with us potentially whenever the speculative intelligibles are potentially present in us, and actually combined with us whenever the intelligibles are actually present in us; and if some of them are potential, others actual, then we say that it is combined with us in part, and in part not; in this case we are said to be moved towards combination. But it is manifest that when some such motion is completed, then the intellect is at once joined to us in every part.' In the fragment of the *Epistola Averroës de Intellectu* which was published by Renan (1852b), 348, the process is described as follows: 'And it is the actual intellect [manifest concept?] that man ultimately apprehends within himself, and this is the so-called acquired intellect. It is a whole formed from the act and that [part] of matter which is called its first potency. And for this reason, whenever a form is repeated, the potency of the different forms is also repeated at the same time so long as it descends or ascends from one whole to another whole, and from one form to another that is more noble and nearer to the act, so that it eventually arrives at that whole and at that act that has no further admixture of potency.' The fragment, quite generally speaking, contains many obscure passages that must be attributed to the poor quality of the translation and the corruption of the text; this passage is no exception, and I at least do not fully understand it.

61. Averroës (1953), 501: 'And from this it also becomes clear why we are not united with that intellect from the beginning, but only in the end. The reason is that potency is part of us so long as there is in us form that exists only potentially. And so long as potency is still part of us, we cannot know anything through [this intellect] unless it [the thing known?] becomes actual form, and this takes place through its being united in an act. And then we know through it all we know (it knows?) and carry out through it the action appropriate to it.'

62. Averroës (1550), ix. 65ra–66vb.

63. *Opusculum* 15: 'De unitate intellectus contra Averroistas Parisienses' [(1949), 70–120].

64. At the outset of the above *Opusculum* he says that (Averroës) 'endeavours to posit as separate the intellect that *Aristotle calls potential*, but he himself by the unsuitable name "material [intellect]"...' [ibid. 71]. Without doubt, he relates this to *DA* 429^{a}21: 'It can have no nature of its own other than that of having a certain capacity.'

65. *DA* 429^{b}5; 430^{a}17.

66. Aquinas (1948), 167: 'He says that the intellect is separate [from the body] since, unlike sense, it does not have an organ. This follows from the fact that because of its dignity the soul surpasses the faculties of the material body and cannot be wholly included in it. Therefore there is in it a certain kind of action which is not connected with the corporeal. Hence its capacity for that activity does not have a bodily organ. And in this sense the intellect is separate [from the body].'

67. *DA* 429^{a}13.

68. *ST* I, q. 78, a. 2, *passim*.

69. e.g. *APo.* 100^{a}10.

70. *DA* 431^{a}16.

71. *DA* 430^{a}18.

72. *ST* I, q. 84, a. 2, *passim*.

73. *ST* I, q. 85, a. 1, ad 4.

74. Durandus of Saint-Pourcain, *Commentaria in Quattuor Libros Sententiarum* 1. 3. 5.

[There are many editions, e.g. Paris, 1508, 1515, etc. It is not certain which of these Brentano used. No modern edition or translation exists.]

75. *DA* 432^{a}8.

76. Suárez (1856–61), iii. 713 ff.

77. One cannot fail to notice how much this is none the less the case if one compares the following faithful description of Suárez's opinion (which we quote verbatim from Kleutgen 1860, 63) with statements of St Thomas, e.g. *ST* I, q. 79, a. 3, and *ScG* II, 77: [(1961), ii. 226]: 'Hence in the intellective soul there is a power whose activity is directed toward the images and which makes them into something actually intelligible, and this capacity of the soul is called active intellect.'

78. Kleutgen (1860), 125.

79. *Metaph.* 993^{a}7.

80. See above, n. 70, and *DA* 432^{a}8.

81. [Brentano gives his reasons in a later chapter, not included in this selection: Book II, Pt. 1. 15, Brentano (1867), 62 f. To document that striving is attributed even to unconscious nature, he cites *DA* 415^{b}1, *GC* 336^{b}27. Other passages cited in support are *Metaph.* 1046^{b}4, 1047^{b}35, *DA* 433^{a}30.]

82. *Metaph.* 1048^{a}5. Hence Aristotle says in *Ph.* 251^{b}5: 'So, if the motion was not always in process, it is clear that they cannot have been in a condition such as to render them capable respectively of being moved and of causing motion, but one or the other of them first had to undergo a change.'

83. *Metaph.* 1072^{a}29.

84. *DA* 429^{b}5; cf. also *Metaph.* 1074^{b}35.

85. Cf. Prantl, (1855–70), 1. 108 ff., and the special literature listed in Ueberweg (1926), i. 115* ff. [Cf. also Totok (1964), 1. 242 ff.]

86. Trendelenburg in Aristotle (1833), 168.

87. Ibid. p. 493.

88. Ibid. 173.

89. Ibid. 492.

90. Ibid. 493.

91. Ibid. 496.

92. Ibid. 494, 495, 173.

93. Ibid. 173.

94. *Metaph.* 1064^{a}7 (cf. 1025^{b}10).

95. Trendelenburg in Aristotle (1833), 495.

96. *Metaph.* 1072^{b}18–30.

97. Trendelenburg in Aristotle (1833), 492 ff.

98. Ibid. 175.

99. Ibid. 496.

100. Such a transition cannot be discerned anywhere; but quite aside from this, there are certain expressions in the subsequent parts which unequivocally describe the *nous* that becomes all things. In the final paragraph of the chapter, as in the beginning, knowledge is called an affection (cf. with 429^{a}13 the passages 429^{b}24 and ^{b}29), and the metaphor of the *tabula rasa* is found at the very end; no one will relate this metaphor to the *nous poiētikos* (429^{b}31). Finally, in the attributes given in the middle of the chapter, one clearly recognizes characteristics of the *nous* that becomes all things; for example, it is called (at 429^{a}29 and ^{b}8) something that has potential being.

101. Zeller, too, has attacked Trendelenburg's interpretation for this reason: Zeller (1856–68), ii/2. 442 n. 1. [= (1963), ii/2. 572 ff.].

102. Cf. also Brandis, (1835–60), II, ii/2. 1177.

103. Ibid. 1178.

104. Brandis (1862–4), 518.

105. *DA* 430^{a}5: 'Why mind is not always thinking, we must consider later.' *APo.* 2, 19. 99^{b}26.

106. *DA* 430^{a}14: 'And there is an intellect that is of this kind by becoming all things' (Hamlyn).

107. Ibid. 431^{b}22; cf. also 429^{a}17, 429^{b}30.

108. Ravaisson-Mollien (1837–46), i. 586–7; cf. ii. 17, 19.

109. *EE* 1248^{a}24.

110. Renan (1852*b*), 96: 'What results from this is that it is a theory somewhat analogous to that of Malebranche.'

111. Aristotle explicitly objects that Anaxagoras gives no account whatever of mode and ground of the knowledge of *nous*: *DA* 405^{b}21.

112. Renan (1852*b*), 97.

113. Zeller (1856–68), ii/2. 441, where the domains of the passible *nous* and of the *nous poiētikos* are delimited. Ibid. 438, *nous* is said to grasp in immediate cognition the highest principles, which cannot be the object of mediating thought, and the subsequent remarks show that this must be applied to the *nous poiētikos*. Hence [it is alleged that] in Aristotle's view we men think these highest principles within the divine intellect. This is strange in itself, but even more strange if, as Zeller interprets the doctrine of Aristotle, this divine intellect by no means contemplates the principles of our knowledge, or even a multiplicity of principles, but solely itself!

114. Ibid. 441 n. 3.

115. Ibid. 443 n. 4.

116. Ibid. 442 n. 1.

18

WHAT DOES THE MAKER MIND MAKE?

L. A. KOSMAN

I. The Question

THE title of this essay is the first half of a question unattested in late antiquity and in the Greek commentators but easily imagined: *Ti pote poiei ho nous ho poiētikos, kai ti pote estin?*—what does the maker mind make, and what is it, anyway? The rendering of *nous poiētikos* as 'maker mind' is meant to suggest the inadequacy of the more usual translation of this phrase as 'active mind' or 'active intellect'. Although it is true that *nous poiētikos* is active and that it is therefore proper to call it 'active intellect', it is odd to think of this as an Englishing of the Aristotelian idiom; surely we should expect Aristotle's Greek for *active intellect* or *active mind* to use some form of his favourite word *energeia* rather than of *poiein*.

Poiein may carry a more general sense of *acting* or *doing*, almost equivalent to *prattein*; a notable Aristotelian example of this use is in the categorical pair *poiein/paschein*, echoes of which are clearly felt in the opening discussion of *nous poiētikos*. But the sense that Aristotle wishes to give *poiein* in this discussion is clear when he explains that *nous poiētikos* is so called *tōi panta poiein*—by virtue of making all things, 'like some state [*hexis*] such as light; for in a sense light makes what are potentially colours actually colours'.[1] The fact that the *nous* elliptically discussed in *DA* 3. 5 may properly be called active *nous* since it may already have been introduced in 3. 4 should therefore not make us forget that if it is also called *poiētikos*, it is appropriate to ask this essay's question: *ti poiei?* what does it make?[2]

I will begin this essay by sketching a series of moves leading to what I take to be a standard answer to this question; then I will raise some further questions concerning this view and finally suggest what I take to be an interesting alternative account.

---

[1] *DA* 3. 5 430ª15 ff.

[2] To say that the problematic *nous* of *DA* 3. 5 is called *nous poiētikos* is true of course, only if we mean *called by later commentators*; any interpretation of the phrase *nous poiētikos* must take account of the fact that it is not Aristotle's phrase. Every inquiry into the nature of such mind thus depends on an act of creative inscription: the writing into Aristotle's text of a concept that is present only implicitly and allusively. The *nous poiētikos* is in a sense a construction of the Aristotelian hermeneutical tradition, successful in so far as the conceptual pattern that it actualizes in construing Aristotle's laconic text is actually potentially present in that text.

II. Some Answers

So what *does* the maker mind make? Perhaps the most obvious answer is this:

the maker mind makes everything.   (1)

This suggestion has much to recommend it. It fits well with the description in our text, in which, as we saw, the *nous* in question is said to be what it is *tōi panta poiein*—by virtue of making all things.[3] And it fits well with other views concerning *nous*; for example, those we find in Plotinus and his followers. The notion that there is a mind which creates the world by thinking the ideas of all things has a rich history in Western philosophical thought, from the earliest of post-classical thinkers such as Albinus, through the Middle Ages, through Berkeley and Leibniz, and up to such modern philosophers as Fichte and Hegel.

But it does not follow that it is the notion that Aristotle had in mind, nor that it is what he envisaged in 3. 5 specifically as the office of mind. And surely the attentive reader of Aristotle's text will balk at the generality of 'everything'. Of course *panta* in *tō panta poiein* does not mean 'everything' *simpliciter*; the phrase is prefaced by the qualification *hekastō genei*, which makes clear that what we are talking about is what makes things be of a particular sort, and the sort is clearly specified in two respects. (i) The context of Aristotle's remarks makes clear that the discussion of *nous*, like the discussion of *psychē* in general, is a discussion of faculties and their activities, and is therefore governed by the distinction between potentiality and actuality; the *nous poiētikos* makes what is *potential* to be *actual*. (ii) In 3. 5, Aristotle is concerned specifically with thought and what can think, or with what is thought and what is thinkable; the *genos* in question is clearly that governed by the concept of *nous*, the power and activity of *thought*. So we might say that:

the maker mind makes everything that is potentially thought actually thought.   (2)

III. More Questions and Answers

This reply seems more adequate than our first attempt, but it leaves unresolved two questions, the answers to which are hidden by the ambiguity of *actually thought* and of *potentially*. (i) The distinction Aristotle's doctrine articulates is between what is capable of becoming *thinking* and that which brings it into its being as thinking, or between what is capable of becoming *thought* and that which brings it into its being as thought. But which of these is operative in the case of the maker mind? What is it that is actualized by *nous poiētikos*—thinking or being thought?

(ii) As Aristotle makes clear throughout *De Anima* and elsewhere, the structure of potentiality and actuality is a complex one; in his discussion of soul and its

[3] *DA* 3. 430ª15.

powers and activities, including *nous*, he thinks of potentiality and actuality specifically in terms of his well-known *Dreistufenlehre*: the distinction among (*a*) first potentiality, (*b*) second potentiality/first actuality, and (*c*) second actuality.[4] We ought to expect to find, in the case of *nous*, the features generally found in those modes of being that are characterized by Aristotle's scheme. Among these features is the fact that first actuality is actual relative to first potentiality, just as second actuality is in turn actual relative to first actuality. Something's 'being made actual', therefore, may signal a development either from first potentiality to first actuality *or* from first actuality to second actuality; which of these is referred to in (2) when we say that the maker mind makes actual what is potential?

Given these two questions, (2) is still not clear; we need to resolve the ambiguities they reveal: (i) According to (2), does the maker mind make the potential *thinkable* actual, or does it make potential *nous* actual? (ii) According to (2), does the maker mind make actual whatever it makes actual in the sense of actualization from first potentiality to first actuality or in the sense of actualization from first actuality to second actuality? In other words, does the maker mind (*a*) make the potentially *thinkable actually* thinkable or does it (*b*) make the already actually thinkable actually *thought*? Or alternatively, depending on our answer to (i) does it (*c*) make our native faculty of thought, a faculty possessed by the most naïve neonate, into the developed ability to think, an ability that might characterize, for example, a sleeping scientist, or does it (*b*) realize that developed ability to think in actual acts of thinking?

It is easy to overlook the ambiguity revealed by question (i): is it thinking or is it being thought that's actualized? Hicks, for example, in his extensive notes on the *De Anima*, begins his explanation of the office of *nous poiētikos* by remarking that

Aristotle has to find an efficient cause by which the transition of *nous* from potentiality to actuality, which is implied in the foregoing chapter, is effected.[5]

On the very next page, however, he tells a different story, one which suggests that *nous poiētikos* actualizes not mind but what mind thinks:

The word *panta* refers strictly to *ta noēta*, as the simile from light shows. Light makes potential colours actual colours, *nous* makes potential *noēta* actual *noēta*.[6]

There is, however, a simple explanation for what looks like interpretative fickleness on Hicks's part, an explanation that provides an interestingly simple answer to the question: is it thinking or what is thought that is actualized? It is this: question (i) is a specious question, and results from disregarding a simple but important fact concerning Aristotle's views on thought. For Aristotle the activity of the subject of consciousness and the activity of the object of consciousness are, in the actuality of consciousness, one and the same entity. Compare the parallel case of perception; when the light shines on an object so that I see it, my seeing and the object's being seen are actualized together; indeed

---

[4] *DA* 417[a]21 ff.   [5] Hicks in Aristotle (1907), 499.   [6] Ibid, 500 f.

they are, as Aristotle says, one actuality, although their being is different.[7] This is
exactly what we learn in 3. 4 about mind; in the case of actual thinking, the subject thinking and the object being thought are one and the same; the actuality of
the one is the same entity as the actuality of the other.

It is not surprising, therefore, that in his commentary Hicks should shift with
such ease between understanding the maker mind as responsible for the actuality
of thinking and understanding it as responsible for the actuality of what is
thought. For there is in fact no such ambiguity as (i) invites us to think needs
resolution; thinking and what is thought are one in the act of the mind's thinking
what is thought.

Consider now the second question; does the *nous poiētikos* actualize from first
potentiality to first actuality or from first actuality to second actuality? It is
unlikely that this question will disappear in the same way, but it does seem to
many commentators to have an equally clear answer. A dominant group of voices
within the tradition speak for the former alternative; they hold that the office
of the *nous poiētikos* is the development of material *nous* into *nous* as *hexis*, the
actualization, that is, of our native ability to think into the developed *skill* of intelligent thought. Alexander expresses this view as follows:

For as light is the cause of colours that are potentially visible becoming actually visible, so
this third *nous* makes potential, that is, material *nous*, into actual *nous* by producing within
it the power to think (*hexis noētikē*).[8]

To see whether Alexander is correct, it may be useful to consider the analogy
in terms of which Aristotle introduces *nous poiētikos* and which Alexander here
invokes, the analogy with light. *Nous poiētikos*, we remember, is said to be

a kind of hexis, like light; for in a sense light also makes what are potentially colours
actually colours.[9]

It will help, therefore, to ask: in what sense may light be said to make potential
colour into actual colour, and what sort of a transformation is this?

We might reason like this: since, as we read earlier in the *De Anima*,[10] colour is
the visible, it follows that in making what is potentially a colour actually a colour,
light is making what is potentially visible actually visible. And since visibility is
itself a first actuality, that is, a realized structure of potentiality relative to the
further actuality of being seen, light brings into being a first actuality: it makes
things visible.

It is easy to see why Aristotle understands light as effecting a transition from

---

[7] *DA* 425[b]26 ff.
[8] Alexander (1887), 107, l. 31. Compare Kahn, (1981), 400: 'What is regarded as problematic and
requiring explanation [by *nous poiētikos*] is the acquisition, not the exercise, of *nous* as *hexis*. This is
clearest in III 4, where potential intellect is compared to a blank tablet on which nothing is written,
and this mode of potentiality ("before it has learned or discovered anything") is contrasted with the
potency of an intellect which "has become all things, like someone actually in possession of science
(*epistēmōn*)". It is the transition from the former to the latter stage of potentiality that Aristotle
attempts to explain, and it is for this explanation that he requires the agent intellect'.
[9] *DA* 430[a]15 ff.   [10] *DA* 418[a]26,28. Cf. *Ph.* 201[b]4.

first potentiality to first actuality. We distinguish entities such as the surface of a table or the hand of a judge, part of whose nature is to able to be seen, from entities such as the square root of seven, or the hand of justice, which are invisible, and this distinction remains a real distinction even when there is no light present. They are not all alike in the dark, even though none of them can be seen. This is due to the fact that visibility, like so many of the structures of potentiality that Aristotle finds interesting, is subject to an iteration of the potentiality–actuality distinction; in the dark, the visible is only, as we might say, potentially visible. Light effects the actualization of *that* potentiality; it makes what it shines upon actually visible, and thus potentially seen.

Since, therefore, the *nous poiētikos* is said to be like light, it is inviting to suppose that Alexander is correct. Aristotle means that it makes actual in the same sense in which light makes actual and that it therefore brings into being a state of first actuality; it makes things thinkable, not actually thought, or it brings into being the (as yet still potential) acquired intellect, the *ability* to think.

Here's a bonus: this view might explain the sense in which *nous* is said by Aristotle, in the *Posterior Analytics* as well as in his discussion of the intellectual powers in the *Ethics*, to be the *archē* of *epistēmē*.[11] For here *nous* is being described as the active agency by which a person with the potentiality *for* understanding comes actually to have the power *of* understanding. The actualization achieved is that by which someone who has understanding only in the sense in which a human being is the sort of animal capable of understanding comes to have the actual ability to understand and to explain: comes, in other words, to have the *hexis* which is *epistēmē*.

Equipped then with these two responses, we may offer the following as an appropriate answer to our initial question:

> The maker mind makes both potential intellect and what is potentially thinkable in the sense of first potentiality, into actual intellect and what is actually thinkable in the sense of first actuality: that is, into what is actually *able* to think and what is actually think*able*. (3)

I will call (3) the Standard View. I use capital letters in order to redirect the semantic force of the phrase and thus (cravenly) to evade the issue of whether it in fact is *the* standard view. It is, in any case, a commonly held understanding of the productive activity of *nous poiētikos*, although it is clear that not all who hold it have chosen it from the Talmudic matrix of possibilities I have offered. It is, furthermore, a limited view about *nous poiētikos*, which leaves unresolved the wide variety of important and ramified differences concerning the *nature* of *nous poiētikos* which has characterized the hermeneutical tradition.

It is this view about which I will now raise more questions, and which I hope thereby to call back into question. I will not mean finally to deny that *nous* is the source and principle of concept formation, or to put it more traditionally, that the activity of *nous* is instrumental in the formation and development of that faculty.

[11] As e.g. in *APo.* 100ᵇ16. See Bonitz, *Index Aristotelicus*, 491ᵃ42 ff.

My suggestion will be, however, that that is not what is being argued in our text, and that the office of *nous poiētikos* described in *DA* 3. 5 is a different though importantly related one. Here then are some questions that I think should cause us uncertainty about the Standard View as expressed in (3).

IV. Still More Questions

(i) Consider first a problem about the consistency of the two answers which have led to the Standard View. If we say in reply to question (ii) that the actualization effected by the maker mind is from first potentiality to first actuality, then our answer to question (i), according to which the choice between *nous* and *noēton* was seen to be an unnecessary choice, becomes problematic. That reply depends on the claim that the actualities of *nous* and *noēton* are materially, although not formally, equivalent to one another. But such a claim requires that the actualizing at issue be not, as our answer to (ii) suggests, from first potentiality to first actuality, but from first actuality to second actuality; for it is only in complete second actuality that subject and object are identical. Consider again perception; it is not the two related powers of *aisthētikon* and *aisthēton*, the perceptual and the perceptible, that are identical, any more than are the sense organ and the sensible entity. It is only the full actuality of *aisthēsis*, the perceiving-and-being-perceived, which, although distinguishable as two beings, is one identical actuality. Isn't the same true in the case of thinking with respect to *nous* and *noēton*? My mind is not identical to the world's intelligibility—until, that is, it thinks it.

This concern may make us wish to deny that the actual identity of the respective first actualities is required for their actualization to be linked in the way the view we have been looking at demands. We may want to argue that since those actualities are essentially potentialities toward one and the same second actuality, that fact alone may be sufficient to guarantee the desired parallel.

In order to see this, we will need to reconsider Aristotle's characterization of light. The description of light in a number of passages we looked at suggests, I proposed, that Aristotle thinks of light as creating the first actuality of visibility. But Aristotle does not always speak this way; sometimes he appears to claim not that light creates *visibility*, but that it creates *vision*. In the short treatise *On Perception and the Perceived*, for example, he links a special feature of light to an analogous special feature of seeing with the explanation that 'light makes vision' (*to phōs poiei to horan*).[12] He does not say, we may note, that light makes the visible (*to phōs poiei to horaton*): light here seems to be thought of as bringing into existence the full actuality of being seen, and not merely the first actuality of visibility.

In *DA* 2. 7, we find Aristotle speaking the same way in the course of explaining phosphorescent objects:

[12] *Sens.* 447[a]11.

The reason why these things are seen [*horatai*] is another story. This much at least is clear: that in the light we see colour; that's why it is not seen without light: *ouch horatai aneu phōtos*.[13]

Again, where Aristotle might have said that something is not *visible* without light (*ouch horaton aneu phōtos*), we find him saying that it is not *seen* (*ouch horatai*).[14]

In these passages, Aristotle's view seems to conflict with the view we saw earlier. This conflict emerges, however, only if we assume that light cannot serve to effect *both* actualizations; we might be lead to this assumption by presupposing that light is uniquely positioned within a linear and one-dimensional model of Aristotle's doctrine. But suppose we relinquish that presupposition; suppose we say that there are three and not merely two necessary conditions for the joint actuality of seeing and being seen to take place. What is needed is not simply the visibility of the object and the visual capacity of the eye, *horaton* and *horatikos*, but light as well. On this view, light is a third *hexis* necessary to the activity of vision and on a par with the other two. No decision of the sort about which I have asked us to worry will then be required; for while light could be said to make the object of sight visible if the seeing eye is not yet at hand, it could be said *either* to make it visible *or* actually envisioned if it is.

But it is because light, when other conditions are fulfilled, causes things to be seen, that we are also willing to say that it causes visibility. If I am looking at a judge in the dark, turning on the lights will make her seen and therefore visible; if I am in the next room, it will make her visible because only my looking at her will be required for her to be seen. (No amount of *light*, on the other hand, will succeed in making visible the square root of seven or the hand of justice or, needless to say, Justice Itself.)

We may be able better to appreciate this model if we invite into our considerations a text whose absence should have been from the first noticeable: the discussion of light and the visible in the sixth book of the *Republic*.[15] This discussion is interesting in a number of respects. In the first place, we may wish simply to note how like Aristotle's discussion it is: here (as in the *Theaetetus*) one can see how deeply Aristotle's theory of perception and cognition is grounded in Platonic discussions. Note in particular (as again in the *Theaetetus*) the symmetrical model of perception which attributes potentiality and actuality to both subject and object; in a critical exchange between Socrates and Glaucon, Plato has Socrates explain:

When sight is in the eye, and the person who has it tries to use it, and colour is in the things he is trying to see, then if there is not present a third sort of thing which is

---

[13] *DA* 419ᵃ7.

[14] Two of the manuscripts do have *horata*, but the better reading, and the one that the commentators clearly had before them, is *horatai*. It may be that *horata* was the result of someone being perplexed by just what's now perplexing us. This perplexity may explain the fact that in Philoponus' commentary on the first half of this passage we find *horatai* in the body of the comment-ary, but *horata* in the lemma (Philoponus (1887), 348, ll. 9 ff.).

[15] *Republic* 6. 507 ff.

specifically and naturally directed to just this purpose, you know that the sight will see nothing, and that the colours will be unseen.

What is this thing of which you speak? he said.

It is, I replied, that which you call light.

What you say is true, he said.

It is, therefore, in no small way true that the perceptual faculty of seeing and the power of being seen (*hē tou horan aisthēsis kai hē tou horasthai dunamis*) are linked together by a link more honourable than that linking other pairs, if indeed light is not without honour.[16]

At the end of this exchange, light is pictured as linking together entities which are Aristotelian first actualities. And so in the conceit that follows; there the fact that without the idea of the good we are unable to understand and the world is unintelligible is figured by the fact that without light we are blind and the world cannot be seen; light thus creates *powers* of vision.

You know that eyes,…when one no longer turns them toward those things on whose colours is directed the light of day, but rather the gleams of night, are dimmed and seem almost blind, as if there were in them no clear sight.[17]

But we are able to talk that way about light only because the *primary* actualization which it effects is from first to second actuality; it is by virtue of *that* actualization that the eye is then said to have sight, and things said to be visible. Since light is what makes possible *seeing*, and since *being able* to see is defined by reference to seeing, light is said to make visibility actual as well. We might thus save, with these hints from Plato, the consistency of what initially seemed two conflicting Aristotelian views of light by stressing the primacy of second actuality to first actuality, the consequent primacy of the actualization from first actuality to second actuality, and the logical dependency on that actualization of the secondary actualization from first potentiality to first actuality.

This fact should suggest to us, as we read out the light analogy, that the same analysis may be appropriate for *nous*. And indeed, exactly the same structure is found in the ensuing discussion in the *Republic* as Socrates reads out the analogy of vision to mind.

The same is true of the eye by which the soul thinks.[18] When it fixes upon that on which shines truth and being, it thinks and knows and seems to possess *nous*. But when it is fixed on what is diluted with darkness, on coming to be and passing away, it opines and is dimmed, changing its opinions back and forth, and then seems not to possess *nous*.[19]

And so with Aristotle's mind. It is because *nous poiētikos* effects the actualization of *nous* in the actual activity of thinking, that is, because it brings about the realization of second-actuality thought, that we are able to describe it with equal facility as actualizing *nous* and *noēton*. Thus we can save the consistency of our two earlier answers by stressing the primacy of second actuality to

[16] *Republic* 6. 507 D 11 ff.   [17] *Republic* 6. 508 C 4 ff.
[18] Reading with Proclus *kai to omma tēs psuchēs hōi dē noei*.   [19] *Republic* 6. 508 D 4 ff.

first actuality, and the consequent primacy of the actualization from first actuality to second actuality. So perhaps Alexander's emphasis is mistaken; it is actual *thinking*, that is, second-actuality thinking, that the maker mind brings into being.

(ii) The second issue I want to raise concerns the characterization earlier alluded to of *nous* as the *archē* of that important human faculty Aristotle calls *epistēmē* or understanding, the reasoned ability to explain phenomena and make actual their intelligibility by revealing them for what they are. *Epistēmē* is, as Aristotle puts it, the *hexis*, or established capacity, for *apodeixis*, which is in turn described as 'a piece of reasoning that brings to light the causes and reasons for something being the case'.[20] It is well known that for a piece of reasoning to qualify as *apodeixis*, there must be understanding in turn of these causes and reasons, and thus eventually of first principles. It is equally well known that Aristotle assigns an important role to *nous* in this understanding; but it is clear, as much recent scholarship has argued, that *nous* is not a faculty for the *discovery* of the principles of scientific understanding, nor a method for the acquisition of scientific understanding.

It will therefore be misleading to claim that *nous poiētikos* effects the transition to the first stage of concept mastery. To do so will encourage us to continue to think of *nous* as a virtually miraculous power that provides us with a magical intuitive grasp of scientific principles.[21] Far the better teaching is that the first actuality of *nous* is acquired by *learning*, by the various forms of *epagōgē* which include above all the activities of science themselves. So it will be inaccurate to say in any *simple* sense that *nous poiētikos* is responsible for bringing about the first actuality of our ability to think and understand. I stress 'simple' in part because those who have held this doctrine have never claimed that it was simple, but more because on the developing view according to which *nous poiētikos* effects the transition to *second* actuality, there will remain a sense in which it is as well responsible, thought only mediately responsible, for the bringing into being of first actuality.

(iii) Finally, the Standard View should occasion in us a question about the rhetorical structure of the chapters of *De Anima* which Aristotle devotes to a discussion of *nous*. For the Standard View suggests not only that Aristotle views the maker mind as the cause of the development of *nous* as *hexis*, but also that he devotes to setting forth and explaining that fact a central chapter of his discussion. That fact follows, however, fairly straightforwardly from features quite general to Aristotle's theory of faculties and their activity. Of course the perfected *habitus* of *nous* is developed by the active agency of *nous*. For in general a *hexis* is

---

[20] *EN* 1139[b]31; *APo*. 85[b]23.

[21] In so far as readers have thought this way, the doctrine of *nous* has often seemed to them an unnatural grafting of an alien teaching on to Aristotle's considered empiricism. This has usually been part of that morality play about Platonism and Aristotelianism that still, even against our better judgement, repeatedly captures our imagination.

established by those very activities for which it is a dispositional capacity.[22] We might, therefore, find it odd that Aristotle should have devoted a chapter at the heart of his discussion of *nous* to spelling out a specific application of this general feature of acquired habits. If he had felt it necessary to give a specific account of the development of *nous* as first actuality, wouldn't the obvious point for him to do so have been in the heart of ch. 4 when first-actuality *nous* is initially introduced?[23]

V. Different Answers to Our Initial Question

Let us make, as Aristotle would say, a fresh start, and consider more generally where the discussion of mind stands at the beginning of ch. 5. To do this, we need to be aware of another important earlier text, besides the *Republic*, which Aristotle has before him: the apparently short but influential book of Anaxagoras (or as he was affectionately called in antiquity, Mr Mind).[24] Aristotle, as we know, in spite of his unhappiness with Anaxagoras' occasional introduction of *nous* as *intellectus ex machina*,[25] had great respect for his use of mind in cosmic explanation. A man who says that the presence of *nous* in the cosmos as a whole as well as in living things is the cause of all order and arrangement, Aristotle tells us only a few pages before his criticism of Anaxagoras, must have appeared sober as a judge in relation to those wild talkers who went before him.[26] And it is clear that from the beginning of his discussion of *nous*, Anaxagoras is very much on Aristotle's mind.

Ch. 4 begins with an account of mind explicitly patterned on that of Anaxagoras, and filled with quotations from and paraphrases of Anaxagoras' discussion. But Aristotle's purpose, as it generally is in his discussion of his philosophical precursors, is not a simple appropriation, but a hermeneutical restructuring and critique of Anaxagoras' position. Thus he quotes Anaxagoras, only to give immediately a gloss on how we are to understand his predecessor's view in the context of the present discussion:

Mind, since it thinks all things, must be unmixed, as Anaxagoras says 'in order that it may rule', that is, in order that it may know: *hina kratēi, touto d' estin hina gnōrizēi.*[27]

More importantly, Aristotle makes clear that however correct Anaxagoras was in thinking of mind as a cosmic principle, the present discussion must first come to terms with the nature of mind as determined by the functional psychic definition of Aristotle's treatise. So he continues:

---

[22] I find Kahn's reasoning here exactly backwards: 'If the transition from *hexis* to exercise does not require separate attention, that is perhaps because Aristotle does not think of it as constituting a distinct problem. It is, after all, only by repeated acts of *noēsis* that we acquire the *hexis* of *nous*' Kahn (1981), 400.

[23] *DA* 429[b]5.   [24] Diog. Laert. 2. 6.   [25] *Metaph.* 985[a]18 ff.   [26] *Metaph.* 984[b]15 ff.

[27] *DA* 429[a]18 ff. Philoponus innocently explains (1897, 523 l. 2); ' "To rule" for Anaxagoras is "to know" for Aristotle.'

that part of the soul that is called *nous*—and by *nous* I here mean that by which the soul reasons and conceives—is nothing at all in actuality before it thinks.[28]

This is not simply a repetition of the functional definition of mind with which the chapter begins, but a strong statement of the fact that although Aristotle's discussion of mind means to take account of those features that were important to Anaxagoras, what he is talking about is mind as a particular faculty of the human *psuchē*.

Ch. 4 then gives an account of this faculty on the basis of those features that Aristotle agrees with Anaxagoras are important, but restricted to mind as a feature of the human soul. At the end of this chapter, it looks as though a number of problems in Anaxagoras' theory have been dealt with, but without any account of that aspect of mind central in Anaxagoras, its function as that by virtue of which the intelligible structure of the cosmos is both ordered and apprehended.

In a sense, ch. 5 may be thought of as turning to that function of mind, mind as the principle of cosmic ordering and apprehending, that is, of intelligibility and intelligizing *en hapasēi tēi phusei*, to redirect the words Aristotle uses at the beginning of the chapter. In this sense, *nous poiētikos* is, as the intrepid half of the tradition has always understood, divine, a fact to which we should be alerted by its description, with clear echoes of *Metaphysics*, as a being 'whose *ousia* is *energeia*'.[29] For just as light is (though in a special sense) most visible, and thus the source of seeing and therefore of visibility, so is the divine most thinkable and thus the source of thinking and therefore of thinkability; light is never in the dark, and God is always, as we know, busy thinking.

This is not, however, the entire story; to see this, let us return to ch. 4. At the end of that chapter, Aristotle raises several *aporiai*:

If *nous* is something simple and unaffected and has nothing in common with anything, as Anaxagoras says, how will it think, if thinking is *paschein ti*—being affected in some way?[30]

A second question is whether *nous*

can itself be thought? For then either *nous* will belong to all other things, if it is not thought because of something else, and that which is thought is one in form, or it will have something mixed in it which makes it itself be thought as other things are.[31]

Two responses are then offered to these two problems:

Mind is in a sense potentially what is thought, although it is actually nothing until it thinks.[32]

Mind is itself thought exactly as what is thought is. For in the case of things which are without matter, the thinker and the thought are the same; for actual understanding [*epistēmē theōrētikē*] and the object of that understanding are the same.[33]

---

[28] *DA* 429[a]22 ff.   [29] *DA* 430[a]18; *Metaph.* 1071[b]20.   [30] *DA* 429[b]23 ff.
[31] *DA* 429[b]26 ff.   [32] *DA* 429[b]30 f.
[33] *DA* 430[a]2 ff. For the translation of *epistēmē theōrētikē* as actual understanding, see below, n. 40.

This solution itself, however, poses another *aporia* in the form of a question which is raised but not resolved in ch. 4, and which therefore remains unanswered at the beginning of ch. 5. Given that mind thus knows itself, and therefore does not, as the perceptual faculty does, depend on the existence of an external object, why is it that thinking is not always actively taking place?

This question is raised by Aristotle in the next sentence:

The reason why [mind] does not always think needs to be considered.[34]

Once we have acquired the *hexis* of *nous*, in other words, how is it—given that mind is, as Philoponus points out,[35] always present to itself—that sometimes we are actualizing that *hexis* in *theōria* and sometimes not? Hicks describes this remark as parenthetical, and Ross is of the opinion, shared by other commentators, that 'Aristotle does not appear to discuss this question anywhere.'[36] Let me suggest rather than it is this question to which Aristotle turns in the opening lines of ch. 5, and which he elucidates by reference to the analogy of light.

For we have, in light and vision, an appropriate model in terms of which to elucidate it. The situation is like that of seeing, where, as we saw, the main characters in the drama can be in place—the power of vision and the power of visibility—but without light, there will be no appropriate second actuality— nothing will get visualized. So with the maker mind; here is a principle like light which explains noetic *second* actuality—the intellect actually *intelligizing* and the intelligible actually *being intelligized*. And as we saw with light, we will also be able to describe this principle as the principle of the intelligible being *intelligible*.

On this account, our earlier suspicions will turn out to have been correct. It is not wrong to say that *nous poiētikos* brings into being first-actuality mind and first-actuality thinkable, and is therefore the source of *epistēmē*, but misleading; for it masks the fact that this happens by virtue of *nous poiētikos* being the source of those acts of thinking by which *nous* and *noēton* alike are brought to second actuality.

But our account is still not complete, as can be seen in the remarks with which Aristotle concludes this discussion at the end of ch. 4:

But in the case of those things which have matter, each of them is potentially thought. Therefore *nous* will not belong to those things; for mind is a potentiality of such things only without matter. But being thought will belong to it.[37]

What these remarks suggest, I think, is that there is a further *aporia* in this

[34] *DA* 430ᵃ5.   [35] Philoponus, (1897), 528. 1. 11.
[36] Hicks in Aristotle (1907), 497; Ross in Aristotle (1961a), 295.
[37] *DA* 430ᵃ6 ff. Does 'it' in the final sentence refer to mind, or to each of the things potentially thought? Both readings give a reasonable sense to the passage. The latter, according to which Aristotle is stressing that although not everything that is thought is mind, mind is nevertheless among the things thought, is the common understanding. The variant reading in one manuscript and in Simplicius of *ekeinois* for *ekeinoi* perhaps supports the latter reading and therefore the interpretation which follows, though it is not one Simplicius agrees with.

concluding discussion, first raised at 429^{b}37, which concerns the question of the universal presence of *nous*. This question should remind us of the similar *aporia* with respect to perception at the conclusion of book 2 of the *De Anima*.[38] There Aristotle asks this question: if to perceive is to be affected by a sensible form, why not say that the air, which is affected, for example, by the sensible form of the odorous, smells it? And what would then prevent us from saying (as some earlier thinker might) that air and many other such things are sensitive and therefore *empsuchon*? Aristotle's answer to this question, introduced at the end of book 2 and developed in a complex argument in the beginning of book 3, is that in being affected by the sensible form of the odorous, air becomes *sensible* but does not thereby become *sensitive*; what distinguishes smelling from merely being affected by odour as air is, and thus what in general distinguishes perception from the mere fact of being so affected as to become perceptible, is that the latter is, but the former is not, a mode of *consciousness*. Aristotle offers his readers little by way of further explanation of this fact; the beginning of book 3 argues only against a certain mode of explanation, one which would locate the seat of awareness in some unique meta-sense whose operation upon the senses generates conscious perception.[39]

A similar problem here presents itself with respect to mind; if the activity of thought is affection by the intelligible, why should we not say that air thinks, given that its intelligible form is present to itself. And why should we not then say, as someone might think Anaxagoras said, that all that is intelligible is mind?

The question which is left unanswered at the end of ch. 4 and to which I earlier suggested the introduction of *nous poiētikos* is in part an answer, is thus not simply the question: why are we not always thinking? but the more general question: why is thinking not always taking place? Aristotle's move at the beginning of ch. 5 is then to offer an indication of the distinction between the merely intelligible, and *nous*, which we now understand to be at once intelligible and, more significantly, capable of *actual thinking*, that is, capable of *theōria*, the fully realized second actuality of *nous*[40]

I say *indication*, since Aristotle does not here offer, any more than he does in the case of perception in the early chapters of book 3, an elaborated explanation of the phenomenon of consciousness which distinguishes the merely intelligible from the intelligent. In particular, it is not his claim that *nous poiētikos* is a separate faculty that explains our capacity for active *nous*. *Theōria* indeed is not located in a separate faculty, any more than perceptual consciousness, as *DA* 3. 2 argues, is located in a separate faculty. *Nous poiētikos*, therefore, does not, strictly speaking, make consciousness, by action for example upon a pathetic mind incapable of

---

[38] *DA* 424^{b}2 ff.

[39] I have argued in favour of this reading of the beginning of book 3 in Kosman (1975).

[40] I use the term *theōria* here in the marked sense it often has for Aristotle as second-actuality *energeia* in contrast to first-actually structures of cognitive capacity. Three central examples of this usage are in *DA* 412^{a}10 f., 417^{a}28 ff. and *Metaph.* 1048^{a}33 ff. See Bonitz, *Index Aristotelicus*, 328^{a}54 ff.: '*theōrein* ab *epistēmē* perinde distinguitur atque *energeia* a *dunamei*.'

thinking by itself. It is simply *nous* understood in its role of self-actualization in *theōria*; in this sense, it is correct, despite my earlier remarks, to call *nous poiētikos* active mind.

What emerges from these indications, however, is at least the following:

(i) It is important to remember that *nous* is not simply a principle of intelligibility, but a principle of active consciousness. (ii) This active consciousness is (an admittedly intermittent) capacity of human *psuchē*. (iii) The paradigm of this *activity* of mind is that divine mind whose substance is *energeia*, and specifically the *energeia* of *theōria*—*noēsis noēseōs noēsis* as it is called in the *Metaphysics*: thinking thinking thinking.[41] It is finally, I suggest, that active thinking, thinking as *theōria*, which the maker mind makes, a thinking most fully exemplified in the unremittingly active thinking of the divine mind.

The maker mind is therefore not simply an element in Aristotle's psychological theory, but an element in his theology as well, and the question we might ask is not simply: what does it mean that Aristotle describes mind in this perplexing and cryptic way? but what does it mean that Aristotle thinks that the divine source of the world's order is mind, and why does he here as in the *Metaphysics* link the divine to that capacity that human beings have to think and to understand?

I will not attempt to answer that question in this essay; I have made moves in that direction elsewhere.[42] But let me say this much. Aristotle's god is not a scientist, nor a philosopher, and divine thought is not a form of cosmic ratiocination or brilliantly articulated scientific theory. For *theōria* is not theory; it is simply the principle of *awareness* (prior to its later thematization as interiority), the (divine) full self-manifesting and self-capturing activity of *consciousness*, of which scientific activity and philosophical speculation are to be sure particularly subtle forms, but of which the ruder and more incorporate activities of perception and nutrition are equally images, if meaner and less noble, and of which indeed—and this is after all simply the doctrine of *Metaphysics*, culminating in Λ—the essential being of all things, the formal principle of their being what they are which constitutes their intelligible essence, is also a mode.

I will take this recognition of the fact that divine *nous* in *Metaphysics* Λ is the principle of all being as licence to end with some more general remarks on *nous*. There is not, as should be clear, a single story to be told about *nous*, or at least not a single story which will make sense of *nous* apart from its deep connections to the entire philosophical-scientific picture Aristotle wants to draw. In one sense, *nous* is the human capacity to think; in another it is the *archē* of that developed cognitive perceptual capacity we have to recognize things for what they are and to construct logically connected bodies of rational discourse that explain and make intelligible the world about us, the *archē*, in other words, of *epistēme*. In yet another sense it is, as I have argued, the *archē* of consciousness in general;

---

[41] *Metaph.* 1074ᵇ34.   [42] Kosman (1988).

thus Aristotle's hint at the end of the *Posterior Analytics* that animals have a rudimentary form of *nous* in the general capacity of discrimination which is *aisthēsis*.[43] I think this must mean that *nous* is only the purest form of that general power of cognitive awareness and discrimination that is increasingly revealed in *scala naturae*.

But in yet another and broader sense *nous* is the *archē* of substance, and therefore of *psuchē*, the form and principle of those living beings which are above all substances. For thinking, and consciousness in general, is the ideal mode of a defining feature of living substances, their capacity to be open to further determination by virtue of that determinacy of essential being that characterizes them in the first instance as substances. A basic ingredient of Aristotle's ontology is the relation between determinacy and openness to determination. It is because and only because substances are the determinate beings they are that they are capable of exhibiting that *malista idion*, that most characteristic feature of substance identified early in the *Categories* as the ability to take on further determination without being overwhelmed by it, the ability to remain one and the same individual while undergoing accidental affection.[44]

For human beings, this openness to further determination is centred in perception and thought, but it is a general feature of human psychic powers as set forth in *De Anima*. The nutritive capacity— the capacity to eat—is a capacity to take in other matter (the power of ingestion) and to transform it into oneself (the power of digestion); thus *De Anima* begins its discussion of psychic powers with an account of nutrition, and specifically of nutriment, that is, of food. In the same way, the capacity to perceive is a power to take in the sensible forms of the world and transform them into consciousness.

Such transformations are grounded in the bodily nature of the nutritional and perceptive powers. A significantly different story will therefore have to be told about knowing, and particularly about *nous*, which is the *archē* of the perceptive and knowing powers in general, the highest form of consciousness. But the story will be similar in that the knower will become the object known without relinquishing its own determinate identity. The activity of knowing is precisely this act of becoming determined by the object of knowledge while remaining oneself, and *nous* is the psychic power so to be determined without relinquishing determinate identity. This is what it means that for Aristotle, as for Anaxagoras, *nous* is *apathēs*, and why it is that God is the principle of both *ousia* and *nous*, and finally of all the cognitive powers including perceptive.

The activities of life are activities which depend upon the separability of form from matter. Thus the reproductive faculty is the ability to recreate the form of the animal in another individual, that is in different matter, and the threptic the ability to take the nutritive power of food and make it one's own. Similarly, the activities of consciousness are activities of taking on form; thus the aisthetic faculty is said to be the power of receiving selectively form without substratum.[45]

---

[43] *APo.* 100ᵃ34 ff.   [44] *Cate.* 4ᵃ10 ff.   [45] *DA* 424ᵃ17 ff.

Behind this general power of *psuchē* to grasp, as it were, the *qua* of being, to separate, distinguish, and discriminate, is the power of *nous*, the capacity to separate out being and, as it were, to dematerialize it; so it is that *hē nou energeia zōē*—life is the activity of mind.[46] *Nous* is also therefore divine being and therefore the *archē* of that principle which orders the world in its fundamental order, that of intelligibility. In this sense Anaxagoras was not so wrong, nor indeed was Plotinus.

Last but not least, *nous* is the *archē* of our capacity to do that very act of reading we have here been doing. For reading the *endoxa* is merely a special instance of reading the *phainomena*, and therefore takes place insofar as we are activated by *nous poiētikos*. This fact should remind us that the *unio mystica* of *theōria*, so important as a theme in earlier discussions of *nous poiētikos*, can take place in the most quotidian of our enterprises, whenever we are engaged in the activity of seeing how things are, as I hope has happened in this essay on *nous poiētikos*.

---

[46] *Metaph.* 1072[b]27.

19

ARISTOTLE ON THINKING

CHARLES H. KAHN

MY aim here will be to clarify some aspects of Aristotle's theory of the intellect (*nous*) which seem to me often neglected or misunderstood. So this paper is presented as a kind of complement to my earlier article on sense perception in Aristotle.[1] But I can now bring into the open the philosophical motivation left unspoken in the earlier piece, since it was only then beginning to take shape. This motivation is best expressed as an answer to my own variant on Myles Burnyeat's question, namely, is an Aristotelian philosophy of mind still possible? My answer is that it is not only possible but necessary, since Aristotle offers us the best alternative to the dualist and anti-dualist theories of mind that have plagued philosophy with persistent and fruitless conflict for more than three centuries. Hence, although the body of my paper will consist of detailed exegesis of Aristotelian texts and doctrines, I begin and end with some comments on the larger issues.

I think it would be a mistake to frame these large questions in terms of the mind–body problem and to ask, for example, is Aristotle a dualist? The interpreter of Aristotle who wants to present his view as philosophically relevant today is obliged to take for granted the scientific advances of the last few centuries. But we are not obliged to take for granted the terms that have been imposed upon this new scientific knowledge by the post-Cartesian tradition of philosophical dualism and anti-dualism. On the contrary, to do so seems to me to kill the philosophic relevance of Aristotle by eliminating his chief advantage, namely that he stands *outside* this post-Cartesian tradition, and hence that a sympathetic understanding of his position may allow us also to step outside this tradition long enough to subject it to critical scrutiny. His real advantage, as I see it, is to be exempt from the Cartesian curse of mind–body opposition with all the baffling paradoxes and philosophical blind alleys that this antithesis gives rise to. It should not, I submit, be regarded as a friendly act to ask Aristotle what his position is on the mind–body question.

As we all know, Aristotle is not a dualist but a quaternist: he treats the issues of thought and perception not within the dual categories of mind and matter but within the fourfold scheme of natural bodies, living things, sentient animals, and rational animals (i.e. humans). And it would be a mistake to suppose that two of his categories (the bodily and the living) could be assigned to 'body' while

© Charles H. Kahn, 1992.
[1] Kahn (1966).

the other two (sentience and rationality) correspond to 'mind'. Aristotle's four divisions are neither opposed to one another nor mutually exclusive, as in our distinction between the mental and the physical. His four levels represent an ascending scale or pyramid in which the 'higher' levels presuppose and rest upon the levels below: a human is a special kind of animal, as an animal is a special kind of living thing, and a living thing a special kind of physical body. Of course we know that the ground-floor level of this scheme, Aristotle's account of in-animate bodies, has been wholly superseded by the development of modern chemistry and physics. But it does not follow that his account of the upper storeys is undermined by this development. Since each level is qualitatively distinct, each calls for its own autonomous level of understanding and expla-nation. On Aristotle's view, the levels below provide a necessary condition, a *sine qua non*, for what lies above. Thus the mechanism required for perception and thought must be understood in terms of modern physiology; but the understand-ing of perception and thought is not to be identified with the understanding of this mechanism. For Aristotle there is no question of reduction or bottom-up explanation. There are, however, complex problems of interaction between these levels, as we shall see in the case of sense and intellect.

My discussion will focus on two doctrines in the theory of intellect or ration-ality (*nous*), which I call Doctrine One (D1) and Doctrine Two (D2). Doctrine One is the claim that *nous* is essentially incorporeal and has no bodily organ. Doctrine Two is the thesis that the intellect in act is identical with its intelligible object.

I

D1, the claim that *nous* has no bodily organ and hence that the faculty of intellect (*to noētikon*) is not only logically distinct but essentially separable from the body and from the rest of the *psuchē*,[2] is an embarrassment to many of Aristotle's mod-ern admirers, who fear that it commits him to some form of Cartesian dualism; I hope to show that this fear is quite unjustified. But D1 might equally seem to be an embarrassment for Aristotle himself. For it seems flatly incompatible with his general definition of the *psuchē* as form and actualization of the body; and it also appears to contradict his insistence that we cannot think without phantasms, since phantasms are derived from sense-perception which is directly dependent upon a bodily organ. I will argue (i) that D1 is in fact incompatible with the general definition of *psuchē*, and that Aristotle is fully aware of this, but (ii) that one can remove the appearance of conflict between D1 and our need for phantasms by drawing a clear distinction between our noetic faculty as such and our concrete acts of human thinking. This is a distinction which Aristotle hardly makes explicit (expect in the extreme case of disembodied *nous* in *DA* 3. 5) but

[2] *DA* 429ᵃ24–7, ᵇ5; cf. 2. 413ᵇ24–7.

which is required to make sense of his position and which, I believe, he everywhere takes for granted.

(i) If *nous* has no bodily organ and is essentially separable from the human body, then it cannot be defined as form or *entelecheia* of that body. Aristotle did not need to wait for contemporary philosophers to call his attention to this consequence. His entire treatment of *nous* is informed by a recognition of this discrepancy. From the very first chapter of the *De Anima* he remarks that 'if there is any act or passion proper to the soul, it could be separated (from the body)' (403ᵃ10). In 1. 4, in an important context to which we will return, Aristotle describes *nous* as entering the soul as a complete substance (*ousia tis ousa*) which is imperishable. Its possessor, the compound of body and soul, will perish 'but *nous* is probably something more divine and impassive (*apathes*)' (408ᵇ18–29). So when the hylomorphic definition of the *psuchē* is introduced in 2. 1–2 it is immediately accompanied by qualifications on the status of *nous*.

It is clear then that the soul is not separable from the body, or that parts of it are not separable if it is divisible into parts...But nothing prevents some parts from being separable, *because they are not the actualization of any body.* (413ᵃ4.)

Thus by anticipation Aristotle denies that his definition of psyche applies to *nous*. In the second chapter of book 2, after the *dianoētikon* has been listed among the basic psychic capacities (413ᵇ13), Aristotle is even more explicit.

Concerning *nous* and the power of contemplation nothing is clear as yet, but this seems to be a different kind of soul (*psuchēs genos heteron*), and this alone can be separated, as the eternal from the perishable. (413ᵇ24.)

By describing *nous* as 'a different *genos* of soul' Aristotle clearly means to exclude it from the hylomorphic definition. And since this definition is not intended to apply to *nous*, there is no question of a literal contradiction between the definition and D1.

But of course there is still a problem. If *nous* is so radically different, how is it connected to the other parts of the soul which *are* the actualizations of bodily structures? We are sentient animals in virtue of our hylomorphic soul. Are we rational animals in virtue of two distinct souls, the one that makes us animals and 'a different kind' that makes us rational? Is human nature constituted by one essence or by two?

I do not see that there is any genuine resolution for this tension within Aristotle's account of the *psuchē*. But I want to suggest that this is not so much an inconsistency in his theory as a systematic attempt on his part to do justice to our split nature as human beings. On the one hand we are part of nature, a functioning organism like any animal, and that is what is covered by the hylomorphic definition. On the other hand we somehow transcend the animal's position within nature by our access to the noetic domain (in modern terms, roughly the domain of culture): the realm of science and ethics, art and technology. It is not as animals but as possessors of language and intellect, *logos* and *nous*, that we are capable of activity in these areas. In Aristotle's terms, it is in virtue of the divine element in us that we are *rational* animals. So his theory of the human *psuchē* requires both the hylomorphic definition *and* an account of incorporeal *nous*. (It remains to be seen—and I will briefly discuss in the conclusion—how far our modern conceptions of language and culture can make it unnecessary to think of the intellect as incorporeal.) So the lack of unity in Aristotle's account of the soul can be seen as an accurate reflection of the complex, paradoxical structure of the human condition.

Whether or not this is an accurate account of human nature, I think it is clearly Aristotle's view. In order to show that this view is a coherent one we must do more than he has done to clarify the relationship between *nous* and the other parts of the soul. Which brings us to the phantasms.

(ii) If *nous* is intrinsically incorporeal and separable from the body, why does Aristotle insist that we cannot think without phantasms? My answer to this question is simple enough, but it may seem very strange, for Aristotle's view has become profoundly unfamiliar to us, because of the prevalence of Cartesian and anti-Cartesian philosophies of mind.

Aristotle assumes that there are two necessary conditions that must be satisfied for our ordinary acts of thinking to occur, where 'thinking' (*dianoeisthai*) is taken in the broadest sense for anything that includes *phantasia* but goes beyond it, any minimally rational train of thought that can eventuate in what he calls a *hupolēpsis*, a judgement or belief that may be true or false and that can be formulated in a *logos* or statement. In order for thinking in this sense to take place the first condition—call it Condition A—is empirical consciousness or sentience, what human beings share with the animals. (We might say: with the 'higher' animals, but Aristotle is not so exclusive.) Sentience for Aristotle is the subjective side of *aisthēsis*, the faculty of sense; its objective side is perception, receiving information about the world. The second condition, Condition B, is the specific human capacity of *nous*, access to the noetic domain (which remains to be specified). What makes us human is the joint possession of these two capacities, and our conscious life is the continuous experience of their interaction.

If this is correct, there is no incompatibility between our need for phantasms and the incorporeality of *nous*. The requirement of phantasms is a direct consequence of Condition A, our existence as sentient animals. As sentient, embodied beings, we cannot think even of *noēta*, intelligible objects, except by way of phantasms, the hylomorphic basis of our thought. (In modern terms phantasms may be thought of either as mental events or as brain states; since for Aristotle phantasms are hylomorphic items, they will correspond to both.) On the other hand, the incorporeality of *nous* is for Aristotle an essential feature of Condition B, our access to the noetic domain. Why *noēsis* must be incorporeal is a separate point, to be discussed below. For the moment I only wish to show that, because of Aristotle's *two* conditions on thinking, there is no contradiction between our dependence upon phantasms, corresponding to Condition A, and the incorporeality of *nous*, corresponding to Condition B. It is not the disembodied principle of *nous* that requires phantasms; it is our use of *nous*, the penetration of *nous* into our embodied activity as sentient animals, which must take place by means of the phantasms, that is, through the neurophysiological mechanism of sense and the mental imagery of conscious thought.[3]

My distinction between Conditions A and B is directly based upon Aristotle's distinction between *aisthēsis* and *nous*, between the sensory and noetic faculties. According to Aristotle, this distinction is fundamental for any understanding of the human *psuchē*. The emergence of the concept of the 'mental' in post-Cartesian philosophy represents from this point of view a catastrophic loss in philosophical clarity, since our modern notion of the mental is founded upon a systematic confusion of the sensory and the noetic. Descartes himself, as the chief initiator of the new view, retains some trace of the older conception. Thus he can contrast *intellectio pura*, 'pure intellection', with sense-perception, imagination, and emotion. For Descartes these sensory and emotive powers represent impure or 'confused' intellection, because they have a non-accidental relation to the body. Hence it is only pure intellection that belongs 'to the essence of my mind'.[4] We might suppose that here Descartes was following Aristotle, but in fact his view is quite different. For Descartes clearly regards the *cogito* itself, the recognition of one's own existence in the *Second Meditation*, as an exercise in *intellectio pura*, since he conceives it as carried out by a 'thinking being' who might not have a body at all; whereas Aristotle would have recognized such self-awareness as an act of *aisthēsis*, our 'perceiving that we think', and hence as an essentially embodied act.[5] This marks the radical discontinuity between Aristotelian and modern philosophies of mind, and it shows why, for all the incorporeality of *nous*, Aristotle cannot be a Cartesian dualist. Since our ordinary intellectual activity is for Aristotle a joint action of sentience and intellect and hence necessarily embodied, Descartes's conception of thought as disembodied consciousness, as activity that is purely 'mental', breaks entirely new ground.[6] By the fatal move of including sensation and emotion among (impure) acts of 'thinking', Descartes has obliterated the Aristotelian line between the capacities of perception and intellect and in their place set the new category of the mental defined by opposition to the bodily-physical.

To return to Aristotle, we must give up the post-Cartesian notion of the mental. On Aristotle's view our conscious awareness, including our feelings and emotional states, belongs to the animal principle of sentience; the noetic faculty represents not so much a different kind of awareness as a different category of conceptual content and a different logical status for what is conceived.

---

[3] Aristotle has a theory of disembodied *nous* in his account of the active intellect and the divine thought of the prime mover. I shall be concerned here only with the activity of *nous* as it occurs in human beings.

[4] Descartes, *Meditation* VI, Adam–Tannery vii. 73. 7; cf. 78. 5.

[5] See the quotation below from *EN* 9. 9 (reference in n. 9).

[6] I ignore here the Neoplatonic and Augustinian antecedents for Descartes's *cogito*, but I doubt whether either the Greek or the Latin tradition has a concept as wide as Cartesian *cogitationes* and the modern concept of the 'mental'.

This distinction calls for clarification and support, not only because Aristotle's position is so unfamiliar to us but also because he has said so little about the interaction between these two principles in human psychology. I can deal briefly here with the sensory principle, since I have discussed this topic at length in the earlier paper. An understanding of *nous* will prove more difficult.

II

First of all, *aisthēsis*. I have argued elsewhere that Aristotle attributes to one and the same faculty of sense (i) the objective perception of qualities and other sensory features of the natural world and (ii) the subjective awareness of ourselves as perceiving, feeling (including feelings of pleasure and pain), and thinking, so that for Aristotle it is *aisthēsis*, not *nous* as such, that carries out most of the activity of the Cartesian *cogito* as defined in *Meditation* II.[7] What we call consciousness is what Aristotle envisages as the unified power of sentience, the capacity that is put out of commission in sleep or when we fall (as we say) unconscious, 'the common power accompanying all the senses, by which we perceive that we are seeing and hearing' (*Somn. Vig.* 455[a]15). This is the subjective side of the faculty located in the central sensorium, in modern terms in the brain. (Note that the noetic faculty as such is not located *anywhere*, since it has no bodily organ, although the phantasms or 'images' that it employs will also be located in the brain.) Not only *phantasia* or imagination but memory too belongs to this power of sentience, the direct realization (*entelecheia*) of our neurophysiology. Thus memory even of intelligible matters (*ta noēta*) requires a phantasm, says Aristotle, and the phantasm is an affect (*pathos*) of the common faculty of sentience (*koinē aisthēsis*). So the memory of an intellectual content 'belongs to *nous* incidentally but it belongs *per se* to the primary power of sense'.[8] It is the same faculty that perceives when we carry out any action, so that 'if we are perceiving, it notices that we are perceiving, and if we are thinking, it notices that we are thinking (*hoti nooumen*)'.[9] Thus although on the objective, external side *aisthēsis* seems to be restricted to a rather narrow range of objects, on the subjective, internal side it expands to cover the whole range of self-awareness and introspection.

Such was the view I presented some twenty years ago. Actually the situation is more complicated, because of a whole series of ambiguities in Aristotle's use of the term *aisthēsis*. There is, first of all, the basic distinction just mentioned, for which Aristotle has no terminological equivalent: between (i) *aisthēsis* as perception objectively understood, receiving information about the environment, and (ii) *aisthēsis* subjectively understood as awareness, feeling, or reflexive consciousness. The external perspective (i) tends to predominate, as when the senses and

---

[7] Kahn (1966). For self-awareness see especially *Sens.* 448[a]26–30, cited there p. 80 n. 86.

[8] *Mem.* 450[a]12–14. In this context *to proton aisthetikon* may refer to the central sensorium or to the common faculty of sense or, better still, to both.

[9] *EN* 1170[a]31, with Bywater's emendation. For discussion see Kahn (1966), 78.

other faculties are defined in terms of their objects.[10] But the internal or subjective side, the 'raw feel', of perceptual experience is also in play when Aristotle emphasizes the necessary link between *aisthēsis* and pleasure, pain, and desire (*DA* 2. 2 413ᵇ23, etc.), or when he speaks of the reflexive experience of 'perceiving that we are seeing and hearing' (3. 2). Hence what we call empirical consciousness is located for Aristotle in the primary *aisthētikon*, the 'common power accompanying all the senses' which ceases its normal function in sleep, although it is affected in a secondary way in dreaming. For full clarity, however, this basic distinction between (i) and (ii) must be further subdivided into a narrow and a broader sense of *aisthēsis*, as follows. On the subjective side we can distinguish (ii*a*) perceptual experience in the narrow sense: seeing, hearing, exercising one or more of the sensory modalities; and (ii*b*) the broader notion of awareness. Thus in 'we perceive that we are seeing and hearing', 'we perceive' properly refers not to (ii*a*) but to (ii*b*), awareness more broadly understood. This genus–species ambiguity is harmless enough. But a corresponding ambiguity on the objective side is potentially misleading, and hence of greater theoretical importance. We must distinguish (i*a*) the reception of sensory forms through the diverse sense organs, perceiving the *aisthēta* ('objects of sense') narrowly understood as shapes, colours, sounds, etc, from (i*b*), perceiving 'sensible things', *aisthēta* broadly understood as the objects of the visible world, such as trees, dogs, and people. And in this case Aristotle himself is careful to draw a terminological distinction. In *DA* 2. 6 our narrow *aisthēta* (i*a*) are Aristotle's *per se* sense-objects, whereas our *aisthēta* broadly conceived (i*b*) are his incidental objects of sense, the sensibles *per accidens*. The importance of this will be seen in a moment.

In principle, this whole range of sensibility is something we share with the animals. But of course as noetic animals our awareness is more complex. We can observe and recall our acts of noetic thought; and even our self-perception (our perceiving that we are perceiving or that we are feeling emotion) will often involve a noetic element, although Aristotle does not mention this. More generally, our perceptual experience is penetrated through and through by conceptual elements that derive from *nous*. This is a point which Aristotle takes for granted but rarely discusses in any detail. A full treatment would require a special study; I must be satisfied here with a few suggestions.

III

First of all we must distinguish more carefully than Aristotle himself does between *nous* strictly speaking, the noetic faculty as such, and *noeisthai* or *dianoeisthai* broadly construed as acts of thinking. 'By *nous*', says Aristotle, 'I

---

[10] *DA* 2. 4 415ᵃ16–22 and 2. 6–12 *passim*. This corresponds to what Deborah Modrak calls the Actuality Principle: 'a cognitive faculty is potentially what its object is actually'. See Modrak (1987*a*), 24 ff.

mean that by which the soul thinks (*dianoeitai*) and forms judgements (*hupolambanei*)'; (429ª23). What he does not say or not so clearly, is that these acts will normally, perhaps always, involve the sensory faculty as well, since these are in fact acts of the whole human being, the embodied individual.

It is perhaps better not to say that the soul feels pity or learns or thinks (*dianoeisthai*), but that the human being does so by means of the soul....Thinking (*noein*) and contemplative activity (*theōrein*) are dulled when something decays inside, but the psychic principle itself [namely *nous*] is unaffected. Thinking (*dianoeisthai*) and loving and hating are not affects of this principle [*nous*? *psuchē*?] but of the individual who possesses it, insofar as he possesses it. Hence when the possessor perishes it neither remembers nor loves. For these activities did not belong to it, but to the compound (*to koinon*) which has perished. But *nous* is perhaps something more divine and unaffected.   (1. 4, 408ᵇ13–29.)

This passage is needlessly obscure, because Aristotle's thought shifts back and forth between two points, the first of which refers to the whole *psuchē* while the second is specifically concerned with *nous*.

(i) For the *psuchē* as a whole Aristotle wants to deny that, as a form, it is properly subject to local motion or change; it is only moved incidentally when the body is moved, whose form it is. To say that the soul is moved by anger 'would be like saying the soul weaves or builds houses' (408ᵇ11–13). The *heart* is of course moved in anger, and some comparable change occurs in the body even when one thinks.[11] Such changes can be traced to, but do not occur in, the soul, for the psyche is localized only by its relation to the body which it informs.

(ii) The point concerning *nous* is quite different, but connected with the previous point by reference to the hylomorphic or bodily aspect of thinking. When the heart (or brain) decays, such hylomorphic activities are impeded, just as in sleep. When the whole human being perishes, no activities of the complex *psuchē* can survive. Thus consciousness in the ordinary sense, as percipient awareness, comes to an end. But the principle of *nous* itself, which never really formed part of the hylomorphic *entelecheia*, survives intact.[12]

What is noteworthy here is that thinking is listed next to pity, anger, love, and hate as activities of the complex *psuchē*, involving a bodily change, and even the terms for the highest use of reason (*noein* and *theōrein*) refer here to activities

[11] *dianoeisthai* 408ᵇ9. In mentioning bodily change in connection with thinking, Aristotle must be referring to the phantasms.
[12] The textual obscurities are due to the fact that Aristotle begins by referring to the whole *psuchē* and ends by referring to *nous* alone, while a number of references in between are desperately ambiguous. In 408ᵇ25 *auto de apathes estin* seems to refer to *nous*, but *ekeinou* in ᵇ26, 28 seems to refer to the compound soul, which is responsible not only for thinking but for loving, hating, and remembering. (This is the suggestion of Hicks in Aristotle 1907, 278 on 408ᵇ26.) Partly as a result of such ambiguities, both Hicks and Rodier think that the argument proves too much: if it shows that the intellect is immortal and impassive, why does it not establish the same result for the whole soul? (Rodier in Aristotle 1900, ii. 137.) But I think the confusion here is one of expression only and not of thought. (1) above is a purely logical point about the soul as a form not being strictly mobile or subject to change; (2) is the metaphysical point about *nous*. The two points are so closely linked for Aristotle just because thinking (*dianoeisthai*) is an activity of the complex *psuchē*, and its reliance on phantasms involves a bodily process in the sensorium.

that deteriorate when bodily decay takes place. And these remarks occur in the very same context when Aristotle declares *nous* to be imperishable, impassive, and 'more divine'! But the appearance of contradiction is easy enough to dispel if we bear in mind the distinction that must be drawn between the principle or faculty of *nous* as such and its concrete activity in us, in human acts of thinking. The latter are of course inextricably combined with the action of the sensory soul, since 'the rational faculty (*to noētikon*) thinks the forms *in the phantasms*'.[13]

But if the noetic and sensory capacities are in practice so intimately fused, why does Aristotle insist upon such a radical distinction between them in principle? And why does he regard *nous* as intrinsically incorporeal? There are two questions here, and I take them one at a time.

IV

Why the fundamental distinction between sense and intellect? For Aristotle two faculties can be discriminated only by reference to their objects, so the difference between sense and intellect is ultimately the difference between *aisthēta* and *noēta*.[14] The *aisthēta* strictly understood are the sensible forms, that is (*a*) the proper objects of the special senses: colour, smell, sound, taste, hot and cold, dry and wet, hard and soft, and suchlike qualities, together with (*b*) the properties that are perceived by more than one sense: motion, shape, size, and number. Strictly speaking, these are the *only* properties perceived by the sense faculty, and even here we must take account of major restrictions. For example, it is only red in its particularity, as the visible quality of a given object, that is a sensible *per se*. Red as a general notion, as a member of the genus *colour* or of the category *quality*, is already conceived as a *noēton*, not as a proper object of the sense-faculty. Furthermore, taken as common sensibles such properties as number and shape will designate only very rough discriminations. For the precision of geometry or the sequence and generality of counting we need a great deal more than sense-perception. So the cognitive grasp of the world that comes from *aisthēsis* alone is extremely limited and fragmentary.[15] All interesting perceptual judgements extend well beyond the strict objects of sense to what Aristotle calls 'sensibles *per accidens*', the incidental objects of sense-perception, as in his example: 'that white shape there is the son of Diares' (418ᵃ21). What is not always noted by the commentators is that the incidental sensibles represent the overlap

---

[13] *DA* 3.7, 431ᵇ2. So also *Mem.* 449ᵇ31: 'there is no *noein* without a phantasm.' By the incorporeal principle of *nous* as such I mean not only the Agent Intellect of *DA* 3. 5, but also the passive or potential intellect insofar as it becomes identical with the *noēta* in the act of *noein*.

[14] See the texts cited in n. 10.

[15] Even for animals much more is required, since they can perceive dangers of different sorts and react to their environments in complex ways. Apparently Aristotle thinks of such behaviour as the work of *phantasia*; the medievals introduce the *vis aestimativa* as a sub-rational form of intelligence, 'evaluating' the data of perception. Aristotle is much more concerned to mark out the gap between *nous* and *aisthēsis* strictly conceived than to fill it by an account of intermediate capacities.

or conjoined action of sense and intellect. 'The son of Diares' is already a *noēton*, a complex conception involving the notions of human being and fatherhood, as well as the notion of an individual substance corresponding to the use here of a proper name and an individuating description.[16] If we run through Aristotle's scheme of categories as a kind of catalogue of basic concepts for information about the world, we see how very little of all this is covered by *aisthēta* strictly understood, the proper and common sensibles. With the exception of movement, the sensible forms recognized by Aristotle all fall within the categories of quality and quantity, and they are far from exhausting either of these categories. So it is not only the opposition particular–universal that defines the dichotomy between sense and intellect. Sense-perception *per se* cannot recognize even individual substances as such, since it has no access to any sortal concepts like *man, horse, tree*. Within relational concepts it can only detect differences of degree (for quality and quantity) and relative location (a common sensible Aristotle seems to have omitted, unless he thought of it as covered by motion). No social relations, no conceptual relations, and no physical relations of acting or being-acted-upon fall within the domain of sense strictly defined.

These narrow limits of sense-perception *per se* are not generally recognized by commentators, not even by the ancient commentators (as we will see in a moment). The ancients seem to have been misled by Aristotle's frequent use of *aisthēta* in the broader, Platonic sense of 'sensible things' which includes the incidental sensibles. Modern authors, on the other hand, are prone to an exaggerated account of sensory capacity by way of what I would describe (following a point made by Geach) as the empiricist myth of abstraction. This is the view that universal concepts are somehow latent in sensory data and need only be isolated by stripping away the irrelevant features. In at least two cases this over-generous view of sense-perception leads to a misreading of Aristotelian texts that are crucial for the distinction between sense and intellect.

(i) The first case consists of *Metaph.* A1 and *APo.* 2. 19, where Aristotle traces the growth of knowledge from *aisthēsis* through memory and 'experience' to the grasp of universals. Here the tempting error is to suppose that the crucial steps in the process are marked by a difference of degree rather than kind, that they represent a continuous series of stages of widening generality. It is true and important that in these two contexts Aristotle's interest is focused on the appearance of the universal, 'the one besides the many, that is present as one and the same in all of them' (*APo.* 100ᵃ7), which makes possible 'a single universal judgement about similar cases' (*Metaph.* 981ᵃ6). The mistake would be to assume that the *empeiria* which precedes this final stage could possibly be the work of sense-perception alone. For the 'experience' of animals who possess *logos* is radically different from that of those without it (*APo.* 100ᵃ1). The individual judgement 'this remedy helped Callias when he was sick with this disease', which belongs to

---

[16] For an interpretation of incidental sensibles along these lines, see Bernard (1988), 75–86. For a quite different view, see Modrak (1987a), 69 f.

empeiria and precedes the stage of universal judgement (*Metaph.* 981ᵃ9), does not contain a single term that could be provided by *aisthēsis* alone; the relevant capacity of judgement is a prerogative of *nous* (or *logos*, which for our purposes is equivalent). It is precisely here that the myth of abstraction will lead some readers to suppose that the universal is already 'given' in the raw data of sense and can simply be extracted by ignoring or subtracting part of those data. But Aristotle has no theory of abstraction in this sense. For him the universal is present in sense-experience only if we include the incidental sensibles with their noetic component, and it is made available only if the percipient subject possesses the *nous* or *logos* required to detect it. As Aristotle sees it, the whole process of *epagōgē* or 'induction' which he describes in these two texts is made possible for sense-perception only in the human case, since only here is the sense informed by a noetic capacity. That is why he can say: 'one perceives an individual, but perception (*aisthēsis*) is of the universal, for example of a man, and not of the man Callias' (100ᵃ17). It is only in the case of *human* perception, enriched by the conceptual resources provided by its marriage with *nous*, that Aristotle can speak of us as *perceiving a man*. If we were restricted to the reception of sensible forms, all we could perceive would be colours and shapes.¹⁷

This account of concept-formation in *APo.* 2. 19 contains a promissory note: 'the soul is so constituted as to be capable of this process' (100ᵃ14). The appropriate place to look for payment on the promise is in the treatise *On the Soul*, where Aristotle describes the objects of the two faculties. Here *nous* is implicitly defined as the principle that accounts for our ability to grasp *noēta*, intelligible forms. But what are the *noēta*? Aristotle does not tell us as much about these as we would like, and what he does tell us is not crystal-clear.¹⁸ He does say that the *aisthēta* and the *noēta* together comprise 'everything there is' (*panta ta onta* 413ᵇ21), but that is not much help. (Furthermore, in this context *ta aisthēta* must refer to sensible things, i.e. to incidental sensibles, not merely to sensible forms strictly understood: Aristotle's example is a stone, not a sense-quality, 431ᵇ29. And similarly for 'the states and properties of *ta aisthēta*' at 432ᵃ6, cited below.) More informative is the statement that 'each of the *noēta* is potentially present in things possessing matter' (430ᵃ6), and that, 'since, as it seems, there is nothing separate besides sensible magnitudes, the *noēta* are present in sensible forms, both the abstract *noēta* (sc. of mathematics) and those which are states and properties of sensible things' (423ᵃ3–6).¹⁹

¹⁷ Here again there is a major problem for the interpretation of animal perception. Clearly animals need to 'make sense' of their perceptions. Do they have something corresponding to sortal classifications like *man*, *dog*, or *my master*, *my sibling*? Aristotle has apparently nothing to say on this question except that, lacking *logos*, animals cannot have *our* way of understanding what they perceive. The 'incidental sensibles' for animals must be interpreted quite differently.

¹⁸ There is probably a reason for his discretion in the *De Anima*. This is a physical treatise, and the *noēta* do not properly belong to physics. See *PA* 641ᵃ32–ᵇ10.

¹⁹ This passage (432ᵃ3–6) calls for a number of comments. (i). 'As it seems' (*hōs dokei*) is meant to allow for the 'separate substances' of *Metaph.* Λ (ii) The phrase 'present in sensible forms' must refer not to sensible forms strictly understood (the proper and common sensibles) but to the forms of sensible things in the broader sense noticed above. One apprehends the form *man* in perceiving visible

(ii) This brings us to the second case which lends itself to empiricist misinterpretation, the introduction of essences as object of *nous* in *DA* 3. 4. Aristotle's examples of essences are presented in a context riddled with difficulties and subject to infinite dispute. But the text is a crucial one for the relation of sense to intellect, so we must try to provide a coherent exegesis.

Since a magnitude is different from the being-of-magnitude, and water is different from the being-of-water (and so for many other cases but not for all; for in some cases they are the same), one discerns the being-of-flesh and flesh by a different principle or by the same principle differently disposed. For flesh is not without matter, but it is like the snub: this (form) in this (matter). Now it is by the faculty of sense that one discerns the hot and cold and those things of which flesh is a certain ratio (*logos*). But one discerns the being-of-flesh by a different faculty [i.e. different from sense], either by one that is (entirely) separate [from sense] or by one related as a bent line is related to itself when straightened out. (429^{b}10–17.)

What is clear here is that Aristotle is contrasting at least two kinds of objects, sensible bodies and their essences or *to ti ēn einai*, that he is alluding to the discussion in *Metaph.* Z as to whether a thing is identical with its essence, and that he is taking for granted the conclusion finally reached there, that for all cases of matter-form compounds the thing and its essence are in fact distinct.[20] Difficulties begin when we ask what contrast or contrasts Aristotle means to draw in regard to faculties. Clearly *nous* is the faculty which discerns the essences. But what faculty discerns the sensible bodies? Most (perhaps all) commentators seem inclined to suppose that it is by the sense-faculty that we apprehend water and flesh. But that is not what Aristotle says. He says that it is by sense that we discern hot and cold and other qualities that make up the matter of flesh; he does not say—and how could he say?—that it is sense which discerns the *logos* that is the form of flesh. In fact, it is not clear that this *logos* is distinct from the essence of flesh. (Compare the definition of formal cause at *Ph.* 194^{b}26–9.) The only interpretation that is both coherent with the context and compatible with Aristotle's general view is the following: since it is by *nous* that we discern the essence of flesh, then it is 'by a different faculty (namely sense) or by the same faculty (i.e. *nous*) differently disposed' that we discern the matter-form compound of flesh (429^{b}12–13). 'For flesh is not without matter, but it is like the snub, this (form) in this (matter)' (429^{b}14).[21]

men, not in perceiving colours and shapes alone. (iii): I takes 'states (*hexeis*) and properties (*pathē*) of sensibles' to include both (*a*) sortal essences and (*b*) accidental or non-essential properties of sensible bodies. For these are the basic *noēta*, the properties of sensible substances as classified by the categories, and first of all their essences or substantial forms.

[20] *Metaph.* Z 1037^{b}4–5. I hope I will be pardoned for saying as little as possible about those pure forms or 'primary *ousiai*' that *are* identical with their essences. These are no doubt the true objects of the intellect as such, the *noēta* par excellence, which Aristotle has in view as the optimal case in his conclusion at 429^{b}21: 'in general, according as things are separate from matter, just so is it with *nous*' (i.e. the intellect is separate from matter, or from sensibility, just to the extent that its object is immaterial). But the metaphysical status of these pure essences is too obscure for discussion here.

[21] And so likewise for water at 429^{b}11. The first example, *megethos* at 429^{b}10, is triply ambiguous. (i) If magnitude is taken as the common sensible, then we have a contrast between sense perceiving

So the question which Aristotle here leaves open is whether we discern the concrete compound flesh by a different faculty, namely sense, or by *nous* 'otherwise disposed', in its union with sense in a perceptual judgement. And both alternatives are correct, depending upon whether we take *aisthēsis* narrowly, in which case it cannot perceive flesh as such but only the only the hot and the cold, or whether we take it broadly to include incidental sensibles in conjunction with *nous*. Now this second alternative is really equivalent to '*nous* otherwise disposed'. And it must be this very same possibility, *nous* in combination with sense-perception, that is referred to in the controversial last sentence of the quotation (429^b16-17): 'one discerns the essence of flesh by a faculty other than sense [namely by *nous*], either by this faculty as separate [from sense] or by this faculty [related to itself] as a bent line is related to itself when straightened out.' It must be *nous*, not sense, which operates *either* separately (like a straight line) *or* in conjunction with sense (like a line bent in two).[22] Whereas an essence can be the object only of *nous*, the perception of the corresponding matter–form compound (flesh as a certain ratio of hot and cold, etc.) can be thought of in either of two ways: as the work of sense broadly understood (since the matter of flesh is properly sensible, and the compound body is a 'sensible thing', a sensible *per accidens*); or as the work of *nous* in a complex way (like a line bent in two). On the second alternative, *nous* grasps a noetic form (the essence or *logos*) as present in sensible matter. In acts of thinking *nous* apprehends its forms in the phantasms; in perception it apprehends them as embodied in matter. The whole line of reasoning is designed to display the objects of *nous* in different stages of separation from matter: embodied flesh, the essence of flesh, a straight line (as example of mathematical abstraction, *ta en aphairesei legomena*, 432^a5), and the essence of straight.[23] 'In general then, according as things are separated from matter, it will be the same in regard to *nous*' (429^b21).[24]

magnitude and *nous* discerning its essence, and that may well be what Aristotle intends. (ii) If, however, he means by 'magnitude' any extended body, this will simply be the general case of which water and flesh are particular examples. For *megethos* in the sense of 'extended body' see *DA* 424^a26, 432^a4. (iii) Some commentators (including Aquinas and Hicks) take magnitude here as an example of mathematical form. This seems to me the least likely interpretation of the three, since Aristotle is economical with his examples, and the mathematical case is given immediately afterwards by the straight line (at 429^b18 where *palin de* introduces a *new* consideration).

[22] So rightly Themistius and Simplicius, cited by Rodier in Aristotle (1900), 445. We need not join the interminable debate about the exact force of the geometric simile. What is clear, I think, is that Aristotle is referring to two different ways in which *nous* (not *aisthēsis*) can operate, since the whole point of the passage is to introduce essences as the object of *nous*.

[23] It is again two different functions of *nous* that are distinguished in Aristotle's last example at 429^b18-21, where the contrast is between a straight line and the essence of straight, 'say the number two'. 'One discerns (this essence) by a different faculty or by (the same faculty) differently disposed.' The first alternative, which implies that the straight line is discerned by sense, might seem inappropriate if we are thinking of a line as defined in geometry, since the objects of mathematics, 'defined by abstraction' (432^a5), do not have sensible matter and hence are not perceived by sense. However, Aristotle must also be thinking of the line as *visible*, and this will explain the suggestion that the line and its essence might be objects of different faculties.

[24] If *megethos* at 429^b10 is understood as the common sensible, then the series begins with a form that is so little 'separate' that it can be apprehended without the collaboration of *nous*. Similarly for

Thus *nous* is consistently presented as the capacity to apprehend forms and essences: both forms as embodied and forms alone, both forms in sensible compounds and in mathematical abstraction. There is, however, one other function of *nous* mentioned by Aristotle in this section of the *De Anima* that must be noted before we leave this topic. *Noēsis*, the activity of *nous*, is not only the grasp of 'indivisibles', that is of simple forms; it is also the principle of the synthesis of concepts in a judgement (430ᵃ26–8): 'the cause of unity is *nous* in every case' (430ᵇ5). This is what the medievals called the second operation of the intellect, the act of judgement, in contrast to the 'simple apprehension' of forms and essences. It is here, says Aristotle, in the unifying synthesis of *noēmata*, that truth and falsity are located.[25]

V

Before turning to our final question, why *nous* must be incorporeal, I want briefly to discuss what I called Doctrine Two, the principle that *nous* in act is identical with its object. This doctrine (D2) can shed some light on the relationship between *nous* and empirical consciousness in ordinary thinking, and thus help to sharpen the contrast between Aristotle's view and post-Cartesian philosophy of mind. So far we have discussed *nous* only on the 'objective' side, on the basis of the distinction between sensible and intelligible objects. But what about the subjective side of *nous*: what kind of awareness does it involve and how is that related to our empirical consciousness understood as sentience? This is perhaps the most obscure point in Aristotle's philosophy of mind. But if we can understand Doctrine Two we will be slightly less in the dark.

The thesis that *nous* in act is identical with its object (D2) is prefigured in *DA*

the straight line at 429ᵇ18–20 if it is taken simply as a visible shape. I have analysed this difficult text in such detail because it is important for the definition of *nous* by reference to its object, and because there is a quite different reading (proposed by Hicks and followed e.g. by Modrak (1987a), 118 with n. 18), inspired I think by empiricist assumptions, which tends to blur or even obliterate the systematic distinction between sense and intellect on which I am insisting and on which the doctrine of *DA* 2–3 as I see it is founded. Hicks misreads 429ᵇ15 as saying not that sense apprehends the matter of flesh (hot and cold, etc.) but that it apprehends flesh as such: 'Flesh as *tode ti* or *sunholon* is judged solely by sensibility' (Hicks in Aristotle 1907, 488, on ᵇ15). 'Since we know flesh and the like by sense and forms or quiddities by intellect, A. appears to be discussing the question, are sense and intellect different or are they the same faculty in two different attitudes?…It may seem strange that intellect should after all be sense in a different relation, but many considerations favour such a view' (ibid, 487). I submit that this interpretation makes nonsense of Aristotle's entire discussion of *nous*, and that it cannot be defended as a reading of 429ᵃ12–18. In part the error can be traced back to the Greek commentators, who are misled by the broader, Platonic notion of *aisthēta* as sensible things. Thus Themistius (cit. Rodier in Aristotle 1900, ii. 444 ff.) begins by claiming that the sensitive faculty is sufficient for knowing water and flesh as compound wholes! But nevertheless the Greek commentators, Zeller, and Rodier all agree in recognizing that in 429ᵇ13 'another faculty, or *the same faculty otherwise* disposed', the reference is to two different functions of *nous*, not to some bizarre interpretation of *nous* as 'sense otherwise disposed'.

[25] *DA* 430ᵃ27. Aristotle also finds truth elsewhere, but alone, without falsity, both in the cognition of simple essences and in the perception of proper sensibles.

3. 2 in the claim that the actualization (*energeia*) of the sense and the sensible object are one and the same: the act of hearing occurs together with, and is only conceptually distinct from, the act of sounding.[26] In that connection Aristotle points out that the actualization occurs *in the patient*, that is, in the sense-faculty; the sense-object is a kind of unmoved mover (426^a2-11). Aristotle never says explicitly the same thing about the actualization of *noēta*, but that seems to be implied by his reference to the latter as existing 'potentially in things possessing matter' (430^a6). As colours are fully actualized only in acts of vision, so noetic form as such would be fully actualized only in acts of *noēsis*.

Aristotle prepares the statement of D2 from the very beginning of his discussion of *nous* in *DA* 3. 4, by the comparison between *noein* and perceiving: 'as the sense faculty is related to the sense objects, so is *nous* related to the intelligibles (*ta noēta*)'; in order to receive these forms, it must be *potentially* of the same kind, but not *actually* anything before thinking (*noein*) takes place (429^a13-24). The noetic soul is 'the place of forms' in that it is potentially all of these forms, i.e. the place in which they can be realized. But when *it becomes each form*, like the knower who is a master of his science, which happens when it is able to put itself into action (*energein*), then 'it is still potential in a way, but not in the same way as before learning or discovering. And it is then able to think itself (*hauton noein*)' (429^b9).[27]

Ignoring for the moment the last, enigmatic reference to noetic self-awareness (which has been eliminated from Ross's text by his acceptance of Bywater's unnecessary emendation), we see that Aristotle distinguishes two degrees of actualization of *nous*, corresponding to the distinction made earlier for sense.[28] *Nous* at birth is like a bare tablet, or, as Rodier suggests, it is like the *unwrittenness* of the tablet. More exactly, it is like the capacity of a blank tablet to have anything and everything written on it. (This is what was later called the 'possible' or 'potential' intellect, echoing *dunatos* at 429^a22.) But *nous* when fully trained and educated is at stage one of actualization (or stage two of potentiality): it can actually think of any form when and as it pleases, and thus put itself into the second (final) stage of actuality, the act of contemplation (*theōrein*). Stage one of actualization is what came to be known as the 'acquired intellect'.[29] And we may note that this capacity to contemplate noetic form is *also* said to be the capacity of *nous* to contemplate itself.

What follows immediately in *DA* 3. 4 is the discussion of essences as objects

---

[26] *DA* 425^b26 ff.: *to de einai ou to auto*.

[27] There is no textual justification for Bywater's emendation at 429^b9, which replaces *hauton noein* by a pointless repetition of *di hautou noein* from 429^b7. The theme of self-cognition, introduced here, prepares for the *aporia* developed later in this chapter (429^b26-9). In Ross's text this connection is lost. See the defence of the transmitted text in Wedin (1986), 170 f., who cites further argument for this reading in Owens (1976).

[28] The example of the *epistēmōn* here at 429^b6 refers back to the earlier discussion in 417^a22-^b28, where the parallelism between sense and intellect was carefully prepared by the distinction between successive stages of scientific knowledge.

[29] See Alexander (1887), 82. 1.

of *nous*, the passage we have analysed in the preceding section (429^b10–22). Aristotle then proceeds to develop two *aporiai*: how can *nous* be affected by its object, if it is as he has said 'impassive' (429^b22 ff.)? And how can *nous* be its own object, i.e. be intelligible (*noētos*), unless *all* intelligible objects are also examples of intellect, 'since the intelligible is one in kind' (429^b26–9)? He then offers D2 as the solution to both *aporiai*. '*Nous* itself is intelligible (*noētos*, its own object) in the same way as the intelligible forms (*ta noēta*). For in things without matter the noetic subject (*to nooun*) is the same as the noetic object (*to nooumenon*). For theoretical knowledge and what is known (or knowable, *epistēton*) in this way are the same' (430^a2–5).

These are hard sayings. I offer the following comments by way of partial exegesis.

(i) The reference to *epistēmē* is proposed as a clarification or justification of D2, relying upon the example of the sciences developed in *DA* 2. 5. As a first approximation of Aristotle's meaning we can say that the noetic structure constituted by the truths of geometry is identical with the full mastery of this structure in the geometer's mind, so that geometric truths are not fully *actualized* except in the actual mathematical thought and insight of a practising mathematician. This may well seem plausible, even surprisingly modern, for an abstract science like geometry. But Aristotle's claim in D2 is more perplexing when applied to natural science: the noetic structure that is known in physics and biology—the formal structure of the natural world—will be identical with, and can be fully realized only in, the actual thought of a scientific mind. Whether this is some form of scientific realism or transcendental idealism remains to be seen.

(ii) How does *nous* become aware of itself, that is , how does it become its own object (*noētos*) 'in the same way as it knows the *noēta*'? Here we are helped by a comment in *Metaph.* Λ 9, à propos of the self-knowledge of the divine intellect: 'But knowledge and sense perception and opinion and thought (*dianoia*) seem always to be *of something else*, and of themselves only secondarily' (*en parergōi* 'as a by-product') (1074^b36). Offered as an objection to the concept of divine self-knowing, this *aporia* is again resolved by a statement of D2: in the contemplative knowledge of objects without matter, such as essences, the act of intellection (*noēsis*) is identical with the object cognized (1075^a1–5). The implications of this solution for the objective content of divine *noēsis* seem to me obvious, though they are not generally recognized.[30] For our purposes in understanding the self-awareness of the human intellect we can say this: *nous* in us knows itself *in knowing the intelligible forms*, in comprehending the essences and the formal structure of the natural world, of mathematics, and of any other object of noetic contemplation. For it has no other structure of its own. Hence the self-awareness

---

[30] Namely, it seems obvious that the direct object of divine *noēsis* is the *noēta*, the intelligible forms of the universe; the divine mind knows itself only *en parergōi* in the act of cognizing the forms. If it be objected that Aristotle insists that divine *nous* can know *only* itself and nothing else, the answer is precisely D2: the objects of *nous* are not something else; and they are fully realized only in the act of *noēsis*. That is what Aristotle actually says at *Metaph.* Λ 1075^a2–5.

of *nous* just is the formal structure of the universe *become aware of itself*. This is partially realized in us to the extent that we live the life of *theōria*, fully realized in the divine intellect. We as individuals have no *noetic* awareness of our own intellect *except* as actually understanding more or less of the rational structure of the universe. The individual acts of thinking by which we gain or exercise such understanding are not themselves *noēta*, intelligible forms, and hence not themselves a possible object for our *noetic self-awareness*. We are of course often aware of our mental activity of reasoning or discursive thinking. But this awareness, which Descartes would have regarded as the work of *intellectio pura*, is for Aristotle the proper function of sentience, even though in our case it is the enriched sentience of a noetic animal.

Noetic awareness, then, is strictly parallel to perceptual awareness narrowly understood as the realization of sensory qualities. Noetic awareness is simply the rational structure of the world as realized in human (or divine) thought, just as perceptual awareness on its objective side is the qualitative structure of the world realized in animal sentience. Aristotle's discussion of sense and intellect in the *De Anima* is designed to bring out this parallelism between biological cognition through the anatomically determined sense-modalities and conceptual cognition through the grasp of rational form or essences. His theoretical concern is so consistently focused on these two that much else is left in darkness or in half-light: the interaction of intellect and sense in perceptual knowledge, the interaction of intellect, perception, and desire in voluntary action and choice. On the side of subjective awareness, where post-Cartesian philosophy and psychology have constructed a realm of mental states and mental events, Aristotle has only the barest outline of a theory. Memory, imagination or *phantasia*, feelings of pleasure and pain, desire and emotion are all connected to the unified principle of perception, *to aisthētikon*; but the modes of these connections and the various interactions with *nous* are never systematically discussed. From a few scattered comments, however, we can safely conclude that personal self-awareness is conceived as a function of the *aisthētikon*. There seems to be no corresponding notion of personal or individual subjectivity in the self-awareness of *nous* as such, no place for a noetic ego, no personal 'I' as the proper subject of *noēsis*. That is excluded by the formal, generic, and timeless content of *ta noēta*, the noetic forms with which every act of *noēsis* is identified. The 'I' of my experience is a hylomorphic animal. *Noēsis* is not an act which I perform but an act which takes place in me. But the fact that I am an animal in which such events can, and occasionally do, take place, is a fundamental fact that colours every aspect of my conscious perceptual experience.

VI

Why must *nous* be incorporeal? Aristotle's own arguments here are suprisingly weak and insubstantial, as if, surrounded by Platonists rather than materialists, he did not regard this position as controversial enough to stand in need of a real defence. I shall briefly review Aristotle's own position and then attempt to reconstruct it in the light of contemporary debate.

Aristotle's explicit arguments are limited to a few remarks in *DA* 3. 4. 'The intellect, since it thinks all things, must be unmixed (with any)…for (if it were mixed with some feature, that feature) would intrude and obstruct and prevent (the reception of) what is alien to it; hence *nous* has no nature other than this: the capacity (to receive noetic form)….It is no thing in actuality (*energeia*) before thinking occurs. Therefore it is not plausible that it should be mixed with the body. For then it would become qualified, either cold or hot, or it would even have an organ, like the power of perception (*to aisthētikon*). But in fact it has none' (429ᵃ18–27).

In support of this claim, Aristotle calls attention to what he takes to be an important contrast between sense and intellect: after intense perception such as loud noises or very bright colours, the sense-organ's capacity is dulled or even damaged; but 'when the intellect comprehends something exceptionally intelligible, its ability to understand lesser things is not diminished but increased. For the sensory faculty cannot exist without the body; but *nous* is separable' (429ᵃ29–ᵇ5).

Aristotle's thesis here is a double one. There is, first of all, his general principle of non-reducibility: phenomena at the level of *nous* are not to be explained in terms of sense-perception, just as phenomena at the level of *aisthēsis*, such as qualitative perception, are not to be explained in terms of biology or neurophysiology. But the claim here is a stronger one: the noetic capacity is not simply irreducible to animal sentience; it is in principle independent of the animal body. This stronger claim can be understood only if we recall our earlier distinction between the principle of *nous* as such and concrete acts of human thought. For the latter but not for the former the use of embodied phantasms is a necessary condition.

Before attempting to reconstrue Aristotle's thesis in contemporary terms, let me point out that his position is clearly defensible in the weak sense that no scientific evidence could possibly tell *against* it. Since he admits in principle the dependence of human thinking upon something bodily, he can cheerfully accept any and all discoveries, present and future, concerning the dependence of intellectual activity upon the functioning of the brain. The progress of neurophysiology and computational models for brain function presents no threat to Aristotle's theory. No matter how fully we come to understand the physical and functional basis of rational thought, Aristotle can always say that we are investigating a *sine qua non* (my Condition A) but not a *cause* of thinking, for thought itself in the strict sense (*noēsis* or *theōria*) is not a bodily event and cannot be located in the brain. Neither brain research nor (I think) cognitive psychology as currently understood is even relevant to Condition B, the incorporeal principle of the intellect. In so far as such research is successful, it simply spells out Condition A, the bodily instrument or mechanism of thought.

But if Aristotle's position is in this sense impregnable, what reason could anyone possibly have for occupying it? It is scarcely enough to recommend a philosophical theory to show that it is designed in such a way that no empirical evidence can count against it. What we want is some positive reason for taking seriously the claim that a necessary condition (and in Aristotle's view, the true cause) for rational thought is a principle that has no spatial location and no bodily component and hence cannot even be described in the language of physical science.

I propose to reconstrue Aristotle's thesis concerning *nous* and *logos* as a claim about language and culture. As a first approximation, the thesis can be formulated as follows: no discoveries in neurophysiology and no computational model for brain function can give an appropriate account of the phenomena of normative culture, where this includes linguistic meaning and propositional belief. I emphasize that it is the whole domain of human culture, including the prehistoric development of technology, symbolic art forms, and social institutions, which represents the essential work of Aristotle's noetic principle. (*Nous* may appear in its purest form in *theōria*, but it is also required for *technē* and *praxis*.) But it will be simpler, and closer to contemporary debate, to take sentential meaning and belief as our model for the noetic domain. The incorporeality thesis then states that neither neurophysiology nor computational brain models can account for sentential meaning and belief.

I cannot argue this thesis here. I simply point to three recent studies whose results can be invoked in support of this claim: John Searle's Chinese room story, Hilary Putnam's notion of interpretation, and Arthur Collins's argument about belief.

(i) Searle's Chinese room argument[31] shows (I think) that a mechanical procedure for manipulating formal symbols, as in a computer program, could never be sufficient for (and might not even be relevant to) the understanding of a language, since a human being might follow all the rules for formal manipulation and thus instantiate the program for translating a Chinese text, for answering relevant questions in Chinese, without understanding the language at all.

(ii) Putnam's conclusion is more radical. He seems to suggest circumstances under which our friend in the Chinese room, who does not *understand* Chinese but merely follows a computer program, would never be able even to provide a reliable translation. In Putnam's words: 'it may be possible to give a complete functionalist psychology'...(which includes stating all the 'rules of computation') 'without in any way solving the problem of interpretation, or even the problem of reference-preserving translation.'[32] Putnam's point is that the notion of interpretation (as involved in understanding a language) is 'inseparable from the analysis of either the normative notion of rationality, or from some such notion as Vico's "humanity"'; and that it would be 'totally utopian' to hope for any algorithmic analysis of these notions.[33]

---

[31] Searle (1980).   [32] Putnam (1983), 150.   [33] Ibid, 151 f.

(iii) Collins[34] distinguishes two notions of belief, (*a*) the temporally datable and essentially personal circumstance of someone's believing that p and (*b*) the propositional belief that p, in the sense of a belief that can be true or false and can be shared by many (or by none). Collins shows that the latter notion, the propositional belief, could never be captured by a physicalist model which construes belief as some kind of sentential inscription on the brain. As a datable and localized event, the latter could not be shared by others and hence is not the kind of entity that can be true or false. Although directed primarily against the physicalist conception of belief as neural representation, the argument works equally well against mentalistic accounts of propositional attitudes. What the argument shows is that our beliefs, as a claim about what is the case in the world, could not be represented by *any* state of the believing subject, neither by a neural state nor by a mental state. Propositional belief bring us into the noetic domain proper. Collins's distinction between two notions of belief corresponds exactly to my distinction between the principle of *nous* as such and concrete acts of human thinking.[35]

These considerations are invoked here not to prove that the intellect is incorporeal but to suggest how this thesis can be plausibly construed in contemporary terms. When so construed, Aristotle's thesis does not cease to be controversial, but it becomes recognizable as a kind of Wittgensteinian protest against Cartesian and computational models of thinking as a 'private language', a personal operation in the mind or in the brain. For Aristotle thought and language (*logos*) go hand in hand, and *logos* is essentially public.[36] Aristotle's thesis thus rejoins the anthropologist's claim 'that human thinking is primarily an overt act conducted in terms of the objective materials of the common culture, and only secondarily a private matter'.[37] Since 'what is essential is the existence of an overt symbol system',[38] the brain cannot learn to think without resources provided by the culture. 'The human nervous system relies, inescapably, on the accessibility of public symbolic structures to build up its own autonomous, ongoing pattern of activity.'[39]

The Platonic myth of the *Phaedrus* claims that a soul which is to enter a human body must previously have had a prenatal glimpse of the Forms, since a human being 'must be able to understand what is said in language by reference to some form, passing through many sense perceptions to a unity gathered together and grasped by reason (*logismos*)', (249 B).

The incorporeality of *nous* is Aristotle's prosaic substitute for the doctrine of recollection.[40] Both doctrines, recollection and incorporeality, may be understood

---

[34] Collins (1979).

[35] Propositional belief and the noetic domain in general thus belong to what Popper has called the 'third world' of propositional structures, theories, and the like. But I am not happy with that terminology, since it presupposes the two post-Cartesian worlds of the mental and the physical.

[36] *Pol.* 1253ª7–18.   [37] Geertz (1973), 83.   [38] Ibid. 77.   [39] Ibid. 83.

[40] *DA* 430ᵇ5: 'what makes a unity is *nous* in every case'. So Kurt Gödel compared the concept of a set to Kant's categories of pure understanding: both of them, he said, perform the function of 'synthesis': 'the generating of unities out of manifolds' (Gödel 1964, 272).

as metaphors for something about the human intellect which we do not fully understand—and perhaps inevitably so, since it is by means of the intellect that we understand everything else. It remains to be seen how much of the ancient theory of *nous* can be reconstrued in terms of modern theories of language and culture. At any rate the two domains have this feature of reflexivity in common. For all our attempts at understanding, including the understanding of culture, are only made possible by resources drawn from our culture and limited by a perspective that is also historically and culturally given. So the anthropologist's definition of mankind as the animal with culture is not a wholly inappropriate reconstrual of Aristotle's definition as the animal possessed of *logos* and *nous*.[41]

[41] An earlier version of this chapter was presented at a conference on Aristotle's Philosophy of Mind in spring 1986, at the University of Rochester, organized by Deborah Modrak. I am grateful to Gary Matthews for comments on this earlier version.

20

DESIRE AND THE GOOD IN
DE ANIMA

HENRY S. RICHARDSON

DESIRE (*orexis*) and the good (*to agathon*) are the central notions Aristotle deploys in his account of animal movement in *De Anima* (3. 9–11). While this much is plain, their relative place in this account and their connection with each other need explication. They are mediated in some way by reason (*nous*)—or more generally by animals' capacities of discernment (*ta kritika*), including imagination or appearance (*phantasia*); however, the nature and import of this mediation remain relatively obscure. This essay will put forward an interpretation of the theory of movement in these chapters that stresses the central place Aristotle accords to the good as the object of desire and, as a corollary, the coordinate importance he assigns to desire and discernment.

My attempt to bring to light the precise relations Aristotle sees between discernment, desire, and the good will be guided by the contrast between two competing schematic interpretations. Anticipating my discussion of a crux in ch. 10, the two models diverge initially in terms of whether 'the mover' is desire or is the object of desire, namely the good or apparent good. Although Aristotle holds that there is no desire without an object and that desire's object will always be some good or apparent good, accounts of action based on one or the other of these two coexisting aspects may nonetheless diverge considerably. Throughout, I will use these differences to generate alternative readings.

On the *desire-based model* (D), the shape of the account of any particular action is fixed by some one occurrent desire. Discernment in general helps the animal become aware of ways of achieving that desire's end; in humans, the role of deliberation is to consider how and by what means the end is to be achieved. When various occurrent desires conflict, some way must be found of determining which desire will be the one to govern action—which is predominant or *kurios*. While the actions of animals may be taken to aim at some good (for the aim of every desire is some good), this is not essential. Accordingly, the animal need not desire its objects *as* good. Rather, the connection between action and the good holds only in general, by virtue of the teleological orientation of the animal's soul.[1]

On the *good-based model* (G), by contrast, the account starts from some object aimed at *as* good. At the outset, this may be an object of desire only in the general

© Henry S. Richardson, 1992.

[1] This possibility of a generalized connection between an animal's good and its desires is suggested by some remarks in Irwin (1988), 332.

sense that it is something this animal is apt to desire.[2] Discernment first of all considers the desirable object as good. To non-reasoning animals, it will *appear* as good. Reasoning animals may also *conceive* it as good.[3] Discernment and deliberation will, in addition, have the roles assigned to them in (D), with the difference that for humans considerations can arise that undercut or reinforce the object's initial claim to goodness. Conflicts among these considerations will matter more than conflicts among occurrent desires. Resolving conflicts of the former sort becomes part of the task of deliberation about how (and in the extreme, whether) to achieve the initial aim. On this model, the connection between action and the good holds for each particular action.

In addressing ourselves to the relations between reason and desire, we must begin by pausing over Aristotle's famous sceptical remarks at the outset of ch. 9 about carving up the soul into parts (432^{a}22–^{b}7). Here he notes that 'a puzzle at once arises', for in one sense the parts of the soul appear to be infinite (or without definite limits or boundaries—*apeira*), since the traditional Platonic divisions are less significant than the Aristotelian functional distinction between the nutritive (*threptikon*), perceptual (*aisthētikon*), and thinking (*noētikon* or *logistikon*) capacities. Further, the capacities for appearance (*to phantastikon*) and for desire (*to orektikon*) cannot be identified with any of the above, but rather generate a further cross-cutting classification, giving rise to 'many puzzles' (432^{b}2) of the same sort within his own view.[4] One common reading has it that in this passage Aristotle digresses, consolidating his criticisms of the Platonic 'real' divisions while none the less reaffirming his own alternative 'functional' divisions.[5] While Aristotle of course prefers his own classification to that of Plato, this traditional view of the passage underplays the broader scepticism in Aristotle's remarks, thereby missing their essential contribution to his discussion of animal motion. If this were merely a digression, it would be odd that the same point recurs in the next chapter, at 433^{b}1–5. The difficulties of classification Aristotle raises cast doubt even upon the sort of functional division that he favours. They remind us of his statement earlier in *De Anima* that the activities (*energeiai*) of the soul are prior in definition to its capacities, and the objects (*antikeimena*) of the various activities are similarly prior to the activities (415^{a}18–22). One way to individuate the soul's capacities is in terms of their potential opposition, as Plato sometimes

[2] This interpretation of the object of desire (*to orekton*) is defended by Loenig (1903), 32. Although I will be supporting G, I will not depend upon Loenig's further suggestion that *to orekton* should be translated as 'the desirable' or 'the to-be-desired'. Rather, I seek to make out the connection between desire and the good on the basis of the arguments in these chapters. Further, since I will skirt issues of value realism, I will be satisfied with the degree of normative correction that will enter with the fact that, for Aristotle, the object of desire is the good.

[3] For reasons to prefer marking the contrast between humans and other animals by 'reasoning' and 'non-reasoning', rather than the more traditional 'rational' and 'non-rational', see Labarrière (1984), 17–49. Reasoning involves both deliberation and reason-giving.

[4] Cf. Wedin (1988), who suggests that some of these puzzles are resolved by the fact that for Aristotle *phantasia* is not a distinct faculty. For his comments on 432^{a}22 ff., see 53 n.

[5] See, e.g., Rodier in Aristotle (1900), ii, on 432^{a}24; Hicks in Aristotle (1907), 548–9; and Modrak (1987a), 208 n. 46.

does (*Rep.* 4, 439^B ff.). Since Aristotle, by contrast, does so in terms of each capacity's activity and ultimately its objects, it is relatively easier for him to allow functional co-operation among the various capacities. By the same token, however, if the functional co-operation extends as far as it does, for example, in the case of a human's deliberate movement, in which the object of desire is the starting-point of practical *nous* (433ᵃ15–16; cf. *MA*, 700ᵇ23–4), then the postulated distinction among capacities threatens to disappear.[6]

The upshot, as Aristotle seems to be warning us here, is that we should not be too concerned with distinguishing the individual realizations of the different capacities in a given case. While it is important to understand in general what psychological functions are exercised in animal movement, we will go astray if we try to set out our results in terms of an ontology that precisely individuates the actualizations of the various functions within a particular movement. By implication, Aristotle may also be hinting that we should not be too literally metaphysical in our construal of his quest for the single 'mover' (*to kinoun*) of animal motion. Rather, as in the contrast between D and G, marking out something as 'the mover' will have more to do with the relevant description of movement, the sort of counterfactuals the account will support, and the structure of deliberation.

I. The Mover of Movement and the Aims of Animals

Using a seemingly redundant phrase, Aristotle introduces and frames the topic of chs. 9 and 10 by asking, 'what is it that moves the animal in the case of progressive movement?' (*ti to kinoun to zōion tēn poreutikēn kinēsin*, 432ᵇ13–14; cf. 432ᵃ17, 406ᵃ31, 410ᵇ20–1). We might want to say that it is the animal that moves, period. Aristotle himself is sometimes willing to say that the human animal is the origin (*archē*) of its actions (*EN* 1112ᵇ32, 1139ᵇ5; *EE* 1223ᵃ5). Why not leave it at that? If some further explanation of its movement were wanted, one could look to external conditions. But Aristotle is asking what moves the animal in a way that does not direct him outwards. For Aristotle, as David Furley explains, 'as a whole, a thing may be said to move itself; but within the whole it must always be possible to distinguish a mover and a moved.'[7] Since he thinks of animal movement as self-movement (e.g. 433ᵇ28), he therefore believes that there must be an internal mover. In these chapters of *De Anima* Aristotle plainly starts by looking for the internal mover.

---

[6] Wedin (1988), 13 f., notes that different Aristotelian capacities can share an object in an 'extensional' sense, and argues that the object can none the less still be seen as ultimately individuating these capacities non-extensionally, as a 'formal object'. If this means, however, that one would still distinguish, say, between eating a certain piece of food *as* desired and eating the same piece of food *as* the aim orienting deliberation, then the intentional description simply throws one back to the level of different activities of the soul.

[7] Furley (1978), 166; cf. *Ph.* 257ᵇ26–258ᵃ5; *MA* 700ᵃ6–11. I do not assume that self-movement involves a wholly fresh start in the causal chain: see the criticisms of Furley on this matter by Sorabji (1980), 229–33.

What is the kind of animal motion that Aristotle seeks to explain in a unified way? He initially specifies it as local movement or locomotion: *kinēsis kata topon* (432ᵃ17); and he distinguishes locomotion from growth and decay and from respiration, sleeping, and waking (432ᵇ8–13; cf. *MA* 703ᵇ8–11).[8] What, though, is the basis of the distinction? This emerges when he begins to argue against the possibility that the nutritive capacity (*to threptikon*) could be the mover. It is 'clear' that the *threptikon* is not the mover, he writes at 432ᵇ15–17,

[i] for this motion is always for the sake of something and [ii] is accompanied by *phantasia* or *orexis*, [iii] for nothing moves without desiring [*oregomenon*] or avoiding [*pheugon*], except by compulsion.[9]

None of the clauses of this purported explanation of why the *threptikon* cannot count as the mover provides by itself a sufficient reason for this conclusion. As one would expect given his general natural teleology, Aristotle holds that growth, respiration, and sleeping are in *some* sense 'for the sake of something' (*heneka tou*). In particular, he holds that *to threptikon* is for the sake of something (*DA* 2. 4, 3. 12). Requiring this relation to an end to be expressed in pursuit or avoidance also fails to disqualify the *threptikon* as a mover, for Aristotle is willing to speak of certain movements governed solely by the *threptikon* as being cases of pursuit and avoidance (e.g., *Sens.* 436ᵇ8–437ᵃ3). It is true that the relevant kind of movement is, as Aristotle writes a few lines further on, always classifiable as a pursuit or avoidance (432ᵇ28–9). On these grounds, the skipping of the heart in response to a fearful stimulus and similar sudden movements of other bodily parts do not count as movement of the relevant kind (432ᵇ29–433ᵃ1; cf. *MA* 703ᵇ5–8). These same examples, however, show that *orexis* and *phantasia* can be involved without producing movement of the relevant kind. Aristotle recognizes a class of 'imperfect' (*atelēs*) animals that enjoy only the sense of touch. Although these do not undergo locomotion (*DA* 413ᵇ2–4), they do move 'indefinitely' (*aoristōs*), as Aristotle says at the outset of ch. 11.[10] Accordingly, he there seems willing to attribute to them *phantasia* and *orexis*, albeit in a form similarly 'indefinite' (434ᵃ1–5). In short, no one of the elements in our passage, by itself, can explain what it is about motions prompted by the *threptikon* that falls short of being what Aristotle is concerned with in these chapters.

We should look, therefore, to the way these three requirements interact. It will turn out that together they yield a special sense in which locomotion is 'for the sake of something'. What is most distinctive is the way in which the animal's pur-

---

[8] Martha Nussbaum has correctly noted that *De Motu*, esp. ch. 11, delineates the subject of animal progressive movement more perspicaciously than *De Anima* (1983, 135–6). My account is considerably indebted to this article, which appears in revised form as Nussbaum (1986), ch. 9. As Nussbaum had noted earlier in her commentary on *De Motu* (1978, 379–83), however, *De Anima* treats as peripheral the same sorts of cases as does *De Motu*.

[9] All translations are my own. In this passage, I translate the *ē* found in the MSS between *phantasia* and *orexis*. Ross, on the strength of Themistius' paraphrase, prints *kai*: see Ross in Aristotle (1961a), app. crit. ad loc. Although the *kai* would, as we shall see, better fit Aristotle's positive view, his negative case against the *threptikon* does not require it (as Hicks notes ad loc.).

[10] Although ch. 11 begins by asking about the mover of the imperfect animals, the qualification 'of progressive movement' or 'of movement with respect to place' is missing.

suit of the object of desire is mediated by *phantasia*,[11] allowing us to think of the animal as *aiming* at the end. For this reason, we should not be surprised to find Aristotle using the same verb he habitually uses in describing the aiming of the person of practical wisdom to say that 'since many animals aim at [*stochazesthai*] what is required for the nurture of their young, they do their mating in a precisely appropriate season' (*HA* 542ᵃ30–2). This instance of aiming well exhibits the intentionality built into *phantasia*, implying that a situation is seen in a certain way—*as* an appropriate time for rearing young, *as* a dangerous place to drink, etc. The description filled in after the 'as' helps delimit the range of situations in which the animal will act in the way concerned. It determines which counterfactuals the account will support. If Fido the dog approaches something shaped like a duck as a tasty morsel, he would spurn it on discovering that (being a decoy) it is made of wood. *Phantasia* is to this degree interpretative.[12]

We can illustrate more dramatically how the intentionality of *phantasia* helps define the special teleological orientation of locomotion by considering further the contrast between the perfect and the imperfect animals. The *De Sensu* passage referred to earlier as according pursuit and avoidance to the *threptikon* also (like *DA* 3. 12) elaborates on the role of the senses aside from touch, which are enjoyed only by the perfect animals. Although the senses of touch and taste do give rise to a kind of discrimination, as between pleasant and unpleasant food (436ᵇ15–16), a full discriminative capacity is none the less said to be linked to having the senses that operate through an outside medium (436ᵇ18–437ᵃ3). The nature of this capacity of judgement and its importance in the teleological explanation of animal movement can be illustrated by considering its relation to time. The crucial place Aristotle accords the senses of hearing, smell, and sight in these passages stems from the fact that since they operate through an outside medium they give the animal an 'advance awareness' (*proaisthēsis*: 436ᵇ21) of objects that might sustain or threaten it. If an animal moves from place to place, it must be able to foresee where it will be—or where its prey will be when it leaps.[13] In this paradigm case of animal movement we also find a literal kind of aiming. By contrast, since the imperfect animals cannot see where they want to be, their ends cannot lead them to modulate their movements in the same way. For them, an end does not serve as a 'limit' (*peras*) of which they are aware.[14] Instead, they react merely to the indefinite 'more or less' of immediate pleasure and pain (*Sens.*

[11] Our text at 432ᵇ16 had said 'accompanied by *phantasia* or *orexis*', but as Aristotle notes in the next chapter, the capacity for *orexis* (the *orektikon*) does not exist without *phantasia* (433ᵇ28–9).

[12] The interpretative character of *phantasia* is championed by Nussbaum (1978), Essay 5; and see now Nussbaum (1986), 486 n. 34. She is followed in this respect by Labarrière (1984). Irwin (1988) 594 n. 41, purports to find some difficulty in agreeing with Nussbaum that *phantasia* is 'active or interpretative', yet seems in the body of his argument (e.g. 317, 318) to do just that. The objections to Nussbaum's view raised by Wedin (1988), 90–9, seem to hinge on (i) an over-broad construal of Nussbaum's attack on the suggestion that *phantasmata* are 'images' (see the qualification in Nussbaum 1978, 224 n. 5); and (ii) an animus against purportedly anti-realist aspects of Nussbaum's account (perhaps inferred from her citations of Nelson Goodman) that even if present could be separated from the more general claim that *phantasia* is interpretative.

[13] This example is given by Irwin (1988), 336.

[14] On the connection between limit and end in Aristotle, see e.g. *Metaph.* α2, Δ17; *Pol.* 1. 3.

436ᵇ16–18; cf. *EN* 1173ª15–17).¹⁵ Accordingly, their movement—and so also their *phantasia*—is indefinite.¹⁶

II. The Negative Arguments

I have been focusing my attention on a passage preliminary to Aristotle's strongest argument that the nutritive capacity is not the mover. His main argument against this possibility comes in the next sentence, and takes the same general form as his argument against the claim of the perceptual capacity (*to aisthetikon*) to be the mover. Both are familiar Aristotelian arguments from over-inclusiveness (cf. *EN* 1097ᵇ33–1098ª5). What defeats each of these possibilities is that—as we have already seen—there are kinds of animals that have both nutritive and perceptual capacities and can reproduce yet do not undergo locomotion (432ᵇ17–26).

Aristotle next takes up the possibility that the reasoning capacity (*to logistikon*) and what is called reason (*nous*) is the mover of animal movement (432ᵇ26). Each of these terms is here used broadly, *to logistikon* echoing the mention earlier in the chapter of the Platonic divisions, and *nous* sometimes serving as Aristotle's generic term for intellectual capacities.¹⁷ The arguments now focus on discriminations among the different movements of a given kind of animal, especially man. Aristotle first sets aside theoretical *nous* as having nothing to say about what is to be pursued or avoided (ᵇ27–9). Even uses of *nous* that do concern such objects can fail to call the animal to action, producing instead only the movements of bodily parts that, as we have seen, fall short of the type of progressive movement Aristotle is here analysing (432ᵇ29–433ª1).¹⁸ If *nous* were to be the mover, it would be so only when it commanded the animal to action.

At this point, Aristotle introduces a pair of human cases to which he will return at the outset of the next chapter, those of the akratic and the continent

¹⁵ Cf. Nussbaum (1978), 383. My suggestion would be that the indefinite movements of the imperfect animals are akin to the 'non-voluntary' (*ouch hekousiai*) movements described in *MA* 703ᵇ8–11 as not being unqualifiedly under the control of *phantasia* and *orexis*.

¹⁶ In the text, I have assumed that 434ª1–5 attributes *phantasia* to the imperfect animals. Yet *DA* 415ª10–11 indicates that certain 'perishable creatures'—apparently lower animals, as Labarrière argues (1984, 24)—may lack *phantasia*. Furthermore, 428ª9–11 (in the traditional text) denies *phantasia* to the bee, the ant, and (even in amended versions) the grub. Accordingly, some commentators (e.g. Labarrière 1984, 23; Wedin 1988, 42 n.) refuse to take 434ª1–5 as committal. The explication of 'indefinitely' at 434ª4–5 given in the text suggests a different version of the general interpretative strategy taken by Rodier (ad loc.) and Hicks (on 415ª10), namely to distinguish different levels of *phantasia*, and to read the earlier passages as denying full-blown *phantasia* to the imperfect animals, the ch. 11 passage as attributing to them only an undeveloped, indefinite form of *phantasia*.

¹⁷ For Aristotle's use of *to logistikon* on refer to the Platonic division of the soul, see above in ch. 9 at 432ª25 and ᵇ5; also *Top.* 126ª8, 13; 129ª11 ff.; 138ª34, ᵇ2. For his generic use of *nous*, see *DA* 429ª23 ('by *nous* I mean that by which the soul thinks [*dianoeitai*] and conceives [*hupolambanei*]') and the discussion thereof by Kal (1988), 9.

¹⁸ As Aristotle makes clear at 433ª14–15, *nous praktikos* is distinguished from *nous theōrētikos* by its aiming at some end attainable in action and reasoning about how to pursue it, not by its actually moving the animal.

(*enkratēs*). At the close of ch. 9, these cases appear to be used to eliminate the claims of *nous* and of *orexis* to be the mover. In the akratic's case, because of a contrary pull of appetite, the animal does not move in accordance with the commands of *nous* (433ᵃ1–3). The continent's case is the reverse: the animal does not follow the urgings of desire (*orexis*) but instead follows the command of *nous* (ᵃ6–8).[19] Accordingly, neither *nous* nor *orexis*, neither reason nor desire, is sufficient to move the animal.

Before we go on to examine Aristotle's own answer to his question about the mover, we should pause to ask why he does not also deploy an under-inclusiveness argument against *nous* in parallel with the over-inclusiveness arguments that I have just summarized. Although an argument from silence would be inconclusive, this particular silence points us to other evidence important in understanding Aristotle's claims. The argument from under-inclusiveness is certainly obvious enough: *nous* cannot be the mover, because many animals undergo locomotion and yet lack *nous*. Since Aristotle explicitly mentions other animals besides humans in the immediate context and throughout these chapters, why does he not make this obvious argument? The answer is that for the animals that, strictly speaking, lack *nous* and calculative reason (*logismos*), *phantasia* stands in the place of *nous*, counting as 'some sort of thinking' (*hōs noēsin tina*), as Aristotle writes in the first sentence of ch. 10 (433ᵃ9–12).[20] It is presumably the semantic or interpretative richness of *phantasia* that makes it relevantly similar to *nous* (and perhaps also the fact that it can account for aiming at something *as* good, but that is getting ahead of ourselves). Thus Aristotle introduces his discussion of *phantasia* in *DA* 3. 3 by distinguishing thought (*noēsis*) from *aisthēsis* and dividing thought into *phantasia* and conception (*hupolēpsis*: 427ᵇ27–9). What role these two types of thought play in animal movement remains to be seen.

III. Aristotle's Settled Account of the Mover

While the cases of *akrasia* and continence tend to show that neither *nous* nor *orexis* is sufficient to account for every case of animal movement, neither undercuts the claim of each capacity to a necessary role. Accordingly, ch. 10, which initiates Aristotle's positive answer to his question about the mover of animal movement, sets out necessary roles both for *orexis* and for *noēsis* broadly understood (*nous* or *dianoia* in humans and *phantasia* in other animals). What portion of this chapter actually presents Aristotle's solution is up for debate. There are

[19] As Nussbaum notes in (1983), 135, to avert an inconsistency between this passage and ch. 10's insistence that *orexis* is involved in every action, including those obeying reason, we may eventually correct it in the light of Aristotle's suggestion that actions obeying reason are according to rational wish (*boulēsis*), which is a type of *orexis* (433ᵃ22–5). See also Hicks on 433ᵇ6–7.

[20] Labarrière (1984, 18–21) elaborates and defends this likening of *phantasia* to *nous*, collecting a number of other passages in which Aristotle ascribes to animals the analogues of *dianoia*, *logismos*, and *phronēsis*.

three main structural possibilities. (S1) The first half of the chapter, down to 433^{b}13, answers Aristotle's question from ch. 9 about the internal mover, whereas the remainder uses Aristotle's distinction at 433^{b}14–15 between (relatively) unmoved mover and the moved-and-moving mover to introduce a new distinction between the internal and the external mover.[21] (S2) The first half of the chapter presents further difficulties and preliminary attempts at a solution, but the real solution comes in the second half.[22] (S3) Both halves of the chapter present necessary and important parts of Aristotle's considered solution to his question from ch. 9. In this section, I will argue against (S1), and will present reasons to prefer (S3) to (S2). As will emerge, this question of the structure of this chapter is importantly linked to the choice between an interpretation based on D and one closer to G.

Chapter 10 naturally begins by trying to specify more clearly the relation in animal movement between *nous*, *logismos*, and *phantasia*, on the one hand, and *orexis* on the other. The passage alternates between reasoning animals endowed with *nous* and the non-reasoning animals who have only lesser forms of thought. Let me start with a paraphrase: the relevant sort of *nous* is practical, that which 'calculates for the sake of something' (433^{a}14).[23] Practical *nous* thus takes up the end, the object of pursuit and avoidance, and reasons concerning it. But the starting-point or principle (*archē*) of practical *nous* is the object of desire (433^{a}15–16), while the final stage reached in (or by) deliberation (*to eschaton*, ^{a}16–17; cf. *EN* 1142^{a}24) is the *archē* of action. This suggests that there are two movers, since *orexis*, the object of which provides the *archē* of practical *nous*, is equally involved in explaining animal movement as is *nous* itself (^{a}17–18). Similarly, in the case of the non-reasoning animals, when *phantasia* moves the animals, it does so not without the involvement of desire (^{a}20). Accordingly, if we examine the cases of the akratic and the continent more carefully we will see that while the commands of reason can overcome appetite they do so only through the operation of rational wish (*boulēsis*), a form of *orexis* (^{a}22–5). And while appetite can act contrary to *nous*, this is possible only if we conceive of *nous* narrowly as being necessarily correct, for even in these cases, as Aristotle makes explicit at 433^{b}28–9, appetite moves the animal not without the mediation of *phantasia*, which may or may not be correct (^{a}26–7).[24] Aristotle concludes that 'the object of desire always moves [*aei kinei men to orekton*], and this is either the good or the apparent good' (^{a}27–9). That is, the object of desire is the good as apprehended by veridical *nous* or by *phantasia*.[25]

This passage makes clear that both desire and discernment are necessary

---

[21] This is the view taken by Rodier in Aristotle (1900), ii. 540.

[22] This is the interpretation suggested at least by the emphasis of Skemp (1978), 181–9.

[23] The fact that *nous* here is described as including calculation (*logismos*) indicates that it is still used in a fairly broad sense, encompassing discursive reasoning. Cf. Kal (1988). On 'practical *nous*', see n. 18, above.

[24] In the case of humans, of course, the *noēsis* of the object of desire will be 'not without' *phantasia* as well: cf. *DA* 431^{b}2–10; also Nussbaum (1978), 238.

[25] On the connection between *phantasia* and *phainetai*, which justifies understanding *to phainomenon agathon* as the good as an object of *phantasia*, see Nussbaum (1978), Essay 5.

factors in the account of movement. None the less, some sort of asymmetry between them is introduced by the fact that the object of desire—which receives the title *orekton*—serves as the *archē* of practical *nous*. To understand the import of this asymmetry, we will have to examine further the crucial role of the *orekton*. In particular, we will have to deal with a textual question that arises in a passage ([a]18–22) that my paraphrase skipped: does Aristotle there say (at [a]21) that the single mover is the object of desire (*to orekton*), or that it is the capacity of desire (*to orektikon*)?

The substantive philosophical question at issue here, recall, is that crystallized by the divergence between D, which focuses on the role of desire as the mover, and G, which takes some good (the object of a desire) to be the mover. The choice between these two interpretations of the relation of reason and desire also connects with the proper understanding of the structure of ch. 10, as follows. If one concurs with D in granting a pre-eminent place to the capacity of desire, then one will support S1: the first part of the chapter, with its stress on the asymmetry between *orexis* and *nous*, presents the case for taking *orexis* to be the 'internal' mover, while 433[b]14 17, which explicitly names the practical good (the object of desire) as the (relatively) unmoved mover which moves desire, thereby identifies the 'external' mover. Position G, by contrast, fits better with taking this latter passage as giving Aristotle's considered solution to the question of the (internal) mover of animal movement, and therefore with either S2, which would take the opening of the chapter as a preliminary skirmish, or S3, which would view it as contributing more positively to the solution announced in the later passage.

Since the question of whether 'the mover' is desire or the object of desire depends both upon the expository structure of ch. 10 and more broadly upon the deep philosophical divergence between D and G, it obviously cannot be answered as an isolated textual matter. In emphasizing both the essential interpretative role for *phantasia* in the animal's aiming for the object of desire and the sense in which *phantasia* stands in the same place in the account of action as does *nous*, I have already been building a case to prefer G over D. This case could well survive even if the manuscripts were unanimous at 433[a]21 that the single mover were the *orektikon*. Since they are not, however, we will profit from examining the reasons that have been put forward in favour of this reading and seeing how they may be rebutted.

The relevant line reads: *hen dē ti to kinoun to orekton/orektikon*, 'Hence the mover is some one thing, namely...' in some manuscripts, the object of desire; in others, the capacity of desire. There is a similar divergence between *orekton* and *orektikon* in two places in the lines immediately preceding this conclusion ([a]18, [a]20), in the sentence in which Aristotle explains how the two apparent movers, *orexis* and *nous*, are connected by saying that 'the *orekt[ik]on* moves, and on account of this thought moves, because the *orekt[ik]on* is the *archē* of [practical] thought.' One main family of manuscripts consistently has *orekton* for all three instances, where the other principal family of manuscripts consistently has *orektikon*. Presumably because reading *orekton* in the first two of these instances makes manifestly better sense, as doing so allows an understanding of the *archē* of practical thinking in line with ᵃ15–16, recent editors (e.g. Rodier, Hicks, Ross) follow the first family for these two cases; none the less, these same editors prefer to follow the second family of manuscripts in the crucial concluding line.²⁶ Most of the reasons they give beg the interpretative question at issue between the two broad alternatives set out above.²⁷

Apparently posing greater difficulty for reading *orekton* are questions of consistency with two other passages in which Aristotle seems to speak of the capacity of desire as the mover. The first of these passages immediately follows the discussion of the *orekton* as the practical good that always moves the animal. Aristotle concludes that 'therefore, it is clear that the capacity of the soul of this sort [sc., of the sort that is moved by the *orekton*], namely *orexis*, moves' (433ᵃ31). This sentence is typically translated as implying that *orexis* is the sole mover; however, it could equally be read as saying that *orexis* is *a* mover—for instance in the qualified sense dependent on being moved by the *orekton*, as will shortly be noted at 433ᵇ14–17. The second of these passages, 433ᵇ10–12, seems to provide stronger support for thinking of the *orektikon* as the single mover. There, Aristotle says that 'the mover must be one in form, namely the *orektikon*, as *orektikon*, or rather first of all the *orekton* (for this moves, and is not moved, in being thought or imagined [*noēthēnai ē phantasthēnai*]).' Still, the support this passage offers for thinking of the *orektikon* as the single mover is obviously mitigated by the statement that the *orekton* is 'first of all' the mover. This passage neither says unqualifiedly that the *orektikon* is the single mover nor undercuts the claim of the *orekton* to that status—quite the contrary.

Since no compelling text precludes taking the *orekton* to be the single mover, we may now turn to more positive reasons for thinking that this is what Aristotle should be saying at 433ᵃ21. To begin with, none of the arguments that lead up to this claim about the single mover undercut the reasons Aristotle has given for holding that while both *orexis* and *nous* or its relative *phantasia* are necessary factors in moving an animal, neither is sufficient.²⁸ On account of this logical

²⁶ On ᵃ18, Hicks condescendingly notes that 'Wallace followed the inferior MSS in reading *orektikon*' there; yet Hicks himself follows a subset of the very same 'inferior' manuscripts in preferring *orektikon* three lines later!

²⁷ Thus, Hicks (ad loc., echoing Rodier, in Aristotle 1900, ii, 540) presumes the correctness of S1 regarding the structure of ch. 10. Rodier gives three additional arguments favoring *orektikon* over *orekton*. (i) He notes that desire serves as the point of departure of practical thought; but this fact is inconclusive unless D is presumed correct. (ii) Reading *orektikon* is preferable, he claims, because this statement about the single mover is followed by a discussion in which Aristotle aims to prove that while all practical thinking presupposes desire, the reverse is not true. Yet Rodier's second point does not discriminate between the *orektikon* and the *orekton*: for desire always presupposes an object of desire and—as Aristotle will go on to tell us—is moved by that object of desire. (iii) Rodier also finds some difficulty for reading *orekton* in the fact that at ᵃ16–17 the final term or stage of practical thinking is said to be the *archē* of action. He supposes (what is not obvious) that the *archē* of action is the same as its mover, and declares that the final term cannot in any way be taken to signify the desirable. Can it not? If we follow this equation of the *archē* and the mover and we read *orektikon*, we will have to recognize that the final term (when deliberation proceeds effectively) is a deliberate desire; but since this desire, too, will have an object, and since this object may represent a deliberative specification of the good, Rodier's third argument again does not suffice to discriminate between *orektikon* and *orekton*.

²⁸ See above, p. 388.

symmetry, some commentators who see Aristotle as none the less plumping for (the capacity of) desire as the single mover think that his arguments for this conclusion are bad.[29] But needlessly attributing a bad argument to Aristotle is to be avoided. The second passage considered in the last paragraph gives us the means to do so, and to understand more constructively the suggestion that the *orekton* is the mover. The parenthesis at 433^{b}11–12 gives the needed explanation of how the *orekton* can be the *internal* mover of the animal—namely, by being the object of *nous* or at least *phantasia*.[30] That the mover is the object of desire taken up as the object of thought or appearance is a view that Aristotle also puts forward elsewhere (*MA*, 700^{b}23–4; *Metaph.* 1072^{a}26–7; cf. *EN* 1114^{a}31–^{b}1).

The distinction this passage makes between the mover's being one in form (*eidei*, ^{b}10) and its being many in number (*arithmōi*, ^{b}12) also provides us with the means to answer an ontological objection to the possibility that the *orekton* could be the single mover. This ontological objection goes as follows: for Aristotle, processes or movements (*kinēseis*) that actualize different capacities are necessarily numerically distinct, even if they are conterminous.[31] Since the alternative reading I have been defending supposes that the co-operation of at least two capacities, the *orektikon* and *nous* or *phantasia*, is necessary to yield action, it must recognize that more than one internal process or movement is involved. Only one of these, strictly speaking, can be the one that 'moves' the animal. Further, the distinctions at 433^{b}13–18 indicate how to order the two *kinēseis*: the *orekton* (which one may think of as internal in the way explained, if one likes) moves desire, and desire moves the animal.[32] Desire is the immediate or proximate cause of action.[33] In short, there can only be one capacity that is actualized in immediately producing animal movement, and that capacity is desire. My answer is that this account could be conceded as the correct one, ontologically, without disturbing the claim that Aristotle really means to say that the object of desire is the single mover of animal movement. In saying that the mover is one in form but many in number, Aristotle concedes that he is not trying to establish that the mover is numerically one. As I have argued, he is not here aiming at ontological precision, but at showing how one might give a unified account of animal movement. His is unified around the idea of the practical good.

This idea of the formal (not numerical) unity of the account of movement also

---

[29] See e.g. Hamlyn in Aristotle (1968), 151–2.

[30] It will be objected that even if the *orekton* is 'internal' in the sense I have explained, it does not count as a 'part' (*morion*) of the animal, which is what would be required to fit the requirements of self-movement as set out in *Ph.* 8. 5. My response is that this is to fasten too much importance on the words of this chapter of the *Physics* in contradistinction to its arguments, which should be satisfied by locating something internal that is a (relatively) unmoved mover. In general, my account is quite close to that of Furley (1978), esp. pp. 175–6.

[31] Cf. Charles (1984), 17.   [32] Ibid. 58.

[33] A weak suggestion of this temporal ordering of two processes involved in moving the animal is found in the statement that the *orekton* is the mover that is 'first of all' at 433^{b}11—if 'first' is construed temporally (see also the parallel claim about what comes first in *Metaph.* 1072^{a}24–30). A more explicitly temporal ordering is given in the *De Motu* account (701^{a}4–6, 701^{a}33–6).

occurs earlier in the chapter, in the sentence immediately following the disputed
text about what the single mover is. There, Aristotle writes that 'if there were
two movers, *nous* and *orexis*, they would move according to some common form'
(ᵃ21–2). The juxtaposition of this sentence with the disputed one about the
single mover has provided probably the most influential reason for taking that
single mover to be the *orektikon*.³⁴ For it might be thought that the pattern of
Aristotle's exposition would have to be as follows: 'There is only one mover, A;
for if there were two, A and B, then we'd be in a pretty pickle.' So long as the
orektikon can be identified with *orexis*, then this pattern would support reading
orektikon. There are, however, two reasons why we do not have to understand
this sentence this way. First, I would repeat that a desire always has an object.
Indeed, the two are united in any particular actualization. Hence, if *orexis* refers
to an occurrent desire, the identification of it with the *orektikon* is not much
more likely than an alternative identification with the *orekton*. Secondly, and
more importantly, an alternative pattern of exposition that is at least as plausible
supports reading *orekton*. It is one that my earlier paraphrase of the opening of
ch. 10 has already begun to support; let me recapitulate and continue the paraphrase as follows: Aristotle begins ch. 10 by declaring that there appear to be
two movers, *orexis* and *nous* [sc. *dianoia praktikē* in humans (433ᵃ18–19) and
phantasia in the non-reasoning animals (ᵃ20)], each necessary to account for
movement, but neither alone sufficient (ᵃ9). And there is good reason for this
view (ᵃ17–18). But, he then declares, there really is just one mover, namely the
object of desire (*to orekton*), which mediates between these two. For suppose we
were stuck with the two apparent movers, *nous* and *orexis*: then there would still
have to be some common form by virtue of which the animal was moved; in
other words, our philosophical job would not yet be done, for we would still
need to give unity to the account. Now it is true that both *nous* and *orexis* are
involved in every case of movement, even in the cases of the akratic and the
continent (ᵃ22–6). The difference between these cases has to do with whether the
end is understood correctly; for while (intuitive) *nous* cannot err, *phantasia* can
(ᵃ26–7). But in either case, what matters is that it is the object of desire, the
orekton, that moves the animal, whether this is the true good or the apparent
good (ᵃ27–9). It is the possibility of error that draws our attention to this
'common form' that can, in fact, give unity to our account of animal motion.³⁵
On this alternative reading of the entire passage, then, the two alternatives at
ᵃ21–2 need not include the one mover just declared: rather, Aristotle is returning
to the apparent duality mentioned at ᵃ9 and ᵃ17, which he now will explain away.

---

³⁴ As Hicks reports in his commentary on 433ᵃ21, Torstrik, who led the shift towards reading
orektikon, put forward this argument. I am grateful to Martha Nussbaum for help in understanding it.

³⁵ Philoponus reads *orekton* at 433ᵃ21, but interprets Aristotle as saying that there must be one
moving *capacity* (*dunamis*, 1897, 585, ll. 20, 32; 586, l. 3). On his reading, we may understand 433ᵃ21–
2 as explaining that if *nous* and *orexis* had been identified as two movers, one would have to identify a
capacity that formed a genus of which both of these were members (586, l. 3; cf. 585, l. 21). The reading I have given in the text, however, offers an alternative way of reading oneness in form—one more

If the result of 433ᵃ9–30 is to establish that the object of desire is the single mover, then what is the role of the passage at 433ᵇ13–18, according to which the *orekton* is classed as (relatively) unmoved mover, the *orektikon* as moved and moving, and the animal as moved? Adopting S1, the rival reading would have it that the first passage establishes desire as the internal mover, while the second explains that the object of desire is the external mover. If the two passages are not to be distinguished in terms of the question they are addressing (internal–external), are they merely repetitive of one another? On the reading I am defending, the distinctions of the later passage have an obvious alternative role, namely to resolve the dialectical tension created by the negative arguments of ch. 9. *Nous* and *phantasia* can be given their place as the capacities whereby the *orekton* is first made internal. *Orexis* can be accorded the honor of being the capacity that immediately moves the animal. The negative arguments of ch. 9 are thus respected in the way that they ought to be, for none of these capacities is said to be the mover full stop.[36] None the less, Aristotle does in characteristic fashion claim to pinpoint an ambiguity in the original question that gave rise to the dialectical difficulty, for he suggests that the distinction between the (relatively) unmoved mover and the moved-and-moving mover marks two ways of understanding the term 'mover' (*to de kinoun ditton*, 433ᵇ14). Both the partisans of desire and, by implication, the partisans of reason were focusing on movers of the second sort. Only the *orekton*, however, is a mover in the first, stricter sense. If the role of this later passage is thus to accommodate his considered philosophical account with the positions canvassed in ch. 9, then S3 gives the correct account of the chapter's structure. The opening passage gives the central positive account of the object of desire as the single mover, while the later passage's distinction works the reconciliation.

As the illustrative contrast between D and G was meant to suggest, the difference between the two interpretations of the single mover with which I have been concerned corresponds to quite different roles for *nous* and *phantasia* in guiding action. In arguing that Aristotle thinks the *orekton* is the single internal mover, I am thereby both making room for an important place for *nous* and *phantasia* in apprehending the good and more generally defending the parity of discernment and desire in the account of animal movement.[37] To see the full

in line with Simplicius' view that *nous* and *orexis* operate 'both in one' in causing animal movement (1882, 297, l. 35).

[36] Concerning this conclusion about the structure of the exposition in chs. 9–10 and concerning the overall shape of Aristotle's positive solution I am in general agreement with Hudson (1981), 111–35. While this article contains many insightful comments on the relation between reason and desire in Aristotle, its textual case is marred by the fact that throughout it prints *orekton* for *orektikon*, making it unclear how Hudson would handle the difference between the two.

[37] To be sure, I must concede one obvious but relatively trivial priority of *orexis* over *nous*: for the *orekton* is, after, all, the object of desire. Although this is more than just a coincidence of names, it does depend upon the range of the words *orexis* and *nous*. The point is that any object of desire is a potential mover of the animal; whereas—as Aristotle points out at 432ᵇ27–9—this is not the case with every object of *nous*. For this verbal reason, Simplicius (1882, 298, ll. 8–17) is right that in some sense the *orektikon* is the 'principal' mover, at least compared with any other capacity of the soul.

import of this point, we must examine further Aristotle's statements that the *orekton* is the good and that our apprehension of it can be correct or incorrect.

IV. The Role of the Good as the Object of Desire

Stressing the intentional object of desire will help a teleological account of animal movement avert a potentially vitiating circularity. If the animal aims at something that it conceives or imagines in a certain way, then a needed logical space opens up between the desires we will attribute on the basis of its movements and those movements themselves, for three reasons. First, as in the case of Fido, the object of desire can appear to the animal in a way that was simply mistaken, and the animal can come to recognize this. Second, the semantic complexity introduced by the notion of 'seeing as' is enough to imply that we cannot be sure from observing an isolated case of movement whether it was made for its own sake or as a means to some further end, which was perhaps not achieved.[38] Third, the intentionality of the desire attributed requires that we should also be able to attribute to the animal an awareness that what it wanted is available to it.[39] Still, there would seem to be too many degrees of freedom remaining in this approximation of a belief-desire model fully to dispel the suspicion that one's attributions of beliefs and desires are fictional.[40]

Aristotle gets beyond this impasse by having independent grounds for describing the content of the object of desire, namely in terms of the good of an animal of the kind in question. We may leave aside whether these grounds are metaphysical, biological, ethical, or (in the case of humans, at least) all of the above. What matters is that on his view, an objective account of the good of each type of animal can be developed. Furthermore, it must be developed in terms that look to the essential constitution of the animal as a whole, rather than reducing to the animal's various particular desires, taken severally. Therefore, since the object of desire is the good or the apparent good, the nature of the good provides some independent information that constrains our attributing mental states such as desires, allowing for a less trivial, less fictional account. The fact that these two layers are involved in accounting for movement—both that of particular desires and that of the organism's overall good—perhaps explains why Aristotle is willing to speak alternatively of the person or of the final stage of deliberation as being the origin (*arche*) of human action.

This role for the animal's good in the account of movement presupposes, with G, that animals—even the non-reasoning animals—pursue particular desirable objects *as* good. Yet influential strands of our philosophical tradition would deny that the non-reasoning animals can be guided by the good in a localized way. Thus, it will be suggested, although what they aim at is some aspect of their

---

[38] Cf. Nussbaum (1986), 279.   [39] Ibid.; cf. Loenig (1903), 34.
[40] Cf. Davidson (1982).

good, and they aim at it as pleasant or as tasty, they do not aim at it *as* good. Accordingly, as D also postulates, the connection between an animal's good and its movement does not hold for each of its particular desires (and hence movements), but only for its desires (and hence movements) taken as a whole.[41] This objection can be met with a concession and a distinction. Although it is true that non-reasoning animals lack any general supposition (*hupolēpsis katholou*) about the good, that is just because such animals lack general suppositions altogether (*Metaph.* 981ᵃ7 ff.; *EN* 1147ᵇ3–5). Yet Aristotle's natural teleology gives us a way to understand the good of an organism and the place of pleasure and survival in its good without having to suppose that the animal has any general suppositions about it.[42] Accordingly, animals unable to entertain general suppositions could still have *phantasmata* of objects of desire *as* good, because the content of propositions about the local good is essential to the account of their particular movements. It is true that, as Aristotle explains in ch. 11, a non-reasoning animal lacks the ability to trace out the logical implications of the relevant proposition.[43] None the less, there is no reason to deny the possibility of a particularized intentional connection between its good and its actions.

V. Deliberative *Phantasia* and Measurement by One

If the single mover were the capacity of desire then, as D spells out, it would be necessary to explain how each action could come to be controlled by a single desire. Since in ch. 10, at 433ᵇ5–10, Aristotle recognizes that desires will conflict —at least in humans, who possess *logos*—this interpretation demands a way to resolve conflicts among desires. Into this service it may press Aristotle's account in ch. 11 of deliberative imagination (*phantasia bouleutikē*). This he there distinguishes from perceptual imagination (*phantasia aisthetikē*), which is shared by non-reasoning and reasoning animals alike. The former, however, is peculiar

---

[41] Irwin (1988, 332), suggests that the non-reasoning animals cannot pursue their ends *as* good. To buttress this claim, he cites *DA* 414ᵇ2–6, which characterizes *epithumia* as having as its object the pleasant, while *boulēsis* (which is limited to the reasoning animals: 432ᵇ5–7) is for the good (331). But to pursue pleasure and to avoid pain *is* a way of acting 'towards the good or bad, as such' (431ᵃ11–12; cf. *MA* 700ᵇ28–9). Irwin also cites *Pol.* 1253ᵃ10–18, where Aristotle writes that while animals can use their voices to communicate their pleasure and displeasure, they can neither communicate nor perceive the useful and the harmful, the good and the bad, or the just and the unjust. Against this, however, we must counterpose *Sens.* 436ᵇ20–437ᵃ1, in which Aristotle writes that the senses besides touch and taste, which belong to all animals capable of locomotion, allow the animal to avoid food that is inferior or dangerous. To avoid a contradiction with the statement in the *Politics* passage that the non-reasoning animals do not perceive the harmful, I suggest that we read the latter passage as denying that the non-reasoning animals recognize or 'perceive' the universal (or in terms of the universals) goodness or badness, usefulness or harmfulness, etc., and *not* as saying that particular things cannot appear to them as good or bad, etc.

[42] This aspect of Aristotle's teleology is strongly emphasized by Gotthelf (1989).

[43] I owe this use of the distinction between propositional content and the logical implications of a proposition to Irwin (1988), § 171.

to the reasoning animals (434ª5–7). If Aristotle's point in adjoining this discussion of deliberative *phantasia* to his account of animal movement were to cope
with this problem of the multiplicity of desires, then D could count ch. 11 in its
favour, thereby casting some doubt on my interpretation of chs. 9 and 10,
which more closely follow G. But is it essential to deliberative *phantasia* to settle
conflicts among desires in this way?

Aristotle explains the role of deliberative *phantasia* as follows (434ª7–10):

Deliberative *phantasia* is found in the reasoning animals, for it is already a function of calculative reasoning [to consider] whether to do one thing or another; and it is necessary to
measure by one, for the greater is pursued. Consequently, [a reasoning animal] is able to
make one [*phantasma*] out of many *phantasmata*.

It seems clear that the 'one' by which the reasoning animal measures—whether
or not it is itself an actualization of *phantasia*—is functioning here as a standard
of comparison.[44] Accordingly, even those interpreters who would prefer to see
Aristotle as recognizing the incommensurability of goods have felt forced to
admit that he is here countenancing some form of weak commensurability.[45] Even
a weak commensurability, supposing only the existence of some standard of comparison for each case of deliberative choice (not necessarily the same one for
every case) would address D's need for the adjudication of conflicts among
desires.

Beyond that, the notion of a single measure might also help D with a more
general problem about its fit with Aristotle's texts, namely, what to say about the
good. As I presented D initially, I emphasized that its account of movement
treats as incidental the fact that desire aims at some good. Given the prominence
that Aristotle gives the good, however, someone wishing to interpret him along
the lines of D will not be content to leave it so far on the periphery. Aristotle's
description of deliberative *phantasia* suggests one way that the good may be
integrated into this interpretation, although only for humans, namely via a *strong*
form of commensurability, in which the highest good serves as the standard in
every case.

Interpretation D's appropriation of ch. 11 is unwarranted, however, because
Aristotle does not here commit himself to any kind of commensurability, strong
or weak. Burnyeat has suggestively noted that all Aristotle needs for the purposes
of his argument in *DA* 3. 11 is the minimal achievement of deliberative rationality sufficient to set apart humans from the non-reasoning animals.[46] We might
fill out this hint by recasting the role of this passage as follows: Aristotle is here
concerned to explain the difference, which has shown up throughout his account
of animal movement, between those animals whose discernment is confined to

---

[44] I am grateful to David Charles for discussion of this point and others regarding this passage.

[45] See Wiggins (1980*b*), 256; and Burnyeat (1980*b*), 91 n. 29. Charles (1984, 133–5) is more whole-
hearted in his identification of a weak commensurability in this passage. The distinction between
strong and weak commensurability is Wiggins's.

[46] Burnyeat (1986*b*), 91, n. 29.

phantasia and those that combine *phantasia* with the kind of discursive thinking he goes on to explain in the remainder of ch. 11. At a minimum, he is saying, rational deliberation will involve comparing alternatives in terms of the more and the less.

While this simple capacity suffices to illustrate the distinct contribution of deliberative reasoning, it does not imply any kind of commensurability. To see this, consider a case in which one option yields more of one good and less of another than does the other option; for instance, when one does something shameful and painful for the sake of great and fine results (*EN* 1110^{a}20–22).[47] These cases show that the statement that 'the greater is pursued' has to be filled out with a *ceteris paribus* clause: other things equal, the option that yields the greater pleasure (or honour) is to be pursued (cf. *Top.* 118^{b}27–32). Where goods of different types conflict, one would have to 'measure by one' twice: first to determine which option is more painful, and next to determine which option is more fine. In all cases, one measures in terms of one good at a time, and more particularly in terms of one *metric* at a time.[48] This does not imply, however, that these acts of measurement will settle what to do in cases involving options that differ with respect to more than one good.[49] On this reading, then, 'measurement by one' is not taken to imply even a weak commensurability, if that is understood to mean that for every deliberative choice there is a standard of measurement that is sufficient to determine which action the agent has most reason to do.

Which of these interpretations best fits the present passage?[50] I claim the one not attributing even a weak commensurability, for two reasons. First, 'measurement by one' arises in this passage as a necessary condition of rational deliberation, not as a sufficient condition. Accordingly, there is no reason to think of the measurement referred to as taking a strong enough form to be capable of settling all questions of deliberative choice. Second, while deliberative *phantasia* may be

[47] This passage is illuminatingly discussed in Stocker (1986).

[48] Philoponus focuses on the metric, comparing the one measure to the carpenter's use of a cubit to measure a length of timber (1897, 592, ll. 31–2). None the less, he moves from this simile to the claim that in cases of opposed desires men always measure in terms of 'the same good', choosing the 'greater good' (ll. 32–4). I am arguing that a focus on the metric can reveal an important role for 'measuring by one' that does not imply weak commensurability. Perhaps the peculiarity of carpenters is that they only measure one kind of thing, namely distance. Engineers, however, need to measure both distance and weight. Wiggins (1980b, 256) undercuts his own attempt to minimize the place of commensurability in Aristotle by translating *to meizon gar diōkei* as 'for what one pursues is the greater good'.

[49] Simplicius reads the present passage as concerning measurement confined to the rubric of one or another major category of value, such as the useful or the pleasant, rather than cutting across these; and indeed he implies that the measure will vary depending upon which one of these goods is posited as the relevant end: (1882, 309, ll. 22–6).

[50] I will not here ask which best fits Aristotle's corpus as a whole, for that question would force us to delve deeply into Aristotle's understanding of *eudaimonia*, among other matters. Wedin (1988, 143–5) suggests a reading of 434^{a}7–10 that is even more radical in denying a place for commensurability than mine, for he claims that the difference between *phantasia aisthētikē* and *phantasia bouleutikē* hangs mainly on the fact that humans can be moved by the thought of an object of desire that is not present but, say, future, and hence must be represented universally. While I am somewhat drawn to this reading, it does not seem to do justice to the verb *metrein*.

needed to cope with conflicting desires, the only detailed explanation of such conflicts that Aristotle offers in these chapters concerns the divergence between short-term and longer-term perspectives (433^{b}5–10). Appetite (*epithumia*), in looking to the present, mistakes what is apparently pleasant for what is pleasant unqualifiedly. To correct this skewed perspective on pleasures is the role of *nous*, which looks to the future. This sort of role for deliberative *phantasia* is the one postulated by the second interpretation of measurement: to assess accurately (sc., without temporal bias) the total pleasure yielded by each option. The first interpretation, by contrast, makes little sense in this instance, for the conflict is not between two different kinds of goods, but between pleasure now and pleasure later.[51] Recourse to some overall measure of goodness seems an unnecessarily circuitous approach to this simple case of conflict. Although some of the pleasures that yield future pain are not 'true' pleasures, Benthamic 'fruitfulness' is far from being Aristotle's criterion of true pleasure. Indeed, he notes that the fact that a pleasure yields painful (or unhealthy) results is not enough to make it bad (*EN* 1153^{a}19–20). Therefore, it is more likely that in a case of conflict like the one he diagnoses in *DA* 3. 10, Aristotle has in mind measuring in terms of pleasure rather than goodness.[52] If so, then the second interpretation of measurement, not implying commensurability, better responds to the problem of conflicts of desires as Aristotle here describes it. In short, while nothing in this passage is incompatible with the claim that Aristotle is committed to weak commensurability, nothing implies it; and the alternative reading that denies any commitment to commensurability fits the passage slightly better.[53]

VI. Conclusion

In every particular, I have argued, the text of *DA* 3. 9–11 better fits the good-based model of animal motion (G) than it fits the desire-based model (D). (i) To begin with, Aristotle's account is limited to those movements that aim at some good, rather than ranging more widely. (ii) Chapter 9 puts forward genuine difficulties with building an account of animal movement around any capacity of the soul, including desire or reason. Aristotle seeks instead to explain how the

---

[51] As I point out in Richardson (1990), a similar problem in finding strong commensurability in Plato's *Protagoras* is posed by the mention of temporal nearness and remoteness at 356 B.

[52] Similar reasoning applies to Aristotle's scheme for ranking pairs of opposites in *APr.* 68^{a}25–^{b}7. The fact that it is opposites that are in play already indicates that the options significantly differ only along one dimension of value. Aristotle clearly envisages some sort of cardinal (interval-scale) comparability, but does not imply that this sort of comparability cuts across different types of value.

[53] To read this passage as simply calling attention to the role of comparative measures in deliberation is not to deny that Aristotle thinks that we can form all-things-considered judgements about which of two alternatives is better (cf. *EE* 1226^{b}13 ff.). Indeed, if the argument of the preceding sections is correct, his overall account of animal movement requires him to give an objective account of the good of the animal in terms of which alternatives appear better or worse. In resisting an attribution of (even) weak commensurability to Aristotle here, I am simply opposing the idea that the all-things-considered judgement is to be reached by determining which alternative yields the most of some single commensurating good.

various necessary capacities co-operate. (iii) The first half of ch. 10 confirms that desire and discernment are equally necessary in movement of the relevant kind, and puts forward the object of desire, which is equated with the good or the apparent good, as the single item that can bring a formal unity to the operation of these two sorts of capacity. (iv) For this reason, the *orekton* should be counted as the single mover of animal movement. (v) To reconcile this conclusion with the prima-facie reasons (largely unstated) in favour of declaring either discernment or desire to be the mover, Aristotle introduces in the second half of ch. 10 the distinction between the (relatively) unmoved mover and the moved-and-moving mover. Each of these interpretative conclusions conspires together to exclude the kind of primacy accorded to desire by D and to support something like the central role for the good and the parity of reason (or discernment) and desire that define G. Finally, (vi) I have shown that the sketch of deliberation in ch. 11 can be taken to elaborate on the difference, within an account such as G, between discernment's contribution to the movement of the non-reasoning animals and its role in the reasoning animals' movements.

The special case of human action is the context in which the otherwise rather elusive difference between D and G matters most. Much of my argument has aimed at minimizing the distance between the way Aristotle would account for human action and the way he would account for animal movement generally. Human deliberative capacities mark a departure not because they introduce a new relation to the good, but because they involve abilities to make explicit comparisons and to follow inferences in a way that allows agents to deal rationally with conflicts among different aspects of their good.[54]

If this interpretation is correct, then Aristotle's basic understanding of human movement does not yet carry with it any strong claim to a higher rationality. There are distinctive human achievements, but they pertain not so much to the way our movements are to be explained as to our ability to develop general suppositions about the good and to test these dialectically against each other. In G, value-conflicts for humans do not reduce to what can be measured on a single scale. Rather, we are able to put forward many complexly competing considerations for and against different theories about the good, where what matters more than the mere strength of these considerations is the inferential connections among them. To trace these well is one of the achievements of the person of practical wisdom. Aristotle's common account of animal motion in *De Anima* lays no claim to capturing this particularly human virtue within its bounds. Instead, its goal is at once more modest and more needed: to maintain an open place for this intellectual virtue by defending the essential and coequal role of the discernment of the good.[55]

[54] Cf. the response of Davidson (1982) by Jeffrey (1985).

[55] I am grateful for the many helpful criticisms and suggestions that I received from David Charles, Alfonso Gomez-Lobo, Martha Nussbaum, and Amélie Rorty, as well as for generous research support from Georgetown University and Harvard University's Program in Ethics and the Professions.

BIBLIOGRAPHY ¹

The following abbreviations will be used to indicate the article in which each bibliographical item is cited: **An.** = Annas, **Br.** = Brentano, **Bu.** = Burnyeat, **Co.** = Code and Moravcsik, **Coh.** = Cohen, **Fr.** = D. Frede, **Fre.** = Freeland, **Ka.** = Kahn, **Kos.** = Kosman, **Ll.** = Lloyd, **Ma.** = Matthews, **Nu.** = Nussbaum, **Pu.** = Nussbaum and Putnam, **Ri.** = Richardson, **Sch.** = Schofield, **Sor.** = Sorabji, **Wh.** = Whiting, **Wi.** = Wilkes, **Wit.** = Witt. Items marked with an asterisk (*) are not cited in any of the articles.

I. Editions, Translations, and Commentaries

A. *De Anima*

ARISTOTLE (1495–8). *Opera*, (*editio Aldina*). Venice (*editio princeps*).

——(1531–50). *Opera*, (*editio Basileensis*). Basle: Jo. Bebel.

——(1550–2). *Opera*. Venice: Giunta. Latin translation.

——(1579–87). *Opera, editio Sylburgiana*. Frankfurt: heirs of A. Wechel.

——(1611). *De Anima*, ed. J. Pacius. Hanau: heirs of C. Marnius.

——(1831–70). *Aristoteles Graece*, ed. Immanuel Bekker. Berlin: G. Reimer. (5 vols., Vol. III, *Latine interpretibus variis*. 1831.)

——(1833). *De Anima*, ed. F. A. Trendelenburg. Jena: Walz; 2nd edn. Berlin: W. Weber, 1877; Graz: Akademische Druck-und Verlagsanstalt, 1957.

——(1846). *Psychologie d'Aristote*, trans. J. Barthélemy-Saint-Hilaire. Paris: Ladrange. First French translation of the *De Anima*.

——(1848–74). *Aristotelis opera omnia, Graece et Latine*, ed. U. C. Bussemaker, J. F. Dübner, E. Heitz. Paris: A. F. Didot.

——(1862). *De Anima*, ed. A. Torstrik. Berlin: Weidmann. **Nu.**, **Br.**

——(1872). *Des Aristoteles Schrift über die Seele*, trans. H. Bender. Stuttgart: C. Hoffman. German translation.

——(1882a). *Aristotle's Psychology in Greek and English*, trans. E. Wallace. Cambridge: Cambridge University Press. Text and English translation.

——(1891). *De Anima liber B*, ed. H. Rabe. Berlin: Weber.

——(1896). *De Anima*, ed. G. Biehl. Leipzig: Teubner; repr., 1911.

——(1900). *Aristote, Traité de l'âme*, 2 vols., ed. G. Rodier. Paris: Ernest Leroux; repr. Dubuque: William C. Brown, n.d. Text, commentary, and French translation. **Ka.**, **Pu.**, **Ri.**

——(1901). *Aristoteles' Schrift über die Seele*, trans. E. Rolfes. Bonn: P. Hanstein. German translation and commentary.

——(1907). *Aristotle De Anima*, with translation, introduction, and notes by R. D. Hicks. Cambridge: Cambridge University Press, repr. New York: Arno Press, (1976). Text, translation, and commentary. **Nu.**, **Coh.**, **Ka.**, **Kos.**, **Pu.**, **Ri.**, **Sor.**, **Wit.**

——(1910–52). *The Works of Aristotle Translated into English*, ed. J. A. Smith and W. D. Ross. Oxford: Clarendon Press. English translation [rev. Aristotle (1984)].

——(1912). *De Anima*, ed. A. Förster. Budapest: Academia litterarum Hungaricae.

¹ The editors wish to thank Robert Hardy for his assistance in constructing the bibliography.

402 *Bibliography*

ARISTOTLE(1936). *Aristotle On the Soul*, trans. W. S. Hett. London: Heinemann. Loeb Classical Library.
—— (1956). *De Anima*, ed. W. D. Ross Oxford: Clarendon Press. Oxford Classical Text.
—— (1959). *Aristoteles über die Seele*, trans. W. Theiler. Berlin: Akademie-Verlag.
—— (1961a). *Aristotle De Anima*, ed. W. D. Ross. Oxford: Clarendon Press. Text and Commentary. **Coh., Nu., Kos., Fr., Ri.**
—— (1966). *Aristote De l'âme*, ed. A. Jannone and E. Barbotin. Paris: Budé. Text and French translation.
—— (1968). *Aristotle's De Anima. Books II and III*, trans. D. W. Hamlyn. Oxford: Clarendon Press. Translation and commentary. **Coh., Fre., Fr., Pu., Ri., Sor., Wi.**
—— (1984). *The Complete Works of Aristotle*, ed. Jonathan Barnes. 2 vols. Bollingen Series, 81/2. Princeton: Princeton University Press. The Revised Oxford Translation. **Fre.**
—— (1986). *Aristotle: De Anima (On the Soul)*, trans. H. Lawson-Tancred. New York: Penguin. English translation.

B. *Other Works by Aristotle*

—— (1882b). *Aristotle on the Parts of Animals*, ed. W. Ogle. London: Kegan Paul. Text and commentary. **Fre.**
—— (1898). *Parva Naturalia*, ed. W. Biehl. Leipzig: Teubner.
—— (1906). *Aristotle, De Sensu et De Memoria*, ed. G. R. T. Ross. Cambridge: Cambridge University Press. Text and commentary. **Sor.**
—— (1943). *Aristotle, Generation of Animals*, trans. A. L. Peck. London: Heinemann. Loeb Classical Library. **Ll.**
—— (1947). *De Insomniis et De Divinatione per Somnum*, ed. H. Lulofs. Leiden: E. J. Brill.
—— (1952). *Aristotle, Meteorologica*, trans. H. D. P. Lee. London: Heinemann. Loeb Classical Library. **Fre.**
—— (1955). *Aristotle's Parva Naturalia*, ed. W. D. Ross. Oxford: Clarendon Press. Text and translation. **An.**
—— (1960). *Aristotle: Posterior Analytics*, trans. Hugh Tredennick; *Topica*, trans. E. S. Forster. London: Heinemann. Loeb Classical Library. **Wit.**
—— (1961). *Aristotle, Parts of Animals*, trans. A. L. Peck; *Movement of Animals* and *Progression of Animals*, trans. E. S. Forster. London: Heinemann. Loeb Classical Library. **Fre.**
—— (1965). *Aristotle, Historia Animalium, Books I–III*, trans. A. L. Peck. London: Heinemann. Loeb Classical Library. **Ll.**
—— (1970). *Aristotle's Physics I-II*, trans. W. Charlton. Oxford: Clarendon Press. Translation with notes. **Wh.**
—— (1971). *Aristotle's Metaphysics, Book Γ, Λ, E*, trans. C. Kirwan. Oxford: Clarendon Press. **Sch.**
—— (1972a). *Aristotle's De Partibus Animalium I and De Generatione Animalium I*, ed. D. M. Balme. Oxford: Clarendon Press. Translation with notes. **Ll.**
—— (1972b). *Aristotle on Memory*, trans. R. Sorabji. London: Duckworth. English translation and commentary. **An., Fr., Sch., Sor.**
—— (1975). *Aristotle's Posterior Analytics*, ed. J. Barnes. Oxford: Clarendon Press. Translation with notes. **Fr.**
—— (1976). *Aristotelis Ars Rhetorica*, ed. R. Kassel. Berlin: de Gruyter.
—— (1978). *Aristotle's De Motu Animalium*, ed. Martha C. Nussbaum. Princeton:

Princeton University Press. Text, translation, and commentary. **Coh., Fr., Ll., Pu., Ri., Sor., Wh., Wit.**

——(1982). *Aristotle's De Generatione et Corruptione*, trans. C. J. F. Williams. Oxford: Clarendon Press. Translation and commentary. **Fre.**

——(1985). *Aristotle's Metaphysics, Books Zeta, Eta, Theta, Iota*, trans. M. Furth. Indianapolis, Ind.: Hackett Publishing Company. Translation and commentary. **Coh.**

——(1988). *Aristoteles, Metaphysik Z*, ed. M. Frede and G. Patzig. 2 vols. Munich: C. H. Beck. **Ll.**

II. Ancient and Medieval Commentaries

ALEXANDER OF APHRODISIAS (1875). *In Aristotelis De Sensu*, ed. Thurot. Paris. **Pu.**

——(1887). *De Anima cum Mantissa* and *Aporiai kai Luseis*, ed. I. Bruns. Supplementum Aristotelicum, vol. ii, pt. 1. Berlin: G. Reimer. **Br., Kos., Nu.**

——(1891). *In Aristotelis Metaphysica*, ed. M. Hayduck. Commentaria in Aristotelem Graeca, vol. 1. Berlin: G. Reimer.

——(1892). *Quaestiones. De Fato. De Mixtione*, ed. I. Bruns. Commentaria in Aristotelem Graeca, vol. ii. Berlin: G. Reimer.

——(1901). *In Aristotelis De Sensu*, ed. P. Wendland. Commentaria in Aristotelem Graeca, vol. iii, pt. 1. Berlin: G. Reimer. **Pu.**

ALFARADI (1892). *Alfarabis philosophische Abhandlungen*, trans. Friedrich Dieterici. Leiden: E. J. Brill. **Br.**

AQUINAS, THOMAS (1948). *In Aristotelis librum de Anima commentarium*, ed. M. Pirotta. Rome: Marietti. **Br.**

——(1949). *Opuscula omnia*, ed. R. P. Perrier. Paris: Lethielleux. **Br.**

——(1951). *Aristotle's De Anima in the Version of William of Moerbeke and the Commentary of St. Thomas Aquinas*, ed. K. Foster and S. Humphries. London: Routledge & Kegan Paul.

——(1961). *Summa contra Gentiles*, ed. C. Peria. Rome: Marietti. **Di.**

AVERROES (1550). *Commentarii*, in Aristotle (1550–2). **Br.**

——(1953). *Averrois Cordubensis Commentarium Magnum in Aristotelis de Anima*, ed. F. Stuart Crawford. Corpus Commentariorum in Aristotelem, vol. vii, Cambridge, Mass.: The Mediaeval Academy of America.

——(1961). *Destructio destructionum philosophiae Algazelis*, ed. Beatrice H. Zedler. Milwaukee: Marquette University Press.

AVICENNA (1907). *Die Metaphysik Avicenna's*, trans. Max Hosten. Halle and New York: R. Haupt.

——(1968). *Avicenna Latinus, Liber de Anima, seu sextus de naturalibus, IV–V*, ed. S. Van Riet. Leiden: E. J. Brill. **Br.**

——(1972). *Avicenna Latinus. Liber de Anima, seu sextus de naturalibus I–III*, ed. S. Van Riet. Leiden: E. J. Brill. **Br.**

GIELE, M., VAN STEENBERGHEN, F., and BARZÁN, B. (eds.) (1971). *Trois Commentaires anonymes sur le Traité de l'âme d'Aristote*. Louvain: Publications Universitaires.

MICHAEL OF EPHESUS (1903). *In Parva Naturalia commentaria*, ed. P. Wendland. Commentaria in Aristotelem Graeca, vol. xxii, pt. 1. Berlin: G. Reimer.

——(1904). *In De Partibus Animalium, de Animalium Motione, de Animalium Incessu*, ed. M. Hayduck. Commentaria in Aristotelem Graeca, vol. xxii, pt. 2. Berlin: G. Reimer.

PHILOPONUS (1897). *In Aristotelis de Anima libros commentaria*, ed. M. Hayduck. Commentaria in Aristotelem Graeca, vol. xv. Berlin: G. Reimer. **Kos.**, **Ri.**, **Sor.**

PRISCIANUS LYDUS (1886). *Opera quae extant*, ed. I. Bywater. Supplementum Aristotelicum, vol. i, pt. 2. Berlin: G. Reimer.

SIMPLICIUS (1882). *In libros Aristotelis de Anima commentaria*, ed. M. Hayduck. Commentaria in Aristotelem Graeca, vol. xi. Berlin: G. Reimer. **Kos.**, **Ri.**

SOPHONIAS (1887). *In Aristotelis De Anima*, ed. M. Hayduck. Commentaria in Aristotelem Graeca, vol. xxiii, pt. 1. Berlin: G. Reimer.

THEMISTIUS (1899). *In Aristotelis De Anima*, ed. R. Heinze. Commentaria in Aristotelem Graeca, vol. v, pt. 3. Berlin: G. Reimer. **Br.**

ZABARELLA, J. (1605). *Commentaria in tres Aristotelis libros de Anima*. Venice: F. Bolzetta.

III. Secondary Literature

ACKRILL, J. L. (1965) 'Aristotle's Distinction between *Energeia* and *Kinesis*', in Bambrough (1965). **Wh.**

——(1972–3/1979) 'Aristotle's Definitions of *psuchē*', *Proceedings of the Aristotelian Society*, 73 (1972–3), 119–33=Barnes *et al.* (1979b), 65–75. **Coh.**, **Ll.**, **Sor.**, **Wh.**, **Wi.**

ALPERN, MATHEW, LAWRENCE, MERLE, and WOLSK, DAVID (1967). *Sensory Processes*. Belmont Calif.: Brooks/Cole Publishing Company. **Fre.**

ANDERSEN, ØIVIND (1976). 'Aristotle on Sense-Perception in Plants', *Symbolae Osloenses*, 51, 81–6. **Ll.**, **Sor.**

*ANNAS, JULIA (1986) 'Aristotle on Memory and the Self', in Michael Woods (ed.), *Oxford Studies in Ancient Philosophy* (*A Festschrift for J. L. Ackrill*), Oxford: Oxford University Press, 101–17.

——(forthcoming). 'Epicurus on Agency', in J. Brunschwig and M. Nussbaum (eds.), *Passions & Perceptions: Proceedings of the Fifth International Symposium on Hellenistic Philosophy*. Cambridge: Cambridge University Press.

——and BARNES, JONATHAN (eds.) (1985). *The Modes of Scepticism*. Cambridge and New York: Cambridge University Press. **Fre.**

*ANSCOMBE, G. E. M. (1965). 'Thought and Action in Aristotle', in Bambrough (1965).

*——and GEACH, P. T. (1961). *Three Philosophers*. Oxford: Clarendon Press.

ARMSTRONG, D. M. (1968). *A Materialist Theory of Mind*. London: Routledge, and section repr. in Dancy (1988). **Sor.**

AUSTIN, J. L. (1962). *Sense and Sensibilia*. Oxford: Clarendon Press. **Pu.**, **Sch.**

BALME, D. M. (1961/1975). 'Aristotle's Use of Differentiae in Zoology', originally published in S. MANSION (1961), 195–212, repr. in Barnes *et al.* (1975), 183–93. **Ll.**

——(1962). '*Genos* and *eidos* in Aristotle's Biology', *Classical Quarterly*, NS 12, 81–98. **Ll.**

——(1987a). 'Aristotle's Use of Division and Differentiae' (revised and expanded version of Balme 1961/1975), in Gotthelf–Lennox (1987), 69–89. **Li.**

——(1987b). 'Aristotle's Biology Was Not Essentialist' (revised and expanded version of article originally published in *Archiv für Geschichte der Philosophie*, 62, (1980), 1–12), in Gotthelf–Lennox (1987), 291–312. **Fre.**, **Ll.**

BAMBROUGH, R. (ed.) (1965). *New Essays on Plato and Aristotle*. London: Routledge and Kegan Paul.

*BARBOTIN, E. (1954). *La Théorie aristotélicienne de l'intellect d'après Théophraste.* Louvain: Publications universitaires de Louvain.

BARKER, A. (1981), 'Aristotle on Perception and Ratios', *Phronesis* 26, 148–66. **Fre.**

BARNES, J. (1971–2). 'Aristotle's Concept of Mind', *Proceedings of the Aristotelian Society*, 72, 101–10; repr. in Barnes *et al.* (1979*b*) 32–41. **Coh., Fre., Ll., Sor., Wi., Wit.**

—— SCHOFIELD, M., and SORABJI, R. (eds.) (1975). *Articles on Aristotle*, i: Science. London: Duckworth.

——(1979*a*). *Articles on Aristotle*, iii: *Metaphysics.*

——(1979*b*). *Articles on Aristotle*, iv: *Psychology and Aesthetics.* **Coh., Li., Sor., Wh., Wi.**

*BÄUMKER, C. (1877). *Aristoteles' Lehre von den äußern und innern Sinnesvermögen.* Leipzig: F. Schöningh.

*BEARE, J. I. (1906). *Greek Theories of Elementary Cognition.* Oxford: Clarendon Press.

BENNETT, J. (1968). 'Substance, Reality, and Primary Qualities', in C. B. Martin and D. M. Armstrong (eds.), *Locke and Berkeley: A Collection of Critical Essays*, London: Macmillan, 104–18. **Sch.**

——(1971). *Locke, Berkeley, Hume.* Oxford: Clarendon Press. **Sch.**

BERKELEY, GEORGE (1713). *Three Dialogues between Hylas and Philonous.* London: H. Clements.

BERNARD, WOLFGANG (1988). *Rezeptivität und Spontaneität der Wahrnehmung bei Aristoteles.* Baden-Baden: V. Koerner. **Ka., Sor.**

*BERTI, ENRICO (1978). 'The Intellection of Indivisibles according to Aristotle: *De Anima* III. 6', in Lloyd and Owen (1978), 141–63.

——(ed.) (1981). *Aristotle on Science.* Padua: Editrice Antenore.

*BLOCK, I. (1961*a*). 'The Order of Aristotle's Psychological Writings', *American Journal of Philology*, 82, 50–77.

*——(1961*b*). 'Truth and Error in Aristotle's Theory of Sense Perception', *Philosophical Quarterly*, 11, 1–9.

* (1964). 'Three German Commentators on the Individual Senses and the Common Sense in Aristotle', *Phronesis*, 9, 58–63.

*——(1965). 'On the Commonness of the Common Sensibles', *Australasian Journal of Philosophy*, 43, 189–95.

*——(1969). 'Aristotle and the Physical Object', *Philosophy and Phenomenological Research*, 21, 93–101.

BLOCK, NED (ed.) (1980). *Readings in Philosophy of Psychology*, i. Cambridge, Mass.: Harvard University Press. **Co. Coh. Fre.**

*BLUMENTHAL, H. J. (1976). 'Neoplatonic Elements in the *De Anima* Commentaries', *Phronesis*, 21, 64–87.

——(1977). 'Neo-Platonic Interpretations of Aristotle on Phantasia', *Review of Metaphysics*, 31, 230–41.

——and ROBINSON, H. M. (eds) (1991), *Aristotle and the Later Tradition.* **Sor.**

BOLTON, R. (1978). 'Aristotle's Definitions of the Soul: De Anima II 1–3', *Phronesis*, 23, 258–78. **Ll.**

——(1987). 'Definition and Scientific Method in Aristotle's *Posterior Analytics* and *Generation of Animals*', in Gotthelf–Lennox (1987), 120–66. **Fre., Ll.**

——(1990). 'The Epistemological Basis of Aristotelian Dialectic' in Devereux–Pellegrin (1990). **Fre., Ll.**

*Bonitz, H. (1862–7) *Aristotelische Studien*. 5 vols. Vienna: Kaiserliche Akademie der Wissenschaften. Philosophisch-historische Klasse. Sitzungsberichte. Bände 39, 41, 42, 52, 55.

Brandis, C. A. (1835–60). *Handbuch der Geschichte der griechisch-römischen Philosophie*. Berlin: G. Reimer. **Br.**

——(1862–4). *Geschichte der Entwicklung der griechischen Philosophie*. Berlin: G. Reimer. **Br.**

*Bremmer, Jan (1983). *The Early Greek Concept of the Soul*. Princeton: Princeton University Press.

Brentano, Franz (1867). *Die Psychologie des Aristoteles, inbesondere seine Lehre von NOUS POIĒTIKOS*. Mainz: Franz Kirchheim. **Br., Sor.**

——(1874). *Psychologie vom empirischen Standpunkt*. Leipzig: Duncker and Humblot. 2nd edn. rev. Oskar Kraus, Leipzig: Felix Meiner, 1924, repr. Hamburg: Meiner, 1955–9. **Sor.**

*——(1911). *Aristoteles' Lehre vom Ursprung des menschlichen Geistes*. Leipzig: Veit.

——(1973). *Psychology from an Empirical Standpoint*, trans. C. Rancurello, D. B. Terrell, Linda McAlister. London: Routledge [translation of Brentano (1874)]. **Sor.**

——(1976). *Aristotle and his World View*, ed. and trans. Roderick M. Chisholm and Rolf George. Berkeley: University of California Press. **Pu.**

——(1977). *The Psychology of Aristotle*, trans. Rolf George. Berkeley: University of California Press [translation of Brentano (1867)]. **Br., Soc.**

Burge, Tyler (1986). 'Individualism and Psychology', *Philosophical Review*, 95, 3–45. **Sor.**

Burnyeat, M. (1976). 'Plato on the Grammar of Perceiving', *Classical Quarterly*, NS 26, 29–51. **Sor.**

——(1980a). 'Can the Sceptic Live his Scepticism?', in M. Schofield, M. Burnyeat, J. Barnes (eds.), *Doubt and Dogmatism*. Oxford: Oxford University Press, ch. 2. **Sor.**

——(1980b). 'Aristotle on Learning to be Good', in A. Rorty (1980), 69–92. **Ri.**

——(1981). 'Aristotle on Understanding Knowledge', in Berti (1981), 97–139. **Fr.**

——(1983). *The Skeptical Tradition*. Berkeley: University of California Press.

Byl, S. (1968). 'Note sur la place du cœur et la valorisation de la MESOTES dans la biologie d'Aristote', *L'Antiquité classique*, 37, 467–76. **Ll.**

——(1980). *Recherches sur les grands traités biologiques d'Aristote: Sources écrites et préjugés* (Académie Royale de Belgique, *Mémoires de la Classe des Lettres*, 2nd ser. 64/3). Brussels: Palais des Académies. **Ll.**

*Bynum, Terrell Ward (1987). 'A New Look at Aristotle's Theory of Perception', *History of Philosophy Quarterly*, 4, 163–78. **Fre.**

*Bywater, I. (1888). 'Aristotelia III', *Journal of Philology*, 17, 53–74.

Carriero, J. (1984). 'Descartes and the Autonomy of Human Understanding'. Ph.D. thesis, Harvard University, Cambridge, Mass. **Pu.**

Cashdollar, S. (1973). 'Aristotle's Account of Incidental Perception', *Phronesis*, 18, 156–75. **Fr., Sor.**

*Cassirer, H. (1932). *Aristoteles' Schrift 'Von der Seele'*. Tübingen: J. C. B. Mohr.

*Chaignet, A. E. (1883). *Essai sur la psychologie d'Aristote*. Paris: Hachette.

*——(1887–93). *Histoire de la psychologie des Grecs*. Paris: Hachette.

Charles, David (1984). *Aristotle's Philosophy of Action*. Ithaca, NY: Cornell University Press. **Co., Ri.**

——(1988). 'Aristotle on Hypothetical Necessity and Irreducibility', *Pacific Philosophical Quarterly*, 69, 1–53. **Co., Sor., Fre.**

CHARLTON, WILLIE (1970). *Aristotle's Physics I–II*. Oxford: Clarendon Press. **Wh.**

——(1980). 'Aristotle's Definition of Soul', *Phronesis*, 25, 170–86. **Sor.**

CHERNISS, H. (1935). *Aristotle's Criticism of Presocratic Philosophy*. Baltimore: Johns Hopkins University Press. **Wit.**

CHISHOLM, Roderick (1957). *Perceiving: A Philosophical Study*. Ithaca, NY: Cornell University Press. **Sor.**

——(1976) *Person and Object: A Metaphysical Study*. London: Allen & Unwin. **Pu.**

CHURCHLAND, PATRICIA (1986). *Neurophilosophy: Toward a Unified Science of the Mind-Brain*. Cambridge, Mass.: MIT Press. **Pu.**

CHURCHLAND, PAUL M. (1981). 'Eliminative Materialism and Propositional Attitudes', *Journal of Philosophy*, 78, 67–90. **Pu.**

*CLARK, G. H. (1929). 'Empedocles and Anaxagoras in Aristotle's *De Anima*'. PhD thesis, University of Pennsylvania, Philadelphia.

CLARK, S. R. L. (1975). *Aristotle's Man*. Oxford: Clarendon Press. **Sch.**

*CLAUS, D. B. (1981). *Toward the Soul: An Inquiry into the Meaning of PSUCHĒ before Plato*. New Haven: Yale University Press.

CODE, A. (1976). 'The Persistence of Aristotelian Matter', *Philosophical Studies*, 29, 356–67. **Wh.**

——(1987). 'Soul as Efficient Cause in Aristotle's Embryology', *Philosophical Topics*, 15/2, 51–9. **Co., Fre., Ll.**

——(forthcoming) 'Aristotle, Searle and the Mind–Body Problem', in E. LePore and R. Van Gulick (eds.), *Essays on the Philosophy of John Searle*. Oxford: Blackwell. **Ll.**

*COHEN, S. MARC (1982). 'St. Thomas Aquinas on the Immaterial Reception of Sensible Forms', *Philosophical Review*, 91, 193–209.

——(1984). 'Aristotle's Doctrine of the Material Substrate', *Philosophical Review*, 93, 171–94. **Wh.**

——(1987). 'The Credibility of Aristotle's Philosophy of Mind', in Matthen (1987), 103–25. **Coh., Sor.**

COLLINS, ARTHUR W. (1979). 'Could our Beliefs be Representations in our Brains?', *Journal of Philosophy*, 76, 225–43. **Ka.**

COOPER, J. (1970). 'Plato on Sense Perception and Knowledge: *Theaetetus* 184–186', *Phronesis*, 15, 123–46. **Sor.**

——(1975). Review of Sorabji (1972), *Archiv für Geschichte der Philosophie*, 57, 63–9. **An.**

——(1988). 'Metaphysics in Aristotle's Embryology', *Proceedings of the Cambridge Philological Society*, NS 34, 14–41.

CORNFORD, F. M. (1935). *Plato's Theory of Knowledge*. London: Kegan Paul. **Sch.**

*CORTE, M. DE (1932). 'Notes exégétiques sur la théorie aristotélicienne du Sensus Communis', *New Scholasticism*. 6, 187–214.

CRANE, TIMOTHY (1988). 'The Waterfall Illusion', *Analysis*, 48, 142–7. **Sor.**

——(1989). 'The Content and Causation of Thought'. Ph.D. Diss., Cambridge. **Sor.**

DANCY, JONATHAN (1988). *Perceptual Knowledge*. Oxford: Oxford University Press. **Sor.**

DAVIDSON, DONALD (1982). 'Rational Animals', *Dialectica*, 36, 318–27 [repr. in LePore–McLaughlin (1985), 472–80]. **Ri., Sor.**

——and HINTIKKA, K. J. J. (eds.) (1969). *Words and Objections*. Dordrecht: D. Reidel Publishing Co. **Sch.**

*DeGroot, Jean Christensen (1983). 'Philoponus on *de Anima* II. 5, *Physics* III. 3, and the Propagation of Light', *Phronesis*, 28, 177–96.

Dennett, D. (1976). 'Conditions of Personhood', in A. Rorty (ed.), *The Identities of Persons*. Berkeley and Los Angeles: University of California Press, ch. 7. **Sor.**

——(1987). *The Intentional Stance*. Cambridge, Mass.: MIT Press. **Pu.**

Descartes, R. (1637–41). *The Philosophical Works of Descartes*, ed. and trans. E. S. Haldane and G. R. T. Ross (1967). Cambridge: Cambridge University Press. **Ma., Wi.**

——(1897–1913). *Œuvres de Descartes*, ed. Ch. Adam and P. Tannery. Paris: J. Vrin. **Ka.**

——(1641). *Descartes: Philosophical Letters*, ed. and trans. A. J. P. Kenny (1970). Oxford: Clarendon Press. **Wi.**

Devereux, Daniel T., and Pellegrin, Pierre (eds.). (1990). *Biologie, logique et métaphysique chez Aristote*. Paris: Éditions du CNRS. **Fre., Ll.**

*Dodds, E. R. (1963). *The Greeks and the Irrational*. Berkeley and Los Angeles: University of California Press.

*Dörrie, H. (1961). 'Gedanken zur Methodik des Aristoteles in der Schrift PERI PSUCHĒS', in S. Mansion (1961[a]) 223–44.

Dretske, F. (1981). *Knowledge and the Flow of Information*. Cambridge, Mass.: MIT Press. **Sor.**

Düring, I. (1956). 'Ariston or Hermippus?', *Classica et Mediaevalia*, 17, 11–21. **Nu.**

*Easterling, H. J. (1966). 'A Note on *De Anima* 413^{a}8–9', *Phronesis*, 11, 159–62.

Ebert, Theo (1983). 'Aristotle on What is Done in Perceiving', *Zeitschrift für philosophische Forschung*, 37, 181–98. **Sor.**

Eckardt, B. Von (1988). 'Mental Images and their Explanations', *Philosophical Studies*, 58, 44–60. **Fr.**

Ellis, John (1990). 'The Trouble with Fragrance', *Phronesis*, 35, 290–302. **Sor.**

*Engmann, J. (1976). 'Imagination and Truth in Aristotle', *Journal of the History of Philosophy*, 14, 259–65.

Evans, G. (1982). *The Varieties of Reference*. Oxford: Oxford University Press. **Sor.**

Everson, S. (ed.) (1991). *Psychology*. Companion to Ancient Thought. Cambridge: Cambridge University Press.

Fabricius, Johann Albert (1790–1809). *Bibliotheca Graeca sive notitia scriptorum veterum Graecorum*, 4th edn. rev. Gottlieb Christoph Harles, 12 vols. Hamburg. **Nu.**

*Finamore, J. (1989). 'Intellect and Common Sense in Aristotle's *De Anima* III. 7', *Syllecta Classica*, 1.

Fodor, J. (1981). *Representations*. Brighton: Harvester Press. **Wi.**

——(1983). *The Modularity of Mind*. Cambridge, Mass.: MIT Press. **Sor.**

*Fortenbaugh, W. W. (1968). 'A Note on *De Anima* 412^{b}19–20', *Phronesis*, 13, 88–9.

——(1971). 'Aristotle: Animals, Emotion and Moral Virtue', *Arethusa*, 4, 137–65. **Sor.**

——(1984). *Quellen zur Ethik Theophrasts*. Amsterdam: Grüner. **Sor.**

Frede, M. (1983). 'Stoics and Sceptics on Clear and Distinct Impressions', in M. Burnyeat (1983) [repr. in Frede (1987*a*), 151–76]. **Sor.**

——(1985). 'Substance in Aristotle's Metaphysics', in Gotthelf (1985*a*), 17–26. **Ll.**

——(1987*a*). *Essays in Ancient Philosophy*. Oxford: Oxford University Press.

——(1987*b*). 'Observations on Perception in Plato's Later Dialogues', in Frede (1987*a*), 3–8. **Sor.**

——(1989). 'An Empiricist View of Knowledge: Memorism', in S. Everson (ed.) *A*

Philosophical Introduction to Ancient Epistemology. Cambridge: Cambridge University Press. **Sor.**

——(1990). 'The Definition of Sensible Substance in *Metaphysics* Z', in Devereux–Pellegrin (1990). **Ll.**

FREELAND, CYNTHIA A. (1987*a*). 'Aristotle on Bodies, Matter, and Potentiality', in Gotthelf–Lennox (1987), 392–406.

——(1987*b*). 'Aristotle on Possibilities and Capacities', *Ancient Philosophy*, 6, 69–89. **Fre.**

FREUDENTHAL, J. (1863). *Über den Begriff des Wortes phantasia bei Aristoteles*. Göttingen: A. Rente. **Fr. Sch.**

FURLEY, D. J. (1967). *Two Studies in the Greek Atomists*. Princeton: Princeton University Press.

——(1978). 'Self Movers', in Lloyd–Owen (1978), 165–79, repr. in A. Rorty (1980). **Ri.**

——(1983). 'The Mechanics of *Meteorologica*, iv: A Prolegomenon to Biology', in P. Moraux and J. Weisner (eds.), *Zweifelhaftes im Corpus Aristotelicum: Studien zu einigen Dubia. Akten des 9. Symposium Aristotelicum*. Berlin: de Gruyter. **Wh.**

FURTH, M. (1978). 'Transtemporal Stability in Aristotelian Substances', *Journal of Philosophy*, 75, 625–46. **Wi.**

——(1987). 'Aristotle's Biological Universe: An Overview', in Gotthelf–Lennox (1987), 21–52. **Fre.**

——(1988). *Substance, Form and Psyche: An Aristotelean Metaphysics*. Cambridge: Cambridge University Press.

——(1990). 'Specific and Individual Form in Aristotle', in Devereux–Pellegrin (1990). **Fre.**

*GALLOP, DAVID (1989). 'Aristotle on Sleep, Dreams, and Final Causes', *Proceedings of the Boston Area Colloquium in Ancient Philosophy*, ed. John J. Cleary and D. Sharten. Lanham, Md.: University Press of America, 257–90 (with commentary by Ronald Polansky, 291–302.) **Ll.**

GEACH, PETER (1957). *Mental Acts: Their Content and their Objects*. London: Routledge & Kegan Paul. **Sor.**

GEERTZ, CLIFFORD. (1973). 'The Growth of Culture and the Evolution of Mind', in *The Interpretation of Cultures*. New York: Basic Books. **Ka.**

GIBSON, JAMES J. (1966). *The Senses Considered as Perceptual Systems*. Boston: Houghton Mifflin Company. **Fre.**

GILL, C. (1991). 'Is there a Concept of Person in Greek Philosophy?', in Everson (1991) 266–313. **Sor.**

GILL, M. L. (1989). *Aristotle on Substance: The Paradox of Unity*. Princeton: Princeton University Press. **Wh.**

GLIDDEN, DAVID (1984). 'Aristotelian Perception and the Hellenistic Problem of Representation', *Ancient Philosophy*, 4, 119–31. **Sor.**

GÖDEL, KURT (1964). 'What is Cantor's Continuum Problem?', in P. Benacerraf and H. Putnam (eds.), *Philosophy of Mathematics*, Englewood Cliffs, NJ: Prentice-Hall. **Ka.**

GOODMAN, N. (1972). 'Seven Strictures on Similarity', in *Problems and Projects*. Indianapolis, Ind.: Bobbs Merrill. **Pu.**

GOTTHELF, A. (ed.) (1985*a*). *Aristotle On Nature and Living Things*. Pittsburgh: Mathesis Publications.

——(1985*b*). 'Notes towards a Study of Substance and Essence in Aristotle's *Parts of Animals* ii-iv', in Gotthelf (1985*a*), 27–54. **Ll.**

——(1987). 'First Principles in Aristotle's *Parts of Animals*', in Gotthelf–Lennox (1987), 167–98. **Ll.**

——(1989). 'The Place of the Good in Aristotle's Natural Teleology', *Proceedings of the Boston Area Colloquium in Ancient Philosophy*, ed. John J. Cleary and D. Sharten. Lanham Md.: University Press of America. **Ri.**

——and LENNOX, J. G. (eds.) (1987). *Philosophical Issues in Aristotle's Biology.* Cambridge: Cambridge University Press. **Ll.**

*GOTTSCHALK, H. B. (1964). 'The *De Coloribus* and its Author', *Hermes*, 92, 59–85.

*——(1968). 'The *De Audibilibus* and Peripatetic Acoustics', *Hermes*, 96, 435–60.

*——(1971). 'Soul as Harmonia', *Phronesis*, 16, 179–98.

*GRAESER, ANDREAS (1978). 'On Aristotle's Framework of *Sensibilia*', in Lloyd–Owen (1978), 69–97. **Fre.**

GRICE, H. P. (1961). 'The Causal Theory of Perception', *Proceedings of the Aristotelian Society*, Suppl. vol. 35, 121–6. **Sch.**

HACKFORTH, R. (1945). *Plato's Examination of Pleasure.* Cambridge: Cambridge University Press. **Sch.**

*HAMELIN, O. (1953). *La Théorie de l'intellect d'après Aristote et ses commentateurs.* Paris: J. Vrin.

HAMLYN, D. W. (1959). 'Aristotle's Account of Aisthēsis in the *De Anima*', *Classical Quarterly*, ns 9, 6–16. **Sor.**

*——(1961). *Sensation and Perception.* London: Routledge & Kegan Paul.

*——(1965). 'Seeing Things as they Are', Inaugural Lecture at Birkbeck College, London.

*——(1968). 'Koinē *aisthēsis*', *The Monist*, 52, 195–200.

*HARDIE, W. F. R. (1964). 'Aristotle's Treatment of the Relation between the Soul and the Body', *Philosophical Quarterly*, 14, 53–72.

*——(1964–5) 'Aristotle's Doctrine that Virtue is a Mean', *Proceedings of the Aristotelian Society*, 65, 53–72.

*——(1968). *Aristotle's Ethical Theory.* Oxford: Clarendon Press. 2nd edition, 1980.

*——(1976). 'Concepts of Consciousness in Aristotle', *Mind*, 85, 388–411.

HARMAN, GILBERT (1973). *Thought.* Princeton: Princeton University Press. **Co., Fre.**

HARTMAN, EDWIN (1977). *Substance, Body, and Soul: Aristotelian Investigations.* Princeton: Princeton University Press. **Coh., Sor.**

*HARVEY, P. (1978). 'Aristotle on Truth and Falsity in De Anima 3. 6.', *Journal of the History of Philosophy*, 16, 219–20.

HINTIKKA, K. J. J. (1966). 'Aristotelian Infinity', *Philosophical Review*, 75, 197–218.

HUBEL, D. H., and WIESEL, T. N. (1962). 'Receptive Fields of Single Neurones in the Cat's Striate Cortex', *Journal of Physiology*, 148, 579–91. **Pu.**

——(1974). 'Receptive Fields, Binocular Interaction and Functional Architecture in the Cat's Striate Cortex', *Journal of Physiology*, 160, 106–54. **Pu.**

HUBY, P. (1975). 'Aristotle, *De Insomniis* 462ᵃ18', *Classical Quarterly*, ns 25, 151–2. **Sor.**

HUDSON, STEPHEN D. (1981). 'Reason and Motivation in Aristotle', *Canadian Journal of Philosophy*, 11, 111–35. **Ri.**

HUME, D. (1739–40). *A Treatise of Human Nature*, ed. L. A. Selby-Bigge (1965). Oxford: Clarendon Press. **Wi.**

——(1748). *An Enquiry Concerning Human Understanding*, ed. L. A. Selby-Bigge (1963). Oxford: Clarendon Press. **Wi.**

INWOOD, B. (1985). *Ethics and Human Action in Early Stoicism.* Oxford: Oxford University Press. **Sor.**

IRWIN, T. H. (1981). 'Homonymy in Aristotle', *Review of Metaphysics*, 34, 523–44. **Wh.**

——(1988). *Aristotle's First Principles.* Oxford: Oxford University Press. **Ri., Wh.**

——(1991). 'Aristotle's Philosophy of Mind', in Everson (1991). **Wh.**

ISHIGURO, H. (1966). 'Imagination', in B. Williams and M. Montefiore (eds.), *British Analytical Philosophy.* London: Routledge & Kegan Paul, 244–57. **Sch.**

——(1967). 'Imagination', *Proceedings of the Aristotelian Society.* Suppl. vol. 41, 37–56. **Sch.**

JACKSON, F. (1977). *Perception.* Cambridge: Cambridge University Press. **Sor.**

JEFFREY, RICHARD (1985). 'Animal Interpretation', in LePore–McLaughlin (1985), 481–7. **Ri.**

JONES, B. (1974). 'Aristotle's Introduction of Matter', *Philosophical Review*, 83, 474–500. **Wh.**

JOYNT, R. J. (1981). 'Are Two Heads Better than One?', *Behavioral and Brain Sciences*, 4, 108–9. **Wi.**

KAHN, C. (1966). 'Sensation and Consciousness in Aristotle's Psychology', *Archiv für Geschichte der Philosophie*, 48, 43–81. **Fr., Ka., Wi.**

——(1981). 'The Role of *nous* in the Cognition of First Principles in Posterior Analytics II. 19', in Berti (1981). **Kos.**

KAL, V. (1988). *On Intuition and Discursive Reasoning in Aristotle.* Leiden: E. J. Brill. **Ri.**

KAPLAN, D. (1969). 'Quantifying In', in Davidson–Hintikka (1969), 206–42. **Sch.**

KATZ, DAVID (1925). *Der Aufbau der Tastwelt. Zeitschrift für Psychologie and Physiologie der Sinnesorgane*, Erganzungsband. Leipzig: J. A. Barth.

KEANEY, J. (1963). 'Two Notes on the Tradition of Aristotle's Writings', *American Journal of Philology*, 84, 52–63. **Nu.**

KIM, J. (1982). 'Psychophysical Supervenience', *Philosophical Studies*, 41, 51–71. **Pu.**

——(1984). 'Concepts of Supervenience', *Philosophy and Phenomenological Research*, 14, 153–4. **Pu.**

KITCHER, PATRICIA (1988). 'Marr's Conceptual Theory of Vision', *Philosophy of Science*, 55, 1–25. **Co., Fre.**

KLEUTGEN, J. (1960). *Die Philosophie der Vorzeit vertheidigt.* Münster: Theissingsche Buchhandlung. **Br.**

KNEALE, WILLIAM and MARTHA (1962). *The Development of Logic.* Oxford: Clarendon Press. **Sor.**

*KOSMAN, L. A. (1973). 'Understanding, Explanation and Insight in the *Posterior Analytics*', in E. N. Lee, A. P. D. Mourelatos, and R. M. Rorty (eds.), *Exegesis and Argument. Phronesis*, Suppl. 1, 374–92.

——(1975). 'Perceiving that we Perceive: On the Soul III, 2', *Philosophical Review*, 84, 499–519. **Bu., Coh., Kos.**

——(1984). 'Substance, Being, and *Energeia*', in J. Annas (ed.), *Oxford Studies in Ancient Philosophy*, 2, 121–49. **Wh.**

——(1987). 'Animals and Other Beings in Aristotle', in Gotthelf–Lennox (1987), 360–91. **Fre., Ll.**

——(1988). 'Divine Being and Divine Thinking in *Metaphysics* Lambda', in *Proceedings of the Boston Area Colloquium in Ancient Philosophy*, iii, ed. John J. Cleary. Lanham, Md.: University Press of America. **Kos.**

——(1990). 'Necessity and Explanation in Aristotle's *Analytics*', in Devereux–Pellegrin (1990). **Fre.**

*KUCHARSKI, P. (1954). 'Sur la théorie des couleurs et des saveurs dans le De Sensu aristotélicien', *Revue des études grecques*, 67, 355–90.

KULLMAN, W. (1974). *Wissenschaft und Methode*. Berlin: De Gruyter. **Ll.**

LABARRIERE, JEAN-LOUIS (1984). 'Imagination humaine et imagination animale chez Aristote', *Phronesis*, 29, 17–49. **Fre., Ri., Sch., Sor.**

——(1990). 'De la phronesis animale', in Devereux–Pellegrin (1990). **Fre.**

——(forthcoming), 'Phantasia et logos chez les animaux', in J. Brunschwig and M. Nussbaum, eds., *Passions & Perceptions: Proceedings of the Fifth International Symposium on Hellenistic Philosophy*. Cambridge: Cambridge University Press. **Sor.**

*LANG, HELEN S. (1980). 'On Memory. Aristotle's Corrections of Plato', *Journal of the History of Philosophy*, 18, 379–93.

LEAR, J. (1988). *Aristotle and the Desire to Understand*. Cambridge: Cambridge University Press. **Li., Sor.**

*LEFEVRE, C. (1972). *Sur l'évolution d'Aristote en psychologie*. Louvain: Publications universitaires de Louvain.

*——(1978). 'Sur le statut de l'âme dans le De Anima et les Parva Naturalia', in Lloyd–Owen (1978), 21–67.

*LEIGHTON, STEPHEN (1982). 'Aristotle on the Emotions', *Phronesis*, 27, 144–74.

LENNOX, J. G. (1980). 'Aristotle on Genera, Species, and "the More and the Less"', *Journal of the History of Biology*, 13, 321–46. **Ll.**

——(1985). 'Demarcating Ancient Science: A Discussion of G. E. R. Lloyd, *Science, Folklore and Ideology: The Life Sciences in Ancient Greece*', *Oxford Studies in Ancient Philosophy*, 3, 307–24. **Fre.**

——(1987a). 'Divide and Explain: The *Posterior Analytics* in Practice', in Gotthelf–Lennox (1987) 90–119. **Ll.**

——(1987b). 'Kinds, Forms of Kinds, and the More and the Less in Aristotle's Biology' (revised version of Lennox 1980), in Gotthelf–Lennox (1987), 339–59. **Ll.**

——(forthcoming). 'What is Natural History?', in A. C. Bowen (ed.), *Science and Philosophy in Classical Greece*. Pittsburgh: Mathesis Publications. **Ll.**

LEPORE, ERNEST, and MCLAUGHLIN, BRIAN (eds.) (1985). *Actions and Events: Perspectives on the Philosophy of Donald Davidson*. Oxford: Basil Blackwell. **Ri.**

*LESHER, J. H. (1973). 'The Meaning of *nous* in the *Posterior Analytics*', *Phronesis*, 18, 44–68.

LEWIS, D. (1983). *Philosophical Papers*. Oxford: Oxford University Press. **Pu.**

*LLOYD, A. C. (1962). 'Genus, Species and Ordered Series in Aristotle', *Phronesis*, 7, 69–70.

*——(1964). 'Nosce teipsum and conscientia', *Archiv für Geschichte der Philosophie*, 46, 188–200.

*——(1969–70). 'Non-Discursive Thought—An Enigma of Greek Philosophy', *Proceedings of the Aristotelian Society*, 70, 261–74.

LLOYD, G. E. R. (1966). *Polarity and Analogy*. Cambridge: Cambridge University Press. **Ll.**

——(1978). 'The Empirical Basis of the Physiology of the *Parva Naturalia*', in Lloyd–Owen (1978), 215–39. **Ll.**

——(1979). *Magic, Reason and Experience*. Cambridge: Cambridge Unviersity Press. **Ll.**

——(1983). *Science, Folklore and Ideology*. Cambridge: Cambridge University Press. **Fre., Ll.**

——(1990). 'Aristotle's Zoology and his Metaphysics: The Status Quaestionis', in Devereux–Pellegrin (1990). **Ll.**

LLOYD, G. E. R., and OWEN, G. E. L. (1978). *Aristotle on Mind and the Senses: Proceedings of the Seventh Symposium Aristotelicum*. Cambridge: Cambridge University Press. **Ri.**

LOCKE, JOHN (1706). *An Essay Concerning Human Understanding*. 5th and rev. edn., repr. New York: Everyman's Library, Dutton, 1961.

LOENIG, RICHARD (1903). *Die Zurechnungslehre des Aristoteles*. Jena: G. Fischer, repr. Hildesheim: Georg Olms, 1967. **Ri.**

LONG, A. A. (1971). 'Language and Thought in Stoicism', in id. (ed.), *Problems in Stoicism*. London: Athlone Press, ch. 5. **Sor.**

*——(1982). 'Soul and Body in Stoicism', *Phronesis*, 27, 34–57.

——and SEDLEY, D. N. (1987). *The Hellenistic Philosophers*, i. Cambridge: Cambridge University Press. **Sor.**

*LOUIS, P. (1952). 'Le traité d'Aristote sur la nutrition', *Revue de philologie*, 3rd ser., 26, 29–35.

*LOWE, MALCOLM (1978). 'Aristotle's *De Somno* and his Theory of Causes', *Phronesis*, 23, 279–91.

*——(1983). 'Aristotle on Kinds of Thinking', *Phronesis*, 28, 17–30.

*LYCOS, K. (1964). 'Aristotle and Plato on Appearing', *Mind*, 73, 496–514.

*MANNING, RITA (1985). 'Materialism, Dualism and Functionalism in Aristotle's Philosophy of Mind', *Apeiron*, 19, 11–23.

*MANSION, A. (1953). 'L'immortalité de l'âme et de l'intellect d'après Aristotle', *Revue philosophique de Louvain*, 51, 444–72.

MANSION, S. (ed.) (1961*a*). *Aristote et les problèmes de méthode*. Louvain: Publications universitaires de Louvain.

*——(1961*b*). 'Le rôle de l'exposé et de la critique des philosophes antérieurs chez Aristote', in Mansion (1961*a*), 35 56.

*——(1973). 'Deux définitions différentes de la vie chez Aristote', *Revue philosophique de Louvain*, 71, 425–50.

*——(1978). 'Soul and Life in the *De Anima*', in Lloyd–Owen (1978), 1–20.

MARR, D. C. (1982). *Vision: A Computational Investigation into the Human Representation and Processing of Visual Information*. San Francisco: Freeman. **Pu.**

MATES, BENSON (1961). *Stoic Logic*. Berkeley: University of California Press. **Sor.**

MATSON, WALLACE I. (1966). 'Why isn't the Mind—Body Problem Ancient?', in P. K. Feyerabend and G. Maxwell (eds.), *Mind, Matter and Method*. Minneapolis: University of Minnesota. **Sor.**

MATTHEN, MOHAN (1987). *Aristotle Today: Essays on Aristotle's Ideal of Science*. Edmonton, Alta.: Academic Printing and Publishing. **Coh.**

*MATTHEWS, G. B. (1977). 'Consciousness and Life', *Philosophy*, 52, 13–26.

MAUDLIN, TIM (1986). 'De Anima III, 1: Any Sense Missing?' *Phronesis*, 31, 51–67. **Fre.**

MILLAR, A. (1985–6). 'What's in a Book?' *Proceedings of the Aristotelian Society*, 86, 83–97. **Sor.**

*MODRAK, D. (1976). '*Aisthēsis* in the Practical Syllogism', *Philosophical Studies*, 30, 379–91.

*——(1981*a*). 'An Aristotelian Theory of Consciousness?' *Ancient Philosophy*, 1, 160–70.

*——(1981*b*). 'Aristotle on Knowing First Principles', *Philosophical Inquiry*, 3, 63–83.

*——(1981*c*). '*Koinē Aisthēsis* and the Discrimination of Sensible Differences in *De Anima* III. 2', *Canadian Journal of Philosophy*, 11, 405–23.

MODRAK, D. (1986). '*Phantasia* Reconsidered', *Archiv für Geschichte der Philosophie*, 66, 47–69. **Fr., Sch.**

——(1987*a*). *Aristotle. The Power of Perception.* Chicago: University of Chicago Press. **Fr., Fre., Ka., Pu., Ri., Sch., Wh.**

*——(1987*b*). 'Aristotle on Thinking', *Proceedings of the Boston Area Colloquium in Ancient Philosophy*, ii, ed. John J. Cleary. Lanham, Md.: University Press of America, 209–36 (with commentary by Cynthia Freeland, 237–41).

MORAUX, Paul (1951). *Les Listes anciennes des ouvrages d'Aristote.* Louvain: Publications universitaires de Louvain.

*——(1955). 'A propos de *nous thurathen* chez Aristote', *Autour d'Aristote: Recueil d'études offerts à Mgr. A. Mansion.* Louvain: Publications universitaires de Louvain.

*——(1978). 'Le *De Anima* dans la tradition grecque. Quelques aspects de l'interprétation du traité, de Théophraste à Themistius', in Lloyd–Owen (1978), 281–324.

MORAVCSIK, JULIUS (1974). 'Aristotle on Adequate Explanation', *Synthese*, 28, 3–17. **Co., Fre.**

*MUELLER, I. (1970). 'Aristotle on Geometrical Objects', *Archiv für Geschichte der Philosophie*, 52, 156–7 [repr. in Barnes, *et al.* (1979*a*)].

*NEUHAUSER, J. (1878). *Aristoteles' Lehre von dem sinnlichen Erkenntnißvermögen und seinen Organen.* Leipzig: Weiss.

NUSSBAUM, M. (1975). 'Aristotle's *De Motu Animalium*'. Ph.D. Diss. Harvard University. **Nu.**

——(1976). 'The Text of Aristotle's *De Motu Animalium*', *Harvard Studies in Classical Philology.* **Nu., Pu.**

——(1978). *Aristotle's De Motu Animalium.* Princeton: Princeton University Press. **Bu., Nu., Pu.**

——(1981). Review of Rudolf Kassel, *Der Text der aristotelischen Rhetorik* and id. (ed.), *Aristotelis Ars Rhetorica. Archiv für Geschichte der Philosophie.* 63, 346–51. **Nu.**

——(1982*a*). 'Saving Aristotle's Appearances', in Malcolm Schofield and Martha Nussbaum (eds.), *Language and Logos.* Cambridge: Cambridge University Press. **Pu.**

——(1982*b*). 'Aristotle', in T. J. Luce (ed.) *Ancient Writers.* New York: Charles Scribner's Sons, 377–416. **Pu.**

——(1983). 'The "Common Explanation" of Animal Motion', in P. Moraux and J. Wiesner (eds.), *Zweifelhaftes im Corpus Aristotelicum: Studien zu einigen Dubia, Akten des 9. Symposium Aristotelicum.* Berlin: de Gruyter. **Pu., Ri.**

——(1984). 'Aristotelian Dualism: Reply to Howard Robinson', in J. Annas (ed.), *Oxford Studies in Ancient Philosophy*, 2, 197–207. **Coh., Pu., Wit.**

——(1986). *The Fragility of Goodness: Luck and Ethics in Greek Tragedy and Philosophy.* Cambridge: Cambridge University Press. **Pu., Ri.**

——(1987). 'The Stoics on the Extirpation of the Passions', *Apeiron*, 20, 129–77. **Pu.**

NUYENS, F. (1973) *L'Evolution de la psychologie d'Aristote.* Louvain: Institut Supérieur de Philosophie. (Originally publ. in Dutch, 1939: *Ontwikkelingsmomenten in de zielkunde van Aristoteles: Een historisch-philosophische studie.*) Nijmegen: Dekker & van de Vegt. **Nu.**

*OEHLER, K. (1962). *Die Lehre vom noetischen und dianoetischen Denken bei Platon und*

Aristoteles. Zweither Abschnitt, 'Die Aristotelische Psychologie des Urteils'. *Zetemata*, 29, 151–69. Munich: Beck.

*ONIANS, R. B. (1951). *The Origins of European Thought*. Cambridge: Cambridge University Press.

*OSTENFELD, ERIK (1987). *Ancient Greek Psychology and the Modern Mind–Body Debate*. Aarhus: Aarhus University Press.

OWEN, G. E. L. (1961). 'Tithenai ta phainomena', in S. Mansion (1961), 83–103; repr. in Owen (1986), 239–51. **Pu.**

——(1978–9). 'Particular and General', *Proceedings of the Aristotelian Society*, 79, 1–21; repr. in Owen (1986), 279–94. **Pu.**

——(1986). *Logic, Science, and Dialectic: Collected Papers in Greek Philosophy*. London: Duckworth. **Pu.**

OWENS JOSEPH (1976). 'A Note on Aristotle, *De Anima* III 4, 429^{b}9', *Phoenix*, 30, 109–18. **Ka.**

——(1980). 'Form and Cognition in Aristotle', *Ancient Philosophy*, 1, 17–28.

*PECK, A. L. (1953). 'The Connate Pneuma: An Essential Factor in Aristotle's Solutions to the Problems of Reproduction and Sensation', in E. A. Underwood (ed.), *Science, Medicine and History: Essays in Honour of Charles Singer*. Oxford: Clarendon Press, i. 111–21.

PEACOCKE, CHRISTOPHER (1986). 'Analogue Content', *Proceedings of the Aristotelian Society*, Suppl. vol. 60, 1–17. **Sor.**

——(1989). 'What are Concepts?', *Midwest Studies in Philosophy*, 14, 1–28. **Sor.**

——(forthcoming). 'Perceptual Content', in Festschrift for David Kaplan, ed. J. Almog, J. Perry, H. Wettstein. **Sor.**

PEGIS, A. (1974). 'The Separated Soul and Its Nature in St. Thomas', in Armand A. Maurer (ed.), *St. Thomas Aquinas: 1274–1974, Commemorative Studies*. Toronto: Pontifical Institute of Medieval Studies, i. 131–58. **Pu.**

PELLEGRIN, P. (1986). *Aristotle's Classification of Animals*, trans. A. Preus. Berkeley: University of California Press [originally publ. as *La Classification des animaux chez Aristote*, Paris: Les Belles Lettres, 1982]. **Ll.**

——(1985). 'Aristotle: A Zoology without Species', in Gotthelf (1985a), 95–115. **Ll.**

PITCHER, GEORGE (1971). *A Theory of Perception*. Princeton: Princeton University Press. **Sor.**

PLEZIA, M. (1946). *De Andronici Rhodii Studiis Aristotelicis*. Archiwum Filologiczne, 20. Kraków: Polska Akademia Umiejectności. **Nu.**

*POPPELREUTER, H. (1892). *Zur Psychologie des Aristoteles, Theophrast, Strato*. Leipzig. (Dissertation.)

*PREUS, A. (1968). '*On Dreams* 2, 459^{b}24–460^{a}33, and Aristotle's *Opsis*', *Phronesis*, 13, 175–82.

PRANTL, CARL (1855–70). *Geschichte der Logik*, 4 vols. Munich: Hirzel. **Br.**

PUTNAM, HILARY (1966). 'The Mental Life of Some Machines', repr. in Putnam (1975). **Co., Coh., Fre.**

——(1975). 'Philosophy and our Mental Life', *Mind, Language, and Reality: Philosophical Papers*, ii. 291–303. Cambridge: Cambridge University Press. **Bu., Coh., Pu., Sor., Wh.**

——(1983). 'Computational Psychology and Interpretation Theory', *Philosophical Papers*, iii. Cambridge: Cambridge University Press. **Ka.**

——(1988). *Representation and Reality*. Cambridge, Mass: MIT Press. **Pu.**

QUINE, W. V. (1960). *Word and Object*. Cambridge, Mass: MIT Press. **Nu., Pu.**

——(1969). 'Replies', in Davidson–Hintikka (1969), 292–352. **Sch.**

RAVAISSON-MOLLIEN, F. (1837–46). *Essai sur la métaphysique d'Aristote*. 2 vols. Paris: J. Vrin. [*Fragments de Tome III* published posthumously. Paris: J. Vrin, 1953.]. **Br.**

*REES, D. A. (1957). 'Bipartition of the Soul in the Early Academy', *Journal of Hellenic Studies*, 77, 112–18.

*——(1960). 'Theories of the Soul in the Early Aristotle', in I. Düring and G. E. L. Owen (eds.), *Aristotle and Plato in the Mid-Fourth Century: Papers of the Symposium Aristotelicum held at Oxford in August 1957*. Studia Graeca et Latina Gothoburgensia, ii. Göteborg: Institute of Classical Studies of the University of Göteborg.

*——(1971). 'Aristotle's Treatment of Phantasia', in J. Anton and G. Kustas (eds.), *Essays in Ancient Greek Philosophy*. Albany: State University of New York Press. **Sch.**

RENAN, E. (1852a). *De philosophia peripatetica apud Syros commentatio historica*. Paris: A. Durand. **Br.**

——(1852b). *Averroès et l'averroïsme*. Paris: A. Durand. **Br.**

RICHARDSON, HENRY (1990). 'Measurement, Pleasure, and Practical Science in Plato's *Protagoras*', *Journal of the History of Philosophy*, 28, 7–32. **Ri.**

*RIST, J. (1966). 'Notes on Aristotle, *De Anima* 3. 5', *Classical Philology*, 61, 8–20.

ROBINSON, HOWARD (1978). 'Mind and Body in Aristotle', *Classical Quarterly*, 28, 105–24. **Sor.**

——(1983). 'Aristotelian Dualism', *Oxford Studies in Ancient Philosophy*, i. 123–44. **Sor.**

RORTY, AMÉLIE O. (ed.) (1980). *Essays on Aristotle's Ethics*. Berkeley: University of California Press. **Ri.**

RORTY, R. (1970). 'Cartesian Epistemology and Changes in Ontology', in J. E. Smith (ed.), *Contemporary American Philosophy*, 273–92. London: Allen and Unwin. **Wi.**

——(1980). *Philosophy and the Mirror of Nature*. Oxford: Basil Blackwell. **Wi.**

ROSEN, S. H. (1961). 'Thought and Touch: A Note on Aristotle's *De Anima*', *Phronesis*, 6, 127–37.

ROSENMEYER, T. G. (1986). '*Phantasia* und Einbildungskraft', *Poetica*, 18, 197–248. **Fr.**

ROSS, W. D. (1923). *Aristotle's Man*. London: Methuen. **Sch.**

RÜSCHE, E. (1930). *Blut, Leben und Seele*. Paderborn: F. Schöningh. **Ll.**

RUSSELL, J. (1984). *Explaining Mental Life*. London: Macmillan. **Wi.**

RYLE, G. (1949). *The Concept of Mind*. London: Hutchinson, repr. Harmondsworth: Penguin, 1963. **Sch.**

*SAMBURSKY, S. (1958). 'Philoponus' Interpretation of Aristotle's Theory of Light', *Osiris*, 13, 114–26.

SCHEERER, E. (1984). 'Motor Theories of Cognitive Structure: A Historical Review', in W. Prinz and A. F. Sanders (eds.), *Cognition and Motor Processes*. Berlin: Springer-Verlag, 77–98. **Wi.**

——(1987). 'Muscle Sense and Innervation Feelings: A Chapter in the History of Perception and Action', in H. Heuer and A. F. Sanders (eds.), *Issues in Perception and Action*. Hillsdale, NJ: Erlbaum Associates. **Wi.**

SCHIFF, WILLIAM, and FOULKE, EMERSON (1982). *Tactual Perception: A Sourcebook*. Cambridge: Cambridge University Press. **Fre.**

SCHOFIELD, M. (1979). 'Aristotle on the Imagination', in J. Barnes et al. (1979b), 103–32 (= above, ch. 14). **Fr.**

*SCHOLAR, M. (1971). 'Aristotle's *Metaphysics* 1010^{b}1–3', *Mind*, 80, 266–8.

SCRUTON, R. (1974). *Art and Imagination.* London: Methuen. **Sch.**

SEARLE, JOHN R. (1980). 'Minds, Brains, and Programs', *Behavioral and Brain Sciences* 3, 417–24. **Ka.**

AL-SHAHRASTANI (1846). *Book of Religious and Philosophical Sects,* ed. and trans. William Cureton. London: Society for the Publication of Oriental Texts. **Br.**

SHERRICK, CARL E., and CRAIG, JAMES C. (1982). 'The Psychophysics of Touch', in Schiff and Foulke (1982), 55–81. **Fre.**

SHIELDS, CHRISTOPHER (unpublished). 'The Homonymy of the Body in Aristotle'. **Wh.**

——(1988). 'Soul and Body in Aristotle', in J. Annas (ed.), *Oxford Studies in Ancient Philosophy,* vi. Oxford: Oxford University Press, 103–37. **Wit.**

——(forthcoming). 'The First Functionalist', presented at the APA Pacific Division meetings in Portland Oregon in March 1988, and forthcoming in J.-C. Smith (ed.), *The Historical Foundations of Cognitive Science.* **Coh., Wh.**

SHINER, R. (1970). 'More on Aristotle, *De Anima* 414ª4–14', *Phoenix,* 24, 29–38.

SHORTER, J. M. (1970). 'Imagination', in O. P. Wood and G. Pitcher (eds.), *Ryle.* London: Macmillan, 137–45.

*SIWEK, P. (1930). *La Psychophysique humaine d'après Aristote.* Paris: F. Alcan.

*——(1965). *Le 'De Anima' d'Aristote dans les manuscrits grecs.* Vatican City: Biblioteca Apostolica Vaticana.

SKEMP, J. B. (1978). 'OREXIS in *De Anima* III. 10', in Lloyd Owen (1978), 181–9. **Ri**.

SLAKEY, THOMAS (1961). 'Aristotle on Sense Perception', *Philosophical Review,* 70, 470–84. **Fre., Sor.**

*SNELL, B. (1953). *The Discovery of Mind.* Oxford: Oxford University Press.

*SOLMSEN, FRIEDRICH (1950). 'Tissues and the Soul', *Philosophical Review,* 59, 435–68.

*——(1955). 'Antecedents of Aristotle's Psychology and Scale of Beings', *American Journal of Philology,* 76, 148–64.

*——(1960). *Aristotle's System of the Physical World.* Ithaca, NY: Cornell University Press.

——(1961a). 'Greek Philosophy and the Discovery of the Nerves', *Museum Helveticum,* 18, 150–97. **Sor.**

*——(1961b). 'Aesthesis in Aristotelian and Epicurean Thought', *Mededelingen der Koninklijke Nederlandse Akademie van Wetenschappen, Afd. Letterkunde,* N.R. 24/8, 241–62.

SORABJI, RICHARD (1971). 'Aristotle on Demarcating the Five Senses', *Philosophical Review,* 80, 55–79 [repr. J. Barnes *et al.* (1979b), 76–92]. **Fr., Fre., Ll., Sor.**

*——(1972). 'Aristotle, Mathematics and Colour: Intermediate Colours as Mixtures of Black and White', *Classical Quarterly,* NS, 22, 293–308.

——(1974/1979). 'Body and Soul in Aristotle', *Philosophy,* 49, 1974, 63–89, repr. J. Barnes *et al.,* (1979b), 42–64. **Bu., Coh., Ll., Pu., Sor.**

——(1980). *Necessity, Cause and Blame.* London and Ithaca, NY: Duckworth and Cornell University Press. **Ri., Sor.**

——(1988). *Matter, Space and Motion.* London and Ithaca, NY: Duckworth and Cornell University Press. **Sor.**

——(1990). 'Perceptual Content in the Stoics', *Phronesis,* 35, 307–14. **Sor.**

——(1991). 'From Aristotle to Brentano: The Development of the Concept of Intentionality', in Blumenthal-Robinson. **Sor.**

*SPRAGUE, R. K. (1967). 'Aristotle, De Anima 414. 4–14', *Phoenix,* 21, 102–7.

*——(1972). 'A Parallel with *De Anima* III. 5', *Phronesis*, 17, 250–1.

*——(1977). 'Aristotle and the Metaphysics of Sleep', *Review of Metaphysics*, 31, 230–41.

*SPRAGUE, R. K. (1985). 'Aristotle on Red Mirrors (*On Dreams* II, 459ᵇ24–460ᵃ23)', *Phronesis*, 30, 323–4.

SQUIRES, R. (1971). 'On One's Mind', *Philosophical Quarterly*, 20, 347–56. **Wi**.

*STIGEN, A. (1961). 'On the Alleged Primacy of Sight in Aristotle', *Symbolae Osloenses*, 37, 15–44.

STOCKER, MICHAEL (1986). 'Dirty Hands and Conflicts of Values and of Desires in Aristotle's Ethics', *Pacific Philosophical Quarterly*, 67, 36–61. **Ri**.

*STRATTON, G. M. (1917). *Theophrastus and the Greek Physiological Psychology before Aristotle*. London: Allen & Unwin.

STRAWSON, P. F. (1964). *Individuals*. London: Methuen. **Pu**.

——(1970). 'Imagination and Perception', in L. Foster and J. W. Swanson (eds.), *Experience and Theory*. London: Methuen. **Sch**.

STRIKER, GISELA (1977). 'Epicurus on the Truth of Sense Impressions', *Archiv für Geschichte der Philosophie*, 59, 125–42. **Sor**.

SUÁREZ, FRANCISCO (1856–61). *Opera omnia*, ed. M. André. Paris: L. Vivès. **Br**.

SUPPES, P. (1974). 'Aristotle's Concept of Matter and its Relation to Modern Concepts of Matter', *Synthese*, 28, 27–50. **Pu**.

TERIJOHN, M. (1982). 'Definition and the Two Stages of Aristotelian Demonstration', *Review of Metaphysics*, 36, 375–95.

TOTOK, W. (1964). *Handbuch der Geschichte der Philosophie*. Frankfurt am Main: V. Klostermann. **Br**.

TRACY, THEODORE JAMES (1969). *Physiological Theory and the Doctrine of the Mean in Plato and Aristotle*. Amsterdam: Mouton. **Fre**.

UEBERWEG, FRIEDRICH (1926). *Grundriß der Geschichte der Philosophie*. 12th edn. Berlin: E. S. Mittler und Sohn. **Br**.

VAN RIET, GEORGES (1953). 'La théorie thomiste de la sensation externe', *Revue philosophique de Louvain*, 51, 374–408. **Sor**.

VENDLER, Z. (1972). *Res cogitans*. Ithaca, NY: Cornell University Press. **Sor**.

VERBEKE, G. (1945). *L'Évolution de la doctrine du pneuma*, Paris: Desclée de Brouwer. **Ll**.

——(1978). 'Doctrine du pneuma et entéléchisme chez Aristote', in Lloyd–Owen (1978), 215–39. **Ll**.

*WARD, JULIE K. (1988). 'Perception and LOGOS in *De anima* II. 12', *Ancient Philosophy*, 8, 217–34.

WATERLOW, SARAH (1982). *Nature, Change, and Agency in Aristotle's Physics: A Philosophical Study*. Oxford: Oxford University Press. **Fre**.

WATSON, G. (1982). '*Phantasia* in Aristotle *De Anima* III, 3', *Classical Quarterly*, NS 32, 100–13. **Fr., Sch**.

——(1988). *Phantasia in Classical Thought*. Galway: Galway University Press. **Sch**.

WEDIN, MICHAEL V. (1986). 'Tracking Aristotle's *nous*', in A. Donagan *et al.* (eds.), *Human Nature and Human Knowledge*, 167–97. Dordrecht: D. Reidel Publishing Co. **Ka**.

——(1988). *Mind and Imagination in Aristotle*. New Haven: Yale University Press. **Fre., Ri., Sch**.

*WEISS, F. (1969). *Hegel's Critique of Aristotle's Philosophy of Mind*. The Hague: M. Nijhoff.

WHITING, J. (1984). 'Individual Forms in Aristotle'. PhD. Thesis, Cornell University. **Wh.**

——(1986). 'Form and Individuation in Aristotle', *History of Philosophy Quarterly*, 3, 359–77. **Wh.**

——(1990). 'Form and Generation in Aristotle', *Proceedings of the Boston Area Colloquium of Ancient Philosophy*, v. **Wh.**

——(forthcoming). *Aristotelian Individuals*. Oxford: Blackwell. **Wh.**

WHYTE, L. L. (1962). *The Unconscious before Freud*. London: Tavistock Publications. **Wi.**

*WIESNER, JÜRGEN (1978). 'The Unity of the *De Somno* and the Psychological Explanation of Sleep in Aristotle', in Lloyd–Owen (1978), 241–80.

WIGGINS, D. (1967). *Identity and Spatio-Temporal Continuity*. Oxford: Clarendon Press. **Wh.**

——(1980a). *Sameness and Substance*. Oxford and Cambridge, Mass.; Basil Blackwell and Harvard University Press. **Wh., Pu.**

*——(1980b). 'Weakness of Will, Commensurability, and the Objects of Deliberation and Desire', in A. Rorty (1980). **Ri.**

WILKES, K. V. (1974). 'Is the Unconscious Important?', *British Journal for the Philosophy of Science*, 35, 223–43. **Wi.**

——(1978). *Physicalism*. Atlantic Highlands, NJ: Humanities Press. **Bu., Coh., Sor.**

——(1988a). *Real People*. Oxford: Clarendon Press. **Wi.**

——(1988b). '—, Yìshì, Duh, Um, and Consciousness', in A. Marcel and E. Bisiach (eds.), *Consciousness in Contemporary Science*, 16–41. Oxford: Oxford University Press. **Wi.**

WILLIAMS, BERNARD (1973). *Problems of the Self*. Cambridge: Cambridge University Press. **Sch.**

——(1986). 'Hylomorphism', in J. Annas (ed.), *Oxford Studies in Ancient Philosophy*, 4, 189–99. **Coh., Ll., Sor., Wh.**

*WILLIAMS, C. J. F., and HIRST, R. J. (1965). 'Form and Sensation', *Proceedings of the Aristotelian Society*, Suppl. vol 39, 139–72.

WITTGENSTEIN, L. (1956). *Remarks on the Foundations of Mathematics*, trans. G. E. M. Anscombe. Cambridge, Mass.: MIT Press. **Pu.**

——(1958). *Philosophical Investigations*, trans. G. E. M. Anscombe. Oxford: Blackwell. **Sch.**

——(1967). *Zettel*, ed. G. E. M. Anscombe and G. H. von Wright, trans. G. E. M. Anscombe. Oxford: Blackwell. **Sch.**

YOUNG, CHARLES (1988). 'Aristotle on Temperance', *Philosophical Review*, 97, 521–42. **Fre.**

ZELLER, EDUARD (1856–68). *Die Philosophie der Griechen in ihrer geschichtlichen Entwicklung dargestellt*. 2nd edn. Leipzig, Tübingen: Fues. (Latest edns. repr. Hildesheim: Georg Olms, 1963.) **Br.**

ADDITIONAL ESSAY (1995)

HOW MUCH HAPPENS WHEN ARISTOTLE SEES RED AND HEARS MIDDLE C?
REMARKS ON *DE ANIMA* 2. 7–8

M. F. BURNYEAT

MODERN scholars seldom read chapters 7 and 8 of book 2 of the *De Anima* with the care and attention they give to other parts of that great work. Consequently, they miss several important details in Aristotle's theory of sight and hearing. Among the important details that are liable to be overlooked if one skips *De Anima* 2. 7–8, the most important, in my opinion, is the following:

> According to the Aristotelian theory of perception, there is no physiological process which stands to the awareness of a colour or a sound as matter to form.

Aristotle believes that when he sees a colour or hears a sound, nothing happens save that he sees the colour or hears the sound.

For us, formed as we are by modern science, such a thesis is incredible. It would be quite impossible for us to believe that when we see a colour or hear a sound, nothing happens save that we see the colour or hear the sound. Consequently, many scholars find it difficult to believe that Aristotle could have held a view so difficult to believe. But there is nothing original in my claim that he did.

When Friedrich Solmsen in his well-known article 'Greek Philosophy and the Discovery of the Nerves', came to Aristotle's account of perception, he observed, '. . . it is doubtful whether the movement or the actualization occurring when the eye sees or the ear hears has any physical or physiological aspect'.[1] I cite this article not only because Solmsen is a scholar with whom it is always better to find oneself agreeing than disagreeing, but also because of the *context* in which he made his observation.

---

[1] *Museum Helveticum* 18 (1961), 150–67 and 187–97, at 170. Substitute 'material' for 'physical' and Solmsen's observation has wide support among the ancient commentators, well documented by Richard Sorabji, 'From Aristotle to Brentano: The Development of the Concept of Intentionality', in *Aristotle and the Later Tradition*, ed. Henry Blumenthal and Howard Robinson (Oxford Studies in Ancient Philosophy suppl. vol. 1991), 227–59. Where Sorabji credits the commentators with a revisionary programme for 'dematerializing' the Aristotelian physics of perception, I credit them with understanding Aristotle pretty well.

After extensive research on Hippocratic and Hellenistic doctors, on Plato, on Galen, and other ancient thinkers who maintained a lively interest in what happens inside the body at the moment of perception, Solmsen faced up to the fact that he had nothing to say about Aristotle. He had found nothing in Aristotle to match the stories about the physiological side of perception that prevail from the Hippocratics at one end of his period of study to Galen at the other, and then on into modern psychology labs.[2]

That finding, in that context, has weight. At the very least, the precedent of Solmsen can serve to encourage us, when we read these two chapters, not to exclude in advance the possibility that Aristotle truly did believe something we could not believe.

Let us then pose the question, What are the material conditions—in the technical Aristotelian sense of the word 'material'—which are necessary for the occurrence of an act of perception? By the technical sense of the word 'material' I mean the sense which indicates the Aristotelian contrast between matter and form, not the modern sense in which 'material' is often synonymous with 'physical' in contrast to 'mental'.

In principle, there are three headings under which they should be found:

(a) the material conditions which are necessary for the perceiving subject to have the relevant perceptual capacity (sight, hearing, etc.);
(b) the material conditions which are necessary for the object perceived to be present at a suitable distance and in a state apt to stimulate perception;
(c) the material conditions which are necessary for the stimulus to awaken the capacity into activity.

Under heading (a) Aristotle gives us a list of receptive stuffs: transparent jelly in the eye (*Sens.* 2. 438^{b}5–8), still air walled up in the ear (*DA* 2. 8, 420^{a}9–10), the organ of touch at a mean of temperature and hardness (2. 11, 424^{a}4–10). He insists that the sense-organs are composed either of one simple, homogeneous element or, in the case of touch, of a homogeneous mixture (*PA* 2. 1, 647^{a}5–24; cf. *Sens.* 2, 437^{a}20 ff.; *DA* 3. 13, 435^{b}1–3). 'Homogeneous' here is to be taken in the strict sense of 'homoiomerous': every part, however small, is exactly like the whole. It is true that Aristotle distinguishes certain observable parts within the eye. But he emphasizes that the sensitive part, the part that sees (*tou men ommatos to oratikon*),[3] is the interior of the eye which consists entirely of water; and he describes the other organs in similar terms (*Sens.* 2, 438^{b}18–22 with 9–11).[4] It seems plain that

---

[2] To go from Aristotle to Galen's anatomical refutation, in *De Placitis Hippocratis et Platonis* 1–2, of the Aristotelian/Stoic identification of the heart as the seat of sensation and the source of locomotion is to be transported at once into a different world: our own.

[3] i.e. the part in which and thanks to which the animal sees.

[4] Further references and discussion in G. E. R. Lloyd, 'The Empirical Basis of the Physiology of the *Parva Naturalia*', in *Aristotle on Mind and the Senses* (Proceedings of the Seventh Symposium Aristotelicum), ed. G. E. R. Lloyd and G. E. L. Owen (Cambridge, 1978), 215–39. Where the eye is concerned, Lloyd concludes (p. 221): 'There is, in fact, no mention of most of the parts that seem difficult to identify straightforwardly with water'.

Aristotelian sense-organs lack internal structure. *A fortiori* they lack entirely a microstructure comparable to that which modern science invokes when it speaks of nerves, for example, or retinal cells.[5]

A lack of internal structure is not the same as a lack of qualitative differentiation. In *De Generatione Animalium* 5. 1–2 Aristotle gives a lengthy account of the material causes of differences among animals in the keenness of their sight and hearing: the causes are such things as the colour of the eyes, the consistency of the water composing them, and factors to do with the external protection of the organ (cf. also *DA* 2. 9, 421ª7–16; *PA* 2. 13). But these are all static material conditions. They facilitate or impede accuracy of perception without adding to the processes that take place at the moment of perceiving.

Besides the sense-organs properly so called, the capacity for perception requires a system of passages (*poroi*) linking the sense organs to the central place where a unitary consciousness of all the objects of perception is located.[6] But what happens in these passages is always a continuation or likeness of what happens in the sense-organs,[7] and it is what happens in the sense-organs that interests me here.

Under heading (*b*) are found the varied material conditions necessary for a thing to have colour, to make a sound, to be hard or soft. I shall be dealing later with some of the requirements for sound.

The locus of controversy is heading (*c*). The only condition I find here is a medium in a suitable state. Nothing more. Aristotle insists that the medium of perception, like the organ, lacks microstructure (*GC* 1. 8). If you ask why an animal with eyes open in clear daylight sees the coloured object in front of it, Aristotle's reply, I maintain, is just this: such is the nature of sight and of colour. (His reply to the question 'Why does fire warm a cold room?' follows the same pattern: such is the nature of the hot and the cold—*GC* 1. 7.) Once you understand what sight is and what colour is, you will appreciate that nothing more by way of explanation need or can be said.

That, in sum, is what I find in the two chapters before us. My task now is to help you find it too.

I begin with a central thesis of 2. 7:

Every colour is capable of setting in motion (*kinētikon*) that which is actually transparent, and this is its nature. (418ª31–ᵇ1; tr. Hamlyn)

Two points call for comment.

The first point is that we must not ask why, in virtue of what, colour is capable of setting the transparent in motion. That is the *nature* of colour. Compare 419ª9–11: 'this is just what it is to be colour, to be capable of setting in motion that which

[5] Cf. Deborak K. Modrak, *Aristotle: The Power of Perception* (University of Chicago Press, 1987): 'The structure and organization of the matter that is enformed by the capacity to see and thus constitute a functional eye would of necessity be very complex'. True in our world, false in Aristotle's.

[6] The texts are pretty vague and do not allow a decisive interpretation. Cf. Lloyd, 'The Empirical Basis'.

[7] *DA* 3. 2, 425ᵇ24–5; 3, 428ᵇ10–14; 429ª4–5; *Mem.* 1, 450ª24–ᵇ1; *Insomn.* 1, 459ª14–22; 2, 459ᵇ3 ff.

is actually transparent' (tr. Hamlyn). We are at a terminus of explanation. For Aristotle, a nature or an essence is something that explains other things without needing to be explained itself.[8] That, presumably, is why Aristotle says at 418ᵃ30–1 that a visible object has within itself the cause of its visibility. The cause of the object's visibility is its colour. The colour is the cause of the object's visibility because the colour is by its very nature capable of setting in motion the actually transparent. End of explanation.

The second point is that the translation just quoted from Hamlyn is deeply misleading. As Hicks rightly remarks,[9] we must not understand 'motion' as 'locomotion'. *Kinēsis* in Aristotle's usage is the generic term for all kinds of change, including alteration. *Kinētikon* just means 'productive of a change', not 'productive of spatial movement'. All we have learned so far is that the colour by its own nature produces a certain effect on the medium (air or water), provided this medium is actually transparent.

The actuality of the transparent, we discover a bit later at 418ᵇ9, is light. Light is not fire, nor is it any kind of body or emanation from bodies (418ᵇ14–15); that is to say, it is not anything that moves (Empedocles is criticized for saying that light travels—418ᵇ20 ff.). And it is not a movement either (*Sens.* 6, 446ᵇ30–1). Rather, light is a state or disposition (*hexis*, 418ᵇ19; 3. 5, 430ᵃ15), the transparency of the medium, its being actually transparent.

Thus the condition laid down for a colour to produce its effect on a medium is not an event or process, but a static condition, a state of affairs. And the condition for this condition is static too: in order for the medium to be in the state of actual transparency which is light, it suffices (*a*) that it has a nature or capacity to be transparent (418ᵇ6–11, 31; *Sens.* 3, 439ᵃ24–7), and (*b*) that there is fire present (418ᵇ11–20; *Sens.* 3, 439ᵃ21–2). It is not necessary for the fire to *do* anything. It just has to be there and the transparent nature of the medium realizes itself.

If you find this incredible, I can only say that I do too, but it is what the texts contain. The great commentator Alexander of Aphrodisias puts light in the category of *relation* (in *Sens.* 134. 11–19; cf. 132. 2–16). When the sun rises or a lamp is lit, for the air around us this is a mere change of relation.[10] The statement 'When fire comes to be present in the air, the air is illuminated' is just like the statement 'When I move to the left of my desk, the desk comes to be on my right'.[11] As usual, Alexander understands Aristotle very well.

But light is not only the condition for the colour to produce its effect on the medium. In a way it is also the condition for the colour itself to be present in actuality (3. 5, 430ᵃ15–17). I conclude that the colour produces its effect all the time it is actually present; all the time the coloured object is visible. There is no

---

[8] Cf. *APo* 1. 4, 73ᵇ16–18; 24, 85ᵇ24–5; *Metaph.* 8. 17, 1041ᵇ9–33; *DA* I. 1, 402ᵃ 7–8; ᵇ25–6.

[9] Hicks ad loc. Unfortunately, he restricts the remark to the case of vision.

[10] The type of change that P. T. Geach called 'Cambridge change', 'since it keeps on occurring in Cambridge philosophers of the great days like Russell and McTaggart' (*God and the Soul* (London 1969) 71–2).

[11] Naturally, the fire's *coming to be* present has its causes and involves process: see J. Thorp, 'The Luminousness of the Quintessence', *Phoenix* 36 (1982), 104–23.

event of production. The effect is continually produced, thanks to the presence of the colour in the light, which means, as already explained, thanks to the very nature of colour.

Next, I propose that Aristotle specifies the effect of colour on the illuminated medium at 418^{b}4–6:

I call transparent that which is visible not, strictly speaking, in itself but because of the colour of something else.

This text does, without doubt, specify *an* effect of colour on the medium, and I have not found another text that does as much. The effect is this: colour makes the transparent visible. Now we already know that the visible is colour.[12] So it is no surprise to read later at 418^{b}11 that light is a sort of colour (*hoion chrōma*) of the transparent, a text to which *De Sensu* 3, 439^{a}19–21 refers when it says that light is the colour of the transparent *per accidens*.[13] The transparent does not have within itself the cause of its visibility. That is to say, it has no colour of its own; it is not coloured in the way the visible object is. When it is illuminated, it is visible and coloured in a derivative way, thanks to the presence of a colour which belongs to a body

But what is the meaning of 'coloured in a derivative way'? Here is a very simple reply. The transparent is coloured in a derivative way when the colour of a body appears through it.

When the medium is actually transparent (*diaphanēs*), i.e. when the medium is such that colours can appear through it (*phainesthai dia*), they do appear through it.[14] At the same time, the transparent itself, the light, becomes visible in a way and coloured in a way—without being really coloured and, in consequence, without undergoing a real alteration. This non-real alteration—a quasi-alteration I shall call it—of the transparent consists in the fact that colours appear through it.

Here is a little experiment to help you to understand the idea of quasi-alteration.[15] Fill a transparent glass with water and put it on a table. Hold a red object a short distance away from the glass and look at it through the water. The water in the glass is now serving as a medium *within* another medium (the surrounding air). You will see a red coloration in the water. But unlike the coloration that ensues if you pour red ink into the water, this coloration is not visible to other observers from other angles of vision. Now let the glass expand in your imagination to meet your eye, on one side, and the red object on the other. The water will become the sole medium and you will see the red object directly through it.

---

[12] Let us agree to leave phosphorescence (418^{a}26–8; 419^{a}7) for another day.

[13] *Kata sumbebēkos* here = *ou kath' auto* at *DA* 418^{b}5 in contrast to *kath' auto* at 418^{a}30, which Hicks ad loc. glosses by *to oikeion* in contrast to *allotrion chrōma* at 418^{b}6.

[14] Alex. *in Sens.* 45. 20–1: *di' hou dē tauta phainetai, touto de idiōs kaloumen diaphanes* (for the verb *diaphainesthai*, cf. *Mete.* 1. 5, 342^{b}6; *GA* 5. 1, 780^{a}34–5). Analogously, *to diosmon, to diēches* in the commentators: Ar. Did. *Epit. phys.* fr. 17 (Diels *Dox.* 456. 13–17); Alex. *in Sens.* 88. 19–89. 2; Them. *in de An.* 62. 31–2; Simp. *in de An.* 139. 1–6. Philoponus *in de An.* 354. 12–16 attributes the terminology to Theophrastus.

[15] I am grateful to Tad Brennan for suggesting it to me.

Such is the effect of a colour on a medium which is actually transparent: the colour appears through it. It is visible through the medium. No more, no less.

It is evident, I hope, that this appearance or visibility of the colour through the transparent is a static condition, a state of affairs, not an event or process. Nothing happens. Nothing moves from the coloured object. There is not even a real alteration, only the quasi-alteration which consists in the fact that the colour is visible through the transparent.

You may think there is an objection to be mounted on the basis of $419^{a}18-19$, where Aristotle argues that it is impossible for the affection which is seeing to be produced by the colour seen itself. The only remaining possibility is that it is produced by something in between the colour and the subject seeing it. Hence it is necessary that there be something in between—the medium.

It is dangerously easy for us to suppose that the impossibility of direct action by colour on sight is to be explained by the fact that the colour is situated at a distance. The function of the medium is to join the object perceived to the subject perceiving it. The medium is needed to transmit the colour, or information about it, to the sight of the perceiver. Nowadays we do indeed understand the medium as a medium of communication. And there were ancients who share our view.[16] But let us look at the context in 2. 7.

Aristotle has just repeated the point I began from, that 'this is just what it is to be colour, to be capable of changing that which is actually transparent' ($419^{a}9-10$, tr. now revised). At $419^{a}11$ he offers to confirm this definition: if one places the coloured object directly on the organ of sight, it will not be seen. What Aristotle excludes thereby is a definition of colour as what has a capacity to change the organ of sight. Colour must be defined as what has a capacity to change a transparent medium—for example, air—and it is the air which changes the organ of sight (14–15). This implies that the function of the medium is primarily to *separate* the object perceived from the perceiving subject. Everyone knows that the necessity of such a separation is the premiss on which Aristotle bases his proof that the organ of touch is not the flesh but the heart.[17] And it is the same, I suspect, with what Democritus had to say on this point.[18]

Democritus suggested that, ideally, vision would work best without a medium: if there was a void or vacuum between the perceiving subject and the object perceived, there would be nothing to interfere with perception, which is effected on his theory by the transmission of something material from the object to the

---

[16] See n. 19 below.

[17] *De An.* 2. 7, $419^{a}25-31$, referring forward at 30–1 to 2. 11, $423^{b}20-6$; cf. 2. 9, $421^{b}17-18$; *PA* 2. 8, $653^{b}19-30$. We should be taken aback by the confidence with which Aristotle asserts that, for all sense organs (even the ear, or the nose of a dog), an object placed on the organ is not perceived. I am tempted to think that he does not go into the details of the different cases because he knows in advance, as a matter of principle, that it *must* be so.

[18] Neither Hicks nor Hamlyn translate the *touto* in line 15.

subject.[19] But from Aristotle's point of view, if *per impossibile* there was a void, i.e.
nothing, between subject and object, then so far as explanation goes the situation
would be just like the case where an object is put directly on the eye.

Let us go back for a moment to the affection which is seeing and which is such
that the colour itself cannot produce it. At the beginning of 2. 12 Aristotle will
finally announce that this affection consists in the reception of sensible form
without matter. But it is obvious that when a coloured object is placed directly on
the eye, it affects it, if at all, as a composite of form *with* matter. From this I
conclude that, if my suggestion is correct that the function of the medium is
primarily to separate rather than to join, it is above all the sensible form and the
matter of the object perceived that need to be separated. The separation is an
aspect of the quasi-alteration I spoke of earlier. If the transparent is coloured in a
derivative way, without being really coloured, we can say that the sensible form,
the colour, is present in the transparent by itself, without the material base with
which it is united in the object perceived. The need for separation can be seen as
the reason why colours are seen only in the light (419^a22–3; cf. 7–9), i.e. in the
actually transparent. The visible form can only *appear* to the eye through a medium which separates it from the coloured object.

So much for the question, What is the immediate effect of a colour on the
medium? The next question is: What is the mediate effect of a colour on the eye?

According to Aristotle, the interior of the eye must consist of water or of air,
because (1) for the eye to see there must be light within as well as without, (2) the
(potentially) transparent elements are water and air, but (3) water is easier to
confine (*Sens.* 2, 438^a13–17; $^b6$–12; *PA* 2. 10, 656^a37–$^b2$). In sum, the eye consists
of water because one does not see if the eye is not actually transparent.[20] Given our
earlier discussion about the transparent medium being coloured in a derivative
way, it will come as no surprise to learn that, when we see, the eye is coloured in
a way (3. 2, 425^b22–3). All this implies that the effect on the eye is the same as the
effect on the medium, as one could already infer from lines 419^a13–15 in 2. 7.[21]
The colour appears to the eye of the subject who perceives it. The effect on the eye
is a quasi-alteration just like the quasi-alteration in the transparent, because the eye
too is actually transparent.

[19] Contrast the Stoic-inspired view of Cleomedes (8. 20–4 Ziegler) that empty spaces (*kenōmata*)
inside the cosmos would break the *sumpatheia* of all its parts and would thereby make sight and hearing
impossible. As David Sedley has pointed out to me, we do not need to suppose that Democritus really
thought, contrary to his own theory of perception, that one *could* see through a void. He was emphasizing that the medium of vision is one source of its fallibility. Compare 'In a void a runner could attain
a speed of a hundred miles an hour'. It would be silly to reply, 'But in a void, without air to breathe,
the runner would die'.
[20] Let us not forget that for Aristotle a teleological explanation can take not only the form 'X is
necessary for function Y', but also the form 'X facilitates function Y more than the other available
means' (*PA* 2. 1, 640^a33–$^b4$; 3. 7, 670^b23–7; *GA* 1. 4, 717^a15 ff.; *DA* 3. 1, 425^b4–11).
[21] For confirmation, cf. 3. 12, 434^b26–435^a10.

Now the key doctrinal passage at 3. 2, 425^b26–426^a26, states that the effect of the colour on the eye is identical with seeing. The passage applies to all modes of perception the celebrated model of action and passion that Aristotle elaborated in *De Generatione et Corruptione* I. 7 and *Physics* 3. 1–3.[22] Just as one and the same road is differently described as 'the road from Athens to Thebes' and 'the road from Thebes to Athens', and one and the same achievement is differently described as '*A* learning grammar from *B*' and '*B* teaching grammar to *A*', so it is one and the same state of affairs that is differently described by the following two statements:

(1) The colour appears to me at my eye through the medium.
(2) I see the colour by my eye through the medium.

The sole difference between the effect on the medium and the effect on the eye is the difference adverted to (for the case of smell) in the very last sentence of 2. 12, 424^b16–18: at the eye the effect is seeing, in the medium it is not, because the eye has the capacity to see and the air does not. End of explanation.[23]

To be sure, one can give a more or less extended description of this capacity for seeing which the medium does not possess. In speaking of a capacity to *receive* sensible forms, Aristotle has in mind not only the appearance of colours to the eye, but also the *retention* of these appearances, which continue to guide the behaviour of animals after the perception itself is over (3. 3, 429^a1–8). But such a description gives us information about the role of sight in animal life. It adds nothing to what happens in the eye at the moment of seeing.

We are now in a position to understand what Aristotle means when he speaks, from 2. 5 onwards, of the alteration or assimilation by which the sense organ becomes that which the object perceived already is in actuality. At the end of 2. 5 (418^a1–3) he had declared that we are not to understand 'being affected' and 'being altered' in the proper (*kurios*) sense fixed for them in *De Generatione et Corruptione* I. 7 and *Physics* 3. 1–3.[24] In the case of sight we have now verified that it is not a real coloration or a real assimilation, but only a quasi-alteration/assimilation/coloration. A matter of appearances alone.

According to Richard Sorabji in his deservedly influential paper 'Body and Soul in Aristotle', if scientists had some device which enabled them to see into the interior of my eye when I look at a red object, they would see red in my eye-jelly.[25] According to me, they would see no such thing. The transparent in my eye would behave just like the glass of water in our little experiment. Provided the observations were made from behind my head, the scientists would see the red object

---

[22] 426^a2–6 recalls the general model; 2. 5, 417^a1–2, has already referred us to *GC* I. 7, and 417^a16–20 to *Ph.* 3. 1–3.
[23] For an interpretation in this sense of 2. 12, see my 'Is an Aristotelian Philosophy of Mind still Credible? (A Draft)', in this volume.
[24] See n. 22 above.
[25] Richard Sorabji, 'Body and Soul in Aristotle' (*Philosophy* 49 [1974], 63–89; cited from the reprint with revisions in Barnes, Schofield, and Sorabji (edd.), *Articles on Aristotle* vol. 4 (London, 1979), 42–64) at pp. 49–50 with n. 22.

itself—through my eye! From other angles they would see nothing but the neighbouring parts of my body.

It is in this sense that there is no material or physiological process in the Aristotelian theory of vision. The mediate effect of a colour on the perceiver is simply that the perceiver sees the colour. The alteration of the eye *by* a sensible quality is (i) a quasi-alteration only and (ii) identical with the perceiving *of* the sensible quality in question. And if *x* is identical with *y*, neither can stand to the other in the technical Aristotelian relation of matter to form.[26]

I pass now to 2. 8 on sound and hearing. There is no denying that it is written throughout in the language of spatial movement. Sound is a sort of movement of the air (420^{b}11; cf. 420^{a}9–11; 21–3). But what sort?

According to 419^{b}34–5 the air produces hearing when it is moved in a continuous unitary mass. (The air has to be a continuous unitary mass for vision too—419^{a}14; 3. 12, 435^{a}5–8.) The contrast, I take it, is with a wind. A wind is moving air, or perhaps better: the travelling of air from one place to another (*Top.* 4. 5, 127^{a}3–12). Nothing of that sort happens in the case of sound. The air between me and the place of the blow stays put (*hupomenēi*, 419^{b}21). It rebounds and vibrates as a single whole (*athroun aphallesthai kai seiesthai*, 420^{a}25–6) without being dispersed (*mē diachuthēi*, 419^{b}21–2). And we will see that in the *De Sensu* Aristotle agrees that sound takes time to reach the ear. But if a sound moves from one place to another, while the air does not, we have to side with the ancient commentators who maintained that Aristotle conceives sound as moving *along* the air between the place of the blow and the ear just like a wave or vibration.[27]

So much for a first account of the immediate effect on the medium. According to 420^{a}4–5 the air without and the air within the ear have a common nature, and when the air without is moved, the air within is moved likewise. In this sense the movement which is the sound is transmitted from outside to inside. That is why the air inside the ear must also be immobile (*akinētos*, 420^{a}10), kept still within, so that it can receive (= perceive) a variety of movements from the air outside.[28] Precisely as in the case of perceiving colour, the mediate effect on the organ is the same as the immediate effect on the medium. But here the effect is a movement.

Yes, but unfortunately for the advocates of material processes, this movement, this *kinēsis tis* is not a kind of movement but only a movement of a kind; it is

---

[26] To be sure, matter and form make a unity. But they can do this precisely because they are not identical. Cf. *Metaph.* 7. 17, 8. 6; *DA* 2. 2, 415^{a}13–28.

[27] Alex. *de An.* 50. 12–18; Them. *in de An.* 65. 31–6; cf. Sorabji, 'From Aristotle to Brentano', 230–1. Compare the analogy with eddies (*dinai*) or moving forms (*schēmata*) that Aristotle invokes to explain the distortion of appearances during sleep (*Insomn.* 3, 461^{a}8–11).

[28] 420^{a}15–18 fits with this, provided it is read sensibly, as saying that an internal movement of the ear's own (a constant ringing in the ears) obstructs hearing—exactly as a previous taste still lingering on the tongue interferes with tasting (2. 10, 422^{b}7–10). The ideas retailed from ancient commentators by Rodier and Hicks ad loc. seem to me sheer fantasy: horns and seashells do not hear, and the second *ho* in 420^{a}17 is textually insecure. I maintain, then, that *to ēchein aei . . . oikeian tina kinēsin* is *sēmeion tou mē akouein*, not *sēmeion tou akouein*. 420^{a}17–18 implies that hearing sound is *to ēchein . . . allotrian tina kinēsin*.

movement only in a derivative way, a quasi-movement. Aristotelian physics does not recognize the movement of a wave or a vibration as movement properly so called. Movement properly so called is the passage of a body (a substance) from one place to another (*Ph.* 3. 1, 200^{b}32–201^{a}3; 5. 2, 226^{a}32–^{b}1). But unlike a wind, a wave or vibration is not (the passage of) a body or a substance.[29]

The problem is not peculiar to sound. At *De Sensu* 6, 446^{b}27, Aristotle remarks that sensible forms are not bodies but *pathos kai kinēsis tis*: affection and a sort of change.[30] How then to explain the fact that, save in the case of visible forms, this affection or this change can take time to reach the subject who perceives it? For the case of smell Aristotle develops an analogy with ice moving across a pond (447^{a}3–7). The ice does not really move. This is a *façon de parler* to describe the fact that the water freezes first here, then there. Freezing is real alteration. But the analogy can be applied without difficulty to a quasi-alteration: the smell manifests itself first here, then there.

The same goes for sound. Like the ice, a sound does not really move. Rather, the air resounds (*gegōnei*, 420^{a}1) first here, then there. And for that it is vital, apparently, that the air is prevented from moving in any direction (419^{b}18–420^{a}2). Sound, therefore, is a travelling of form alone, a quasi-movement.

There is a nice illustration of this idea in the example Aristotle gives at *De Sensu* 6, 446^{b}7–10, to prove the point that the 'passage' of sound takes time. It can happen that you do not hear quite the words I uttered, because they get distorted somewhere in the medium between me and you. This distortion Aristotle describes as a reshaping of the phonemes (*metaschēmatisis tōn grammatōn*), and, more significantly, as a reshaping of the air that moves (*metaschēmatizesthai pheromenon ton aera*; cf. 446^{b}33–447^{a}1). But the air does not really move. It is not a wind. What Aristotle must mean, therefore, is that the *grammata*, which are the sounds themselves, i.e. the audible forms, are different in different portions of the air between me and you. There has been a change of forms between me and you. Democritus could have used the same or similar words.[31] But he would not have meant, as Aristotle does, a change solely of forms, a reshaping (*metaschēmatisis*) without any movement or change of matter. The Aristotelian physics of sound is a physics of form alone, without material processes.

We should give this result its full generality, as Aristotle does at the beginning of 2. 12. Here for the first time in the treatise we meet the celebrated formula 'receiving sensible forms without matter', which Aristotle introduces only *after* he has shown, for each of the five senses, that the stimulus which awakens it to activity is the appearance of a sensible quality. Chapters 7–8, which I have examined

[29] Cf. the passage from H. A. Pritchard quoted as an Appendix at the end of this paper. For us an eccentricity from the home of lost causes, it would meet with Aristotle's approval. Aristotle need not deny that a wave involves the air or water moving up and down at each place between A and B, for this movement is not the movement from A to B (hearing can take place in water too: 420^{a}11–13; *HA* 4. 8, 533^{b}4 ff.).

[30] I translate 'change' rather than 'movement' here with an eye to the fact that 446^{b}31–2 proceeds to separate the case of *alloiōsis* from that of *phora*.

[31] For example *metarruthmizesthai* DK 68 A 132.

here, are only one portion of the larger discussion of 2. 7–11, and the results of Aristotle's summing-up at the beginning of 2. 12 ought to hold for all five senses:

> The generalization we should make about all perception is that a sense is what is capable of receiving sensible forms without matter, as wax receives the marking of the ring without the iron or the gold; it takes on the golden or brazen marking, but not insofar as it is gold or insofar as it is bronze. Likewise, the individual sense is affected by some thing that has colour or taste or sound, but not by these insofar as each is said to be such and such a thing; it is affected by them insofar as each is of a certain quality and according to its form. (424^{a}17–24)

When I read these words, the message coming over is that with each of the five senses we have to do with a physics of form alone, without material processes.

Back finally to the mediate effect of sound at the ear. The vibration, resonance, or movement passes from the air outside to the air inside the ear. According to the key doctrinal passage of 3. 2, the vibration or resonance in the ear (*psophēsis*) is identical with the hearing (*akousis*) of the sound. It is one single event that admits of two descriptions. But it is an event on the level of form alone. For us, a vibration or movement is a physical event, hearing a mental event. The fact that for Aristotle 'movement' and 'hearing' are two descriptions of one and the same event demonstrates how badly our categories, which emanate from Descartes, fit his philosophy.[32]

It is no good responding that, if this discussion has shown anything, it is that Aristotle can be classified alongside modern advocates of the view that mental events or states can be type-identified with physical ones. For we have seen that the exterior movement is just like the interior one. But the exterior movement is not a mental event. The explanation of the difference that we found in 2. 12 is very simple: the air of the environment, like the plants at 424^{a}32–^{b}3, does not have the capacity to hear.

This may not sound much like a reason to us; it cites an *explanandum* rather than an *explanans*. Hence the temptation to read a more congenial moral into the last sentence of 2. 12.[33] But that tells us less about Aristotle than about our own predicament as heirs of Descartes and modern science. For Aristotle, reference to the faculty or power of hearing is a paradigm of satisfactory explanation. Indeed, it is a terminus of explanation, and a very good place for me to stop. Accordingly, I shall close by simply mentioning two non-Aristotelian texts which may help modern readers come to terms with the non-material physics of *De Anima* 2. 7–8.

The first is Plato's *Timaeus* 48e–53c, which I take to be Aristotle's inspiration for the idea of quasi-alteration.[34] Like Aristotelian sense-organs, the Receptacle must

---

[32] For a good corrective to the widespread tendency to equate 'physical' vs. 'mental' with 'material' vs. 'formal', see Alan Code, 'Aristotle, Searle, and the Mind-Body Problem', in *John Searle and his Critics*, edited by E. LePore and R. Van Gulick (Oxford, 1991), 105–13, and also Alan Code and Julius Moravcsik, 'Explaining Various Forms of Living', in this volume.

[33] See Sorabji, 'Body and Soul', 47; cf. pp. 46, 54, 56, 60.

[34] My inspiration for this conjecture is Plotinus, *Enneads* 3. 6. Entitled 'On the impassibility of things without body', it is an extended study of the parallels between the *Timaeus* on changes in the Receptacle and *De Anima* 2. 5 on changes in the soul.

be formless itself if it is receive all the elemental forms. Contrary qualities like hot
and cold, light and dark, will appear in it and make it appear different at different
times (*allote alloion*, 50c), so that the Receptacle as medium can be described in the
language of assimilation as moistened here, made fiery there (51b, 52d). But this
language must not be taken to mean that the coming and going of sensible qualities
(forms) brings real change for the medium. The forms appear there, without ever
affecting the formless nature of the thing that receives them (50be). And since
these quasi-alterations occur at the very lowest level of Plato's universe, prior to
the introduction of geometrical atomism at 53c, of necessity there are no underlying processes to point to when the question is pressed, But *how* are the warmings
and moistenings effected?

The second text, from one of the great masterpieces of ancient science, is
Ptolemy's *Optics* 2. 23–4.[35] To describe colour vision, Ptolemy employs language
that recalls the Aristotelian description of the same phenomenon. Sight detects
colour through undergoing an accidental coloration: it recognizes white, for example, because it goes white. None the less, sight itself must remain pure and
colourless in order to be able to perceive the colours outside.[36] In a work of
mathematical optics there is no need to give a physiological meaning to such
language. Optics is the study of visual *appearances*. If colour appearances are to be
included (in Euclid they are not), Aristotelian quasi-alteration—suggestively developed by Ptolemy to make colour a form of luminosity, and modified to let light
travel (2. 16)—is quite a good starting-point.

This helps to explain why Solmsen found nothing to say about Aristotle. He
was looking for a physiology of vision and hearing. But Aristotle's methodology gives
priority to the scientific study of the *objects* of vision and hearing (2. 4, 415ª20–2).
Let it not be said, therefore, that on my account chapters 7 and 8 of book 2 of the
De Anima contribute nothing to science. Their contribution is to make room
within physics for (the application of) two 'intermediate' sciences which in Aristotle's day were both more successful and more prestigious than physiology.

By 'intermediate' I refer to the placing of optics and harmonics in Aristotle's
scheme of the sciences midway, somehow, between pure mathematics and full-
bodied physics, where definitions must specify the matter of the definiendum. We
know from the first chapter of the *De Anima* itself (403ᵇ17–19) that the scientific
definition of anger includes an essential material aspect which is omitted, because
it is not essential, from the scientific definition of line. But what of the official
definiendum of optics, 'line qua physical' (*Ph.* 2. 2, 194ª7–12)?[37] Its intermediate

---

[35] See pp. 23–4 in the magnificent edition by Albert Lejeune (Louvain, 1956; reprinted with a
French translation, Leiden, 1989).

[36] 'Oportet enim ut sensus perspicabilis non habeat qualitatem, sed sit purus et suscipiat qualitatem
ab illis [*sc.* lumen et color], quoniam participat eis et in genere . . . visus cognoscit colorem per colorationem
accidentem; et cognoscit albedinem, verbi gratia, quia dealbat, et nigridinem quia denigrat.'

[37] It is easy to give the most important references (to *Ph.* 2. 2 just cited, add *APo.* 1. 13, 78ᵇ34–79ª16;
Metaph. 13. 3, 1078ª14–21), not easy to extract a consistent doctrine. There may be some vacillation
between optics as currently practised and optics as Aristotle would wish it to be practised. What is not
in doubt is that Aristotle wants to be in a position to apply current optics in his physical works: *Mete.*
3. 2, 372ª29 ff.; *DA* 3. 12, 435ª5–10; *GA* 5. 1, 781ª37.

status strikes me as interestingly like the intermediate status of perception in *De Anima* 1. 1: perception is mentioned in the list of attributes (*pathē*) of soul that require a body (403ᵃ5–7), but not in the list of affections or passions (*pathē* in some narrower sense[38]) that require a concomitant bodily process.

If you ask why perception and its objects should be singled out for special status, I can only guess. What is special about perception is that it is a low-grade form of *knowledge*.[39] As knowledge, it must be of forms—*sensible* forms if they are to be objects of perception. But if, in causing themselves to be perceived, sensible forms cause themselves to be known, they had better do it with the least possible involvement of matter. That much Democritus got right. What he failed to realize is that form is better than nothing.[40]

APPENDIX (cf. n. 29)

(1) I once made what I thought the unquestionable remark to a German mathematician who was also a physicist that only a body could move—so that, for example, the centre of gravity of a body or of a system of bodies, which is a geometrical point, could not move. He, as I rather expected, thought I was just mad. In this case I should certainly have said I was certain that a centre of gravity cannot move, and I think he would have said he was certain that it could. Here I personally should assert he could not possibly have been more than uncertain that it could not, and that, if he had thought a bit more, he would have become certain that it could not; you cannot make a man think, any more than you can make a horse drink.

But (2) I also made the same remark (viz. that only a body could move) to a mathematician here. What was in my mind was that it is mere inaccuracy to say that a wave could move, and that where people talked of a wave as moving, say with the velocity of a foot, or a mile, or 150,000 miles, a second, the real movement consisted of the oscillations of certain particles, each of which took place a little later than a neighbouring oscillation.

He scoffed for quite a different reason. He said that you could illustrate a movement by a noise—that, for example, if an explosion occurred in the middle of Oxford the noise would spread outwards, being heard at different times by people at varying distances from

---

[38] I prefer 'passions' but need only insist on the point that at 403ᵃ3 *pathē* has the wide sense of *sumbebēkota* in contrast to *to ti estin* (402ᵇ25–403ᵃ2 with 402ᵃ7–10), but by 403ᵃ16 these *pathē* have been divided into *erga* and *pathēmata* (403ᵃ10–11; cf. *paschein oude poiein*, 403ᵃ6–7; *erga kai pathē*, 403ᵇ12). Hamlyn translates, very sensibly, 'properties' at 402ᵃ9 and 403ᵃ3, and 'affections' at 403ᵃ10 and 16. It follows that the famous affirmation at 403ᵃ25 that *pathē logoi enuloi eisin* does not take an explicit stand on the *erga* of soul.

[39] So presented from the beginning of the treatise: 1. 2, 404ᵇ9 ff.; 5, 409ᵇ23 ff.

[40] This is an English translation of a paper first published in French (*Revue philosophique de la France et de l'Étranger* 118 [1993] and, with corrections, in *Études sur le De Anima d'Aristote*, edited by Gilbert Romeyer Dherbey (Paris, 1995)), and (the earliest version) in Spanish (*Revista latinoamericana de filosofia* 20 (1994)). I am grateful for the remarks and friendly criticism offered when I presented the first version at the Centre Léon Robin in Paris, and for the quite different criticisms and observations which enlivened seminars on this topic in Harvard, Oxford, Pittsburgh, Princeton, Rutgers, and Sheffield. I owe thanks to G. E. R. Lloyd and Sarah Broadie for their help and encouragement throughout the preparation of this essay. For a profound study of the idea of a theory of perception without material processes, I recommend to my readers Broadie's article 'Aristotle's Perceptual Realism', *Southern Journal of Philosophy* 31 (1993), suppl. vol.: *Spindel Conference 1992: Ancient Minds*, edited by John Ellis, 137–59.

the centre, so that at one moment the noise was at one place and that a little later it was somewhere else, and in the interval it had moved from one place to the other.

Now, of course, it was not in dispute that in the process imagined people in different places each heard a noise at a rather different time. The only question was, 'Was the succession of noises a movement?' and I think that on considering the matter you will have to allow that it was not, and that what happened was that he, being certain of the noises, and wanting to limit the term 'movement' to something he was certain of, used the term 'movement' to designate the succession of noises, implying that this was the real thing of which we were both talking. But if this is what happened, then he was using the term 'movement' in a sense of his own, and in saying that in the imagined case he was certain of a movement, he was being certain of something other than the opposite of what I was certain of.

H. A. Prichard, *Knowledge and Perception* (Oxford, 1950), p. 99.

INDEX LOCORUM[1]

[1] The Editors wish to thank Steven Rutledge for preparing this index.

NAME INDEX